AMERICAN LAW YEARBOOK 2007

AN ANNUAL SOURCE PUBLISHED
BY THOMSON GALE AS A
SUPPLEMENT TO
WEST'S ENCYCLOPEDIA OF
AMERICAN LAW

ISSN 1521-0901

AMERICAN LAW YEARBOOK 2007

AN ANNUAL SOURCE PUBLISHED
BY THOMSON GALE AS A
SUPPLEMENT TO
WEST'S ENCYCLOPEDIA OF
AMERICAN LAW

THOMSON

GALE

Detroit • New York • San Francisco • New Haven, Conn. • Waterville, Maine • London

THOMSON
™
GALE

American Law Yearbook 2007

Project Editor
Jeffrey Wilson

Editorial Support Services
Luann Brennan, Mike Lesniak, Selwa Petrus

Permissions
Margaret Chamberlain-Gaston, Aja Perales

Imaging and Multimedia
Lezlie Light, Robyn Young

Composition and Electronic Capture
Evi Seoud

Manufacturing
Rita Wimberley

ISBN 978-1-4144-0118-8
ISBN 1-4144-0118-3
ISSN 1521-0901

Printed in the United States of America
10 9 8 7 6 5 4 3 2 1

CONTENTS

The need for a layperson's comprehensive, understandable guide to terms, concepts, and historical developments in U.S. law has been well met by *West's Encyclopedia of American Law* (*WEAL*). Published in a second edition in 2004 by The Gale Group, *WEAL* has proved itself a valuable successor to West's 1983 publication, *The Guide to American Law: Everyone's Legal Encyclopedia*. and the 1997 first edition of WEAL.

Since 1998, The Gale Group, a premier reference publisher, has extended the value of *WEAL* with the publication of *American Law Yearbook* (*ALY*). This supplement adds entries on emerging topics not covered in the main set. A legal reference must be current to be authoritative, so *ALY* is a vital companion to a key reference source. Uniform organization by *WEAL* term and cross-referencing make it easy to use the titles together, while inclusion of key definitions and summaries of earlier rulings in supplement entries—whether new or continuations—make it unnecessary to refer to the main set constantly.

Understanding the American Legal System

The U.S. legal system is admired around the world for the freedoms it allows the individual and the fairness with which it attempts to treat all persons. On the surface, it may seem simple, yet those who have delved into it know that this system of federal and state constitutions, statutes, regulations, and common-law decisions is elaborate and complex. It derives from the English common law, but includes principles older than England, along with some principles from other lands. The U.S. legal system, like many others, has a language all its own, but too often it is an unfamiliar language:

many concepts are still phrased in Latin. *WEAL* explains legal terms and concepts in everyday language, however. It covers a wide variety of persons, entities, and events that have shaped the U.S. legal system and influenced public perceptions of it.

FEATURES OF THIS SUPPLEMENT

Entries

ALY 2007 contains 151 entries covering individuals, cases, laws, and concepts significant to U.S. law. Entries are arranged alphabetically and use the same entry title as in *WEAL* or *ALY*—when introduced in an earlier *Yearbook* (e.g., September 11th Attacks). There may be several cases discussed under a given topic.

Profiles of individuals cover interesting and influential people from the world of law, government, and public life, both historic and contemporary. All have contributed to U.S. law as a whole. Each short biography includes a timeline highlighting important moments in the subject's life. Persons whose lives were detailed in *WEAL*, but who have died since publication of that work, receive obituary entries in *ALY*.

Definitions

Each entry on a legal term is preceded by a definition, which is easily distinguished by its sans serif typeface. The back of the book includes a Glossary of Legal Terms containing the definitions for a selection of the most important terms **bolded** in the text of the essays and biographies. Terms bolded but not included in the Glossary of Legal Terms in ALY can be found in the Dictionary volume of WEAL.

Cross References

To facilitate research, *ALY 2007* provides two types of cross-references: within and following entries. Within the entries, terms are set in small capital letters (e.g., FIRST AMENDMENT) to indicate that they have their own entry in *WEAL*. At the end of each entry, additional relevant topics in *ALY 2007* are listed alphabetically by title.

Appendix

This section follows the Glossary of Legal Terms and includes ten organization biographies, covering groups not previously included in prior editions of WEAL or ALY.

Table of Cases Cited and Index by Name and Subject

These features make it quick and easy for users to locate references to cases, people, statutes, events, and other subjects. The Table of Cases Cited traces the influences of legal precedents by identifying cases mentioned throughout the text. In a departure from *WEAL*, references to individuals have been folded into the general index to simplify searches. Litigants, justices, historical and contemporary figures, as well as topical references are included in the Index by Name and Subject.

Citations

Wherever possible, *ALY* includes citations to cases and statutes for readers wishing to do further research. They refer to one or more series, called "reporters," which publish court opinions and related information. Each citation includes a volume number, an abbreviation for the reporter, and the starting page reference. Underscores in a citation indicate that a court opinion has not been officially reported as of *ALY*'s publication. Two sample citations, with explanations, are presented below.

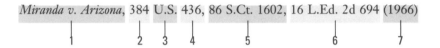

Miranda v. Arizona, 384 U.S. 436, 86 S.Ct. 1602, 16 L.Ed. 2d 694 (1966)

1   2 3 4   5   6   7

1. *Case title.* The title of the case is set in i and indicates the names of the parties. The suit in this sample citation was between Ernesto A. Miranda and the state of Arizona.

2. *Reporter volume number.* The number preceding the reporter abbreviation indicates the reporter volume containing the case. The volume number appears on the spine of the reporter, along with the reporter abbreviation.

3. *Reporter abbreviation.* The suit in the sample citation is from the reporter, or series of books, called *U.S. Reports,* which contains cases from the U.S. Supreme Court. Numerous reporters publish cases from the federal and state courts; consult the Abbreviations list at the back of this volume for full titles.

4. *Reporter page.* The number following the reporter abbreviation indicates the reporter page on which the case begins.

5. *Additional reporter citation.* Many cases may be found in more than one reporter. The suit in the sample citation also appears in volume 86 of the *Supreme Court Reporter,* beginning on page 1602.

6. *Additional reporter citation.* The suit in the sample citation is also reported in volume 16 of the *Lawyer's Edition,* second series, beginning on page 694.

7. *Year of decision.* The year the court issued its decision in the case appears in parentheses at the end of the cite.

Brady Handgun Violence Prevention Act, Pub. L. No. 103-159, 107 Stat. 1536 (18 U.S.C.A. § § 921-925A)

| | 1 | 2 | 3 | 4 | 5 | 6 | 7 | 8 |

1. *Statute title.*

2. *Public law number.* In the sample citation, the number 103 indicates this law was passed by the 103d Congress, and the number 159 indicates it was the 159th law passed by that Congress.

3. *Reporter volume number.* The number preceding the reporter abbreviation indicates the reporter volume containing the statute.

4. *Reporter abbreviation.* The name of the reporter is abbreviated. The statute in the sample citation is from *Statutes at Large.*

5. *Reporter page.* The number following the reporter abbreviation indicates the reporter page on which the statute begins.

6. *Title number.* Federal laws are divided into major sections with specific titles. The number preceding a reference to the U.S. Code stands for the section called Crimes and Criminal Procedure.

7. *Additional reporter.* The statute in the sample citation may also be found in the *U.S. Code Annotated.*

8. *Section numbers.* The section numbers following a reference to the *U.S. Code Annotated* indicate where the statute appears in that reporter.

COMMENTS WELCOME

Considerable efforts were expended at the time of publication to ensure the accuracy of the information presented in *American Law Yearbook 2007.* The editor welcomes your comments and suggestions for enhancing and improving future editions of this supplement to *West's*

Encyclopedia of American Law. Send comments and suggestions to:

> *American Law Yearbook*
> The Gale Group
> 27500 Drake Rd.
> Farmington Hills, MI 48331-3535

SPECIAL THANKS

The editor wishes to acknowledge the contributions of the writers and copyeditors who aided in the compilation of *American Law Yearbook*. The editor gratefully thanks Matthew Cordon, Frederick K. Grittner, Lauri R. Harding, and Mary Hertz Scarbrough. Furthermore, valuable content review of entries came from: Matthew Cordon, Frederick K. Grittner, and Lauri R. Harding.

PHOTOGRAPHIC CREDITS

The editor wishes to thank the permission managers of the companies that assisted in securing reprint rights. The following list—in order of appearance—acknowledges the copyright holders who have granted us permission to reprint material in this edition of *American Law Yearbook*:

A dose of the vaccine Gardasil, used the prevention of cervical cancer, photograph. AP Images—A still image of a computer screen showing the You Tube Web site, the subject of copyright lawsuits in 2007, photograph. AP Images—An airport sign details new travel regulations, January 2007, photograph. AP Images—Apple CEO Steve Jobs demonstrates the new Apple iPhone, January 9, 2007, photograph. AP Images—Attorney General Alberto Gonzales takes a question during a news conference on March 9, 2007, photograph. AP Images—Avery, Steven, in prison garb, is escorted out of court by a policeman in January 2006, photograph. AP Images—Carhart, Dr LeRoy, in his clinic, December 15, 2006, photograph.

AP Images—Cuomo, Andrew, and wife Carrie-Kennedy-Cuomo, June 10, 2002, photograph. AP Images—Davenport, Gary, sitting at desk in home, January 2007, photograph. AP Images—Exterior view of Genentech headquarters in San Francisco, January 2007, photograph. AP Images—File photos of Jefferson, William and Ney, Bob, Representatives, photograph. AP Images—Fitzgerald, Patrick, speaking at news conference October 28, 2005, photograph. AP Images—Foley, Mark, Representative, speaks at a news conference, March 2004, photograph. AP Images—Former Senator Mark Dayton listens to testimony, May 2006, photograph. AP Images—Former Westar Energy chief executive Wettig, David, leaves court after guilty verdict in his fraud trial, September 2005, photograph. AP Images—Franklin, Massachusetts, police officer Brian Johnson poses with computer displaying Youtube page on which he posted surveillance tape in hopes of gathering leads, photograph. AP Images—Lewis "Scooter" Libby (center) leaves federal court, flanked by his attorneys, March 2007, photograph. AP Images—Majority Leader Jerry Keen, center, discusses details of a proposed bill that would strengthen Georgia law against sex offenders, photograph. AP Images—McDarby, David, right, following guilty verdict against Merck and Co in Vioxx liability trial, photograph. AP Images—Michigan Governor Jennifer Granholm signs legislation making rental of adult-rated video games illegal to those under 17 years of age, photograph. AP Images—National Intelligence Director-designate Michael McConnell, testifying on Capitol Hill, Feb 1, 2007, photograph. AP Images—**New Jersey Governor Jon Corzine, sitting, signs civil union legislation on December 21, 2006, photograph.** AP Images—**Ney, Bob, center, leaving federal courthouse in Washington, October 2006, photograph.** AP Images—**Panetti, Scott, Texas Department of Criminal Justice, photograph.** AP Images—**Peters, Steve, April 2007, photograph.** AP Images—**Players at the San Miguel Indian Bingo and Casino play slot machines, June 2006, photograph.** AP Images—**President George W, Bush speaking June 7, 2006 about immigration reform in Omaha, NE, photograph.** AP Images—**Protesters demonstrate outside Philadelphia city hall against eminent domain, June 23, 2006, photograph.** AP Images—**Rambus Inc headquarters in August 2006, photograph.** AP Images—Scalia, Antonin, speaking at ACLU conference, October 2006, photograph. AP Images—**Seung-Hui, Cho, the shooter in the Virginia Tech shootings of April 16, 2007, photograph.** AP Images—**Smith, Kay and Phil, in their retail clothing store, March 2007, photograph.** AP Images—**Students demonstrate outside US Supreme Court, March 2007, photograph.** AP Images—**Studer, Jim, displays the button with the picture of his slain brother worn during the trial of Matthew Musladin, photograph.** AP Images—**Supreme Court Justice Anthony Kennedy testifies on Capitol Hill on March 8, 2007, photograph.** AP Images—**Texas Department of Corrections shots of Smith, Laroyce, Brewer, Brent Ray, and Abdul-Kamir, Jalil, photograph.** AP Images—**Three Kansas board of education members during voting on evolution measures, February 2007, photograph.** AP Images—**US Army Lt Colonel Steven Jordan arrives at military court for a hearing in the Abu Ghraib prison scandal, October 2006, photograph.** AP Images—**US House Speaker Nancy Pelosi, left, with Syrian Foreign Minister Walid al-Moallem in Damascus, April 4, 2007, photograph.** AP Images—**Yoo, John, law professor undated photograph.** AP Images.

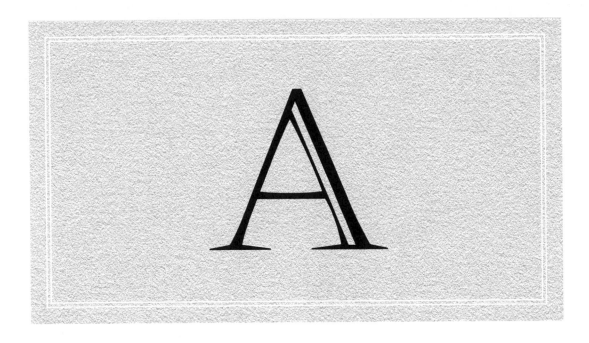

ABORTION

The spontaneous or artificially induced expulsion of an embryo or fetus. As used in legal context, usually refers to induced abortion.

Gonzales v. Carhart

Without question the issue of abortion has been one of the most controversial in recent U.S. History. Since the Supreme Court decided in *Roe v. Wade*, 410 U.S. 113, 93 S. Ct. 705, 35 L. Ed. 2d 147 (1973), that women have the right to have an abortion, opponents of the decision have sought to overturn it or, in the alternative, limit the procedure. In the late 1990s abortion foes succeeded in having several state legislatures outlaw what they labeled partial-birth abortion, a procedure in which a fetus is partially delivered, generally in the second or third trimester, before being aborted. Though Supreme Court overturned a Nebraska partial-birth abortion law in 2000, Congress passed the Partial-Birth Abortion Act of 202, 18 U.S.C.A. §1531, which tried to be more specific than the Nebraska **statute**. The U.S. SUPREME COURT, in *Gonzales v. Carhart*, __U.S.__, 127 S.Ct. 610, __L.Ed.2d __ (2007), upheld the act, ruling that it did impose an undue burden on a woman's right to end a pregnancy. The two newest members of the Court, Chief Justice JOHN ROBERTS and Justice SAMUEL ALITO, voted in the majority, confirming that the recent appointees had solidified the conservative base on the Court. The decision also revealed a new interest in the mother's health and safety.

LeRoy Carhart and three other doctors who performed second-trimester abortions filed suit in Nebraska federal **district court**, challenging the constitutionality of the act and seeking a permanent injunction against its enforcement. The court granted the injunction and prohibited the government from enforcing the act in all cases but those in which there was no dispute that the fetus was viable. It found the act unconstitutional because it lacked an exception allowing the procedure where it was necessary for the health of the mother. The 8th **Circuit Court** of Appeals affirmed this decision, relying on the Supreme Court's ruling on the Nebraska partial-birth abortion law in *Stenberg v. Carhart*, 530 U.S. 914, 120 S.Ct. 2597, 147 L.Ed.2d 743 (U.S. 2000). The Court had struck it down in part for the lack of a health exception for the mother.

The Supreme Court, in a 5–4 decision, overturned the Eight Circuit ruling. Justice ANTHONY KENNEDY, writing for the majority, held that the act did not violate a woman's right to an abortion. By doing so the Court endorsed Congress's view that this specific procedure was not necessary. Justice Kennedy described in graphic detail the nature of the banned procedure known as "intact dilation and extraction; the fetus remains unharmed until the end of the procedure when its skull is crush or the contents extracted to permit its removal. Opponents of the procedure argued that this was similar to infanticide because the unborn child could be alive when it was being removed. Of the 1.3 million abortions performed each year in the United States, 85 to 90 percent occur in the first trimester, which places these abortions outside the reach of the 2003 act.

Justice Kennedy stated that the government has "an interest in promoting respect for human life at all stages of pregnancy. The law need

Dr. LeRoy Carhart in his clinic, December 15, 2006.

AP IMAGES

Justices ANTONIN SCALIA and CLARENCE THOMAS filed a concurring opinion, reiterating their conclusion that *Roe* had "no basis" in the Constitution.

South Dakota Anti-Abortion Law Defeated

In March 2006, Governor Michael Rounds of South Dakota signed into law The Women's Health and Human Life Protection Act, the most sweeping yet of several state anti-abortion measures. House Bill 1215, overwhelmingly approved by the state legislature, banned all abortions excepting those involving **jeopardy** to the life of the mother. No exceptions were made for the circumstances of the pregnancy (e.g., incest or rape) or for general health considerations of the mother. Instead, the law focused on the sanctity of life, irrespective of how that life began, expressly recognizing "that each human being is totally unique immediately at fertilization." The Act further noted that under the state's constitution, "a pregnant mother and her unborn child, each possess a natural and inalienable right to life." (Section 1, H.B. 1215). The Act was to take effect in July 2006. Violations of the Act were punishable as felonies.

Immediately after it was signed into law, abortion rights advocates mobilized. Under South Dakota law, if opponents petition and collect 16,728 signatures from registered voters (the number applicable for the present controversy), a statute's effective date will be delayed until after it is placed on a the general election ballot for a statewide vote in November. By approximately a 55–45 percent margin, South Dakota voters rejected the new law in November 2006. Combined spending on the opposing campaigns exceeded $4 million in a state with a population of approximately 750,000. Campaign finance reports also indicated that an unidentified donor had single-handedly contributed $750,000 in support of the law. The debate split not only the general public but also the medical community, with public advertisements featuring doctors who offered differing interpretations of the law.

not give abortion doctors unfettered choice in the course of their medical practice." One possible outcome from the act was that it would "encourage" women to carry the fetus to full term, thereby reducing the absolute number of late-term abortions. Kennedy also posited a new concern: the well-being of the mother. Some women regret their decision to have an abortion and some would suffer "grief more anguished and sorrow more profound when she learns, only after the event, that she allowed a doctor to pierce the skull and vacuum the fast-developing brain of her unborn child." As to the legal arguments, Justice Kennedy found that the act would not be unconstitutional in most "relevant" cases. In addition, opponents of the act failed to show that it was "void for vagueness, an undue burden on a woman's right to an abortion based on overbreadth or lack of a health exception."

Justice RUTH BADER GINSBURG, in a dissenting opinion joined by Justices JOHN PAUL STEVENS, DAVID SOUTER, and STEPHEN BREYER, called it an "alarming decision" that was part of an effort to "chip away" at a woman's right to an abortion. Justice Ginsburg lamented that the decision endorsed federal intervention to ban a procedure "found necessary and proper in certain cases by the American College of Obstetricians and Gynecologists." Moreover, the Court's failure to require a health exception meant it had abandoned a long-held principle. As to the majority's claim that most abortions are performed early in pregnancy, Justice Ginsburg noted that adolescents and poor women have a hard time obtaining an early abortion, so the decision could put them at a disadvantage.

The legislature had admittedly passed the law in an effort to prompt a court challenge aimed at *Roe v. Wade*, the 1973 landmark decision recognizing the right of women to choose an abortion. More recently, in *Gonzales v. Carhart*, No. 05-380 (2007), the U.S. SUPREME COURT upheld the U.S. Congress' Partial Birth Abortion Act of 2003 that prohibits certain methods of terminating fetal life in later stages of pregnancy, but *Roe v. Wade* was left untouched.

Although opponents generally found the new law too severe, in retrospect, the language contained in the **statute** did invite alternative interpretations. For example, the bill provided that "nothing . . . may be construed to prohibit the sale, use, prescription, or administration of a contraceptive measure, drug or chemical, if it is administered prior to the time when a pregnancy could be determined through conventional medical testing . . ."

However, it generally takes approximately seven days for a fertilized egg to develop into a blastocyst capable of implanting itself in the lining of a woman's uterus. Once it is thus implanted, another week or so may be needed before even the most sensitive of commercially-available pregnancy tests can determine if a pregnancy has begun. Therefore, "conventional medical testing" might not be able to detect pregnancy until two weeks after fertilization (conception).

As a result, it would not be unreasonable to read the statute as permitting a two-week window following "fertilization" during which the administration of "contraceptive measures" would be legal, e.g., Plan B or intrauterine devices (IUDs) that work to prevent the implantation of an already fertilized egg. In the alternative, a strict reading of the language might have outlawed several previously-legal contraceptive methods.

Opponents to the law argued that it did not except abortions in cases of rape or incest. Supporters responded that the law would have allowed physicians to prioritize the lives of pregnant women with medical conditions or problems. They further argued that rape and incest victims were protected by one of the law's provisions expressly clarifying that nothing in the statute would prevent women from getting emergency contraceptives up to the point at which a pregnancy could be medically determined, e.g. "morning after pills."

Notwithstanding the ultimate outcome, several states were emboldened and encouraged by South Dakota's initiative. Legislators in Ohio, Georgia, Missouri, Mississippi, and Tennessee were working on language for similar bans in those states. However, some anti-abortion groups disagreed with the timing, instead opting to channel efforts into more widely-accepted abortion-reducing measures, such as parental and spousal notification laws and new clinic regulations.

South Dakota already bans human embryonic stem cell research and all human cloning and/or treatments or medicines derived from human cloning. (It does allow embryos to be created via *in vitro* fertilization.) The state also took the lead in the national debate regarding a pharmacist's right to refuse dispensing medication based upon his or her conscience. South Dakota law provides that pharmacists may refuse to dispense emergency contraception to women on this basis, notwithstanding if such emergency contraception is legally prescribed.

ADMINISTRATIVE LAW AND PROCEDURE

Administrative law is the body of law that allows for the creation of public regulatory agencies and contains all the statutes, judicial decisions, and regulations that govern them. It is the body of law created by administrative agencies to implement their powers and duties in the form of rules, regulations, orders, and decisions. *Administrative procedure* constitutes the methods and processes before administrative agencies, as distinguished from judicial procedure, which applies to courts.

President Approves Executive Order on Federal Environmental, Energy, and Transportation Management

President GEORGE W. BUSH on January 24, 2007 issued an executive order that establishes goals for energy efficiency, renewable energy, and water conservation, among other areas. President Bush approved the Executive Order 13423, entitled Strengthening Federal Environmental, Energy, and Transportation Management, as part of an agenda to reduce dependence on foreign oil. Several of the provisions in the new order correspond to requirements found in the Energy Policy Act of 2005, Pub. L. No. 109-58, 119 Stat. 594.

This new order consolidates the provisions of five executive orders that were issued between 1998 and 2000 by former President BILL CLINTON. These previous orders had established a series of goals, many of which had been exceeded by the federal government. However, a number of these goals had since expired by the terms of the orders themselves.

One of the primary goals of this order is to increase energy efficiency. The order specifies that the federal government should increase energy efficiency by three percent annually through 2015 or by an overall total of 30 percent by 2015. These numbers represent that same level of improvement that federal agencies achieved between 1985 and 2005 (29.6 percent during that period). The goals of the new executive order are 50 percent higher than those specified in the Energy Policy Act.

The order also addresses the issue of increased use of renewable energy. Executive Order 13123, issued on June 3, 1999, established a goal specifying that 2.5 percent of power needs must come from renewable sources. The Energy Policy Act of 2005 also established a renewable energy goal, but the **statute** does not require that any specific percentage come from new sources. Under the new order, at least 50 percent of current renewable energy purchases must come from renewable sources that have been in service since January 1, 1999.

The area of water efficiency is likewise an important part of the order, given that water efficiency and energy efficiency are closely related to one another due to the energy needs for pumping, treating, heating, and processing water. The order focuses on improving water efficiency by reducing water consumption by two percent annually. Water efficiency itself was not expressly included in the Energy Policy Act.

Executive Order 13149, issued on April 21, 2000, sought to ensure that the federal government encouraged reduced petroleum consumption by increasing the use of alternative fuel vehicles (AFVs) and alternative fuels themselves. The agencies were required to establish a compliance strategy that would reduce annual petroleum consumption by 20 percent in **fiscal** year 2005 as compared with fiscal year 2000. Executive Order 13423 updates the now-expired goals of E.O. 13149 by requiring a reduction of petroleum consumption in certain federal vehicles by two percent annually. The new order also mandates an increase in alternative fuel consumption by at least 10 percent annually and requires an increase in the purchase of AFVs when these vehicles become commercially available.

Building performance is another area addressed by the new order. Between 1985 and 2005, energy use in federal buildings decreased by 12.9 percent. On January 24, 2006, officials with the ENVIRONMENTAL PROTECTION AGENCY, along with representatives of several federal agencies, signed a memorandum of understanding entitled "Federal Leadership in High Performance and Sustainable Buildings," which commits these agencies to designing design, construct, and operate buildings in an energy-efficiency and sustainable manner. The new order seeks to continue to decrease building energy use by making mandatory the elements in the 2006 EPA memorandum.

Another memorandum of understanding related to electronic assets was also incorporated into the new order. In 2004, the Executive Office of the President and 12 federal agencies signed a memorandum entitled Promoting Sustainable Environmental Stewardship of Federal Electronic Assets, which focused in large part on the reduction of electronic waste. The memorandum defined "stewardship" to include "those concepts, strategies, tools, practices, and approaches that lead to environmental improvement in a manner that is sustainable over time; considers the long term effects as well as the shorter term, more immediate effect; and that contribute positively, even if indirectly, to the social and economic condition." Under Executive Order 13423, 95 percent of electronic products that are purchased by the federal government must meet electronic product environmental assessment standards. Moreover, every computer and monitor must have Energy Star features, and federal agencies must reuse, donate, sell, or recycle 100 percent of the electronic products by using environmentally sound practices.

Federal agencies additionally must expand purchases of environmentally-sound goods and services, and must take steps to reduce the use of chemicals and toxic materials. In order to implement the order, the roles of several federal agencies and offices, including the White House Council on Environmental Quality, the Office of the Federal Environmental Executive, the OFFICE OF MANAGEMENT AND BUDGET, have been clarified and expanded. Existing and new working groups will provide federal agencies with more detailed instructions about how to implement the new requirements.

ADOPTION

A two-step judicial process in conformance to state statutory provisions in which the legal obligations and rights of a child toward the biological parents are terminated and new rights and obligations are created in the acquired parents.

Custody Returned to Biological Parents After Seven Years

It started in 1999 when little Anna Mae He was only weeks old (she is referred to in court documents as "AMH"). At that time, an American couple was granted open-ended "temporary" custody of her, with hopes of eventual adoption. However, in 2007, the Tennessee Supreme Court returned custody of Anna Mae (now a young girl) to her biological parents, Chinese nationals who planned to take her back to China. The primary reasoning behind the court's decision was its conclusion that the biological parents, because of language barriers, did not understand the consequences of their earlier waiver of custody and parental rights to the American couple. *In Re Adoption of A.M.H.*, No. W2004-01225-SC-R11-PT, (2007).

Anna Mae's father, Shao-Qiang, moved to the United States in 1995 to attend Arizona State University, but ended up at the University of Memphis (Tennessee) on an economics scholarship, along with a graduate assistant position and small stipend. The mother of Anna Mae, although unmarried, nonetheless obtained a visa by representing that she was the father's wife and arrived in the United States in June 1998. One month later, she became pregnant with Anna Mae.

Shortly thereafter, in October 1998, a student at the University of Memphis filed charges of attempted rape against the father. During the pendency of the investigation and litigation, he lost his scholarship and graduate assistant position, along with the stipend. Unemployed and uninsured, he and the mother sought public assistance for their unborn child and met with a "birth-parent counselor" at Mid-South Christian Services in Tennessee. At trial several years later, one counselor testified that the parents, back in 1998 and 1999, desired that their unborn child be adopted by a financially stable family, but another testified that they wanted social assistance only.

In any event, on January 28, 1999, Anna Mae was born, and hospital records stated that she was not available for adoption. Instead, the parents sought temporary help with the care of their baby for six to twelve months, until they could regain financial stability. Just weeks after the birth, they appeared in juvenile court and asked for temporary foster care. The juvenile court office contacted Mid-South, which agreed to provide temporary foster care for Anna Mae. She was placed in the home of the Bakers, the American couple that would later seek termination of parental rights and adoption of the girl.

The parents did regularly visit Anna Mae at the home of the foster parents until April 1999, when the father was arrested on the attempted rape charge and (although released on bail the next day) again lost the part-time job he had obtained. At that time, the parents entered into an oral agreement with the Bakers, and in June 1999, both couples, along with an attorney from Mid-South, appeared in juvenile court for a consent order transferring custody of Anna Mae to the Bakers. A guardianship provision was added to the order so that the Bakers could obtain medical insurance and care for Anna Mae, as needed. The consent order did not mention child support or visitation. Moreover, later testimony would greatly vary as to the length of time contemplated by the couples for the "temporary" custody. The Bakers would later testify that the couples agreed that the Bakers would raise Anna Mae until she was eighteen, and that the parents agreed that Anna Mae could refer to the Bakers as "mommy" and "daddy."

In September 1999, the University of Memphis suspended the father and required him to attend sexual abuse classes. The father, having lost his status as a student, was subject to deportation. A series of failed communications between foster and birth parents ensued over the next six months, with the parents asking for their child back and the Bakers resisting. In May 2000, the parents filed a petition to have their daughter returned to them, but were denied based on income and the pending criminal charges against the father for sexual **battery**.

In February 2002, the father was acquitted of the criminal charges. During the pendency of the criminal charges and for two years thereafter, the biological parents attempted to see Anna Mae, but police kept them away from the Bakers' residence on the complaint of the Bakers, who were able to show authorities that they had custody and controlled visitation.

Memphis **Circuit Court** Judge Robert Childers terminated the parental rights of the biological parents in May 2004, on the Bakers' petition for same. The ruling was premised on the ground that the parents abandoned Anna Mae by willfully failing to visit her for four months. The parents appealed but the decision was upheld in November 2005. Again, the parents appealed and the Tennessee Supreme Court took up the case in October 2006.

In January 2007, the Tennessee Supreme Court reversed the lower courts. The court noted that parties seeking to terminate parental rights must prove two elements. First, they must prove **statutory** grounds for termination (in this case, alleged abandonment). Second, they must prove that a termination of parental rights is in the best interest of the child. According to court records, the sole ground for termination presented by the Bakers was the claim that the parents failed to visit Anna Mae for the four months preceding the filing of the petition for termination, which constituted abandonment of the child. A person who has abandoned a child by willfully failing to visit is "unfit" under state constitutional standards.

But the Tennessee Supreme Court, in reviewing the record, first found that the alleged abandonment was not "willful." Undisputed evidence showed the continued animosity between the two couples, and that the parents were actively pursuing custody through **legal proceedings** during the four-month period immediately preceding the filing of Bakers' petition. Accordingly, the court reversed the termination of parental rights.

But that was not enough to return the child to the parents. The 1999 temporary custody order still prevailed, unless that, too, could be reversed. After thorough review of the entire **appellate** record, the court found that, because of language barriers, the parents' consent to transfer custody and guardianship of Anna Mae was not made with a full knowledge or appreciation of the consequences. As such, the parents had a superior right to the custody of their child. Only a showing of substantial harm to the child would prevent returned custody. In fact, concluded the court, "the only evidence of substantial harm arises from the delay caused by protracted litigation and the failure of the court system to protect the parent-child relationship." The court ordered return of the child to her biological parents.

In May 2007, the Bakers announced that they would appeal the decision to the U.S. SU-PREME COURT.

AGRICULTURAL LAW

The body of law governing the cultivation of various crops and the raising and management of livestock to provide a food and fabric supply for human and animal consumption.

Jones v. Gale

The family farm in the United States has an enduring place in American history and culture, both as a means of agricultural production and as a way of life. The rise of corporate farming after WORLD WAR II worried many people, for the connection between the individual and the land was replaced with a faceless business **entity**. The state of Nebraska expressed its opposition to corporate and absentee ownership agriculture when its citizens in 1982 passed a state constitutional amendment that prohibited corporations or syndicates (non-family-owned limited partnerships) from acquiring an interest in "real estate used for farming or ranching" in Nebraska or "engage[ing] in farming or ranching." Almost 25 years later a group of Nebraska farmers filed a federal lawsuit, alleging that the amendment, known as Initiative 300, violated the U.S. Constitution's **Commerce Clause**. The Eighth **Circuit Court** of Appeals in *Jones v. Gale*, 470 F.3d(8th Cir. 2006), agreed with the plaintiffs and struck down the amendment as unconstitutional.

Initiative 300 clearly addressed the issue of corporate farming. An explanatory statement presented with the initiative stated that a vote for it would "create a constitutional prohibition against further purchase of Nebraska farm and ranch lands by any corporation or syndicate other than a Nebraska family farm corporation." The initiative defined a family farm or ranch corporation as one "engaged in farming or ranching or the ownership of agricultural land, in which the majority of the voting stock is held by members of a family . . . at least one of whom is a person residing on or actively engaged in the day to day labor and management of the farm or ranch."

Jim Jones and five other people with interests in Nebraska farm and ranch land operations filed a lawsuit against the state, alleging that the amendment violated their constitutional rights. One plaintiff who lived in Colorado but who had an ownership interest in several parcels of Nebraska farmland wanted to transfer his land to a limited liability entity so he could improve his **fiscal** planning and management of the farms. The amendment prevented him from creating this entity, which had led to economic losses. Another plaintiff operated a cattle feedlot that provided for the daily care and feeding of cattle owned by customers, some of whom did not live in Nebraska. The feedlot operator could not contract with non-exempt out-of-state corporations for the purpose of raising and feeding livestock for slaughter. This had hurt his business and prevented him from gaining free access to the national cattle market.

The Nebraska federal **district court** agreed with the plaintiffs and ruled the amendment unconstitutional. The state appealed but a three-judge panel of the Eighth Circuit Court of Appeals unanimously affirmed the decision. Judge Morris Arnold, writing for the court, first ruled that the plaintiffs had standing to bring the lawsuit. To demonstrate standing to bring a lawsuit the plaintiffs must show they suffered an actual injury that was traceable to the defendant's challenged actions. They also had to show that if they prevailed their injuries would be redressed. Judge Arnold noted the economic harm visited upon the plaintiffs because of the legal restrictions on nonresidents and corporations owning farmland and concluded that these were actual injuries that could be cured if they were successful in having the constitutional amendment struck down.

The substantive issue before the Eighth Circuit was whether the amendment violated the U.S. Constitution's Commerce Clause. The plaintiffs alleged a violation of the "dormant" commerce clause, which refers to the negative implications of the constitutional provision. The Commerce Clause gives Congress the power to enact laws effecting interstate commerce. The dormant commerce clause is the other side of the issue, prohibiting a state from passing legislation that discriminates or improperly burdens interstate commerce. In this context discrimination refers to differential treatment of in-state and out-of-state economic interests, with the in-state interests treated more favorably than the out-of-state interests. Judge Arnold concluded that the amendment was discriminatory on its face because its "prohibition against farming by corporations and syndicates does not apply to family farm corporations and limited partnerships in which at least one family member resides or engages in the daily labor and management of the farm." The amendment favored Nebraska residents and those nonresidents who live close to Nebraska and who could commute daily to the farm. The 1982 ballot language that accompanied the initiative clearly stated this point. In addition, the Nebraska Supreme Court had read the language of the amendment to mean that it prohibited "absentee ownership and operation of farm and ranch land by a corporate entity." The appeals court also found discriminatory intent in the amendment. The 1982 advertising campaign supporting Initiative 300 demonstrated this fact. In the court's view it was "clear beyond cavil that these ads bristle with an **animus** against out-of-state corporations." Therefore, the court ruled the entire amendment unconstitutional.

Tainted Spinach Leads to Sickness and Death

An outbreak of Escherichia coli (widely known by its abbreviation, E. coli) contamination in prepackaged spinach led to three deaths and left nearly 200 others sickened during the fall of 2006. Several months after the outbreak occurred, state and federal official determined that the source was a small cattle ranch about 30 miles from the central coastline in California.

Ingesting E. coli generally causes diarrhea and often results in bloody stools. Most healthy adult victims can recover after about a week. However, E. coli can cause hemolytic uremic syndrome, which is a condition that can lead to kidney failure, especially in cases involving those who are very young or very old. The bacteria reside in the intestines of cattle and other animals, and an outbreak of E. coli is often associated with contamination by fecal matter. The Centers for the Disease Control and Prevention estimates that 73,000 cases of infection occur each year and that an average of 61 deaths result from these infections. According to the CDC, major sources for the bacteria include meat (especially undercooked or raw hamburger), uncooked produce, raw milk, unpasteurized juice, and contaminated water.

The packaged lettuce and spinach industry, which has annual revenues of about $4 billion per year, has adopted safety measures to kill bacteria. This process involves washing lettuce and spinach in chlorinated water. However, this process kills only 90 to 99 percent of the bacteria, assuming that the process is conducted properly. Moreover, there are no means of completely killing all of the microbes on leafy greens that would be as effective as pasteurizing milk or juice without seriously damaging the lettuce or spinach product.

The outbreak in 2006 first surfaced on August 23, according to the FOOD AND DRUG ADMINISTRATION. However, the agency did not identify spinach as the cause of the outbreak until September 13. By that time, 50 people from eight states had become ill. Twenty of those who had become ill were from Wisconsin, including the first person to die as a result of tainted spinach. Consumers from Connecticut, Idaho, Indiana, Michigan, New Mexico, Oregon, and Utah also became ill after eating spinach. Most of the victims were older women. Federal health officials at that point warned consumers not to each bagged fresh spinach.

California was targeted as the likely source of the outbreak. About 75 percent of the nation's spinach supply comes from Salinas Valley in California, which produces a crop worth an estimated $200 million a year. Two of the largest companies that produce spinach include Natural Selection Foods and River Ranch. These companies supply their spinach to brands that package it. As news of the outbreak became widely known, a total of 37 of these brands of bagged spinach were recalled. The recall involved both organic and conventionally grown spinach products. Natural Selection is the larger of the two companies, and federal officials acknowledged that the company's production of spinach was the focal point of the investigation.

Less than a week after the report of the first death, the number of cases increased to 114 in 21 states. The FDA expanded its warning to consumers that they should not consume any fresh spinach. According to Dr. Robert Brackett, the director of the FDA's Center for Food Safety and Applied Nutrition, "That's because we learned that some of the companies that produced the consumer bag spinach also produced larger food-service size. We want to make sure consumers are aware that they don't consume any of the fresh spinach. We don't know whether it came from the bag or another state. We just don't have the focus down that much yet."

Spinach remained off the shelves until early October. CDC statistics indicate that a total of 199 cases arose in 26 states. Nearly 47 percent of the individual outbreaks occurred in three states, including Wisconsin (49 victims), Ohio (25 victims), and Utah (19 victims). Somewhat ironically, only two individuals from California were infected with the outbreak strain.

In March 2007, health officials announced that they had determined that the source of the outbreak was a small cattle ranch in San Benito County in California. The ranch is located near a field leached to spinach grower Mission Organics. Officials determined that E. coli found in river water and cattle and pig feces were "indistinguishable from the outbreak strain," though they were unable to determine how the bacteria contaminated the spinach that was sold. The ranch, which breeds cattle and horses, indicated that it was not under investigation at the outbreak. Mission Organics also indicated that although wild animals are present on the property, the company had not found animal tracks near the spinach fields.

Previous outbreaks have resulted from such sources as a Washington dairy that had distributed raw milk, pre-packaged salads, and undercooked Jack in the Box hamburgers. Between 1998 and 2004, the FDA inspected 36 domestic and foreign produce farms and determined that one-third of those used insufficient cleaning methods. The outbreak in 2006, along with pre-vious outbreaks, has led to calls for improved measures for cleaning produce.

ANTITERRORISM AND EFFECTIVE DEATH PENALTY ACT OF 1996

Roper v. Weaver

By a 6–3 vote, the U.S. SUPREME COURT ultimately dismissed its previously-granted **writ** of **certiorari** as "improvidently granted" in the case of *Roper v. Weaver*, No. 06-313, 550 U.S. ___ (2007). This case involved the Eighth **Circuit Court** of Appeals' questionable granting of *habeas corpus* relief in light of previous precedent as well as the Antiterrorism and Effective Death Penalty Act of 1996 (AEDPA), 110 Stat. 1214, 28 USC §2254.

As background, the AEDPA has a stated goal "to deter terrorism, provide justice for victims, provide for an effective death penalty, and for other purposes." By 'provid[ing] for an effective death penalty,' Congress intended to limit lengthy appeals that typically precede executions, to limit unwarranted federal intrusion into state **criminal law**, and to promote finality of state court decisions. Under AEDPA, **federal courts** cannot grant habeas relief in criminal cases unless the state court's decision "was contrary to, or involved an unreasonable application of, clearly established federal law, as determined by the Supreme Court of the United States."

Shortly after granting certiorari and hearing oral arguments in the present case, the Supreme Court issued its *per curiam* decision(by the Court and not written by any particular justice), characterizing the issue before it as follows: "We grant certiorari in this case . . . to decide whether the Court of Appeals had exceeded its authority under 28 U.S.C. USC §2254(d)(1) by setting aside a capital sentence on the ground that the prosecutor's closing statement was "unfairly inflammatory." . . . Our primary concern was whether the Court of Appeals' application of the more stringent standard of review mandated by the Antiterrorism and Effective Death Penalty Act of 1996 (AEDPA) 110 Stat. 1214, was consistent with our interpretation of that **statute**. Cf *Carey v. Musladin*, 549 U.S. ___ (2006). We are now aware of circumstances that persuade us that dismissal of the writ is the appropriate manner in which to dispose of this case."

The "circumstances" alluded to in the Court's opening paragraph involved two other capital punishment cases in which the same prosecutor made the same **closing argument** to the jury (one of the cases involved Weaver's co-defendant). Also, in each of the other cases (as in the present case), the defendant filed a petition seeking habeas relief *before* the effective date of AEDPA. In those cases, the courts granted habeas review, as the Eighth Circuit had done in this (Weaver's) case. However, in Weaver's case, it came in a roundabout way. His first petition was dismissed by the **district court** as premature, because Weaver's petition to the U.S. Supreme Court for review of his state courts' decisions (the Missouri Supreme Court) was pending. Once the Supreme Court denied his petition for state court review, Weaver then re-filed his habeas request. By this time, AEDPA had already gone into effect, imposing the stricter standard mentioned above. The district court denied relief again.

Although relief had been granted in the other two cases based on the more lenient pre-AEDPA standard for review, in Weaver's case, the Eighth Circuit (in reviewing the Missouri Supreme Court's decision) applied the stricter AEDPA standard. It nonetheless found that, since there was some Supreme Court precedent on guilt-phase closing arguments and penalty-phase closing arguments, there was "clearly-established federal law" that the prosecutor in Weaver's case violated.

Now it appeared that there were two errors. First, the district court did not have cause to dismiss Weaver's original pre-AEDPA petition. In *Lawrence v. Florida*, 549 U.S ___ (2007), the Supreme Court dispositively established that a district court was wrong in concluding that, if a person sought certiorari review (of state court decisions), he had to exhaust that remedy before filing a federal habeas petition. The Court in that case said that "[s]tate review ends when the state courts have finally resolved an application for state post-conviction relief."

Second, regarding the Eighth Circuit's substantive ruling that the Missouri Supreme Court had unreasonably applied "clearly established law," the Supreme Court has never ruled on whether closing argument statements, similar to the ones in these three cases, were inflammatory and required reversal of a sentence. Therefore, there was unlikely "clearly established law," as required under the stricter AEDPA standard.

But the Court's *per curiam* opinion did not address the question of whether the Eighth Circuit had substantively erred in its application of the AEDPA. Instead the Court dismissed the writ as 'improvidently granted." A decision on the

Eighth Circuit's application of AEDPA may have been "outcome-determinative," meaning that the outcome of the other two cases (that were not appealed) could affect the outcome of this one. The Court's dismissal let stand the Eighth Circuit's grant of habeas relief to Weaver, effectively setting aside his death sentence.

". . . [W]e find it appropriate to exercise our discretion to prevent these three virtually identically situated litigants from being treated in a needlessly disparate manner, simply because the District Court erroneously dismissed respondent's pre-AEDPA petition," said the Court."

Chief Justice JOHN ROBERTS concurred in the dismissal, although he "[did] not agree with all the reasons given in the *per curiam . . .*" (He did not expound.)

However, Justice ANTONIN SCALIA, joined in dissent by Justices Thomas and Alito, opined that the Court should have addressed the Eighth Circuit's application of AEDPA. While the dissent agreed that the district court had erred, the nature of that error had been clear way before *Lawrence v. Florida*. Weaver failed to raise this issue until the Supreme Court's merit briefing stage. As a result (opined the dissent), Weaver had been "rewarded" for failing to previously raise the issue of the prior erroneous dismissal, and this alone would have precluded Supreme Court review because Weaver had not "exhausted" his appeals on this issue.

But the dissent disliked that the majority had relied on this fact for dismissing the case. Justice Scalia pointed out that, in any event, no legal principle, i.e. "clearly established law," would have entitled Weaver to relief from the **collateral** consequences of an uncorrected judicial error. He clearly implied that the Eighth Circuit's application of AEDPA was erroneous, and cautioned other courts not to follow.

ANTITRUST LAW

Legislation enacted by the federal and various state governments to regulate trade and commerce by preventing unlawful restraints, price-fixing, and monopolies, to promote competition, and to encourage the production of quality goods and services at the lowest prices, with the primary goal of safeguarding public welfare by ensuring that consumer demands will be met by the manufacture and sale of goods at reasonable prices.

Bell Atlantic Corporation v. Twombly

When a plaintiff starts a civil lawsuit by filing a complaint, the plaintiff needs to include a short and plain statement about the claim that shows that the plaintiff is entitled to relief. The complaint does not need to include detailed factual allegations but labels, conclusions, and generic recitations of the elements of a cause action will not suffice. The rules of **civil procedure** do not seek to make it hard to initiate an action but they do mandate that the defendant is given fair notice about the claim and the grounds for it. In antitrust lawsuits where a conspiracy among companies is alleged the courts have had difficulty divining what a complaint must contain to allow the action to go forward. The U.S. SUPREME COURT, in *Bell Atlantic Corporation v. Twombly*, __U.S.__, 127 S.Ct., __L.Ed.2d__ 2007 WL 1461066 (2007), dismissed such an antitrust lawsuit because the complaint failed to provide facts that the companies agreed to take anti-competitive actions.

The case grew out of major changes in the telecommunication industry that began with the breakup in 1984 of AT&T into regional phone companies popularly known as "Baby Bells." These regional monopolies, known within the industry as "Incumbent Local Exchange Carriers" (ILECs), were excluded from competing with long-distance **carriers**. Congress altered this arrangement when it passed the Telecommunications Act of 1996, 110 Stat. 56, ordering ILECs to share their networks with "competitive local exchange carriers" (CLECs). CLECs were intended to foster competition in the local phone network business but the ILECs vigorously fought for changes in FEDERAL COMMUNICATIONS COMMISSION (FCC) regulations that limited the range of network elements that had to be shared with CLECs.

William Twombly and Lawrence Marcus filed suit in New York federal **district court** in 2003 against a group of ILECs, alleging that the companies had conspired to restrain trade in violation of §1 of the Sherman Act, 15 U.S.C.A. §1. The plaintiffs also asked the court to make the case a **class action** representing subscribers of local telephone and high speed internet services from 1996 to the present. The complaint alleged that the ILECs conspired to restrain trade in two ways. First, the ILECs engaged in "parallel conduct" in their respective service areas to prevent the growth of CLECs. They did so by allegedly making unfair agreements with CLECs, providing inferior service to them, and billing in ways that hurt the CLECs' relations with their own customers. This common motivation to damage the chances of CLECs succeeding led the ILECs to form a conspiracy. If any one ILEC had treated a CLEC fairly it would have exposed the anti-competitive behavior of the other ILECs. The plaintiffs' second allegation charged that the ILECs did make agreements to refrain from competing with each other. This was to be inferred from the fact that ILECs did not seek to become CLECs' in other ILEC markets.

The ILECs moved the district court to dismiss the lawsuit. The court agreed, dismissing the complaint for failure to state a claim upon which relief could be granted. Although the plaintiffs had used circumstantial evidence to show consciously parallel behavior, "conscious parallelism" was not by itself a conspiracy under the Sherman Act. The plaintiffs needed to allege additional facts that tended to exclude independent self-interested conduct for the defendants' parallel behavior. As presented, the ILECS had their own self-interest in defending their territories from CLECs. The court also rejected the second allegation, finding no alleged facts that showed the ILECs refrained from competing in other territories as CLECs contrary to the ILECs' "apparent economic interest." The Second **Circuit Court** of Appeals affirmed the dismissal and the Supreme Court agreed to hear the plaintiffs' appeal to address the proper standard for pleading an antitrust conspiracy.

The Supreme Court, in a 7–2 decision, upheld the Second Circuit. Justice DAVID SOUTER, writing for the majority, held that stating a Sherman Act conspiracy claim required "a complaint with enough factual matter (taken as true) to suggest that an agreement was made." There must be "enough fact to raise a reasonable expectation that discovery with reveal evidence of illegal agreement." Bare assertions would not be enough. Justice Souter raised the factor of legal costs when an antitrust complaint is allowed to proceed to the discovery phase. The potential expense for the defendants in this case would be enormous, for the potential class would have included at least 90 percent of telephone subscribers and the period of time covered occurred over a period of seven years. As to the two allegations in the present case, the Court agreed with the district court's conclusions. There was nothing in the complaint that "invests either the action or inaction alleged with a plausible suggestion of conspiracy." The actions of the ILECs could be explained by independent economic self-interest. The case must be dismissed because the plaintiffs "have not nudged their claims across the line from conceivable to plausible."

Justice JOHN PAUL STEVENS, in a dissenting opinion joined by RUTH BADER GINSBURG, was disturbed that the complaint had been dismissed before the allegations were admitted or denied by the ILECs. A court should not dismiss a case because it believes the allegations are not "plausible." Stevens believed the district court should have required the defendants to respond to the allegations using sworn depositions or other limited discovery methods. The parallel conduct might not have been the product of a conspiracy but that conduct was also "entirely consistent with the *presence* of the illegal agreement alleged in the complaint. The majority went too far in protecting the interests of antitrust defendants.

Credit Suisse First Boston v. Billing

Antitrust laws generally protect trade and commerce from such unfair practices as monopolies that impede or eliminate competition in capital markets, **price-fixing**, price-gouging, etc. In *Credit Suisse First Boston Ltd. v. Billing*, No. 05-1157, 551 U.S. ___ (2007), the Supreme Court was asked to decide whether defendant Credit Suisse First Boston Ltd. ("Credit Suisse"), a securities underwriter, was immune from private lawsuits filed by investors alleging violations of state and federal antitrust laws. Credit Suisse argued that those laws were effectively "trumped" by federal securities laws. In a very technical and lengthy decision, the Supreme Court agreed with Credit Suisse, holding that securities laws impliedly precluded the application of antitrust laws for the alleged wrongful conduct in this case. The high court's decision reversed that of the Second **Circuit Court** of Appeals, which had ruled in favor of the investors.

Several investors including Billing, the named plaintiff, sued sixteen of the largest national underwriting firms and institutional investors, including Credit Suisse, for violations of the Sherman [Antitrust] Act, the ROBINSON-PATMAN ACT, and state antitrust laws.

The gist of the allegations was that defendants violated antitrust laws when they formed syndicates and got involved in assisting several hundred technology-related companies with their initial public offerings (IPOs). The plaintiffs alleged that the defendants entered into illegal contract deals with potential purchasers of securities, holding back purchases unless (1) the purchasers committed to buy additional shares at a later date, at an escalated price (known as "laddering"); (2) the purchasers paid high commissions on subsequent purchases from the defendants; and (3) the purchasers agreed to purchase from defendants other less desirable securities (known as "tying"). The plaintiffs alleged that after the IPO, the purchase price of the securities was grossly and artificially inflated by defendants for their own profit and at the expense of the public.

In the **district court**, defendant underwriters (including Credit Suisse) moved for dismissal, claiming that even if plaintiffs' allegations were true, only securities laws and not antitrust laws could provide a remedy. Therefore, they were immune from private investor lawsuits under these antitrust laws. The district court agreed and dismissed plaintiffs' case.

The Second Circuit Court of Appeals, however, reversed. It reasoned that Credit Suisse and other defendants did not have implied immunity because the alleged illegal conduct, e.g., "tie-in" agreements that would require purchasers to pay inflated commissions, to purchase more shares in the aftermarket (following the IPO), and to purchase less desirable securities, was not authorized by securities laws. Therefore, there was no implied **repeal** of antitrust laws as applied to tie-in agreements. The defendants appealed and the Supreme Court accepted review.

Justice Breyer delivered the opinion of the Court, and he was joined by five others (Justice Kennedy took no part in the decision).

The Court characterized the issue before it as whether there was a "plain repugnancy" between the antitrust claims and the federal securities laws. The Court cited its relevant prior holdings, including that in *Gordon v. New York Stock Exchange, Inc.*, 422 U.S. 659 (1975), (quoting *United States v. Philadelphia National Bank*, 374 U.S. 321 (1963). Justice Breyer noted that these cases explained the need for "plain repugnancy," meaning that securities laws must be interpreted as implicitly repugnant or incompatible with the application of antitrust laws (as they relate to specific conduct) in order to preclude application of antitrust laws.

The Court noted that where regulatory statutes are silent about antitrust issues, courts must determine whether, and to what extent, if any, they might preclude the application of antitrust laws to fill the gap. *Gordon* (cited above) and other cases made clear that in making this determination, courts must decide whether, within context and consequence, there is a "clear repugnancy" between the two bodies; that is to say, whether they are clearly incompatible. A finding of incompatibility (i.e. **repugnancy**) would warrant an implication of preclusion.

In making this determination, it was critical to look at (1) the existence of regulatory authority under securities laws to supervise the activities in question; (2) any evidence that the responsible regulatory entities exercised that authority; (3) the resulting risk, if both securities and antitrust laws were applied, of having conflicting requirements, duties, privileges, or standards of conduct; and (4) whether the possible conflict would affect practices that lie squarely within an area of financial markets that securities laws seek to regulate.

The Court went on to detail the complexity and finer points of promoting and selling newly issued securities to keep a proper functioning and well-regulated capital market running smoothly. Clearly, Congress granted to the federal SECURITIES AND EXCHANGE COMMISSION (SEC) the authority to regulate and supervise such activities. The Court's analysis left it with the conclusion that, using the above analysis in conjunction with the alleged conduct in the present case, Nos. 1, 2, and 4 above were satisfied. However, the third consideration, i.e., whether any potential conflict would rise to the level of incompatibility, needed further review.

Looking to the plaintiffs' complaint, the allegations contained therein essentially attacked the *manner* in which the defendants were conducting practices clearly regulated by the SEC. Since a very complex line separates activity that the SEC permits or encourages, from activity that it forbids, the SEC is in the best position, i.e., has the most expertise, to distinguish where that line exists. Therefore, it would be incompatible and repugnant to that authority and expertise for antitrust laws to prevail.

Having found that all four conditions were satisfied, the Court held that securities laws generally policed by the SEC, and not the broader antitrust laws, controlled the alleged conduct in this case. The Court reversed the Second Circuit and remanded for further action consistent with its ruling.

Justice Thomas was the lone dissenter, who disagreed with the basic premise that the Court felt it had to decide upon. He argued that the securities laws were not silent, but rather contained "broad saving clauses that preserve rights and remedies existing outside of the securities laws."

Leegin Creative Leather Products v. PSKS

In an important antitrust case involving minimum **price-fixing**, the U.S. SUPREME COURT overruled a 96-year-old earlier case and held that such "vertical price restraints" are now to be judged by the rule of reason. *Leegin Creative Leather Products v. PSKS*, No. 06-480, 551 U.S. —— (2007). Overruled was the 1911 case of *Dr. Miles Medical Co. v. John D. Park & Sons Co.*, 220 U.S. 373, which had made such restraints *per se* illegal violations of the Sherman [Antitrust] Act, 15 USC §1. Antitrust laws generally protect trade and commerce from such unfair practices as monopolies that impede or eliminate competition in capital markets, price-fixing, price-gouging, etc.

Leegin Creative Leather Products (Leegin) was a small California manufacturer of women's specialty fashion and leather accessories. It wanted to keep its products more exclusive to trendy boutiques and shops with more personalized service. In 1997, Leegin instituted a pricing policy requiring its retailers to adhere to a minimum price, in particular for its Brighton line of products. One of its retailer clients, PSKS, dba Kay's Closet, refused to adhere to this policy and consistently priced Brighton products below the minimum set by Leegin. In return, Leegin suspended all shipments of Brighton products to PSKS in 2002, causing retail losses for Kay's Closet.

PSKS then sued Leegin, claiming that it entered into illegal agreements with retailers to fix prices, an automatic violation of the Sherman Act. It sought damages for past and future lost profits. At trial, Leegin tried to offer expert testimony about the pricing policy's pre-competitive effects, but the court excluded it. The jury returned a verdict for PSKS, awarding $1.2 million in lost profits, which was automatically tripled under **antitrust law**.

On appeal before the U.S. Court of Appeals for the Fifth Circuit, Leegin did not dispute that its policy amounted to price-fixing. Rather, it argued that consumers stood to benefit from the extra care and **personal service**, which the retailers, in return, could afford to expend on consumers because of their guaranteed profit margin. Leegin tried to urge the court to adopt the rule of reason, a familiar concept in antitrust law that calls for courts to evaluate the anti-competition effect of marketing restrictions on a case-by-case basis. However the Fifth Circuit declined. The Court stated that any pre-competitive justifications for Leegin's policy were rendered moot because the court was

Kay and Phil Smith in their retail clothing store, Kay's Closet, March 2007.

AP IMAGES

bound by Supreme Court precedent (the *Dr. Miles* case, above), which makes Leegin's policy a *per se* violation.

The U.S. Supreme Court accepted **certiorari**, and at the end of its 2006-2007 term, rendered a 5–4 divided opinion in the case. Justice Kennedy, writing for the majority, found Leegin's distinctions relevant and overruled the Court's previous decision in *Dr. Miles*. From now on, such vertical price restraints are to be judged by the rule of reason, said the Court.

The accepted standard for gauging whether a trade practice serves to restrain trade under §1 of the Sherman Act is the rule of reason, the Court held. This requires the fact-finder to weigh all of the circumstances, including specific information about the relevant business, as well as the restraint's history, nature, and effect.

Incorporating Leegin's argument, the Court noted that the rule of reason distinguishes between restraints with anti-competitive effect, which are harmful to consumers, and restraints with pre-competitive effect, which are in the consumers' best interest. A straight *per se* rule eliminates the need (and opportunity) to study a particular restraint's reasonableness in light of real market forces.

Looking to *Dr. Miles* as existing precedent, the Court found it necessary to examine the economic effects of vertical restraints or agreements that purported to fix minimum resale (retail) prices, in order to determine whether the

per se rule would still be appropriate. Upon examination, the Court found numerous justifications for pre-competitive restraints expounded upon in economics literature.

Vertical restraints pass down from manufacturers/producers to distributors and retailers. They affect *intra-* brand competition between retailers carrying the same brand. On the other hand, they may spread horizontally to affect *inter-* brand competition among manufacturers selling different brands of the same product.

The Court noted that minimum resale price maintenance can stimulate interbrand competition by reducing intrabrand competition among retailers selling the same brand. This is important because the primary purpose of antitrust laws "... is to protect interbrand competition." (The Court quoted from *State Oil Co. v. Khan*, 522 U.S. 3.

Notwithstanding, the use of minimum resale prices can also have anticompetitive effects, resulting in unlawful price-fixing, which is an ever-present temptation for powerful manufacturers or retailers.

Both sides considered, the Court concluded that it cannot be said that retail price maintenance always or almost always tended to restrict competition and decrease output. Vertical agreements have either precompetitive or anticompetitive effects, depending on the circumstances under which they were formed. The rule of reason is designed to accommodate both analyses, and therefore a preferred rule. Down the road, noted the Court, as trial and **appellate** courts become more familiar with such restraints by applying the rule of reason over the course of their decisions, they will more ably establish a litigation structure that ensures the elimination of anticompetitive restraints in the market.

Finally, the Court addressed the issue of *stare decisis*, i.e., the value of case precedent to abide by and adhere to. Because the Sherman Act is treated as a **common law statute**, said the Court, its prohibition on restraints of trade evolves to meet the demands and dynamics of present-day economic markets and conditions. Accordingly, *Dr. Miles* is overruled to facilitate that "evolving" prohibition without regard to precedent or *stare decisis*.

Justice Breyer filed a dissenting opinion, joined by Justices Stevens, Souter, and Ginsburg. They resisted the need to overrule *Dr. Miles*, finding Leegin's arguments not persuasive enough to erase such well-established precedent.

Weyerhaeuser Company v. Ross-Simmons Hardwood Lumber Co., Inc.

Federal antitrust laws are most frequently used to prevent a company from having **monopoly** power. If a company does acquire monopoly power the company can set prices that are not subject to competition. Companies are often accused of setting artificially low prices to drive other companies out of the market or out of business. However, there are situations where a company is accused of bidding up prices of raw materials so that other companies cannot acquire these materials and thus are drive out of the market. This practice of predatory bidding is called monopsony. The Supreme Court, in *Weyerhaeuser Company v. Ross-Simmons Hardwood Lumber Co., Inc.*, __U.S.__, 127 S.Ct. 1069, __L.Ed.2d __ (2007), was called on to decide whether the same legal principles needed to prove predatory pricing (monopoly) should be applied to predatory bidding (monopsony). The Court concluded that the same principles should apply, making it very hard for plaintiffs to prevail in such an antitrust action.

Ross-Simmons Hardwood Lumber Company started operating a sawmill in Longview, Washington in 1962. Weyerhaeuser Lumber purchased an existing sawmill in 1980 and steadily increased the size of its hardwood operation. In 2007 it owned six hardwood sawmills in the region. During this period Weyerhaeuser made large capital investments in the sawmills, using new technology to increase production. Ross-Simmons, Weyerhaeuser, and other hardwood mills obtain red alder sawlogs that are found in the Pacific Northwest. The mills acquire these logs in one of three ways. Some logs are harvested from land owned by the mills, others are obtained through short-and-long-term agreements with timberland owners, and others are purchased in the open bidding market. By 2001 Weyerhaeuser was acquiring bout 65 percent of the alder logs available on the open market in the region. From 1998 to 2001 the price of alder logs increased while the prices for finished hardwood lumber fell. This placed a strain on smaller sawmill companies because the cost of logs represents up to 75 percent of a mill's total costs. As a result Ross-Simmons saw its profit margin disappear. After several years of red ink that amounted to several million dollars, Ross-Simmons closed its sawmill in May 2001.

Ross-Simmons believed the bidding practices of Weyerhaeuser drove it out of business. It filed an antitrust lawsuit against Weyerhaeuser, arguing that the company had monopolized or attempted to monopolize in violation of §2 of the Sherman Act, 26 Stat. 209. Ross-Simmons claimed that Weyerhaeuser drove up the prices of alder logs to levels that severely reduced or eliminated the profit margins of the other competing sawmills. By overpaying for the logs Weyerhaeuser caused the log prices to rise to an artificially high level. Ross-Simmons pointed to the fact Weyerhaeuser's profits declined during the period it purchased a larger share of the logs at the higher prices. This chain of events was characterized as "predatory-bidding."

At the close of trial, Weyerhaeuser asked that the case be dismissed. The motion was denied. It then asked the court to use a proposed jury instruction on predatory bidding that incorporated the standards set out by the Supreme Court to determine if a company had violated **antitrust law** through "predatory pricing" practices. The court rejected Weyerhaeuser's proposal, issuing a jury instruction that said Ross-Simmons could prove that Weyerhaeuser's bidding practices were anticompetitive acts if the jury concluded that Weyerhaeuser "purchased more logs than it needed, or paid a higher price for logs than necessary, in order to prevent [Ross-Simmons] from obtaining the logs they needed at a fair price." The jury concluded that this was the case and awarded Ross-Simons $26 million, which was trebled under the Sherman Act to almost $79 million. The Ninth Circuit upheld the verdict, finding that "buy side predatory bidding" and "sell-side predatory pricing" were different enough to justify a different standard of proof.

The Supreme Court, in a unanimous decision, overruled the Ninth Circuit. Justice CLARENCE THOMAS, writing for the Court, noted that it had established two prerequisites to recovery on claims of predatory pricing. A plaintiff seeking to establish competitive injury from a rival's low prices "must prove that the prices complained of are below an appropriate measure of its rivals' costs." Second, the plaintiff must show that the competitor had a "dangerous probability of recouping its investment in below-cost prices." Thomas concluded that predatory-pricing and predatory-bidding claims were analytically similar. Both claims "involve the deliberate use of unilateral pricing measures for anticompetitive purposes." Both claims "logically require firms to incur short-term losses on the chance that they might reap supracompetitive profits in the future." Thomas noted that like predatory pricing, predatory bidding schemes were rarely tried and rarely successful, for a "rational business will rarely make this sacrifice." Moreover, the actions of a company like Weyerhaeuser could be seen as the "very essence of competition." The company could have had a "myriad" of legitimate reasons for paying the higher prices, for "this sort of high bidding is essential to competition and innovation on the buy side of the market." Therefore, the judgment was vacated and the case was remanded for a trial using the two requirements used for predatory pricing actions. These elements would be hard for Ross-Simmons to prove because it would have to show that Weyerhaeuser had a dangerous probability of recouping the bidding losses. Without proof of **recoupment** "a strategy of predatory bidding makes no economic sense."

APPELLATE REVIEW

Osborn v. Haley

The FEDERAL TORT CLAIMS ACT (FTCA), 28 U.S.C.A. §1346 waives the federal government's **sovereign immunity** in certain circumstances to permit persons to sue it for damages. Plaintiffs who sue federal employees in tort must also contend with the Federal Employees Liability and Tort Compensation Act of 1998, commonly called the Westfall Act, 28 U.S.C.A. §2679, which grants absolute immunity to federal employees for common-law torts. However, this immunity is limited to acts employees un-

dertake in the course of their official duties. The Supreme Court was called upon to interpret several issues involving the Westfall Act in *Osborn v. Haley*, __U.S.__, 127 S.Ct. 881, 166 L.Ed.2d 819 (2007).

Pat Osborn worked for a private company that contracted with the U.S. Forest Service to provide staff for a recreation area in Kentucky. While employed by the private company, Osborn applied for a trainee position with the Forest Service. Barry Haley, the Forest Service employee responsible for the hiring process, announced at a meeting that he had hired someone else for job that Osborn wanted. Osborn asked why she had not been informed of the decision before the meeting and Osborn made a joke at Haley's expense. After the meeting Osborn's supervisor told her to apologize to Haley but she refused. A few weeks later Osborn filed a complaint with the U.S. DEPARTMENT OF LABOR, asking that it investigate the hiring decision. She alleged that the Forest Service had not given her the appropriate veterans' preference points. The LABOR DEPARTMENT investigator interviewed Haley and concluded that the process had been conducted correctly and informed Osborn of the decision. That same day Osborn's supervisor again ordered her to apologize to Haley. Osborn refused and two days later she was fired.

Osborn filed a civil lawsuit in a Kentucky state court against Haley, her supervisor, and her employer, alleging that Haley tortiously interfered with her employment relationship and conspired to cause her **wrongful discharge**. Osborn specifically charged that Haley's action were in retaliation for her filing the Department of Labor complaint. The U.S. Attorney promptly invoked the Westfall Act. He certified on behalf of the Attorney General that Haley was acting within the scope of his employment at the time of the conduct alleged in Osborn's complaint. As is customary in Westfall Act proceedings, the certification did not state reasons for this determination. Having made the certification, Haley was dismissed from the lawsuit, the United States was substituted as the defendant, and the United States removed (transferred) the case to the U.S. **District Court** for Western Kentucky. The United States then moved to dismiss Osborn's case on the ground that she had not exhausted her administrative remedies under the FTCA.

Osborn challenged the substitution and the motion to dismiss. She contended that Haley's actions were outside the scope of his employment, which negated Westfall Act immunity.

The U.S. district court sided with Osborn because the United States had denied there had been any communication between Haley and Osborn's supervisor involving Osborn's dismissal. The judge reasoned that the government had to admit to the event central to the proof of Osborn's claim. Based on this reasoning the court declared the Westfall Act certification invalid and sent the case back to state court. The Sixth **Circuit Court** of Appeals reversed this decision, concluding that a Westfall Act certification is conclusive for establishing the **scope of employment** needed for removal to federal court. In addition, a district court must resolve the factual dispute over scope of employment at trial.

The Supreme Court, in a 7–2 decision, upheld the Sixth Circuit. Justice RUTH BADER GINSBURG, writing for the majority, first disposed of two jurisdictional issues. The district court's order rejecting certification and substitution was a reviewable **final decision** and the appeals court had jurisdiction to review this order. One federal **statute** forbade **appellate** review of Westfall Act decisions, yet Ginsburg found that the district court had no authority to send a certified case back to the state court. It made no sense to bar review of an improper decision. Therefore, the Court allowed appellate review in this "extraordinary case in which Congress ordered the intercourt shuttle to travel just one way-from state to federal court."

Turning to the substantive issues, Justice Ginsburg examined whether the U.S. Attorney validly certified that Haley was acting within the scope of his employment at the time of the conduct alleged in the complaint. Two Courts of Appeals had held Westfall Act certification was improper if the government denied the occurrence of the alleged injury-causing action. Several other courts sided with the Sixth Circuit's reasoning. Justice Ginsburg concluded that certification is proper even when the government determines that the action or episode never occurred. The term "scope of employment" encompassed "an employee on duty at the time and place of an 'incident' alleged in a complaint who denies that the incident occurred." To find otherwise would strip a federal employee of immunity "not by what the court finds, but by what the complaint alleges." Justice Ginsburg pointed out the absurdity of thinking Congress would have intended to protect a guilty employee but desert innocent ones.

Finally, Justice Ginsburg stated that the core purpose of the Westfall Act was to relieve employees from "the cost and effort of defending the lawsuit, and to place those burdens on the Government's shoulders." Therefore, immunity issues must be decided at the earliest opportunity.

Justice ANTONIN SCALIA, in a dissenting opinion joined by Justice CLARENCE THOMAS, argued that the statute barring appellate review of Westfall Act certification decisions should have been honored, even if the decision was erroneous.

ASYLUM

A sanctuary, or place of refuge and protection; in relation to aliens, asylum may be claimed in a foreign country if the alien has a well-founded fear of persecution and reprisals in his or her country of origin.

U.S. Asylum Process Needs Further Reform, According to Commission Report

The U.S. Commission on International Religious Freedom concluded that the HOMELAND SECURITY DEPARTMENT has failed to protect those who seek asylum in the United States. The report was a follow-up to one issued in 2005 in which the commission concluded that U.S. agencies treated those seeking asylum as if they were criminals. The report renewed calls by some organizations for Congress to approve legislation that would improve the asylum system.

Congress established the U.S. Commission on International Religious Freedom (USCIRF) as part of the International Religious Freedom Act of 1998, Pub. L. No. 105-292, 112 Stat. 2787. The USCIRF was created to monitor religious freedom in foreign countries and to provide advice as to how to promote religious freedom domestically. The **statute** also authorized the commission to appoint experts to study whether prior legislation interfered with the ability of those suffering from persecution to seek asylum in the United States.

The commission focused its study on the expedited removal procedures that were part of the Illegal Immigration Reform and Immigrant Responsibility Act of 1996 (IIRAIRA), Pub. L. No. 104-208, 110 Stat. 3009. Prior to its enactment, immigration inspectors could not legally require an improperly documented alien from leaving the country without following certain procedures, such as referring the alien to an immigration judge for a hearing. Under the IIRAIRA, the inspectors can summarily remove aliens who lack proper travel documents. However, the statute also includes provisions that prevent the expedited removal of refugees who flee persecution. Refugees who state that they intend to apply for asylum or who fear return to their place of origin are entitled to a "credible fear interview" by an asylum officer.

The report that the USCIRF issued in 2005 revealed that while those who seek refuge from persecution were being evaluated, they were treated much like criminals. They were subjected to strip searches, shackling, and solitary confinement. Moreover, the report indicated great disparities in who was granted or denied asylum, depending on such factors as where the aliens was located, the place from where the alien originated, and whether the alien was represented by a lawyer. For instance, a person seeking asylum who was in a detention center in New York or New Jersey faced much harsher treatment and was much less likely to be freed than a person detained in such places as Chicago or San Antonio. Similarly, more than 80 percent of Cubans were granted a permanent right to stay, compared with the fewer than five percent of those from El Salvador who are given the same right. This disparity was due in large part to the political power that Cubans possess in some parts of the country.

The 2005 report received extensive coverage from the media and has been used a valuable resource by both lawmakers and scholars, due largely to the access that the commission's experts had to the process. Members of the commission met with the Secretary of the Department of Homeland Security as well as with the Director of the Executive Office for Immigration Review to discuss the report's findings and recommendations. The report's overarching message was that expedited removal should not be expanded by the federal agencies until the many problems identified in the report were resolved.

Although the Senate Appropriations Committee asked the Department of Homeland Security to consult with the Executive Office of Immigration Review and report by February 2006 about how it would implement the study's recommendation, the Department never responded publicly to the study. The House of Representatives' Appropriation Committee made a similar request, to which the Department also failed to respond. The lack of response led members of Congress to draft legislative proposals that would make implementation of the study's findings mandatory.

Before any legislation was introduced, however, the USCIRF issued a report card that reviewed the expedited removal process in the two years that followed the release of the 2005 report. The report card, issued in February 2007, concluded that the Department of Homeland Security had not only failed to resolve the problem, but had also expanded expedited removal. The commission organized the report card by agency and included a summary of the original questions posed by Congress as well as summaries of the findings from the 2005 study. The agencies include Customs and Border Protection (CBP), which is part of the Department of Homeland Security; Immigration and Customs Enforcement (ICE), part of Homeland Security; U.S. Citizenship and Immigration Services (USCIS), part of Homeland Security; the Department of Homeland Security as a whole; the Executive Office of Immigration Review, a part of the Department of Justice; and the Departments of Homeland Security and Justice jointly. Each department or agency received a letter grade ranging from A to F.

The Homeland Security Department did not provide any information about steps that CBP has taken to implement the study's recommendations, and so CBP received an F in every category. ICE and the Department of Homeland Security both received D grades for having implemented only a few of the recommended changes. The Executive Office of Immigration Review and the USCIS both fared better, earning grades of C+ and B respectively. The report card credited the USCIS with implementing quality assurance review for certain determinations.

The commission's report card prompted the National Immigrant Justice Center, as well as other groups, to call for legislation that would mandate implementation of the 2005 study's recommendations. Senator Joe Lieberman (Ind.-Conn.) has expressed support for the introduction of such a bill.

BANKS AND BANKING

Authorized financial institutions and the business in which they engage, which encompasses the receipt of money for deposit, to be payable according to the terms of the account; collection of checks presented for payment; issuance of loans to individuals who meet certain requirements; discount of commercial paper; and other money-related functions.

Watters v. Wachovia Bank, N.A.

The federal government regulates federally chartered banks, while the states have the authority to regulate state chartered banks. States that seek to regulate federally chartered banks are prohibited through the doctrine of **preemption**, which recognizes the constitutional authority to completely control areas such as interstate commerce. Despite this apparently clear demarcation in state and federal bank regulatory powers, the state of Michigan challenged a ruling that it could not regulate a subsidiary of a national bank that had originally been states chartered. The U.S. SUPREME COURT, in *Watters v. Wachovia Bank, N.A.*, __U.S.__, 127 S.Ct. 1559, __L.Ed.2d __ (2007), ruled that a national bank's mortgage business, whether conducted by the bank itself or through the bank's operating subsidiary, was subject only to federal regulation.

The State of Michigan banking laws required mortgage lenders were subsidiaries of national banks to register with the state's Office of Insurance and Financial Services (OIFS) and submit to state supervision. From 1997 to 2003,

Wachovia Mortgage was registered with OIFS, paying an annual fee and opening its books and records for inspection by OIFS examiners. In 2003 the company became a wholly owned subsidiary of Wachovia Bank, a federally chartered bank with corporate headquarters in North Carolina. Soon after the acquisition Wachovia Mortgage notified OIFS that it was surrendering its mortgage lending registration. As an operating subsidiary of a national bank it contended that the state's registration and inspection requirements were preempted. Linda Watters, the commissioner of OIFS, responded in a letter, advising Wachovia Mortgage it would not be authorize to conduct further mortgage lending in Michigan.

Wachovia Mortgage and Wachovia Bank filed suit in Michigan federal **district court**, asking it to prohibit Watters from enforcing Michigan's registration prescriptions. They argued that under federal banking law, the Office of the **Comptroller** of the Currency (OCC) was the only **entity** that had supervisory authority over Wachovia Mortgage. Watters countered by claiming that Wachovia Mortgage was not itself a national bank and thus the state was not preempted from regulating it. In addition, Watters claimed the TENTH AMENDMENT prohibited OCC's exclusive oversight of lending activities conducted through national bank operating subsidiaries. The district court sided with Wachovia, deferring to OCC's determination that an operating subsidiary is subject to state regulation only to the extent that the parent bank would be if it performed the same functions. The district court also rejected Watter's Tenth Amendment claim. The Sixth **Circuit Court** of Appeals affirmed the district court.

The Supreme Court, in a 5 to 3 decision (Justice CLARENCE THOMAS did not participate because members of his family were employed by Wachovia Bank), upheld the Tenth Circuit ruling. Justice RUTH BADER GINSBURG, writing for the majority, noted that the National Bank Act (NBA), first enacted in 1864, established a system of national banking that was still in force. One provision stated that "No national bank shall be subject to any visitorial powers except as authorized by Federal law." 12. U.S.C.A. §484(a). Visitorial powers include the power to regulate and the authority to examine bank records and books. In addition, Justice Ginsburg cited prior cases where the Court made clear that "federal control shields national banking from unduly burdensome and duplicative state regulation." These facts were buttressed by an NBA provision that authorized national banks to engage in mortgage lending, subject to OCC regulation.

Though Michigan law did exempt national banks from OIFS oversight, Watters argued that state regulation survived preemption when the institution was a national bank's operating subsidiary. Because Wachovia Mortgage had been chartered under state law, it was not an operating subsidiary but merely an "affiliate" of the national bank. Such affiliates could be regulated by both the OCC and the state. Justice Ginsburg rejected this argument. Since 1966 the OCC had recognized the authority of national banks to do business through operating subsidiaries. In 1999 Congress defined and regulated financial subsidiaries, distinguishing national bank affiliates from operating subsidies as defined by the OCC. The latter were subject to the same terms and conditions that govern national banks. The OCC regulations, which treated national banks and their operating subsidiaries as a single economic unit, were reasonable. Therefore, the Court must defer to the OCC's interpretation. As to the Tenth Amendment, Justice Ginsburg found Watters' claim meritless. If a power is delegated to Congress in the Constitution, the Tenth Amendment "expressly disclaims any reservation of that power to the States."

Justice JOHN PAUL STEVENS, in a dissenting opinion joined by Chief Justice JOHN ROBERTS and Justice ANTONIN SCALIA, contended that Congress had not enacted a law that immunized "national bank subsidiaries from compliance with nondiscriminatory state laws regulating the business activities of mortgage brokers and lenders." Therefore, the OCC did not have the power to preempt state law through its regulations.

BANKRUPTCY

A federally authorized procedure by which a debtor—an individual, corporation, or municipality—is relieved of total liability for its debts by making court-approved arrangements for their partial repayment.

Marrama v. Citizens Bank of Massachussetts

Under the federal Bankruptcy Code an insolvent individual may file a petition for protection under either Chapter 7 or Chapter 13 of the code. Chapter 7 authorizes a discharge of debts following the **liquidation** of the debtor's assets by a bankruptcy **trustee**. The trustee uses the proceeds to pay the creditors. Chapter 13 authorizes an individual with regular income to obtain a discharge after the successful completion of a payment plan approved by the bankruptcy court. Unlike Chapter 7, where the trustee controls the debtor's assets, Chapter 13 allows the debtor to retain possession of the debtor's property. In addition, a Chapter 7 proceeding may be converted into a Chapter 13 proceeding and vice versa. However, questions arose in the **federal courts** over whether a Chapter 7 debtor who acts in **bad faith** may convert the proceeding to a Chapter 13 case. The Supreme Court, in *Marrama v. Citizens Bank of Massachusetts*, ___U.S.___, 127 S.Ct. 1105, ___L.Ed.2d ___ (2007), ruled that a bad-faith Chapter 7 debtor forfeits the right to convert the bankruptcy into a Chapter 13 proceeding.

In March 2003 Robert Marrama filed a Chapter 7 petition and the bankruptcy court appointed a trustee to manage his assets. In his petition Marrama made misleading or inaccurate statements about his principal asset, a house in Maine. Though he was sole beneficiary of the trust that owned the property, he listed its value as zero. He denied transferring the Maine property other than in the ordinary course of business but he later admitted he had transferred it to protect it from creditors. At the meeting of the creditors the trustee informed Marrama that he intended to recover the Maine house as an estate asset to be used to pay his creditors. After the meeting Marrama filed a notice to convert the Chapter 7 action into a Chapter 13 proceeding. The trustee and Citizens Bank of Massachusetts, the principal creditor, filed objections, arguing that Marrama's attempt to conceal the Maine property was made in bad faith and was an abuse of the bankruptcy process. At a hearing on the conversion issue Marrama's lawyer attributed the misstatements about the Maine property to **clerical error** and stated that his client sought Chapter 13 status because he had recently become employed, which is a Chapter 13 requirement. The bankruptcy judge rejected Marrama's explanations and concluded that the facts established a bad faith case. The judge denied the conversion to Chapter 13. Marrama appealed to the Bankruptcy **Appellate** Panel for the First Circuit, contending that he had an absolute right under §706(a) of the Code to convert his case from Chapter 7 to Chapter 13. The panel affirmed the bankruptcy court's decision, holding that petitioners had an absolute right to convert from Chapter 7 to Chapter "only in the absence of extreme circumstances." The record disclosed such circumstances, including the concealment of the Maine property, an attempt to obtain a **homestead** exemption on rental property in Massachusetts, and the nondisclosure of an anticipated tax refund. The First **Circuit Court** of Appeals affirmed the panel decision, noting that §706(a) uses the word "may" rather than "shall."

The Supreme Court, in a 5–4 decision, agreed with the First Circuit ruling. Justice JOHN PAUL STEVENS, writing for the majority, looked to §706(d) to condition the apparent absolute right of a Chapter 7 petitioner to convert it into a Chapter 13 case. This provision stated that "Notwithstanding any other provisions, a case may not be converted to a case under another chapter of this title unless the debtor maybe a debtor under such chapter." Justice Stevens interpreted this to mean Marrama's right to convert was conditioned on his ability to qualify as a debtor under Chapter 13. In addition, §1307(c) of the Code gives the bankruptcy court the authority to dismiss or convert a Chapter 13 proceeding to a Chapter 7 proceeding for cause. Though bad faith is not listed in the code as a cause justifying this relief, Justice Stevens noted that bankruptcy courts "routinely treat dismissal for prepetition bad-faith conduct as implicitly authorized by the words "for cause." Such a Chapter 13 dismissal or conversion to Chapter 7 was "tantamount to a ruling that the individual does not qualify as a debtor under Chapter 13." Therefore, there was no absolute right to convert from Chapter 7 to Chapter 13.

Justice Samuel Alito, in a dissenting opinion joined by Chief Justice JOHN ROBERTS, ANTONIN SCALIA, and CLARENCE THOMAS, contended that under the "clear terms" of the Code a debtor under Chapter 7 had an absolute right to convert the case. Marrama should have been permitted to convert his plan to Chapter 13. At that point the bankruptcy court could have reconverted the case to a Chapter 7 liquidation, or required him to file a repayment plan that satisfied the creditors. Alito pointed out that Marrama's asset schedules were filed under penalty of perjury and that in Chapter 13 cases a trustee is empowered to investigate the debtor's financial affairs, make reports, and, if necessary, object to the debtor's discharge from bankruptcy. These provisions, rather than the "good faith" test announced by the majority, were the way Congress intended the courts to police abuse.

Travelers Casualty & Surety Co. of America v. Pacific Gas & Electric Co.

On March 20, 2007, the U.S. SUPREME COURT vacated a decision of the Ninth **Circuit Court** of appeals regarding the award of attorney's fees that were incurred by a creditor during a bankruptcy proceeding. The Ninth Circuit had applied a rule that prohibited recovery of attorney's fees during litigation of issues "peculiar to bankruptcy law," as opposed to the law of contracts. The Supreme Court determined that this rule had no basis in the Bankruptcy Code.

Travelers Casualty and Surety Company issued a $100 million surety bond on behalf of Pacific Gas and Electronic Company (PG & E) to the California Department of Industrial Relations. The bond was necessary to guarantee the utility company's payment of workers compensation benefits to employees who were injured at work. PG & E also executed a series of agreements to indemnify Travelers should the utility company default on its workers compensation obligations. These indemnity agreements provided that PG & E would pay any attorney's fees that Travelers incurred while pursuing, protecting, or litigating Travelers' rights in connection with the bonds.

On April 6, 2001, subsequent to the issuance of the bond and the signing of the indemnification agreements, PG & E filed Chapter 11 bankruptcy. PG & E did not default on its workers compensation obligations and in fact obtained an order from the bankruptcy court allowing the company to continue making its workers compensation payments. Five months after PG & E filed for bankruptcy, Travelers filed a protective proof of claim to assert its rights for future reimbursement and **subrogation** rights under the agreements it signed with PG & E. In other words, Travelers sought to protect its rights in the event that PG & E defaulted on its workers compensation payments in the future. If PG & E had defaulted, Travelers would have been obligated under its bond to make payments.

Travelers objected to the first plan of reorganization that PG & E filed with the bankruptcy court on September 20, 2001. Travelers argued that the plan did not provide adequate information about the **disposition** of the bonds and PG & E's obligations to Travelers under those bonds. Throughout much of 2002, Travelers and PG & E continued to have disagreements about PG & E's reorganization plans.

The parties ultimately agreed that because PG & E had not defaulted on its workers compensation obligations, Travelers' claims should be disallowed. However, the parties also agreed that Travelers could assert its claim for attorney's fees under the indemnity agreements as a general unsecured creditor. After this stipulation was accepted by the bankruptcy court, Travelers submitted a proof of claim on January 6, 2003, for attorney's fees and costs totaling more than $167,000. PG & E objected to this claim on for a variety of reasons, asserting that Travelers had not provided sufficient documentation to support the claim and that the fees were not compensable under the various agreements that the parties had signed. PG & E also argued that the fees were not reimbursable under controlling bankruptcy law.

The bankruptcy court held a hearing on the issue of Travelers' claim for attorney's fees. On July 11, 2003, the court disallowed Travelers' claim. Travelers then appealed the decision of the bankruptcy court to the U.S. **District Court** for the Northern District of California. The district court reviewed the framework of the Bankruptcy Code and determined attorney's fees may be allowed when state law governs a substantive issue that is being litigated by the parties. However, the court determined that attorney's fees are not recoverable when the substantive issues raise federal bankruptcy law issues rather than state law issues. Because the court ruled that Travelers had raised federal bankruptcy issues, the court affirmed the bankruptcy court's decision. *In re Pacific Gas & Elec. Co.*, NO. C-03-3499 PJH, 2004 WL 5167592 (N.D. Cal. 2004).

Travelers appealed the decision to the Ninth Circuit Court of Appeals. The Ninth Circuit determined that its prior decision in *In re Fobian*, 951 F.2d 1149 (9th Cir. 1991) governed this issue. In that case, the Ninth Circuit held that "where the litigated issues involve not basic contract enforcement questions, but issues peculiar to federal bankruptcy law, attorney's fees will not be awarded absent **bad faith** or harassment by the losing party." In a brief opinion, the Ninth Circuit affirmed the district court's decision. *Travelers Cas. & Sur. Co. of Am. v. Pac. Gas & Elec. Co.*, 167 F. Appx., 2006 WL 285977 (9th Cir. 2006).

The Supreme Court agreed to hear the case due to a split among federal circuits about the issue of attorney's fees. In an unanimous decision, the Court reversed the Ninth Circuit's decision in an opinion written by Justice Samuel Alito. Alito's opinion focused on the language of the Bankruptcy Code, specifically on the provisions in 11 U.S.C. §502(b)(1) (2000), which disallows certain claims. Under this section, the Code disallows a claim that is "unenforceable against the debtor and property of the debtor, under any agreement or applicable law for a reason other than because such claim is continent or unmatured." According to the Court, disallowance of attorney's fees would have to be based on §502(b)(1).

The Court noted that the Ninth Circuit had relied on a rule of its own creation rather than relying on the text of the Bankruptcy Code. The Court determined that neither *Fobian* nor other cases on which *Fobian* relied was based on the language in §502(b)(1). "Significantly, in none of those cases did the court identify any basis for disallowing a contractual claim for attorney's fees incurred litigating issues of federal bankruptcy law," Alito wrote. "Nor did the court have occasion to do so; in each of those cases, the claim for attorney's fees failed as a matter of state law."

Because the Ninth Circuit's rule was inconsistent with the text of the Bankruptcy Code, the court vacated the lower court's decision and remanded the case to the Ninth Circuit for further proceedings. *Travelers Cas. & Sur. Co. of Am. v. Pac. Gas & Elec. Co.*, ___ U.S. ___, 127 S. Ct. 1199, ___ L. Ed. 2d ___ (2007).

BRIBERY

The offering, giving, receiving, or soliciting of something of value for the purpose of influencing the action of an official in the discharge of his or her public or legal duties.

Representatives Robert Ney, William Jefferson Face Bribery Charges

It started with an announcement, in August 2006, that Representative Robert W. Ney

(R-Ohio) would not seek a seventh term in the U.S. House of Representatives. Ney, 52, was the last of three House members to fall under an ongoing federal investigation into widespread bribery and influence-peddling in Congress. Representative Randy "Duke" Cunningham (R-Cal.) had pleaded guilty to accepting more than $2.4 million in bribes from defense contractors, and Representative Tom DeLay (R-Tex.) resigned from the House after two of his former aides pleaded guilty to corruption charges. Ney and his former longtime chief of staff, Neil G. Volz were implicated in several guilty pleas entered by former lobbyist Jack Abramoff and three co-conspirators, whose activities triggered the expanding investigation two years earlier.

Abramoff and Volz (who had since joined Abramoff's lobbying firm) had already pleaded guilty to related charges, and as part of that plea, agreed to help investigators. (Volz's confession included language that he had conspired to unjustly enrich himself by providing "a stream of things of value with the intent to influence and reward official acts.") Moreover, three senior Ney aides had already resigned when a fourth was ordered by federal prosecutors to provide documents and testify before a federal **grand jury** regarding Ney's dealings with Abramoff. Buckling under the investigation and at the behest of House Speaker Dennis Hastert, Ney had given up the chairmanship of the Administration Committee in January 2006. Notwithstanding, Ney denied and wrongdoing and stated that he resigned for political and personal family reasons, not legal considerations. According to filed campaign reports, Ney spent nearly $300,000 in campaign funds to pay for legal expenses.

Court documents alleged that, at Abramoff's request, Ney helped secure government contracts, promoted the gambling interests of Indian tribes, and helped delay minimum wage legislation helpful to a garment maker in the Northern Mariana Islands. He did this mostly by making floor speeches in Congress helpful to these causes and inserting favorable statements in the **Congressional Record**. In return, Ney accepted lavish gifts from Abramoff and his associates, including a golf vacation to Scotland, a trip to the Fiesta Bowl in Arizona, trips to New Orleans and Lake George, New York, meals and entertainment, and tickets to a U2 concert, the value of which was estimated at well over $170,000. Other charges included his acceptance of thousands of dollars in campaign contributions in return for

Jefferson   Ney

official favors for Abramoff clients. He also allegedly accepted more than $50,000 in gambling chips from a foreign businessman seeking to gain an exemption from U.S. laws that prohibit the selling of domestically-manufactured aircraft and aircraft parts in a foreign country. A Senate Indian Affairs Committee report suggested that Ney had made untrue statements to committee investigators as well.

In September 2006, news broke that Ney had agreed to enter guilty pleas to criminal charges of conspiracy and making false statements in the U.S. **District Court** in Washington, DC. He was the first member of Congress to confess to crimes in the Abramoff scandal. As part of his guilty plea, Ney admitted to concealing gifts by filing false reports with U.S. Customs and false travel and financial disclosure reports required by the U.S. House. He also admitted to encouraging Volz ("conspiring") to violate the one-year ban against lobbying by former staff members. Ney further admitted that he attempted to insert four provisions into a 2002 campaign finance bill in order to help a Texas Indian tribe and Abramoff client reopen a casino; helping another Abramoff client, a foreign beverage distiller, to improperly label its imported products; causing the GENERAL SERVICES ADMINISTRATION (GSA) to transfer property to a religious school founded by Abramoff; helping another Abramoff client secure a wireless communications contract at the Capitol; and inserting statements in the Congressional Record to help Abramoff and a partner purchase the SunCruz casino ship line.

Following the announcement that Ney had agreed to plead guilty to one count each of con-

File photos of Representatives William Jefferson and Bob Ney, both subjects of ethics investigations.
AP IMAGES

spiracy and making false statement charges, Ney's formal plea was delayed while he voluntarily entered a one-month alcohol treatment program. Upon completion, he appeared in federal court to enter formal plea before U.S. District Court Judge Ellen S. Huvelle. He made no statement in court, but repeatedly answered, "That's accurate, Your Honor," as she read his admissions. With the acceptance of the guilty pleas, Ney became the eighth person convicted in connection with the Abramoff investigation. After his court appearance, Ney issued a formal statement that he was "ashamed" that his long career in public service had ended this way.

Ironically, in early 2006, Ney's committee passed ethics legislation intended to strip **pension** benefits from convicted members of Congress, but the bill died in the House. Ney had personally championed the bill.

One month after entering his guilty pleas, and only days before the November elections, Ney resigned his seat in Congress. Printed under his House letterhead, his resignation letter stated: "Having completed all outstanding work in my congressional office, I now hereby resign from the United States House of Representatives effective close of business on Friday, Nov. 3, 2006."

In January 2007, Judge Huvelle sentenced Ney to 30 months in prison and a $6,000 fine. The sentence was three months more than the 27-month imprisonment requested by prosecutors, because Ney had violated the trust placed in him as a public official, Huvelle said. She also ordered his enrollment in a prison alcohol treatment program. Ney was to serve his time at a federal prison in Morgantown, West Virginia and complete two years' probation upon release.

Born in Wheeling, West Virginia, Ney is a former teacher (B.S. Ohio State University) who previously served as program manager of health and education for the Ohio Office of Appalachia. He also served for several years as an Ohio state legislator prior to being elected to the U.S. House of Representatives

Ney was not the only Congressman to face bribery charges. William Jefferson, a Democratic congressman from Louisiana. Jefferson, who had faced called for ethics committee investigations in Congress, was finally indicted in June 2007 on charges that he had solicited bribes and used his office to make business deals for himself and family members. His indictment includes 16 charges, including racketeering and wire fraud, and could lead to a maximum of 235 years in prison. FBI videotape shows Jefferson accepting a box of cash from an informer, and a later raid of his home found $90,000 in a box in his freezer.

Jefferson claimed complete innocence, pleading not guilty to all the charges and pledging to fight them to the fullest. Upon his indictment, the House Ethics Committee announced it would also begin an investigation of Jefferson. Jefferson had resigned from his position on the Small Business Committee before he could be voted off of it. Jefferson's situation became another field of verbal battle between Democrats and Republicans, as both sides tried to paint the other as hypocritical over the handling, or lack thereof, of Jefferson's case. Jefferson is expected to go on trial in January of 2008.

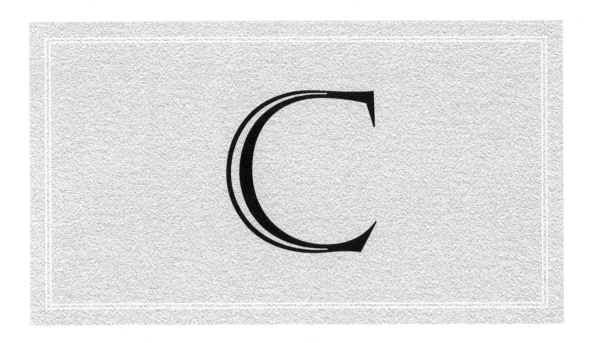

CAMPAIGN FINANCING

2008 Race Could Be the First Billion Dollar Campaign

Thanks to record-setting fundraising efforts by several Democrat and Republican candidates for president in 2008, the presidential race could become the first billion-dollar race in U.S. history. This phenomenon has been due largely to the ability of Democratic frontrunners HILLARY RODHAM CLINTON and Barack Obama to acquire substantial funds, even during the early stages of the campaign. A number of commentators have suggested that the system for using public election funds may come to an end with this election, and critics have noted that many candidates will not be able to compete simply due to financial constraints.

The Federal Election Campaign Act Amendments of 1974, Pub. L. No. 93-443, 88 Stat. 1263 established a public financing system for presidential elections designed to avoid the corruption often associated with money that is used for such a campaign. The voluntary system that the act created establishes spending limits for those candidates who rely on public money to run their campaigns. This system has been hailed as a means to level the playing field for the major candidates and to limit the influence that individual donors can have on the political process.

Since the program was first implemented in 1976, no candidate has forgone public money for both the primary and the general election. However, the fundraising efforts of GEORGE W. BUSH began to change the landscape for presidential hopefuls. Despite having limitations on the total amounts that individual donors could give, Bush's supporters helped him to raise a record $296.3 million between 1998 and 2004. In both the 2000 and 2004 elections, Bush's funds gave him a major advantage over Democratic opponents AL GORE and John Kerry, although Kerry's camp raised an estimated $235 million for the 2004 campaign. According to some estimates, at least a third of Bush's money came from a total of 631 people. Both Bush and Kerry refused to accept public funding for the 2004 primaries due to the spending limits, but they did accept this money for the general election.

Unlike the past two elections, the Democratic hopefuls have led the charge in terms of raising money for the 2008 campaign. Clinton has been the leader since she announced her candidacy, and she announced that she would not accept public financing for either the primary or the general election. Accepting public funds would have limited her spending to roughly $150 million. Many believed that Clinton would pull away with the Democratic nod early the process due to the amount of funds that she has been able to raise.

Obama, however, had a strong showing on the fund raising front for the first quarter of 2007 and very nearly overtook Clinton in terms of the total number of dollars raised. Even though he did not begin his fund raising efforts until mid-January in 2007, between that time and March 31 he had twice as many individual donors and raised about $3.5 million more than Clinton. Some insiders said that the Clinton camp has simply been too aggressive and too arrogant, and some of Clinton's early supporters have moved over to the Obama camp. Moreover, some of the consultants on whom the Clinton camp expected to rely have said that they will support both Clinton and Obama. According to statistics supplied by the FEDERAL ELECTION COMMISSION, Clinton had raised $26.1 million as of March 31, compared with $25.7 by Obama. The next closest competitor is John Edwards, who had raised $14 million.

Unlike the aggressive Clinton, Obama has challenged opponents to limit fund-raising and spending for the campaign. Although Obama stated that he would not accept public funding, he also left open the possibility that he could return the money at a later date in order to accept the public funding. Commentators noted that if Obama should win the election, he could strike a deal with the Republican nominee to ensure that both sides use only the public financing. According to a filing by Obama with the Federal Election Commission, "Should both major party nominees elect to receive public funding, this would preserve the public financing system, now in danger of collapse, and facilitate the conduct of campaigns freed from any dependence on private fund-raising."

Republican nominees have also been aggressive on the fund-raising front, though they have not been as successful. Former Massachusetts Governor W. Mitt Romney led the pack for the Republican candidates, according to the FEC, by having raised $21 million. Former New York City Major Rudy Giuliani had raised $16 million. Even former campaign finance reformer JOHN McCAIN (R.-Ariz.) has been actively pursuing funds, having raised $13.7.

McCain has been criticized in some circles for relying on donors who were the subjects of some of his attacks when he was a leading spokesperson for campaign finance reform. He led the charge in Congress to end the so-called "soft money" donations by co-sponsoring a bill in 2002 that also placed strict limits on donations. Moreover, he has introduced legislation that would prevent nonprofit political groups, known as 527s, from using their unlimited donations to spend money on elections. Despite these efforts, however, McCain himself is relying on certain big donors and these 527 groups to fund his own campaign.

The race for the candidacies in both parties most likely will continue to focus more on fund-raising that on other substantive issues. According to Michael E. Toner, a commissioner with the FEC, "The 2008 race will be the longest and most expensive presidential election in American history. Top-tier candidates are going to have to raise $100 million by the end of 2007 to be a serious candidate. We are looking at a $100 million entry fee."

CAPITAL PUNISHMENT

The lawful infliction of death as a punishment; the death penalty.

Ayers v. Belmontes

The Supreme Court has reviewed numerous capital punishment cases that involve challenges about jury instructions. Because death penalty appeals can go on for decades, the Court is sometimes called on to determine whether a now defunct instruction should lead to the invalidation of a death sentence. In *Ayers v. Belmontes*, __U.S.__, 127 S.Ct. 469, 166 L.Ed.2d 334 (2006), the Court examined a California jury instruction that suggested jurors only consider mitigating evidence from the defendant that extenuated the gravity of the crime and to ignore evidence that showed the defendant might lead a constructive life if given a life sentence.

Fernando Belmontes was tried in 1982 in a California trial court for first degree murder. In March 1981 Belmontes burglarized a home and encountered a 19-year-old woman. He struck her head 15 to 20 times with a steel dumbbell bar he had brought with him. He was convicted of the crime and then the jury considered whether he should be sentenced to death during the sentencing phase of the trial. Belmontes introduced mitigating evidence that sought to show that he would make positive contributions to society in a prison environment. He testified that he done well when he was under the California Youth Authority (CYA), eventually becoming the number two person on a fire crew in the youth camp. In addition, Belmontes became friendly with a married couple who counseled him on religion while he was in the CYA. Though his commitment to religion lapsed after he was released from the CYA, Belmontes told the jury that he would rededicated himself to following a spiritual life. He buttressed this argument with testimony from his CYA chaplain, who called Belmontes' conversion genuine, and from the married couple who said he had participated in church activities. Despite this mitigating evidence the jury sentenced Belmontes to death.

Belmontes appealed his sentence through the California courts and then to the **federal courts**, arguing that the jury was given an instruction which prevented it from considering his forward-looking mitigating evidence. The jury instruction directed the jury to consider "any other circumstance which extenuates the gravity of the crime even though it is not a legal excuse for the crime." This general or catchall factor was referred to as "factor k." Belmontes contended that factor k limited the jurors to consider mitigating factors surrounding the crime itself rather than evidence relating to his character and background. The Ninth **Circuit Court** of Appeals agreed with Belmontes and overturned his sentence in 2005.

The Supreme Court, in a 5–4 decision, reversed the Ninth Circuit, concluding that there was no reasonable likelihood that the jurors interepreted factor k to exclude considering Belmontes' **character evidence** during the penalty phase. Justice ANTHONY KENNEDY, writing for the majority, noted that the Court had examined factor k in two prior cases and had found that the proper inquiry was "whether there is a reasonable likelihood that the jury has applied the challenged instruction in a way that prevents the consideration of constitutionally relevant evidence." In this case the Ninth Circuit had mistakenly applied "a narrow, and we conclude, an unrealistic interpretation of factor k." The instruction did not limit the jury's consideration to any other circumstance of the crime which extenuates the gravity of the crime, rather it directed the jury to consider "any other circumstance that might excuse the crime." Justice Kennedy concluded that the Ninth Circuit's narrow reading of factor k required "the surprising conclusion that remorse could never serve to lessen or excuse a crime."

Justice Kennedy found it "improbable" that jurors believed Belmontes' presentation of mitigating evidence was an exercise of futility because of factor k. Both the prosecution and the defense assumed the evidence was relevant. For example, the prosecutor argued that the evidence of Belmontes' religious beliefs was proper but that the evidence was weak. The prosecutor never argued that the jury could not consider the evidence. Justice Kennedy also noted that Belmontes' personal pleas to the jury "were consistent with a trial in which the jury would assess his future prospects in determining what sentence to impose." The final argument of defense counsel reinforced this conclusion. In the end, Justice Kenney found it "implausible" that the jury concluded it could not consider the mitigating evidence. The judge had directed the jury to consider all the evidence presented. From the record there was no reasonable likelihood that

the jury failed to consider all evidence. Therefore, the death penalty was proper.

Justice JOHN PAUL STEVENS, in a dissenting opinion joined by Justice DAVID SOUTER, RUTH BADER GINSBURG, and STEPHEN BREYER, argued that factor k "sent the unmistakable message that California juries could properly give no mitigating weight to evidence that did not extenuate the severity of the crime."

Brewer v. Quarterman

This U.S. SUPREME COURT case is companion to another decided the same day (*Abdul-Kabir v. Quarterman*, No. 05-112874,), both presenting overlapping issues before the Court. As in the companion case, the petitioner in the present case, *Brewer v. Quarterman*, No. 05-11287, 550 U.S.___ (2007), claimed that jury instructions provided pursuant to the Texas capital sentencing **statute** prevented his sentencing jury from giving meaningful consideration to his constitutionally relevant mitigating evidence. (The "special issue" jury instructions have not been used since 1991, the year of Brewer's conviction.) A narrowly-divided U.S. Supreme Court threw out Brewer's death sentence based on the defective jury instructions. The high court's decision reversed the ruling of the Fifth **Circuit Court** of Appeals, which had denied such relief.

The majority opinion essentially relied on an earlier case, *Penry v. Lynaugh*, 492 U.S. 302 (1989), in which the Supreme Court had considered the same Texas "special issue" jury instructions. It concluded at that time that giving these instructions without directing a jury to consider mitigating evidence as it bears on personal culpability, did not provide a jury with an adequate opportunity to decide whether that evidence might provide a legitimate basis for imposing a sentence other than death.

Brewer was convicted of murder committed during the course of a **robbery**. At the sentencing hearing, he introduced evidence of an abusive father and his substance abuse. The trial judge rejected all of Brewer's proposed jury instructions designed to give effect to his mitigating evidence, and instructed the jury to answer two special issues (essentially asking whether the defendant committed the crime "deliberately," and whether the defendant was likely to be a "continuing threat to society"). In closing arguments, the prosecutor discouraged jurors from considering Brewer's mitigating evidence, instead advising them to focus on

Brewer   Abdul-Kabir

Texas Department of Corrections shots of Brent Ray Brewer and Jalil Abdul-Kamir

AP IMAGES

whether the facts objectively supported findings of deliberateness and future dangerousness (the special issues) and not on their personal views as to what might be an appropriate punishment for this particular defendant. The jury answered both in the affirmative, and Brewer was sentenced to death.

After the Texas Court of Criminal Appeals (CCA) affirmed the sentence and a state habeas petition was denied, Brewer filed a petition for **habeas corpus** in federal **district court**. He argued that he was entitled to federal habeas relief because the two special issues did not allow the jury to fully consider mitigating evidence presented on his behalf. He further argued that such limitation on the jury's ability to consider mitigating evidence was a violation under the EIGHTH AMENDMENT to the U.S. Constitution, resulting in **cruel and unusual punishment**.

The Anti-terrorism and Effective Death Penalty Act of 1996 (AEDPA), 28 USC §2254, AEDPA (see above) grants federal habeas relief only if a state court's decision is contrary to, or involves an unreasonable application of, "clearly established federal law as determined by the Supreme Court of the United States." The federal district court granted conditional relief but the Fifth Circuit Court of Appeals reversed. The U.S. Supreme Court granted **certiorari**.

Justice Stevens delivered the narrow 5–4 majority opinion of the Court, citing its previous decision in *Penry*. In that case, the Court characterized Penry's abuse and mental impairment evidence as a "two-edged sword" that might diminish blameworthiness while at the same

time indicate a probability of his dangerousness to society. When the possibility of that inference exists, the evidence is as likely to be viewed as aggravating as it is mitigating, and Texas' two special issue questions are too confining to allow proper consideration of mitigating evidence as it bears on the defendant's personal culpability. This, in turn, results in a decision that is contrary to, or involves an unreasonable application of, clearly established federal law as determined by the Supreme Court.

Even though Brewer's mitigating evidence was less convincing than Penry's, the Court noted that this was insufficient to support the CCA's refusal to consider the case under *Penry*'s guidelines. Also, the fact that Brewer did not offer expert testimony did not excuse analysis under *Penry*, as nothing in that decision requires this. Further, the Fifth Circuit's mischaracterization of the law as requiring only that such mitigating evidence be given "sufficient mitigating effect" is not consistent with the "full effect" standard of *Penry*.

A strong dissent by Chief Justice Roberts, joined by Justices Scalia, Alito, and Stevens, opined that "We give ourselves far too much credit in claiming that our sharply divided, ebbing and flowing decisions in this area gave rise to 'clearly-established' federal law. If the law were indeed clearly established . . . it should not take the Court more than a dozen pages of close analysis. . . ." to articulate what that 'clearly established law' was. Instead, noted the dissent, the precedents relied upon offered state courts "a dog's breakfast of divided, conflicting, and ever-changing analyses."

Justice Scalia, with whom Justices Thomas, Alito (as to Part I), and Chief Justice Roberts also joined, wrote a separate dissent as well. He repeated his view "that limiting a jury's discretion to consider all mitigating evidence does not violate the Eighth Amendment."

Abdul-Kabir v. Quarterman

As background, one of the main reasons that Congress passed the Anti-terrorism and Effective Death Penalty Act of 1996 (AEDPA), 28 USC §2254, was to limit lengthy appeals that typically precede executions. However, the AEDPA does afford certain protections for capital punishment convictees, and became the procedural vehicle (via a petition for its federal **habeas corpus** relief) used to access the U.S. SUPREME COURT in *Abdul-Kabir v. Quarterman*, No. 05-11284, 550 U.S.___ (2007). A narrowly-divided U.S. Supreme Court, in this and two other separate but related cases, threw out death sentences based on defective jury instructions given in Texas state courts. (See also, *Brewer v. Quarterman*, No. 05-11287, ___U.S.___ (2007), and *Smith v. Texas*, No. 05-11304 ___U.S.___ (2007).) The high court's decision reversed the ruling of the Fifth **Circuit Court** of Appeals, which had denied such relief.

Jalil Abdul-Kabir (formerly known, prosecuted, and convicted as Ted Calvin Cole),joined his stepbrother and stepbrother's wife in robbing and murdering the wife's grandfather. Cole strangled him with a dog leash, and the three spent the stolen $20 on beer and food.

Cole's accomplices surrendered and confessed, but Cole was tried by a jury and convicted of capital murder in a Texas state court. At the sentencing phase, prosecutors presented copious evidence including a prior murder conviction and guilty pleas to aggravated sexual assault on two boys. In response, Cole presented mitigating evidence regarding his childhood neglect and abandonment, as well as expert testimony related to neurological damage that might have caused his violent propensities. The trial judge instructed the jury to answer two special issues (essentially asking whether the defendant committed the crime "deliberately," and whether the defendant was likely to be a "continuing threat to society"). However, the prosecutor had discouraged jurors from considering Cole's mitigating evidence, instead advising them to focus on whether the facts objectively supported findings of deliberateness and future dangerousness (the special issues) and not on their personal views as to what might be an appropriate punishment for this particular defendant. The jury answered both in the affirmative, and Cole was sentenced to death.

After the Texas Court of Criminal Appeals (CCA) affirmed the sentence and a state habeas petition was denied, Cole filed a petition for habeas **corpus** in federal **district court**. The AEDPA (see above) grants federal habeas relief only if a state court's decision is contrary to, or involves an unreasonable application of, "clearly established federal law as determined by the Supreme Court of the United States."

The Supreme Court had previously ruled, in *Penry v. Lynaugh*, 492 U.S. 302 (2001), that juries must be given instructions that allow them to give full consideration and meaningful effect to a defendant's mitigating evidence, and to express their reasoned moral response to that evidence in determining an appropriate sentence.

Accordingly, Cole argued that he was entitled to federal habeas relief under the AEDPA because the two special issues did not allow the jury to fully consider mitigating evidence presented on his behalf. He argued that such limitation on the jury's ability to consider mitigating evidence was a violation under the EIGHTH AMENDMENT to the U.S. Constitution, resulting in **cruel and unusual punishment**.

The federal district court, however, denied Cole's petition, relying on the Fifth Circuit Court of Appeals' analysis for evaluating *Penry* claims. Under Fifth Circuit analysis, a defendant was required to show that he or she suffered from a severe, permanent, or untreatable mental disorder, and further show a nexus between this disorder and the criminal act attributed to it. It was determined that Cole did not meet that standard, and his petition was denied. The Fifth Circuit affirmed, but the U.S. Supreme Court rejected this analysis in another Fifth Circuit case, *Tennard v. Dretke*, 542 U.S. 274, effectively vacating the denial of Cole's application as well.

On remand, the Fifth Circuit considered the two special issue questions, especially the one addressing the future dangerousness of a defendant. The **appellate court** found that Cole's neurological damage (ostensibly affecting his impulse control) did qualify as mitigating evidence, but that this evidence could be fully considered and weighed under the two special jury questions. Therefore, the Fifth Circuit concluded that the state court decision was not contrary to, nor did it misapply, federal law, and Cole was not entitled to federal habeas relief under the AEDPA.

Now fully before the U.S. Supreme Court, Cole's fortunes changed. By a narrow 5–4 vote, the Court held that there was a reasonable likelihood that the Texas trial court's instructions (the two special issues) prevented jurors from giving meaningful consideration to constitutionally relevant mitigating evidence. This, in turn, resulted in a decision that was contrary to, or involved an unreasonable application of, clearly established federal law as determined by the Supreme Court, invoking the AEDPA. Accordingly, Cole's death sentence was reversed, and the case remanded.

However, in pointing to the relevant "clearly established federal law" as established by the Supreme Court, the Court referred to multiple previous rulings and cases, including *Penry* (see above)and *Tennard*, (see above), as well as *Lockett v. Ohio*, 438 U.S. 586, and *Franklin v. Lynaugh*, 487 U.S. 164. Essentially, the Court delineated a holding based on all these prior cases, repeating that where mitigating evidence served as a "two-edged sword" that might diminish blameworthiness while at the same time indicate dangerousness to society (as in mental impairment), the two special issue instructions did not allow jurors an ability to adequately consider the evidence. This was because the evidence was as likely to be viewed as aggravating as it was as mitigating, and the two special issue questions were too confining to allow proper consideration.

That it took the majority such lengthy and scrupulous reasoning in coming to the above decision was precisely what triggered the strong dissent from Chief Justice JOHN ROBERTS, joined by Justices Alito, Scalia, and Thomas. Justice Roberts referred to the majority opinion as "revisionist," since, according to the dissent, there was no "clearly established federal law," as evidenced by the Court's own deliberations in the present case. Justice Scalia also wrote a separate dissent in which he cautioned that "this Court's vacillating pronouncements" would produce grossly inequitable treatment of death row inmates.

Although 47 death row inmates were sentenced under the subject Texas rules, the jury instructions were abandoned by the state in 1991. (Cole was convicted in 1988.)

Panetti v. Quarterman

Under the EIGHTH AMENDMENT to the U.S. Constitution, a state cannot carry out the death sentence on a prisoner who is insane. This rule, established in *Ford v. Wainwright*, 477 U.S. 399, 106 S. Ct. 2595, 91 L. Ed. 2d 335 (1986), applies though a court has determined that the prisoner is competent to stand trial for the crime. Thus, even when a prisoner has previously been found to be competent, the prisoner may later prove that he or she is incompetent to be executed. Once the prisoner has shown in a **preliminary hearing** that the prisoner's mental state would bar his or her execution, the prisoner is then entitled to an **adjudication** about whether he is competent to be executed.

In 2007, the U.S. SUPREME COURT clarified the procedures that must be followed when a court determines whether a prisoner is competent to be put to death. In *Panetti v. Quarterman*, No. 06-6407, 2007 WL 1836653 (June 28, 2007), the Court held that both state and **federal courts** had failed to provide the proper procedures to an inmate who had claimed **incompetency**.

In 1992, Scott Louis Panetti, dressed in camouflage, drove to the house of his estranged wife's parents. He broke the front door lock and proceeded to kill his wife's mother and father in front of his wife and daughter. He thereafter kidnapped his wife and daughter before surrendering to police the following day.

He was tried for capital murder in 1995, and Panetti chose to represent himself. The court ordered Panetti to undergo a psychiatric evaluation, which showed that he suffered from a fragmented personality, delusions, and hallucinations. He had previously been hospitalized for these disorders, and doctors had prescribed **mediation** for these mental disorders. According to one expert, it would have been difficult for anyone who did not suffer from extreme psychosis to tolerate. Panetti's wife also testified that he had psychotic episodes during their marriage, including an incident where he believed that the devil and possessed their home.

Despite this evidence, however, the court allowed Panetti to stand trial. During this trial, Panetti's behavior was described as "bizarre," "scary," and "trance-like." According to an attorney present during the case, his behavior both before the jury and in private evidenced that he was suffering from mental incompetence. Moreover, the attorney said that his behavior was "truly a judicial farce, and a mockery of self-representation." Evidence presented at trial showed that Panetti had stopped taking his medication a few months prior to the trial. An expert testified that the failure to take this medication would exacerbate the mental problems. Panetti's condition appeared to worsen before the end of the trial.

A jury in a Texas state court found Panetti guilty of murder and sentenced him to death. Panetti appealed his conviction on direct appeal to the Texas Court of Criminal Appeals, but the court denied his request for relief. Panetti also sought relief through a state **habeas corpus** action but was again denied relief. The U.S. Supreme Court denied Panetti's petitions for **certiorari** on two occasions in 1998.

Pursuant to 28 U.S.C. §2254, Panetti subsequently filed a **writ** of habeas **corpus** in the U.S. **District Court** for the Western District of Texas. In 2001, the district court rejected his claims. Two years later, the Fifth **Circuit Court** of Appeals also denied relief. The Supreme Court for a third time denied certiorari to review Panetti's case. At both the state and federal level, Panetti focused his argument on the alleged fact that he was incompetent to stand trial and to waive his right to counsel.

In 2003, a state judge set Panetti's execution date for February 5, 2004. Panetti at that time filed a motion claiming that he was incompetent to be executed. The judge denied this motion. Panetti then appealed this denial to the Court of Criminal Appeals, but the **appellate court** concluded that it did not have the power to review a decision about whether a prisoner is competent to be put to death.

Panetti returned to the federal courts, filing a motion for stay of execution and arguing that the state had violated the procedures established in *Ford*. Panetti initially failed to include evidence of his mental state at the time that he filed his habeas request. After submitting this evidence, the district court stayed his execution so that a state court could consider his mental state at that time. Evidence presented at that time showed that Panetti did not understand the reasons why he was being executed. After a series of procedural moves, the court appointed two experts to evaluate Panetti. These experts concluded that Panetti's behavior was due to "calculated design," meaning that he acted insane in order to manipulate the proceedings.

The federal district court concluded that the state court's proceedings were inadequate under the Constitution, but the court nevertheless denied relief. *Panetti v. Dretke*, 401 F. Supp. 2d 702 (W.D. Tex. 2004). The district court concluded that Panetti had failed to prove incompetency as the Fifth Circuit had defined it. The Fifth Circuit subsequently affirmed the district court's conclusion, and the Supreme Court then agreed to review the case.

In an opinion by Justice ANTHONY KENNEDY, the Court reversed the decision of the lower federal courts. The Court first concluded that the Antiterrorism and Effective Death Penalty Act of 1996 (AEDPA), Pub. L. No. 104-132, 110 Stat. 1214, did not preclude habeas review of Panetti's case. The Court then reviewed the procedures that the state courts had followed to determine Panetti's competency. Under *Ford*, the determination of whether Panetti was insane could not be made solely on the basis of examinations performed by state-appointed psychiatrists. Other evidence, such as the state court's refusal to transcribe its proceedings regarding the competency hearing, further showed that the procedures had been inadequate.

The Court likewise reviewed the Fifth Circuit's standard of incompetency and determined

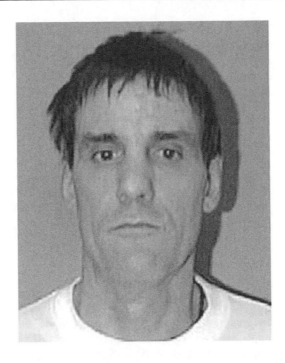

Texas Department of Criminal Justice photo of Scott Panetti.
AP IMAGES

that it was too restrictive. According to the Supreme Court, the prisoner's delusions should have been considered when the court determined competency. Under the Fifth Circuit's standard, the lower courts did not consider the delusions to be relevant so long as the defendant was aware that the state had identified a link between the crime and the punishment that was inflicted.

Justice CLARENCE THOMAS, joined by three other justices, dissented. According to Thomas, the case should have been "simple" because Panetti's arguments had been heard numerous times by the lower courts. Moreover, Thomas concluded that the AEDPA barred this case because the claim did not meet the **statutory** requirements for filing a "second or successive" habeas application under the **statute**. Thomas also criticized the majority for imposing a new standard for determining incompetency without engaging in any sort of Eighth Amendment analysis.

Smith V. Texas (Smith II)

This was the second time before the U.S. SUPREME COURT for LaRoyce Smith, a Dallas County, Texas inmate who was sentenced to death in 1991 following a first-degree murder conviction. At the original criminal trial, Smith's attorney had presented extensive mitigating evidence regarding Smith's diminished intellectual capacity, learning disabilities, special education, and troubling family background. Following conviction, Smith petitioned for **habeas corpus** relief, claiming that the jury instructions provided pursuant to the Texas capital sentencing **statute** prevented his sentencing jury from giving meaningful consideration to his constitutionally relevant mitigating evidence. The U.S. Supreme Court agreed and remanded his case in *Smith v. Texas*, 543 U.S. 37 (2004) (*Smith I.*

On remand, the Texas Court of Criminal Appeals nonetheless found that the possible constitutional error in the jury instruction was not so "egregiously injurious" to Smith as to make his trial fundamentally unfair. It therefore denied relief once more and let stand Smith's death sentence. *Ex Parte Smith*, 185 S.W.3d 455 (Tex. Crim. App. 2006). It is this *second* decision that came before the Court in the present case, *Smith v. Texas*, No. 05-11304, 550 U.S.___ (2007).).

The subject jury instructions have not been used since 1991 and have stimulated numerous appeals before the U.S. Supreme Court. The Supreme Court had previously ruled, in *Penry v. Lynaugh*, 492 U.S. 302 (2001), that juries must be given instructions that allow them to give full consideration and meaningful effect to a defendant's mitigating evidence, and to express their reasoned moral response to that evidence in determining an appropriate sentence. (See also, *Brewer v. Quarterman*, No. 05-11287, (2007), and *Abdul-Kabir v. Quarterman*, No. 05-112874, (2007).)

Texas tried to cure the instructions by modifying them only to the point that juries could effectively "nullify" the parts that were struck down by the Supreme Court. However, that remedy (the "nullification instruction") was also shot down by the Supreme Court in *Penry v. Johnson*, 532 U.S. 782, (*Penry II.*)

Smith's sentencing took place between *Penry I* and *Penry II*. When Smith's second appeal was heard, the Texas Court of Criminal Appeals held that Smith had not preserved a *Penry II* challenge to the nullification jury instruction. Smith had only made a *Penry I* challenge at trial. Under Texas law, in determining whether reversal is warranted for an error in jury instructions, Smith was required to show "egregious harm." Therefore, finding that he did not meet his burden, the court denied relief.

But the U.S. Supreme Court disagreed. It held that the Texas Criminal Court had predicated the "egregious harm" requirement on a mistaken understanding of the federal right Smith was asserting. The **appellate court** mistook the Supreme Court's holding in *Smith I* as granting relief based on the nullification in-

struction. It then concluded that since Smith had never objected to the nullification charge, he had not preserved that claim for *Smith II.*

Justice Kennedy delivered the opinion of the majority, in which he was joined by Justices Stevens, Souter, Ginsburg, and Breyer. The opinion concluded that the Texas **appellate** court's misinterpretation of federal law on remand from *Smith I* could not form a basis for imposing upon Smith the higher standard of "egregious harm." Because Smith did challenge as unconstitutional the special issue jury instructions, he was entitled to relief under the state's "harmless error" standard instead.

Justice Alito, joined by Chief Justice Roberts and Justices Thomas and Scalia, dissented. The dissent began with the statement, "The issue in this case is less complicated than the opinion of the Court suggests." The dissent went on to opine that the case could have been dismissed for want of jurisdiction. The constitutional error in *Smith I* could have been avoided by changing the instructions. But defense counsel never objected to the text of the instructions nor proffered modifications, instead choosing to argue that *Penry I* precluded a death sentence for Smith. As a result of this failure to object, the Texas Criminal Court was entitled to use a stricter procedural rule "that represents an adequate and independent state-law ground for [its] decision."

CIVIL RIGHTS

Personal liberties that belong to an individual owing to his or her status as a citizen or resident of a particular country or community.

Andrews v. City of West Branch Iowa

Law enforcement officers have the authority to kill animals such as dogs that are a menace to the public but they may be subject to civil liability if they act unreasonably in killing a pet. The federal civil rights **tort law** 42 U.S.C.A. §1983 gives individuals the right to sue a police officer for injuries caused by the officer's unconstitutional actions. Though most 1983 lawsuits involve injuries to the suing individual, in some cases the injuries may be related to the killing of a pet by a police officer. In these cases the plaintiff claims the killing was an unreasonable **search and seizure** in violation of the FOURTH AMENDMENT. In *Andrews v. City of West Branch, Iowa*, 454 F.3d 914(8th cir.2006), the Eighth **Circuit Court** of Appeals ruled that a police could be sued for the killing of a dog. The officer did not have immunity because his actions were unreasonable and did not conform to state law and local regulations.

The actions at the heart of the case unfolded on February 28, 2002 in West Branch, Iowa, when the city administrator received a phone call from a local resident complaining about a large black dog loose in the neighborhood that was harassing her dog. The administrator passed on the information to police chief Dan Knight, who drove to the neighborhood and tried to catch the dog. Though he saw the dog several times during his pursuit, the dog managed to elude him. Knight finally parked his car in the driveway of a home because he had seen a large black dog in the backyard of the home. As he approached the fenced backyard he fired two shots at the dog. He immediately realized he had shot the wrong dog—the owner of Riker, Jana Andrew, was standing outside just a few feet away from her dog. She had just let Riker out to go to the bathroom inside the fenced backyard. Knight, seeing that Riker was badly injured, fired a third shot to end his suffering. Riker had not been wearing his collar and tags when he was shot but he was current on his rabies and distemper booster vaccines. Knight had not given any warning before he shot and had not attempted to ask Andrews whether Riker had been running free prior to the shooting. Andrews and her husband responded by filing a 1983 lawsuit against Knight and the city that alleged the killing was an unreasonable search and seizure.

The federal **district court** dismissed the lawsuit against the city and dismissed the claims against Knight because he was entitled to qualified immunity. Qualified immunity is a doctrine developed by the U.S. SUPREME COURT that protects police officers when the officers' actions were reasonable and the constitutional right supposedly violated was not clearly established under the law. The court concluded that Knight's actions were lawful under an Iowa **statute** dealing with dangerous animals. The Andrews then appealed to the Eighth Circuit Court of Appeals.

A three-judge panel of the appeals court decided, on a 2–1 vote, that the city was properly dismissed from the appeal but Knight was not entitled to qualified immunity. Judge Gerald Heaney, writing for the majority, first looked at whether Knight was authorized by state law or local regulation to shoot Riker. The city **ordinance** regulated dogs "running at large" but the plain meaning of that phrase meant that Riker, a fenced-in dog, was not at large. That meant that Knight did not have animal control jurisdiction over the dog at the time of the shooting. Knight argued that he was justified in shooting Riker because he was not wearing his rabies tag, which is a state law requirement. However, Judge Heaney pointed out that this **statutory** requirement did not apply if the local jurisdiction had regulations for the seizure and impoundment of dogs. West Branch did have such an ordinance, which stated that the discharge of a firearm at an animal was a last resort, so Knight's plain meaning argument was ineffective. The appeals court found that this seizure and impoundment policy "logically extended to a fenced-in, passive dog." Therefore, a reasonable jury could conclude that Knight's shooting of Riker was premature. He had not exhausted other means of dealing with the dog before he discharged his firearm.

As to the Andrewses' contention that Knight violated their Fourth Amendment rights by his unreasonable shooting and killing of Riker, Judge Heaney found ample evidence for this argument. To seize property a person must interfere with another person's possessory interest in that property. Knight clearly seized the dog, so the only remaining issue was whether his seizure was reasonable. The appeals court held that his seizure was unreasonable, for Knight could not claim that Riker posed an imminent danger to the public. Riker was "not on the loose, growling, acting fiercely, or harassing anyone at the time Knight killed him." Knight knew that state law and local regulations required him to use all means of capturing an at-large dog before resorting to killing the animal. Knight could not claim qualified immunity because at the time he shot Riker he knew he was violating the Andrewses' clearly established right to be free of unreasonable searches and seizures. Judge Dianna Murphy dissented, believing Knight was entitled to qualified immunity.

Wallace v. Kato

The federal rights **statute** 42 U.S.C.A. §1983 is recognized as one of the most important civil rights law, allowing a person to sue state and local government officials for damages and equitable relief based on the alleged deprivations by the officials of the plaintiff's constitutional rights. Though §1983 is a federal law, in some areas state law may have a bearing on the case. This is particularly true in terms of statutes of limitation, which govern the amount of time a plaintiff has to file a civil rights lawsuit. The U.S. SUPREME COURT has ruled that all §1983 actions are to be classified for **statute of limita-**

tions purposes as actions to recover damages for injury to the person, and the appropriate state statute of limitations for such claims are to be applied. However, the Court, in *Wallace v. Kato*, ___U.S.___, 127 S.Ct. 1091, ___L.Ed.2d ___ (2007), ruled that the accrual date, i.e., the date the clock starts ticking to file the lawsuit, is a question of federal law that is not resolved by reference to state law. It further held that the accrual date begins when the plaintiff becomes detained pursuant to legal process, making it more difficult to pursue a §1983 action.

Andre Wallace, a fifteen-year-old Chicago resident, was picked up by the Chicago police in January 1994 in connection with the murder of a man. After a lengthy interrogation at the police station Wallace confessed to the murder. He signed a statement prepared by an assistant state's attorney and waived his *Miranda* rights. Before trial Wallace sought to suppress his confession, arguing that it was the product of an unlawful arrest. The judge rejected the suppression motion and Wallace was convicted of first-degree murder and sentenced to 26 years in prison. The **Appellate Court** of Illinois overturned his conviction, ruling that the police officers had arrested Wallace without **probable cause**, in violation of the FOURTH AMENDMENT. Another round of appeals ensued but in August 2001 the appeals court reaffirmed its ruling and remanded the case for a new trial. In April 2002 the prosecutors dropped all charges against Wallace.

In April 2003 Wallace filed a §1983 lawsuit against the city of Chicago and several police officers, seeking damages for his unlawful arrest. The federal **district court** dismissed the lawsuit and the Seventh **Circuit Court** of Appeals affirmed. The Seventh Circuit concluded that the action was barred by the statutes of limitations (two years in Illinois) because the accrual date began at the time of his arrest in 1994 and not when his conviction was set aside in 2002. If the court had measured the time period from the dismissal of Wallace's case the lawsuit would have been timely. Wallace then appealed this decision to the U.S. Supreme Court.

The Court, in a 7–2 decision, upheld the Seventh Circuit ruling. Justice ANTONIN SCALIA, writing for the majority, stated that the accrual date of a §1983 action is a question of federal law that is not resolved by reference to state law. The Court is guided by federal rules that conform "in general to common-law principles." It was clear to Scalia that Wallace could have filed his lawsuit "as soon as the allegedly

wrongful arrest occurred, subjecting him to the harm of involuntary detention, so the statute of limitations would normally commence to run from that date." However, the tort of **false imprisonment**, which was Wallace's essential claim, gave the Court more direction. Under the tort of false imprisonment Wallace could only sue for the period he was detained "without legal process." Acknowledging the reality that a victim may not be able to sue while still imprisoned, Scalia sought to pinpoint the beginning of the limitations period. The crucial inquiry was when Wallace's false imprisonment ended. Scalia concluded that Wallace's false imprisonment ended when he was arraigned on the murder charge before a state court judge and bound over for trial. That occurred in 1994, which meant that Wallace's filing was seven years too late.

Wallace argued that the **false arrest** and imprisonment led to his coerced confession, conviction, and incarceration. Therefore, the accrual date for his lawsuit began the date he was released from custody in 2002, a full year under the two-year statute of limitations. Justice Scalia rejected this claim, finding that neither Court precedent nor state law authorized the tolling (suspension) of the statute of limitations until the conviction was set aside.

Justice STEPHEN BREYER, in a dissenting opinion joined by Justice RUTH BADER GINSBURG, argued that the Court should have applied the doctrine of "equitable tolling," which "tolls the running of the limitations period until the disabling circumstance[in this case, Wallace's incarceration] can be overcome." He believed that equitable tolling would remove the need for an individual to immediately file a §1983 lawsuit. It would permit "the criminal proceedings to winnow the constitutional wheat from chaff, and thereby increase the likelihood that the constitutionally meritless claims will never (in a §1983 action) see the light of day.

CLEAN AIR ACT

Environmental Defense v. Duke Energy Corporation

The Clean Air Act (CAA), which is enforced by the ENVIRONMENTAL PROTECTION AGENCY (EPA), regulates the release of air pollutants. Since its enactment in 1963 the CAA has been amended by Congress several times to strengthen its regulatory powers. The regulation of power plant emissions has been a major component of EPA oversight because coal has been the fuel of choice for most power plants.

Despite statutes and regulations that seek to define the scope of environmental oversight, energy producers sometimes run afoul and trigger legal controversies. Such was the case in *Environmental Defense v. Duke Energy Corporation*, __U.S.__, 127 S.Ct. 1423, __L.Ed.2d __ (2007), where the U.S. SUPREME COURT held that the EPA could interpret the word "modification" differently in two sets of air quality regulations. In addition, a power company seeking to force a uniform interpretation of the word was essentially challenging one of the regulations. This approach was not acceptable because challenges to regulations must be addressed within 60 days of the rulemaking in a specific **circuit court** of appeals.

Duke Energy Corporation operates 30 coal-fired power plants in North and South Carolina which provide power to over two million people. Beginning in 1988 Duke Energy started to modernize more than 24 of these unites. They were refurbished and the central sections of the generators were either rebuilt or replaced. The modernization was long overdue for some of the equipment, which had gone into operation in the 1940s. Between 1988 and 2000 the company updated the boilers to extend the life of the units and to allow them to run longer each day. The EPA filed a lawsuit against Duke Energy in 2000, alleging that the company had not obtained EPA permits and that the modernization program violated a 1977 amendment to the CAA known as the Prevention of Significant Deterioration or PSD. Under the PSD a permit is required before a "major emitting facility" can be constructed; modification of a facility was included in this requirement. Following the enactment of this amendment the EPA issued PSD regulations which limited the need for a review and permit to any "major modification." This was defined as a change in the method of operation that would result "in a significant net emissions increase of any pollutant subject to regulation under the Act." Complications arose because the CAA contained an earlier amendment entitled New Source Performance Standards or NSPS. Under NSPS regulations the word "modification" had a different meaning. A source would not need to use the best pollution-limiting technology if the modification would not increase the rate of discharge of pollutants measured in kilograms per hour.

Duke moved for **summary judgment**, contending that none of its projects were "major modifications" requiring a PSD permit because none increased hourly rates of emission under NSPS. The EPA and a group of environmental organizations that intervened in the lawsuit contended that the increased use of the units, which can more hours per day, contravened the language of the PSD regulations. The **district court** ruled in favor of Duke Energy and the case moved to the Fourth Circuit Court of Appeals. The appeals court upheld the lower court, finding that identical **statutory** definitions of the term "modification" in the NSPS and PSD provisions "mandated that this term be interpreted identically" in the regulations for these two provisions. Therefore, the PSD regulations must use an increase in the hourly rate of emissions as its guide for determining whether a permit is required.

The Supreme Court, in a unanimous decision, overruled the Fourth Circuit. Justice DAVID SOUTER, writing for the Court, concluded that the appeals court's effort to harmonize the two statutes and sets of regulations and "trim the PSD regulations to match their different NSPS counterparts can only be seen as an implicit declaration that the PSD regulations were invalid as written." This approach was in error for several reasons. First, he pointed out that a given term in a **statute** may take on a different character when associated with "distinct statutory objects calling for different implementation strategies." Contrary to the appeals court, there was no "irrebuttable" presumption that the same defined term in different provisions of the same law must be interpreted identically. The PSD regulations use of the term "major modification" clearly was not defined to mean an increase in hourly emissions rate. On its face the PSD regulations did not specify a rate, "merely requiring a physical or operational change that would result in significant net emissions. Justice Souter held that the Fourth Circuit's equation of the NSPS and PSD regulations served as "an implicit invalidation" of the PSD regulations. This was incorrect because **judicial review** of CAA regulations is limited during enforcement proceedings when review could have been obtained by Duke Power in the Court of Appeals for the DISTRICT OF COLUMBIA within 60 days of EPA rulemaking. Therefore, the case was remanded to the district court for further consideration.

Massachusetts v. Environmental Protection Agency (EPA)

The prospect that human activity has significantly contributed to an increase in "greenhouse gases," which, in turn, causes global warming, has suffered from less-than-convincing consensus over the years. It has only been since 2006-2007 that at least a clear majority of respected scientific opinions has so concluded, despite the existence of impressive data supporting that conclusion for at least two decades.

In *Massachusetts v. ENVIRONMENTAL PROTECTION AGENCY (EPA)*, No. 05-1120, 549 U.S.___ (2007), the U.S. SUPREME COURT was asked to determine whether the U.S. Environmental Protection Agency (EPA) had the **statutory** authority to regulate greenhouse gas emissions from new motor vehicles; and if so, whether EPA's stated reasons for declining to act were consistent with the **statute**. In a narrow 5–4 landmark decision, the Court found that gases which cause global warming were pollutants under the federal *Clean Air Act*; that EPA did indeed have the statutory authority to regulate them; and that it had acted arbitrarily and capriciously in refusing to exercise that authority.

This long-winded controversy centered on Section 202(a)(1) of the Clean Air Act, specifically, 42 USC §7521(a)(1), which states in relevant part:

> The [EPA] Administrator shall by regulation prescribe (and from time to time revise) in accordance with the provisions of this section, standards applicable to the emission of any air pollutant from any class or classes of new motor vehicles or new motor vehicle engines, which in his judgment cause, or contribute to, air pollution which may reasonably be anticipated to endanger public health or welfare . . .

The Act defines air pollutants to include "any air pollution agent . . . including any physical, chemical . . . substance . . . emitted into . . . the ambient air." [§7602(g)].

In 1999, various environmental groups filed an administrative "rule-making" petition formally requesting that EPA establish standards for motor vehicle "greenhouse gas" emissions (primarily carbon dioxide and other heat-trapping gases). Four years later, in 2003, the EPA denied the administrative petition, stating that it lacked authority to regulate such gases. It argued, in part, that carbon dioxide and other greenhouse gases were naturally occurring substances in the atmosphere and therefore did not constitute "air pollutants" within the meaning of the Clean Air Act. Further, even if it did have authority, *arguendo*, it would discretionarily decline in favor of voluntary programs and further research. The EPA noted that a causal link between greenhouse gases and increased global surface temperatures had not been dispositively established. Therefore, such a piecemeal approach would conflict with the President's more comprehensive environmental package, which included non-regulatory private-sector voluntary reductions and technologically innovative research into other climate-change alternatives.

Next, the State of Massachusetts joined the original petitioners as an intervening party and sought review of EPA's administrative decision in the Court of Appeals for the D.C. Circuit. Although each of the judges wrote a separate opinion, the ultimate decision let stand the EPA's decision and denied **appellate** review. The U.S. Supreme Court granted review (**certiorari**).

In response, the EPA, joined by ten intervening states and six trade associations, argued that the Supreme Court first needed to address whether the petitioners even had legal standing to invoke the Court's jurisdiction. The Court agreed. In order for the petitioners (at least one) to have standing, there needed to be a **justiciable** controversy under Art. III of the U.S. Constitution, which means that petitioners needed to show that they suffered particular injury (actual or imminent) because of EPA's actions (or failure to act). The Supreme Court found that the petitioners did have standing, particularly Massachusetts, as Congress had ordered EPA to protect Massachusetts and other states; and that EPA's refusal to regulate greenhouse gas emissions presented a risk of actual and imminent harm. This preliminary question being resolved in favor of petitioners, the Court went on to address the case on its merits.

The Court found that greenhouse gases fit well within the definition of "air pollutants" contemplated by the Clean Air Act. Therefore, EPA does have the authority to regulate them. Even though regulating motor vehicle emissions may not by itself reverse global warming, this does not mean that the Court does not have jurisdiction to decide whether EPA has a duty to act to slow or reduce it.

Next, the Court noted that under the Act's clear terms, EPA can decline to promulgate regulations only if it determines that greenhouse gases do not contribute to global climate change, or if it provides explanation as to why it cannot or will not exercise its discretion to determine whether such gases do contribute to climate change. If scientific uncertainty prevents EPA from making such a determination, it must state so. It had not. Nor did the Court find

EPA's other arguments persuasive, for example, that regulation of motor vehicle carbon dioxide emissions would require it to tighten mileage standards, which was really the **purview** of the U.S. Department of Transportation. The Court held that even if there was overlap in responsibilities, EPA may not shirk its duty to protect the public health and welfare under the Clean Air Act. Having found EPA's responsive reasons less than acceptable, the Court held that EPA had acted arbitrarily, capriciously, or otherwise not in accordance with law [§7607(d)(9) of the Act]. Accordingly, the Court remanded the matter for EPA to specifically articulate plausible reasons for its action or inaction.

Justice Stevens delivered the opinion of the court, in which he was joined by Justices Kennedy, Souter, Ginsburg, and Breyer. Chief Justice Roberts filed a dissenting opinion, joined by Justices Scalia, Alito, and Thomas. The dissent addressed the justiciability issue, arguing that the Court used "the dire nature of global warming itself as a bootstrap for finding causation and redressability." Since domestic automobile emissions are but a miniscule part of global greenhouse gas emissions, linking those emissions to Massachusetts' alleged injury was "far too speculative to establish causation."

Justice Scalia also filed a separate dissenting opinion, joined by the same dissenting justices. Justice Scalia addressed the substantive merits of distinguishing air pollutants from air pollution agents. However, he ended his dissent by noting that this was a straightforward administrative-law case for which Congress had given broad agency discretion. No matter how important the issue of global warming, said his dissent, it was not incumbent upon the Supreme Court to substitute its own desired outcome for the judgment of the delegated agency (EPA).

COMMERCE CLAUSE

The provision of the U.S. Constitution that gives Congress exclusive power over trade activities between the states and with foreign countries and Indian tribes.

United Haulers Ass'n v. Oneida-Herkimer Solid Waste Management Authority

During its 2006 term, the U.S. SUPREME COURT agreed to consider a case involving the application of the so-called "dormant Commerce Clause." The case concerned the constitutionality of a county **ordinance** that regulated the hauling of waste. The ordinance in question required waste haulers to direct their trash to a publicly-owned waste facility. A sharply divided Court decided that the ordinance did not violate the **Commerce Clause**.

Article I, §8 of the U.S. Constitution provides that "Congress shall have the power ... [t]o regulate Commerce with foreign nations, and among the several States." Throughout most of its history, the Court has interpreted this clause to establish an implicit restraint on the authority of the individual states to regulate interstate commerce, even where Congress has not acted. This restraint is referred to as the "dormant" Commerce Clause. Under this doctrine, the Court first considers whether the state law in question discriminates on its face against interstate commerce. This type of discrimination occurs when a state treats in-state economic interests differently than out-of-state interests in a manner that benefits the in-state interests and burdens the out-of-state interests.

In *C&A Carbone, Inc. v. Clarkstown*, 511 U.S. 383, 114 S. Ct. 1677, 128 L. Ed. 2d 399 (1994), the Court considered a waste flow control ordinance enacted by a New York town. Prior to enacting the ordinance, the town had hired a private contractor to construct a waste transfer station. The ordinance required all of the town's nonhazardous waste to be deposited at the station. In a 6–3 decision, the Court struck down the ordinance as a violation of the dormant Commerce Clause because it required haulers to deposit the waste at a preferred processing facility for the benefit of that facility. Since the time that the Court decided *Carbone*, commentators have generally agreed that local authorities are restricted in their ability to enact flow control ordinances.

During the 1980s, Oneida and Herkimer Counties in New York faced a crisis. Many of the local landfills, which were owned by private companies, operated without permits and in violation of state regulations. State officials required several of these landfills to close, and the federal government later brought an action to require the cleanup of an Oneida landfill. Both counties also experienced problems with local waste management companies, some of which were engaged in price fixing and overcharging.

At the request of these counties, the New York Legislature addressed these problems by creating the Oneida-Herkimer Solid Waste Management Authority as a public benefit corporation. The **statute** that created this authority empowered the corporation to collect, process, and dispose of solid waste in the counties, and also permitted the counties to impose "appropriate and reasonable limitations on competition," including the enactment of local laws that require solid waste to sent to a solid waste management facility.

The Authority and the two counties in 1989 entered into an agreement that allowed the Authority to manage all solid waste within the counties. Under the agreement, the Authority was required to purchase and develop facilities to process and dispose of solid waste and recyclables. To generate revenues, the Authority charged a "tipping fee," which was levied against trash collectors who dropped off their waste at a processing facility ("tipping" refers to the act of a garbage truck tipping its back end to dump the trash at the facility). The Authority charged higher tipping fees than those charged on the open market. However, these greater fees allowed the Authority to offer additional services that a private waste disposer might be able to provide.

In 1995, United Haulers Association, Inc., which is a trade association made up of several solid waste management companies, and six trash haulers brought suit against the counties and the Authority. According to the plaintiffs, the flow control laws passed by the counties violated the Commerce Clause because the laws favored the local **entity**. United Haulers argued that *Carbone* governed this type of case.

The U.S. **District Court** for the Northern District of New York agreed with the plaintiffs, holding that *Carbone* categorically rejected these types of flow control laws. On appeal, the Second **Circuit Court** of Appeals reversed. According to the **appellate court**, the Supreme Court's precedent had established a distinction between laws that benefit public entities as compared with laws that benefit private entities. The Second Circuit thus reversed the district court's decision. *United Haulers Ass'n v. Oneida-Herkimer Solid Waste Mgmt. Auth.*, 261 F.3d 245 (2d Cir. 2001). The case was remanded to the district court, which determined that the ordinances did not impose any relevant burden on interstate commerce. On appeal for the second time, the Second Circuit affirmed the district court's decision. *United Haulers Ass'n v. Oneida-Herkimer Solid Waste Mgmt. Auth.*, 438 F.3d 150 (2d Cir. 2006).

The Supreme Court granted **certiorari** to resolve a conflict between the Second Circuit's decision and a conflicting holding rendered by the Sixth Circuit Court of Appeals. Chief Justice Roberts delivered the opinion of the Court,

though only three other justices joined his opinion. Roberts acknowledged that the only significant difference between the New York law and the one invalidated in *Carbone* is that the New York law required the haulers to take their waste to a public benefit corporation. According to Roberts' opinion, this difference was enough to reach a different conclusion than the one in *Carbone*. Roberts noted that a publicly-owned facility benefits the community and allows the local governmental entity to fulfill its responsibilities of protecting "the health, safety, and welfare of its citizens." For these reasons, the distinction between the public facility and a private facility was enough to lead the Court to uphold the ordinance.

Justice CLARENCE THOMAS wrote a concurrence in which he argued that the dormant Commerce Clause has proven to be "unworkable in practice." Justice ANTONIN SCALIA also criticized the doctrine and argued that he would limit the application of the rule "beyond its existing domain." Samuel Alito, who was joined by two other justices, dissented, saying that the case should have been controlled by *Carbone*.

CONSTITUTIONAL LAW

The written text of the state and federal constitutions. The body of judicial PRECEDENT that has gradually developed through a process in which courts interpret, apply, and explain the meaning of particular constitutional provisions and principles during a legal proceeding. Executive, legislative, and judicial actions that conform with the norms prescribed by a constitutional provision.

Justice Scalia Debates President of American Civil Liberties Union

In October 2006, Justice ANTONIN SCALIA engaged in a debate with Nadine Strossen, the president of the AMERICAN CIVIL LIBERTIES UNION, during which Scalia defended his approach to interpreting the Constitution. The one-hour debate, which was considered a cordial affair, was televised on C-SPAN. During this time, the two exchanged their views on such issues as the role of the federal judiciary, abortion rights, race questions, and religious issues.

The 70-year-old Scalia was appointed to the Supreme Court by President RONALD REAGAN in 1986. In the 20 years since that time, Scalia has become one of the most outspoken members of the Court. The conservative maintains a staunch stance that the Constitution should be interpreted rigidly and strictly, and that the meaning of the text should be derived from the 18th-century context when it was written. Scalia has clashed with both liberal and moderate justices in the past.

Strossen criticized Scalia for protecting certain privacy rights, such as those found in the FOURTH AMENDMENT, while failing to protect others, such as the right of consenting adults to engage in sexual relations. "Many people, and including those of us in the ACLU, are very distressed at your failure to find within the constitution protection for what we think is at least as important a type of privacy, namely the right of consenting individuals—mature individuals in their own homes—to decide what they are going to see, or read, to decide with whom they are going to live, what kind of sexual intimacies or relationships they are going to engage in," she said. "Isn't this, in fact, a confluence of the FIRST AMENDMENT and the Fourth Amendment? That government should not have the right to criminalize certain materials that we read, and should not have the right to criminalize certain sexual intimacies."

Scalia responded by saying that it was not up to the federal judiciary to make decisions about what the law should be. "I'm in the business of enforcing the laws," Scalia, who also rejected the notion that he is a "strict constructionist," said. "What democracy means is that on controversial issues, even stuff like homosexual rights, abortion, whatever, we debate with each other, and persuade each other, and vote on it. Either our representatives, or through a constitutional amendment in the states, we decide the question."

Scalia also argued against the notion that the Constitution is an evolving document, saying that such an approach puts the justices in the position of having to decide how the Constitution evolves. "Why in the world would you want nine people from a very uncharacteristic class of society—to whit, nine lawyers—to decide how the constitution evolves?," he said. "It means whatever they think it ought to mean."

Strossen responded by stressing that federal judges were precisely the best individuals to interpret the text of the Constitution. "There are some rights that are so fundamental that no majority can take them away from any minority, no matter how small or unpopular that minority might be," she said. "And who is better positioned to represent and defend and be the ultimate backstop for rights of individuals and

Antonin Scalia, speaking at ACLU conference, October 2006.
AP IMAGES

minorities than those who are not directly accountable in the electoral process, namely federal judges?"

With respect to abortion rights, Scalia has maintained that the decision in *Roe v. Wade*, 410 U.S. 113, 93 S. Ct. 705, 35 L. Ed. 2d 147 (1973) should be overruled. He also dissented from the decision in *Lawrence v. Texas*, 539 U.S. 558, 123 S. Ct. 2472, 156 L. Ed. 2d 508 (2003), in which the Court struck down a Texas **statute** proscribing homosexual **sodomy**. In his debate with Strossen, Scalia again stressed that these are issues that should be addressed by legislative bodies. "Nobody ever thought that [abortion or gay rights] had been included in the rights contained in the Bill of Rights, which is why abortion and homosexual sodomy were criminal for 200 years. Now whether that's a good idea or a bad is not what I'm talking about. That's not my job to say that. It is my job to say whether the Bill of Rights has taken it out of the realm of democratic debate. Just because you feel strongly about it, it isn't necessarily in the Bill of Rights."

Scalia has similarly taken a hard stance against using race as a factor for diversity in schools. He dissented in the 2003 case of *Grutter v. Bollinger*, 539 U.S. 306, 123 S. Ct. 2325, 156 S. Ct. 304, in which the Court upheld the University of Michigan Law School's policy of considering race as a factor for achieving a diverse student body. In the debate, Scalia noted, "The Constitution very clearly forbids discrimination on the basis of race. It doesn't seem to me to allow Michigan to say we think it's good to discriminate on the basis of race when you want to make sure everyone is exposed to different backgrounds. We cannot use race as the test of diversity."

The debate took place at the beginning of a term where the Court would consider some significant cases addressing abortion and school integration. In a series of abortion cases in the past, Scalia often voted with the minority, while moderate justice Sandra Day O'Connor famously served as the swing vote. However, the Court's two newest members, Chief Justice JOHN ROBERTS and Samuel Alito, are both more conservative than O'Connor, and commentators expected some cases heard during the 2006 term to provide clear indications of how conservative the Court may have become.

Six months after the debate, Scalia voted with the majority in *Gonzales v. Carhart*, Nos. 05-380, 05-1382, 2007 WL 1135596 (Apr. 18, 2007), in which the Court upheld a partial-birth abortion ban. The decision was immediately criticized by women's rights groups as having damaged the rights established in *Roe v. Wade*.

CONSUMER CREDIT

Short-term loans made to enable people to purchase goods or services primarily for personal, family, or household purposes.

Safeco Insurance Co. of America v. Burr

Under the FAIR CREDIT REPORTING ACT (FCRA), 15 U.S.C. §§1681 **et seq.**, establishes that a consumer who is subjected to an "adverse action" based on the consumer's credit report is entitled to notice of this action. A consumer who is entitled to, but does not receive, this notice may recover from the business that failed to give notice in a **civil action**. The U.S. SUPREME COURT during its 2006 term considered the circumstances in which an insurance company might be liable under the FCRA. In *Safeco Insurance Co. of America v. Burr*, ___ U.S. ___, 127 S. Ct. 2201, ___ L. Ed. 2d ___ (2007), the Court determined that two well-known insurers were not liable to consumers even though they had used information in the consumers' credit reports.

The FCRA provides that "any person [who] takes any adverse action with respect to any consumer that is based in whole or in part on any information contained in a consumer report" must provide notice to the affected consumer. This notice must state what the adverse action is, explain how to contact the business that took the action, and explain to the consumer that he or she can obtain a copy of a credit report and can dispute its accuracy.

The FRCA applies to insurance companies as well as other types of businesses. The **statute** directly addresses what an "adverse action" is in the business of insurance, defining such an action as "a denial or cancellation of, an increase in any charge for, or a reduction or other adverse or unfavorable change in the terms of coverage or amount of, any insurance, existing or applied for." Under the FCRA, a consumer may bring a civil action against a business that uses a consumer report but fails to notify the consumer of having done so. If the business is negligent in failing to provide notice, the consumer is entitled to actual damages. However, where a business has willfully failed to provide notice, the consumer may be entitled to actual, **statutory**, or **punitive damages**.

GEICO provides automobile insurance through one of four subsidiaries. Potential customers can call the company on a toll-free number. The company's agent takes the customer's information as well as the applicant's credit score, with the permission of the applicant. Based on this information, GEICO's computer system determines the appropriate rate that at which the policy should be issued. The rate determines which of GEICO's subsidiary will issue the policy. For instance, GEICO Casualty sells policies at higher rates to high-risk customers.

GEICO's practice at one time was to send adverse action notices to any applicant that was not offered a "preferred," low-rate policy. The company altered its practice by adopting a method where it would "neutralize" the credit score of an applicant. Under this method, the company compared the applicant's rate that it received with the applicant's current credit score with the rate that the applicant would have received with a "neutral" score, meaning one that was calculated without reference to the credit history. If using the neutral credit score would have resulted in the applicant receiving a lower rate, then the company would notify the customer. However, the company did not send notice if the applicant would have received a better rate had the customer had a better credit rating.

Ajene Edo applied for insurance coverage with GEICO. The company checked Edo's credit report and offered him a policy that the company provides to moderate-risk customers. GEICO determined that had it used a neutral score, it would have offered the same rate to Edo. Thus, the company did not provide an adverse action notice to him. Edo filed a **class action** suit, arguing that he was entitled to statutory and punitive damages for the company's failure to provide notice. The U.S. **District Court** for the District of Oregon issued **summary judgment** in favor of GEICO, holding that there was no adverse action because the premium that the company charged to Edo "would have been the same even if GEICO Indemnity did not consider information in [his] **consumer credit** history."

The court in the District of Oregon also ordered summary judgment in a separate case involving Safeco, another insurer that determined insurance rates based on each customer's credit score. The Safeco case arose when the company offered a customer higher rates than the best ones available, due to the customer's credit rating. When the company did not send an adverse action notice, the customer sued. The court ordered summary judgment in favor of Safeco, determining that that the offering of a single, initial rate for insurance was not an adverse action.

The Ninth **Circuit Court** of Appeals reversed both decisions by the district court. According to the Ninth Circuit, when a customer "would have received a lower rate for his insurance had the information in his consumer report been more favorable, an adverse action has been taken against him." In GEICO's case, if Edo had a better credit score, he would have been placed with a different subsidiary. Thus, the court held that GEICO had violated the FCRA for failing to not sending the adverse action notice. The court applied this rationale to the Safeco case, concluding that Safeco had also violated the FCRA. The Ninth Circuit remanded the case to the district court to determine whether the insurance companies had willfully failed to comply with the statute.

The Supreme Court agreed to review the case. An opinion by Justice DAVID SOUTER focused first on what a willful failure to comply with the FCRA means. According to the Court, the term "willful" is generally synonymous with terms such as "wanton" and "reckless." Thus, if either company had acted recklessly in failing to comply with the statute, the company would have violated the statute. The Court, however, concluded that neither company had acted recklessly. In GEICO's case, because the company had offered Edo the same rate that he would have received with a neutral credit score, the Court concluded that the company had not violated the statute in failing to provide adverse

action notice. In Safeco's case, the Court determined that even if the company had violated the statute, it had not done so willfully. Thus, the Court reversed the Ninth Circuit's decision.

COPYRIGHT

An intangible right granted by statute to the author or originator of certain literary or artistic productions, whereby, for a limited period, the exclusive privilege is given to the person to make copies of the same for publication and sale.

Video Sharing Sites Face Major Copyright Issues

In 2006, the founders of the popular video-sharing site YouTube had a significant payday when Google purchased the company for $1.65 billion in stock in October. This news came at a time when YouTube faced allegations of copyright infringement, which led the site to remove tens of thousands of its video clips. By 2007, both YouTube and Google were named as defendants in a $1 billion lawsuit filed by Viacom.

YouTube launched in February 2005 and quickly became one of the Internet's most popular sites. Users on the site may upload their own video clips, which are then processed by the site so that other users may view them in a standard media form. The company estimates that 100 million of its videos are viewed every day, and the site has more than 70 million individual visitors per day. Many commentators note that YouTube has been a major part of what is commonly referred to as Web 2.0, a new generation of web-based communities.

After its first year, YouTube already faced copyright concerns. In its original form, YouTube did not place limits on the length of the videos that could be uploaded. A number of users posted full-length clips of certain shows, often in violation of the content owner's copyright. In March 2006, the company announced that it would limit the length of most clips to 10 minutes, a preemptive move designed to avoid litigation over the copyright concerns. According to one media analyst, "They're trying to avoid becoming the Napster of video."

YouTube continued to grow in popularity, even with the limitations on the lengths of the clips. Many of the clips are short clips created by users themselves, and these are often the most popular clips. The content ranges considerably. In some clips, users simply speak into the camera, creating what is known as a video blog.

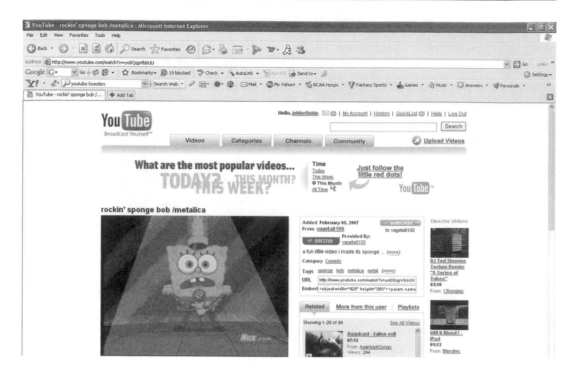

A still image of a computer screen showing the YouTube Web site, the subject of copyright lawsuits in 2007.

AP IMAGES

Other amateur producers create fictional scenes. Videos that the site highlights can often have tens of thousands of viewers in just a few days.

A significant number of clips, however, are copyrighted by others. Some of the most popular clips on the site were clips from such shows as "South Park" and "The Daily Show with John Stewart," both owned by Viacom. Sports videos, including highlight clips from major sporting events, were also quite popular, as were music videos. Although a number of commentators suggested that YouTube was bound to run into copyright problems, the company nevertheless flourished.

Less than two years after its founding, YouTube was purchased by Google. YouTube's three founders and its financial backer, Sequoia Capital, benefited the most. Sequoia received 941,027 shares of Google, valued at approximately $442 million. Chad Hurley, YouTube's chief executive, received stock worth about $345 million. Two other founders, including Steven Chen and Jawed Karim, received $326 million and $64.6 million worth of stock, respectively. The $1.65 billion deal was Google's largest acquisition in its history.

Less than two weeks after the purchase was announced, copyright problems again emerged. In October 2006, YouTube deleted nearly 30,000 video clips owned by a Japanese firm. Shortly after that time, the site removed hundreds of sports video clips, namely those featur-

ing highlights from the National Football League. Despite the removal of these videos, new copyrighted videos soon replaced those that were deleted, prompting those in the media industry to demand that YouTube devise a system for screening videos before they are posted to the site.

Although both YouTube and Google reportedly promised to adopt copyright protection mechanisms, by the beginning of 2007 they had still failed to do so. Of particular concern to the copyright owners is the ability of YouTube users to embed clips from YouTube on their own sites and sell advertisements that appear next to the clips. According to one industry source, "When you sell children's programming, you get a little sensitive about what ads are sold next to it, and you hope that it's not Girls Gone Wild."

By February 2007, Viacom had asked YouTube to remove more than 160,000 videos, which had been viewed approximately 1.2 billion times. Following this demand, Viacom filed a $1 billion suit against both YouTube and Google. "YouTube continues in its unlawful business model," a Viacom spokesperson said. "Therefore, we must turn to the courts to prevent Google and YouTube from continuing to steal value from artists and to obtain compensation for the significant damage they have caused." Viacom claimed that YouTube applied content filters selectively, noting that clips showing pornography and criminal acts are removed immediately, while other clips that infringe copyrights are allowed to remain.

The popularity of YouTube led to the creation of dozens of clone sites, such as Meta-Cafe and Revver. Google and Yahoo also have their own video-sharing sites, and sites such as MySpace allow users to post videos in a manner similar to YouTube. Many of these sites are now scrambling to develop new business models to allow them to remain in business. YouTube has entered into partnerships with such media entities as NBC and CBS, allowing the site to show authorized clips that are produced by these networks.

In the meantime, companies are spending thousands of dollars to search the Web for copyrighted videos in an effort to remove as much of the content as possible. Other entities, such as the Motion Picture Association of America, are evaluating copyright-detection software that could be used to screen the sites for infringing materials.

COURT MARTIAL

A tribunal that tries violations of military criminal law. Often, the entire military justice process, from actual court proceedings to punishment.

Court Martial of Military Officer in Abu Ghraib Prison Scandal

In April 2006, U.S. Army Lieutenant Colonel Steven L. Jordan became the first and only military officer to be criminally charged for abuse and mistreatment of Iraqi prisoners at Baghdad's now infamous Abu Ghraib facility. The prison scandal stems from incidents that took place in 2004, when photographs of the prisoner abuse were leaked to the media. They included images of naked prisoners with dog leashes around their necks, being intimidated and forced into various demeaning and/or sexual positions and acts. Some of the more disturbing photographs showed detainees smeared with excrement, posing to be lynched, and cowering under attack from U.S. military dogs. President GEORGE W. BUSH referred to the scandal as the "biggest mistake" made by the United States in Iraq, even as the images were continually transmitted via Internet around the world, evoking anger and global condemnation.

Jordan, the second-highest ranking intelligence officer at the prison at the time of the alleged incident(s), was initially charged with multiple violations of the UNIFORM CODE OF

U.S. Army Lt. Colonel Steven Jordan arrives at military court for a hearing in the Abu Ghraib prison scandal, October 2006.

AP IMAGES

MILITARY JUSTICE (UCMJ), including cruelty and maltreatment of prisoners, interfering with an investigation (obstruction of justice), disobeying a superior commissioned officer, dereliction of duty, false swearing, and failure to obey a regulation.

Some of the charges were dismissed in October 2006 following an Article 32 hearing (the equivalent of a civilian **preliminary hearing**) at Fort McNair in Washington. The presiding judge at the hearing ordered court martial of Jordan for the remaining charges. (Jordan's defense lawyers had argued at the hearing that all charges should be dropped because he was never properly advised of his rights by investigators.) Originally scheduled for July 2007, the actual court martial was delayed until August to allow additional time for the review of documents and e-mails from the prison. If convicted, Jordan faced up to 16 years in prison. In the interim, Jordan remained on active duty at the intelligence and security command at Fort Belvoir, Virginia.

Jordan, a reservist from South Dakota on active duty, was formally trained as a civil affairs officer before serving as head of the interrogation operation at the Baghdad prison. He reported to another officer, Colonel Thomas Pappas, who officially was in charge of the Joint Interrogation Debriefing Center at Abu Ghraib. Pappas was the most senior official to receive punishment for the abuses, but unlike Jordan, was not criminally charged. Instead, he received a formal reprimand in addition to an $8,000 fine for approving the use of dogs on a high-value detainee without obtaining permission from top officers at Baghdad. He later was granted immunity for testifying against Jordan and military dog handlers. In March 2006, Army dog handler Michael J. Smith was sentenced to six months in prison for using his snarling canine to intimidate prisoners. The most infamous convictees included the alleged ringleader in the abuse, Specialist Charles Graner, Jr., who was photographed smiling with thumbs up over the body of an Iraqi (and who received a ten-year prison sentence) and his then-girlfriend, Private Lynndie England, pictured holding a naked prisoner at the end of a dog leash (sentenced to three years).

Results from Army investigations that supported the charges against Jordan included a finding that he, in one incident, had given military police "tacit approval" for violence against some prisoners, which ultimately contributed to the downward spiral of their treatment. Major General Antonio Taguba, who investigated the Abu Ghraib abuses, recommended that Jordan be relieved from duty for "failing to ensure that Soldiers under his direct control knew, understood, and followed the protections afforded to detainees in the Geneva Convention Relative to the Treatment of Prisoners of War."

Moreover, Taguba accused Jordan of "making material misrepresentations" when he told Taguba that he "never saw nude detainees [and] never knew of dogs being used in interrogations." Two lengthy unpublished interviews later obtained by the media revealed that the Army's Criminal Investigation Command questioned Graner and Staff Sergeant Ivan Frederick II, both serving prison terms for their roles in the scandal. They independently told investigators that Jordan had seen nude detainees handcuffed to prison doors as well as sexual humiliation and abuse of other prisoners, but made no comment. Jordan also allegedly helped Graner erect a plywood wall to obscure the view of prisoner abuse from the corridor hallway. When asked about the plywood wall, Jordan apparently told General Taguba that it was erected to protect prisoner privacy. However, an independent interview with another prisoner collaborated the true purpose of the wall. Jordan was also implicated for his knowledge of mistreatment of "ghost detainees," who were delivered to the prison by CIA operatives and interrogated "off the books." Jordan earlier told General Taguba that he "never imagined anything going on other than normal operations." The Army referred to his statements as "totally false."

Jordan remained the only officer to face court-martial on criminal charges related to Abu Ghraib. At least eleven U.S. enlisted soldiers were convicted and several officers were reprimanded or demoted, including Colonel Janis Karpinski, prison commander at the time, who was demoted from brigadier general to colonel, but faced no charges. In a related matter, the AMERICAN CIVIL LIBERTIES UNION (ACLU) expressed disappointment at the dismissal of a case against former Secretary of Defense Donald Rumsfeld, brought by nine Iraqi and Afghan former detainees for alleged "torture" endured while in U.S. military custody. "We believe that the law and constitution require more, and that the former secretary of defense must be held accountable for his policies that led to this abuse," ACLU attorney Lucas Guttentag told an AFP news reporter.

CRIMINAL LAW

A body of rules and statutes that defines conduct prohibited by the government because it threatens and harms public safety and welfare and that establishes punishment to be imposed for the commission of such acts.

Whorton v. Bockting

The U.S. SUPREME COURT periodically announces a new rule of **criminal law** or procedure that could affect thousands of persons previously convicted under the old **rule of law**. The Court has established standards for determining whether those previously convicted, and whose direct appeals had been exhausted before the date of the ruling, may seek to reverse their convictions. The Supreme Court, in *Whorton v. Bockting*, __U.S.__, 127 S.Ct. 1173, __L.Ed.2d __ (2007), held that a 2004 rule dealing with the Sixth Amendment's Confrontation Clause was not a "watershed rule" that implicated the fairness and accuracy of criminal proceedings. Therefore, those persons convicted under the old rule could not collaterally attack their convictions using the new rule.

Marvin Bockting collaterally attacked his conviction for the sexual assault of the six-year-old daughter of his wife. Bockting and his wife Laura lived in Las Vegas, Nevada with their three-year-old daughter Honesty and Laura's daughter Autumn. Autumn told her mother that Bockting had forced her to engage in numerous sex acts with him. Laura kicked Marvin out of the house and took Autumn to the hospital for a physical examination. The Las Vegas police department's investigator for sexual assaults tried to interview Autumn but found her too upset to talk about the assaults. The officer then ordered a rape examination, which revealed strong physical evidence of sexual assault. Two days later the investigator interviewed Autumn in the presence of her mother. This time she gave detailed descriptions of the sexual assaults committed by Bockting. The police then arrested him for sexual assault. At the **preliminary hearing** Autumn testified but she became upset when asked about the assaults. She first said that Bockting had touched her in way that was wrong but then backtracked, saying she couldn't remember how he had touched her or what she had told the mother or the investigator. The court was persuaded by the testimony of the mother and the investigator to hold Bockting for trial.

At trial the judge determined that Autumn was too distressed to testify. Under Nevada state law the judge found sufficient evidence of reliability to allow the investigator and Laura Bockting to recount Autumn's statements. Marvin Bockting's lawyer had objected, arguing that the Confrontation Clause barred the admission of this evidence. The defendant took the stand in his own defense and denied that he had assaulted Autumn. He claimed that Autumn had acquired some knowledge about sexual acts because she had seen him and her mother engaging in sexual intercourse and had become familiar with sexual terms. The jury convicted Bockting on three counts of sexual assault on a minor under the age of 14 and he was given a life sentence.

Bockting's conviction was upheld by the Nevada Supreme Court in 1993. The court applied a U.S. Supreme Court precedent concerning the admission of out-of-court statements. This precedent held that the Confrontation Clause permitted the admission of a **hearsay** statement where the circumstances surrounding the making of the statements provided "particularized guarantees of trustworthiness." The Nevada Supreme Court believed Autumn's initial statements to her mother, her recitations to the investigator, and her use of anatomically correct dolls to demonstrate the assaults justified the admission of the statements. Bockting then filed for a **writ** of **habeas corpus** in federal court, again arguing that the state court decision violated his Confrontation Clause rights. The **district court** rejected his argument and Bockting appealed to the Ninth **Circuit Court** of Appeals. While his appeal was pending the Su-

preme Court overruled its Confrontation Clause precedent in *Crawford v. Washington*, 541 U.S. 36, 124 S.Ct. 1354, 158 L.Ed.2d 177 (2004). The Court held that "statements of witnesses absent from trial" were admissible "only where the declarant is unavailable, and only where the defendant has had a prior opportunity to cross-examine [the witness]." Bockting argued to the Ninth Circuit that if *Crawford* had been applied to his case Autumn's out-of-court statements would not have been admitted and the jury would not have convicted him. The Ninth Circuit ruled that *Crawford* could be applied retroactively to cases on **collateral** review and granted Bockting his petition. The Supreme Court agreed to review this decision because it conflicted with every other circuit court of appeals and every state supreme court that had addressed the issue.

The Court, in a unanimous decision, reversed the Ninth Circuit. Justice Samuel Alito, writing for the Court, noted that the Court had laid out a framework for determining whether a rule should be applied retroactively to judgments in criminal cases that are already final on direct review. A new rule is generally applicable only to cases that are still on direct review. In this case *Crawford* was a new rule because "it was not dictated by the governing precedent at the time when the respondent's conviction became final." Having established that *Crawford* was a new rule, Alito stated that under the framework the rule cannot be applied to a **collateral attack** on a Bockting's conviction unless it is a "watershed rule of **criminal procedure** implicating the fundamental fairness and accuracy of the criminal proceeding." Since the framework had been established no new rule had achieved watershed status.

The *Crawford* rule failed to satisfy the requirement that it prevent an "impermissibly large risk of an inaccurate conviction." It was not enough if the rule improved the accuracy of trial or enhanced the reliability of evidence. In this case *Crawford* had overruled the prior precedent because the old rule was "inconsistent with the original understanding of the meaning of the Confrontation Clause." The Court did not make the new rule to improve the "accuracy of fact finding in criminal trials. The *Crawford* rule also did not change the Court's "bedrock procedural elements essential to the fairness of a proceeding." A new procedural rule could not meet this requirement if it was based on a "bedrock" right. Though this new rule was "certainly important" it did not approach the establishment

Franklin, Massachusetts, police officer Brian Johnson poses with computer displaying Youtube page on which he posted a surveillance tape in hopes of gathering leads.

of the right of indigents charged with felonies to have a court-appointed lawyer announced in *Gideon v. Wainwright*, 372 U.S. 335, 83 S.Ct. 792, 9 L.Ed.2d 799 (1963). Therefore the new rule in *Crawford* could not be applied to Bockting's case.

Law Enforcement Using YouTube to Catch Criminals

Law enforcement officials in some areas are taking advantage of the popularity of online video sites, such as YouTube, to catch criminals. These officials post such information as the clips of surveillance cameras, and then send the link to groups of people who might be able to identify suspects that have been captured on the video. In some instances, several thousand people have seen the video clips, and the tactic has led to successful arrests.

The founders of YouTube launched the site in February 2005, and it was an instant hit on the Internet. The site allows user to upload video clips, which are then processed and converted to a format that can be seen on most Web browsers. By some estimates, the site has more than 70 million unique viewers per day. YouTube became so popular that Internet giant Google bought the company in October 2006 for $1.65 billion. Dozens of clone sites have also popped up on the Internet since the birth of YouTube.

Postings of mug shots and other pictures of suspects for the public to see is, of course, a tactic long used by law enforcement. It is also common for police to share videos and photos between departments. However, broadcasts of these videos and photos on the Internet has not been a common practice. In such places as

Franklin, Massachusetts, which has a population of about 30,000, the Internet can broaden the range of people who might be able to identify suspects in videos shot by security cameras.

In December 2006, the Franklin police department posted on YouTube one of these videos showing two suspects in a stolen credit card case. The clip shows the two men standing in line at a Home Depot less than an hour after stealing a credit card from a car parked outside a fitness center. The faces of the two men are not clear on the 30-second clip, but it provides enough detail that the men are identifiable. After posting the clip, officers emailed the link to the clip to about 300 people and organizations, indicating that the department sought these men in connection with the crime.

"You don't have to be a technology wizard to figure out how to watch a video on YouTube," said officer Brian Johnson of the Franklin Police Department. He also noted, "You never know who is going to say, 'Hey, I know that guy.'" The suspects in the case were ultimately arrested, though officers credited old-fashioned police work for the capture.

Franklin's use of the Internet in that case was relatively small-scale compared with departments elsewhere. In Hamilton, Ontario, offices posted a 72-second surveillance video on YouTube after a fatal shooting outside of a hip-hop concert. The clip attracted about 35,000 hits, and the police had enough information within two weeks to arrest a suspect. A detective working on the case sought to increase awareness by placing an announcement on websites that are visited by hip-hop fans. According to the detective, "We hoped there would be enough buzz created that people on their own would go to YouTube."

YouTube allows officers to post a description of the scene on the site, along with the telephone number of the department. In a video posted by the Billerica, Maine police department, the clip contains the following description: "Suspects smash the front window of the convenient store and steal some beer. Incident occurred on 3/14/07 in Billerica, MA. This appears to be very similar to another incident which occurred on 12/25/06 of last year. We believe the vehicle to be a dark Toyota Matrix or similar small wagon. Anyone who may know anything about the suspect sin the video, please call the Billerica Police Department. . . ."

Despite the promise, some commentators have expressed concern about the use of sites such as YouTube for these purposes. A video that is viewed by several thousand people might lead to numerous false leads, thus hampering the ability of police officers to track down legitimate leads. One detective noted, "There is a concern that if we use this option often that we would unnecessarily tie up our investigators who'd be looking into hundreds or thousands of leads that would be produced." Others have expressed privacy concerns. For instance, some have noted that victims and innocent bystanders should consent before the videos are posted. Similarly, some experts have said that the videos should be removed once the court proceedings have closed.

One irony in the use of the videos is that police are using a medium that has been employed to demonstrate police misconduct. Some groups and users use YouTube and other sites to post videos showing instances of police abuse or excessive force. In one instance, a clip on YouTube showed an officer punching a suspect repeatedly in the face, prompting an investigation by the FEDERAL BUREAU OF INVESTIGATION.

A growing number of departments now consider YouTube as one of many options that may be used during investigations. Departments are also using other popular sites for a similar purpose. For example, social networking sites such as MySpace have been used to benefit investigations due to the type of information that can be exchanged there.

CUOMO, ANDREW

Andrew Cuomo, son of former New York Governor Mario Cuomo, is noted for his work on housing issues. Once the secretary of housing and urban development (HUD), he also attracted attention with his marriage to (and eventual divorce from) a daughter of assassinated New York Senator Robert F. Kennedy. He mounted a failed bid for governor of New York in 2002, but rebounded to become New York's attorney general in the 2006 election.

He worked his way through Fordham University (B.A. 1979) and Albany Law School (1982). And then his life changed considerably. Fresh out of law school in 1982, Cuomo was tapped by his father to run the latter's first campaign for governor. It was successful and he spent the next two years as special advisor to his dad—at a salary of a dollar a year. Leaving the elder Cuomo safely ensconced in Albany (for three terms), he headed back to New York City in 1984 to practice law. Cuomo began to focus

---

ANDREW CUOMO

1997: Became Secretary of Housing and Urban Development

2002: Failed in bid for New York governorship

2006: Elected attorney general of New York

---

his considerable energies on housing issues in 1984, when he started the Genesis Project, an urban renewal and community development enterprise. He went on to found the Housing Enterprise for the Less Privileged (H.E.L.P.) in 1986. It was designed to build transitional housing and provide guidance to those in need. These efforts laid the groundwork for much of his career.

In 1988, Cuomo met Kerry Kennedy, a daughter of the late Senator Robert F. Kennedy. The two were married in 1990—a much-heralded match between two powerful Democratic families. They had three children before the marriage broke up with an equal amount of ballyhoo in 2003. Meanwhile, Cuomo began to attract national attention on his own. After serving as then-mayor David Dinkins' head of New York City's Commission on the Homeless in 1991, he went to Washington D.C. to be assistant secretary of HUD. He moved into the top job there in January of 1997 and began to clean house. Among his controversial changes were internal restructuring, job cuts, and a first-time audit of 29,000 properties. He also got HUD its largest budgets in years. Although effective, however, Cuomo was not always liked.

Since running his father's campaign in 1982, Cuomo has been variously described as brilliant, vindictive, effective, ambitious, and volatile. His tenure at HUD did little to change these opinions. Neither did his unsuccessful run for New York governor in 2002 (from which he withdrew in the week just before the primary). However one felt about his personal style, though, few doubted his convictions. Jay Nordlinger of the *National Review* quoted Cuomo's then-wife's comments in this regard. "He has a serious commitment to helping the most vulnerable, the poorest people in our

Andrew Cuomo
AP IMAGES

society. . . . He's their advocate. He speaks for the people . . . who have no other voice."

Cuomo surprised many with his campaign for the influential position of New York's attorney general in 2006. His complete failure in 2002, coupled with what was perceived as an alienating personality, led many to assume he would fail again. However, superior fundraising and a less abrasive personal style led to an easy victory over Republican Jeanine Pirro. Following in the footsteps of predecessor Eliot Spitzer, Cuomo has pursued a reform-oriented agenda, including a major investigation of the college loan industry, targeting banks and schools that preyed on students.

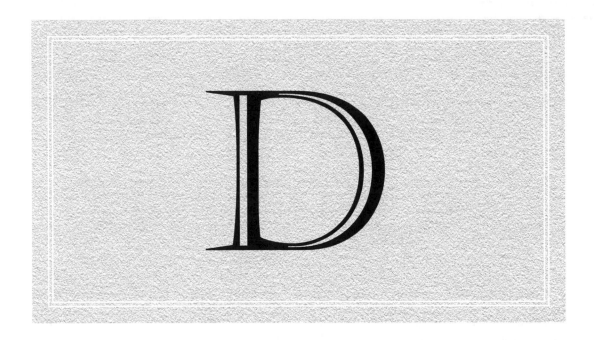

DAMAGES

Monetary compensation that is awarded by a court in a civil action to an individual who has been injured through the wrongful conduct of another party.

Christopher v. Florida

When a jury awards a plaintiff damages for injuries caused by the defendant, the defendant has the right to file post-trial motions that ask the judge to either ignore the jury verdict and declare that the defendant was not liable for the injuries, grant the defendant a new trial, or reduce the amount of the damages using a procedure called **remittitur**. It is rare that a judge will find the defendant not liable by granting a judgment as a matter of law (JMOL), for the judge must find that there were no facts to justify liability. It is more common to give the plaintiff the option of receiving a lower amount of damages (remittitur) or retrying the case to a new jury. Typically, the plaintiff accepts the reduced damages award. In *Christopher v. Florida*, 449 F.3d 1360 (11th Cir.2006), the Eleventh **Circuit Court** of Appeals ruled that a trial judge had improperly issued a JMOL and that both defendants must receive a new trial. The appeals court buttressed this decision by concluding that the "gross excessiveness" of the jury awards cast doubt on the validity of the entire verdict.

Kenrick Christopher sued two Florida Highway Patrol officers, Barry Tierney and Jose Hernandez, for a severe brain injury he received when the officers conducted a drug raid pursuant to a search warrant naming the owner of the house, but not Christopher. At trial Christopher alleged that he was lying on his bed when two masked man armed with guns burst into his room. He was ordered to get off the bed and when he did not immediately comply he was pushed to the floor. He landed face down and felt an officer put his knee into his back and pull his right arm back until he felt his shoulder snap. When Christopher asked what the officer was doing he was told to shut up and then hit in the back of his head with a sharp object. He felt a warm tingling and could not stand and walk out of the house when ordered by the two officers. An ambulance was called and during the ride to the hospital Christopher told the EMT that had been assaulted by police. Doctors discovered that a blood vessel had ruptured in his brain and performed surgery. Christopher spent three weeks in the hospital and was permanently disabled.

Officers Tierney and Gonzalez offered different accounts of what went on in the room with Christopher. Tierney claimed that a second man was in the room and that he scuffled with him and not Christopher. (No second man was ever charged in the case.) Tierney said he never touched Christopher and did not know what Gonzalez said or did while in the room. Gonzalez testified that he did not recall touching Christopher and had no recollection who handcuffed Christopher or what Tierney said or did while in the room.

Doctors called as expert witnesses disagreed as to what caused the brain trauma. Christopher's doctor said he had been born with a brain malformation that made vessels susceptible to rupture, but concluded the injury was caused by a blow to the back of the head. The defendants' doctor testified that the injury was most likely caused by heightened blood pressure attributable to surprise or apprehension. Another expert for Christopher stated that the plaintiff's memory was not intact when he arrived at the hospital and that his memories were likely reconstructed by others. The judge, before trial, dismissed all of Christopher's excessive force claims except the alleged blow to the head. Defendants would only be liable if an officer intentionally hit Christopher. The jury found both officers liable and awarded Christopher $6.725 million in damages. The officers filed post-trial motions asking either for a new trial or a JMOL. The judge granted Hernandez a new trial and granted Tierney a JMOL.

The Eleventh Circuit Court of Appeals, in a 2–1 vote, ruled that the trial court should not have granted Tierney a JOML. Instead, the appeals court concluded that both Hernandez and Tierney were entitled to a new trial on both the issue of liability and the amount of damages. Judge J.L. Edmondson, writing for the majority, stated that the JOML was unwarranted because the jury was entitled to weigh the highly contradictory statements of the plaintiff and Tierney. As to the need for a new trial, the court focused both on the conduct of the plaintiff's lawyer and the size of the damages awarded by the jury. In his **closing argument**, Christopher's lawyer lamented that the case had been reduced to whether the defendants had intentionally inflicted a blow to his client's head, rather than the broader issue of excessive force. Though defense counsel did not object to this statement, Judge Edmondson believed this and other statements were a "clear invitation to the jury to hold Defendants liable based on conduct other than an intentional blow to head."

The court also examined the jury award. Edmondson believed the award was "manifestly excessive and swayed by passion." Christopher received 40 percent more in future medical expenses than the highest number given by his expert witness and twice as much in past, documented medical expenses. This, along with the pain-and-suffering award was clearly improper. Therefore, both defendants were entitled to a new trial.

Judge Rosemary Barkett, in a dissenting opinion, agreed that the defendant's were entitled to a new trial, but only on the question of damages. The closing argument by Christopher's lawyer was not improper and the failure of defense counsel to object foreclosed the appeals court from considering this issue. Therefore, the new trial should have been limited to determining the amount of damages.

DECLARATORY JUDGMENT

Statutory remedy for the determination of a justiciable controversy where the plaintiff is in doubt as to his or her legal rights. A binding adjudication of the rights and status of litigants even though no consequential relief is awarded.

MedImmune, Inc. v. Genentech, Inc.

It is a fundamental constitutional principle under Article III that the U.S. court system may only hear "cases" and "controversies." Courts may not entertain lawsuits where the plaintiff does not have a personal stake in the outcome or has not suffered an actual injury. Courts may not issue advisory opinions. The enactment of state and federal **declaratory judgment** acts in the 1920s and 1930s seemed to challenge these principles, as a plaintiff was authorized to ask a court to interpret a legal provision, usually a **statute** or a contract, and have the court issue a ruling on the matter. However, the court may only declare the rights and other legal relations; it cannot award damages or issue an injunction. Though the U.S. SUPREME COURT upheld the constitutionality of the Declaratory Judgment Act, 28 U.S.C.A. § 2201, in 1937, it has been called on to define the act's relation to specific substantive areas of the law. In *MedImmune, Inc. v. Genentech, Inc.*, —U.S.—, 127 S.Ct. 764, 166 L.Ed.2d 604 (2007), the Court was called on to decide whether a patent licensee must terminate or breach its license agreement before it can seek a declaratory judgment that the underlying patent is invalid, unenforceable, or not infringed.

MedImmune, Inc. manufactured Synagis, a drug used to prevent respiratory disease in infants and young children. In 1997 it contracted with Genentech, Inc., to obtain a patent license for two processes. One of the processes, dealing with the production of "chimeric antibodies," was under patent, while the other process involving "the coexpression of immunoglobulin chains" was under a pending patent application. MedImmune agreed to pay royalties on the sales of licensed products and Genentech granted MedImmune the right to make, use, and sell these products using its two processes. In December 2001 Genentech was awarded a patent for the coexpression process. Genentech then contacted MedImmune and stated its belief that Synagis was covered by the new "Cabilly II" patent and that MedImmune was to start paying royalties beginning March 1, 2002.

This communication raised great concerns with MedImmune, as Synagis accounted for

Exterior view of Genentech headquarters in San Francisco, January 2007.

AP IMAGES

80 percent of its revenues since 1999. If MedImmune did not pay the royalties it feared that Genentech would terminate the 1997 licensing agreement and sue for patent infringement. If Genentech prevailed in an infringement lawsuit, MedImmune could bee ordered to pay treble (triple) damages and attorney's fees, and to stop the production and sale of Synagis. MedImmune paid the royalties under protest and reserved all its legal rights. It then filed a declaratory judgment action seeking a declaratory judgment on the contractual rights and obligations contained in the 1997 agreement. MedImmune also challenged the Cabilly II patent, arguing it was invalid and unenforceable. The U.S. **District Court** dismissed the lawsuit, concluding it did not have subject-matter jurisdiction because of a ruling by the Federal **Circuit Court** of Appeals. In that case the appeals court held that a patent licensee cannot establish an Article III **case or controversy** dealing with the validity, enforceability, or scope of the patent because the license agreement "obliterates any reasonable apprehension" that the licensee will be sued for infringement." The Federal Circuit applied this precedent on MedIummune's appeal and upheld the lower court.

The Supreme Court, in an 8–1 decision, overturned the Federal Circuit decision and precedent. Justice ANTONIN SCALIA, writing for the majority, reviewed the history of declaratory judgment law in the Supreme Court and admitted that the decisions did not "draw the brightest of lines between those declaratory judgment actions that satisfy the case-or-controversy requirement" and those that did not. Scalia concluded that MedImmune would have met without question the requirement if it had refused to make the royalty payments under the 1997 licensing agreement. By paying the royalty MedImmune was under no risk of legal action from Genentech because MedImmune's own acts eliminated the "imminent threat of harm."

Justice Scalia pointed out that when the government threatens an action the Court does not require a plaintiff "to expose himself to liability before bringing suit to challenge the basis for the threat." Where there is a "genuine threat of enforcement" the Court did not require the plaintiff to "bet the farm, so to speak, by taking the violative action." The very point of enacting the Declaratory Judgment Act was to ameliorate the dilemma facing a plaintiff—abandon his rights or risk prosecution. Turning to private parties, Scalia found that lower **federal courts** had long accepted jurisdiction where the "plaintiff's self-avoidance of imminent injury is coerced by threatened enforcement action." Therefore, MedImmune was not required to violate or terminate its 1997 agreement before seeking a declaratory judgment that the patent was invalid, unenforceable, or not infringed.

Justice CLARENCE THOMAS, in a dissenting opinion, contended that the Court had mistakenly extended its government-threatened action **jurisprudence** to private contractual obligations.

Attorney general Alberto Gonzales takes a question during a news conference on March 9, 2007.

AP IMAGES

DEPARTMENT OF JUSTICE

Firing of Nine U.S. Attorneys

United States Attorneys are federal prosecutors who represent the U.S. government in federal court cases. There are 93 U.S. Attorneys nationwide, one for each federal judicial district. U.S. Attorneys are appointed by the U.S. President, subject to Senate confirmation (28 USC §541), and generally serve four-year terms. Since 1986, the Attorney General of the United States has had the authority to appoint interim U.S. Attorneys to fill a vacancy (28 USC §546). This **statutory** section formerly provided that an interim appointee could continue to serve until either the confirmation of a presidential appointee, or the expiration of 120 days, whichever occurred first. Subsection (d) of the above provision states that if a 120-day interim appointment expires, the **district court** may appoint a U.S. Attorney until the vacancy is filled.

On March 9, 2006, President GEORGE W. BUSH signed into law the USA PATRIOT Act (P.L. 109-177). A provision of the Act struck the existing interim appointment procedures (above) and replaced them with new statutory language that allows an interim appointee to remain in that position until the confirmation of a presidential appointee to fill the vacancy. This new provision effectively changed 120-day interim appointments to indefinite ones. It also meant that if a president failed to nominate an appointee for Senate confirmation, Senate con-

firmation was avoided and the interim appointee could serve indefinitely.

In December 2006, the Bush Administration dismissed seven U.S. Attorneys and replaced them with interim appointees (by June 2007, a total of nine had been dismissed). At first blush, this was not worthy of media attention, as all U.S. Attorneys serve at the pleasure of the President, and can be fired for good, bad, or no reason at all. In 1993, President Clinton fired all 93 U.S. Attorneys, an unprecedented move that created enormous outcry among Republicans in Congress, but received little media attention.

The Bush Administration's action was therefore neither improper nor unusual on its face. But what started as an exercise of clearly-authorized executive power quickly eroded into a showdown between legislative and executive branches, as a newly-Democratic-controlled Congress sought to prove political motivation behind the firings.

Quickly, the story started to unravel, raising questions about who really instigated the firings, and what the true motivations may have been. The momentum went into high gear following February 2007 testimony of Deputy Attorney General Paul J. McNulty before the SENATE JUDICIARY COMMITTEE that most of the U.S. Attorneys were fired for "performance-related" reasons. After later reports showed that several of the attorneys actually had received good performance reviews, the controversy began to spread out in different directions. Democrats in Congress were swift to focus on what appeared to be shifting explanations from the JUSTICE DEPARTMENT, and the Senate Judiciary Committee began to issue subpoenas to various administration officials, as well as some of the removed attorneys.

In fact, the Bush Administration was within its authority to effect the firings, even if there were some political underpinnings. But testimony from a few of the fired attorneys and other witnesses began to suggest that at least some of them had been fired for not cooperating with three Republican members of Congress. The fired attorneys claimed that the legislators contacted them to inquire if they were planning on indicting some public officials (Democrats) in an ongoing public corruption investigation. Attempting to influence public corruption investigations violates congressional ethics rules.

Amid calls for his immediate resignation, U.S. Attorney General Alberto Gonzales, already an unpopular Bush appointee, appeared in a Senate panel hearing and distanced his involvement in the firings. The *Washington Post* quoted him as saying, "I know that I did not-and would not-ask for the resignation of any U.S. Attorney for an improper reason. Furthermore, I have no basis to believe that anyone involved in this process sought the removal of a U.S. Attorney for an improper reason."

Within days of the clash between Congress and the White House, the Senate Judiciary Committee approved a bill sponsored by Senator Feinstein (D-Calif.) that would revoke the amendatory language in the U.S. Patriot Act giving the executive branch the power to appoint interim U.S. Attorneys without Senate confirmation. However, as of June 2007, no bill from either the House or Senate had been presented to the President for signature into law,—something that could be vetoed in any event.

In early July 2007, the White House announced it was asserting **executive privilege** in response to congressional demands for documents and testimony in the ongoing investigation. It reiterated its very early position that White House officials, including strategist Karl Rove, former White House counsel Harriet Meirs, and political operative Sara Taylor were available for questioning by Congress behind closed doors and without transcripts, but they would invoke privilege if subpoenaed.

The controversy was now spreading into uncharted legal and political terrain, with un-

predictable outcomes. Congress was left to decide whether to move forward with contempt proceedings against administration officials, or attempt to further negotiate an offer of renewed cooperation received in early July from White House counsel Fred Fielding.

DISCRIMINATION

In constitutional law, the grant by statute of particular privileges to a class arbitrarily designated from a sizable number of persons, where no reasonable distinction exists between the favored and disfavored classes. Federal laws, supplemented by court decisions, prohibit discrimination in such areas as employment, housing, voting rights, education, and access to public facilities. They also proscribe discrimination on the basis of race, age, sex, nationality, disability, or religion. In addition, state and local laws can prohibit discrimination in these areas and in others not covered by federal laws.

Jury Verdict Enhanced to $334 Million in Corporate Discrimination Case

In November 2006, a federal jury in Illinois awarded $48 million against Virginia Beach, Va.-based Amerigroup Corporation and subsidiary Amerigroup Illinois ("Amerigroup")for discrimination against pregnant women and other high-risk patients in their managed-care health maintenance organization (HMO) plan enrollments. Amerigroup was hired by the U.S. government to provide health care coverage for Medicaid-eligible needy persons. Instead, the jury found, Amerigroup pocketed the money and offered its services only to healthy clients within that group, intentionally avoiding those with health issues, including pregnancy. The original jury verdict was automatically tripled to $144 million pursuant to the federal False Claims Act and the Illinois Whistleblower Reward and Protection Act, which permit the award of treble damages for such extensive and systematic **fraud**. (Whistleblower acts generally protect employees from retaliatory employment actions for having reported illegal or wrongful conduct of their employers to appropriate authorities.)

In March 2007, the federal judge raised defendants' total liability to $334 million by adding civil penalties of $10,500 to each of 18,130 false **Medicaid** claims. The jury verdict followed a three-week trial and nearly four years of litigation originally stemming from a whistleblower's case filed by Cleveland Tyson, corporate lobbyist and former head of government relations for Amerigroup Illinois. In 2005, the Illinois Attorney General and the U.S. JUSTICE DEPARTMENT joined the case. Under applicable law, Tyson was entitled to receive between 15 and 25 percent of the total damages awarded. *United States, ex rel. Cleveland Tyson, et al. vs. Amerigroup Illinois, et al.*, 02C6074 (N.D. IL) 2006.

Tyson was fired from his position at Amerigroup in 2002 before filing a federal lawsuit alleging that Amerigroup had been filing false Medicaid claims with the state. The suit alleged that from 2002 to 2003,Amerigroup was paid $243 million in Medicaid money in return for providing health care to economically-eligible state applicants without regard to their health status. However, evidence presented at trial showed that Amerigroup trained its marketing representatives to avoid persons with medical conditions who could represent high corporate pay-outs for medical bills. Ultimately, the company spent less than half of the funds it was paid by the state and federal government on providing healthcare.

According to testimony and **documentary evidence** presented at trial, Amerigroup had a policy of "cherry-picking" healthy clients. Particularly damaging were e-mails and internal memoranda from the company. In one 2001 e-mail from Amerigroup's Illinois director of medical management, corporate officials were advised to "Please keep up the good work with the marketing reps of not trying to sign up pregnant women." In another e-mail, the director advised that the company had continued to build experience in not signing up pregnant women or people from areas where drug abuse was prevalent. Still another Amerigroup executive admitted that it was always his policy "to go after the healthies," and Dwight Jones, Amerigroup's corporate representative at trial, acknowledged that a large drop in the number of pregnant women as enrollees was the direct result of an active effort to avoid them in the first place.

Defense counsel denied the allegations that Amerigroup discriminated against pregnant women. While the company admitted that it did attempt to reduce its enrollment of women in their third trimester of pregnancy, the stated reason was to ensure "continuity of care" so that women would not be forced to switch doctors after having switched health plans. Defense also argued that state authorities had knowledge of and even encouraged such a policy.

Technically and procedurally, the initial 2002 complaint alleged that Amerigroup Illinois submitted false claims under the Medicaid program. The first amended complaint added a charge that Amerigroup maintained a scheme to discourage or avoid the enrollment of pregnant women and other Medicaid recipients with special needs. The third amended complaint alleged that Amerigroup Corporation was liable as the alter-ego of Amerigroup Illinois, Inc., and that Amerigroup Corporation was also liable for making false claims or causing false claims to be made.

Jury findings were that (1)the HMO (Amerigroup) actively discriminated against and sought to prevent the enrollment of pregnant women and sick individuals; and (2) the HMO (Amerigroup) had falsified its certification that it complied with anti-discrimination statutes and policies. This certification was made individually on each enrollment form submitted to the government between 2000 and 2003. Thus, each falsely-certified enrollment form constituted a separate "false claim" (18,130 in all).

Managed-care HMO health plans, such as those run by Amerigroup, are generally less expensive than fee-for-service Medicaid plans, because HMOs place restrictions on doctor and hospital choices to their networks. Medicaid is funded jointly by federal and state governments, which have supported the creations of HMOs to save money.

Amerigroup no longer operates is Illinois but continues to provide Medicaid-based HMO services in nine other states. At the time of the litigation, Amerigroup was posting between $2.3 and $3 billion in revenue annually.

DRUGS AND NARCOTICS

Drugs are articles intended for use in the diagnosis, cure, mitigation, treatment, or prevention of disease in humans or animals, and any articles other than food intended to affect the mental or body function of humans or animals. *Narcotics* are any drugs that dull the senses and commonly become addictive after prolonged use.

Raid of Drug Ring Could Expose Athletes' Steroid Use

An investigation by a prosecutor in Albany, New York uncovered the presence of a vast ring of doctors and pharmacists who allegedly distributed steroids, human growth hormone, and similar drugs to thousands of individuals who order these drugs on the Internet. Several prominent professional athletes have been identified as possible customers in this ring, and some commentators have said that this could be one of the more important steroid investigations in recent history.

The use of anabolic steroids and other performance-enhancing drugs has been a problem in professional sports for much of the past fifty years. Though most sports have developed testing procedures to which athletes much subject themselves, many critics and commentators have speculated that use of steroids is more widespread that the general public might suspect. Athletes that have commonly been suspected of use include bodybuilders, weightlifters, football players, and other athletes who rely on bulk and strength to excel. However, recent events have indicated that the use of steroids may be prevalent in a wide range of sports, including baseball and track and field.

In 2003 and 2004, an investigation into a California laboratory, Bay Area Laboratory Co-Operative (BALCO), led to allegations that a large number of professional baseball players had used a previously undetectable steroid. Dozens of athletes testified before a federal **grand jury** that investigated the BALCO scandal. This later led to a Congressional hearing at which several prominent baseball and football players spoke. In 2006 and 2007, several athletes continued to face legal problems from the BALCO scandal.

On the heels of the BALCO controversy, David Soares, the district attorney in Albany, began an investigation when officials discovered that an estimated $250,000 worth of steroids had been sold in Albany County. The investigation uncovered a wide-spread scheme of steroid distribution that involved several "anti-aging" clinics located in New York, Texas, and Florida. Soares discovered that some New York doctors had engaged in the practice of signing prescriptions for steroids and other drugs for patients with whom the doctors had never evaluated. Many of these transactions occurred through sales over the Internet.

The investigation later led Soares to some pharmacies in Florida. On February 27, 2007, police raided Signature Pharmacy in Orlando. The officers confiscated what was described as truck loads of drugs and other evidence. The search led to the arrest of four individuals connected with Signature, including a **husband and wife** who are both pharmacists. These four were

charged with 20 counts each of criminal diversion of prescription medications and prescriptions, criminal sale of a controlled substance, and insurance **fraud**. Two others were also arrested in connection with the Signature raid in February, including a doctor at an anti-aging clinic. She was charged with criminal sale of a controlled substance, as was a sixth person. All six individuals who were charged with offenses related to the activities at Signature pleaded not guilty in March 2007.

In an unusual twist to the raid, officers reported that employees of the pharmacy had in their possession cards with phone numbers of lawyers. Officers referred to these as "raid cards" and suggested that the company anticipated that it could be raided at some point. Signature's sales rose from $550,000 in 2000 to $21 million in 2005, which the owners attributed to the sale of human growth hormone prescribed by doctors as an anti-aging remedy. One of the names on the customer list for Signature was a doctor for the Pittsburgh Steelers, who reportedly purchased $150,000 worth of testosterone and human growth hormone on this personal credit card. Officials forwarded the relevant information to the National Football League.

Other agents raided a pharmacy in Mobile, Alabama as part of the same investigation. Officers discovered the names of several athletes on the pharmacy's customer list. These athletes included Major League Baseball players Gary Matthews Jr. and Jerry Hairston Jr., former baseball player Jose Canseco, and former heavyweight boxing champion Evander Holyfield. Another name that arose during the investigation was former baseball pitcher Jason Grimsley, who was released by the Arizona Diamondbacks in 2006 after admitting to using human growth hormone, steroids and amphetamines.

In March 2007, Ana Maria Santi, a former New York doctor, pleaded guilty to signing prescriptions for patients with whom she never met. Santi received the prescriptions by fax from Oasis Longevity & Rejuvenation Center in Delray Beach, Florida, another **entity** that was subject to the investigation. As part of a plea bargain, Santi pleaded guilty to a count of criminal diversion of prescription medications and prescriptions. She will spend at least two to four years in prison, according to the terms of the agreement. She also faces charges in connection with a related federal prosecution.

A ruling by a Florida judge in April 2007 stalled the progress of the investigation. Circuit Judge JOHN MARSHALL Kest of Osceola

David McDarby,
right, following the
guilty verdict
against Merck and
Co in his Vioxx
liability trial.

AP IMAGES

County, Florida ruled that several thousand people across the U.S. who purchased drugs from Signature must be notified that their records were seized. Kest ordered police to stop sifting through documents until the medical privacy issues had been resolved. Commentators noted that the ruling could allow many of the athletes to avoid having their names appear in public records. One of the prosecutors indicated that about 300,000 prescriptions were seized from Signature in February.

Vioxx Producer Continues to Face Litigation

The company that produced the arthritis medication Vioxx continued to defend itself in a several cases throughout the United States in 2006 and 2007. Although the producer, Merck & Co., has successfully defended several of these suits, it faces tens of thousands of others, most of which are based on allegations that Vioxx caused heart attacks. The company must also defend against more than 200 **class action** suits that have been brought on a variety of theories for recovery.

The firm of Merck & Co., Inc. can be traced back as far as the seventeenth century in Europe. Its more recent history began in 1891 when George Merck established a fine chemical supplies company in New York. By the 1930s, Merck & Co. had entered into the field of pharmaceutical research. The company merged with Sharp & Dohme to create Merck Sharp & Dohme, and it has grown ever since. The company produces numerous well-known drugs, in-

cluding Zocor for reducing cholesterol and Propecia for treating male-pattern baldness.

In May 1999, the FOOD AND DRUG ADMINISTRATION (FDA) approved distribution of Vioxx. This drug is a COX-2 inhibitor that reduces inflammation and is used in treatments for arthritis and acute pain in adults. About a year after its approval, Merck provided the FDA with the results of its own study of Vioxx, known as the Vioxx Gastrointestinal Outcomes Research, or VIGOR. In this study, researchers determined that patients who took the drug were five times more likely to suffer from heart problems than those who took naproxen, an older pain medication. These researchers determined that naproxen had certain effects that prevented users from having heart problems. By September 2001, the FDA had warned Merck that its promotional campaign "minimizes the potentially serious cardiovascular findings" and "misrepresents the safety profile of Vioxx." Seven months later, the FDA altered the inserts in Vioxx packages to reflect the VIGOR findings.

Vioxx, which reportedly earned $2.5 billion for Merck in sales per year, remained in circulation until September 2004, after a long-term study showed that Vioxx doubled a user's risk of a heart attack or a stroke after prolonged use. (The company's conclusion that the risk of heart problems arose after uses of longer than 18 months was refuted by an article published in 2006 in the *New England Journal of Medicine*, which indicated that the risk of heart problems were immediate). The FDA in February 2005 issued a report indicating that though Vioxx and similar drugs posed heart risks, the drug should be available to users.

Numerous lawsuits arose from Vioxx users and their heirs for heart problems allegedly caused by the drug. The first case related to Vioxx to go to trial concerned the death of 59-year-old Robert Ernst, a resident of Keene, Texas. Ernst ran marathons and triathlons and taught aerobics. He began taking Vioxx to relieve pain and stiffness in his hands and remained on the drug for eight months prior to his death. About a week after participating in a 100K bicycle race, Ernst died suddenly from cardiac arrhythmia. His wife sued Merck, and an Angelton, Texas court agreed with the plaintiff, awarding $253.4 million in damages. Though this award was later reduced due to caps on **punitive damages** in Texas, it led to the filing of large numbers of other suits.

New Jersey courts have considered several cases related to Vioxx. In November 2005, a court in Atlantic City ruled in favor of Merck in a case arising from the death of Federick "Mike" Humeston, a Boise, Idaho postal worker who took the drug. Less than a year later, a state judge overruled the decision, finding that Merck had omitted some of the data about heart attacks that was found in the VIGOR report. In at least two other cases, courts in Atlantic City ruled against plaintiffs who had taken Vioxx for at least two years. However, in April 2006, the Atlantic City court ruled in favor of 77-year-old John McDarby, who had suffered a heart attack after taking Vioxx for approximately four years.

In addition to the New Jersey cases, Merck has successfully defended suits in other venues such as New Orleans, Los Angeles, and Kentucky. In the cases that the company has lost, however, the jury verdicts have been significant, such as a $51 million award given to Gerald Barnett by a court in New Orleans in August 2006. Barnett suffered a heart attack after being on the drug for about two years. The judge in the case ordered a new trial shortly after the verdict was announced, finding that $50 million in **compensatory damages** was "grossly excessive."

Commentators have noted that in the cases in which Merck has prevailed, the plaintiffs have had certain common characteristics. For instance, in a case arising in Madison County, Illinois (which is well-known as a **venue** that favors plaintiffs against corporate defendants), a jury ruled in favor of Merck after the company was sued by a woman who had taken the drug for about 20 months and who had suffered a heart attack. The woman, Patricia Schwaller, possessed several risk factors for heart problems, including a family history of heart disease, obesity, and high blood pressure. By comparison, in another case that is pending in Madison County, the plaintiff is a truck driver who underwent regular physicals and who had no risk factors for a heart attack. After taking the drug for about a year, he had a heart attack and required triple bypass surgery. Plaintiffs with these types of characteristics have tended to be more successful in the Vioxx cases.

As of April 2007, approximately 27,000 Vioxx cases against Merck were pending. In addition, about 200 class action suits were also pending. In addition to the grounds of personal injury and consumer **fraud**, some of these class action suits also represent Merck shareholders as well as plaintiffs who seek medical monitoring.

DUE PROCESS

A fundamental, constitutional guarantee that all legal proceedings will be fair and that one will be given notice of the proceedings and an opportunity to be heard before the government acts to take away one's life, liberty, or property. Also, a constitutional guarantee that a law shall not be unreasonable, arbitrary, or capricious.

Brown v. City of Michigan City, Indiana

The Fourteenth Amendment's Due Process Clause applies to state and local governments in the same way the Fifth Amendment's Due Process Clause applies to the federal government. The clause prohibits state governments from arbitrarily or unfairly depriving individuals of their basic constitutional rights to life, liberty, and property. Procedural due process is concerned with the methods used by the legal system to carry out its work. In cases where an individual has claimed a violation of due process rights, the court must determine whether a citizen is being deprived of "life, liberty, or property" and what procedural protections are due that individual. In addition, the U.S. SUPREME COURT has recognized the existence of **substantive due process**, which evaluates the importance of the right or the severity of the infringement. The Seventh **Circuit Court** of Appeals dealt with both types of due process in *Brown v. City of Michigan City, Indiana*, 462 F.3d 720(7th Cir.2006), ruling that a city could constitutionally deny a convicted sex offender access to city parks. The appeals court concluded that the ban did not implicate a constitutionally protected liberty interest.

Robert Brown, a resident of Michigan City, Indiana, frequented Washington Park, a large park on the shores of Lake Michigan, on a regular basis. Brown entered the park free of charge with a resident pass issued by the city. Brown began visiting the park on a daily basis in 1988 with his wife. After her death that year he continued his daily visits for 14 years. He would park his R.V. near the lake, drink coffee, smoke cigarettes, and watch people at the beach, sometimes with binoculars. Brown usually remained in his van. In early July 2002 a park official received a phone call from the recreation director in LaPorte, Indiana concerning Brown's presence and behavior at a beach in that city. Brown had been observed watching beach patrons through his binoculars. The LaPorte police investigated and discovered that Brown had been convicted of one count of child molestation in 1995 and had spent three years in prison. He had been placed on probation and had completed a counseling program after his release. Armed with this information, Michigan City park employees watched and logged Brown's visits to the park. They alleged that he had watched children at a day camp within the park and sometimes entered the park twice daily. In late July Brown was approached in the park by police officers and a city attorney. The attorney confiscated Brown's park pass and was informed he was no longer allowed in the park. If he returned he would be charged with trespass. The city parks and recreation board met several days later and passed a resolution deny access to city parks to Brown and to any other person convicted of child molestation. The board rescinded the resolution in late August after Brown commenced a federal civil rights lawsuit and sought to make it a **class action**. It removed the clause dealing with sex offenders in general and limited its action to the prohibition of Brown from entering city parks. Brown then dropped his request for a class action.

In his lawsuit Brown alleged that the city had denied him procedural and substantive due process. He claimed he was denied procedural due process because the park board conducted its meetings in the park office inside Washington Park. He had been warned he would be charged with trespass if he entered the park, making attendance at the hearing risky for him. Though the city told a friend of his that he would not be charged if he attended, the city refused to put this promise in writing. Brown also a contended that the right to enter public spaces like public parks is a fundamental and basic right and that the ban was arbitrary and irrational. The federal **district court** rejected Brown's claims and granted **summary judgment** to the city, ending the litigation. The court ruled that Brown did not have a protected property interest in being permitted to enter the city parks, which negated his procedural due process claim. The court also rejected his liberty interest claim, finding that Brown's reputation

may have been damaged by being labeled a threat to children but he could not show the "alteration of a legal status." To meet this burden he would need to show an injury in addition to his damaged reputation, such as finding it impossible to find employment in his chosen field. As to the substantive due process claim, Brown had failed show that access to public parks was a fundamental right. The city's ban was rationally related to its compelling interest in protecting children in its parks.

Brown's appeal to the Seventh Circuit Court of Appeals was unsuccessful. The appeals court agreed with the lower court that Brown had failed to point to a state law or other independent source that guaranteed him access to the park. More importantly, the state had delegated to the city parks and recreation board the authority to exercise supervision over the parks and to establish park rules. Therefore, the board had the discretion to decide "whether and under what conditions members of the public can access the City's parks." His reputation may have been damaged but he could not point to an actual injury related to this ban. Therefore, he could not claim a due process right violation.

As to Brown's substantive due process claim the appeals court was similarly dismissive. The court noted that the Supreme Court has recognized a narrow category of "fundamental" rights. They included the rights to marry, to have children, to direct the education and upbringing of children, to marital privacy, to use contraception, to bodily integrity, and to abortion. The "right to enter a public park is not among this list" and the appeals court refused to expand the list. Though Brown's "right" to enter a park for innocent purposes was "certainly important," it was not fundamental. The court agreed with the lower court that the ban was rationally related to a legitimate government purposed: the protection of children. Brown was "not just another patron of the public parks" but a convicted child molester whose "frequency of attendance and atypical behavior while in the park" justified the concerns of park officials.

EDUCATION LAW

The body of state and federal constitutional provisions; local, state, and federal statutes; court opinions; and government regulations that provide the legal framework for educational institutions.

Winkelman v. Parma City School District

The Individuals with Disabilities Education Act (IDEA), 20 U.S.C.A. §1400 *et seq.*, seeks to ensure that children with disabilities have available to them a "free appropriate education," while making sure that the rights of children with disabilities and their parents are protected. IDEA provides an administrative appeal process if children and parents disagree with the individualized education program (IEP) proposed by the school. However, it had been unclear whether parents could pursue a review in a federal **district court** on their own behalf or as representatives of the child if they were not represented by a lawyer. The U.S. SUPREME COURT, in *Winkelman v. Parma City School District*, __U.S.__, 127 S.Ct., __L.Ed.2d __ 2007 WL 1461151 (2007), resolved this issue, holding that parents have independent, enforceable rights that they may vindicate in federal court without a lawyer. If the ruling had gone the other way, parents who could not afford a lawyer would not be allowed to litigate IDEA issues in court.

Jeff and Sandee Winkelman, the parents of Jacob Winkelman, worked with the Parma City School District in Parma, Ohio, to develop an IEP for their six-year-old son, who has autism spectrum disorder. The school district proposed that Jacob attend a public elementary school but the parents disagreed. They filed an administrative appeal that alleged the district had failed to provide Jacob with a free appropriate education. The hearing officer rejected the appeal and the Winkelmans brought their complaint to a state-level review officer. After this appeal was unsuccessful they filed a complaint in Ohio federal district court on their own behalf and on behalf of Jacob. In their complaint they alleged that Jacob had been denied a free appropriate education as mandated by the IDEA, that his IEP was inadequate, and that the school district had not followed the proper administrative procedures required by the act. While these reviews were proceeding the Winkelmans enrolled Jacob in a private school at their own expense. They asked the court to reverse the administrative decision and reimburse them for the private school tuition.

The Winkelmans did not get the opportunity to argue these issues. The school district asked the court to rule in its favor on the pleadings that they had complied with the IDEA and the court agreed. The parents then filed an appeal, without a lawyer, with the Sixth **Circuit Court** of Appeals. The appeals court issued an order that dismissed the appeal unless they retained legal counsel. The parents could not proceed with an IDEA appeal by themselves because the right to a free appropriate education belonged only to the child. Therefore, any rights the parents might have flowed out of the child's rights. This meant that the parents were not appearing on their own behalf; a court will not allow a nonlawyer to represent another person, hence the exclusion of the Winkelmans. The Supreme Court agreed to hear the Winkelmans appeal, which they prepared themselves, to resolve a conflict among the circuit courts of appeals on this issue.

The Supreme Court, in a 7–2 decision, overturned the Sixth Circuit ruling. Justice ANTHONY KENNEDY, writing for the majority, agreed that there was no specific language in the IDEA granting parents individual rights. However, he concluded that the "entire **statutory** scheme" demonstrated that parents have independent, enforceable rights that they may bring in federal court. In doing so he rejected the school district's claims that the only redressable rights under the IDEA belonged to the children. Justice Kennedy noted that the word "parents" was mentioned throughout the IDEA. Parents served as members of the IEP team that develops the IEP and parents have the right to lodge an administrative complaint and have an administrative appeal. In addition, parents may be reimbursed for the cost of private school enrollment and for attorney's fees if a court or hearing officer determines a child was denied a free appropriate education. These provisions demonstrated that parents have enforceable rights at the administrative stage. It would be "inconsistent with the statutory scheme to bar them from continuing to assert these rights in federal court."

The school district rejected this broad reading of the IDEA, arguing that those provisions limited parental involvement to the representation of their child's interests. Justice Kennedy found no merit in this narrow reading and believed this position would frustrate the will of Congress to convey rights to parents as well as to children. He also dismissed the position of some appeals courts that parents had limited independents rights, including reimbursement of school expenses and violations of their own procedural rights. He believed "incongruous results would follow" if parents' IDEA rights were limited to certain nonsubstantive matters. This theory would require parents to prove the inadequacy of their child's education before they could win reimbursement, yet it would prevent them from obtaining a ruling that the school district must provide their child with an appropriate education program. In the Court's view the "potential for injustice in this result is apparent." Therefore, the Winkelmans enjoyed rights under the IDEA that allowed them to prosecute their IDEA claims on their own behalf.

Justice ANTONIN SCALIA, in a concurring and dissenting opinion joined by Justice CLARENCE THOMAS, agreed with the district's position that the parents could only sue on their own behalf for reimbursement and violations of their

procedural rights. He believed the Winkelmans were entitled to seek reimbursement for their private school costs but they did not have the right to seek a judicial determination that their child's free appropriate education was substantively inadequate.

Zuni Public School District 89 v. Dept. of Education

In *Zuni Public School District No. 89 v. DEPARTMENT OF EDUCATION*, No. 05-1508 (2007), the U.S. SUPREME COURT was asked to rule on the meaning of certain **statutory** language. The quintessential holding of the majority opinion is that statutory intent trumps gaps in statutory language.

The Federal Impact Aid Program, 20 USC §7701 *et seq.* (the "Act"), was enacted to financially assist local state school districts that have a "federal presence" within their districts (e.g., military bases, federal public housing, or in this case, Indian reservations). The financial assistance, in the form of a subsidy, is to offset losses in tax revenues suffered from the fact that affected school districts cannot impose school taxes on such federal entities occupying land within their districts. Hence, the program's name literally reflects a form of aid to offset the impact of federal use of local land.

Impact aid funds, sent directly to affected school districts, are intended to supplement the district's general fund for operational expenses, purchases of text books, computers, utilities, salaries, etc. Generally, a state may not reduce its aid to a school district because that district is already receiving federal aid. But under certain provisions of the Act, states may reduce their own aid to schools if the Department of Education certifies that the state "equalizes" expenditures throughout the state. The Act contains express language setting forth a method that the Secretary of Education is to use when determining whether a state's public school funding program has equalized expenditures.

The formula spelled out in the Act instructs the Secretary of Education to compare the local school district with the greatest per-pupil expenditures to the school district with the smallest per-pupil expenditures, to determine whether the former exceeds the latter by more than 25 percent. If not, then the state aid program qualifies as one that equalizes expenditures, and the state may reduce its own local funding to districts receiving federal aid under the Act.

In applying this formula under the Act, the Secretary must "disregard" school districts with per-pupil expenditures above the 95th percentile (in the wealthiest districts) or below the 5th percentile (in the poorest districts). If the remaining districts are within the 25 percent range, the Secretary may deem the state system as "equalized" and the state can take Impact Aid payments into account when calculating state aid to districts.

Accordingly, and relating to the present case, Department of Education officials ranked New Mexico's 89 local school districts by per-pupil spending for **fiscal** year 1998. This resulted in the exclusion of 17 school districts at the top and six districts at the bottom. The remaining 66 districts constituted 90 percent of the state's student population, and because the disparity among these was less than 25 percent, the state's program "equalized expenditures" and the state could offset federal impact aid by reducing funds to individual districts.

Zuni Public School District, located within the Pueblo of Zuni Reservation, and Gallup-McKinley County School District, located on Navajo Reservation lands, are two public school districts within the state of New Mexico. They challenged the reduction of funds to their districts, which amounted to several million dollars. Specifically, they challenged an aspect of the "formula" used for the cutoff point at the 95th and 5th percentile. The challenge addressed interpretation of the statutory language found in the Act.

20 USC §7709(b)(2)(B)(i) (last amended in 1994) provides that the Secretary of Education is to "disregard" school districts "with per-pupil expenditures . . . above the 95th percentile or below the 5th percentile of such expenditures . . . in the State." The precise question before the Supreme Court was whether the above language permits the Secretary, in applying this language, to "disregard" school districts by looking to the *number of pupils* as well as to the size of the district's expenditure per pupil. The Court, in a very tight 5–4 decision with scathing dissent, held that it did.

Zuni's argument challenged the fact that in New Mexico, the Secretary considered student populations in "disregarding" the five percent at the top (the "95th percentile") and the five percent at the bottom (the "5th percentile). This, argued Zuni, was correct under the Secretary's regulation, dated and used since 1976, but not under the **statute** (last updated in 1994). In the statute, Congress used specific language that mentions only "school districts," not student populations within the districts. In 1996, the

Secretary, by regulation, reinstated his equalization formula that provides the latitude to consider both district and population within that district.

Justice Breyer, writing for the narrow majority (in which he was joined by Justices Alito, Ginsburg, Kennedy, and Stevens), upheld the Secretary's formula as "a reasonable method that carries out Congress' intent." The Court took great pains to consider the longstanding history and use of the Secretary's regulatory method, and found no express language in the statute that would defeat it. Therefore, viewed in terms of purpose, the Secretary's method fell within the scope of the statute's plain language.

Justice Scalia's dissent was long and powerful, and he was joined by the Chief Justice as well as Justices Thomas and (as to Part I) Souter. "The plain language of the federal Impact Aid statute clearly and unambiguously forecloses the Secretary of Education's preferred methodology for determining whether a State's school-funding system is equalized," he wrote. "This case is not a scary math problem; it is a straightforward matter of statutory interpretation."

ELECTION CAMPAIGN FINANCING

Wisconsin Right to Life v. Federal Election Commission

It all started with the Bipartisan Campaign Reform Act of 2002 (BCRA), 116 Stat.91 (also known as the McCain-Feingold Act, [the "Act"] named after its bipartisan sponsors). It was ostensibly created to assuage the general public's growing wariness and distrust of "special interest groups" and the widely held perception of their influence and control over political election processes. Various provisions of the Act address these and related issues. The Act is enforced by the FEDERAL ELECTION COMMISSION (FEC).

After a very lengthy and protracted court battle, the U.S. SUPREME COURT, in an opinion approaching 100 pages, affirmed a lower district court's ruling that §203 of the Act was unconstitutional as applied to three television advertisements paid for and sponsored by the Wisconsin Right to Life (WRTL) in 2004. *Federal Election Commission v. Wisconsin Right to Life*, No. 06-969, 551 U.S. ___ (2007). This follows an earlier decision in which the Supreme Court had remanded the matter back to the **district court**. Wisconsin Right to Life, Inc. v. FEC (WRTL I), 546 U.S.410(2006).

Section §203 of the Act prohibits corporations and labor unions from using their corporate or general funds to pay for political "electioneering communications," including certain paid political advertisements. Technically, Section 201 of the BCRA defines "electioneering communications" as any broadcast, cable, or satellite communication that refers to a candidate for federal office and that is broadcast within 30 days of a federal primary election or 60 days of a federal general election in the jurisdiction in which that candidate is running for office. 2 USC 434(f)(3).

Back in July 2004, WRTL paid for and aired a series of television advertisements. These ads encouraged viewers to contact Wisconsin's two Democratic senators (expressly identified by name in the advertisements) for the purpose of urging them to oppose efforts in Congress (mostly by Democrats) to **filibuster** President George Bush's federal judicial nominees. The advertisements were intended to run for several weeks, up to and including the weeks preceding the November 2004 general elections. One of the senators was running for reelection in November (less than 60 days away).

As a preemptive move, the WRTL sought a **preliminary injunction** barring the FEC from enforcing the BCRA against the pending television advertisements. Its legal argument urged the court to find the BCRA unconstitutional *as applied* to the advertisements. The organization did not dispute that the advertisements were covered by the BCRA's definition of prohibited "electioneering communications," which had previously withstood constitutional challenge in *McConnell v. Federal Election Commission*, 540 U.S. 93, (2003). Instead, the WRTL argued that the BCRA could not be applied to its advertisements because they constituted "grassroots lobbying advertisements" not related to electoral campaigning. The communications merely encouraged citizens to contact Congress to influence legislation, and not to influence the electoral process.

The U.S. District Court for the DISTRICT OF COLUMBIA denied the motion for preliminary injunction and later dismissed the WTRL's complaint in an unpublished opinion.

The U.S. Supreme Court, in a 9–0 *per curiam* opinion *WRTL I*, noting probable jurisdiction after the D.C. **appellate court** ruled that it lacked jurisdiction, vacated the opinion of the district court dismissing the challenge, then remanded the matter back to that court for consideration on the merits.

The significant holding in the *WRTL I* opinion was in noting that the district court had misinterpreted the relevance of (i.e., had incorrectly read) a footnote in *McConnell* as barring any "as-applied" challenges to the BCRA's prohibition on electioneering communications. The Court in its opinion (*WRTL I*) stated,

> "Contrary to the understanding of the District Court, that footnote merely notes that because we found BCRA's primary definition of 'electioneering communication' facially valid when used with regard to BCRA's disclosure and funding requirements, it was unnecessary to consider the constitutionality of the backup definition Congress provided.*Ibid*. In upholding §203 against a facial challenge, we did not purport to resolve future as-applied challenges."

For its part, the FEC had argued that the district court had rested its decision on the ground that the facts of this case "suggest that WRTL's advertisements may fit the very type of activity *McConnell* found Congress had a compelling interest in regulating." The district court expressly found that WRTL's 'as-applied' challenge to BCRA was foreclosed by the *McConnell* decision.

On remand and on the merits, the district court concluded that the advertisements were genuine issue ads and *not* express advocacy ads or their "functional equivalents" under *McConnell*. It further held that no compelling interest had been shown to justify BCRA's regulation of such ads. The FEC appealed.

Now again before the U.S. Supreme Court (*WRTL II*), the decision of the district court was affirmed. The Chief Justice delivered the opinion of the Court, holding that because WTRL's ads could reasonably be interpreted as something other than appeals to vote for or against a specific candidate, they were not the "functional equivalent" of express campaign speech or express advocacy. Therefore, they fell outside of *McConnell's* scope or application. (The Court noted that when defining speech that qualifies as the functional equivalent of express advocacy subject to such a ban, the Court should give the benefit of the doubt to speech and not censorship.)

Since WRTL's ads did not constitute express advocacy or its functional equivalent, a **strict scrutiny** test would apply. Under that constitutional test, BCRA §203 would have to be narrowly tailored to further a compelling interest. However, since the FEC identified no compelling interest to justify burdening WRTL's speech, BCRA §203 was unconstitutional as applied to the ads.

Finally, the Court addressed two other issues raised by FEC. First, FEC argued that the matter had now become moot, as the 2004 elections had passed. But the Court noted that these cases precisely fit into the exception to mootness that addresses disputes capable of repetition, yet evading review. Additionally, FEC argued that WRTC carried the burden to show that BCRA §203 was unconstitutional. To the contrary, said the Court. Because §203 burdens political speech, it was the *government* that needed to prove not only its compelling interest at stake, but also that the BCRA section was narrowly tailored to achieve that interest.

ELEVENTH AMENDMENT

Thomas v. St. Louis Board of Police Commissioners

The ELEVENTH AMENDMENT bars individuals from suing state governments unless a state consents to such a lawsuit. In addition, the U.S. SUPREME COURT has recognized that states possess **sovereign immunity**, which bars damages suits against state governments unless they consent to be sued. However, the Supreme Court has made clear that only states and "arms of the state" possess sovereign immunity from suits authorized by federal law. Legal questions arise when an apparently "local" unit of government is authorized by a state law and the state retains authority over most functions of this unit of government. Is it "local" and thus vulnerable to lawsuits or is it an "arm of the state" that renders it immune from lawsuits under the Eleventh Amendment? In *Thomas v. St. Louis Board of Police Commissioners*, 447 F.3d 1082 (8th Cir. 2006), the Eighth **Circuit Court** of Appeals reluctantly ruled that a police oversight board created by the state of Missouri to govern the St. Louis Police Department was not an arm of the state. The appeals court recognized that the board was most likely a unit of state government but it was forced to honor a Supreme Court precedent that held it was a municipal body.

The case arose of out the way the St. Louis Police Department treated Yvonne Thomas. In June 2002 two St. Louis police officers entered Thomas' yard without her permission and performed a warrantless search. Thomas objected to the search and threatened to report the incident to the officers' supervisor. The two officers then arrested her and took her to a psychiatric center where she was admitted against her will. Thomas sued the St. Louis Board of Police Commissioners under the federal civil rights law 42 U.S.C.A §1983, alleging that she was falsely arrested. The federal **district court** dismissed her lawsuit, concluding that the board was entitled to Eleventh Amendment immunity from suit in federal court. The court ruled that the board was an agency of the state, for judgments obtained against the board would be paid from state funds. In addition, the state law that authorized police boards for St. Louis and Kansas City imposed many requirements that limited local control. Therefore, the board could not be sued because it was entitled to Eleventh Amendment immunity.

The Eighth Circuit Court of Appeals reversed the district court. The appeals court acknowledged that the issue was whether the board was a state or local agency. To determine this status the **federal courts** must look at the provisions of state law that define the agency's character, examining the degree of autonomy and control over its own affairs and "more importantly, whether a money judgment against the agency will be paid with state funds." The pointed out that a number of factors suggested the St. Louis board was an arm of the state. The board was established by the state to address political corruption issues in St. Louis and Kansas City. State money was used to pay at least a portion of legal judgment against the board. In addition, the governor appointed four of the five board members and had the power to removed commissioners for misconduct. The qualifications and salaries for the commissioners were determined by the state and St. Louis was prohibited from passing ordinances that interfered with the powers of the board. These and other provisions underscored the conclusion that the board was an arm of the state, yet in the end the appeals court ruled that it could not endorse this position.

The Eighth Circuit declined to grant Eleventh Amendment immunity because the U.S. Supreme Court had addressed the issue of the St. Louis Board's status in a 1997 case involving overtime pay under the FAIR LABOR STANDARDS ACT of 1938. In that case the Court rejected the board's claim for Eleventh Amendment immunity, ruling that the board was not an arm of the state. Though the state had great authority over the board the Court found that the city of St. Louis was responsible for its financial liabilities and that "the board is not subject to the State's direction or control in any other respect." The appeals court pointed out that it had applied this precedent in a 2002 case involving the Kansas City Board of Police Commissioners because it was indistinguishable from the St. Louis board. This decision was buttressed by a 2001 Missouri Court of Appeals case that held that the state had no obligation to pay judgments rendered against the St. Louis board.

The appeals court acknowledged that recent developments appeared to have eroded the analysis in the prior cases. The Missouri Supreme Court reversed the Missouri Court of Appeals and held that the St. Louis board was an arm of the state. Following this decision the Missouri Legislature passed a law limiting the state's obligation to pay judgments lodged against the two police boards. Though the Eighth Circuit agreed that these changes in the "legal landscape" suggested the St. Louis board was an arm of the state, it felt compelled to honor the 1997 Supreme Court precedent. The Supreme Court has advised the circuit courts of appeals that if its precedent has direct application in a case the court of appeals "should follow the case which directly controls, leaving to this Court the prerogative of overruling its own case." Therefore, the case was reinstated and sent back to the district court for further litigation.

EMINENT DOMAIN

The power to take private property for public use by a state, municipality, or private person or corporation authorized to exercise functions of public character, following the payment of just compensation to the owner of that property.

Mendota Golf v. City of Mendota Heights

In the wake of the U.S. Supreme Court's landmark decision in *Kelo v. City of New London*, 125 S. Ct. 2655 (2005), (allowing the use of **eminent domain** to acquire non-blighted property for economic development by private developers), at least 43 of 44 state legislatures in session considered legislation to restrict the use of eminent domain in an economic development context. (In *Kelo*, the majority opinion stressed that "nothing in our opinion precludes any State from placing further restrictions on its exercise of the takings power." *Id.* at 2668.

In an unusual twist to this expanded understanding of the law, the owners of Mendota Golf (in Mendota Heights, a suburb of St. Paul, Minnesota) tried very hard to sell their golf course for economic development, but the City of Mendota wanted to keep it as a golf course for public recreation. Could the City exercise eminent domain and "take" the property to keep it as a golf course, when in fact, the property had been zoned for development?

The Minnesota Supreme Court, in *Mendota Golf v. City of Mendota Heights*, No. A04-206 (2006), effectively said 'yes.' However, the real issue before the court was whether a private party, by **mandamus** (an order by a higher court to compel a governmental **entity** or lower court to act) could compel a city to change its comprehensive development plan when that plan conflicted with a **zoning ordinance**. The Minnesota high court held that a mandamus action was *not* appropriate to challenge a city's exercise of legislative discretion in denying a proposed amendment to its comprehensive plan, when there were other alternatives available to resolve the conflict. One of the ways to resolve the conflict was for the city to exercise its eminent domain power.

The 17.5-acre Mendota Heights Par 3 Golf Course was privately owned by Michael Cashill and Alan Spaulding. The property had been used as a nine-hole par 3 golf course at least since the 1960s. When the owners purchased the golf course in January 1995, the property was actually zoned as "R-1," or one-family residential property (as was the neighborhood surrounding the golf course). Under R-1 zoning, one-family detached dwellings are a "permitted use," while golf courses are a "conditional use." At that time, the city's comprehensive plan designated the property as a golf course. The state's Metropolitan Land Planning Act (MLPA), Minn. Stat. §473.858 (1994) provided that a city's zoning designations took priority over conflicting comprehensive plan designations.

However, later in 1995, the Minnesota legislature amended the MLPA to direct local governments to reconcile conflicts between zoning ordinances and comprehensive plans. Specifically, the amendment provided that if a comprehensive municipal plan conflicted with a zoning ordinance, "the zoning ordinance shall be brought into conformance with the plan . . . and if necessary, amendment of its comprehensive plan . . ."

In 2003, owners Cashill and Spaulding decided to sell Mendota Golf Course for $2.35 million to a developer who planned to convert the property to R-1 single-family residences. They entered into a purchase agreement that contained a contingency requiring "the buyer's obtaining necessary governmental approvals for proposed residential development." The developer then submitted a design concept plan to the city, but according to the minutes of the related city council meeting, the mayor and several council members indicated they would not support a plan to change the comprehensive plan to allow residential development of the property.

Cashill and Spaulding (Mendota Golf, LLP) then formally applied to have the city's comprehensive plan amended, arguing that the property was already zoned for R-1 residences. In June 2003, after holding a public hearing on the matter, the city's planning commission recommended denial of the application to amend, expressly finding that "the golf course is the best use of the property consistent with the surrounding use of the neighborhood." The city took no further action.

At this point, Mendota Golf filed a mandamus action in the local **district court**, asking the court to compel the city to reconcile its zoning ordinance with its comprehensive plan by approving the amendment to the comprehensive plan. The district court agreed with the owners, concluding that the city had acted in an arbitrary and capricious manner in denying the amendment. The court ordered the city to amend its comprehensive plan. The ruling was affirmed by the Minnesota Court of Appeals. The city appealed to the state's highest court.

The Minnesota Supreme Court reversed. First, it noted that a mandamus was a serious and **extraordinary remedy** for a court to invoke. Notwithstanding, the Court agreed that there was a conflict between the city's comprehensive plan and its zoning ordinance. More importantly, the court agreed that the city had failed to reconcile this conflict as required under the MLPA.

However, decided the Court, the answer was not to compel the city to amend its plan. Rather, noted the court, the discretionary power to zone and develop plans rested with the city council and not the courts. While mandamus was *not* appropriate to control or interfere with the manner in which a city exercised its discretion, mandamus *was* appropriate "to set the exercise of that discretion in motion."

The city did not contest its obligation to reconcile conflicts between the comprehensive plan and zoning ordinance. Rather, it objected to the mandamus that removed its discretion as to how it intended to reconcile the conflict. The

Minnesota Supreme Court agreed. It remanded the matter to the district court to issue a new **writ** of mandamus directing the city to reconcile the conflict (rather than directing the city to amend its comprehensive plan, as the first mandamus did). A strong dissent by three of the judges noted that if the city denied a change in "use" and required the owners to operate the unprofitable golf course, this would be tantamount to an eminent domain "taking."

Ultimately, in April 2007, the city held a special election. By a narrow margin (254 votes), residents approved the city's purchase of the property to run it as a municipal golf course. Residents will pay $50 a year for the next 15 years to pay for the property.

Kelo Decision Continues to Cause Controversy

Many state and local governments continued in 2006 and 2007 to consider measures in response to the U.S. Supreme Court's decision in *Kelo v. City of New London*, 545 U.S. 469, 125 S. Ct. 2655, 162 L. Ed. 2d 439 (2005). The Court in that decision ruled that governmental units may seize private property for the purpose of economic development and prompted widespread calls for legislation that would curb use of **eminent domain** powers. However, several commentators have noted that much of the legislation that has passed will do little to protect the rights of property owners.

The *Kelo* decision arose when the city of New London, Connecticut approved a development plan that called for the acquisition of several pieces of private property along the Thames River. Although the plan was expected to increase tax revenue and jobs for the area, parts of the property would not be open to the general public. The Supreme Court agreed with the Connecticut Supreme Court that use of the private property for an economic development plan constituted "public use" under the law of eminent domain. The Court emphasized that its decision did not preclude states from enacting their own laws to restrict the use of eminent domain.

Critics of the *Kelo* decision note that the action of the city of New London represents a common practice among local governments. "By our own count, over a five-year period, we have found about 10,000 instances where a local government either used or threatened to use eminent domain in order to take a home or parcel of property from one person and give it to another," said Dana Berliner, an attorney with

Protesters demonstrate outside Philadelphia city hall against eminent domain, June 23, 2006.

AP IMAGES

the Institute for Justice. "It is obviously more widespread and commonly practiced than most people could ever imagine. And it is a power that essentially allows a government **entity** to take any person's home away from them, to ruin their businesses or destroy their lives, whatever the case may be."

Various polls have shown that between 80 and 95 percent of Americans oppose the Court's decision, spreading across political, gender, and racial lines. By April 2006, legislators in 47 states had introduced more than 325 measures that were designed to protect private property from seizure through the use of eminent domain. Congress also expressed its disapproval, passing a bill that prohibits a private developer who obtains lands through eminent domain from receiving transportation funds. Pub. L. No. 109-115, 119 Stat. 2396 (2005).

Despite the opposition, the direct fallout has not been as severe as it might appear. Commentators note that only 14 states have enacted laws that significantly increase protection of property rights. Several other states have enacted statutes that appear to restrict the use of eminent domain but actually accomplish little. For instance, the Texas legislature enacted a **statute** that forbids use of eminent domain for "economic development," but it allows takings under other names, such as "community development." A number of states allow takings when the use of eminent domain will alleviate "blight," but even this tactic does not provide a significant level of protection for private land-

owners. One commentator noted that previous cases have identified both downtown Las Vegas in Nevada and Times Square in New York City as "blighted" areas.

According to the Institute of Justice, which represented the property owners in *Kelo*, more than half of the 20 states that have the largest number of condemnations similar to those in *Kelo* have either passed no legislation or have passed ineffective legislation limiting the use of eminent domain. Other states, such as Pennsylvania and Minnesota, have passed effective reforms but have exempted large areas where condemnations are likely to occur, such as Pittsburgh, Philadelphia, and the Twin Cities area. According to critics, even an executive order signed by President GEORGE W. BUSH on June 23, 2006 that bans the use of eminent domain for private development does little to protect private property because it allows takings where the use will be for both private and public development.

Developers have begun to defend the use of eminent domain, noting that it has been in use since the beginning of the Republic. In some instances, it is the only tool that cities and state can use to improve run-down areas that may include numerous abandoned properties. According to William J. Kearns, general counsel to the New Jersey State League of Municipalities, "Every city has within its borders large areas of land that are sitting there unused or are in a deteriorated or dangerous condition. It would be nice if the owners of these kinds of properties would step forward and arrive at a fair market price for what they own and then sell it. But all too often, owners can't be found or have not concern about the condition the property is in, and feel no responsibility to the surrounding area. To take away a city's power to change that means huge areas of blight would remain just that, and would probably only grow larger."

Some of those who acknowledge that use of eminent domain is beneficial argue that states need to establish better criteria that the states must meet before using eminent domain for redevelopment. These individuals are concerned more with people being evicted from their homes, as was the case with the *Kelo* plaintiffs. Commentators have noted that though many of the state statutes are ineffective efforts to restrict eminent domain, reforms that have been enacted as part of referendums have had more success. Voters in 12 states considered **referendum** measures that would ban or curtail condemnation of private property to promote economic development, and these measures were passed in ten of those states. In the majority of these states, the referendums are worded strongly enough that they provide real protection for property owners.

EMPLOYMENT LAW

The body of law that governs the employer-employee relationship, including individual employment contracts, the application of tort and contract doctrines, and a large group of statutory regulations on issues such as the right to organize and negotiate collective bargaining agreements, protection from discrimination, wages and hours, and health and safety.

Ledbetter v. Goodyear Tire & Rubber Company, Inc.

Title VII of the Civil Rights Act of 1963 bars employment practices that discriminate against any individual with respect to compensation because of the individual's race, religion, national origin, age, disability, or sex. 42 U.S.C.A. §2000e-2(a)(1). An individual must file a charge of discrimination with the EQUAL EMPLOYMENT OPPORTUNITY COMMISSION (EEOC) within 180 days of the date that the alleged unlawful employment practice occurred. If the employee fails to file a charge with the EEOC during this time period the employee may not sue the employer in court. It is easy to establish a date of injury when an employee is hired, fired, transferred, or demoted. Dating pay disparities is much more difficult, for compensation information is often kept confidential by employers. The EEOC and many **federal courts** allowed employees to sue their employers for unequal pay caused by discrimination that was alleged to have occurred years earlier. In a major decision the U.S. SUPREME COURT, in *Ledbetter v. Goodyear Tire & Rubber Company, Inc.*, __U.S.__, 127 S.Ct. 2162, __L.Ed.2d __ (2007), reversed course, ruled that employees had to file within 180 days of a specific allegedly discriminatory event, such as receiving a smaller raise because of her gender. Employees can no longer recover by establishing a pattern of discrimination that reaches back many years. Though the case involved sex discrimination, the ruling applies to Title VII's other protected classes.

Lilly Ledbetter worked as a supervisor at Goodyear Tire and Rubber's plant in Gadsden, Alabama from 1979 to her retirement in 1998.

During her tenure she worked as an area manager, a position dominated by men. When she started in 1979 her salary was equal to men who did substantially similar work but over time she earned less than other managers. By 1997 Ledbetter was the only female area manager, with a monthly salary of approximately $3,700. The lowest paid male area manager earned $4,300 while the highest paid manager earned $5,200. In July 1998 Ledbetter filed a charge of discrimination with the EEOC, alleging she was underpaid because of her sex. After she took an early retirement in November 1998, Ledbetter filed a federal civil rights lawsuit under Title VII and the Equal Pay Act (EPA), 29 U.S.C.A. §206(d). The federal **district court** dismissed her EPA claim but allowed the Title VII claim to proceed to trial. At trial she introduced evidence that suggested she had been given poor job evaluations because she was a woman. These evaluations result in lower raises than her male counterparts. The jury found in Ledbetter's favor and awarded her backpay and damages. The company appealed to the Eleventh **Circuit Court** of Appeals, which reversed the verdict. The appeals court held that the company had not discriminated against Ledbetter in 1997 and 1998 during the EEOC charging period. The remainder of her claims was barred by the 180-day **statute of limitations**, thereby eliminating almost 20 years of alleged discrimination. Ledbetter appealed to the Supreme Court.

The Supreme Court, in a 5–4 decision, upheld the Eleventh Circuit ruling. Justice Samuel Alito, writing for the majority, concluded that a line of Title VII cases supported the conclusion that unequal pay claims must be filed within 180 days of the allegedly discriminatory act. In doing so Alito rejected the EEOC's position that each paycheck that reflects the initial discrimination was a new act that restarted the 180-day clock. Alito stated that this "paycheck accrual" rule was wrong because Congress had set a "short deadline" for making discrimination claims to promote the "prompt resolution" of the matter. Though he admitted the 180-day deadline is "short by any measure," the Congress had made its intent clear that prompt resolution of these type of claims was important.

Ledbetter had argued that Goodyear had intentionally discriminated against her. It would be unfair for employers to try to defend themselves for actions that allegedly occurred many years before. The better course was to acknowledge that "strict adherence to the procedural requirements specified by the legislature is the best guarantee of evenhanded administration of the law." Ledbetter should have filed an EEOC charge within 180 days after "each allegedly discriminatory pay decision was communicated made and communicated to her." Because she had failed to show that Goodyear had intentionally discriminated against her in the 180-day period before she complained to the EEOC, she could not recover under Title VII. Justice Alito noted that alleged sex discrimination in pay could be pursued under the Equal Pay Act, which does allow plaintiffs to show a long pattern of unfair pay disparity.

Justice RUTH BADER GINSBURG, in a dissenting opinion joined by Justices JOHN PAUL STEVENS, DAVID SOUTER, and STEPHEN BREYER, argued that the Court had ignored the realities of the workplace. Employees rarely know the pay of the co-workers and may only find out many years later. Ginsburg contended that the Court "does not comprehend, or is indifferent to, the insidious way in which women can be victims of pay discrimination." Pay disparities often grew in small increments that, over time, lead a person to suspect that discrimination is the cause. For an employee like Ledbetter, who is trying to succeed "in a male-dominated workplace, in a job filled only by men before she was hired, understandably may be anxious to avoid making waves." The ruling was even more troubling because the "same denial of relief" would apply to individuals alleging discrimination based on race, religion, national origin, age, or disability. Justice Ginsberg, noting that the majority believed it was upholding the intent of Congress, suggested that this "cramped interpretation of Title VII" should be corrected by Congress. The 1991 Civil Rights Act overruled several Supreme Court decisions and Justice Ginsburg stated that "Once again, the ball is in Congress' court.

BCI Coca-Cola Bottling Co. of L.A. v. EEOC

One week before the U.S. SUPREME COURT was scheduled to hear a major employment discrimination case, the company involved with the case asked the Court to dismiss the suit. The EQUAL EMPLOYMENT OPPORTUNITY COMMISSION, which had filed an action for racial discrimination against the company, BCI Coca-Cola Bottling Co. of Los Angeles, did not object to the dismissal. The dismissal meant that a decision by the Tenth **Circuit Court** of Appeals, which ruled in favor of the EEOC, was allowed to stand.

BCI is a wholly owned subsidiary of Coca-Cola Bottlers, which is the world's largest bottler of Coca-Cola products. Stephen Peters worked for BCI as a merchandiser at the company's plant in Albuquerque, New Mexico. A merchandiser is an hourly employee who is responsible for arranging, cleaning, and rotating product displays and promotional materials. Merchandisers generally work five days a week, but because the grocery stores where the displays appear are usually open seven days per week, the merchandisers' schedules were usually staggered, and sometimes they had to work overtime.

Peters, who is black, was the senior-most merchandiser in his district. He had the most desirable schedule, with Saturdays and Sundays off. He received commendations from the company for his service and for "being a team player." He was occasionally asked to work on one of his scheduled off days. This occurred eight times during the first nine months of 2001. Other merchandisers also worked on days in which they were not originally scheduled. However, Peters had been warned in 1999 about refusing to work on a scheduled day off, which the company considered an act of insubordination. The file did not indicate the reason why Peters had refused to work, which was because his fiancée's son had died in a car accident and Peters had to serve as a pallbearer.

More than 60 percent of the facility's 200 employees were Hispanic, while fewer than two percent were black. Peters reported to Cesar Grado, an Hispanic district sales manager. Grado also supervised five other merchandisers as well as two account sales representatives. The other merchandisers account representatives were either Hispanic or white. Grado had broad discretion to bring facts about an employee's performance to the attention of BCI's human resources department, but Grado was not authorized to terminate an employee. The highest ranking human resources official in BCI's human resources office was Sherry Pederson. Pederson's supervisor was Pat Edgar, who worked in BCI's office in Phoenix, Arizona.

Grado faced a scheduling problem during the weekend of September 29 and 30, 2001. He needed an extra merchandiser but learned on the morning of September 29 that the one who usually worked extra shifts had been injured on the job and would not be available. Later that day, Grado told Peters' immediate supervisor to fill a shift on Sunday, September 30. Peters told the other supervisor, who was one of the account managers, that he could not work the shift because he was busy. Subsequently, Grado con-

Steven Peters, in an April 2007 photograph.
AP IMAGES

tacted BCI's human resources office to determine whether he could require Peters to work the shift. Grado later contacted Peters and ordered him to work on September 30. Although the parties dispute the specific conversations that took place, both agreed that Grado told Peters that if the latter did not work on the 30th, it would be considered an act of insubordination.

Peters went to an urgent care clinic on the evening of September 29, complaining of a headache, sinus pain, and a cough. He was diagnosed with a sinus infection, and his doctor told him not to return to work until Monday, October 1. Peters called his direct supervisor to inform him that he could not work on September 30. The supervisor attempted to call Grado, but Grado did not respond to the calls. After Peters did not work on September 30, Edgar had telephone conversations with both Grado and Pederson about Peters' conduct. Edgar then pulled Peters' file and discovered the notice from 1999. With this information in hand, Edgar decided on October 2 to terminate Peters' employment, which was announced at a meeting attended by Peters, Grado, Pederson, and Grado's supervisor. Until this meeting, neither Pederson nor Edgar knew that Peters was black.

Peters filed a complaint with the EEOC on October 11, 2001, alleging that his termination was the result of racial discrimination. Peters alleged that Grado treated African American employees less favorably than employees of other racial groups. The EEOC acquired three affidavits from BCI employees indicating that Grado treated black employees worse than employees of other races. At least one BCI employee said that Grado made disparaging remarks about African-Americans during working hours.

The EEOC filed suit on Peters behalf on December 30, 2002. BCI argued that it could not be liable for racial discrimination, because the person who made the decision to fire Peters did not know that he was black. EEOC countered by arguing that this claim arose under the "cat's paw" or "rubber stamp" theory, under which an employer may be liable for the act of a racially biased subordinate, even if the subordinate is not the one who made the actual decision.

The U.S. **District Court** for the District of New Mexico agreed with BCI. According the district court, the EEOC had established a **prima facie** case of discrimination because Peters is a member of a protected class, he was qualified for his position with the company, he was discharged despite the fact that he was qualified, and the company did not eliminate the position after discharging him. However, the district court held that BCI had shown a legitimate, nondiscriminatory reason for terminating Peters' employment, which was because Peters had been insubordinate toward Grado. Accordingly, the district court granted **summary judgment** in favor of BCI. *EEOC v. BCI Coca-Cola*

Bottling Co. of L.A., No. Civ. 02-1644 JB/RHS, 2004 WL 3426757 (D.N.M. June 10, 2004).

EEOC appealed the decision to the Tenth Circuit Court of Appeals, which reversed the district court's ruling. According to the **appellate court**, the EEOC produced enough evidence to raise a question about Grado's racial **animus** that should have been answered by a jury. Moreover, the company's conflicting statements about the reasons for Peters' termination led the court to conclude that genuine issue of material fact existed as to whether BCI's actions were a pretext for racial discrimination. Accordingly, the court remanded the case for further proceedings. *EEOC v. BCI Coca-Cola Bottling Co. of L.A.*, 450 F.3d 476 (10th Cir. 2006).

BCI's petition for **writ** of **certiorari** was granted on January 5, 2007. Oral argument was originally schedule for April 18, 2007, but about a week prior to the scheduled date, BCI decided to request for the dismissal of the writ. Five parties filed amici briefs in support of BCI, while EEOC had none, showing that employers had concerns about the outcome of the case. However, commentators noted that the facts of the case were such that BCI was likely to lose, and so instead of risking another adverse decision from the high court, the company decided to maintain status quo.

ENVIRONMENTAL LAW

An amalgam of state and federal statutes, regulations, and common-law principles covering air pollution, water pollution, hazardous waste, the wilderness, and endangered wildlife.

United States v. Atlantic Research Corporation

Following the 1970s, when Americans started getting serious about environmental cleanup, Congress passed the Comprehensive Environmental Response Compensation and Liability Act of 1980 (CERCLA). The Act was intended to encourage private citizens to report environmentally-contaminated dump sites, to encourage corporations to clean up sites, and to allow the recovery of expenses associated with cleaning up contaminated sites.

At issue in *United States v. Atlantic Research Corporation*, No. 06-562, 551 U.S. ___ (2007) were two specific sections of the Act that relate to the right to seek recovery for expenses and costs of cleanup. Section §107(a) of the Act provides that potentially responsible parties (PRPs) are

liable for all costs of removal or remedial action undertaken by the federal or a state government or an Indian tribe in cleaning up the site, that are not inconsistent with the national contingency plan. It further states that PRPs are liable for "any other necessary costs of response incurred by any other person consistent with [such] plan."

Some courts initially interpreted §107(a) to provide a **cause of action** for private parties to recover clean-up costs and/or seek *contribution* if they were sued. (Under the principle of contribution, one who is found liable for damages is entitled to recover a proportional share of the damages from other joint tortfeasors whose negligence or wrongful conduct also contributed to the damage.)

However, Congress later added §113(f) to CERCLA as part of the Superfund Amendments and Reauthorization Act of 1986. This new section expressly authorized one PRP to sue another for contribution. Many courts then found this section to be the exclusive remedy for contribution. Then in *Cooper Industries v. Aviall Services, Inc.*, 543 U.S. 157 (2004), the Supreme Court held that a private party could seek contribution under §113(f) only after being sued under §106 or §107(a).

Atlantic Research Corporation leased property held by the Department of Defense after being awarded a government contract to build rocket motors. In the course of its work, Atlantic Research contaminated the site with runoff and/or burnt rocket fuel. It voluntarily cleaned up the toxic material, then sought contribution from the government for the clean-up costs, filing suit under both §§107(a) and 113(f).

§113(f) states in relevant part,

"Any person may seek contribution from any other person who is liable or potentially liable under section 9607(a) [§107(a)] of this title, during or following any **civil action** under section 9606[§106] or under section 9607(a) of this title. . . . Nothing in this subsection shall diminish the right of any person to bring an action for contribution in the absence of a civil action under section 9606 of this title or section 9607 of this title."

The **district court** dismissed the case. First, it found that §113(f) was inapplicable, as a party can only bring a claim under that section if it is already the subject of an action under §107(a) (or under §106). Since Atlantic had not been sued by anyone, and voluntarily cleaned up the site, it was not entitled to seek contribution under § 113(f).

The district court also found no cause of action under § 107(a), the cost recovery section. The court held that § 107(a) did not create a cause of action entitling one PRP to sue another for voluntary clean-ups. Atlantic Research appealed.

The Eighth **Circuit Court** of Appeals agreed that Atlantic Research had no cause of action for contribution under § 113(f). However, it reversed the dismissal of the § 107(a) claim, holding that this section indeed provided a cause of action to PRPs, i.e., "potentially liable parties" against other PRPs. This time, the government appealed.

A unanimous Supreme Court upheld the Eighth Circuit's interpretation of the relevant sections. Justice Thomas, writing for the Court, quite simply held that because the plain language of § 107(a)(4)(B) allows a PRP to recover costs from other PRPs, the **statute** provides a pre-lawsuit cause of action, in this case, for Atlantic Research.

The Court recognized two separate and legitimate causes of action to recover cleanup expenses: a § 107(a) claim prior to civil action for voluntary cleanups of contaminated sites; and a § 113(f) contribution claim during or following a lawsuit or enforcement action under §§ 106 and 107(a).

The Court briefly addressed the government's concern that PRPs could avoid the shorter three-year **statute of limitations** under § 113(f) by filing § 107(a) actions instead (with a six-year statute of limitation). The Court reiterated that each section created its own distinct remedy. A PRP cannot seek contribution under § 107(a) and can only recover the costs actually "incurred" in cleaning up the site.

Conversely, the Court noted that:

". . . a PRP that pays money to satisfy a settlement agreement or a court judgment may pursue § 113(f) contribution. But by reimbursing response costs paid by other parties, the PRP has not incurred its own costs of response and therefore cannot recover under § 107(a). As a result, though eligible to seek contribution under § 113(f)(1), the PRP cannot simultaneously seek to recover the same expenses under § 107(a)."

EPA Issues New Rules to Cut Toxic Emissions

During the Clinton Administration, Congress, under provisions of the Clean Air Act,), had required the ENVIRONMENTAL PROTECTION AGENCY (EPA) to issue regulations (in the form of rules or standards) controlling toxic emissions from "mobile sources" by 1995. This primarily affected the motor vehicle industry, and nothing much happened for the next ten years. In 2005, environmental groups SIERRA CLUB and U.S. Public Interest Research Group, represented by environmental law firm Earthsource, won a federal court order (in the form of a consent decree) compelling EPA to issue a preliminary proposal for new regulations no later than 2006, with a final rule by early February 2007.

On February 26, 2007, the EPA published its final rule for the regulation of benzene, a naturally-occurring but highly toxic and cancer-causing substance found in crude oil, gasoline, and exhaust fumes emitted from vehicles. The rule, published as *Control of Hazardous Air Pollutants from Mobile Sources*, (72 FR 8428) requires sequential implementation between 2009 and 2011, and is estimated to reduce toxic emissions of benzene and other pollutants by up to 80 percent over the next two decades. The new requirements were expected to reduce total emissions of mobile source air toxics by 330,000 tons, and VOC emissions (precursors to ozone and "PM2.5") by more than one million tons.

The new rule was designed to meet the court order's requirement that EPA force oil refineries to meet an average 0.62 percent limit of benzene in all fuel produced for consumption by 2011. The current content of benzene in gasoline is just under one percent, averaging 0.97 percent.

The rule also regulates evaporation of fuel, and sets standards for evaporation limits for all fuel containers starting in 2009. Finally, by 2010, passenger vehicle engines started up at cold temperatures (the time when vehicles emit the most toxic fumes) must emit fewer benzene and other pollutants.

The new standards were expected to cost consumers about $400 million, mostly attached to the price of new vehicles. However, the extra cost would average out to less than $1 per vehicle, an EPA spokesperson reported to the Associated Press.

Environmentalists and others were infuriated over another less publicized provision in the new rule, which would allow some refineries to purchase emissions credits to meet the new regional standards. Essentially, by adopting regional standards, EPA would allow several gasoline refineries, particularly in the Northwest, to avoid the limits by "trading" pollution credits with other refineries elsewhere in the country that were below the regional standard.

But EPA defended the credit-trading program as more fair. It adopted regional benzene standards ranging from 0.52 percent along the East Coast to 0.9 percent in the Rocky Mountains. The credit-trade program would mostly affect the Pacific Northwest, where benzene emissions run nearly twice the national average. This is because much of the region's gasoline comes from Alaska's benzene-rich oil. For this Northwest region, the new regulations require that benzene fuel limits drop from the current level of 1.8 percent to 0.69 by 2011 (just above the national level of 0.62).

In parts of the country where reformulated gasoline (RFG) products are required, benzene levels have been reduced by 50 percent or more. In areas that have not adopted RFG, average benzene levels remain about twice the national average, while in the Pacific Northwest, levels have run nearly three times as high.

In addition to the reduction of benzene, EPA issued new regulations to control pollutants such as hydrocarbons, particulate matter, and nitrogen oxides. Other regulations addressed emissions from highway and off-road vehicles, and new programs were under development to address standards for small non-road gasoline engines (such as used in lawn mowers and tractors), diesel locomotives, and marine engines. Other related EPA program initiatives included its "Clean School Bus USA," "The Volunteer Diesel Retrofit Program," and "Best Workplaces for Computers." By 2010, EPA's existing programs are expected to reduce all mobile source air toxics by over one million tons from 1999 levels.

At the same time that EPA published its new benzene rule, the United States Senate Committee on Environment and Public Works, chaired by Senator Barbara Boxer (D-CA) planned to conduct an oversight hearing on recent decisions of the EPA, including the credit-purchasing program of the Mobile Source rule, which would essentially allow several industries and refineries to increase rather than decrease their toxic emissions. As of early 2007, other pollutants such as mercury (mostly from cement kilns), dioxins, and PCBs continued to be emitted without restriction from many unregulated industries across the country.

National Association of Home Builders v. Defenders of Wildlife

In June 2007, the U.S. SUPREME COURT resolved a case involving the interrelationship between two federal environmental statutes. In *National Association of Home Builders v. Defenders of Wildlife*, the Court determined that the ENVIRONMENTAL PROTECTION AGENCY (EPA) was not required by the ENDANGERED SPECIES ACT (ESA) to consider whether the agency's transfer of authority regarding water pollution to a state agency may jeopardize endangered species. The Court's decision reversed an opinion by the Ninth **Circuit Court** of Appeals, which had held that the EPA's transfer power under the Clean Water Act was limited by the ESA.

Congress enacted the Clean Water Act of 1972 (CWA), 33 U.S.C. §1251, to prevent pollution of the nation's waters through the National Pollution Discharge Elimination System (NPDES). It allows the EPA to issue permits for discharging pollutants into water. Where a state has met certain requirements under the **statute**, the state may request that EPA transfer permitting authority to state officials. If the EPA determines that the state has met nine criteria set forth in the CWA, then it is required to transfer permitting authority to the state. Once this authority has been transferred, the state then has the **primary authority** to review and approve NPDES permits, though the EPA retains oversight.

The Endangered Species Act, 16 U.S.C. §1531, which is a completely separate environmental statute, protects and conserves endangered species and their habitats. Section 7 of this statute establishes steps that all federal agencies must take to ensure that their actions do not jeopardize endangered species. More specifically, the statute requires that "[e]ach Federal agency shall, in consultation with and with the assistance of the Secretary [of Commerce or the Interior], insure that any action authorized, funded, or carried out" by such an agency "is not likely to jeopardize the continued existence of any endangered species." The ESA does not specifically refer to the CWA, and state agencies are not bound to follow the directives established in Section 7 of the ESA.

In 2002, officials in the State of Arizona submitted an application to administer the NPDES program in that state. The EPA consulted with the Fish and Wildlife Service (FWS) to determine whether the transfer of permitting authority to the State of Arizona would have an impact on water quality that would, in turn, have an adverse effect on endangered species. The FWS decided that the transfer of authority would not have an adverse impact on a listed species, but the agency expressed concern that the transfer could have an indirect adverse impact. The primary reason for this conclusion was that because section 7 of the ESA does not apply to state agencies, that Arizona officials could issue permits without considering the impact on endangered species. The EPA later determined that the CWA did not allow it to disapprove a transfer of authority based on considerations other than those found in the CWA itself. The national office of the FWS later issued an opinion concluding that the transfer of permitting authority would not have an adverse effect on listed species under the ESA.

Defenders of Wildlife filed a petition with the Ninth Circuit Court of Appeals pursuant to 33 U.S.C. §1369, which permits private parties to seek direct review of the EPA's decisions regarding the transfer of permitting authority. The National Association of Home Builders intervened in the case. Defenders of Wildlife also brought suit against the FWS for its opinion, which the Defenders of Wildlife said failed to comply with standards set forth in the ESA. The Ninth Circuit subsequently consolidated the case with the other case pending before the **appellate court**.

A split panel of the Ninth Circuit ruled that the EPA had acted in an arbitrarily and capriciously because the agency had "relied during the administrative proceedings on legally contradictory positions regarding its section 7 obligations." *Defenders of Wildlife v. U.S. EPA*, 420 F.3d 946 (9th Cir. 2005). According to the opinion by circuit judge Marsha Berzon, the EPA did not "understand its own authority" under section 7 in the agency's failure to act on behalf of endangered species. More specifically, the court noted that the EPA's decision contradicted itself because the agency had first acknowledged that it was required to consider the impact of transferring authority on endangered species (when it submitted the decision to FWS) and then later determined that the agency could not consider ESA concerns when it made the decision about transferring the permitting authority.

The majority panel reviewed the statutes in question and determined that the ESA not only gave the EPA power to determine the impact of the transfer on endangered species but also required the EPA to make this determination. This decision effectively added a tenth criterion to the nine that are set forth in the CWA itself.

According to the dissent by Judge David R. Thompson, the panel's decision was incorrect because the language in the CWA clearly states that if the nine listed criteria are met, "the EPA administrator 'shall approve' the program." Nevertheless, the Ninth Circuit sitting **en banc** ruled denied a request to rehear the case.

The Supreme Court agreed to review the case, and in a 5–4 decision, reversed the Ninth Circuit. *Nat'l Ass'n of Home Builders v. Defenders of Wildlife*, Nos. 06-340, 06-549, 2007 WL 1801745 (June 25, 2007). In an opinion by Justice Samuel Alito, the majority noted that the Ninth Circuit had erroneously considered statements made during the EPA's review process when it should have only reviewed the agency's final action. The fact that officials at a higher level had overruled a prior decision made at the local agency level did not render the decision of the agency arbitrary and capricious. The Court also determined that the language of the CWA was such that the decision as to whether to grant a transfer of permitting authority was not a discretionary one on the part of the EPA. Based on the language of the statutes, the Court concluded that the EPA did not have to consider the provisions of the ESA when determining whether to transfer permitting authority and that once the EPA determined that the nine criteria in the CWA were met, the agency was required to transfer that authority.

Justice JOHN PAUL STEVENS, joined by three other justices, dissented. He argued that because the EPA was faced with competing **statutory** mandates, the Court should have found a way to give full effect to both.

ERISA

The name of federal legislation, popularly abbreviated as ERISA (29 U.S.C.A. §1001 et seq. [1974]), which regulates the financing, vesting, and administration of pension plans for workers in private business and industry.

Beck v. Pace International Union

One of the protections of The EMPLOYEE RETIREMENT INCOME SECURITY ACT of 1974 (ERISA) is a requirement that private sector **pension** plan managers discharge their managerial duties solely in the interests of their plan participants and beneficiaries. In *Beck v. Pace International Union*, No. 05-1448, 551 U.S. ___ (2007), the U.S. SUPREME COURT held that bankrupt employer Crown Vantage Inc.

(through its liquidating **trustee**, Jeffrey Beck) did not breach its **fiduciary** duty to plan participants and beneficiaries for failing to consider a merger with the labor union's plan, as one of its options when terminating the plans. This was true even though the company stood to retain a $5 million **reversion** after satisfying its obligations to plan participants and beneficiaries, by choosing a standard termination and purchasing annuities. The Court's decision was unanimous, reversing the Ninth **Circuit Court** of appeals

Crown Paper and its parent **entity**, Crown Vantage ("Crown") operated seven paper mills, employing approximately 2,600. PACE International Union ("PACE") represented employees covered by 17 of Crown's defined-benefit pension plans (under which retired employees were entitled to fixed periodic payments).

In March 2000, Crown filed for bankruptcy and began liquidating its assets. Under such circumstances, ERISA permits employers to terminate pension plans voluntarily, as long as the terminated plans have sufficient assets to cover benefit liabilities (a "standard termination"). As Crown explored the possibility of this option, PACE interjected itself into the discussions and proposed that Crown, instead, merge the plans (covering PACE union members) with PACE's own multi-employer pension fund, PIUMPF. Under this option, Crown would be required to turn over all plan assets to PIUMPF and PIUMPF would assume all plan liabilities. Crown took the offer under advisement.

AS Crown looked into **annuity** options, it discovered it had actually over-funded certain pension plans, so that converting them to annuities would allow Crown to retain an estimated $5 million. This money could be used toward satisfying its bankruptcy creditors after it had satisfied its obligations to pension plan participants and beneficiaries. Conversely, under the PIUMPF merger proposal, the $5 million excess would go to PIUMPF. Crown chose the annuities.

PACE then filed suit in federal **district court**. It claimed that Crown had breached its fiduciary duty to plan participants and beneficiaries under ERISA by neglecting to give adequate or diligent consideration to the proposed merger of plans with PIUMPF. The district court ruled in favor of PACE, and the bankruptcy trustee, Beck, appealed first to the district court, and then to the Ninth Circuit.

The Ninth Circuit affirmed in relevant part. Importantly, the court acknowledged that a decision to terminate a pension plan is generally a business decision *not* subject to ERISA's fiduciary obligations. Notwithstanding, the **appellate court** reasoned that the *implementation* of a termination decision was fiduciary in nature.

Writing for an unanimous Supreme Court, Justice Scalia reversed and remanded. The Court noted that it is well established that a decision by an employer to terminate an ERISA plan is a **settlor** rather than administrative function, not subject to ERISA's fiduciary obligations. Still, the Court did not totally dismiss the possibility that, under certain circumstances, a decision whether to merge plans could switch from being a settlor to a fiduciary function, since both options involve the **transfer of assets** and liabilities.

However, to find that a fiduciary duty was involved, the Court said it would have to find that the merger option was a permissible form of plan termination under ERISA.

To the contrary, the Court concluded that merger was not a method of termination. Timing played into its ruling. At the time PACE proposed the merger, Crown had already made a decision to terminate its pension plans; it was merely deliberating over whether to put the money into annuities.

Justice Scalia enumerated several other reasons why a "termination" under ERISA should not encompass mergers. They included the fact that terminating a plan through purchase of annuities formally severs the applicability of ERISA to plan assets. Moreover, the Pension Benefit Guarantee Corporation (PBGC), an independent governmental agency created under ERISA to protect pensions, would no longer be liable for deficiencies if the plan became insolvent. Also, risks associated with annuities related solely to the **solvency** of insurance companies and not to the performance of merged fund investments. Still another reason was that following a merger, merged plan assets could be used to satisfy the benefits liabilities of participants and beneficiaries other than those in the original plan. (The Court listed several more reasons.)

In summary, the Court noted that PBGC takes the position that ERISA does not permit merger as a method of termination of plans, because merger is an alternative to, rather than a form of, plan termination. The Court had historically deferred to the PBGC when interpreting ERISA, and now again, found PBGC's policy not only permissible and reasonable but more plausible. Termination by merger could have exposed plan participants and beneficiaries to more risks, with detrimental financial consequences.

Retail Industry Leaders Association v. Fielder

Many states have seen the cost of their medical assistance programs, including **Medicaid**, rise dramatically in the past five years. In analyzing why the costs have risen so sharply, states discovered that employees of Wal-Mart Stores, Inc. have ended up on public health programs. It has been alleged that Wal-Mart provides substandard health care benefits to its employees. As a result several states, including Maryland and California, have enacted "play or pay" laws that require large employers to either spend a specific percentage of their payroll on employee healthcare benefits or pay the amount that their spending falls short to a state healthcare fund. Wal-Mart, which has been the chief target of these laws, mobilized a trade association group made up of large corporations to challenge the Maryland law. The Fourth **Circuit Court** of Appeals, in *Retail Industry Leaders Association v. Fielder*, 475 F.3d 180(4th Cir. 2007), dealt a blow to these state efforts when it ruled that the federal EMPLOYEE RETIREMENT INCOME SECURITY ACT (ERISA) preempted the Maryland law. The court held that such state laws would undermine the national uniformity of employee benefit plans that Congress intended when it passed ERISA.

The Maryland legislature enacted the Fair Share Health Care Fund Act (Fair Share) in 2006 because state medical assistance costs had risen from $3.46 billion to $4.7 billion in just three **fiscal** years. It believed Wal-Mart, one of the four largest employers in Maryland, provided substandard employee healthcare benefits. Studies in Georgia and North Carolina supported this conclusion, demonstrating that substantial numbers of Wal-Mart employees and their children have joined public health programs. The legislature concluded that state tax dollars were subsidizing Wal-Mart. Therefore, Fair Share required employers with 10,000 or more Maryland employees to spend at least 8 percent of their total payrolls on employees' heath insurance costs or pay the amount their spending fell short to the state. Wal-Mart, which has 16,000 Maryland employees, was one of four employers covered by Fair Share. However, the other three employers did not feel the effect of the law for various reasons. Johns Hopkins University, a nonprofit corporation, was subject to a 6 percent contribution

which it already satisfied. Giant Foods, which employed unionized workers, spent more than 8 percent on employee health insurance, while Northrup Grumman, a defense contractor, was eventually excluded from the program by legislative amendment. A corporation was also required to file an annual report disclosing its health care costs. If a corporation failed to make the required payment to the state for the difference between its health insurance costs and an amount equal to 8 percent of the total wages paid to employees, it could be subject to a $250,000 civil penalty.

Soon after Fair Share was enacted, and before it went into effect, the Retail Industry Leaders Association (RILA) filed suit against the state of Maryland. RILA, a trade association whose members include Best Buy Company, Target Corporation, Lowe's Companies, IKEA and Wal-Mart, alleged that Fair Share was preempted by ERISA. ERISA is an extremely complex and technical set of provisions that seek to protect employee benefit programs by preventing the states from regulating plan design and administration. This is particularly important for multi-state employers, who would incur increased costs if they were required to administer their plans differently in each state. Therefore, Congress included broad **preemption** provisions that prohibit states from regulating benefit employee plans. RILA alleged that Fair Share was exactly the type of scheme that ERISA was meant to prevent. If the courts failed to strike Fair Share other states would be emboldened to do the same. In time large employers like Wal-Mart would be spending time and money administering 50 different plans. The state countered that ERISA was not an issue because employers could choose to pay into the fund rather than modify their health insurance plans to increase spending. The federal **district court** sided with RILA, ruling that the Maryland law was preempted by ERISA.

A three-judge panel of the Fourth Circuit Court of Appeals upheld the lower court ruling on a 2–1 vote. Judge Paul Niemeyer, writing for the majority, found that Fair Share would undermine ERISA's goal to have national uniform administration of employee benefit plans. The Maryland "opt out" provision was not a meaningful option because "any reasonable employer" would choose to spend money on increasing employees' heath care, for to do otherwise would hurt employees' morale. The Fair Share reporting requirements also burdened employers by forcing them to alter their national administration plans. If Fair Share and other similar plans were permitted it would force employers to tailor their benefit plans to "each specific State, and even to specific cities and counties. This is precisely the regulatory balkanization that Congress sought to avoid by enacting ERISA's preemptive provision." Though Maryland might have had a "noble purpose," the law would have undermined ERISA's "foundational policy" and encourage other states and local governments to follow suit. Such laws were preempted by ERISA.

Judge M. Blane Michael dissented, arguing that the **statute** was not preempted by ERISA because employers could opt out and pay into the special fund. Congress intended for the states to find "innovative ways to solve the Medicaid funding crisis" and Fair Share was a legitimate response.

ESTABLISHMENT CLAUSE

Hein v. Freedom From Religion Foundation

In order to file suit against another party, a plaintiff must have standing to sue ("standing"), meaning that the plaintiff must have a sufficient stake or interest in the controversy to be granted relief. Under the traditional doctrine of standing, ordinary taxpayers do not have sufficient standing to sue the government over how their tax dollars are spent. This is because each taxpayer's monetary contribution toward a particular congressional expenditure would be considered miniscule, and certainly the government cannot have every taxpayer challenging each or any government program he or she disagrees with.

There has been an exception to this general rule. In the 1968 Supreme Court decision of *Flast v. Cohen, 392 U.S.83*, the Court held that taxpayers who alleged that a government program violated the Establishment Clause of the U.S. Constitution could have standing to challenge the government in a lawsuit. (The "Establishment Clause" refers to that clause in the FIRST AMENDMENT to the Constitution that states, "Congress shall make no law respecting an establishment of religion . . ." This clause is also invoked when persons speak of "separation of church and state.")

In *Hein v. Freedom From Religion Foundation*, No. 06-157, 551 U.S. ___ (2007), the Foundation and three of its members (invoking their standing as individual taxpayers) filed suit against Hein, the director of the White House Office of Faith-Based and Community Initia-

tives (and several other executive agencies of the government) in an Establishment Clause challenge. Specifically, the plaintiffs complained that parts of President Bush's "faith-based" initiative, which sought to increase the participation of religious and private charitable groups in providing government social services, violated the Establishment Clause.

Shortly after taking office, President Bush, in an attempt to get local communities more involved in social welfare, created, by executive order, the Office of Faith-Based and Community Initiatives. Acknowledging that at the local community level, "private and charitable groups, including religious ones" often played key roles in social service and community welfare, another presidential executive order created a White House office and several centers within federal agencies to ensure that faith-based community groups were eligible to compete alongside nonreligious groups for federal funds.

In the lawsuit, the Foundation complained that these "centers," their directors, and the conferences they organized were designed to promote, and had the effect of promoting, religious community groups in violation of the Establishment Clause. The complaint alleged that the conferences actually favored religious organizations over non-religious ones, and in reality, functioned as propaganda vehicles to promote religion.

The government responded to the suit by first arguing that the Foundation, et al., had no standing to sue, because the Foundation suffered no harm by way of the conferences or the initiative, and therefore lacked standing. Even though the Foundation's members were taxpayers and it was an Establishment Clause challenge, the government countered that creation of the faith-based initiative and the conference centers was all done by executive order through the government's executive branch, *not by congressional act or appropriation of funds.*

The **district court** dismissed the suit for lack of standing. It held that the exceptions (under *Flast*, above) encompassed only challenges to specific congressional expenditures, not executive-branch actions funded by "general funds" allocated by Congress to the executive branch and its departments.

The Seventh **Circuit Court** of Appeals reversed the decision and sided with the Foundation. The **appellate court** held that any taxpayer had standing to bring an Establishment Clause challenge against an executive branch program, whether it was funded by specific congressional appropriation or by discretionary use of a general fund. Hein and the government agencies appealed. Thirteen states also filed a brief in the case, requesting that the Seventh Circuit decision be overturned, for fear of states being flooded with lawsuits over state executive-branch actions.

By a 5–4 **plurality** vote, the U.S. SUPREME COURT reversed the Seventh Circuit decision. Justice Alito, writing for the plurality, ruled that citizens do not have standing, even under the Establishment Clause, to challenge executive branch programs funded by general administrative appropriations. The Court rejected the Seventh Circuit's broad expansion of the *Flast* exception, instead saying that *Flast* represented a "narrow exception" that accommodates taxpayers only when they bring an Establishment Clause challenge against a congressional expenditure. To extend *Flast* to executive actions and programs would not only violate separation of powers, but also would turn **federal courts** into "general complaint bureaus."

The Court noted that the link between congressional action and constitutional violation was missing in the present case. The Foundation had argued that any distinction between expenditures pursuant to congressional appropriation versus expenditures made in the course of executive discretion was arbitrary, because the injury to taxpayers was the same. But the Court rejected this argument, saying that *Flast* focused only on congressional expenditures, and the invitation to expand or extend its holding to executive branch expenditures must be declined. In summary, when plaintiffs challenge no act of the legislative branch (Congress), and the executive branch action being challenged was financed only indirectly through general appropriations, and no funds were disbursed to any entities or persons outside the government, individual taxpayers have no standing to challenge the action.

Justice Kennedy filed a separate concurring opinion. Justice Scalia, joined by Justice Thomas, concurred in the judgment, but felt that *Flast* should be overruled. Justice Souter, joined by Justices Stevens, Ginsburg, and Breyer, filed a dissenting opinion that would have given taxpayers standing in such a challenge.

EXTRADITION

The transfer of an accused from one state or country to another state or country that seeks to place the accused on trial.

United States and United Kingdom Ratify New Extradition Treaty

Three years after negotiating its provisions, the United States Senate ratified a new extradition treaty with the United Kingdom in September 2006. The new treaty replaces two others that have been the subject of controversy for several years. Of particular interest to commentators are revised provisions related to the extradition of those who are accused of committing political offenses.

The U.S. and the U.K. negotiated the first modern version of extradition treaty between the two nations on June 8, 1972. The Senate did not ratify it until June 21, 1976, and the treaty was finally entered into force on January 21, 1977. One of the major causes of controversy over the original **statute** was the so-called "political offense exception." Article V of the original treaty provided, "Extradition shall not be granted if . . . (i) the offense for which extradition is requested is regarded by the requested Party as one of a political character; or (ii) the person sought proves that the request for his extradition has in fact been made with a view to try or punish him for an offense of a political character."

Several other extradition treaties include political offense exceptions, and **federal courts** in the U.S. had developed judicial standards for determining whether a person facing extradition was accused of committing a political offense. Under this judicial standard, the treaties precluded extradition on the basis of criminal charges growing out of conduct "committed in the course of and incidental to a violent political disturbance, such as war, revolution, or rebellion." *Eain v. Wilkes*, 641 F.2d 504 (7th Cir. 1981).

A controversy arose surrounding the treatment of four members of the Provisional Irish Republican Army. Federal courts in New York and California refused to extradite these individuals based on the political offense exception. The uproar that ensued led the U.S. and the U.K. to negotiate a supplemental treaty, which was signed on June 25, 1985. This supplemental treaty curtailed the political offense exception and also revised other provisions, including easing the **statute of limitations** in the original treaty. The U.S. Senate produced a compromise under which the political offense exception allowed the extradition of terrorists in most cases, among other changes. The effect of the changes on the individuals from the Provisional Irish Republican Army was that all four were returned to Ireland, either through extradition or through deportation.

Extradition treaties that were ratified after the Supplemental Treaty of 1985 have generally had more most exemption to the extradition bar for political offenses. Most of these new treaties allow extradition where the political offense involves a crime of violence against the head of a state or that person's family. Likewise, these treaties permit extradition when the crime is covered by a treaty that obligates a nation to extradite the offender. Some extradition treaties, however, have retained the exemptions to the political offense ban that are found in the Supplemental Treaty.

The United States and the United Kingdom entered into negotiations to draft a new treaty that would replace both the 1977 version and the Supplemental Treaty of 1985. On March 31, 2003, former U.S. Attorney General JOHN ASHCROFT and U.K. Home Secretary David Blunkett announced that the two nations had agreed to the new pact, pending the **ratification** by appropriate bodies of the two governments. Later that year, the United Kingdom incorporated the treaty into British law through the passage of the Extradition Act of 2003.

Under the terms of the 2003 agreement, federal courts in the U.S. would retain the authority to bar extradition requests when the request fails to meet the demands of the treaty. Moreover, the treaty does not require the United States to take any action that is forbidden by the U.S. Constitution. The accord urges the U.S. Secretary of State to consider any requests for the extradition of a fugitive who has been previously acquitted, and it requires annual reports from the Secretary of State about the number and **disposition** of extradition requests brought under the treaty.

The 2003 agreement received criticism on a number of grounds. Most notably, the treaty eliminates the ban on extradition for political offenses for any offense that allegedly involves violence or weapons. The treaty also transfers responsibility for determination of whether a request is politically-motivated from the judiciary to the executive branch. Moreover, the agreement eliminates any statute of limitations.

A controversy surrounding three bankers led to the ratification of the treaty by the United States. Three bankers associated with NatWest were accused of **fraud** offenses in connection with Enron, the now infamous energy trading company that went bankrupt in 2001. According to allegations, the three conspired with former Enron executives over the sale of part of the company in 2000, which earned them a total of $7.3 million. The U.S. wanted to extradite the three bankers, but because the U.K. had ratified the treaty and the U.S. had not, critics in the United Kingdom said that the two nations did not have a reciprocal legal arrangement.

The bankers were extradited during the summer of 2006. In July 2006, British Home Minister Baroness Scotland traveled to the U.S. to urge the U.S. to ratify the 2003 treaty. On September 29, the Senate finally approved the pact. According to Robert Tuttle, the U.S. ambassador to the U.K., "I am extremely gratified at the unanimous support of the United States Senate for this extremely important Treaty. With the Senate's action, we can now have a fully modernized extradition relationship that helps to protect citizens of both of our countries and to improve the administration of justice."

A fact sheet about the extradition treaty is available from the Secretary of State's website at <http://www.state.gov/p/eur/rls/fs/34885.htm>.

FALSE CLAIMS ACT

Rockwell International, Corp. v. United States

Under the federal False Claims Act (FCA), 31 U.S.C.A. §§3729-3733, those who knowingly submit, or cause another person or **entity** to submit, false claims for payment of government funds are liable for three times the government's damages plus civil penalties of $5,500 to $11,000 per false claim. The FCA contains "qui tam", or whistleblower, provisions. Qui tam allows citizens with evidence of **fraud** against government contracts and programs to sue, on behalf of the government, in order to recover the fraudulently paid funds. In compensation for the risk and effort of filing a case, the whistleblower may be awarded a portion of the funds recovered. To limit these lawsuits Congress mandated that the whistleblower must be the "original source" of the information that leads to the recovery of the funds. The U.S. SUPREME COURT, in *Rockwell International, Corp. v. United States*, __U.S.__, 127 S.Ct.1397, __L.Ed.2d __ (2007), tightened this requirement by ruling that a qui tam informant cannot receive compensation if he lacked "direct and independent knowledge of the information upon which his allegations were based."

James Stone worked for Rockwell International Corp. at the Rocky Flats, Colorado nuclear weapons plant from 1980 to 1986. Rockwell, which managed the plant from 1975 to 1989 under a management contract with the DEPARTMENT OF ENERGY (DOE), was given a semi-annual award fee based on a list of categories including environmental, safety, and health concerns. In 1982 Stone reviewed a plan to dispose of toxic pond sludge by mixing it with cement and making "pondcrete" blocks that could be stored onsite or transported to other sites for disposal. Stone concluded that the proposed manufacturing process was flawed and would not work. He put his concerns in writing, contending that the mixture would be unstable and the blocks would deteriorate, releasing unwanted toxic wastes. Rockwell ignored his concerns and began manufacturing pondcrete blocks. Several months after Stone was laid off in 1986, Rockwell learned that many of the blocks were not stable. However, DOE did not become aware of the problem until 1988, when some of the blocks began to leak. The news media reported these problems and attributed it to the reduction of the ratio of concrete to sludge in the mixture. In June 1987 Stone went to the FBI with allegations of environmental crimes at Rocky Flats. The FBI and DOE conducted a search of the plant in 1989 and found evidence that Rockwell broken environmental laws. The company pleaded guilty to 10 violations, including the knowing storage of defective pondcrete blocks, and paid a fine of $18.5 million.

In 1989 Stone filed a qui tam suit under the FCA, alleging that Rockwell presented false and **fraudulent** claims about its environmental records in order to get paid. As required by the FCA, Stone delivered his complaint to the federal government, which detailed 26 environmental and safety issues; the pondcrete blocks constituted just one issue. He alleged that he had foreseen that the piping system would not produce an adequate mixture of sludge and cement. The government initially declined to join the lawsuit but changed its mind in 1996. The government and Stone then amended the complaint, removing the piping system allegation and substituting the allegation that Rockwell had violated regulations by storing leaky blocks. In 1999 a jury awarded the government and Stone of almost $1.4 million. The **district court** tripled the amount of damages, which is allowed under the FCA. The Tenth **Circuit Court** of Appeals upheld the verdict. However, the only false claims found by the jury involved failed processes discovered after Stone had left Rockwell. Stone's prediction of failure based on the piping problem turned out to be wrong

The Supreme Court, in an 6–2 decision (Justice STEPHEN BREYER did not participate in the case), overruled the Tenth Circuit, finding that Stone could not claim 25 percent of the damages under the FCA because he was not the original source of the information used to implicate Rockwell. Justice ANTONIN SCALIA, writing for the majority, was concerned that Stone had changed his approach during the lawsuit, dropping claims that proved weak. Scalia concluded that the Court could not look at his original complaint and Stone had to satisfy the original source requirement through all stages of litigation. To hold otherwise would encourage a plaintiff "to plead a trivial theory of fraud for which he had some direct and independent knowledge and later amend the complaint to include theories copied from the **public domain** or from materials in the Government's possession." Stone could not receive damages because he had merely made a prediction, which turned out incorrect, about the solidity of the pondcrete blocks. He did not have direct and independent knowledge about the lack of solidity in the blocks because he was not employed by Rockwell at the time this was detected. The Court did, however, uphold the verdict and awarded the government the entire damages amount.

The decision makes it more difficult for a whistleblower to litigate a qui tam action under the FCA, as highly specific knowledge will be required to succeed.

FEDERAL COMMUNICATIONS COMMISSION

Global Crossing Telecommunications, Inc. v. Metrophones Telecommunications, Inc.

The FEDERAL COMMUNICATIONS COMMISSION (FCC) regulates long-distance telephone **carriers** through statutes and its own regulations. In 1990 Congress directed the FCC to establish a per call compensation plan to compensate payphone operators when callers use a payphone to obtain access to a carrier's lines by using a calling card with a 1-800 number and an access code. When a carrier failed to pay a payphone operator, the operator sued the carrier for violations of FCC regulations. The Supreme Court, in *Global Crossing Telecommunications, Inc. v. Metrophones Telecommunications, Inc.,* __U.S.__, 127 S.Ct. 1513, __L.Ed.2d __ (2007), rejected the carrier's claims that no such private **right of action** existed for violations of FCC regulations.

Prior to 1990 a payphone operator had great control over the placing of long-distance calls using its phones. The operator could require the caller to use a long-distance carrier favored by the operator while blocking access to the caller's preferred carrier. In 1990 Congress enacted the Telephone Operator Consumers Services Improvement Act, 47 U.S.C.A. §226. The act required payphone operators to allow users "free" access to the carrier of his or her choice. This meant that a long-distance call could be made without the depositing coins. In return, Congress directed the FCC to impose regulations that would pay the payphone operators a fee for each of these "free" calls. The FCC drafted regulations that directed long-distance carriers to reimburse payphone operators $0.24 per call; this amount could be passed on to the long-distance carrier's customers. If a carrier refused to compensate a payphone operator this refusal constituted an "unreasonable practice" under the terms of the Communications Act of 1934, 47 U.S.C.A. §201(b). Such a determination would allow a private party, the payphone operator, to bring a federal lawsuit under §207 of the act to collect the compensation owed.

In 2003, Metrophones Telecommunications, Inc., a payphone operator, filed a **civil action** in federal **district court**, alleging that Global Crossing Telecommunications, Inc., a long-distance carrier, had failed to pay $30,000 in "free calls" reimbursements. Metrophones argued that the failure to pay was an unreasonable practice under §201(b), thereby permitting it to sue under §207. The federal district court agreed and this decision was upheld by the Ninth **Circuit Court** of Appeals.

The Supreme Court, in a 7–2 decision, affirmed the Ninth Circuit ruling. Justice STEPHEN BREYER, writing for the majority, found that the clear purpose of §207 was to allow persons injured by §201(b) violations to bring an action for damages in federal court. The question in this case was whether the FCC regulation lawfully implemented §201(b)'s "unreasonable practice" prohibition. The Court concluded that that FCC's unreasonable practice determination was a reasonable one. Using ordinary English, the refusal to pay FCC-ordered compensation despite having received a benefit from the payphone operator was clearly unreasonable. The payphone operator provided an "integral part of the total long-distance service" and the carrier's refusal to pay, despite the FCC regulation, was a "practice" that was "unreasonable."

Global Crossing had argued that §207 only authorizes actions for **statutory** violations and not for regulations imposed to carry out statutory objectives. Justice Breyer rejected this claim, for the lawsuit sought damages for a statutory violation, "namely, a violation of §201(b)'s prohibition of an "unreasonable practice.""

Justice ANTONIN SCALIA, in a dissenting opinion, claimed that the decision "conflicts with the Communications Act's carefully delineated remedial scheme." He saw a difference between private actions to enforce interpretive regulations, which construe a **statute** by itself, with private actions to enforce substantive regulations. Substantive regulations were promulgated "pursuant to an express delegation of authority to impose freestanding legal obligations beyond those created by the statute itself." In his view substantive regulations could not trigger a §207 lawsuit.

Justice CLARENCE THOMAS, in a separate dissenting opinion, argued that the FCC had contradicted provisions of the Communications Act when it imposed the compensation plan and the consequences for non-payment by long-distance carriers. The law was intended to deal with practices that harm carrier customers, not carrier suppliers.

FEDERAL TORT CLAIMS ACT

A federal statute enacted in 1946 that removed the inherent immunity of the federal government from most tort actions brought against it and established the conditions for the commencement of such suits.

Barrett v. United States

The FEDERAL TORT CLAIMS ACT (FTCA), 28 U.S.C.A. §1346, waives the federal government's **sovereign immunity** in certain circumstances to permit persons to sue it for damages. Though the government voluntary waives its immunity in the FTCA, it places conditions on

when a person may sue. One requirement is that the person must exhaust all administrative remedies with the federal government before filing suit. A failure to exhaust these remedies can lead to the dismissal of the lawsuit. The First **Circuit Court** of Appeals in, *Barrett v. United States*, 462 F.3d 28(1st Cir.2006), reaffirmed this consequence, ruling that a lawsuit filed by a murder victim's wife must be dismissed for failure to exhaust administrative remedies. This defect, coupled with other procedural errors, meant that the lawsuit would not be heard.

The case arose out the Federal Bureau of Investigation's (FBI) mishandling of informants involved in organized crime. Arthur Barrett was kidnapped and murdered in 1983 by James Bulger, Stephen Flemmi, and Kevin Weeks. The FBI protected Bulger and Flemmi from the investigation and prosecution of these crimes because they were confidential informants. A 1999 criminal case discussed the FBI's relationship with the two informants and noted that the FBI had been informed Bulger killed Barrett. Barrett's body was exhumed from a ditch next to a Massachusetts highway in January 2000. His identity was confirmed in March 2000 when Elaine Barrett, Arthur Barrett's widow, told the press that the government was responsible for his death by allowing the informants to continue their criminal ways while serving as informants. Barrett's body was released to her in April 2000. In January 2003 Elaine Barrett filed an administrative tort claim under the FTCA, alleging that her husband's injuries and death were caused by the negligent and wrongful acts of the FBI. On April 3, 2003, before the government ruled on the claim, Barrett filed a lawsuit in federal **district court** seeking damages from the government under the FTCA and damages from eight FBI agents, Bulger, Flemmi, and Weeks. They were sued under a federal civil rights **cause of action** and a Massachusetts **wrongful death statute**. On April 15, 2003 the Department of Justice denied Barrett's FTCA administrative claim as untimely based on the FTCA's two-year **statute of limitations**. In November 2003 the government filed a motion to dismiss the court case and two of the agents filed similar motions over the next two months. The district court dismissed the government from the case in September 2004, ruling that Barrett had missed the two-year statute of limitations under the FTCA. It also dismissed the two agents from the lawsuit because she had missed the three-year statute of limitations for the federal civil rights and wrongful death claims. By April 2005, the court had dismissed Barrett's claims against the remaining agents. Barrett filed an appeal in June 2005 that sought to challenge all the dismissal orders from 2004 and 2005.

The First Circuit Court of Appeals upheld the dismissal of the claims against the government and the agents. Though the appeals court broadly construed its jurisdiction to consider all of the orders (the appeal of the 2004 orders could have been viewed as untimely), it concluded that Barrett had made several procedural errors that doomed her case. As to the FTCA claim, the waiver of government sovereignty was "closely circumscribed by the terms of the statute." The statute stated that a court action could not be instituted until the claimant filed an administrative claim and received a written **disposition** from the federal agency within six months of the filing. If the agency failed to respond within six months this inaction would be treated as a denial of the claim. The government argued that the district court had no jurisdiction to consider Barrett's FTCA claim because she filed the lawsuit 12 days before the Department of Justice issued its formal denial. Barrett countered that though she had filed the lawsuit in early April she had not served the defendants with the complaint until September 2003, well past the issuance of the administrative claim denial. The appeals court rejected Barrett's argument because it was unsupported by any **case law** that indicated a service date rather than a filing date determined whether she had exhausted her administrative remedies.

The appeals court then looked at the timeliness of Barrett's civil rights and wrongful death claims. Both claims were governed by a three-year statute of limitations. The clock started running on Barrett's appeal time when an action "accrued." This meant that an action began to run when Barrett knew or had reason to know of the existence and cause of the injuries committed upon her husband. Either actual knowledge or constructive knowledge of who killed her husband was sufficient to start the clock. The government argued that she missed the deadline by approximately one month. She had filed her complaint on April 2, 2003. Therefore, her lawsuit would be untimely if she had reason to know who killed her husband prior to April 2, 2000. Barrett's statement to the press in early March 2000 proved her downfall. The appeals court found that her statement indicated that she believed the government was responsible for the killing of Arthur Barrett. She appeared to have actual knowledge at that time, thus making her remaining claims untimely.

Though the court acknowledged the FBI's misconduct was a "tragedy" and that the FTCA exhaustion requirement as well as the statute of limitations rules might have defeated a meritorious claim, these requirements served important purposes. The fact that other plaintiffs had followed these requirements demonstrated that they were not intended to frustrate diligent litigants.

FIRST AMENDMENT

Davenport v. Washington Education Association

The U.S. SUPREME COURT in June 2007 ruled that under the FIRST AMENDMENT, a state may properly require its public sector labor unions to receive affirmative authorization from a nonmember before spending the nonmember's fees for election-related purposes. In doing so, the unanimous Court reversed the holding of two Washington state courts that had determined that the **statute** was unconstitutional.

The National Labor Relations Act (NLRA), 29 U.S.C. § 152(2) allows states to regulate their labor relationships with public employees. Many states, including Washington, have enacted states that allow unions and government employers to enter into so-called "agency-shop" agreements. These agreements allow unions to impose fees on the government employees who are not members of the union but who are still represented by a union during the collective bargaining process. The purpose behind these agreements is to prevent employees who are not members of the union to share the benefits of collective bargaining without having to share the costs of this bargaining.

In the past, the Supreme Court has considered objections to these types of agreements. Nonunion employees have argued that the agreements violate the First Amendment because they require these employees to contribute money as a condition of their government employment. In one case, the Court held that public-sector unions could not use fees of nonunion employees for certain ideological purposes unrelated to the union's collective bargaining duties, where the employee objects to such use of the fees. *Abbod v. Detroit Bd. of Educ.*, 431 U.S. 209, 97 S. Ct. 1782, 52 L. Ed. 2d 261 (1977). Another case established procedural requirements that public-sector unions must follow to ensure that an objecting nonmember can prevent the fees from being used for improper purposes. *Teachers v. Hudson*, 475 U.S. 292, 106 S. Ct. 1066, 89 L. Ed. 2d 232 (1986).

About 12 million workers in both the public and the private sector must pay union fees even if these members do not decide to join a union. Opponents of unions have argued that mandating payment of these dues is unconstitutional, and Republicans have supported limitations on the political use of union dues. These funds have traditionally been a major source of funding for Democratic candidates.

Under Washington law, a union may charge nonmembers a fee that is equivalent to the dues paid by union members, and the union can collect this fee from the employer through payroll deductions. The statute also provides that a union "may not use agency shop fees paid by an individual who is not a member of the organization to make contributions or expenditures to influence an election or to operate a political committee, unless affirmatively authorized by the individual." Wash. Rev. Code §42.17.760.

The Washington Education Association (WEA) served as the exclusive **bargaining agent** for about 70,000 state employees in public education in the state of Washington. Pursuant to the requirements of the Supreme Court's decision in *Hudson*, the union sent a packet to all nonmembers twice per year, informing these nonmembers that they had the right to object to certain expenditures. According to the packet, nonmembers had several options that would allow them to object to these expenditures.

Both the State of Washington and nonmembers of the union brought actions against the WEA. Both suits alleged that the WEA had violated the Washington statute because the union had used nonmember dues for election-related purposes without receiving authorization from the nonmembers. Two trial courts ruled against the WEA, holding that the WEA had indeed violated the statute.

An intermediate **appellate court** reversed the trial court's decision, and the plaintiffs appealed to the Washington Supreme Court. The state's high court determined that the U.S. Supreme Court's prior decisions had balanced the constitutional rights of both unions and nonmembers, focusing on language that requires nonmembers to objecting to the expenditures before the union could be barred from spending the fees. According to the Washington Supreme Court, the Washington statute infringed on the union's First Amendment rights because it re-

quired the union to send the packet of information to the nonmembers and to confirm that each nonmember does not object to the use of the fees. The state court decided that these requirements imposed an unconstitutional burden on the union. *State ex rel. Wash. State Public Disclosure Comm'n v. Wash. Ed. Ass'n*, 130 P.3d 352 (Wash. 2006).

A unanimous Supreme Court reversed the Washington Supreme Court. In an opinion by Justice ANTONIN SCALIA, the Court determined that the Washington Supreme Court's interpretation of the previous agency-fee cases "extends them well beyond their proper ambit." According to Scalia, the cases never balanced the rights of unions with the rights of nonmember employees, and the Court has never established a principle that a union has a constitutional entitlement to the nonmember fees. Because the requirements of the Washington statute did not implicate the First Amendment rights of the WEA, the Court determined that the statute was constitutional. *Davenport v. Wash. Educ. Ass'n* Nos. 05-1589, 05-1657, 2007 WL 1703022 (2007).

Leonard v. Robinson

The FIRST AMENDMENT gives citizens the right to voice their views about politics, religion, morality, and other matters without fear of prosecution by the government. However, **freedom of speech** is not unlimited and the courts have ruled that "fighting words," which are intended to inflict injury or incite an immediate **breach of the peace**, are not protected by the First Amendment. These narrow restrictions on freedom of speech demonstrate that most speech is protected, even if it is **libelous** or profane. The

Gary Davenport sits at a desk in his home, January 2007.
AP IMAGES

Seventh **Circuit Court** of Appeals reaffirmed these principles in *Leonard v. Robinson*, 477 F.3d 347 (7th Cir.2006), ruling that a police officer who arrested a man at a township board meeting after he uttered the phrase "God damn" could be sued for violating the man's First Amendment rights.

Sarah Leonard owned a towing company in the township of Montrose, Michigan. Leonard's Auto Works was the exclusive towing company for the township for a number of years but she lost her business with the township after she had a falling out with the township Chief of Police, Charles Abraham. Abraham had sought to extend township police jurisdiction to include the city of Montrose as well as the surrounding township. Leonard's mother was on the city council and opposed this plan. After Leonard refused Abraham's request that she lobby her mother to support the plan, Auto Works lost its business with the township. Leonard sued the township and Abraham for violating her First Amendment rights and secured a settlement with both parties in 2003. As a result, Leonard and her husband Thomas Leonard believed Abraham hated them. In October 2002, before the settlement of the lawsuit, the Leonards attended a township board meeting. Abraham ordered one of his officers, Stephen Robinson, to attend the meeting. Robinson sat at the back of the meeting hall and when asked by another attendee why he was there, lied, saying he just liked to see what was going on. Sarah Leonard addressed the council and complained about the losses her business had suffered since losing the towing contract. Thomas then addressed the council and made several emotionally-charged statements that culminated in him telling a council member that "That's why you're in a God damn lawsuit." After he sat down Officer Robinson directed him to leave the meeting room. Once outside Robinson placed him under arrest, charging him with violations of Michigan state law involving **disorderly conduct** and obscenity. Leonard was released after one hour in detention and one month later the charges were dismissed.

Thomas Leonard filed a federal civil rights lawsuit under 42 U.S.C.A. § 1983 against Robinson, alleging that he violated his First and FOURTH AMENDMENT rights when he arrested him. Robinson filed a motion with the federal **district court**, arguing that he was entitled to qualified immunity. Qualified immunity is a doctrine developed by the U.S. SUPREME COURT that protects police officers when the officers' actions were reasonable and the constitutional right supposedly violated was not clearly established under the law. Robinson contended that the arrest was reasonable under the Fourth Amendment because the laws supporting the charges had not been invalidated by the Michigan Supreme Court. The court agreed with Robinson, concluding that he had **probable cause** to arrest Leonard because he had violated the plain language of those statutes and Robinson was "to enforce laws until and unless they are declared unconstitutional." The district court also denied Leonard's First Amendment retaliation claim because there was no causal connection between Leonard's protected speech and his arrest. The court ignored Leonard's allegations that his wife's lawsuit against Abraham was the motive behind the arrest.

The Seventh Circuit Court of Appeals reversed the district court decision. The appeals court concluded that Robinson was not entitled to qualified immunity because First Amendment law, "established for a generation," precluded a finding of probable cause because the laws cited by Robinson were "either facially invalid, vague, or overbroad when applied to speech (as opposed to conduct) at a democratic assembly where the speaker is not out of order." Though the Michigan state court had not ruled on the constitutionality of the laws used by Robinson to justify the arrest, the federal appeals court pointed to another **statute** that had been ruled unconstitutional by the state supreme court. This law had made it a crime to use indecent or obscene language in the presence of women and children. The state supreme court had called the statute as so vague as to be unenforceable. The appeals court concluded that the statutes invoked by Robinson were also vague and that no reasonable police officer would believe they were constitutional "as applied to Leonard's political speech during a democratic assembly." This meant that Robinson did not have probable cause to arrest Leonard.

As to the First Amendment retaliation claim, the appeals court found that the district court had failed to properly evaluate Robinson's motive for the arrest. Although it was a close case, the court ruled that a reasonable factfinder could conclude that Leonard was arrested in retaliation for constitutionally protected conduct. The turmoil surrounding Sarah Leonard's feud with the police chief, the loss of business, and her lawsuit, all suggested that Robinson's reason for attending the meeting was to settle a score for the police chief. Therefore, Robinson was not entitled to qualified immunity and Leonard was allowed to proceed with his lawsuit.

Morse v. Frederick

In a landmark FIRST AMENDMENT case receiving much media attention, the U.S. SUPREME COURT ruled that a student's free speech rights were not violated when school officials suspended him for displaying a "Bong Hits 4 Jesus" banner. *Morse v. Frederick*, No. 06-278, 551 U.S. ___ (2007). The event which is the subject matter of the case took place in 2002. As of the date of the Supreme Court decision five years later, Joseph Frederick was a senior in college, still waiting for the ultimate **disposition** of his high school free-speech challenge. He lost.

Frederick had had previous run-ins with teachers and officials at Juneau-Douglas High School in Juneau, Alaska. He planned this particular challenge in advance, even creating an Internet page that read in part, "This is the story of a high school senior who refused to bow down in submission before an authority . . ."

On the day of the event, January 24, 2002, Frederick and the entire student body were released from school to attend a school-sponsored event. The Olympic Torch was passing through Juneau, part of a 50-state relay leading to the winter games in Salt Lake City, Utah. As television and media cameras rolled during the ensuing parade, Frederick and a few others jumped in front of the camera and unfurled a large banner, reading "Bong Hits 4 Jesus."

Morse, the high school principal, saw him from across the street. She perceived the message as promoting illegal drug use. Consistent with school policy prohibiting such messages at school events, she crossed the road and directed the students to take down the banner. Frederick refused. The principal confiscated the banner and later suspended him.

Frederick tried twice to administratively appeal his suspension, but both school superintendent and school board upheld the suspension. He then filed suit against Morse and the school board under 42 USC § 1983, which protects persons from state actions that violate constitutional rights.

The **district court** granted **summary judgment** to defendants school board and principal, ruling that they were entitled to *qualified immunity* and that they had not infringed on Frederick's First Amendment rights. However, the Ninth **Circuit Court** of Appeals reversed. It found that, even if Frederick's action occurred

Students demonstrate outside U.S. Supreme Court, March 2007.

AP IMAGES

during a school-authorized event, and even if the banner promoted marijuana use, there nonetheless was a First Amendment violation. Importantly, in coming to this conclusion, the Ninth Circuit relied on *Tinker v. Des Moines Independent Community School District*, 393 U.S. 503, a case which held that a school policy prohibiting the wearing of antiwar armbands by students violated the First Amendment. In that case, the Court ruled that student expression could not be suppressed unless school officials reasonably concluded that it would "materially and substantially disrupt the work and discipline of the school."

The Ninth Circuit reasoned that Morse could not have been concerned about disruption of school or educational activities. Therefore, she could not discipline or punish Frederick's off-site, non-disruptive expressive speech, even though he was a student entrusted to the school's care, the speech took place during a school-sponsored activity, and the speech promoted a social message contrary to that of the school. Finally, finding that Frederick's right was "clearly established by law" (a condition needed to prevail in a claim under 42 USC § 1983), the **appellate court** held that Morse was not entitled to qualified immunity.

Not so, said the Supreme Court in reversing the Ninth Circuit. Chief Justice Roberts wrote the lengthy Court opinion. The Court held that schools have every right to safeguard students entrusted to their care from speech that can reasonably be regarded as promoting illegal drug use. Therefore, neither the confiscation of the banner nor the ensuing punishment of suspension violated Frederick's free speech.

Frederick's argument that this was not "school speech" was also rejected. The event occurred during school hours and was part of a school-sanctioned activity, supervised off-site by teachers and other school officials. Frederick stood across the street from the school and pointed the banner toward the school, making it clearly visible to most students. He could not, therefore, claim that it was not school speech.

The Court also agreed with Morse that the message conveyed on the banner would most likely be interpreted by those reading it as promoting illegal drug use. The record on appeal contained little proffered evidence of other possible meanings. Therefore, a principal may, consistent with the First Amendment, restrict speech that is reasonably perceived to promote illegal drug use.

In another previous case, *Bethel School District v. Fraser*, 478 U.S. 675, the Court upheld the suspension of a student who delivered a graphic and sexually-charged metaphor as part of a high school assembly speech. The lower courts found no "disruption" and therefore no basis for discipline. But in reversing, the Supreme Court held that the school was "within its permissible authority in imposing sanctions . . . in response to . . . offensively lewd and indecent speech."

Now, in the present case, the Court said there were two things that could be gleaned from the above case. First, the constitutional rights of students in public school were not automatically equal to the rights of adults in other settings. Student rights were delineated "in light of the special characteristics of the school environment," (quoting from *Tinker*, above). Second, the "substantial disruption" test is not absolute. Rather, while children do not shed their constitutional rights at the school's gate, the nature of those rights are defined by what is appropriate "for children in school." Thus, the "special characteristics of the school environment," in which students are entrusted to the care of others, allows schools to restrict student expression that they reasonably regard as promoting illegal drug abuse.

Justice Stevens filed a dissenting opinion, joined by Justices Ginsburg and Souter. They agreed that Morse should not be held liable. However, they rejected the school's interest in protecting students from drug-promoting speech as justification for disciplining Frederick "for his attempt to make an ambiguous statement to a television audience simply because it contained an oblique reference to drugs."

Tennessee Secondary School Athletic Assn. v. Brentwood

In *Tennessee Secondary School Association v. Brentwood*, No. 06-427, 551 U.S. ___ (2007), the U.S. SUPREME COURT was asked to determine the extent to which the FIRST AMENDMENT might protect a private school's ability to recruit students, given an anti-recruiting rule imposed by the area's athletic association. The Supreme Court, in a **plurality** opinion, held that the rule, which prohibited high school coaches from recruiting middle school athletes, was constitutional. In so holding, the Court reversed a decision by the Sixth **Circuit Court** of Appeals.

The Tennessee Secondary School Athletic Association (TSSAA) was a voluntary association of member schools, primarily public schools, that adopted rules governing athletic competition between member schools. Brentwood Academy was one of the few private schools that voluntarily became a member of TSSAA. In accepting membership, Brentwood agreed to abide by the association's rules.

TSSAA prohibited member schools from exercising "undue influence" in recruiting middle school students for their athletic programs. In 1997, Brentwood's football coach sent a letter to a group of eighth-grade boys inviting them to attend spring football practice sessions. The letter offered the use of all equipment and further stated that "getting involved as soon as possible would definitely be to your advantage." It was signed, "Your coach."

Although the boys receiving the letter had previously indicated their intent to attend Brentwood, the case came to the Supreme Court with the stipulation that all parties agreed that Brentwood's coach violated TSSAA's rule, and that he knew in advance that his conduct was prohibited. This stipulation was the result of two internal reviews conducted by TSSAA.

Rather, Brentwood staked its claim on two other premises. First, it filed suit against TSSAA under 42 USC §1983, claiming that enforcement of the rule was **state action** that violated its First Amendment rights, applicable to it through the FOURTEENTH AMENDMENT. Second, Brentwood alleged that TSSAA's internal review/adjudication of Brentwood's appeal deprived it of **due process of law**.

The **district court** agreed and granted relief to Brentwood, but the Sixth Circuit Court of Appeals reversed, holding that TSSAA was a private voluntary association, not acting under the **color of law**, i.e., not taking a "state action."

On the case's first trip to the U.S. Supreme Court, that "threshold issue" determination was reversed. Brentwood Academy v. Tennessee Secondary School Association, 531 U.S. 288 (2001).

On remand, the District Court ruled for Brentwood. TSSAA appealed, and this time the Sixth Circuit affirmed, finding that the anti-recruiting rule was a content-based regulation of speech that was not narrowly tailored to serve its permissible uses. Further, it found that TSSAA's appeals procedure impermissibly considered *ex parte* evidence, thereby violating Brentwood's due process rights.

Back before the Supreme Court, the Sixth Circuit was again reversed. Justice Stevens, writing for the Court, held that the rule did not violate the First Amendment. TSSAA's interest in enforcing its rules could warrant curtailing some speech, to which its voluntary members had agreed. While it did not have unbounded authority to curtail all speech as a condition of membership, it could impose those conditions necessary to managing an efficient and effective state-sponsored high school athletic league. Its rule was intended to discourage precisely the type of conduct which brought the case into litigation.

The Court also held that Brentwood's due process rights were not violated. The evidence allegedly considered on an *ex parte* basis (behind closed doors and involving a separate incident not related to the coach's letter), was, at best, harmless **beyond a reasonable doubt**. Brentwood alleged that it would have handled the case differently at the board hearing had it been given an opportunity to object to the evidence or cross-examine witnesses. But Brentwood failed to show that any *ex parte* evidence presented to TSSAA was not already known to it.

Justice Kennedy wrote a separate opinion, concurring in part and concurring with the judgment. He did not agree with the majority's reliance on *Ohralik v. Ohio State Bar Assn*, 436 U.S. 447 (1978), which had to do with an attorney's right to solicit clients. He felt that the present majority's invoking of *Ohralik* would be a "dramatic expansion" of *Ohralik's* holding, now encompassing free-standing state regulation of speech by coaches and other representatives of nonmember schools. He was joined in this concern by the Chief Justice as well as Justices Scalia and Alito.

Justice Thomas also wrote a separate opinion concurring in the judgment. His opinion also took exception to what he believed to be an expansion of the original holding in yet another case cited by the majority, *Pickering v. Board of Ed. of Township H.S. District 205 Will City*, 391 U.S. 563 (1968), determining the speech rights of government employees and contractors.

FITZGERALD, PATRICK

Patrick Fitzgerald.
AP IMAGES

Patrick J. Fitzgerald was a relatively unknown government attorney in late 2003 when he was appointed special counsel in charge of a criminal investigation that, two years later, would implicate senior staffers at the White House. He was charged with uncovering the source of a leak, or disclosure of classified information, involving the identity of a Central Intelligence Agency operative. Fitzgerald, who had served as U.S. Attorney for the Northern District of Illinois since 2001, won praise from both sides of the ideological fence for his handling of the investigation that became known as "Plamegate," after the agent, Valerie Plame.

Born in December of 1960, Fitzgerald grew up in the Flatbush neighborhood of Brooklyn, New York. His parents were Irish immigrants, and his father worked as a doorman for a Manhattan residential building. One of four siblings in the Roman Catholic family, Fitzgerald attended Regis High School in Manhattan, known for its rigorous academic program. At Regis he emerged as a talented member of the debate team before heading on to Amherst College, where he majored in economics and mathematics. He earned tuition money during the summer months by working as a doorman at a building down the street from his father's post, and also by serving as a deckhand on the commuter ferries that plied New York harbor.

Fitzgerald went on to Harvard Law School, and practiced at a firm for three years after earning his degree in 1985. In 1988, he was hired as an assistant U.S. Attorney for the district that includes New York City, and spent the next several years prosecuting drug-trafficking and organized-crime cases. He was involved in the trials related to the Gambino crime family, which resulted in several convictions, including that of notorious mob boss John Gotti. Fitzgerald soon developed a reputation as a brilliant legal strategist who possessed a photographic memory as well as a talent for unearthing obscure laws on the books which inevitably resulted in jury convictions.

One of the prime examples of that latter skill was Fitzgerald's work on the 1993 World

PATRICK J. FITZGERALD

1960: Born in New York, NY

1985: Received law degree from Harvard School of Law

1996: Named National Security Coordinator for the Office of the U.S. Attorney for the Southern District of New York

2001: Named U.S. Attorney for the Northern District of Illinois

2003: Appointed special counsel for White House investigation

Trade Center bombing case. With a blind Egyptian cleric, Sheikh Omar Abdel Rahman, and eleven other defendants in the dock, Fitzgerald applied a rarely used sedition law dating back to the Civil War era to convict them. The prosecutor eventually became somewhat of an expert in Islamic fundamentalist groups, and in 1996 was named National Security Coordinator for the Office of the U.S. Attorney for the Southern District of New York. An early predictor of the dangers posed by Osama bin Laden and the al-Qaeda network, Fitzgerald was designated to serve as chief counsel in prosecutions of those suspected of carrying out bombings on U.S. embassies in Africa in 1998, which again resulted in successful convictions.

Fitzgerald was nominated to become U.S. Attorney for the Northern District of Illinois on September 1, 2001. His appointment was confirmed by the Senate several weeks later, and Fitzgerald moved to Chicago, where he and his team of 160 attorneys launched a major probe of government corruption in the state. Less than five years later, former Illinois governor George Ryan had been prosecuted and faced up to 20 years in prison for bribery and lying to investigators. Fitzgerald's campaign, which netted a bipartisan roster of wrongdoers, also reached into the Chicago mayor's office, and in this case he relied on a mail-fraud statute usually deployed for organized-crime cases in order to prosecute some of the defendants.

Fitzgerald was still technically in charge of the U.S. Attorney's office in the northern half of

Illinois when he was named special counsel for the White House leak investigation in December of 2003, which the U.S. Department of Justice had launched at the request of the Central Intelligence Agency (CIA). The Plamegate story had unfolded over several months, beginning in February of 2002, when Vice President Dick Cheney asked Joseph Wilson, a former U.S. ambassador with a distinguished career, to undertake a secret mission to Niger in order to confirm reports that in the late 1990s Iraqi leader Saddam Hussein had purchased uranium yellowcake from the country. The material is a lightly processed ore that can be refined into making weapons-grade plutonium. Wilson made the trip and found no truth to the report, which he delivered to administration officials. The claims persisted, however, and were repeated by Cheney and President George W. Bush, and became one of the Administration's series of justifications for the invasion of Iraq in March of 2003. Four months later, irate that the yellowcake rumors were still being repeated by the White House, Wilson penned a blistering op-ed piece for the July 6, 2003, edition of the New York Times headlined, "What I Didn't Find in Africa."

Within days, conservative commentator Robert Novak had mentioned the name of Wilson's wife, Valerie Plame, in his widely syndicated column, noting that she worked for the Central Intelligence Agency. But Plame was a covert operative—in other words, under no circumstances was it to be revealed that she worked for the agency, lest the lives of foreign nationals who provide intelligence information to the United States be endangered—and it was a violation of federal law to reveal such identities. Fitzgerald's investigation into who leaked her name to Novak resulted in the indictment of Lewis "Scooter" Libby, chief of staff for U.S. Vice President Dick Cheney, in October of 2005 on multiple counts of giving false statements to investigators, perjury, and obstruction of justice. Libby resigned, and Fitzgerald's team prepared for trial. The leak investigation also threatened to involve Karl Rove, a high-ranking White House official.

Fitzgerald rarely makes statements to the press or gives interviews. Friends and former colleagues divulge that he works long hours, once owned a cat but was rarely home to feed it, and occasionally takes mountain climbing or hang-gliding vacations. Unmarried, Fitzgerald is the subject of speculation that he may one day seek public office, but others note a more likely scenario is a future appointment as head of the Federal Bureau of Investigation.

FOOD AND DRUG ADMINISTRATION

FDA Approves Silicone Breast Implants After 14-Year Ban

The FOOD AND DRUG ADMINISTRATION in November 2006 lifted restrictions on the use of silicone breast implants for cosmetic augmentation. The decision came 14 years after the agency had limited the use of these implants to reconstructive surgery and clinical testing. The reason for the change in the FDA's decision was that the newer types of implants were less prone to tears that could cause the implants to leak, which was a major problem when the agency decided to limit the use of the implants in 1992. The FDA now requires manufacturers to warn consumers that the implants are not lifetime devices, and that the vast majority of women to receive the implants will need to replace or remove them at some point in time.

In November 1991, the FDA held a panel meeting to review information about the safety and effectiveness of breast implants that were filled with silicone gel. After the meeting, the agency asked the industry to cease marketing these types of implants until the FDA could review the information that had been submitted. Within months of this meeting, the FDA denied approval of the marketing of the silicone implants for purposes of augmentation. However, the agency determined that these devices should be available for those who underwent breast reconstruction or replacement of existing silicone implants. Since this time, saline-filled implants have remained on the market.

In 1998, a major manufacturer of silicone implants, Dow Corning of Midland, Michigan, agreed to pay $3.2 billion over a 16-year period to settle the claims of more than 300,000 women who alleged that the silicone implants had harmed them due to leakage and ruptures. Some claimed that these devices were linked with connective tissue disease or cancer. Since the 1990s, several independent studies, including one by the Institute of Medicine, tested these claims. However, these studies have concluded that there is no convincing evidence that the implants were associated with either of these diseases. According to Daniel Schultz, the director for the Center for Devices and Radiological Health of the FDA, "The silicone breast implant is one of the most extensively studied medical devices. We now have a good understanding of what complications of can occur and at what rates."

Between 1998 and 2005, the FDA approved several applications by private companies to study the use of silicone implants. These companies, which include Allergan Corp. (formerly Inamed Corp.) of Irvine, California and Mentor Corp. of Santa Barbara, conducted numerous clinical trials of women who had received the implants. The companies compiled a body of scientific evidence that detailed the benefits and risks of silicone implants. The FDA reviewed these companies' studies, tests completed by independent scientific bodies, and reports from advisory bodies made up of outside experts. The agency also conducted thorough inspections each of the companies' manufacturing facilities to determine whether they comply with FDA standards.

The majority of the women in the studies reported that they were satisfied with the implants. However, the studies also identified some complications that women would need to consider when deciding whether to received these implants. Some of the problems include the following: many of the changes to the women's breasts are irreversible; rupture of a silicone implant is usually silent, which means that neither the woman nor her doctor will know that the implant has ruptured; and the woman will need regular MRI examinations to determine whether a silent rupture has occurred. Moreover, some women in the studies complained of hardening of the area around the implant, change in nipple sensation, and breast pain.

Despite some concerns expressed by health advocates, the FDA on November 17, 2006 approved the marketing of silicone implants. Women of all ages may receive implants for reconstructive purposes. However, only women ages 22 and up can receive implants for augmentation purposes. The FDA has maintained that the decision is in the best interests of woman. "FDA has reviewed an extensive amount of data from clinical trials of women studied up to four years, as well as a wealth of other information to determine the benefits and risks of these products," Schultz said. "The extensive body of scientific evidence provides reasonable assurance of the benefits and risks of these devices. This information is available in the product labeling and will enable women and their physicians to make informed decisions."

The agency attached several conditions to its approval. The companies that market these implants must conduct patient and laboratory studies to determine the failure rates of the devices. These companies must also track each implant in order to notify patients and their doctors of updated product information, as well as other purposes. The FDA stressed that breast implants are not lifetime devices and that a woman receiving an implant will likely need at least one additional surgery during her lifetime. Researchers with the FDA point out that the implants are prone to breakdown within the body.

Commentators expect the reintroduction of silicone implants to increase the number of women who seek breast augmentation. In 2005, plastic surgeons reportedly performed 291,000 augmentations, representing a 37 percent increase from 2000. An additional 58,000 women had breast reconstructions last year. The typical cost for an augmentation procedure is about $8,000.

Critics of the FDA's decision point out that women must not only pay the cost for the initial implant, but must also pay tens of thousands more for the regular MRI screenings as well as the replacement surgeries that will be necessary once the implants have reached their life spans. Moreover, the fact that the FDA has mandated further studies proves that the FDA is aware of the dangers associated with the implants, according to these critics.

FORUM NON CONVENIENS

A doctrine whereby a court that has jurisdiction may decline to exercise it when the parties and the interest of justice would benefitif the action were heard in another court that also has jurisdiction over the matter.

Sinochem International v. Malaysia International Shipping

In *Sinochem International Co. v. Malaysia International Shipping*, No. 06-102, 549 U.S. ___ (2007), the U.S. SUPREME COURT addressed the issue of whether a court must first establish its own jurisdiction before dismissing a suit on the grounds of forum non conveniens. The doctrine of forum non conveniens is employed by courts when determining whether a court chosen by plaintiff(s) is convenient for witnesses and defendant(s) as the most suitable **arbiter** of the merits of the case. In this case, the Supreme Court ruled that a **district court** has immediate discretion to respond to a defendant's forum non conveniens plea, without first taking up any other threshold objection. Specifically, a court

need not first establish its jurisdiction over the matter or parties if it determines, in any event, that a foreign **tribunal** is the more suitable arbiter of the case. Justice Ruth Bader Ginsberg wrote the opinion for an unanimous Court.

The underlying facts of the case involved two foreign corporations. In 2003, Chinese chemical company Sinochem had contracted with Pennsylvania-based Triorient International (not a party to the dispute) for the purchase and shipment of steel coils. A specific term in the contract gave Sinochem the right to stop payment and/or renegotiate the contract if shipment were not made by April 30, 2003. Triorient then subcontracted/subchartered a shipping vessel from Malaysian International Shipping Company (MISC), a Malaysian shipping company, to transport the coils.

The **bill of lading** (issued by a transportation carrier to the shipper) indicated that the coils had been loaded by the specified date. However, the vessel did not set sail from the Port of Philadelphia for another two days (May 2, 2003).

On June 8, 2003, Sinochem filed for preservation of a claim against MISC in a Chinese admiralty court, alleging **fraudulent backdating** of the bill of lading for the shipment, which cost Sinochem its ability to stop payment and/or renegotiate the contract. The Chinese court rejected MISC's jurisdictional objections and ordered the ship to be arrested upon arrival. Its decision was upheld on appeal. Sinochem then filed full suit against MISC in that court.

Shortly after the order for arrest, MISC filed its own suit in a federal district court in Pennsylvania. Sinochem filed a motion in the Pennsylvania court for dismissal of the case for lack of subject matter and **personal jurisdiction** of the court, and for forum non conveniens.

The district court found that it had **subject matter jurisdiction** but not personal jurisdiction over Sinochem unless such became evident with further discovery. However, it did not order further discovery or argument because it concluded that dismissal was appropriate, in any event, based on forum non conveniens. This was because sources of proof and key witnesses were based in China. Besides, reasoned the court, witnesses located in the United States would have had to travel to China anyway, because of the ongoing case in the Chinese admiralty court. (The court acknowledged that its decision was inconsistent with the interests of judicial economy because it would likely be appealed and would be a case of **first impression** before the U.S. **Circuit Court** of Appeals for the Third Circuit.)

Indeed, MISC filed its appeal with the U.S. Circuit Court of Appeals for the Third Circuit. A divided Third Circuit panel ruled, in February 2006, that the district court should have first determined whether it had personal jurisdiction before ruling on the forum non conveniens motion. Because of disagreement among circuit courts of appeal regarding this issue, the U.S. Supreme Court accepted review.

Justice Ginsberg, writing for the Court, noted, "This is a textbook case for immediate *forum non conveniens* dismissal." The Court stated that while a federal court generally may not rule on the merits of a case without first determining that it has jurisdiction over the subject matter and parties, there is no mandatory sequencing of *non-merit* issues. A court has leeway "to choose among threshold grounds for denying audience to a case on the merits," (quoting from one of the Court's previous decisions in *Ruhrgas AG v. Marathon Oil Co*, 526 U.S. 574.

The Court went on to note that *forum non conveniens* is a non-merits ground for dismissal. For the district court to have ordered discovery concerning personal jurisdiction over Sinochem would have cost that company expense and delay to no good purpose, since the district court inevitably would dismiss the case without reaching the merits, based on its well-considered *forum non conveniens* appraisal. Further, even looking at the basis for MISC's complaint—i.e. that Sinochem had misrepresented facts to the Chinese admiralty court in order to secure arrest of the vessel—these issues were best addressed on the merits by the Chinese court. In conclusion, the Supreme Court reversed and remanded, finding that the district court had taken the less burdensome but proper course in dismissing the case based on *forum non conveniens*.

FOURTH AMENDMENT

Unlawful Shooting of Pet Dog Constitutes Fourth Amendment Seizure

In *Andrews v. City of West Branch (IA)*, No. 05-1188, 454 F.3d 914 (2006), the U.S. Court of Appeals for the Eighth Circuit held that a policeman's shooting of a dog in an enclosed fence on the owner's property constituted an unreasonable seizure under the FOURTH AMENDMENT to the U.S. Constitution. The policeman

mistakenly assumed that the dog was the one he had been chasing after the district received a complaint about a dog at large. Because the policeman failed to exhaust other means of capturing the dog prior to shooting it (e.g., leash, tranquilizing dart gun, etc.), he was not entitled to **summary judgment** based on qualified immunity, and the case would go to a jury for verdict on that issue, among others.

At approximately 8:00 a.m. one morning in 2002, West Branch Police Chief Dan Knight received a resident complaint (forwarded to him by the city administrator) regarding a large black dog running at large through a neighborhood. Knight responded by driving around in his squad car and spotted the dog several times, but would then lose sight of it again. Finally, he parked the car in the Andrew's driveway because he had seen a large black dog in their backyard. Although he had a dog leash in his pocket, he walked toward the enclosed fence and shot the dog twice. The dog was urinating at the time it was shot.

Knight realized immediately that he mistakenly shot the wrong dog. The dog's owner was standing just a few feet away from the dog, on her back patio, when it was shot. She had just let the dog, a family pet named Riker, out for his morning bathroom break in the family's enclosed, fenced-in backyard. Because the dog had been badly injured by the first two shots, Knight decided to shoot Riker a third time to end his suffering.

The U.S. **District Court** for the Northern District of Iowa granted summary judgment to Knight and the City of West Branch, based on immunity. The Andrews had filed their suit under 42 USC §1983, under which a plaintiff must establish a constitutional violation committed "under color of state law." The Andrews based their suit on three claims: constitutional **substantive due process**, illegal seizure under the Fourth Amendment, and **vicarious liability** of the City of West Branch for Knight's conduct. On appeal, the Eighth Circuit affirmed the district court's dismissal of the substantive due process and vicarious liability claims.

However, the **appellate court** reversed the district court's dismissal of the Fourth Amendment claim. In analyzing that claim (in a light most favorable to the Andrews, the appealing party), the court first considered whether Knight even had any authority, by **statute** or local regulation, to shoot Riker. It cited Iowa Code §351.26, which declared, in relevant part, that no animal shall be deemed "at large" if it was "tethered or on the enclosed premises of the owner (which Riker was). Second, the Code of Ordinances for West Branch, Chapter 55.11 stated, in relevant part, that officers should utilize all available methods to obtain the capture of animals running at large. Specifically, "[t]he discharging of a firearm at an animal should be considered as a last resort . . ."

It was clear from facts on record that before shooting Riker, Chief Knight had neither given warning nor made any effort to inquire if Riker had been running at large prior to the shooting, or whether the Andrdews' yard was completely enclosed (which it was). Although Riker was not wearing his collar and "tags" at the time, Knight made no effort to attempt to leash him or subdue him (e.g., using a tranquilizer).

Because a jury could reasonably conclude that Riker posed no greater threat to public safety than a stray dog running at large, and because a jury could reasonable conclude that Knight's shooting of the dog was, at a minimum, premature. Further, Knight's decision to shoot Riker did not comport with requirements under the relevant local Code or ordinances.

Having so determined, the court next considered the Andrews' constitutional claim. The Fourth Amendment protects against unreasonable searches and seizures. Previous **case law** has already established that a dog is considered personal property for Fourth Amendment purposes. For purposes of analyzing violations, a "seizure" occurs when there is some meaningful interference with a person's possessory interest in that property. The question before the court was whether the "seizure" of Riker was reasonable under the circumstances.

"Reasonableness" must be judged from the standpoint and perspective of the actor, in this case, Knight. The court concluded that, in enacting the Code and local ordinances, the state of Iowa and the City of West Branch outlined "reasonable" action when confronted with stray dogs. Even if Knight mistakenly assumed that Riker was the stray dog complained of, he was not permitted, by **ordinance** or statute, to destroy it when it posed no immediate danger and the owner was present. Riker was not growling, acting fierce, harassing anyone, or even on the loose. He was urinating a few feet from his owner. Accordingly, a reasonable jury could conclude that Knight acted unreasonably when he seized and killed Riker.

Finally, qualified immunity is available to an officer only when he can show that a reasonable officer with the same information as that which he possessed at the time of the shooting, could have believed that his conduct was lawful under clearly established law. A right is clearly established if a reasonable officer would understand that what he was doing violated that right. If the facts asserted by the Andrews were true, Knight could not have concluded that his actions to destroy a pet that posed no immediate threat or danger, and whose owners were known and available, were reasonable. Therefore, Knight knew at the time he shot Riker that he was violating the Andrews' clearly established right to be free from unreasonable seizures of property.

Sanchez v. County of San Diego

The Fourth Amendment's prohibition against unreasonable searches and seizures deals with an essential element of **criminal procedure**. However, questions have been raised about government programs that require individuals to consent to warrantless searches of their homes to obtain government benefits. In *Sanchez v. County of San Diego*, 464 F.3d 916 (9th. Cir. 2006), the Ninth **Circuit Court** of Appeals ruled that requiring welfare applicants to consent to warrantless home visits by an investigator for the district attorney's office in order to qualify for welfare benefits did not amount to searches covered by the FOURTH AMENDMENT.

In 1997 the San Diego County Attorney (DA) established the Project 100% program for county residents who applied for welfare. Under the program all applicants receive a home visit from an investigator in the DA's Public Assistance **Fraud** Division. The home visit has two parts: an interview with the applicant concerning the information submitted during the intake process and a "walk through" of the home. The visit takes from 15 minutes to an hour, with the walk through taking only 5 to 10 minutes. When applicants submit their applications for welfare benefits they are told about the mandatory home visit and the fact that the visit must take place before benefits are awarded. Applicants are not given notice of the exact date and time of the visit but they usually occur within 10 days of receipt of the application. If the applicant refuses to allow a home visit or stops it before the investigator has finished the inspection, the investigator will report the applicant failed to cooperate. Welfare benefits are then denied but there are no criminal sanctions imposed for refusing to consent to the visit. If the visit goes forward the investigator has the applicant lead the walk through and open closets and cabinets.

The investigator is trained to look for items in plain view. An investigator is required to report any evidence of potential criminal wrongdoing but San Diego claimed that there was no evidence that any prosecutions for welfare fraud stemmed from evidence uncovered during the home visits.

Rocio Sanchez and other San Diego County welfare recipients filed a federal civil rights **class action** lawsuit against the county, alleging that the mandatory home visits were warrantless searches that violated the Fourth Amendment. The federal **district court** dismissed the lawsuit, ruling that the walk through visits did not violate the Constitution.

A panel of the Ninth Circuit Court of Appeals, in a 2–1 decision, upheld the lower court. Judge A. Wallace Tashima, writing for the majority, noted that the threshold question in the case was whether the home visits qualified as searches within the meaning of the Fourth Amendment. The plaintiffs argued that the visits were highly intrusive and that they were meant to discover evidence of welfare fraud. Judge Tashima concluded that a U.S. SUPREME COURT case. *Wyman v. James*, 400 U.S. 309, 91 S.Ct. 381, 27 L.Ed.2d 408 (1971), settled the matter. The Court in *Wyman* held that home visits by social workers as part of New York's welfare program were not searches because the visits were made to verify welfare eligibility and not to investigate for crimes. As with the San Diego program the visits were not compelled and the beneficiary's denial of permission was not a criminal act. Moreover, the visits were not searches because if the beneficiary withheld consent the social worker could not enter the home and search it. Though the Supreme Court agreed that the nature of the visit was "both rehabilitative and investigative," the visits were not conducted as part of a criminal investigation. Therefore, the visits did not rise to the level of a "search in the traditional **criminal law** context." Judge Tashima found that *Wyman* directly controlled the San Diego case.

The appeals court also held that even if the home visits did rise to the level of searches, they were reasonable searches. The home visits served an important government interest in verifying the eligibility of a welfare applicant and preventing fraud. The visits were also reasonable because applicants are notified about the mandatory home visit and are given the opportunity to withhold consent to the visit. It also made no administrative sense to require the county to obtain a warrant to make the home

visits. Judge Tashima believed a warrant requirement "would make home visits more intrusive than the County's current suspicionless home visit program because welfare applicants' rights and privacy would be subject to greater infringement." The appeals court rejected for similar reasons the plaintiffs' claims under the California constitution's **search and seizure** provision.

Judge Raymond Fisher dissented, arguing that *Wyman* did not directly control the case because it dealt home visits that were "primarily rehabilitative." This was a much different situation than the San Diego County home visits. The law enforcement agent who conducted the visit was trained not to give advice but to search for physical evidence of ineligibility "that could lead to criminal prosecution either for welfare fraud or other crimes unrelated to the welfare application." Therefore, the home visits did rise to a search covered by the Fourth Amendment. Judge Fisher concluded that the searches were unreasonable and violated a persons' right to privacy.

FRAUD

A false representation of a matter of fact—whether by words or by conduct, by false or misleading allegations, or by concealment of what should have been disclosed—that deceives and is intended to deceive another so that the individual will act upon it to her or his legal injury.

Legal Woes of Former CEO of Westar Energy Continue

David Wittig, the former chief executive officer of Westar Energy in Topeka, Kansas, was sentenced to 24 months in prison in February 2007 on charges of bank **fraud**, **money laundering**, and conspiracy. It was the third time that Wittig had been sentenced, after panels of the 10th **Circuit Court** of Appeals reversed two previous sentences due to errors that the trial judge had made in computing his sentence. In January, Wittig successfully appealed his conviction of other fraud charges also stemming from his role with Westar and awaits retrial on those charges.

Wittig worked at a Wall Street investment bank before taking over as CEO and chairman of the board of Westar Energy, the largest public utility in the state of Kansas. He was also a borrower from Capital Bank in Topeka. At that time, Clinton Odell Weidner II was the presi-

Former Westar Energy chief executive David Wettig leaves court after guilty verdict in his fraud tiral, September 2005.

AP IMAGES

dent of Capital Bank and also served as Wittig's loan officer. According to court records, Wittig had a net worth of more than $33 million. He had borrowed several million from the bank to purchase and to renovate his home in Topeka.

In April 2001, a bank customer brought to Weidner's attention a real estate project in Scottsdale, Arizona, which would require an investment of $1.5 million. Weidner asked Wittig if the latter would like to enter into the transaction, but Wittig declined. However, Wittig said that he would loan Weidner the $1.5 million if Weidner would increase Wittig's **line of credit** at Capital City by the same amount. Weidner increased Wittig's line of credit, and then on April 30, 2001 transferred $1.5 million from Wittig's account to make the down payment for the real estate development project. Weidner later provided Wittig with a **promissory note** for the $1.5 million.

Both Weidner and Wittig attempted to conceal the fact that the extension of Wittig's credit was used to make Weidner's down payment on the Arizona property. The men did not disclose the loan in various documents that were filed with the bank. Bank officers finally discovered the loan in late 2001. At that time, Weidner asked a friend to forward funds to Weidner's partner in Arizona, who in turn transferred funds to Wittig's bank account. Wittig subsequently paid down his line of credit at Capital Bank by $1.6 million. The bank finally discovered the true nature of the loan on March 16, 2002, at which time the bank placed Weidner on

administrative leave. The bank asked Wittig to increase the **collateral** for his line of credit, which he did. He paid off the line of credit three months later.

A federal **grand jury** with the U.S. **District Court** in Topeka indicted Wittig and Weidner on November 7, 2002. The men faced a total of six counts, including four counts of making a false bank entry, one count of conspiracy to submit false entries to a federally insured bank and to launder money, and one count of money laundering. Wittig announced his resignation from Westar on November 22, 2002.

After Wittig's resignation, some of his other illicit activities more directly related to Westar came to light. He and former chief strategy officer Douglas Lake were accused of engineering extravagant salaries and benefits for themselves while hiding their actions from Westar's board of directors and federal regulators. Prosecutors charged Wittig with 39 counts on charges that included conspiracy, wire fraud, and money laundering. Lake was charged with 30 similar counts.

Wittig has faced a somewhat confusing series of trials and appeals between 2003 and 2007. In 2003, a federal court convicted Wittig on all six counts related to the transactions with Weidner. The trial court applied the Federal Sentencing Guidelines and determined that his sentencing range was between 51 and 63 months. The court sentenced him to 51 months' imprisonment followed by three years of unsupervised release. The court also ordered Wittig to pay a $1 million fine.

In February 2006, the 10th Circuit Court of Appeals affirmed the conviction, but vacated and remanded the sentence because the **appellate court** determined that the trial court had miscalculated Wittig's sentence. *United States v. Weidner*, 437 F.3d 1023 (10th Cir. 2006). On remand, U.S. District Judge Julie Robinson sentenced Wittig to 60 months. The 10th Circuit in November 2006 vacated this sentence on grounds similar to the February opinion. *United States v. Wittig*, No. 06-3166, 2006 WL 3378451 (10th Cir. Nov. 22, 2006). After the second remand, Robinson in February 2007 reduced the sentence to 24 months. *United States v. Wittig*, 474 F. Supp. 2d 1215 (D. Kan. 2007).

Wittig and Lake were convicted in September 2005 on charges stemming from the allegations that the men stole millions from Westar. They were sentenced to 18 years and 15 years, respectively, for their involvement in the scheme.

However, the 10th Circuit in January 2007 reversed the convictions. The **appellate** court ruled that prosecutors had failed to prove that Wittig and Lake were required to disclose certain activities on forms filed with the SECURITIES AND EXCHANGE COMMISSION, and thus the court determined that the men had not supplied false or **fraudulent** information in those reports. Moreover, the court determined that the prosecution had not proven that the Wittig and Lake had engaged in unlawful wire fraud, which precluded convictions for money laundering. The court remanded the case for a retrial. *United States v. Lake*, 472 F.3d 1247 (10th Cir. 2007).

Wittig was imprisoned from January 2006 until February 2007 because he violated the terms of his release from prison. After his conviction for corporate fraud, the trial court allowed Wittig to remain free until his attorneys exhausted the appeals process, provided that he did nothing to hide the value of his assets. Prosecutors persuaded Judge Robinson that Wittig had manipulated bank accounts and sold stocks since the time of his conviction in order to transfer wealth to his wife. Robinson ordered Wittig to return to detention. Wittig was released on bond on February 12.

FREEDOM OF INFORMATION ACT

A federal law (5 U.S.C.A. §552 et seq.) providing for the disclosure of information held by administrative agencies to the public, unless the documents requested fall into one of the specific exemptions set forth in the statute.

Davis v. Department of Justice

Although the FREEDOM OF INFORMATION ACT (FOIA) gives citizens a way to obtain federal government information and documents, the government may deny access for various **statutory** reasons. However, efforts to use the FOIA may also be frustrated by internal agency policies that make finding the information virtually impossible. An information seeker may sue the agency for release of the data but litigation can be lengthy and costly. Such was the case in *Davis v. Department of Justice*, 460 F.3d 92 (D.C. Cir.2006), where an author sought the release of undercover audiotapes made by the FEDERAL BUREAU OF INVESTIGATION (FBI) for 20 years. The case went between the federal **district court** and the **Circuit Court** of Appeals for the DISTRICT OF COLUMBIA four times. The appeals court ruled that the FBI must abandon several search methods that virtually guaranteed

the information would never be found, even though it was apparent the FBI could locate the identities of two individuals very easily.

John Davis, an author, submitted an FOIA request in 1986, asking for all audiotapes recorded during an FBI criminal investigation called "BRILAB." The investigation was conducted during 1979 and 1980 in Louisiana, with the FBI examining bribery and racketeering activities among organized crime figures, labor unions, and politicians. Five individuals were indicted and two men were convicted, including reputed Mafia boss Carlos Marcello. Prosecutors played portions of 130 BRILAB tape recordings during the defendants' 1981 trial. Davis filed his FOIA request for a book he was writing on Marcello. The book, *Mafia Kingfish: Carlos Marcello and the Assassination of John F. Kennedy*, was published in 1989 but Davis did not give up his fight to obtain the audiotapes. After the FBI refused to release the tapes, Davis filed a lawsuit under the FOIA demanding their release. The government contended that the recordings were confidential under several FOIA exemptions but the federal district court rejected this argument, concluding that the tapes, once played in court, were in the **public domain** and could not be withheld. The FBI asserted that it could not determine which parts of the tapes were played at trial but the court ruled that the government bore the burden of showing the tapes had not entered the public domain. The Circuit Court of Appeals for the District of Columbia reversed this decision in 1992, finding that Davis carried the burden of showing which tapes were in the public domain. The case was remanded to the district court to give Davis the opportunity to show the tapes were played at trial.

Davis produced trial records that led the FBI to release 157 of the 163 tapes. The FBI stated that it had lost several of the remaining tapes and that the five remaining tapes were not disclosable under an FOIA exemption that prevented release where it could be reasonably expected to constitute an unwarranted invasion of personal privacy. The district court agreed with the FBI on this issue but the appeals court returned the case to the district court to determine if portions of the tapes could be released without impinging upon anyone's privacy. The FBI conducted further review and released one of the five tapes because the bureau determined the principal speaker on the tape had died and therefore that person's privacy interest was extinguished. The bureau stated that the other four tapes could not be released because it could not determine whether the speakers were alive or dead. The FBI stated in an affidavit it had made "adequate efforts" to determine if the speakers on the tapes were not dead. Davis appealed again and the appeals court again sent the case back to the district court, asking that the FBI specify what methods it used to determine whether a person was alive or dead.

The FBI filed two affidavits that revealed the bureau's research methods into determining whether a "prominent individual" and the "undercover informant" were living or dead. These methods included examining a book on famous individuals called *Who Was Who*, and reviewing the audiotapes in question to learn if the individuals disclosed their birth dates or social security numbers. If a birth record was present the FBI would only conclude a person was deceased if the individual would be over 100 years of age. The district court concluded that these methods were adequate and dismissed the FOIA request.

Davis appealed a fourth time and the appeals court found these research methods unsatisfactory. The circuit court concluded that these procedures could not reasonably be expected to answer whether an individual was dead. The court noted that the FBI had access to databases that could easily answer the question yet the bureau held fast to limiting its review to the contents of the audiotapes. The court believed there were BRILAB investigative reports that would have disclosed the names of persons under investigation and identifying information about them. The use of *Who Was Who* made no sense in the Internet age. The court pointedly asked "Why, in short, doesn't the FBI just Google the two names?" Internet search engines provided links to hundreds of websites that collect obituaries. Though the court did not order the FBI to use these search methods, it questioned whether the bureau's methods were reasonable. Therefore, the appeals court returned the case yet again to the district court. The FBI was directed to "evaluate alternative methods" for determining whether the speakers on the tapes were dead. The district court then was ordered to determine if FBI's "chosen course is reasonable."

FREEDOM OF THE PRESS

The right, guaranteed by the First Amendment to the U.S. Constitution, to gather, publish, and distribute information and ideas without government restriction; this right encompasses freedom from prior restraints on publication and freedom from censorship.

The New York Times Company v. Gonzales

Though journalists believe they have the FIRST AMENDMENT right to protect their confidential sources, the courts have made clear that in certain circumstances reporters must surrender this information. The courts are particularly reluctant to deny prosecutors access to press records when serious crimes are under investigation. This reluctance was expressed again in *The New York Times Company v. Gonzales*, 459 F.3d 160 (2nd Cir. 2006), where the Second **Circuit Court** of Appeals ruled that reporters' telephone records that are in the hands of telephone providers could be subpoenaed by a federal prosecutor. The court held that the First Amendment's guarantee of **freedom of the press** did not protect these records because the reporters may have obstructed justice.

Chicago U.S. Attorney Patrick Fitzgerald empanelled a **grand jury** to investigate how two *New York Times* reporters obtained information about the government's plan to freeze the assets and search the offices of Holy Land Foundation (HLF) and Global Relief Foundation (GRF) on December 4 and 14, 2001, respectively. Fitzgerald also wanted to know why the reporters, Judith Miller and Philip Shenon, disclosed this information to the two foundations by seeking comment from them ahead of the search. The government suspected the foundations of terrorist activities in the wake of the September 11, 2001 attacks on the World Trade Center and the Pentagon. Because of the reporters' disclosures the government alleged that its investigation was compromised. In addition, Fitzgerald noted that no government agent was authorized to disclose this information prior to the execution of the searches. Such an unauthorized disclosure can subject a government agent to prosecution for obstruction of justice.

Judith Miller published a story on October 1, 2001 that stated the government was considering adding GRF to a list of organizations with suspected ties to terrorism. Miller later acknowledged that she received this information from confidential sources. On December 3, 2001 Miller called an HLF representative for comment on the government's intent to freeze HLF's assets. The next day the government searched the HLF offices. The government alleged that Miller's call put HLF on notice that a search was imminent and that HLF took actions to reduce the effectiveness of the search.

Philip Shenon contacted GRF on December 13, 2001 seeking comment on the government's apparent intent to freeze its assets. The next day government agents searched the GRF offices. Fitzgerald later stated the GRF acted with alarm to Shenon's tip and took certain actions before the search. When agents entered the offices to begin the search it was apparent that GRF employees were expecting them and had sufficient time to remove items.

Fitzgerald then began his investigation into who leaked the information to the reporters. In August 2002 he wrote *New York Times*, requesting a voluntary interview with Shenon and voluntary production of Shenon's telephone records for one week in late September and one week in December. In his letter Fitzgerald told the newspaper that the leaks may have compromised national security and hurt the government's attempts to investigate terrorist organizations. The newspaper refused the requests. Fitzgerald renewed his requests in July 2004 and enlarged it, asking for Miller's phone records from the pertinent times in 2001. The *Times* again refused and eventually filed a suit in New York federal **district court** in September 24, asking for a **declaratory judgment** that the reporters' telephone records could not be subpoenaed by Fitzgerald because of the First Amendment. The district court ruled in favor of the *Times*. The government then appealed to the Second Circuit Court of Appeals.

The three-judge panel ruled 2–1 in favor of the government's right to subpoena the telephone records. Judge Ralph Winter, writing for the majority, agreed with the newspaper that under Second Circuit precedent the government does not have an absolute right to subpoena third-party providers of phone records. If the **third party** plays an "integral role" in reporters' work and the reporters are granted the privilege of not disclosing confidential sources, then the third party's information is privileged. Therefore the key issue was whether Miller and Shenon could successfully assert such a privilege. Judge Winter concluded that the reporters did not have a **common law** or First Amendment privilege to withhold information. The government had a "compelling interest in maintaining the secrecy of imminent asset freezes or searches lest the targets be informed and spirit away those assets or incriminating evidence." Apart from the importance of maintaining secrecy was "a set of facts—informing the targets of those impending actions—that may constitute a serious obstruction of justice." A grand jury would not be able to pursue the investigation further without the reporters' evidence. Freedom of the press was in no danger because the leaking of imminent law enforcement searches and freezes and informing the targets of these actions "is not an actively essential, or even common, to journalism." In addition, the grand jury was not seeking the testimony of the two reporters.

FREEDOM OF SPEECH

The right, guaranteed by the First Amendment to the U.S. Constitution, to express beliefs and ideas without unwarranted government restriction.

Video Game Industry Defeats Bans on Sales of Video Games

A number of state legislatures in the recent past have attempted to combat what is perceived as a problem with violence in video games. These states have enacted statutes that ban the sale of certain games, especially those that depict sexual or violent acts, to minors. The video game industry, acting through trade associations, have challenged these statutes by arguing that they violate the FIRST AMENDMENT the United States Constitution. In 2006 and 2007, the video game industry was successful in challenging several of these statutes in various **federal courts**.

Michigan Governor Jennifer Granholm signed a bill in September 2005 that regulated the distribution of sexually explicit and "ultra-violent" explicit video games to individuals under the age of 17. The **statute** defined an "ultra-violent explicit video game as one that "continually and repetitively depicts extreme and loathsome violence." The act in turn defines "extreme and loathsome violence" as "real or simulated graphic depictions of physical injuries or physical violence against parties who realistically appear to be human beings, including actions causing death, inflicting cruelty, dismemberment, decapitation, maiming, disfigurement, or other mutilation of body parts, murder, criminal sexual conduct, or torture."

The Michigan legislature stated several concerns about the nature of these video games as the reason for enacting the statute. The concerns were that children who play ultra-violent video games are more likely to exhibit aggressive and violent behavior, that there are causal connections between media violence and aggressive behavior in children, and that minors in that

Michigan Governor Jennifer Granholm signs legislation making rental of adult-rated video games illegal to those under 17 years of age.

AP IMAGES

state were capable of purchasing ultra-violent games. The legislature's goals included: "(1) safeguarding both the physical and psychological well being of minors, (2) preventing violent, aggressive, and asocial behavior from manifesting itself in minors, and (3) directly and substantially alleviating the real-life harms perpetrated by minors who play ultra-violent explicit video games."

The Entertainment Software Association (ESA), along with the Video Software Dealers Association and the Michigan Retailers Association, brought suit to challenge the statute, arguing that it violated protections of free speech, **equal protection**, and due process. On November 9, 2005, the U.S. **District Court** for the Eastern District of Michigan issued a **preliminary injunction** that barred enforcement of the statute. Four months later, the court issued a permanent injunction, ruling that the statute could not pass muster under the First Amendment. *Entertainment Software Ass'n v. Granholm*, 426 F. Supp. 2d 646 (E.D. Mich. 2006). According to the court, the state could not prove that it had substantial evidence that linked ultra-violent video games with violent behavior in children. The state also could not prove that the statute materially advance the state's goal of reducing aggressive behavior in children. Moreover, the court determined that the statute was unconstitutionally vague.

The Minnesota legislature enacted a statute in 2006 that incorporated the video game industry's voluntary rating system as part of the statute. The video game industry has established the Entertainment Software Rating Board (ESRB), to which video games are submitted voluntarily

for review. Ratings are made based on reviews by three trained individuals. A game that is reviewed receives one of six classifications, including EC (Early Childhood), E (Everyone), E + 10 (Everyone 10 and Older), T (Teen), M (Mature), and AO (Adults Only). Under the Minnesota statute, a person under the age of 17 could not rent or purchase a video game rated AO or M.

The ESA and the Entertainment Merchants Association (EMA) challenged the statute on First Amendment and due process grounds. The U.S. District Court for the District of Minnesota agreed with the plaintiffs. According to the court, the statute violated the First Amendment because it regulated the distribution of video games based on content, and the state could not meet the requisite standard for imposing such a regulation. The court also ruled that the state's incorporation of the ESRB standard violated due process. Accordingly, the court enjoined enforcement of the statute. *Entertainment Software Ass'n v. Hatch*, 443 F. Supp. 2d 1065 (D. Minn. 2006).

The state of Louisiana in 2006 passed a statute that prohibited and criminalized the sale, lease, or rental of video or computer games that "appeal to a minor's morbid interest in violence." The ESA and EMA challenged the statute on First Amendment grounds, and the U.S. District Court for the Middle District of Louisiana enjoined the enforcement of the statute. In its decision, the court noted that the evidence presented by the legislature in support of its bill was "sparse and could hardly be called in any sense reliable." The judge also noted that studies cited by the state, which included those attempting to link violence in video games with aggressive behavior in children, had "been considered by numerous courts and in each case the connection was found to be tenuous and speculative." The district court granted a preliminary injunction on August 24, 2006, *Entertainment Software Ass'n v. Foti*, 451 F. Supp. 823 (M.D. La. 2006), and then issued a permanent injunction in November.

The Oklahoma legislature enacted a bill in 2006 that prohibited the sale of an interactive video game or software that displayed "inappropriate violence." The ESA and EMA challenged the statute in the U.S. District Court for the Western District of Oklahoma, and the court issued a preliminary injunction on October 11, 2006. *Entertainment Merchants Ass'n v. Henry*, No. CIV-06-675-C, 2006 WL 2927884 (W.D. Okla. Oct. 11, 2006).

In 2005, the Illinois legislature enacted two statutes related to video games, including the Violent Video Game Law (VVGL) and the Sexually Explicit Video Game Law (SEVGL). The SEVGL defined "sexually explicit" video games as "those that the average person, applying contemporary community standards, would find, with respect to minors, is designed to appeal or **pander** to the prurient interest and depict or represent in a manner patently offensive with respect to minors, an actual or simulated sexual act or sexual contact, an actual or simulated normal or perverted sexual act or a lewd exhibition of the genitals or post-pubescent female breast." Under the SEVGL, retailers were required to place labels on video games indicating that the games were sexually explicit, and the statute prohibited the sale or rental of these games to minors.

The ESA, the Video Software Dealers Association, and the Illinois Retail Merchants Association brought suit in the U.S. District Court for the Northern District of Illinois. In December 2005, the court struck down the law as a violation of free speech. *Entertainment Software Ass'n v. Blagojevich*, 404 F. Supp. 2d 1051 (N.D. Ill. 2005). The court also determined that a labeling requirement in the statute violated free speech as a form of compelled speech. Eight months later, the court ruled that the State of Illinois had to pay $510,528.64 in attorney's fees resulting from the litigation.

The State of Illinois appealed the decision to the Seventh **Circuit Court** of Appeals. In November 2006, the court affirmed the trial court's decision, finding that the SEVGL was not narrowly tailored to achieve a compelling **state interest** in protecting children from indecent sexual material, and also that the labeling requirements constituted compelled speech. *Entertainment Software Ass'n v. Blagojevich*, 469 F.3d 641 (7th Cir. 2006).

GAY AND LESBIAN RIGHTS

The goal of full legal and social equality for gay men and lesbians sought by the gay movement in the United States and other Western countries.

New Jersey Passes Law Offering Civil Unions

In February 2007, New Jersey became the third state in the nation (following Connecticut and Vermont) to offer civil unions for gay and lesbian couples. Further, the new law automatically granted civil unions to New Jersey gay couples who had previously gone through civil unions or marriages in other states or nations. The state had been permitting "domestic partnerships" since 2004. (As of early 2007, in addition to the three states offering civil unions, only California offered domestic partnerships and Massachusetts was the lone state permitting marriage. Forty-five states had legal or constitutional bans on same-sex marriages.)

The distinction between terms is more than linguistic. Under the new civil union law, couples gained the rights to adoption and child custody, as well as the right to visit a hospitalized partner and/or make medical decisions on behalf of that partner. They also gained the right not to testify against a partner in state court (parallel to state rules of evidence regarding marital or spousal privilege).

However, because the federal government and most states do not recognize civil unions or marriages between same-sex partners, a surviving member of such a union would not be entitled to a deceased partner's Social Security benefits and/or other federal or state privileges or rights regarding survivorship, inheritance, etc. He or she also may not have automatic visitation rights if a partner were hospitalized in one of these states.

The New Jersey **statute** was hastily drafted following an October 2006 court decision by the Supreme Court of New Jersey. In that case, *Lewis, et al. v. Harris, et al.*, No. A-68 (2006), the court found that it could not justify a distinction between same and opposite-sex unions, and that gay couples had a right to the same benefits as married couples. Said Justice Barry T. Albin, writing for the four-member majority opinion,

> "Although we cannot find that a fundamental right to same-sex marriage exists in this state, the unequal dispensation of rights and benefits to committed same-sex partners can no longer be tolerated under our state Constitution."

the justices gave legislators 180 days to come up with a law consistent with this ruling. But the ruling fell short of what either side wanted. It did not demand that New Jersey create the **entity** of gay marriage, but rather, that New Jersey create a law that entitles homosexual couples to the same rights and privileges as heterosexual married couples. The court stated that the legislature "must either amend the marriage statutes to include same-sex couples or create a parallel **statutory** structure . . ." The court further noted that the name given to such statutory scheme, whether called a marriage or some other term, was a matter left to the democratic process.

The lawsuit, filed by Mark Lewis and Dennis Winslow, joined by other representative couples, was filed against Gwendolyn L. Harris, Commissioner of the New Jersey Department of Human Services; Clifton R. Lacy, Commissioner of the New Jersey Department of Health and Senior Services; and Joseph Komosinski, Acting State **Registrar** of Vital Statistics of the New Jersey STATE DEPARTMENT of Health and Senior Services. In the suit, the plaintiffs alleged that laws denying same-sex marriage violated the liberty and **equal protection** guarantees of Article I, Paragraph 1 of the New Jersey Constitution.

In coming to its conclusion, the court relied on a standard for "fundamental" substantive rights adopted by the U.S. SUPREME COURT. First, the asserted liberty must be clearly identified; in this case, the right of same-sex couples to marry. Second, the liberty interest in same-sex marriage must be objectively and deeply rooted in the traditions, history, and conscience of the people of the State.

The plaintiffs had cited several federal cases to support a fundamental right to same-sex marriage, but the Supreme Court of New Jersey found those cases far short of establishing a right "deeply rooted in the traditions, history, and conscience of the people of this State." Further, as to state history, New Jersey's 1912 marriage law expressly limited marriage to heterosexual couples. The court further noted that the

framers of the 1947 state constitution could not have imagined that the liberty right protected in Article I embraced same-sex marriage. Thus, while acknowledging the existence of changing times and attitudes, the court could not find such a fundamental right under the state's constitution.

As to the equal protection claim, the court applied a flexible three-factor test: the nature of the right at stake; the extent to which the challenged statutory scheme restricted that right; and the public need for the statutory restriction. Since the court had already decided that there was no fundamental liberty right to same-sex marriage, it merely answered the question of whether same-sex couples were entitled, under equal protection, to the same rights and benefits afforded to married heterosexual couples. To this, the court concluded they did, finding that "equality of treatment" was a dominant theme in the state's laws and constitution. The court said that Article I of the state constitution protected not only the rights of the majority, but also the rights of the disfavored and the disadvantaged; they too were promised a fair opportunity for "pursuing and obtaining safety and happiness."

The three dissenting judges would have gone further and found a fundamental right—by those exercising their autonomous liberty interest to choose same-sex partners—to participate in state-sanctioned civil marriage.

HABEAS CORPUS

[*Latin, You have the body.*] A writ (court order) that commands an individual or a government official who has restrained another to produce the prisoner at a designated time and place so that the court can determine the legality of custody and decide whether to order the prisoner's release.

Bowles v. Russell

In *Bowles v. Russell*, No. 06-5306, 551 U.S. ___(2007), the U.S. SUPREME COURT upheld the Sixth **Circuit Court** of Appeals' ruling that it lacked jurisdiction to hear an appeal regarding denial of a **habeas corpus** petition. The notice of appeal had been filed too late. However, it had been filed within the time frame mistakenly given to it by the district court's order. Notwithstanding, the high court said that taking an appeal within the prescribed **statutory** time frame was "mandatory and jurisdictional." Therefore, the Sixth Circuit was correct in holding that it lacked jurisdiction to review the matter.

Petitioner Keith Bowles was convicted of murder in the beating death of a man. An Ohio jury sentenced him to 15 years to life imprisonment. His conviction and sentence were upheld by state **appellate** courts.

In 2002, Bowles filed for federal habeas **corpus** relief. The **district court** denied relief on September 9, 2003. By federal **statute** 28 USC §2107(a), Bowles had 30 days from the date of entry of the district court's judgment of denial to file a notice of appeal.

Bowles then asked the district court for an extension to file the notice of appeal. Federal Rule of Appellate Procedure 4(a)(6) allows a district court to grant a 14-day extension under certain conditions (taken from 28 USC §2107(c)). Bowles apparently alleged that he did not receive notice from the district court of the **entry of judgment** of denial.

The district court granted Bowles' motion for a 14-day extension under Rule 4(a)(6). However, the district court mistakenly gave him 17 days to file his notice of appeal instead of fourteen. He filed his notice of appeal on the 16th day, i.e., one day before the date given to him by the district court order, but two days past the 14-day limit under the federal appellate rule.

On appeal to the Sixth Circuit, Russell (the warden) argued that Bowles' appeal was untimely and that the **appellate court** therefore lacked jurisdiction to hear the case. The Sixth Circuit agreed, expressly noting that the U.S. Supreme Court had consistently held that the time limitations for filing notices of appeal were "mandatory and jurisdictional" (See, e.g., *Browder v. Director, Dept. of Corrections of Illinois*, 434 U.S. 257 (1978). The Sixth Circuit also noted that courts of appeal have uniformly held the other time periods under Rule 4(a)(6) to be mandatory and not susceptible to equitable modification. Therefore, the 14-day period under that same rule should be treated as likewise mandatory and not susceptible to equitable modification. The Sixth Circuit then concluded that it had no jurisdiction to hear a case not timely filed.

Justice Thomas, writing for the majority of the Supreme Court, affirmed. Succinctly, the question before the Court was whether the Sixth Circuit had jurisdiction to hear an appeal filed after the statutory period but within the period allowed by the district court's order. Equally succinctly, the Court noted,

> "We have long and repeatedly held that the time limits for filing a notice of appeal are jurisdictional in nature. Accordingly, we hold that the petitioner's untimely notice-even though filed in reliance upon a District Court's order-deprived the Court of Appeals of jurisdiction."

The Court distinguished between time limitations set by a statute such as §2107, which are jurisdictional, and those that are based on court rules, which are not. Because Congress decides (within its constitutional power) what cases are heard, it can also determine under what conditions **federal courts** can hear them: that is the uncompromising power of statute.

Bowles cited two previous Supreme Court cases that, on the surface, appeared similar in fact to his own: *Harris Truck Lines v. Cherry Meat Packers*, 371 U.S. 215, as applied in *Thompson v. INS*, 375 U.S. 384. In those cases, the Court appeared to rely on equitable doctrine to grant relief. Without substantively distinguishing the present case, the Court rejected Bowles' reliance on these cases. Instead, the Court noted that it has no authority to create equitable exceptions to jurisdictional requirements. Finally and importantly, the Court stated that *Harris Truck Lines* and *Thompson* (above) were both now overruled to the extent that they purported to authorize an equitable exception to a jurisdictional rule.

The Court's 5–4 decision drew sharp dissent from Justice Souter, joined in dissent by Justices Stevens, Ginsburg, and Breyer. Justice Souter noted that Bowles had followed the order of the district court, filing one day before the date the district court gave him. "It is intolerable for the judicial system to treat people this way," Souter wrote, "and there is not even a technical justification for condoning this bait and switch." The dissenting opinion took great exception to the seeming expansive then narrowing definition (and "misuse") of the "jurisdiction" label. "The stakes are high in treating time limits as jurisdictional," the dissent noted.

Burton v. Stewart

The **federal courts** have continued to grapple with the procedural rules governing petitions for writs of **habeas corpus**. Congress enacted the Anti-Terrorism and Effective Death Penalty Act of 1996 (AEDPA), Pub. L. No.

104-132, to AEDPA sought to reduce the number of habeas filings by imposing strict rules on when and how a prisoner is entitled to use the federal courts for habeas relief. The U.S. SU-PREME COURT, in *Burton v. Stewart*, __U.S.__, 127 S.Ct. 793, 166 L.Ed.2d 628 (2007), issued another ruling that sought to instruct the lower federal courts on how to interpret provisions of the AEDPA. The decision also made clear that prisoners risk forfeiting their right to petition for habeas **corpus** if they ignore or misunderstand this often confusing body of law.

In 1994, a Washington state jury convicted Lonnie Burton of rape, **robbery**, and **burglary**. The state trial court entered judgment and sentence in December 1994, sentencing Burton to 562 months in prison (the 1994 judgment). The judge rested the sentence on two alternative grounds under the state's determinate sentencing system. The first ground was sentencing Burton to 153 months for robbery, 105 months for burglary, and 304 months for rape, with Burton serving the sentences consecutively for a total of 562 months (almost 47 years). The second ground was running the sentences concurrently but imposing an exceptional sentence of 562 months under the state sentencing law solely for the rape conviction. Burton challenged an unrelated conviction and it was overturned. He then asked the judge in the 1994 case to recalculate his offender scores and resentence him. The court did so but relied only on the 562-month exceptional sentence, running concurrently with the other two sentences (the 1996 judgment). The Washington Court of Appeals upheld Burton's conviction on direct review but remanded the case to the trial judge for resentencing because it appeared vindictive. In March 1998 the trial court entered a second amended judgment, sentencing Burton to 562 months based on the original ground of having the prisoner serve the three sentences consecutively. Burton exhausted his state appeal rights on direct review and in state postconviction proceedings.

In late December 1998, while his sentencing appeal was still pending in state court, Burton filed a petition for habeas corpus in Washington federal **district court**. He filled out a standard form that warned applicants that must ordinarily exhaust all their state court remedies as to each ground on which they sought federal relief or risk being barred from presenting additional grounds at a later date. Burton proceeded to complete and file the form but he only challenged his three convictions, not his sentencing claims. He stated that he was challenging his 1994 judgment and that he had a pending sentencing appeal in state court. Ultimately the court denied Burton's petition. In 2002 Burton filed another habeas petition, contesting the 1998 judgment and the constitutionality of his sentence. The district court and the Ninth **Circuit Court** of Appeals heard Burton's case, despite the fact that the state alleged he had failed to comply with the AEDPA rules for second petitions. Under the AEDPA a prisoner seeking to petition two or more times must obtain authorization from the circuit court of appeals before he could file in district court. The Ninth Circuit ruled against Burton on the substantive issues he raised and Burton appealed to the U.S. Supreme Court.

The Court, in a *per curiam* opinion (no justice signs the opinion as author), ruled that the lower federal courts should never have considered Burton's second habeas petition because he had not obtained prior authorization from the Ninth Circuit. Under AEDPA a three-judge panel of appeals judges may authorize such petitions. The Ninth Circuit, in its opinion, contended that this procedure was not needed because Burton had a legitimate reason for not raising his sentencing challenges in his 1998 petition. The appeals court reasoned that because he had not exhausted his sentencing claims in state court when he filed his first petition they were not ripe for federal habeas review. The Supreme Court ruled that this reasoning was "inconsistent with the precise practice" the Court had explained in prior decisions. District courts should dismiss "mixed petitions" that contain exhausted and unexhausted claims. At that point the petitioner can either exhaust the remaining claims and return to the court with a fully exhausted petition or proceed only on the exhausted claims, as Burton did, and "risk subjecting later petitions that raise new claims to rigorous procedural obstacles." Therefore, Burton's failure to seek or receive authorization from the Ninth Circuit before filing his 2002 petition meant the district court was without jurisdiction to entertain it. The Court reversed the Ninth Circuit decision and ordered the district court to dismiss the petition.

Lawrence v. Florida

Congress passed the Anti-Terrorism and Effective Death Penalty Act of 1996 (AEDPA), Pub. L. No. 104-132, seeking to reduce the number of **habeas corpus** filings by imposing strict timelines on petitions. Because of the ambiguities in some of the AEDPA provisions the **federal courts** have wrestled with how to interpret them. The U.S. SUPREME COURT issued its latest interpretation in *Lawrence v. Florida*, __U.S.__, 127 S.Ct. 1079, __L.Ed.2d __ (2007), ruling that the filing of a petition of **certiorari** to the Court does not stop the running of the 1-year **statute of limitations** on federal habeas petitions.

Gary Lawrence was convicted of first-degree murder and several other crimes by a Florida jury and sentenced to death. The Florida Supreme Court upheld his conviction and death penalty and the U.S. Supreme Court denied his **writ** of certiorari on January 20, 1998. On January 19, 1999, 364 days later, Lawrence filed a postconviction application in the Florida trial court. The court denied him relief and the Florida Supreme Court upheld the postconviction decision on November 18, 2002. Lawrence filed another petition with the U.S. Supreme Court but it denied review on March 24, 2003.

While this petition was pending before the U.S. Supreme Court, Lawrence filed an application for a writ of habeas **corpus**. The federal **district court** dismissed it as untimely, for he had filed it past the 1-year limitations period. All but one day of the limitations period had lapsed during the 364 days between the time his conviction became final and when Lawrence filed for state postconviction relief. The limitations period was tolled (suspended) while the Florida courts reviewed his case. After the Florida Supreme Court issued its decision, Lawrence waited 113 days before filing his federal habeas application. This was well past the one day left to file the habeas application. The only way Lawrence could have his application considered timely was if limitations period continued to be tolled while the Supreme Court reviewed his certiorari petition. The Eleventh **Circuit Court** of Appeals rejected this possibility, noting that §2244 of AEDPA applied only to pending state postconviction proceedings.

The Supreme Court, in a 5–4 decision, upheld the Eleventh Circuit ruling. Justice CLARENCE THOMAS, writing for the majority, noted that §2244 clearly stated the 1-year limitations period for filing a federal habeas application was tolled during the time the state courts considered a post-conviction proceeding. The **statute** said nothing about a federal proceeding staying the 1-year limitations period. Justice Thomas stated that an application for state postconviction review is not pending after the state's postconviction review is complete. Moreover, it did not toll the 1-year limitations period. Another provision of AEDPA used much different language involving direct review of a case to calculate the limitations period. Lawrence had argued that the meaning of this provision should be applied to §2244 but Thomas found that the language was too different to justify an identical meaning.

Lawrence also argued that limiting the tolling period to state postconviction proceedings would result in the prisoner having to file a federal habeas application while the certiorari petition from the postconviction proceeding was pending before the U.S. Supreme Court. Justice Thomas concluded that Congress was not concerned with this potential awkward situation, so the Court did not need to remedy it. Thomas discounted the idea that there were practical problems with this approach. He found the likelihood "quite small" that a federal district court would duplicate the work or analysis "that might be done by this Court if we granted certiorari to review the state postconviction proceeding." In addition, if the district court was concerned about duplicative work it could stay the proceeding until the Supreme Court resolved the case.

Lawrence also was concerned about a situation where the prisoner prevailed at the postconviction proceeding and the state filed for certiorari with the Court. The prisoner would "arguably lack standing to file a federal habeas application" but would later be barred by the statute of limitations if the Court granted certiorari and state won. Justice Thomas viewed this possibility as "extremely rare" but speculated that "equitable tolling" (the court suspends the limitation period based on its own inherent powers) could be made available "in light of the arguably extraordinary circumstances and the prisoner's diligence." For Thomas a more serious problem would occur if the Court allowed tolling for certiorari petitions. He envisioned prisoners filing such petitions as a delaying tactic, giving them more time to file their habeas applications. This would undercut the purposes of AEDPA.

Justice RUTH BADER GINSBURG filed a dissenting opinion that was joined by Justices JOHN PAUL STEVENS, DAVID SOUTER, and STEPHEN BREYER. Ginsburg argued that pending certiorari petitions should toll the habeas time period. Her reading of other AEDPA provisions led her to conclude that Congress had not explicitly excluded Supreme Court review from the tolling period. The practical problems dismissed by the majority were very real: a prisoner denied relief by the state's highest court will now have to file at the same time a habeas application and a certiorari petition. Otherwise the prisoner would risk going beyond the 1-year period while the Supreme Court considers a petition.

HARMLESS ERROR

A legal doctrine in criminal law that allows verdicts to stand without new trials being ordered despite errors of law at trial as long as all errors were insufficient to affect the final outcome. Rule 52(a) of the Federal Code of Criminal Procedure explains it as, "Any error, defect, irregularity or variance which does not affect substantial rights shall be disregarded."

Fry v. Pliler

Certain errors often occur during criminal trials that relate to which or what evidence may be admitted for jury consideration. Not all these errors warrant a new trial. In determining if the "error" (most often in the form of admitting or excluding certain evidence) prejudiced a defendant's right to a fair trial, courts apply a certain standard of review, referred to as the "harmless error standard." An error is generally deemed harmless if, upon review of all evidence, the reviewing court determines that its admission or exclusion would not have affected the ultimate outcome of the trial or case anyway.

In *Fry v. Pliler*, No. 06-5247, 551 U.S. ___ (2007), the U.S. SUPREME COURT was asked to determine which standard must be used by **federal courts**, in 28 USC §2254 proceedings (federal **habeas corpus** petitions)to assess **harmless error** in a state court criminal trial. The Court affirmed the holdings of a majority of the circuit courts of appeals, that the "substantial and injurious effect" standard articulated in its earlier case of *Brecht v. Abrahamson*, 507 U.S. 619 (1993) was the applicable standard. The Court rejected defendant Fry's argument that the more stringent standard of "harmless beyond a reasonable doubt," as articulated in *Chapman v. California*, 386 U.S. 18 (1967), should be used. By a 5–4 majority, the Court declined to decide the question as to whether the exclusion of witness testimony in Fry's case amounted to harmless error under the appropriate *Brecht* standard.

Following two hung juries and five weeks of deliberation, a California state court jury convicted John Fry for his role in the 1992 double murders of Cynthia and James Bell. At the [third] criminal trial, defense strategy focused on attempting to implicate one or more other persons in the murders. Defense counsel offered testimony from several witnesses who linked "Anthony Hurtz" to the killings. But the trial court excluded the testimony of defense witness Pamela Maples, who was planning to testify that she overheard a conversation in which Hurtz discussed homicides bearing some resemblance to the murders of the Bells. The trial court excluded Maples' testimony as "cumulative" (redundant with other testimony; not adding anything new) under California's evidence rules, and concluded that the defense had failed to provide sufficient evidence linking Hurtz's alleged comments to the murders.

Fry appealed to the California **Court of Appeal**, arguing (among other things) that the trial court's exclusion of Maples' testimony deprived him of a constitutional due process right to a fair trial. Without specifying which "harmless error" standard it was using, the state **appellate court** held that the trial court had not abused its discretion in excluding Maples' testimony, adding that "no possible prejudice" could have occurred, given the "merely cumulative nature" of the testimony. The Supreme Court of California denied review, effectively letting the **appellate** court's decision stand.

Fry next applied for a **writ** of habeas **corpus** in federal **district court**, raising the same underlying claim. The district court, adopting a magistrate's recommendations, found that there had been insufficient showing that the exclusion of Maples' testimony, even if improper, had a "substantial and injurious effect on the jury's verdict" (using the *Brecht* standard. A divided panel of the Ninth **Circuit Court** of Appeals affirmed.

Now before the U.S. Supreme Court, the Ninth Circuit decision was affirmed. Justice Scalia wrote the opinion for a unanimous Court on nearly all points (excepting Justice Stevens' separate concurring and dissenting opinion, below). All justices agreed that a federal court must assess prejudicial impact of a constitutional error in a state court criminal trial under the *Brecht* "substantial and injurious effect" standard. This was true whether or not the state appellate court had recognized the error and reviewed it under the "harmless beyond a reasonable doubt" standard of *Chapman*. According to the Court, neither the Court's previous case precedents, nor the Antiterrorism and Effective Death Penalty Act of 1996 (AEDPA) required the use of the more stringent *Chapman* standard. The Court also noted that, as the government had conceded, the state had the **burden of persuasion** on the question of how substantial and injurious was the effect (of any error).

Justice Stevens, concurring in the appropriate standard, nonetheless believed that the Court should have "answer[ed] the question whether the constitutional error was harmless under the standard announced in *"Brecht."*

IMMIGRATION

The entrance into a country of foreigners for purposes of permanent residence. The correlative term *emigration* denotes the act of such persons in leaving their former country.

Bush Administration's Immigration Reform Fails

On June 28, 2007, the U.S. Senate essentially "killed" the Bush Administration's comprehensive immigration reform bill intended to fortify the nation's borders while creating a vehicle toward citizenship for an estimated 12 million current illegal immigrants. The bill had essentially failed three weeks prior, but was revived at the last minute by bi-partisan lobbying to reconsider a revised version. A **cloture** motion received a 64–35 vote to allow continued debate, but that success was short-lived. After considering three more amendments, the votes fell 14 short of the 60 needed for a final cloture (ending debate and clearing the way for final passage of the legislation). The topic was considered so volatile that it was unlikely to be revisited again before 2009, or at a minimum, after 2008 elections.

In the wake of a failed foreign policy centered on the Iraq war, the President had hoped for more success with domestic policy, and immigration reform became the flagship for both his 2000 and 2004 policy platforms. Despite the defeat, Mr. Bush had important bi-partisan backing from Democrats, including Senator Edward M. Kennedy (D-Mass.), the party's key negotiator. Senator Kennedy called the defeat "enormously disappointing for Congress and for the country," but added that, "[w]e will be back." He and others had worked hard to find common ground for an immigration compromise which they referred to as "an imperfect but necessary fix" to the current system.

The "current system," had not been seriously overhauled in 20 years, resulting in a sagging policy under which millions of illegal immigrants used forged and counterfeit documents or lapsed visas to live and work in the United States. Mr. Bush's proposed plan would have made those millions eventually eligible for legal status over time, while immediately focusing on tightening border security and creating an employee verification system intended to weed out illegal workers from jobs in the United States. The bill also would have created a temporary worker ("guest worker") program and a system that based future legal immigration on employment rather than family ties.

Opposition to the bill primarily centered on what many referred to as "amnesty" for existing illegal immigrants, primarily through the temporary guest worker program. A mainstay of the Bush bill, the guest worker program was premised on a few principles that should have accommodated criticism: (1)American workers were to be given priority over guest workers for employment; (2)participation in the program was to be temporary; (3)(the most controversial) undocumented workers seeking citizenship could be eligible in the future. To that end, no undocumented alien would be given citizenship ahead of those who had followed procedural channels and were in a waiting status. In other words, said the President, they would have to go to "the back of the line." Part of the program would

President George W, Bush speaking June 7, 2006 about immigration reform in Omaha, Nebraska.

AP IMAGES

have made workers entering illegally or overstaying their visas pay a substantial monetary penalty, learn the English language, pay taxes, pass a background check, and hold a job for a number of years before being considered eligible for legal status.

However, Republican conservatives strongly opposed any provisions in the bill that would have ultimately led to legal status, and continued to use the word 'amnesty" when referring to the provisions. They insisted that the national priority was to secure the borders before even thinking about giving the millions of illegal aliens already present a path to legal status. Some carried the sentiment that existing laws were more than adequate, but lacked enforcement. As Representative Duncan Hunter (R-Calif.) told Associated Press reporters, there should be "a very strong sense of urgency in this country to simply carry out the law, the mandate, for 854 miles of fence that we passed [in the previous 109th Congress] . . . They've only built 13 miles of the fence so far. Let's get it built before the next hot season."

In the end, 33 Democrats, 12 Republicans, and Independent Joseph Lieberman (Conn.) voted to allow the bill to proceed for a vote (by ending debate). Voting to block the bill by not limiting debate were 37 Republicans, 15 Democrats, and Independent Bernard Sanders (Vt.)

The Senators ultimately rejected a proposed amendment to the bill sponsored by Senator Christopher Bond of Missouri, which would have eliminated the contentious "path to legal status" provision. Earlier, they likewise rejected an amendment offered by Senator Kay Hutchi-

son of Texas that included what became known as the "touchback requirement," mandating that illegal immigrants return to their home countries before they could obtain even temporary legal status. Still another rejected amendment offered by Senator Robert Menendez of New Jersey would have made it easier for relatives of citizens and legal permanent residents to get "green cards," ostensibly discouraging illegal activity. Overall, the senators considered more than 20 amendments to the bill before the final **filibuster** that led to its demise.

Notwithstanding, hours after the bill's failure, lawmakers and lobbyists began seeking ways to selectively advance bits and pieces found within the bill. For example, the "Ag jobs" component of the bill would have granted temporary legal status to approximately one million undocumented agricultural workers, whose work was needed to prevent unharvested crops from rotting in the fields. Another more popular program under the President's plan was for the DREAM Act, or Development, Relief and Education for Alien Minors Act, which would have created a path to legal status for those committed to attending college or joining the military, who had come to the United States with their families before they turned 16 years old.

Gonzales v. Duenas-Alvarez

U.S. immigration law contains provisions that authorize the federal government to remove aliens from the United States who have been convicted of certain crimes. The **federal courts** have reviewed these provisions to determine if state and federal criminal statutes should be applied. The Supreme Court, in *Gonzales v. Duenas-Alvarez*, __U.S.__, 127 S.Ct. 815, 166 L.Ed.2d 683 (2007), examined whether the crime of "aiding and abetting" a theft offense qualifies as a theft offense for which an alien may be removed from the United States. The Court concluded that aiding and **abetting** a theft offense is included in the federal removal **statute**.

Luis Duenas-Alvarez, a permanent resident alien, was convicted of violating a California criminal statute dealing with auto theft. The statute imposes criminal liability on "any person who is a party or an accessory to or an accomplice in the driving or unauthorized taking or stealing" of a motor vehicle. Following his conviction the federal government concluded that the conviction was for a generic theft offense and began removal proceedings. The federal immigration judge and the Board of Immigration Appeals concurred with the government's position because it was a theft offense and the term of imprisonment was at least one year. These two elements are found in 8 U.S.C.A. §1101(a)(43)(G). Duenas-Alvarez then appealed to the Ninth **Circuit Court** of Appeals. The Ninth Circuit overruled the immigration courts, finding that the California auto theft statute swept more broadly than generic theft. The court stated that generic theft has as an element of the crime the taking or control of others' property. The California statute accomplice or accessory language would permit conviction for aiding and abetting a theft without taking or controlling property. Therefore, the accomplice and accessory parts of the California statute fell outside the term "theft" in the immigration statute.

The Supreme Court, in an 8–1 decision, overruled the Ninth Circuit decision. Justice STEPHEN BREYER, writing for the majority, concluded that a person "who aids or abets a theft falls, like a principal, within the scope" of the generic definition of theft. This generic definition of theft is the "taking of property or an exercise of control over property without consent with the criminal intent to deprive the owner of rights and benefits of ownership, even if such deprivation is less than total or permanent." During the Twentieth Century U.S. court eliminated the distinction among the person who actually committed the crime, aiders and abettors present at the scene of the crime, and accessories before the fact who helped the person who committed the crime before the crime took place. Since **criminal law** treats persons who call into these categories alike, the generic definition of theft "covers aiders and abettors as well as principals." Therefore, aiding and abetting theft falls within the scope of the term "theft" in the federal immigration statute.

Duenas-Alvarez did not contest this conclusion but argued that the California provision reached beyond generic theft to cover certain nongeneric crimes in other ways. He noted that California makes aiders and abettors criminally responsible not just for the crimes they intend but also for any crime that "naturally and probably" results from the intended crime. Justice Breyer found that this fact alone did not show the statute covered a nongeneric theft crime. For Duenas-Alvarez to prevail he had to show something special about the California natural-and probable law that would demonstrate California criminalized conduct "that most other States would not consider theft." Duenas-Alvarez would, for example, have to show that California made a defendant criminally liable for

conduct that other states would not consider theft. Justice Breyer examined several California cases but found no merit in this argument. California's law was not special. It was not enough for Duenas-Alvarez to apply "legal imagination to a state statute's language." He needed to show a "realistic probability, not a theoretical possibility" that California would apply its statute to conduct that was outside the generic definition of a crime. Justice Breyer concluded that Duenas-Alvarez had failed to meet this burden; the **natural and probable consequences** doctrine had not been applied to create a "subspecies" of the auto theft statute that would all outside the generic definition of theft.

Justice Stevens filed an opinion that concurred in the decision to send the case back to the lower courts. However, he dissented in part because he believed it would have been better for the Ninth Circuit to review California law on the natural and probable consequences doctrine.

Lopez v. Gonzales

U.S. immigration law gives the federal government the power to remove aliens from the country if they commit serious crimes. One provision provides a list of offenses that are termed "aggravated felonies," which limits the ability of the attorney general to cancel the removal of an alien. Drug trafficking crimes are part of this list. The Supreme Court, in *Lopez v. Gonzales*, __U.S.__, 127 S.Ct. 625, 166 L.Ed.2d 462(2006), was confronted with the question of whether a state drug trafficking conviction counted as an aggravated **felony** when the same conduct was a **misdemeanor** under federal drug control laws. The Court concluded that the state conviction could not be classified as an aggravated felony for removal proceedings.

Jose Antonio Lopez entered the United States illegally in 1986 but in 1990 he became a legal permanent resident. In 1997 South Dakota police arrested Lopez on state drug charges, pleading guilty to aiding and **abetting** another person's possession of cocaine. He was sentenced to five years in prison but Lopez was released for good conduct in 15 months. The Immigration and Naturalization Service (INS), now called the Bureau of Immigration and Customs Enforcement (ICE), started removal proceedings against Lopez because he had been convicted of a controlled substance violation that was an aggravated felony under federal immigration law. Lopez did not contest the controlled substance violation but did challenge the aggravated felony determination because it would disqualify him from discretionary cancellation of removal. The immigration judge initially agreed with Lopez because the proscribed state conduct was not treated as a felony under federal drug laws. However, he reversed his ruling when the Board of Immigration Appeals (BIA) changed its position on the issue. As long as the conviction was a felony under state law, it must be treated as an aggravated felony under federal law. The judge order Lopez removed from the United States. This ruling was upheld by the BIA and the Eighth **Circuit Court** of Appeals. The Supreme Court accepted Lopez's appeal to resolve a conflict over this issue in the circuit courts.

The Supreme Court, in an 8–1 decision, reversed the Eighth Circuit, holding that a state felony conviction cannot be counted as an aggravated felony if the conduct is a misdemeanor under federal drug laws. Justice DAVID SOUTER, in his majority opinion, noted that Lopez's state conviction was for helping someone else possess cocaine. The mere possession of cocaine is not a felony under federal **criminal law** unless the defendant possessed more than what one person would have for himself. The federal government argued that federal law required only that the drug offense be punishable, not that it be punishable as a federal felony. Under this theory a conviction in state court would satisfy the felony element of the immigration **statute** because the state treated possession that way.

Justice Souter discounted this theory on several grounds. He concluded that the use of the term "trafficking" in the immigration statute should be given a commonsense reading. The ordinary meaning of the word refers to some type of commercial dealing. In Lopez's conduct there was no allegation of commercial dealing; he only aided someone else to possess cocaine. It made no sense to "turn simple possession into trafficking," which was "just what the English language tells us not to expect." Congress has the right to define illicit trafficking "in an unexpected way," but "it would need to tell us so, and there are good reasons to think it was doing no such thing here." Turning to the statute, Justice Souter pointed out that Congress had in some places referred to guilt under state law but that the provision in question referred only to felonies under the federal Controlled Substance Act (CSA). The rules of **statutory** construction mandate that when Congress includes particular language in one section of a law but omits it in another section of the same act, it is generally presumed Congress acted "intentionally and purposely" in making the inclusion

or exclusion. Therefore, Justice Souter held that "Unless a state offense is punishable as a federal felony it does not count."

The law of alien removal was also implicated in the government's troublesome theory. Justice Souter stated that this part of immigration law would be dependent on varying state criminal classifications, despite the fact that Congress had matched the immigration statutes to the classifications it had chosen. It was hard to "imagine that Congress took the trouble to incorporate its own statutory scheme of felonies and misdemeanors if it meant courts to ignore it whenever a State chose to punish a given act more heavily." The government's reading meant that a state could make it a felony to possess a gram of marijuana and the state convict would be subject to mandatory deportation because the alien would be ineligible for cancellation of removal. The reverse could also be true: the state could classify a drug crime as a misdemeanor that is a felony under federal law, thus barring the federal government from using the aggravated felony standard for removal. Therefore, state drug conviction cannot be classified as a felony unless the proscribed conduct is punishable as a felony under federal law.

Justice CLARENCE THOMAS, in a dissenting opinion, disagreed with Souter's analysis. Lopez's state felony conviction was punishable under the CSA, even if it was treated as a misdemeanor. He contended that the majority's decision would have a significant effect on removal proceedings involving state possession offenses.

IMMUNITY

Exemption from performing duties that the law generally requires other citizens to perform, or from a penalty or burden that the law generally places on other citizens.

Rogers v. City of Kennewick

Under 42 U.S.C.A. §1983, a person may sue a police officer for violating a constitutional right or statute. Over the course of 30 years, the U.S. Supreme Court has developed the doctrine of qualified immunity for police officers as a way to shield them from civil liability. Under this doctrine a police officer who is sued for excessive force may not be sued if the officer's actions were reasonable and the constitutional right supposedly violated was not clearly established under the law. Qualified immunity is asserted immediately after a person sues an officer by a motion to the court, thereby forcing a judge to make a determination before the litigation accelerates and legal bills begin to rise. If the officer is denied qualified immunity by the trial court, the matter is subject to immediate appeal.

These procedures were reviewed by the Ninth **Circuit Court** of Appeals in *Rogers v. City of Kennewick*, 205 Fed. Appx. 491 (9th Cir. 2006), where several police officers challenged the denial of qualified immunity. The court upheld the lower court, finding that the officers were did not act reasonably in deploying a police dog on a suspect who was severely bitten by the dog.

At 1:00 a.m. on July 13, 2003, a suspect on a moped was being pursued in the city of Kennewick, Washington for two traffic infractions and a misdemeanor violation for failing to stop when signaled by police. Police did not have any evidence that he was armed or dangerous, yet they treated these minor crimes as a serious matter. That night Ken Rogers, a 50-year-old salesman, had gone to his daughter's house to stay but she had inadvertently locked the house with the dead bolt. Rogers decided to sleep in the fenced backyard. Sgt. Richard Dopke, who had chased the moped driver, tracked him to a garage next to where Rogers was sleeping. He requested police dog backup.

Officer R.B. Kohn arrived with his dog Deke. Kohn sent Deke into the yard where Rogers was sleeping, believing that he might be the suspect. Rogers was awakened by noises coming from the house and suspected that it was being burglarized. He yelled and asked what was going on. A few seconds later Deke attacked him. As he fought off the dog, which was biting into his left arm, Rogers was hit with a baton or blunt object by one of the officers. He was arrested but later released when police discovered he was not the moped driver. Rogers suffered permanent injuries, including hearing loss. He then sued the two officers and the city under § 1983, alleging that they had committed an unconstitutional search and seizure under the **Fourth Amendment**.

Dopke and Kohn immediately filed motions to dismiss the case, claiming they were entitled to qualified immunity. The district court denied the motions, finding that the officers made an unconstitutional seizure of Rogers in violation of the Fourth Amendment. The officers then appealed to the Ninth Circuit Court of Appeals.

A three-judge panel of the Ninth Circuit upheld the district court. The appeals rejected the officers' claim that they had not violated the Fourth Amendment because they did not intend to seize Rogers. The court noted that a seizure occurs even when an unintended person is the object of detention and the officer acts willfully in detaining the person. Kohn acted intentionally because he had control over the dog when it bit Rogers and he had "effectively ordered the dog to find and bite the individual he was tracking." Therefore, it was of "no legal consequence" whether the officers intended to restrain Rogers or an unidentified person. The court then examined the two-part immunity test: whether a constitutional right violated, and, if so, whether the right was clearly established.

The key in Rogers' case was whether the seizure was reasonable; if unreasonable the search would violate the Fourth Amendment. The court cited the minor severity of the crime, the lack of any evidence that the suspect posed a threat to the safety of the officers, and the fact the suspect was not trying to evade arrest by flight to sustain its ruling that the seizure of Rogers was unreasonable. As to whether this right was clearly established, case law demonstrated that the failure to give a warning before releasing a police dog to bite and hold is unreasonable. Moreover, releasing the dog into the yard without a warrant was unreasonable as was allowing the dog to bite Rogers for over one minute. Therefore, the district court properly denied the officers qualified immunity.

In addition, Sgt. Dopke had argued he should not be liable because he was not present when the dog attacked Rogers. The appeals court found that clearly established law made a supervisor liable for the actions of subordinates if he "sets in motion a series of acts by others." Department policy prohibited officers from "pursuits" of suspects of traffic misdemeanors, which Dopke violated. Therefore, Rogers must be allowed to pursue the officers in the civil lawsuit.

Scott v. Harris

In *Scott v. Harris*, No. 05-1631, 550 U.S. ___ (2007), the U.S. SUPREME COURT held that a high speed police chase ending in a serious crash after police forced the vehicle off the road, did not constitute an unreasonable seizure under the FOURTH AMENDMENT to the U.S. Constitution. Accordingly, the police officer was entitled to qualified immunity and **summary judgment**. The decision reversed the ruling of the U.S. Court of Appeals for the 11th Circuit.

On the night of March 21, 2001, a police officer clocked Victor Harris' vehicle traveling at a high rate of speed and pursued him in his police vehicle, with lights flashing. Harris refused to stop, continuing at speeds between 80 and 90 m.p.h. He ran several red lights as well as crossed over double-yellow traffic lines in order to pass other drivers.

Another officer, Deputy Timothy Scott, heard about the pursuit on his dispatch radio and joined the chase without knowing why Harris was being pursued. After Harris' vehicle entered a highway, Scott radioed his supervisor for permission to perform a Precision Intervention Technique (PIT) maneuver on Harris's car. When done correctly, the maneuver's impact causes a fleeing car into a spin before eventually bringing it to a stop. Scott's supervisor responded to "[g]o ahead and take him out."

However, Scott (or any police officer in the county) was not trained in how to execute a PIT maneuver. He had the foresight to wait until other motorists were out of the area, then rammed his front bumper into Harris' vehicle. Harris' car went out of control and rolled down an embankment. Harris, who was not wearing a seatbelt, sustained serious injuries which rendered him a quadriplegic.

Harris filed suit in the U.S. **District Court** for the Northern District of Georgia, charging that under *Tennessee v. Garner*, 471 U.S. 1 (1985), Scott's use of force was unreasonable and unconstitutional under the Fourth Amendment. The district court denied Scott's motion for summary judgment based on qualified immunity. The Eleventh **Circuit Court** of Appeals affirmed on **interlocutory** appeal, concluding that Scott's actions could constitute "deadly force" under *Tennessee v. Garner*. Further, held the **appellate court**, a reasonable jury could find that use of such force in this context was a violation of Harris' constitutional right to be free from excessive force during a seizure. As such, Scott's qualified immunity in this case was a matter of factual dispute and not one of law, so dismissal by summary judgment was inappropriate.

In reversing the 11th Circuit, Justice Scalia delivered the opinion of the Court. Qualified immunity, noted the Court, requires resolution of a threshold question: taken in the light most favorable to the injured party, do the alleged facts show the officer's conduct violated a constitutional right?

However, as a preliminary issue, the Court further noted that a videotape capturing the chase unequivocally contradicted Harris' rendition of facts, to the point that no reasonable jury

would believe Harris' version. Therefore, the above test for qualified immunity should be done by viewing the facts in the light depicted by the videotape.

Next, the matter of Harris' cited precedent regarding deadly force, *Tennessee v. Garner*. In that case, the Supreme Court stated that "deadly force" could be used when (1)an officer had **probable cause** to believe that a suspect posed a threat of serious harm to the officer or others; or the suspect uses a weapon to threaten the officer; or there was probable cause to believe that the suspect committed a crime involving the infliction or threat of infliction of serious physical harm; (2)the force was necessary to prevent escape; and (3) some warning had been given.

Viewing the facts in the light as depicted by the videotape, the Court concluded, it was clear that Deputy Scott did not violate the Fourth Amendment. The car chase initiated by Harris posed a substantial and immediate risk of serious physical injury to others. Scott's attempt to force Harris off the road was reasonable under the facts, and Scott was entitled to summary judgment.

The Court's opinion also noted that *Tennessee v. Garner* did not establish a magical on/off switch triggering rigid preconditions whenever an officer's actions constituted "deadly force." The *Garner* Court simply applied the Fourth Amendment's 'reasonableness' test to the use of particular force in those particular circumstances. This case had vastly different facts. Whether or not Scott's actions constituted deadly force, those actions were reasonable in this case.

Justice Stevens was the lone dissenter. He essentially characterized the issue as one where the officer was placing the *fleeing motorist* at risk of serious injury or death in order to stop the motorist's flight from endangering the lives of innocent bystanders. The answer could be yes or no, and the question of reasonableness should be decided by a jury. Stevens also objected to the *de novo* (for the first time) review of the videotape to establish the facts.

INDICTMENT

A written accusation charging that an individual named therein has committed an act or omitted to do something that is punishable by law.

United States v. Resendiz-Ponce

A criminal indictment is a written charge that states the time, place, and manner in which the defendant is alleged to have committed an offense. By detailing how the alleged actions violated the law, the indictment gives the defendant an opportunity to prepare a defense. Sometimes prosecutors issue faulty indictments, which fail to provide enough specific details on what actions the defendant took that violated a **criminal law**. The U.S. SUPREME COURT considered whether a criminal indictment was defective in *United States v. Resendiz-Ponce*, __U.S.__, 127 S.Ct.782, 166 L.Ed.2d 591 (2007). The Court concluded that the indictment's failure to provide detailed allegations did not violate the defendant's constitutional rights.

Juan Resendiz-Ponce illegally entered the United States from Mexico twice and was twice deported in 1988 and 2002. On June 1, 2003 he walked up to a port of entry near San Luis, Arizona. He presented a photo identification of his cousin to the border agent and told the agent that he was a legal resident traveling to Calexico, California. The agent noted the discrepancy between the photo and Resendiz's features, questioned him, and eventually took him into custody. Resendiz was charged with violating a federal criminal law that makes it a **felony** to attempt to enter the United States illegally. The indictment against Resendiz stated that he was an alien who "knowingly and intentionally attempted to enter" the United States near San Luis, Arizona after having been deported in October 2002. Resendiz moved the U.S. **district court** to dismiss the indictment because it failed to allege "an essential element, an overt act, or to state the essential facts of such overt act." The district court rejected this motion and a jury found him guilty of the crime. He was sentenced to 63 months in prison.

Resendiz appealed his conviction to the Ninth **Circuit Court** of Appeals. The Ninth Circuit reversed his conviction, concluding that an indictment's omission of an essential element of the offense was a fatal flaw." The indictment had failed because it did not allege "any specific overt act that is a substantial step" toward the completion of the unlawful entry." Resendiz had a right to be informed of what overt act the government would try to prove at trial. The physical crossing into the government inspection area was but one of a number of other acts that the government could have alleged as a substantial step toward entry into the United States. The Ninth Circuit noted that the indictment could have alleged the tendering of a false identification card, the successful clearance of the inspection area, or lying to an inspection officer with the purpose of being admitted. The

grand jury that issued the indictment "never passed on a specific overt act, and Resendiz was never given notice of what specific overt act would be proved at trial."

The Supreme Court, in an 8–1 decision, overruled the Ninth Circuit. Justice JOHN PAUL STEVENS, writing for the majority, acknowledged that both **common law** and federal law hold that "the mere intent to violate a federal criminal **statute** is not punishable as an attempt unless it is also accompanied by significant conduct." The government argued that the indictment against Resendiz implicitly alleged that he engaged in the necessary overt act simply by alleging that he attempted to enter the United States. Justice Stevens agreed with the government position, finding that the word "attempt" encompasses both the overt act and intent elements. Therefore, an indictment alleging illegal reentry does not have to specifically allege a particular overt act or any other component of the offense. The indictment was legally sufficient because it alleged that Resendiz attempted to enter the United States near San Luis, Arizona on or about June 1, 2003. This time and place information provided Resendiz "with more adequate notice than would an indictment describing particular overt acts," for the defendant might have approached the border or lied to a border-patrol agent "in the course of countless attempts on innumerable occasions." The time and place information in the indictment "provided ample protection against the risk of multiple prosecutions for the same crime."

Justice Steven's rejected Resendiz's claim that the government needed to allege any one of three overt acts: that he walked into the inspection area, that he presented a misleading identification card, or that he lied to the inspector. Stevens rule that those three acts were "part of a single course of conduct culminating in the charged 'attempt.'" Though some crimes require more specificity in an indictment, in this case the crime of attempted illegal entry did not depend "so crucially" on specifically identified facts. Moreover, Congress had modified common law principles by moving away from rules of technical and formalized pleading. The indictment met the criteria of the Federal Rules of **Criminal Procedure** by being a "plain, concise, and definite written statement of the essential facts constituting the offense charged."

Justice ANTONIN SCALIA, in a dissenting opinion, argued that the Court had ignored fundamental rules principles of criminal procedure. The crime of attempt required the government to allege that the defendant had the intent to commit the crime "and that he took some action toward its commission. Any rule to the contrary would be an exception to the standard practice."

INSURANCE

A contract whereby, for a specified consideration, one party undertakes to compensate the other for a loss relating to a particular subject as a result of the occurrence of designated hazards.

$2.5 Million in Punitive Damages Against State Farm

In January 2007, a Mississippi jury awarded a married couple $2.5 million in **punitive damages** against State Farm Insurance Company stemming from its denial of a Hurricane Katrina-related homeowners' claim. Although a judge later reduced the punitive damages to $1 million (remittitur,) as more reasonably related to the $223,000 in actual damages, this was but a drop in the bucket for State Farm. It still faced more than 600 other Katrina-related lawsuits and 35,000 pending claims still unresolved.

The actual damage award was the result of U.S. **District Court** Judge L.T. Senter Jr.'s directed verdict. He ruled that State Farm had failed to carry its burden, under Mississippi law, of proving that the damage to the Broussard's home was caused by storm-surged water rather than wind, and therefore excluded from coverage. State Farm had argued that the homeowners' policy covered damage from wind but not from water. Further, the policy ostensibly excluded damages that could have been caused by a combination of both, even if the hurricane winds preceded the storm's water damage.

The Broussard home was reduced to its cement slab. Because Judge Senter found that State Farm failed to show how much, if any, of the damage was caused by water versus wind, he directed that State Farm pay the maximum $212,000 policy limit. He then handed the case over to the jury to decide whether to award punitive damages. One of Broussards' attorneys, William Walker, told the jury in closing arguments that State Farm had breached its contract with the Broussards "in a bad way" and had "acted like a chiseler," listening to the pocketbook and not the clients.

State Farm also argued that the policy at issue categorically excluded any damage caused by negligence. (The storm surge and flooding in the aftermath of Hurricane Katrina are widely believed to have resulted from negligent engineering of levees.) But in the first Katrina-related lawsuit to go to trial (August 2006), a federal judge had ruled that Nationwide Insurance Company was not liable for payment on a policyholder's claims for water damage caused by the hurricane. Later, in November 2006, another federal judge held that water and flood damage caused by Katrina may be covered under those policies that did not specifically exclude damage caused by negligence.

State Farm saw the writing on the wall and finally announced that it would pay at least $50 million to settle the pending **class action** involving 35,000 policyholders, and offered another $80 million to settle 640 existing lawsuits.

The settlements had been pending before Judge Senter, who withheld approval and demanded more information. Meanwhile, State Attorney General Jim Hood had repeatedly called for a statewide settlement between all Mississippi policyholders and all insurance companies. Its office had agreed in January 2007 to drop State Farm from the lawsuit it had filed against several insurance companies for their refusal to cover such Katrina damages, in return for State Farm's agreement to settle those claims.

In March 2007, more than a year and a half after the storm, State Farm announced that it would bypass the court and work directly with the state insurance commissioner, George Dale, to reopen pending claims and attempt settlement. This, hopefully, would speed the flow of money to approved claimants. Meanwhile, Judge Senter denied class-action status to the approximately 640 related lawsuits still pending against State Farm.

Following denial of class-action status, State Farm continued to settle the pending lawsuits individually, either during or shortly before trials were scheduled to start, in order to avoid the possibility of punitive damages being awarded. In some cases, State Farm agreed to settle the lawsuits after the jury had awarded actual damages to the homeowners, but prior to any determination of punitive damages. The dollar amount of these settlements remained undisclosed.

But the 35,000 pending pre-lawsuit claims remained unresolved and unsettled, many of the policyholders still living in government-issued trailers. In addition to the failed court settlement of these claims, State Farm also failed to make good on the deal with the state insurance commissioner (which was not subject to court review).

As of June 2007, State Farm was still handling both individual claims and lawsuits on a case by case basis, disputing whether homeowners' damages were caused by water or wind from the August 2005 storm. In a last minute twist to the matter, state Attorney General Jim Hood filed suit against State Farm in June 2007, stating that it had failed to honor its agreement for a mass settlement of these pending claims. He declined to rule out the possibility of re-opening a criminal investigation that he also ended in January as part of the agreement. His office had been investigating allegations of criminal **fraud** in State Farm's denial of policyholders' claims.

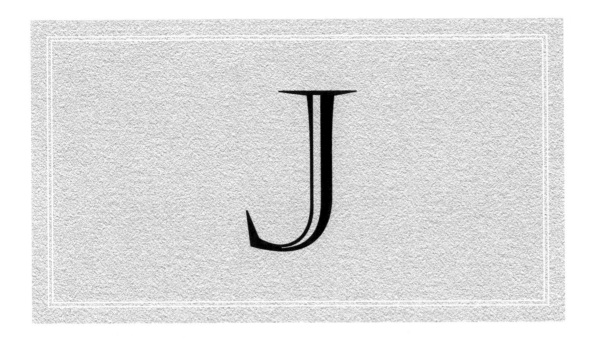

JUDGE

A public officer chosen or elected to preside over and to administer the law in a court of justice; one who controls the proceedings in a courtroom and decides questions of law or discretion.

ABA House of Delegates Approves New Model Code of Judicial Conduct

The AMERICAN BAR ASSOCIATION House of Delegates on February 14, 2007 unanimously approved a revised Model CODE OF JUDICIAL CONDUCT, which establishes standards of professional responsibility for judges. The new code replaces one that was last approved in full in 1990. The revisions included a restructuring of the provisions from the previous Code and a number of changes designed to clarify guidelines under which judges must act.

The ABA has had a long history of establishing standards by which judges and attorneys much conduct themselves. In 1908, the ABA approved the first ethical guidelines for members of the bar with the approval of the Canons of Professional Ethics. These canons did not apply to judges, and efforts in 1909 and 1917 to include judicial standards failed. However, concerns regarding conflicts of interest among some judges arose, and by 1922, the ABA had appointed a commission on judicial ethics. Chaired by former President and Chief Justice of the U.S. SUPREME COURT WILLIAM HOWARD TAFT, the committee was charged with drafting a code of judicial ethics. The ABA approved the Canons of Judicial Ethics in 1924. This document, which consisted of 36 canons, was intended to serve as a guide for the states.

In 1969, the ABA began a comprehensive process to review, evaluate, and update these canons. Three years later, the ABA approved the Model Code of Judicial Conduct, which changed the style and form of the old rules. More specifically, the new code reduced the number of canons from 36 to seven and also cleaned up much of the language. The ABA again conducted a comprehensive study the model code in 1988. This led to the adoption of the 1990 Model Code of Judicial Conduct, which reduced the number of canons from seven to five. As was the case with the 1972 Model Code, the 1990 version was designed to be enforceable and incorporated mandatory language.

In recent years, the ABA has considered additional revisions to the Model Code. In 1998, the organization approved revisions related to campaign contributions for judges running for positions on the bench. A report from an **ad hoc** committee in 2002 concluded that new rules related to public financing for judicial elections were necessary. The Supreme Court's decision in *Republican Party of Minnesota v. White*, 536 U.S. 765, 122 S. Ct. 2528; 153 L. Ed. 2d 694 (2002) also affected judicial rules. In that case, the Court determined that a law prohibiting judges from discussing political issues.

In September 2003, ABA President Dennis W. Archer, Jr. announced the appointment of a joint committee that was charged to evaluate the 1990 Model Code. This committee was formed under the auspices of the ABA standing committees on judicial independence and professional responsibility. Phoenix lawyer Mark I. Harrison was appointed as chair of the committee. The committee planned to hold public hearings in

2004 and 2005, with completion of the project expected by February 2007.

"Judicial ethics are not static," Archer said when he formed the committee. "It has been 12 years since the ABA took a good, hard look at the code to see if it provides adequate guidance to judges about their conduct, and to the public about what to expect from judges. In the meantime, judges are facing growing pressures from interest groups participating in the judicial election process and initiatives in Congress that would restrict judicial independence, and other factors are coming into play that can bear on the conduct of judges performing their duties in office."

In the first 22 months after the committee's formation, the committee met a dozen times in person and an additional 17 times in conference calls. The committee completed two drafts in 2005 and invited public comment at hearings. The committee continued to meet and consider revisions in 2006, leading to the submission of a final report to the ABA on December 20, 2006.

The new Model Code reduces the total number of canons from five to four. Under the 1990 Model Code, each Canon was subdivided into additional canons. Thus, the specific canon governing use of nonpublic information by judges was Canon 3B(12). Under the new code, the canons remain as broad statements, but the specific provisions now exist as rules. Thus, the same provision regarding use of nonpublic information is now contained in Rule 3.5.

One provision that gave rise to controversy was a proposal that would have downgraded the proscription against a judge engaging in an activity that would present an "appearance of impropriety." One of the previous drafts included this language as a guideline, but did not establish that violation of this provision alone could give rise to disciplinary action. In the final version, however, the ABA chose to retain the language from the 1990 Code. Under the new code, "A judge shall uphold and promote the independence, integrity, and impartiality of the judiciary, and shall avoid impropriety and the appearance of impropriety."

The committee's decision to reduce this proscription in the first place led some critics to charge that the ABA looked too closely at internal politics rather than sound legal principles. Even though the ABA reversed its position, according to an editorial in the *New York Times*, "the proposed code revisions have serious deficiencies. They fall well short of ending the festering scandal of expense-paid judicial seminars that are held at desirable resorts and underwritten by private interests. If the House of Delegates lacks the resolve to ban these junkets, it should at least limit reimbursements for accompanying spouses. There should be no free rides or free lunches (or breakfasts or dinners)."

The ABA approved the Model Code by a unanimous vote on February 14. The Model Code itself is not binding law, but it serves as a persuasive guide for the states to use when developing their own codes. In practice, almost all states adopt the ABA's model codes in a wholesale manner.

Lopez Torres v. New York State Board of Elections

The election of state judges is part of the U.S. political process, involving the participation of political parties in some jurisdictions. Unlike federal judges, who are appointed for life, state judges must face the electorate when their terms near an end. The state of New York's system of electing judges was one of the most complicated in the nation, making it virtually impossible for judicial candidates not endorsed by the Democratic or Republican parties to get on the ballot. Frustrated by this system, a group of judicial candidates, voters, and a non-profit organization challenged the constitutionality in a federal civil rights suit. The Second **Circuit Court** of Appeals, in *Lopez Torres v. New York State Board of Elections*, 462 F.3d 161 (2nd Cir. 2006), agreed with the plaintiffs that the system violated their political association rights and directed the state to hold direct primary elections for judges until the state legislature enacted corrective legislation.

New York state trial judges who work in the state's **general jurisdiction** trial courts are called "Supreme Court Justices." In 1921 the New York legislature revamped the electoral process for Supreme Court justices, enacting a three-part scheme that includes a primary election, a nominating convention, and a general election. Justices are elected from New York's 12 judicial districts, which are very large. In each of the judicial districts are a number of assembly districts. During the first phase the state held a primary election at which rank-and-file party members elected judicial delegates. Judicial candidates needed to assemble a slate of delegates to run on their behalf, so these delegates could vote for their candidates at the judicial nominating convention. Small subgroups of delegates stood for election in each assembly district but before they appeared on the ballot they first circulated petitions within the district. Within a span of 37 days each slate of delegates had to gather 500 valid signatures from party members residing in the assembly district. Each party member could sign only one petition, which meant the number of available signatories shrunk each time a party member signed a petition. Because these petitions were routinely challenged based on the one-signature rule, each delegate slate needed to collect 1,000 to 1,500 signatures. Once a delegate slate was approved it was placed on the primary ballot by the State Board of Elections. However, the ballot did not disclose the name of the judicial candidate that was linked to the delegates. Therefore, a candidate would have to run a voter education campaign in each assembly district.

The political parties held their judicial nominating conventions one to two weeks after a slate of delegates was elected. In theory any judicial candidate could lobby the delegates for support but in practice only candidates who had the backing of the party's leadership would be nominated. The nominating conventions rubber-stamped the party candidates. Between 1990 and 2002 over 96 percent of nominations went uncontested and delegate absenteeism was high. The final phase of the process, the general election, was equally an uncontested affair, as one-party rule was the norm in most judicial districts. Between 1990 and 2002 almost half of the elections for Supreme Court Justice were uncontested.

Brooklyn Civil Court Judge Margarita Lopez Torres first won election in 1992. She immediately offended powerful Democratic officials by refusing to hire their friends and relatives for her office. A few years later Lopez Torres expressed her interest in becoming a Supreme Court Justice but the officials blocked her. She tried two more times, the last time in 2003, but the three-step process made it virtually impossible for her to assemble and elect a slate of delegates. It became clear that only a candidate with the backing of a political party would have the resources to mount an effective campaign. Therefore, in 2004 Lopez Torres and others filed suit against the Board of Elections, alleging that the election system violated their FIRST AMENDMENT guarantee of political association. The New York federal **district court** agreed with the plaintiffs and issued a **preliminary injunction** prohibiting the board from enforcing the judicial nominating system and directed the state to conduct open primary elections until the legislature overhauled the system. The order was stayed until after the 2006 general election.

The state appealed but the Second Circuit Court of Appeals upheld the injunction. The Court found that the district court had conducted an exhaustive evidentiary inquiry that demonstrated beyond doubt that the political parties controlled the election of Supreme Court justices. The scheme frustrated the First Amendment rights of judicial candidates and voters, for the amendment guaranteed them a "realistic opportunity to participate in the nominating phase free from severe and unnecessary burdens." The state could not show a compelling **state interest** for a scheme that did not "merely deprive a candidate of a realistic chance to prevail; rather, through the use of overlapping and severe burdens, it deprives a candidate of access altogether."

Justice Kennedy Urges Congress to Raise Judicial Salaries

Speaking before the SENATE JUDICIARY COMMITTEE in February 2007, U.S. SUPREME COURT Justice ANTHONY M. KENNEDY urged Congress to increase the salaries of all federal judges or else risk the possibility that fewer talented judges will accept appointments to the bench. According to Kennedy, if judicial salaries do not improve, it will increasingly become more difficult to attract top lawyers from **private law** firms to accept positions on the bench because many of those lawyers make several times the amount that judges make. Moreover, said Kennedy, judges will become more likely to accept positions outside of the judiciary, such as in academia, due to the salary disparity.

The Judiciary Committee invited Kennedy to speak at a hearing entitled "Judicial Security and Independence." Although members of the Supreme Court were reportedly skeptical when the committee asked Chief Justice JOHN ROBERTS if one of the associate justices could speak, the justices eventually perceived a benefit in having a justice testify. Joining Kennedy were Judge Brock Hornby, who serves as U.S. **District Court** for the District of Maine and also as the Chair of the Judicial Branch Committee of the JUDICIAL CONFERENCE OF THE UNITED STATES; James Duff, Director of the ADMINISTRATIVE OFFICE OF THE UNITED STATES COURTS; and Jeffrey Minear, Administrative Assistant to the Chief Justice of the United States.

Congress establishes the salaries of federal judges by way of legislation. As of 2007, federal district court judges earn $165,200. Judges from the courts of appeals make $175,100. Supreme Court associate justices make $203,000, while

Supreme Court Justice Anthony Kennedy testifies on Capitol Hill on March 8, 2007.
AP IMAGES

the chief justice earns $212,100. In his testimony, Kennedy acknowledged that those amounts are large compared with the wages of the average American. However, this level of salary "is insufficient to attract the finest members of the practicing bar to the bench," he said.

Kennedy noted that judges now hear a substantially larger number of cases than judges hear 30 years ago. When Kennedy began serving as a judge with the Ninth **Circuit Court** of Appeals in 1975, approximately 17,000 cases were filed. By 2005, this number had quadrupled to 70,000. He said that without the work of dedicated senior judges, federal dockets could become "dangerously congested." Judicial salaries have not kept pace.

"Despite the increase in workload, the real compensation of federal judges has diminished substantially over the years," Kennedy testified. "Between 1969 and 2006, the real pay of district judges declined by about 25 percent. In the same period, the real pay of the average American worker increased by eighteen percent. The resulting disparity is a forty-three percent disadvantage to the district judges. If judges' salaries had kept pace with the increase in the wages of the average American worker during this time period, the district judge salary would be $261,000. That salary is large compared to the average wages of citizens, but it is still far less than the salary of a highly qualified individual in private practice or academia would give up to become a judge."

Congress considered legislation in 2006 that would have given judges a 16 percent increase in salary, but that proposal died. Some members of the Judiciary Committee, including Dick Durbin (D.-Ill.) noted that even though financial rewards may be driving some judges to accept jobs with private firms, judges still earn more money than 95 percent of the population. Other members of the committee appeared to agree with Kennedy. Committee chairman Patrick Leahy (D.-Vt.) indicated that he had already introduced a bill that called for cost-of-living increases for judges, and he agreed with Kennedy that Congress needed to end its reluctance to give raises to judges without also giving raises for themselves.

Kennedy stressed that he has never seen colleagues in the judiciary more dispirited in the past three decades than they are right now. "The blunt fact is that the past Congressional policy with respect to judicial salaries has been one of neglect," he said. "As a consequence, the nation is in danger of having a judiciary that is no longer considered one of the leading judiciaries in the world. This is particularly discordant and disheartening, in light of the care and consideration Congress has generally given in respect to other matters of judiciary resources and administration."

Some critics noted that the statistics cited by Kennedy and others may be misleading. "Unfortunately, the evidence cited by Justice Kennedy . . . amounts to very little when it comes to figuring out whether current federal judicial salaries are dissuading fine lawyers from taking seats on the federal bench," wrote one writer for the nonprofit Center for Individual Freedom. "Justice Kennedy's admittedly anecdotal evidence is exceptionally weak when you think about it. He pointed to only ten judges leaving the federal bench in more than a year, and some of those were due to retirements. Remember that is ten out of hundreds of federal judges sitting across these United States."

Between 2004 and 2007, a total of 19 judges left their positions, with several taking higher-paying jobs. Kennedy used the situation of David Levi as an example of how the judiciary is losing its members to the higher pay of other positions. Levi announced in January 2007 that he would leave his federal judicial position in the Eastern District of California in order to become dean at Duke University Law School. However, critics point out that Kennedy and others who complain about the judicial salaries cannot give examples of individuals who refuse to leave private practice for the prestige of a position on the federal bench.

South Dakota Voters Defeat Judicial Accountability Proposal

A ballot initiative in South Dakota that would have held judges civilly and even criminally liable for their actions on the bench was defeated by voters in 2006. Leading this effort was a group based in California that believes that the judges need to be held accountable for their actions on the bench. The group reportedly wanted to test the initiative in several small states before attempting to include the matter on a ballot in California.

A judge is generally immune from any lawsuit that is based on the official actions of the judge. A judge is protected by absolute immunity for an act that is considered judicial in nature, even where that act has been done maliciously or corruptly. This immunity does not extend to all cases in which a judge is a defendant, however. Where a judge serves an executive, legislative, or administrative function, the judge is not entitled to **judicial immunity**, although other types of immunity may apply in those situations. Judicial immunity is often viewed as necessary in order to ensure an independent judiciary.

Critics of the judiciary have taken aim at the concept of judicial immunity, claiming that judges need to be held accountable to improve the performance of judges. One such critic is Ron Branson, a Baptist minister, former prison guard, and former party official with the REPUBLICAN PARTY in the Los Angeles area. He has also been an unsuccessful litigant in state and **federal courts** in California. Branson formed an organization known as Judicial Accountability Initiative Law, or JAIL for Judges, which has focused its attention on enacting state laws that would limit the application of judicial immunity.

JAIL for Judges describes itself as "a single-issue national grassroots organization designed to end the rampant and pervasive judicial corruption in the legal system of the United States." According to the organization, this corruption "can be achieved only through making the Judicial Branch of government answerable and accountable to an **entity** other than itself." Because the judicial branch is not accountable, says the group, judicial immunity leaves the people "without recourse when their inherent rights are violated by judges." Branson first proposed the idea of limiting judicial immunity in California in 1996, but he was only able to gather 5,000

to 6,000 signatures. According to Branson, he lacked the money or help to gain more support.

In 2005, JAIL for Judges drafted a ballot initiative to include its proposal as a constitutional amendment in South Dakota. In order to qualify for a vote, the initiative needed 33,456 votes. With financial backing from a South Dakota businessman, the initiative gained more than the minimum number of votes to place the issue on the ballot. Branson indicated that he hoped that a successful vote in that state would lead to initiatives in other states, including Nevada and Idaho. The text of the South Dakota initiative was nearly identical to the one submitted in California in 1996.

The organization proposed an amendment to the South Dakota Constitution that would create a special **grand jury** to hear complaints about judges. This grand jury would have the power to set aside judicial immunity in specified instances in civil suits brought by parties against whom the judge has ruled. Moreover, this special grand jury could levy fines or issue indictments against judges, who would be subject to criminal proceedings before special trial juries. The initiative would have waived immunity for "any deliberate violation of law, **fraud** or conspiracy, intentional violation of **due process of law**, deliberate disregard of material facts, judicial acts without jurisdiction, blocking of a lawful conclusion of a case, or any deliberate violation of the Constitutions of South Dakota or the United States." The initiative defines "blocking" as "any act that impedes the lawful conclusion of a case, to include unreasonable delay and willful rendering of an unlawful or void judgment or order."

Subsequent to the filing of the South Dakota initiative, the group in South Dakota that supported the initiative separated itself from Branson's group. The South Dakota campaign became known as Amendment E. The spokeswoman for Amendment E referred to Branson as a "clown" and said that he was bad for the campaign. Moreover, she noted that opponents of the South Dakota measure used him to discredit the movement.

Legislators in South Dakota attacked the initiative prior to the November 2006 election. In a unanimous vote, the South Dakota Legislature approved a **concurrent resolution** that denounced the initiative. According to the resolution, supporters of the initiative told South Dakota voters that the initiative simply provided a remedy for intentional judicial misconduct. The resolution further emphasized that the amendment "would actually allow lawsuits against all South Dakota citizen boards, including county commissioners, school board members, city council members, planning and **zoning** board members, township board members, public utilities commissioners, professional licensing board members, jurors, judges, prosecutors, and all other citizen boards. . . ."

Members of the judiciary and legal community also spoke out against the proposal. Ronald M. George, chief justice of the California Supreme Court, said that he viewed the effort as a threat to democratic government. The chief justice of the Missouri Supreme Court made similar statements. The executive director the State Bar of South Dakota called the proposal a "devious attack on both our criminal and civil justice system," noting that it would likely increase litigation associated with the special tribunals.

Supporters of the South Dakota measure conducted a poll two months prior to the November election to determine the level of support for the amendment. According to the poll, 67 percent of those responding said that they would support the initiative. The poll question noted that "[t]he amendment would allow the creation of a citizen's oversight committee or special grand jury which would hear complaints of alleged judicial misconduct against judges." It also referred to the provision that would make a judge ineligible for office if the judge is found guilty of misconduct three times. However, the question did not mention that the measure was an effort to eliminate judicial immunity for bad decisions as well as for intentional misconduct.

Support for the amendment fell apart during the November election. Of 330,387 voters, only 35,640—11 percent— voted in favor of the amendment. Despite allegations by JAIL for Judges that the result occurred through "vote fraud," most commentators agreed that the election represented a devastating defeat for the initiative and called into question the viability of the initiatives in other states.

JURISDICTION

The geographic area over which authority extends; legal authority; the authority to hear and determine causes of action.

Powerex Corp. v. Reliant Energy Services, Inc.

Congress enacted the Foreign Sovereign Immunities Act of 1976 (FSIA), 28 U.S.C.A. §1603, to codify protections and immunities for foreign governments and the entities of those governments. In doing so Congress gave foreign entities the right to remove state lawsuits against them to federal **district court** and to have trials before judges rather then juries. However, a federal district court may decide that it lacks jurisdiction to hear the case if it decides the party did not qualify as a foreign sovereign. The litigation is then returned to the state court. In contrast to standard civil rules, when a district court acts in this way, a federal law, 28 U.S.C.A. §1447(d), prohibits a federal **circuit court** of appeals from reviewing the decision to return the matter to state court. In *Powerex Corp. v. Reliant Energy Services, Inc.*, __U.S.__, 127 S.Ct., __L.Ed.2d __ 2007 WL 1731097 (2007), the U.S. SU-PREME COURT rejected the claim that in FSIA cases §1447(d) did not apply and could be reviewed by an **appellate court**. The Supreme Court found that Congress had made no such exception and it declined to create one despite the problems this created for foreign governments denied federal jurisdiction.

The State of California, along with private individuals and corporations, filed suits in California state courts against a host of energy companies that had allegedly conspired to fix prices. Some of these defendants then filed cross-claims against two federal power agencies, the British Columbia Hydro and Power Authority (BC Hydro), and Powerex Corporation, a wholly owned subsidiary of BC Hydro. BC Hydro itself is wholly owned by the province of British Columbia and therefore qualified as a "foreign state" under the FSIA. The federal agencies, BC Hydro, and Powerex removed the entire case to federal court, citing two different statutes that permitted such removal. The plaintiffs contested the removal, arguing before the federal district court that Powerex was not a foreign state and that the cross-claims were barred by **sovereign immunity**.

The district court ruled that BC Hydro enjoyed sovereign immunity under FSIA and the two federal power agencies were immune from suit in state court. It also ruled that Powerex did not qualify for protection under FSIA. Having come to these conclusions the court found that it had no subject-matter jurisdiction to hear the Powerex issue. Therefore, it remanded the entire case to state court. Powerex appealed to the Ninth Circuit Court of Appeals, contending that the district court had erred when it said it was not a foreign sovereign entitled to FSIA protection. The plaintiffs argued that the appeals court did not have jurisdiction to hear the merits of Powerex's case because §1447(d) barred such appeals. The Ninth Circuit rejected this argument, holding that it had the authority to review substantive issues of law that preceded the remand order. However, it agreed that Powerex was not protected by FSIA.

The Supreme Court reversed the Ninth Circuit's ruling that it had jurisdiction to hear the appeal. In a 7–2 decision the Court declined to rule on the merits of whether Powerex was an organ of a foreign state under FSIA, limiting the ruling to **appellate** jurisdiction over the remand of removed cases to state court. Justice Antonin, writing for the majority, acknowledged that a "mere reading" of §1447(d) would not settle the matter because the Court had previously interpreted it to "cover less than its words alone suggest." These prior decisions precluded review only of remands for lack of subject-matter jurisdiction and for defects in removal procedure. Powerex did not claim any procedural defects, thereby shifting the inquiry to the question of whether there was or was not subject-matter jurisdiction. Powerex contended §1447(d) only applied when there was a defect in subject-matter jurisdiction at the time of removal that made removal jurisdictionally improper. Following this argument, the district court's remand order was not based on a lack of subject-matter jurisdiction since the federal agencies and BC Hydro were statutorily authorized to remove the entire case because of their sovereign status.

Justice Scalia found no merit in this construction of the jurisdiction statutes. His reading of the laws "unambiguously demonstrates that a case can be properly removed and yet suffer from a failing in *subject-matter jurisdiction* that requires remand." In the present case the district had repeatedly stated in denying a stay of remand that a lack of subject-matter jurisdiction required remand. Justice Scalia declined to analyze the jurisdictional grounds at issue because would frustrate the purpose of in preventing delay in the resolution of litigation. Because the line between misclassifying and misapplying grounds was "sometimes elusively thin," the Court held "that when, as here, the District Court relied upon a ground that is colorably characterized as subject-matter jurisdiction, appellate review is barred by §1447(d)." Justice Scalia noted that the Court was aware that erroneous remands would have "undesirable consequences in the FSIA context," but stated that it was up to Congress to exempt this type of case from §1447(d).

Justice STEPHEN BREYER, in a dissenting opinion joined by Justice JOHN PAUL STEVENS, believed the Court should have, as it had done in the past, find an exception to §1447(d). The special status of FSIA and the importance of foreign sovereign immunity provided sufficient bases for such an exception. Turning to the merits of the case, Breyer concluded that Powerex was an organ of the government of British Columbia, and thus entitled to immunity under FSIA.

JURY

In trials, a group of people selected and sworn to inquire into matters of fact and to reach a verdict on the basis of the evidence presented to it.

Uttecht v. Brown

In *Uttecht v. Brown*, the U.S. SUPREME COURT reversed the Ninth **Circuit Court** of Appeals and reinstated the decision of a trial court judge to dismiss a potential juror and uphold the jury's decision to impose a death sentence. The convicted defendant had argued that the potential juror, who expressed equivocal feelings about the death penalty, might have been helpful to the defendant. But the Supreme Court found it well within the proper purview of the trial judge to determine that a potential juror should be dismissed because of possible prejudicial statements in favor of the defendant.

Defendant Cal Coburn Brown had robbed, raped, tortured, then murdered a woman in the state of Washington. Two days later, he robbed, raped, tortured, and attempted to murder a second woman in California, but was apprehended by police. He confessed to the crimes and pleaded guilty in California, for which he received life imprisonment. However, the State of Washington brought him to trial. Following the jury's guilty verdict, Brown was sentenced to death. Both conviction and death sentence were affirmed on appeal to the state Supreme Court of Washington.

On federal habeas appeal, Brown argued that the state trial court had violated his Sixth and FOURTEENTH AMENDMENT rights to a fair trial by excusing three potential jurors (whom the **appellate court** referred to as Jurors X,Y, and Z) for cause. At trial, state prosecutors had moved to dismiss these jurors due to a concern that they could not be impartial in deciding to impose a death sentence.

Back in 1968, the Supreme Court held, in Witherspoon v. Illinois, 391 U.S. 510, that a juror cannot be dismissed from serving simply because he or she has a general moral or religious objection to the death penalty. The relevant question was whether that objection would interfere with an ability to follow the law and responsibility of a juror.

Carrying that holding further, in *Wainwright v. Witt*, 469 U.S. 412 (1985), the Supreme Court ruled that a juror may be excused if his or her views would "prevent or substantially impair" an ability to follow instructions and act in accordance with a juror's responsibilities and oath of service.

In the present case, all three jurors were questioned during *voir dire*) for their views on the death penalty. All three were dismissed. On appeal, the Ninth Circuit panel agreed with the dismissals of Jurors X and Y. But it reversed the dismissal of Juror Z. At voir dire, Juror Z had indicated that he was willing to follow the law, had reservations about the death penalty, but agreed that the death penalty might be appropriate under certain circumstances, such as when a defendant is incorrigible and likely to commit crimes again if released. The jurors were told prior to voir dire that Brown was only eligible for the death penalty or life without possibility of release or parole.

The state prosecutors then moved to remove the juror for cause because he seemed to believe in the death penalty only when there was a chance that the defendant could commit more crimes. Defense counsel was asked and responded "No objection" to the dismissal.

But on appeal, Brown wanted his death sentence set aside, claiming that the dismissal violated his right to a fair trial under the SIXTH AMENDMENT, applicable to states under the Fourteenth Amendment.

Justice Kennedy, in writing for the majority of the Court, summarized the law. Under *Witherspoon*, (above), a criminal defendant had the right to an impartial jury, not one that had been tilted toward capital punishment from selective challenges for cause by state prosecutors. On the other hand, under *Witt*, (above), the state has a strong interest in having jurors who are able to apply capital punishment where state law requires it. In balancing these interests, a juror who is substantially impaired in an ability to impose the death sentence may be excused for cause, but if the juror is not so impaired, removal for cause is impermissible.

In determining whether a potential juror should be dismissed for cause, the trial court bases its judgment in part on the juror's demeanor, said Justice Kennedy. And this judgment is owed deference, under the Anti-terrorism and Effective Death Penalty Act of 1996 (AEDPA), 28 USC §2254, AEDPA. Under AEDPA, courts may grant federal habeas relief only if a state court's decision is contrary to, or involves an unreasonable application of, "clearly established federal law as determined by the Supreme Court of the United States."

The trial court is in the best position to judge a potential juror's demeanor. This is a critical factor in assessing the juror's attitude and qualifications to serve on a capital jury, and that assessment must be given deference.

In the present case, Juror Z clearly appeared confused about his responsibilities as a juror. Further, his attitude toward capital punishment could have prevented him from returning a death sentence under the facts of the case. Review of the trial record clearly showed that he was told at least four times that Brown could not be released from prison, and therefore posed no threat for **recidivism**. The juror stated six times that he could follow the law. But he continued to give equivocal statements about imposing the death penalty only if Brown might be released and could commit crimes again. The state properly challenged Juror Z on these grounds, and defense counsel failed to object. The trial court's dismissal for cause was proper.

The Court held that the Ninth Circuit had erred in holding that the state courts' affirming the dismissal of Juror Z was contrary to, or involved an unreasonable application of, "clearly established federal law as determined by the Supreme Court of the United States." It reversed and remanded, effectively upholding the death sentence for Brown.

There was strong dissent from Justice Stevens, joined by Justices Souter, Ginsburg, and Breyer. The dissent felt that the juror's demeanor, even if equivocal, could not overcome his actual responses during voir dire. The best reading of his responses was that, while he had reservations about the death penalty, he would consider it and impose it where appropriate. His mention of the possibility of recidivism, or repeat offenses, was only an example. Further, under Washington law, defense counsel's failure to object did not serve to bar his ability to raise the issue on appeal.

MCCONNELL, JOHN MICHAEL

John Michael "Mike" McConnell was sworn in as Director of Nation Intelligence on February 13, 2007. McConnell was born on July 26, 1943, in Greenville, South Carolina. He earned a bachelor's degree from Furman University in 1966, majoring in Economics. McConnell later earned advanced degrees from George Washington University (MPA, 1986) and Defense Intelligence College (PhD, 1992). McConnell joined the U.S. Navy, where he advanced to numerous positions, culminating in his becoming a vice admiral.

McConnell moved to the Pentagon in 1990, serving as the intelligence director for Joint Chiefs of Staff until 1992. Following that post, he became the director of the National Security Agency, serving in that position from 1992-96. He then left government service to take a position with the consulting firm Booz Allen Hamilton, specializing in the areas of national security and intelligence work. He also served as chairman of the Intelligence and National Security Alliance, an independent lobbying group.

That firm was at the heart of a controversial program to mine data from U.S. citizens for anti-terrorism purposes called "Total Information Awareness." McConnell was a key player in getting the program running, a program decried by many as a serious threat to personal privacy. The cancellation of the program came after Democratic congressmen questioned the privacy issues it ignited.

When President George W. Bush nominated McConnell to succeed John Negroponte as Director of National Intelligence, many pointed to this affair as a reason to regard him as a questionable selection. Despite these questions, McConnell was confirmed as Director on February 13, 2007. Afterwards, in a article printed in the July/August 2007 edition of *Foreign Affairs*, he wrote of U.S. intelligence:

Although the United States is improving the nuts and bolts of its intelligence system, it must not lose sight of the strategic conditions that will determine the ultimate success of those efforts. The United States must comprehend the profound threats of the times and position its institutions to meet those challenges. The intelligence community understands the threats posed by

Michael McConnell.
AP IMAGES

JOHN MICHAEL MCCONNELL

1966: Earned BA from Furman University

1990: Intelligence Director of Joint Chiefs of Staff

1992–96: Director of NSA

1996: Joined Booz Allen Hamilton consulting firm

2007: Confirmed as National Director of Intelligence

terrorists inside and outside the United States, nuclear proliferators, and rogue and failed states. Now, it must set its priorities to meet these threats.

MILITARY LAW

The body of laws, rules, and regulations developed to meet the needs of the military. It encompasses service in the military, the constitutional rights of service members, the military criminal justice system, and the international law of armed conflict.

U.S. Soldiers Guilty of Murder and Rape in Iraq

President GEORGE W. BUSH referred to the 2004 scandal involving abuse and mistreatment of Iraqi prisoners at Baghdad's now infamous Abu Ghraib facility as the "biggest mistake" made by the United States in Iraq. Little did he know that another horror was looming. In July 2006, six U.S. soldiers were charged in the rape and murder of an innocent 14-year-old Iraqi girl and the murder of her entire family. The March 12, 2006 incident took place in Mahmoudiya, a little town 20 miles south of Baghdad.

The soldiers, all from the 101st Airborne Division based in Fort Campbell, Kentucky, faced court-martial after an Article 32 hearing was held in Baghdad (parallel to a **grand jury** or **preliminary hearing** in civilian law). Specialist James P Barker, 23; Sergeant Paul Cortez, 23; Private First Class (Pfc) Jesse V. Spielman, 21; and Pfc. Bryan L. Howard, 19, were charged with participation in the rape and murder of the girl and her family. A fifth soldier, Sgt. Anthony W. Yribe, was charged with dereliction of duty for failing to report the incident.

Additionally, all five were charged with conspiring with former Pfc. Steven D. Green to commit the atrocities. Green, who was considered the ringleader in the incident, was discharged from the Army in May 2006 because of an "anti-social personality disorder" prior to his superiors knowing of his involvement. He was separately charged in a civilian federal court in Kentucky.

The sordid details of the incident were brought forward in the soldiers' own statements to military authorities. In their own words, they told of drinking whiskey, playing cards, and hitting golf balls when Green suggested they go to a house near the checkpoint where they were stationed and rape the young girl that lived there. They took the time to change into dark clothing and cover their faces, even providing a two-way radio for one of them who served as a lookout. The four remaining soldiers then entered the house. One rounded up a five-year-old child and the parents, herding them all into a bedroom. Then while one soldier pushed the young girl down, the other held her hands as they switched positions and raped her.

At this point, according to their statements, they heard gunshots coming from the bedroom. Green allegedly exited from the bedroom in an agitated state, announced he had killed the family, laid down the AK-47 he had been carrying, then raped the girl while another held her down. He then picked up the gun and shot her several times. Green then allegedly went into the kitchen. When he emerged from that room, he told the soldiers to get out of the house because he had opened a propane tank and the house would explode. One of the soldiers then poured kerosene from a lamp onto the girl's body to hide evidence. One of the soldiers later burned all the bloodstained clothes they were wearing and threw the AK-47 into a nearby canal.

The incident was originally reported as the work of insurgents. However, Pfc. Justin Watt, a soldier not connected with the murders, testified at the Article 32 hearing that a fellow soldier, Yribe, confided to him that Green had been bragging about the rape and killings. Watt then asked Howard what had happened, and Howard confirmed the plan to rape the girl and his role as the lookout. Howard told Watt that when he saw a Humvee, he radioed the others frantically, but when they returned from the house, their clothes were covered with blood. Watt then pieced the information together and reported it to authorities. Yribe was charged with dereliction of duty for failing to report the incident. The others faced court-martial and the possibility of a death sentence.

At the start of his court martial in November 2006, Sgt. James Barker pleaded guilty to rape and murder, and agreed to cooperate with prosecutors by testifying against the others. He did not receive the death penalty but was sentenced to 90 years in military prison with the possibility of parole in 20 years.

Not until February 2007 did the second soldier, Sgt. Paul Cortez, plead guilty at the start of his court martial to four counts of murder, rape, and conspiracy to rape. He was sentenced to 100 years in military prison. In March 2007, Pfc. Bryan Howard (the "lookout") pleaded guilty to being an accessory to the rape and murders as well as conspiracy to obstruct justice for lying to authorities and superiors about the atrocity. He received 27 months in military prison.

Also in March 2007, the court martial of Pfc. Jesse Spielman was delayed until July 23, 2007 at the request of defense counsel, who ostensibly received "new information" regarding witnesses. There was no **direct evidence** that Spielman participated in the rape or murders, but the other soldiers identified him as being present and being the one who burned their clothes and threw the gun into the canal. Also pending was the civilian court trial of ex-soldier Steven Green, the alleged key player in the incident, in the U.S. **District Court** for the Western District of Kentucky, Case No. 3:06-MJ-230-R.

When asked by a military judge why he participated in the shocking events, Spec. Barker, who wept during his closing statement, responded that the violence in Iraq had had left him "angry and mean." He accepted responsibility for the rape and killings, but told the judge, "I hated Iraqis, your honor. They can smile at you, then shoot you in the face without even thinking about it." Pfc. Watt (who had reported information to authorities) had also testified that the stressful conditions the soldiers experienced were affecting everyone. He said they had been living in the basement of a "dilapidated, abandoned water treatment facility" and had gone 30 days without being able to take a shower. "I was going to get a memorial tattoo of all the guys [who were killed], but there's not enough room on my arm," he told CNN reporters.

The Military Commissions Act of 2006

In Hamdan v. Rumsfeld, 126 S.Ct. 2749 (2005), the U.S. SUPREME COURT held that neither the U.S. Constitution (including the inherent powers of the Executive) nor any act of Congress expressly authorized the type of "military commissions" created by the Bush Administration to try detained enemy combatants for war crimes. Absent that express authorization, the commissions had to comply with the ordinary laws of the United States and the laws of war, including parts of the Geneva Convention and the **statutory** UNIFORM CODE OF MILITARY JUSTICE (UCMJ). However, nothing in the Court's decision gave detainees direct access to **federal courts**; they need only have access to a fair and impartial hearing in a **tribunal** constitutionally authorized by Congress and proceeding with certain due process guarantees.

In response to the Court's ruling, Congress enacted the U.S. Military Commissions Act, Pub. L. 109-366, 120 Stat. 2600, on September 29, 2006 (the "Act"). (President Bush signed it on October 10, 2006.) Its stated purpose was to "facilitate bringing to justice terrorists and other unlawful enemy combatants through full and fair trials by military commissions, and for other purposes."

The Act expressly provides the President with the authority not only to establish military commissions, but also to determine what constitutes breaches of the Geneva Conventions other than those already constituting "grave breaches." Further, the Act expressly prohibits U.S. courts from using foreign or international sources of law to interpret provisions of 18 USC §2441 on war crimes, —grave breaches of the Geneva Convention.

Importantly, the Act specifically defines an "unlawful enemy combatant" as a person who engaged in hostilities or purposefully and materially supported such acts against the United States or our allies who is not an enemy combatant (including a member of the Taliban, al Qaeda, or associated groups); or someone who, after the date of enactment of the Act, was determined to be an unlawful enemy combatant by a Combatant Status Review Tribunal or another competent tribunal established pursuant to the authority of the President or of the Secretary of Defense.

Conversely, and equally importantly, a "lawful enemy combatant" is defined as a member of regular forces of a state party engaged in hostilities against the United States; or a member of a militia, volunteer corps, or organized resistance movement belonging to a state party participating in hostilities under a responsible command, wearing a distinctive sign recognizable at a distance, carrying arms openly, and following "the law of war," or a member of a regular armed force professing allegiance to a government engaged in such hostilities, but not recognized by the United States.

Another key provision of the Act is that it specifically exempts military commissions from having to follow a number of requirements found in the UCMJ. Unlawful enemy combatants are not permitted to avail themselves of speedy trials, nor can they invoke the Geneva Convention as a source of rights. Further, no precedental weight is to be accorded findings, holdings, interpretations, or other determinations in military commissions.

A less publicized provision follows the tradition of allowing military commissions (as was done in WORLD WAR II and is currently done in most modern European criminal courts and the International Criminal Court) to consider **hearsay** evidence or information gathered without a search warrant. These may be used as admissible evidence if the military judge determines they have **probative** value.

One of the more controversial provisions of the Act is its amendment of the federal *habeas corpus* statute, 28 USC §2241. The new subsection (e) prevents courts from exercising jurisdiction to consider applications for writs of habeas **corpus** filed by or on behalf of aliens detained by the United States who have been determined to be detained as enemy combatants or those who are awaiting such determination.

However, the Act does provide some protections, including the prohibition of **cruel and unusual punishment**, including flogging, branding, marking, or tattooing, as well as the use of either single or double restraining irons, except for safe custody. Finally, the Act provides double **jeopardy** protection for military commission proceedings.

Almost immediately upon its enactment, legal challenges to some of the Act's provisions were filed. On April 2, 2007, the U.S. Supreme Court declined **certiorari** in two cases involving Guantanamo Bay detainees seeking habeas corpus review of their detainment (not permitted under the Act) in Boumedienne v. Bush, and Odah v. United States. Three weeks later, on April 30, 2007, the Court denied certiorari of two more Guantanamo Bay detainees in Hamdan v. Gates, and Khadr v. Bush. These latter cases had a new twist. The same Salim Ahmed Hamdan who had prevailed in the 2005 case of Hamdan v. Rumsfeld, (see above) was now facing the possibility of being tried under the new Act. This time he attempted to challenge the *constitutionality* of Congress' decision to deny habeas relief under the Act. His lawyers unsuccessfully argued that the new tribunal system was substantially similar to the old one. As of June 2007, several cases were still pending in lower courts in which detainees were challenging their status as "enemy combatants" under the Act.

MONOPOLY

An economic advantage held by one or more persons or companies deriving from the exclusive power to carry on a particular business or trade or to manufacture and sell a particular item, thereby suppressing competition and allowing such persons or companies to raise the price of a product or service substantially above the price that would be established by a free market.

FTC Rules That Rambus Illegally Acquired Monopoly Power

The FEDERAL TRADE COMMISSION in 2006 ruled that Rambus Inc., a technology licensing company, had acquired **monopoly** power related to computer memory technologies. The case arose from the activities of Rambus during the 1990s when Rambus convinced various trade groups to adopt a standard technology for memory used in computers and other devices without informing those groups that Rambus owned the patents for those technologies. Despite the ruling, however, the FTC withdrew part of its order related to penalties that it imposed on Rambus, and the company said it would appeal the remainder of the order.

Two developers founded Rambus in 1990 as a technology licensing company. Rambus specializes in the invention and design of high-speed chip interfaces that are used in computers and other electronic devices. More specifically, the company designs, develops, licenses, and markets the chip technology to enhance performance of the computers and other devices. Rambus licenses its technology to semiconductor companies to use in their products. As of 2006, Rambus owned the rights to 480 issued patents, and the company had 485 pending patent applications. During 2006, Rambus earned $194.2 million in revenues, up 24 percent from the previous year.

Rambus has been involved with the development of dynamic random access memory (DRAM). This standard has been a competitor with another type of memory, known as static random access memory, or SRAM, for much of the past two decades. Early in the 1990s, the company became involved with the development of its own DRAM standard, known as Rambus DRAM or RDRAM. Rambus hoped that this would become the industry standard. This did not occur, however, and manufacturers instead resorted to a standard-setting industry body known as the Joint Electronic Device Engineering Council, or JEDEC, to develop the next-generation technology for DRAM.

Throughout much of the decade, JEDEC worked to establish newer standards. These efforts eventually resulted in the development of synchronous dynamic random access memory, or SDRAM, which was adopted as an industry standard. Rambus participated in the JEDEC DRAM process along with the DRAM manufacturers. During this process, Rambus' patent applications for its own DRAM technologies were still pending, and the company changed its patent applications to incorporate the changes that were being discussed as part of the JEDEC process. Others that were involved in this process were not aware that Rambus had made these changes.

Once the standards had been finalized, various manufacturers began using them in their memory chips. In 2000, Rambus sued these manufacturers, claiming patent infringement. In one case involving a German DRAM manufacturer, a jury in the U.S. **District Court** for the Eastern District of Virginia decided that Rambus had committee **fraud** for failing to disclose its patents and patent applications related to the SDRAM standards. On appeal, the Federal **Circuit Court** of Appeals disagreed, ruling that Rambus was not required to disclose its patents. The **appellate court** reviewed the JEDEC's disclosure policy and determined that Rambus was under no duty to disclose the changes in the patent applications. Thus, according to the court, even if Rambus' actions may have been unethical, these actions did not constitute a breach of duty. *Rambus Inc. v. Infineon Technologies, A.G.*, 318 F.3d 1081 (Fed. Cir. 2003).

Chip manufacturers in 2002 raised a different argument when they filed a complaint with the FTC in 2002. The manufacturer argued that the Rambus had engaged in monopolistic behavior in violation of federal law. An administrative law judge that reviewed the case ruled in favor of Rambus, reaching a conclusion similar to the one in the Federal Circuit. According to the judge, Rambus was only required to disclose the existence of certain "essential" patents that could be read onto the JEDEC DRAM standard. Because Rambus did not have any such patents or patent applications, the judge ruled in favor of the company.

On August 2, 2006, the FTC reversed the judge's decision, finding that Rambus had acted deceptively, and in doing so, acquired monopoly power. *In re Rambus*, No. 9302, 2006 WL 2330117 (Aug. 2, 2006). The commission determined that Rambus misled other JEDEC committee members to believe that the company was not seeking patents that would cover the technologies. However, Rambus was secretly amending its applications so that they would

Rambus Inc. headquarters in August 2006.
AP IMAGES

cover the technology that was being discussed in the JEDEC committee meetings. "'Rambus's conduct was calculated to mislead JEDEC members by fostering the belief that Rambus neither had, nor was seeking, relevant patents that would be enforced against JEDEC-compliant products," the commission wrote. "Rambus's silence, in the face of members' expectations of disclosure, created a misimpression that Rambus would not obtain and/or enforce such patents."

Despite the ruling, the FTC was more lenient than some commentators expected when the commission levied penalties on Rambus in February 2007. The commission established limits on the amount of royalties that Rambus could receive for some of its older chip designs, but it did not place limitations on designs that were developed after the JEDEC process had concluded. The February ruling also placed bookkeeping and record-keeping requirements on Rambus to ensure that the company was complying with the order. Despite the fact that the order was not as harsh as expected, Rambus officials expressed disappointment, claiming that the commission disregarded part of the record when reaching its decision.

About one month after issuing its ruling, the FTC modified the order to allow Rambus to continue to collect royalties for all past uses of the DRAM technology. Under an order issued in March, the FTC limited the amount of royalties that Rambus can collect on future uses of the technology. Rambus officials indicated that they were satisfied with modified part of the order but would appeal the rest of the February order that remained intact.

Steven Avery is escorted out of court by a policeman in January 2006.

AP IMAGES

MURDER

The unlawful killing of another human being without justification or excuse.

Wisconsin Man Exonerated Through DNA Evidence Subsequently Convicted of Murder

Steven Avery, a Wisconsin man who was exonerated in 2003 after spending 18 years in prison for attempted murder and sexual assault, returned to prison in 2007 after being convicted of the murder of a photographer. Even more disturbing was the charge against Avery's 16-year-old nephew for participating in the murder. The case represented the first time in U.S. history that a person has been convicted of murder after being freed through DNA testing.

Avery was convicted in December 1985 with the attempted murder and sexual assault of a 36-year-old woman on a beach in Manitowoc County in Wisconsin. At his trial, 16 alibi witnesses testified on behalf of Avery, but a jury still found him guilty based on the testimony of a single eyewitness. Avery received a 32-year sentence in 1986. He appealed his conviction, but the Wisconsin court of appeals affirmed his conviction and the Wisconsin Supreme Court refused to review it.

Ten years after the conviction, Avery requested DNA testing of fingernail scrapings taken from the victim. Although the tests showed genetic markers that were consistent with both Avery and the victim, and so the laboratory that conducted the test could not ex-

clude Avery as the perpetrator. At the same time, however, the tests revealed the DNA of person other than Avery. Despite this evidence, Wisconsin courts refused to order a new trial based on this new evidence.

Avery's case caught the attention of Wisconsin Innocence Project, which was founded in 1998 at the University of Wisconsin's law school. This project investigates certain cases where a person may have been wrongly convicted of a crime by working to complete testing of DNA evidence from various cases. Lawyers working for this project obtained a court order to test one of the hairs that had been collected from the victim using technology that was more powerful than the technology used in 1995. These tests showed that the hair belonged to Gregory A. Allen, who was then serving a 60-year sentence for a sexual assault committed after the Manitowoc woman was assaulted.

Avery was released in September 2003 after this evidence proved his innocence. He was the third person in state history to be exonerated of a crime through DNA evidence and the 137th person to be freed nationwide. He was the first person who was freed through efforts of the Wisconsin Innocence Project, and his story and photograph were prominent on the project's website. Avery's story received extensive coverage by newspapers and television stations in Milwaukee and elsewhere in Wisconsin.

According to several news reports, Avery had a difficult time adjusting to life after prison. Under Wisconsin law, he was entitled to receive only $25,000 in compensation for the time he spent in prison. His wife at the time of his conviction later divorced him, and he was estranged from his two youngest children. He returned to work at his family's auto salvage yard, but admitted in newspaper accounts in 2003 that he frequently would become frustrated and angered about his situation. He even talked about thoughts of returning to prison.

In October 2005, Avery was questioned in connection with the disappearance of Teresa Halbach, a photographer who worked for *Auto Trader* magazine. Halbach had an appointment to take a picture of a car at Avery's home on the day of her disappearance. Five days after officials questioned Avery, police found Halbach's car hidden underneath brush at Avery's family salvage yard. Police also found charred remains of a body on Avery's property. On November 15, DNA tests showed that the remains belonged to Halbach, and Avery was charged with the murder.

Avery was charged with first-degree intentional homicide, which carries an automatic life sentence. Police found the DNA of both Avery and Halbach in Halbach's car. Officers also found the key to Halbach's car in Avery's possession and with Avery's DNA on it. Due to the circumstances of the case, much of the state of Wisconsin followed the case closely. The Wisconsin Innocence Project eventually removed most of the pictures of and references to Avery, later saying that the nature of the story was such that the organization did not want to upset the victim's family.

In March 2006, prosecutors charged 16-year-old Brendan Dassey, Avery's nephew, with helping Avery to sexually assault and kill Halbach. According to the criminal complaint filed against Dassey, the boy received a note from Avery when the former returned home from school. He went to Avery's trailer, where he heard screams from a woman inside. Avery allegedly asked Dassey if the boy wanted to have sex with the woman, and the boy then sexually assaulted Halbach. Subsequently, Avery and Dassey stabbed and then strangled Halbach, before finally shooting her at least 10 times. She was burned with other debris behind the trailer. Avery covered her car at the salvage yard, removed the license plates, and hid the key to the car.

Avery was convicted on the intentional homicide charge on March 18, 2007. He became the second person in U.S. history to be convicted of a serious crime after being exonerated through DNA testing. He was also the first person to be subsequently convicted of killing another person. The jury additionally convicted him of being a felon in possession of a firearm, but acquitted him of mutilating Halbach's corpse.

In October 2004, Avery filed suit against officials in Manitowoc County, asking for $36 million for his wrongful conviction. He filed suit in the U.S. **District Court** in Milwaukee. He later settled the case for $400,000, though the proceeds he received went to lawyers fees for the homicide trial. Avery claimed that he would be exonerated again, and his lawyers filed a motion for a new trial.

Virginia Tech Massacre

Virginia Tech is the commonly-used name for Virginia Polytechnic Institute and State University, located in Blacksburg, Virginia, southwest of Roanoke, and home to more than 25,000 full-time students. On the morning of April 16, 2007, a deranged student, Seung-Hui Cho, opened fire in a dormitory and crowded class-

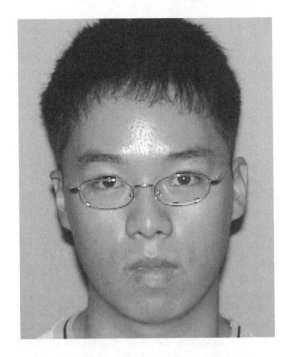

Cho Seung-Hui, the shooter in the Virginia Tech shootings of April 16, 2007.
AP IMAGES

room on Virginia Tech's campus, killing 27 students and five faculty members before committing suicide.

Although the funerals and memorial services took place in the ensuing weeks following the unspeakable tragedy, the legal fallout was just beginning. Could this have been prevented? What did school officials know, or should have known, about Cho's medical and/or mental health history? What about campus security? What about emergency warning systems? What about gun control, on campus and in general?

In the aftermath of the incident, details emerged from several witnesses that raised multiple issues and questions. The killings had occurred in two separate incidents on campus. The first occurred at approximately 7:15 a.m. in one of the dormitories. Two students, one male and one female, were fatally shot. The second attack occurred more than two and a half hours later, when Cho entered classrooms in Norris Hall, a science and engineering building. Thirty more people were killed in or near the building, and several more wounded.

Police could not immediately identify Cho as the gunman, as his unidentified body lay among those of victims at the scene after he apparently shot himself in the head. Two handguns were found near his body and investigators immediately began tracing purchase records.

Following the initial shock of the incident, Wendell Flinchum, campus chief of police, held a news conference that evening, under heavy fire to explain why authorities did not act to secure the campus in the two-plus hours following the two dormitory fatalities. Chief Flinchum responded that campus officials initially thought the dormitory shooting was an isolated "domestic" incident, suggesting that it involved people who knew each other. The campus was not shut down because authorities believed the attacker may have left the campus or even the state. However, the involved building and the immediate crime scene were secured. Flinchum told *New York Times* reporters, "We acted on the best information we had at the time."

Unfortunately, Cho, a disgruntled student with prior mental health problems, had not left the campus or the state. It was later learned that in the two-hour interim between shootings, he video-taped a violent message for the media and loaded bullet magazines for the two automatic high-powered guns he brought with him. Investigators also learned that Cho had taken the time to chain the doors shut in Norris Hall before opening fire inside several classrooms.

At 9:45 a.m., campus police received another 911 call about shootings at Norris Hall, just as university officials were meeting to discuss the earlier dormitory shootings. By the time officers arrived at Norris Hall, the shootings were over and Cho was among the dead. Ballistics analyses later confirmed that the two separate incidents were related, and that Cho was the gunman in both.

In the aftermath of the killings and questions raised, Virginia State Governor Timothy M. Kaine announced that the state would form a panel commission to investigate Virginia Tech's response to the massacre, as well as the circumstances that might have caused it, including Cho's mental health history. He promised the public that the investigation would be fair, impartial, and free of political interference. He named eight experts with various backgrounds in academia, law enforcement, mental health, psychology, and victim services to the panel.

But almost immediately, new questions were raised about the panel's impartiality, muddled with real or perceived conflicts of interest. At the first meeting, a retired state police superintendent who was the panel's chairman held a private meeting with state and federal law enforcement officials, then announced to panel members that they "should be proud" of the response by authorities on the day of the incident, suggesting favorable bias even before the panel's work was done. By June 2007, several victims' families had organized and released a statement to the media, complaining about their lack of representation on the panel and other issues. The statement, released to Associated Press reporters, was presented to the review board and said in part, "We are angry about being ostracized from a government-chartered panel investigating a government-sponsored university, and about how the university has used the names and images of our loved ones to raise millions of dollars without any consultation."

Meanwhile, the media was criticized for focusing on Cho, his background, and his story, while the 32 victims remained virtually nameless and faceless in news stories. One psychiatrist made a public plea on national television, urging the media to stop immortalizing the gunman and instead tell the stories of victims. Cho's violent messages and self-promoting video images soon began to disappear from cover pages and Internet web sites.

In early July 2007, panel members announced that they had received tape recordings and transcripts from Cho's mental health hearing in December 2005. It was revealed that the judge conducting the hearing ruled that Cho was a danger to himself but not to others, and ordered Cho to seek treatment; there was no indication that Cho had ever sought treatment. He had been referred to Virginia Tech's Cook Counseling Center. However, the center did not accept "ordered" treatment of patients and was not required by state law to report to courts whether patients ever received treatments. Cho's personal medical records had not been released, but court records and transcripts were.

In early July 2007, Governor Kaine announced the appointment of Kenneth R. Feinberg, the Washington lawyer who directed the federal compensation program for relatives of victims of the September 11, 2001 terrorist attacks, to oversee the $7 million in private donations used to set up the Hokie Spirit Memorial Fund. Feinberg stated that approximately $1 million of the total donations had been designated by donors toward specific uses, but the balance would go to general use. The school announced it would use $3.2 million of the fund to establish 32 separate $100,000 funds to honor each of the victims. The remaining money was to be distributed to victims and their families. Feinberg announced that he would establish eligibility criteria by the end of July. Victims were also likely eligible for funds through the state's compensation fund for victims of violent crimes.

NATIVE AMERICAN RIGHTS

San Manuel Indian Bingo and Casino v. National Labor Relations Board

Though American Indian Tribes are recognized by the federal government as sovereign entities, Congress and the courts have created exceptions that allow state and federal governments to regulate certain activities on tribal lands. With the explosive growth of Indian casinos, a host of legal issues concerning the application of business and labor rights have come into the courts. In *San Manuel Indian Bingo and Casino v. National Labor Relations Board*, 475 F.3d 1306(D.C. Cir. 2007), the **Circuit Court** of Appeals for the DISTRICT OF COLUMBIA ruled that that the National Labor Relations Act (NLRA) 29 U.S.C.A. §§ 151 *et seq.* applies to employment at Indian casinos.

The San Manuel Band of Serrano Mission Indians opened a casino on its reservation in San Bernardino County, California in 1986. The tribe, which has endure decades of poverty and unemployment, soon had millions of dollars of gambling profits that it could distribute for the benefit of the tribe. Unlike other Indian casinos, San Manuel does not contract with an independent management company to operate the casino, choosing instead to have tribal members work in key positions. The casino, which is about an hour's drive from Los Angeles, employed many non-Indians and drew most of its customers from outside the reservation.

In the late 1990s, two rival unions, the Communications Workers of America (CWA) and the Hotel Employees and Restaurant Employees International Union (HERE), set their sights on organizing casino employees. In 1999, HERE filed an unfair labor practice charge with the National Labor Relations Board (NLRB), the **administrative agency** that enforces the NLRA. HERE charged that the casino had interfered with their attempt to organize workers, using threats and coercion against casino workers. In addition, HERE alleged that the casino had thrown its support to CWA by allowing CWA representatives access to casino property. The casino permitted CWA to place a trailer on its property to use as its headquarters and to hand out leaflets and talk to employees during working hours. CWA also alleged that casino security guards denied its representatives equal access to employees.

The tribe sought to dismiss the complaint, contending that Indian reservations are not subject to the NLRA. The NLRB issued a ruling in 2004 that the tribal casino was subject to the NLRA and that the tribe had committed an unfair labor practice. It ordered the tribe to give access to HERE and to post notices in the casino describing the rights of employees under the NLRA. The tribe then petitioned the Circuit Court for the District Columbia, which reviews NLRB appeals, arguing that the NLRB had no jurisdiction to hear the case.

A three-judge panel of the appeals court upheld the NLRB decision. Judge Janice Rogers Brown, writing for the court, acknowledged that the case was complicated because of issues involving tribal sovereignty, congressional intent, and the lack of clear legal precedent. The key issue was tribal sovereignty and how it related to the NLRA. The court posed two questions: would application of the NLRA violate federal

Players at the San Miguel Indian Bingo and Casino play slot machines, June 2006.
AP IMAGES

Indian law by impinging upon protected tribal sovereignty, and, if the answer to the first question was negative, does the term "employer" in the NLRA apply to Indian tribal governments operating commercial enterprises? Judge Brown reviewed a host of conflicting decision on tribal sovereignty and concluded that it was "far from absolute." Tribal sovereignty was strongest when explicitly established by treaty or when the tribal government acted on matters of concern only to tribal members. Judge Brown stated that the "determinative consideration appears to be the extent to which application of the general law will constrain the tribe with respect to its governmental functions." In this case impairment of tribal sovereignty was slight because the operation of a casino was not a traditional element of self-government and because most of the casino's employees were not tribal members and they lived off the reservation. Applying the NLRA to the casino would not impair tribal sovereignty.

Having removed the sovereignty issue, the court reviewed whether the word "employer" in the NLRA applied to Indian governments operating commercial enterprises. The NLRA does not define "employer," but does list certain specific entities that are not employers. Judge Brown noted the common definition of the word meant a person who controls and directs a worker under a contract and pays the worker's salary or wages. Using this definition the casino clearly was an employer; in its brief the casino

even referred to its workers as employees. Finally, there was nothing in the law governing Indian gaming that foreclosed application of the NLRA to tribal enterprises.

NEGLIGENCE

Norfolk Southern Railway Company v. Sorrell

Working for a railroad in the early Twentieth Century was a very dangerous occupation. Workers injured on the job faced numerous legal hurdles if they attempted to sue railroads for negligence. A Nineteenth-Century legal doctrine called **assumption of risk** held that workers who knowingly went to work in a dangerous industry could not sue their employers for damages. Even if a court of law ignored the assumption of risk doctrine a worker could lose if the employer proved that the worker contributed to the negligent action. It did not matter if the employee was only 5 percent negligent because such a finding barred the worker from recovering any damages. Public concern over number and severity of railroad employee uncompensated injuries led Congress in 1908 to enact the Federal Employers' Liability Act (FELA), 45 U.S.C.A. §§ 51-60. FELA established a compensation scheme for railroad workplace injuries and pre-empted state tort remedies. The common-law assumption of risk doctrine was abolished and contributory negligence was replaced with comparative negligence. Workers who were negligent would have the damages award reduced by the proportion of their fault. FELA provisions have been litigated for almost one hundred years and the Supreme Court issued another FELA ruling in *Norfolk Southern Railway Company v. Sorrell*, __U.S.__, 127 S.Ct. 799, 166 L.Ed.2d 638 (2007), holding that the state of Missouri had improperly provided a more lenient causation standard for railroad negligence than for employee comparative negligence. The Court ruled that the FELA causation standard must be the same for both categories of negligence.

Timothy Sorrell injured his back and neck while working as a trackman for the Norfolk Southern Railway Company. In 1999 Sorrell was working for Norfolk in Indiana, driving a dump truck filled with asphalt to be used to repair railroad crossings. While driving on a gravel road between crossings another Norfolk dump truck approached Sorrell's truck. Sorrell and the driver of the other truck gave different accounts of what happened next but Sorrell's truck veered off the road and tipped on it side. Sorrell testified that the other driver forced him off the road, while the other driver said Sorrell drove his truck into the ditch.

In 2002 Sorrell filed suit in Missouri state court under FELA, which makes railroads liable to their employees for injuries "resulting in whole or part from the negligence" of the railroad. Sorrell alleged that Norfolk had failed to provide him with a reasonably safe place to work and that its negligence caused his injuries. Norfolk countered by claiming Sorrell's own negligence caused his injuries. When the time came for the judge to issue jury instructions a legal controversy arose. Under Missouri law a jury was to apply two different standards of causation to railroad and employee contributory negligence. The instructions directed the jury to find an employee contributory negligent if the employee was negligent and his negligence "directly contributed to cause" the injury. The jury was also instructed to find the railroad negligent if the railroad was negligent and its negligence contributed "in whole or in part" to the injury. Norfolk objected to these instructions, arguing that the same causation standard should be applied to employee and employer, for the standard applied to the railroad was a "much more exacting" standard. The judge overruled the objection and Sorrell recovered $1.5 million in damages. Norfolk appealed but the Missouri Court of Appeals affirmed the dual causation

standards. After the Missouri Supreme Court rejected Norfolk's petition to appeal Norfolk petitioned the U.S. SUPREME COURT. Norfolk argued that Missouri was the only jurisdiction to apply different standards. The Supreme Court granted review.

The Supreme Court, in a unanimous decision, overturned the Missouri appeals court decision. Chief Justice JOHN ROBERTS, writing for the Court (four justices joined in concurring opinions), rejected Norfolk's attempt to broaden the question before the Court to include what the standard of causation under FELA should be. Norfolk not only sought to enlarge the question but it took a position that was contrary to the position it took in the Missouri courts. In the lower courts Norfolk urged that the less rigorous negligence standard applied to railroads be applied to employee negligence. Before the U.S. Supreme Court Norfolk urged the Court to apply the more rigorous contributory negligence standard to the railroad's negligence as well. Chief Roberts concluded that "we should stick to the question on which **certiorari** was sought and granted," for the Court is reluctant to let parties "smuggle additional questions into the case."

Turning to the issue of dual standards of negligence, Chief Justice Roberts agreed with Norfolk that Missouri was the only jurisdiction to apply differing causation standards in a FELA action. Though it was possible that "everyone is out of step except Missouri," Roberts found that Congress did not intend to allow disparate causation standards. Common-law principles that have not been expressly rejected under FELA are given "great weight" by the Court in analyzing issues. In this case the **common law** applied the same causation to defendant and plaintiff negligence and FELA "did not expressly depart from this approach." Roberts thought that allowing more than one standard of causation would have been a "peculiar approach for Congress to take in FELA." Moreover, as a practical matter it would be difficult to reduce damages "in proportion" to the employee's negligence if "the relevance of each party's negligence to the injury is measured by a different standard of causation." It would be simpler for the jury to apportion negligence if "the jury compares like with like-apples to apples." Other courts supported this position, leading the Supreme Court to reject Missouri's "idiosyncratic approach" that "unduly muddies what may, to a jury, be already murky waters."

PASSPORTS

A document that indicates permission granted by a sovereign to its citizen to travel to foreign countries and return and requests foreign governments to allow that citizen to pass freely and safely.

New U.S. Passport Requirements

The Western Hemisphere Travel Initiative (WHTI) was enacted by Congress as part of the Intelligence Reform and Terrorism Prevention Act of 2004. Its primary purpose was to strengthen border security and yet facilitate legal entry into the United States for citizens and legitimate international visitors. WHTI directives, requiring U.S. citizens to have passports when entering the United States from Canada, Mexico, and the Caribbean by air, became effective on January 23, 2007.

Beginning in June 2007, overwhelmed with new passport demands, the U.S. Departments of State and Homeland Security reluctantly relaxed the new requirement on a 90-day temporary basis (through September 30, 2007), mostly to accommodate vacation travel for Americans. The new passport applications had overwhelmed government processors, creating up to a four-month backlog that defeated applicants' purpose for the passports in the first place.

On June 15, 2007, the U.S. House of Representatives overwhelmingly voted (379-45) to delay the new rules for 17 months. However, the Department of Homeland Security still intended to press forward with passport requirements for all land travel (vehicle, bicycle, pedestrian, etc.) at the Canadian and Mexican borders beginning in January 2008.

Importantly, the above temporary accommodations did *not* relax the entry requirements imposed by other hemispheric countries, e.g., Canada, Mexico, Bermuda, or Caribbean countries. Existing entry requirements for those countries remained in effect, as they were self-determined by each country. However, U.S. officials were working with governments of countries affected by WHTI to consult about the relaxed U.S. requirement.

Under the temporary relaxed requirements, U.S. citizens traveling to Canada, Mexico, Bermuda, or Caribbean countries who had applied for, but not yet received passports, could re-enter the United States by air if they presented government-issued photo identification and official proof from the DEPARTMENT OF STATE that they had applied for a passport.

Children under the age of 16 who traveled with their parents or legal **guardian** needed proof of passport application status, while children older than 16 additionally needed official photo identification. Children traveling alone needed a copy of their birth certificate, baptismal record or a hospital record of birth in the United States, in addition to official proof that their passport application was pending.

For U.S. citizens traveling to countries not included in the WHTI whose passports were still pending as of two weeks prior to travel departure, the Department of State had special contacts to facilitate expediting the passports' release.

Also new, as of October 2006, was the implementation of *e-Passports* for all travel between Visa Waiver Program (VWP) countries (primarily 27 countries in Western Europe) or

travel to the United States from a VWP country. E-Passports contain electronic chips holding the same information as that found on a passport's data page, including name, date of birth, and other biographic information. Uniquely, the e-Passports are equipped with biometric identifiers. The United States requires that the electronic chip contain a digital photograph of the passport-holder as well.

All e-Passports issued by VWP countries and the United States have special security features designed to prevent the unauthorized reading or "skimming" of data stored on the e-Passport chip. The inspection process upon entry into the United States is different for holders of e-Passports than previously-issued ones, and all U.S. ports of entry were to be equipped with signs and/or special personnel to direct e-Passport holders to the appropriate U.S. Customs and Border Protection booth to process through.

As of October 26, 2006, all new passports issued by VWP countries must be e-Passports. Persons issued non-e-Passports on or after October 26, 2006 must obtain a visa.

Older but still valid passports issued by VWP countries between October 26, 2005 and October 26, 2006 must include a digital photograph printed on the data page; otherwise, the traveler will be required to obtain a visa. Passports issued prior to October 26, 2005 may still be valid as well, if they contain a "machine-readable zone," two lines of text data at the bottom of the personal information page, along with the bearer's identifying photograph. Persons without one of the above-required passports could either obtain a qualifying passport or get a visa.

Government reports indicated in mid-2007 that approximately six million Americans would need formal documents to travel to the Caribbean, Canada, or Mexico by air or sea. Another 27 million Americans would need these for land crossings over the next five years. These estimates did not include regular yearly demands for passports. In 2006, the STATE DEPARTMENT processed 12.1 million passports. The number was expected to reach 18 million in 2007, based on the monthly applications received in the first few months of the year.

PATENTS

Rights, granted to inventors by the federal government, pursuant to its power under Article I, Section 8, Clause 8, of the U.S. Constitution, that permit them to exclude others from making, using, or selling an invention for a definite, or restricted, period of time.

KSR International Co. v. Teleflex Inc.

Patent protection is designed to foster innovation and creativity by giving inventors a **monopoly** for the fruits of their labor. Armed with a U.S. patent, a patent holder is entitled to sue those who do not pay a license fee to use the patented product or process. Alleged infringers typically respond by alleging that the patent is invalid. One such defense is the issue of obviousness. If the combining of parts is obvious and the elements being combined are obvious, then a patent should not be granted because it lacks novelty. The U.S. SUPREME COURT, in *KSR International Co. v. Teleflex Inc.*, __U.S.__, 127 S.Ct. 1727, __L.Ed.2d __ (2007), restated its test for obviousness and ruled that a test used by the Federal **Circuit Court** of Appeals was wrong and could not be used. The ruling favored more stringent standards for obtaining a patent where the innovation is "obvious."

Teleflex Incorporated licensed the rights to a patent held by Steven Engelgau, which was entitled "Adjustable Pedal Assembly with Electronics Throttle Control." The patent described a mechanism for combining an electronic sensor with an automobile accelerator pedal so the pedal's position can be sent to a computer that controls the throttle in the vehicle's engine. The application was filed in 2000 but Engelgau swore in his application that he invented the pedal design in early 1998. KSR International Company, a rival to Teleflex in the design and manufacture of adjustable pedals, was hired in 1998 by Ford Motor Company to supply an adjustable pedal system for various lines of automobiles with cable-actuated throttle controls. In 2000 General Motors hired KSR to supply adjustable pedal systems for Chevrolet and GMC light trucks that used computer-controlled throttles. KSR took the pedal designed for Ford and added a modular sensor system to the pedal. Teleflex accused KSR of infringing the Engelgau patent and filed a suit in federal **district court**. KSR countered by claiming that the patent was invalid because its subject matter was obvious.

The district court reviewed the details of the patent and a number of other patents preceding Engelgau's that dealt with throttle pedal design and relevant prior art. The court applied a test for obviousness developed by the Supreme Court in 1966. The court first determined the level of skill needed for pedal design, finding that an undergraduate degree in mechanical engineering and familiarity with pedal control systems was sufficient. As to the prior art, including patents and pedal designs, the court noted several pedal designs and found little difference between them and Engelgau's. One patent taught everything in Engelgau's except the use of a sensor to detect and transmit the pedal's position to the computer controlling the throttle. That aspect was revealed in another patent preceding Engelgau's. Based on these findings the court ruled the Engelgau design was obvious and the patent was invalid. The Federal Circuit Court of Appeals, which hears all patent appeals, reversed. The appeals court ignored the Supreme Court, applying its own TSM test: teaching, suggestion, or motivation. Under the TSM test a patent claim is obvious if "some motivation or suggestion to combine the prior art teachings" can be found in the prior art, the nature of the problem, or the knowledge of a person having ordinary skill in the art. In this case the appeals court concluded that the prior pedal patents did not teach anything helpful to Engelgau's purpose. The patents would not have led a person of ordinary skill to put a sensor on the type of pedal described in one of the prior patents.

The Supreme Court, in a unanimous decision, reversed the Federal Circuit's decision and the reasoning embodied in the TSM test. Justice ANTHONY KENNEDY, writing for the Court, rejected the "rigid approach" of the appeals court. In its prior cases involving obviousness the Supreme Court had used an "expansive and flexible approach" that allowed courts to look at any "secondary considerations that would prove instructive." Turning to the appeals court's analysis, Justice Kennedy found that the key question was whether the combination was obvious to a person with ordinary skill in the art, not the patentee himself. Second, the appeals court operated on the mistaken assumption that a person of ordinary skill will be led "only to those elements of prior art designed to solve the same problem." This was wrong because in many cases such a person "will be able to fit the teachings of multiple patents together like pieces of a puzzle." Moreover, a person of ordinary skill was also a person of "ordinary creativity, not an automaton." The Federal Circuit continued down the wrong path by worrying too much about applying "hindsight bias;" its "rigid preventative rules" denied factfinders "recourse to common sense." Justice Kennedy agreed with the district court's analysis that at the time Engelegau designed his pedal it was obvious to a person of ordinary skill to combine a prior patented pedal design with a pedal position electronic sensor.

Microsoft Corp. v. AT&T Corp.

The U.S. SUPREME COURT in April 2007 rendered a decision in a patent law case involving two giant corporations that were being represented by high-profile attorneys. In *Microsoft Corp. v. AT&T Corp.*, ___ U.S. ___, 127 S. Ct. 1746, ___ L. Ed. 2d ___ (2007), the Court held that Microsoft had not infringed AT&T's speech compacting software when Microsoft shipped a master copy of its Windows software overseas to be installed in computers that were manufactured and sold in foreign countries. Former **Solicitor General** Theodore B. Olson argued the case on behalf of Microsoft, while another former Solicitor General, Seth P. Waxman, advocated on behalf of AT&T.

In 1972, the Supreme Court rendered a decision in *Deepsouth Packing Co. v. Laitram Corp.*, 406 U.S. 518, 92 S. Ct. 1700, 32 L. Ed. 2d 273 (1972), which involved a patent for a shrimp deveining machine. The patent holder, Laitram, sued a company, Deepsouth, for infringing on Laitram's patent. Deepsouth acknowledged that it could not sell its deveining product in the United States without infringing Laitram's patent, but Deepsouth argued that it could make parts of its deveiner and sell those parts to foreign buyers to assemble overseas. At that time, the federal patent **statute** only applied to inventions made "within the United States," and since the product in that instance would have been assembled and used outside of the United States, the Court held that Deepsouth had not infringed Laitram's patent.

Congress responded to this decision in 1984 by amending the Patent Act to expand the definition of infringement to include acts of supplying a patented invention's components from the United States to a place outside of the U.S. The statute provides that infringement occurs when one "suppl[ies] . . . from the United States," for "combination" abroad, a patented invention's "components." 35 U.S.C. §271(f)(1). The legislative history of the amendment clearly indicated that Congress intended for the change to alter the result that the Court reached in *Deepsouth*.

Microsoft produces Windows, a highly popular software operating system, at the company's plant in Redmond, Washington. The company sells the system to foreign manufacturers to install on computers that are made outside of the United States. To do so, Microsoft provides a master copy of Windows to the manufacturers, either by shipping a disk with the software or by sending the copy via a secured electronic transmission. The manufacturers then use this master disk to produce copies, and the copies are then installed onto the foreign machines that are sold.

AT&T developed a computer that was capable of digitally encoding and compressing recorded speech. Microsoft packaged Windows with software that allows a computer to process speech in a manner that is claimed by AT&T's patent. AT&T initially brought a patent infringement suit against Microsoft in the U.S. **District Court** for the Southern District of New York in 2001. AT&T wanted to recover damages for the foreign and domestic installations of Windows. During the course of the litigation, Microsoft conceded that it infringed on AT&T's patent when it installed Windows on its own systems during software development and also when it licensed copies of Windows to manufacturers of computers sold in the United States.

However, Microsoft challenged the imposition of liability based on the foreign sales of computers that had Windows installed on them. According to AT&T, Microsoft was liable under §271(f) because Microsoft supplied "components" of AT&T's patented speech processor when it sent the master copies outside of the U.S. Microsoft countered that unincorporated software, which is intangible information, cannot be characterized as a "component" within the meaning of that term in §271(f). Moreover, Microsoft argued that if it were liable under §271(f), it "would simply pick up [its] manufacturing operation for the golden master, go [one] hundred miles north to Vancouver, set up the operation in Vancouver, [and] burn [its] golden master CDs [there]."

In 2004, Judge William H. Pauley of the Southern District of New York rejected Microsoft's claims and held the company liable for patent infringement. *AT&T Corp. v. Microsoft Corp.*, No. 01 Civ. 4872, 2004 WL 406640 (S.D.N.Y. March 5, 2004). According to Pauley's opinion, software can be a component of a patented invention or an infringing device. Moreover, the text of the statute does not limit the definition of "component" to exclude software. The court also determined that Microsoft's actions meant that the company had supplied infringing components from the United States.

On appeal, a divided panel of the U.S. Court of Appeals for the Federal Circuit affirmed the district court's decision. *AT&T Corp. v. Microsoft Corp.*, 414 F.3d 1366 (Fed. Cir. 2005). According to the majority opinion, "Were we to hold that Microsoft's supply by exportation of the master versions of the Windows software—specifically for the purpose of foreign replication—avoids infringement, we would be subverting the remedial nature of §271(f), permitting a technical avoidance of the statute by ignoring the advances in a field of technology—and its associated industry practices—that developed after the enactment of §271(f). It would be unsound to construe a **statutory** provision that was originally enacted to encourage advances in technology by closing a loophole, in a manner that allows the very advances in technology thus encouraged to subvert that intent. Section 271(f), if it is to remain effective, must therefore be interpreted in a manner that is appropriate to the nature of the technology at issue."

The Supreme Court granted **certiorari**, and in an opinion by Justice RUTH BADER GINSBURG, reversed the Federal Circuit. Unlike the lower courts, Ginsburg's majority opinion did not conclude that software in the abstract could constitute a component. Instead, only a copy of the computer software on a medium, such as a CD-ROM, could constitute such a component. According to Ginsburg, when the foreign manufacturers created copies of Windows from the master disk and then installed the software onto the foreign computers, the copies themselves had not been supplied from the United States. Thus, Microsoft could not be liable under §271(f) because it had not supplied patented components from the United States.

Justice Samuel Alito concurred with Ginsburg's opinion, but differed in opinion about why the software was not a component under the meaning of §271(f). Justice JOHN PAUL STEVENS dissented, arguing that the software should not be treated differently than components used in other types of devices. "The relevant component in this case is not a physical item like a knife," he wrote. "Both Microsoft and the Court think that means it cannot be a 'component.' But if a disk with software inscribed on it is a 'component,' I find it difficult to understand why the most important ingredient of that component is not also a component. Indeed, the master disk is the functional equivalent of a warehouse of components—components that Microsoft fully expects to be incorporated into foreign-manufactured computers."

Microsoft's victory before the Supreme Court came just over two months after a federal jury in San Diego ordered the company to pay $1.52 billion in damages to Alcatel-Lucent of Paris in a suit related to Microsoft's Windows Media Player. It represented the largest verdict in a patent infringement case in U.S. history, according to the attorney for Alcatel-Lucent.

PELOSI, NANCY

Nancy Pelosi
AP IMAGES

The first woman to serve in a top leadership role in a major U.S. political party, California Congresswoman Nancy Pelosi (born 1940) became the Democratic Party's minority leader of the House of Representatives. Pelosi, known as an outspoken liberal, became a strong critic of the administration of President George W. Bush, but also strove to reunify dispirited Democrats while Republicans controlled both houses of Congress and the White House.

Born as Nancy D'Alesandro in Baltimore, Pelosi inherited her family's political tradition. Her father, Thomas D'Alesandro, Jr., was the ward boss for Baltimore's Little Italy ward, then a city councilman and five-term congressman before becoming Baltimore mayor from 1947 through 1959. Later, her brother, Thomas D'Alesandro III, also became Baltimore's mayor, from 1967 to 1971. The young woman met her future husband, Paul Pelosi, who came from San Francisco, California, while both were attending Trinity College in Washington, D.C. After they married, they moved to San Francisco and started a family. Her husband, who made a living as an investor, also had a family with political leanings, his brother winning a seat on the city's board of supervisors. The Pelosis had five children: Nancy Corinne, Christine, Jacqueline, Paul, and Alexandra. Only when the youngest, Alexandra, entered school did their mother become involved in local Democratic Party politics. Alexandra later became a documentary filmmaker who chronicled political campaigns. Starting at the grass roots with house parties and door-to-door campaigning, Pelosi eventually became Northern California party chairwoman. She became a close ally of a powerful Democratic politician, Congressman Phillip Burton, who represented San Francisco. In 1983, Burton died, and his wife, Sala, won a special election to finish his term in office. But when she was diagnosed with cancer, Sala Burton asked Pelosi to run for her seat. Pelosi won a special election in 1987 and was re-elected every two years after that from California's Eighth District.

Pelosi represents one of the country's most left-leaning Congressional districts, encompassing most of San Francisco. Reflecting the concerns of her constituency, which strongly favors gay rights, Pelosi sponsored a bill creating a special housing opportunities program for people

NANCY PELOSI

1940: Born in Baltimore, MD
1987: Elected to Congress
2002: Named minority leader
2007: Elected Speaker of the House

infected with Acquired Immune Deficiency Syndrome, or AIDS. In related work, she championed programs to expand access to Medicaid for people with the HIV virus that causes AIDS, to increase funding for HIV- and AIDS-related healthcare and to spur development of an HIV vaccine. Pelosi served on the House's powerful Appropriations and Intelligence committees. On the latter, her more than ten years of continuous service was the longest in the committee's history, and for two years she was the ranking Democrat on the panel. Pelosi met with leaders of intelligence services in the United States and in allied countries and advocated stronger efforts to stop nuclear proliferation. After the September 11, 2001 terrorist attacks, Pelosi wrote a bill creating the independent 9/11 commission, and that panel conducted a thorough, high-profile investigation of the U.S. government's intelligence and response efforts before and after the attacks. Despite her liberal stance on domestic matters, Pelosi supported the U.S. Patriot Act.

When Richard Gephardt resigned as the party's minority leader in 2002 to run for president in 2004, Pelosi was selected to replace him. Under Gephardt's leadership, the Democrats had appeared powerless to stop what they saw as the radical conservative agenda of the George W. Bush administration. When Pelosi declared her desire to take over from Gephardt, she said: "We must draw clear distinctions between our vision of the future and the extreme policies put forth by the Republicans. We cannot allow Republicans to pretend they share our values and then legislate against those values without consequence." Despite her liberalism, Pelosi appealed to all wings of the party, working closely with moderate party whip Steny Hoyer and filling a new position of assistant to the leader with another centrist, John Spratt. She also routinely helped junior party members gain media exposure and integrate them into the legislative process.

In the wake of the Democratic takeover of Congree following the 2006 elections, Pelosi was elected the first woman Speaker of the House on January 5, 2007. She commented that "In this House, we may be different parties, but we serve one country," as she pledged to try and work with Republicans after years of partisan warring between the parties.

PERJURY

A crime that occurs when an individual willfully makes a false statement during a judicial proceeding, after he or she has taken an oath to speak the truth.

Libby Convicted for Lying About His Role in CIA Leak

A federal jury in March 2007 convicted I. Lewis "Scooter" Libby, the former chief of staff of Vice President Dick Cheney, on four criminal charges related to his role in the leak of the identify of an undercover agent of the CENTRAL INTELLIGENCE AGENCY. Jurors said after the trial that Libby's defense that he had could not remember facts related to the case was weak. However, members of the jury also indicated that they believed Libby to be the fall guy, taking the blame for other members of the administration of President GEORGE W. BUSH.

The case stemmed from a statement made during Bush's State of the Union address in 2003, where he indicated that former Iraqi dictator Saddam Hussein had bought significant quantities of uranium from Africa. Reporters learned that this information contradicted reports from former ambassador Joseph C. Wilson, who visited Niger in 2002. Wilson later wrote an op-ed piece for the *New York Times* in which he said that Bush had exaggerated the threat of Iraq's nuclear weapons program.

Journalists learned shortly thereafter that Wilson's wife, Valerie Plame, was an operative of the CIA and had been involved with sending her husband to Niger. Robert Novak, a syndicated columnist, revealed Plame's identity in an article published on July 14. He attributed his information to two unidentified "senior administration officials." Shortly after Novak's piece was published, three reporters for *Time* also said that government officials had disclosed Plame's identity to them. In September 2003, the JUSTICE DEPARTMENT authorized the FEDERAL BUREAU OF INVESTIGATION to begin a criminal investigation into the leak of Plame's identify.

The investigation led to the convening of a **grand jury** for the U.S. **District Court** for the DISTRICT OF COLUMBIA. The grand jury called several witnesses, including Bush, Cheney, Presidential Chief of Staff Andrew H. Card, National Security Advisor Stephen J. Hadley, Assistant to the President Dan Bartlett, former press secretary Art Fleischer, and advisor Karen Hughes. Libby testified under oath on two different occasions during March 2004.

The grand jury investigation became embroiled in more controversy when reporters for the *New York Times* and *Time* refused to cooperate. Over the next several months, the reporters and their employers fought subpoenas that the grand jury had issued, and two of the reporters were eventually found in contempt of court. Over the next year, *New York Times* reporter Judith Miller continued to refuse to divulge her sources, even after she was sent to jail for her refusal. *Time* reporter Matthew Cooper faced similar penalties for not cooperating with the grand jury.

Miller finally testified on September 30, 2005. About a month later, the grand jury indicted Libby on charges of obstruction of justice, making false statements, and perjury. Shortly after his indictment was announced, Bob Woodward, editor of the *Washington Post*, said the senior government official who had released Plame's identify was not Libby. By December 2005, special prosecutor Robert Fitzgerald began presenting evidence against Bush advisor

Karl Rove before a new grand jury. Rove was never officially charged in the case.

Throughout much of 2006, Libby's attorneys tried to obtain notes and other information about the CIA leak from various journalists. Judge Reggie B. Walton ruled that Libby was not entitled to know the identity of the official who had revealed information about Plame to two journalists. Reports in March 2006 suggested that the source of the leak was former STATE DEPARTMENT official Richard L. Armitage. However, no other official was charged in the case.

Libby's trial began on January 16, 2007. Libby told investigators that he had forgotten that he had learned about Plame from Cheney in June 2003 that that he mistakenly believed that he learned of her from NBC's Tim Russert about a month later. Miller contradicted Libby's statements by testifying that she had learned of Plame's identity from Libby on June 23, 2003. However, six journalists testified on February 12 that Libby was not the source of information about Plame' identity and that they had learned about her from other sources within the administration.

Evidence at the trial suggested that Cheney was trying to disparage Wilson, who had been openly critical of the war with Iraq. Wilson clearly implied that the results of his findings would have been reported to Cheney, meaning that Cheney would have known that Bush's statement about the alleged uranium connection between Iraq and Niger were false. Defense attorneys had suggested that they were going to call both Libby and Cheney to the stand, but neither of the men testified at the trial.

On March 6, the jury convicted Libby on four of the five charges, including obstruction of justice, making a false statement to the FBI, and two counts of perjury. The jury acquitted Libby on a charge that he made a false statement related to a conversation that Libby allegedly had with Cooper in July 2003. Libby faces a possible prison term of 1 1/2 to three years under the Federal Sentencing Guidelines.

Cheney said in a written statement that he was "disappointed with the verdict." Jurors said that they did not believe Libby's defense that he could not remember the source who told him of Plame's identity. However, one juror said that the jury had a "tremendous amount of sympathy" for Libby and that the members of the jury questioned why other White House officials were not also charged. The juror also indicated that the jury believed that Cheney had told Libby to speak with reporters about Plame's identity.

PREVAILING PARTY

The litigant who successfully brings or defends an action and, as a result, receives a favorable judgment or verdict.

Sole v. Wyner

In one of the more unusual cases before the U.S. SUPREME COURT in its 2006-2007 term, plaintiff nude artist-performers were deemed *not* entitled to "prevailing party" attorneys' fees under 42 USC §1983, even though they succeeded in getting a **preliminary injunction** in the matter before the court. After violating the terms of the preliminary injunction involving their "free expression" speech on a public beach, the plaintiffs in *Sole v. Wyner* No. 06-531, 551 U.S. ___ (2007), later lost their FIRST AMENDMENT case on the merits. Therefore, they were not the "prevailing party" and were not entitled to attorney fees. The Supreme Court's decision reversed decisions by the lower courts.

Although the case on the merits involved First Amendment speech, the appeal before the Supreme Court was limited to that of defining and determining the "prevailing party." In most private (civil) litigation, each party generally pays its own attorney fees and costs. But, in furtherance of promoting fair and effective counsel in civil rights litigation, Congress pro-

vided for a fee-shifting remedy under 42 USC §1983, permitting the award of fees to the **prevailing party**. Actions brought under §1983 generally deal with allegations that a public official or **entity** violated private constitutional rights "under the color of law," i.e., as part of a **state action**.

In January 2003, plaintiff Toni Wyner notified the Florida Department of Environmental Protection of her intention to create, with friends, an anti-war protest in the form of nude individuals forming a peace symbol with their bodies. She intended to do this on the public beach at John D. MacArthur Beach State Park on February 14, 2003. Department officials notified Wyner by mail that her peace symbol would be lawful only if the participants complied with the beach's "Bathing Suit Rule," essentially prohibiting nudity.

Wyner then filed suit under 42 USC §1983 in the U.S. **District Court** for the Southern District of Florida, as a preemptive move to prevent any police interference with her nude display as she planned it. Wyner cited the First Amendment's protection of expressive speech and conduct as legal support for her position, alleging that the "bathing suit rule" violated her First Amendment rights to nude protests and was therefore unconstitutional. She also attached to her complaint a copy of a 1995 settlement with the same defendant in which she was permitted to stage a nude play at MacArthur Beach, with the condition that the stage area was screened off to spare beachgoers who were not interested in seeing her play or the nudity.

The district court found that by separating the nude display behind a curtain or screen from the rest of the beach, the interests of both the state and Wyner would be satisfied. It therefore granted Wyner a preliminary injunction which allowed the protest, under the condition that the "artwork" be shielded from other parts of the beach with a curtain or screen.

On the day of the event, Wyner and her friends ignored the screen barrier that was in place and conducted their nude peace symbol on the outside of the barrier, after which she and the participants romped on the beach and went swimming.

Wyner then went back to the district court seeking a permanent injunction against Florida's bathing suit rule, arguing that it violated the First Amendment. She also announced her intention to stage another nude protest at the beach. The case proceeded through the discovery process, after which her attorney acknowledged that she and her fellow-participants set up in front of, rather than behind, the barrier. Both parties filed motions for **summary judgment**.

The district court denied Wyner's motion for summary judgment and granted defendant state officials and departments theirs. The court found the bathing suit rule to be a reasonable restriction, to protect the experiences and choices of park and beach visitors. Notwithstanding, the court awarded Wyner **statutory** fees based on the preliminary injunction stage of the proceedings, reasoning that she had succeeded in getting the preliminary injunction and was therefore entitled to fees as the prevailing party. The Eleventh **Circuit Court** of Appeals affirmed, further reasoning that Wyner had prevailed because the preliminary order had allowed her to proceed without interference by state action.

The U.S. Supreme Court held otherwise. The Court cited one of its earlier cases, Texas State Teachers Assn. v. Garland Independent School District, 489 U.S. 782, for the holding that "[t]he touchstone of the prevailing party inquiry is the material alteration of the legal relationship of the parties in a manner which Congress sought to promote in the fee statute." A preliminary injunction is just that: "preliminary;" it is not based on discovery or review of documents or presentation of witnesses.

The Court noted that the **final decision** in Wyner's case soundly rejected the substantive argument she presented at the preliminary injunction stage: that state law prohibiting nudity in public parks is unconstitutional as applied to expressive, non-erotic nudity. Writing for the unanimous Court, Justice Ginsburg noted that "At the end of the fray, Florida's Bathing Suit Rule remained intact, and Wyner had gained no enduring 'chang[e] [in] the legal relationship.'"

For these reasons, the Court ended, Wyner was not a prevailing party, and not entitled to attorneys' fees under the **statute**. Her initial victory (preliminary injunction) was "ephemeral;" she might have won the battle but she lost the war, noted the Court.

PRISONERS' RIGHTS

The nature and extent of the privileges afforded to individuals kept in custody or confinement against their will because they were convicted of performing an unlawful act.

Jones v. Bock

Congress enacted the Prison Litigation Reform Act of 1995 (PLRA), 28 U.S.C.A. §1932, to deal with which placed a number of restrictions on prisoners who used the federal civil rights **statute** 42 U.S.C.A. §1983 to pursue actions challenging prison conditions. The goal was to reduce frivolous actions, reduce the workload of the **federal courts**, and give prison administrators the ability to handle disputes through administrative procedures. One provision of the PRLA requires prisoners to exhaust all administrative remedies before they are allowed to file a §1983 lawsuit or any other **civil action** based on a federal law. Another provision requires federal magistrates to screen all prisoner lawsuit filings to determine if they comport with the PLRA. If not, the federal **district court** will dismiss the case.

A number of federal circuit courts of appeal and federal district courts developed procedural rules to work in conjunction with the PRLA. However, some of these rules came under legal attack because they were more stringent than the PRLA provisions. The Supreme Court, in *Jones v. Bock*, __U.S.__, 127 S.Ct. 910, 166 L.Ed.2d 798 (2007), addressed the Sixth **Circuit Court** of Appeals' rules and their effect on §1983 lawsuits filed by three inmates in the custody of the Michigan Department of Corrections (MDOC). The Court held that the procedural rules were not required by the PLRA and exceeded the powers of the judiciary.

The three inmates, Lorenzo Jones, Timothy Williams, and John Walton, were incarcerated in three different facilities. Jones, who had injured his neck and back, was directed to perform work that aggravated his injuries. He unsuccessfully exhausted his MDOC grievance process and then filed a §1983 lawsuit in Michigan federal district court. The district court, using the PLRA and local rules, dismissed his lawsuit because he had failed to attach copies of his grievance forms or describe his claims with specificity. The Sixth Circuit upheld this decision.

Timothy Williams suffered from a serious medical condition that affected his right arm and which had required several surgeries. The MDOC physician recommended another surgery. MDOC's medical advisory committee overruled the recommendation. Williams filed a grievance objecting to his medical care and seeking authorization for the surgery. He filed second grievance after being denied a single-occupancy handicapped cell. After both grievances were denied by MDOC he filed a §1983 lawsuit in Michigan federal district court, naming seven MNDOC staff as defendants. The district court dismissed Williams's case because he had failed to exhaust his administrative remedies because he had not named any of the defendants in his grievance process.

John Walton assaulted a guard at his MDOC facility and was sanctioned with indefinite restrictions while he was confined to his cell. He later learned that other inmates who committed the same infraction received only a three-month restriction. Walton, who is black, filed a grievance that claimed the disparity in discipline was based on racial discrimination because the other inmates who received shorter disciplinary periods were white. His grievance was denied and he too filed a §1983 lawsuit in Michigan federal district court. The lawsuit was dismissed because he had listed six defendants from MDOC in his filing but had only listed one of the staff members in his grievance. His claims against the others were not properly exhausted under the rules crafted by the district court and Sixth Circuit. The Supreme Court agreed to accept the appeals from the three inmates because of numerous conflicts in the lower federal courts on how to interpret and administer the PLRA.

The Supreme Court, in a unanimous decision, overturned the Sixth Circuit rules and interpretation of the PLRA on exhaustion of administrative remedies. Chief Justice JOHN ROBERTS, writing for the Court, agreed that exhaustion is mandatory under the PLRA and that unexhausted claims cannot be brought in court. The issue before the Court was whether the burden is on the prisoner to plead and demonstrate exhaustion in the complaint, or to the defendant to raise lack of exhaustion as an **affirmative defense**. The Sixth Circuit took the minority position by placing the burden on the prisoner. Roberts concluded that exhaustion should be an affirmative defense. He pointed out that Rule 8(a) of the Federal Rules of **Civil Procedure** require only a "short and plain statement of the claim" in a complaint, while Rule 8(c) identified a list of affirmative defenses that must be pleaded in response. The PLRA was silent on this issue but the Court believed that the usual practice under the Federal Rules should be followed.

The Williams and Walton lawsuits had been thrown out because they failed to identify in their initial grievances each defendant they later sued. Chief Justice Roberts could not find a textual basis in the PLRA for this rule. The PLRA stated only that the prisoner exhaust "such administrative remedies as are available."

There was nothing in the statute to support a "name all the defendant's requirement along the lines of the Sixth Circuit's judicially created rule." The court concluded that exhaustion is not automatically inadequate because an individual later sued was not named in the grievance.

Finally, the Court examined whether a federal lawsuit could go forward if the prisoner has failed to exhaust some, but not all, of the claims asserted in the complaint. The Sixth Circuit rule required dismissal of the entire action, while other courts have proceeded with the exhausted claims. Chief Justice Roberts found not **statutory** or policy grounds sufficiently compelling to adopt the Sixth Circuit practice. He raised concerns that such a practice would make more work for prison administrators and the courts. Inmates would likely file "various claims in separate suits to avoid the possibility of an unexhausted claim tainting the others." Moreover, district judges would have to examine the claim twice, first reviewing and dismissing under the total exhaustion rule, and then again when the inmate refiled the action.

PRISONS

California Judge Blocks Effort to Transfer Prisoners Out of the State

A California state superior judge in February 2007 ruled that Governor Arnold Schwarzenegger could not order the transfer of several thousand inmates from California prisons to prisons in other states. Schwarzenegger's move was part of an effort to address an overcrowding crisis in the state's prison system. The judge who ruled on the case determined that Schwarzenegger had inappropriately declared a state of emergency when he made the decision to transfer the prisoners. Schwarzenegger said that he would appeal the ruling.

California has struggled with problems in its prison system for most of Schwarzenegger's term in office. In June 2006, he declared that the prisons were in a crisis, noting that the system was trying to house 171,000 inmates in facilities that were designed to hold only about 100,000. Many of the inmates have had to sleep in such places as gyms, dayrooms, and other areas that were not intended for housing purposes. The state has also had significant problem with **recidivism**, with an estimated 70 percent of inmates ending up back in prison.

Schwarzenegger has introduced a variety of proposals that have been designed to address the trouble that the state has had with its prison population. In 2004, he proposed a change to the state's parole policy that would send parolees who failed drug tests or committee other violations to rehabilitation programs instead of sending them back to prison. However, the state's prison guards union and victims' rights groups protested the move, and officials also admitted that the proposal had not been planned well. Later proposals included a plan to reshuffle responsibilities within the state's corrections department, but that plan was also never implemented.

Legislators have been skeptical of several of Schwarzenegger's proposals. In January 2006, he added the construction of prisons as part of a proposal to issue bonds that would also be used to fund new roads, schools, and levees. Another plan called for the transfer of some female inmates out of prison. The California Legislature rejected both ideas. Some lawmakers suggested that the state needed to change its policies in order to lower the prison population.

In June 2006, a special master working for U.S. District Judge Thelton Henderson criticized Schwarzenegger for bowing to pressure from the state's prison guard union, which has been influential in the California Legislature. According to report from the special master, the governor had begun to retreat from prison reform efforts. Less than a week after the report was issued, Schwarzenegger convened a special legislative session in order to enact legislation that would order construction of new prisons in urban areas and the transfer of several thousand prisoners in an effort to free up beds.

The governor's plan resulted in a $6-billion proposal that called for the use of private facilities to house 4,000 low-security inmates as well as the for the transfer of 5,000 inmates who faced deportation to prisons in other states. Lawmakers, however, reacted critically to the plan, saying that it was hastily assembled and lacked basic pieces of information. Several bills were introduced as alternatives to Schwarzenegger's proposal, but state administrators said that the bills would not do enough to address the immediate need for more beds. "[T]hese bills do not solve the state's short-term capacity problem," said acting corrections secretary James Tilton. "The lack of a short-term solution will create an emergency situation whereby the department will run out of beds by June 2007. When that day comes, the department will be forced to stop accepting inmates, and will notify counties that (the prisons) can no longer accept felons sentenced by the courts."

In October, Schwarzenegger signed an emergency declaration that ordered the corrections department to send several thousand criminals to private prisons in other states in order to relieve the overcrowding. State officials had hoped that as many as 2,200 inmates would volunteer to be transferred, but fewer than 500 did. Thus, the state had to transfer the inmates involuntarily. In signing this declaration, Schwarzenegger acted under the state's Emergency Services Act, Cal. Gov't Code Ann. §8550 et seq..

Two unions, including the California Correctional Peace Officers Association and the Service Employees International Union, challenged Schwarzenegger's actions in state court. The plaintiffs in the case argued that the governor had violated both the emergency act and the state's constitution, the latter of which prohibits the use of private companies to perform jobs that are ordinarily performed by state employees. The suit was brought in the Superior Court in Sacramento County.

Judge Gail Ohanesian agreed with the unions' arguments and ruled that the contracts with the others states were invalid. "Prison overcrowding in California is a crisis creating conditions of extreme peril, she wrote. However, "this is not the type of circumstance generally covered by the Emergency Services Act." Ohanesian also noted that "[t]he control of state prisons is exclusively within the **purview** of state government and not local government. The intent of the Emergency Services Act is not to give the governor extraordinary powers to act without legislative approval in matters such as this that are ordinary and entirely within the control of the state government."

Schwarzenegger said that he would appeal the decision, and members of the governor's administration said publicly that they thought the decision was wrong. Spokespersons for the unions who brought the suit disagreed and argued that the state should instead focus on long-term solutions to the prison problem. According to the unions, the governor's plans to transfer the prisoners would have only alleviated the problem on a short-term basis.

The dispute between Schwarzenegger and the guard union continued for several months after the decision. Commentators suggested that in order for Schwarzenegger to be successful in proposing a reform solution, he may first have to negotiate a new labor contract with the union, which has political power with both of the major parties. At the same time that the legislature was considering Schwarzenegger's proposal, the union was promoting its own proposed plan, which was created after the guards had several meetings with traditional adversaries such as defense attorneys and advocates for inmate rights.

U.S. Prison Population Continues to Rise

According to a report issued by the Justice Department's Bureau of Justice Statistics in November 2006, the prison population in the United States grew 1.9% during 2005, which was less than the average annual growth during the past decade. By the end of 2005, one in every 32 adults was in prison, in jail, on probation, or on parole. Despite the decline in the rate of growth in U.S. prisons, however, another survey showed that the U.S. correctional population reached a total of more than seven million for the first time.

For a number of years, the United States has had the highest incarceration rate in the world. In 2003, the U.S. first released statistical estimates of the number of people imprisoned. According to that report, more than 5.6 million Americans were in prison or had spent time there. At that time, one in 37 adults had served time in prison, which led all nations. Racial minorities made up a significant percentage of the total number of current and former inmates. According to the trends, a black male in the U.S. would have a one in three chance of going to prison during his or her lifetime. For a Hispanic male, the odds were one in six. A white male's odds were one in 17.

Advocates for prison reform have noted that the disparity in the race of prisoners demonstrates an underlying problem in society. "For the generation of black children today, there's almost an inevitable aspect of going to prison," said Marc Mauer, assistant director for an advocacy group that focuses on reforms for sentencing. "We have the wealthiest society in human history, and we maintain the highest level of imprisonment. It's striking what that says about our approach to social problems and equality."

According to the report issued in 2005, the U.S. had a total of more than 2.3 million people incarcerated at the end of 2005. The overall incarceration rate was 491 inmates per 100,000 U.S. residents, which increase from a total of 411 per 100,000 in 1995. More than 1.4 million of those inmates were housed in federal and state prisons, while 747,529 were housed in local jails. Others were incarcerated in territorial prisons, immigration facilities, military facilities, jails in Indian country, or juvenile facilities.

Federal prisons had the highest population, with a total of 187,618 inmates. Among the states, California and Texas had the highest prison populations, with both having close to 170,000. Florida and New York had the third and fourth highest populations, respectively, among the states. Among those four states, only Texas was also among the top five in the number of inmates per 100,000 residents, with 691. Louisiana led the nation with 797 inmates per 100,000. Following Louisiana and Texas were Mississippi (660), Oklahoma (652), and Alabama (591).

Several of the southern states saw their prison populations decrease in 2005, including Georgia (down 4.6 percent), Maryland (down 2.4 percent), Louisiana (down 2.3%), and Mississippi (down 2.2 percent). Meanwhile, fourteen states, including several of the smaller states, saw increases in their prison numbers. These include South Dakota (increase of 11.9 percent), Montana (up 10.9 percent), and Kentucky (up 10.4 percent).

Other small states had the lowest overall prison populations as well as the lowest incarceration rates. North Dakota has the smallest population with 1,385 prisoners. The number was followed by Maine (2,023), Wyoming (2,047), Vermont (2,078), and New Hampshire (2,530). Maine, New Hampshire, and North Dakota were also among five states with the fewest number of prisoners per 100,000 residents. That list also included Minnesota and Rhode Island.

The total number of persons held in state prisons, federal prisons, or local jails increased by an average of 3.3 percent per year. The number of federal prisoners increased at a higher rate per year (7.2 percent) than the total number of state prisoners (2.5 percent) or inmates in local jails (4.0 percent). The percentage of women who made up the total number of inmates increased from 6.1 percent in 1995 to 7.0 percent in 2005. A total of 107,518 females were incarcerated by the end of 2005.

Due to the rise in the number of prisoners, several states operated above capacity. According to the report, federal prisons operated at 134 percent of their highest capacity. Twenty-three other states also operated above their highest capacity. Among those states with overcrowded prisons were Massachusetts and Illinois, which both operated at 133 percent of their highest capacity. Nevada was on the opposite end of the spectrum, operating at 56 percent of its highest capacity.

Commentators have noted that the focus on drug crimes and the imposition of tougher sentences has increased the numbers of prisoners in the U.S. The International Centre for Prison Studies has concluded that the U.S. has by far the highest prison rate of any other country. China (1.5 million prisoners) and Russia (870,000) follow the U.S. About 29 percent of the seven million people who are imprisoned, on probation, or on parole were convicted of drug-related crimes.

Those who advocate a different approach to the war on drugs say that the United States has missed the mark in combating these violations. "The United States has five percent of the world's population and 25 percent of the world's incarcerated population," said Ethan Nadelmann of the Drug Policy Alliance. "We rank first in the world in locking up our fellow citizens. We now imprison more people for drug law violations than all of western Europe, with a much larger population, incarcerates for all offenses."

Supporters of U.S. policies say that the focus on the incarceration statistics misses the point, emphasizing that the increase in criminal convictions has led to a decrease in the overall crime rate.

PRIVACY

In constitutional law, the right of people to make personal decisions regarding intimate matters; under the common law, the right of people to lead their lives in a manner that is reasonably secluded from public scrutiny, whether such scrutiny comes from a neighbor's prying eyes, an investigator's eavesdropping ears, or a news photographer's intrusive camera; and in statutory law, the right of people to be free from unwarranted drug testing and electronic surveillance.

Anderson v. Blake

The right to privacy is a powerful **legal right**, one that is both broad and at times difficult to measure. Government officials who disclose private information that violates an individual's right to privacy may be sued for damages under state and federal laws. However, government officials are protected by one of several immunity doctrines. While judges have absolute immunity, most government officials have a qualified immunity. Officials may claim it by proving that their conduct was not unreasonable in light of clearly established law. In *Anderson v. Blake*, 469 F.3d 910 (10th Cir. 2006), a police officer who released a videotape of a woman's alleged rape to a television reporter, and which was aired on a local news broadcast, sought to claim qualified immunity from a lawsuit filed by the woman on the tape. The Tenth **Circuit Court** of Appeals rejected his claim, finding that a woman's privacy interest in such a videotape was clearly established.

Aundra Anderson, a Norman, Oklahoma resident, alleged she was the victim of rape that occurred while she was unconscious. She later discovered a videotape documenting the sexual assault and reported this information to Norman police detective Don Blake, who took the videotape with him. Anderson alleged that Blake promised to keep the tape confidential and use it only to investigate the alleged assault. At some point after their meeting Blake shared the contents of the tape with an Oklahoma City reporter and her cameraman. Anderson alleged that Blake called her and then put the reporter on the line to interview her about the sexual assault. Portions of the videotape were shown on a news broadcast in a way that obscured Anderson's identity. Anderson sued Blake, the news reporter, and the television station, alleging that they had violated her right to privacy. Blake made a motion in federal **district court** to dismiss him from the case. The district court rejected his motion, finding that Anderson had a legitimate expectation of privacy when she gave Blake the tape. The court also rejected Blake's claims that the criminal activity depicted on tape rendered it beyond constitutional protection and that the video would have eventually been made public. Finally, the court ruled that Blake did not have qualified immunity because Anderson's privacy interest was clearly established under existing law. The denial of qualified immunity made the case immediately appealable.

The Tenth Circuit Court of Appeals upheld the district court rulings. The court noted that at this stage of the proceedings it had to accept Anderson's facts as true and consider them in the light most favorable to her. The key question on appeal was immunity, for if the appeals court sided with Blake he would be dismissed from the litigation. Under U.S. SUPREME COURT immunity doctrine, Anderson needed to show that Blake's actions violated a constitutional or **statutory** right and that this right was clearly established at the time Blake gave the reporter the videotape. The court acknowledged that there was no specific right that protected the release of the videotape but there was a general constitutional rule, the right to privacy, which could be applied with "obvious clarity to the specific conduct in question." Anderson had a constitutionally protected privacy interested because the video was of a "personal nature." Supreme Court and Tenth Circuit cases supported this conclusion, holding that the government could not disclose information of this type unless it had a "compelling state interest" and it used "the least intrusive means of disclosing the information."

Anderson's privacy interests were protected because the video depicted "the most private of matters: namely her body being forcibly violated." The court pointed out cases in which individuals had a legitimate expectation of privacy in a diary, answering questions about their sexual history, or in undressing before a guard. Surely the videotape in question matched those cases. Blake contended that video was not protected by the right of privacy because it contained evidence of a crime, citing a case where the airing of a video documenting a plaintiff's private sexual conduct was not protected for that reason. The appeals court found no merit in the alleged precedent because that plaintiff in that case was the perpetrator of a crime, while Anderson was the victim of a crime.

The court concluded that Anderson's privacy interest was clearly established in law at the time Blake shared the video with the reporter. Supreme Court and Tenth Circuit cases backed up this conclusion. At this stage in the litigation Anderson had demonstrated that Blake lacked a compelling interest to release the video and he did not use the least intrusive means of disclosure. Therefore, Blake was not entitled to qualified immunity and must defend his actions.

Texas Legislature Blocks Effort to Require Vaccines for Cervical Cancer

In February 2007, Texas Governor Rick Perry signed the first order in the United States mandating that girls receive a vaccine for the virus that causes cervical cancer. The order was met immediately with strong opposition from the state's conservative legislature, which questioned the legality of the order. Nearly three months after Perry signed the order, the legislature passed a bill that prevents state officials from requiring the vaccinations for at least four years.

A genital HPV infection is a type of sexually transmitted disease caused by human papillomavirus, or HPV. About 30 of the more than 100 different strains of HPV are sexually transmitted. The virus can infect the genital area of men and women. Although most people who are infected with HPV have no symptoms and are in no danger of serious health problems, some high-risk viruses can lead to certain cancers, including cervical cancer. HPV is fairly common, infecting at least half of sexually-active men and women during their lifetimes. Genital HPV is the most common sexually transmitted disease. In the State of Texas alone, nearly 400 women each year die of cervical cancer caused by HPV.

In 2006, the FOOD AND DRUG ADMINISTRATION approved a new vaccine for HPV, known as the quadrivalent human papillomavirus vaccine. This vaccine is administered via injection in three doses that are given over a six-month period. The vaccine can be given to girls as young as nine years old, though the recommended age is between 11 and 12 years. Although the vaccination cannot eliminate all possibility of a woman developing cervical cancer, it can reduce the possibility significantly. The Centers for Disease Control and the American Cancer Society have recommended this vaccine in order to reduce the risk of cervical cancer. Even the 16,000-member Christian Medical Association agreed that the vaccine should be required, so long as parents could choose to opt their children out of the requirement.

By early 2007, at least thirteen states, in addition to Texas, were considering whether to mandate HPV vaccinations. Among the states to consider the mandatory vaccinations were Arkansas, California, Colorado, Indiana, Kansas, Kentucky, Maryland, Michigan, New Jersey, Pennsylvania, Virginia, West Virginia, and Wisconsin. (Virginia later became the second state to require the vaccination). Supporters of the vaccination stress that it will be far less costly to require the vaccinations than it would to treat cervical cancer later in life.

Perry bypassed consideration of whether to require the vaccination by signing an executive order on February 2, 2007 that required girls to receive the vaccination prior to entering sixth grade. In order to reduce the cost of the vaccine, which runs more than $360 for the series of three shots, the order made the vaccine available through the Texas Vaccines for Children program as well as through **Medicaid**. Under the order, parents could choose to opt out of the mandatory vaccinations by submitting a conscientious objection affidavit through the DEPARTMENT OF STATE Health Services. The order would have taken effect in September 2008.

After signing the order, Perry said that the benefits of requiring the vaccination were great. "The HPV vaccine provides us with an incredible opportunity to effectively target and prevent cervical cancer," he said in a press release. "Requiring young girls to get vaccinated before they come into contact with HPV is responsible health and **fiscal** policy that has the potential to significantly reduce cases of cervical cancer and mitigate future medical costs."

Several Texas lawmakers were not pleased with the order. Shortly after Perry signed the directive, leading members of the legislature criticized Perry's action, saying that the order subverted the legislative process and interfered with the parent-child relationship. Some legislators even asked Texas Attorney General for an opinion about whether the order was within the power of the governor. Moreover, about 26 of the 31 state senators sent a letter to Perry asking him to **rescind** the order so that the legislature could debate the merits of the vaccination requirement.

Perry refused to back down. In his State of the State address delivered a week after he signed the order, Perry addressed the controversy. "I understand the concern some of my good friends have about requiring this vaccine, which is why parents can opt out if they so choose," he said. "But I refuse to look a young woman in the eye ten years from now who suffers from this form of cancer and tell her we could have stopped it, but we didn't. Others may focus on the cause of this cancer. I will stay focused on the cure. And if I err, I will err on the side of protecting life."

Members of the legislature acted quickly to propose legislation that would effectively block Perry's order. Many of those who opposed the requirement are social conservative who fear that the vaccine sends a message to young girls that sex is permissible. Others oppose the requirement because the vaccine is so new, having only been approved about eight months prior to the order. Among those opposing the order was the Texas Medical Association, which expressed concerns about liability and cost.

Less than three weeks after Perry issued the order, the Texas legislature advanced a bill that would explicitly preempt Perry's action. On March 14, the House approved the bill by an overwhelming majority of 118 to 23. About six weeks later, the Texas Senate followed suit, passing the bill by a 30–1 majority. Under the version passed by the Senate, state officials may not require the shots for at least four years.

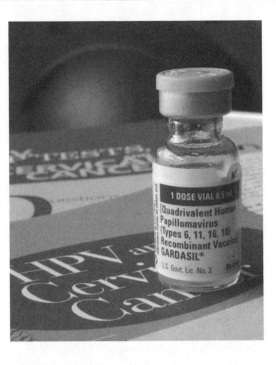

A dose of the vaccine Gardasil, used the prevention of cervical cancer.
AP IMAGES

Perry could veto the bill, though the legislature appeared to have enough votes to override a veto should that occur.

Congress Passes the Telephone Records and Privacy Protection Act of 2006

In an effort to curb the sale of private phone records, Congress in 2006 approve the Telephone Records and Privacy Protection Act of 2006, Pub. L. No. 109-476, 120 Stat. 3568. The act's purpose is to provide "explicit protection for the privacy of confidential telephone records, including call logs, and to establish specific criminal penalties for the **fraudulent** acquisition or disclosure of such records without the consent of the consumer." Legislators referred to the proposal as the "pretexting" bill, referring to a term used to describe a practice whereby individuals obtain private phone records through lying, deceit, or impersonation.

The issue involving the sale of private phone records gained prominence in 2006 with the disclosure that officials with Hewlett-Packard had spied on the company's directors. The controversy started in January 2006, the online technology site CNET published an article about HP's long-term strategy. Although the story was upbeat, it contained information that could have only come from an HP director. The company's chairperson, Patricia Dunn, expressed frustration with leaks from the company and decided to try to find out which director had leaked the information. She hired a team of independent electronic-security experts to spy on the communications of the directors.

The team that Dunn hired did not focus on calls made from the company itself, but rather made from personal accounts. Thus, directors' calls from home phones or cell phones were tracked. Moreover, the team did not review the content of the calls, but rather only reviewed the pattern of contacts. This practice eventually allowed Dunn to identify the director who leaked the information. Dunn confronted the director at a meeting in May 2006, which eventually led to the director's resignation from the board. The SECURITIES AND EXCHANGE COMMISSION began an investigation of the company's actions, and several former officials, along with the investigators, face criminal and civil charges. (Dunn was diagnosed with ovarian cancer after resigning from HP in September; a judge later dropped the criminal charges against her).

Even before news of the HP scandal broke, lawmakers had become concerned with the ease in which phone records could be obtained. Reporters with the *Chicago Sun-Times* obtained phone records of undercover agents with the FEDERAL BUREAU OF INVESTIGATION. This information was available from companies that sold the information on the Internet. Law enforcement officials and others expressed their concerns about the possibility that such information could be used the hinder investigations. Moreover, these officials said that the sale of these records violated privacy rights of those whose records were sold.

"If this were not enough of a privacy violation for the average consumer, the [Senate Judiciary] Committee also learned that criminals were employing these services to learn the identity of undercover law enforcement officers, as well as suspected confidential informants and witnesses," said U.S. Representative James Sensenbrenner (R.-Wisc.). "In addition, this practice also endangers victims of domestic violence and stalking, since stalkers and abusers can use cell record information to track a victim's location and associates. Amazingly enough, none of this is clearly illegal under federal law."

In February 2006, Representative Lamar Smith (R.-Tex.) introduced H.R. 4709, entitled the Telephone Records and Privacy Protection Act of 2006. It was referred to the House Judiciary Committee, which released a report on the bill on March 16, 2006. The report expressed concerns about the ease in which companies can acquire the private telephone records. The House committee also noted that though many companies operate on the Internet, as many as several thousand other companies and individuals may provide these services as well. The committee report noted that the services that provide these records often use fraudulent schemes in order to acquire the information. More specifically, the report expressed concern about the practice of pretexting, which "occurs when an unauthorized individual calls the phone company posing as someone who is authorized to receive the information lawfully, such as the actual phone service subscriber or another employee of the target phone company."

The House of Representatives approved the bill on April 25 by a vote of 409 to zero. The Senate received the bill one day later. On December 2006, the Senate approved the measure by unanimous consent. President GEORGE W. BUSH signed the bill on January 12, 2007.

The act, which became **Public Law** No. 109-476, amends the federal criminal code to prohibit the obtaining of confidential phone records information from a telecommunications carrier (referred to as a "covered entity" in the **statute**) through one of the following means: "(1) making false or fraudulent statements or representations to an employee of a covered **entity**; (2) making such false or fraudulent representations to a customer of a covered entity; (3) providing a document to a covered entity knowing that such document is false or fraudulent; or (4) accessing customer accounts of a covered entity via the Internet . . . without prior authorization from the customer to whom such confidential phone records information relates."

The act imposes fines and imprisonment of up to 10 years for those who violate the statute. The statute also doubles the fines and imposes an additional five-year prison term for violations that occur within a 12-month period and that involve transactions of more than $100,000 or more than 50 customers of a covered entity. Moreover, the act imposes additional five-year terms for those who use confidential phone records information to commit crimes of violence, crimes of domestic violence, and crimes against law enforcement officials and the administration of justice.

Lawfully authorized investigations and intelligence activities are exempted from the act. Congress also exempted certain telecommunications entities from the provisions of the act, when the entity uses public records information for such purposes as billing, protection of property rights, and emergency purposes.

PROBATE

The court process by which a will is proved valid or invalid. The legal process wherein the estate of a decedent is administered.

Death of Anna Nicole Smith Leads to Numerous Legal Disputes

In February 2007, less than one year after she won a case before the U.S. SUPREME COURT, celebrity Anna Nicole Smith died in a Florida hotel room. Her death came only months after she gave birth to a daughter, which occurred just days before her adult son died accidentally from a combination of medications. Smith's death led to a number of legal disputes involving her mother and a number of men claiming to be the father of her child.

Smith was born Vickie Lynn Hogan in Houston, Texas in 1967. She withdrew from school after the 11th grade and began working as a waitress at a fried chicken restaurant in Mexia, Texas. She married a fry cook named Bill Smith in 1985 and had a child with him the next year. She separated from Smith in 1987 and eventually became an exotic dancer. She entered a contest to appear in *Playboy* magazine and was selected for the publication in 1992. The appearance made her a celebrity, as she later became the Playboy Playmate of the Year and a model for Guess? jeans.

Prior to her appearance in *Playboy*, she met 89-year-old oil tycoon J. Howard Marshall II, who was a customer at a strip club at which Smith performed. The two developed a relationship, and a year after her divorce with Billy Smith became final, she married Marshall. Marshall died in 1995, leading to a protracted legal battle over the next decade between Smith and E. Pierce Marshall, the son of the J. Howard Marshall. The elder Marshall had left a fortune of about $1.6 billion, and Smith maintained that he had promised to leave a significant portion to her.

A federal bankruptcy judge in 1996 awarded $474 million to Smith, though a federal district judge later reduced the award to $88 million. In 2004, though, the Ninth **Circuit Court** of Appeals held that the California court did not have jurisdiction over the case and vacated the lower court rulings. Smith appealed the decision to the U.S. Supreme Court, which granted **certiorari** in 2005. On May 1, 2006, the Court held that the federal court had properly asserted jurisdiction over the case and reversed the Ninth Circuit's decision. *Marshall v. Marshall*, 547 U.S. 293, 126 S. Ct. 1735, 164 L. Ed. 2d 480 (2006).

Smith remained in the spotlight despite her legal problems. From 2002 to 2004, she appeared on her own reality show, entitled "The Anna Nicole Smith Show," which also featured her son and her lawyer, Howard K. Stern. She also became a spokesperson for TrimSpa, which produced a diet pill that Smith reportedly used to lose nearly 70 pounds.

Events that occurred after her victory at the Supreme Court were mostly tragic. She gave birth to a daughter named Dannielynn Hope Marshall Stern in the Bahamas September 2006. However, the identity of the child's father was in question even before the baby was born. Celebrity photographer Larry Birkhead claimed paternity several months before Dannielynn's birth, but Stern's name was included on the birth certificate. After the baby was born, Smith's son Daniel, then 20, flew to the Bahamas to see his mother. Three days after the baby was born, Daniel collapsed in his mother's hospital room and died. Tests later revealed that Daniel died of a lethal combination of methadone and the antidepressants Zoloft and Lexapro.

Daniel's death left Smith in disarray. In the wake of Daniel's death, Smith and Stern exchanged informal vows in the Bahamas in a ceremony that did not qualify as a legal marriage. Stern appeared on the talk show Larry King Live and said that he was the true father of Smith's daughter. In October, Birkhead filed a paternity lawsuit against Smith, claiming that Smith was addicted to drugs and that Stern was claiming to be the child's father for his own financial gain. The dispute between Birkhead and Smith continued until Smith's death.

Smith returned to the United States in January after a California judge required Smith to submit the baby to DNA testing. For the next month, Smith's lawyers continued to fight the court ordered test, but on February 8, Smith collapsed in her hotel room in Hollywood, Florida and was rushed to the hospital. She died an hour after her arrival. In the wake of her death, the battle over Dannielynn's custody heated up. An attorney named Richard Millstein was awarded temporary custody of Dannielynn, pending the result of the paternity test.

Disputes about where to bury Smith's body also arose. Smith's estranged mother, Virgie Arthur, wanted to take the body back to Texas, but Stern and others wanted for her to be buried in the Bahamas. On February 23, a Florida judge, Larry Seidlin, settled the question by giving custody of Smith's remains to Millstein, who chose to bury Smith in the Bahamas. Seidlin himself made news with his tearful issuance of the order granting custody to Millstein. Arthur appealed Seidlin's ruling, but a Florida **appellate court** affirmed the decision. Smith was buried in the Bahamas on March 2. Autopsy results later revealed that she died of an accidental overdose of several drugs.

A third name in the custody dispute arose shortly after Smith's death. Prince Frederic Von Anhalt, husband of Zsa Zsa Gabor, claimed that he was the true father of Dannielynn and agreed to submit to paternity testing along with Birkhead and Stern. The three men submitted to the paternity test, which was administered on March 21 (several other men, including Smith's former bodyguard, also claimed to be the child's father). On April 10, results from the DNA test revealed that Birkhead was the true father. A court in the Bahamas granted custody of Dannielynn to Birkhead and allowed him to change her birth certificate to remove Stern's name and add his own. In May, Birkhead took the baby to Kentucky.

Smith's estate will likely remain entangled in litigation for some time to come. In addition to the final resolution of her case against her former husband's estate, Smith was also named as a defendant in a **class action** suit against TrimSpa. Additionally, Smith's will, which was drafted in 2001, has caused significant controversy, because it left all of her assets to her son Daniel. Moreover, the will could be read to exclude future children or spouses, which could mean that Dannielynn would receive nothing from her mother's estate.

PUBLIC UTILITIES

Businesses that provide the public with necessities, such as water, electricity, natural gas, and telephone and telegraph communication.

California Approves Measures Designed to Reduce Greenhouse Gases

The California Public Utilities Commission in January 2007 approved a regulation that prohibits utilities from purchasing electricity that is produced by power plants that produce greenhouse gases. The rule was adopted pursuant to an emissions control bill that the California Legislature passed in 2006. Under the new rule, utilities will not be able to purchase power from most coal-burning plants, because few of these plants are able to meet the new guidelines.

Scientists have proven that carbon dioxide and other greenhouse gases contribute to the problem of global warming. Despite this fact, increased use of alternative energy sources has been slow. In 2006, plans for more than 20 power plants had been introduced for construction in the Rocky Mountain states as well as the southwest. Plans called for these plants to burn coal, which is plentiful and relatively inexpensive, and much of the energy produced by the plants would be sent to California. These coal-burning plants would produce high quantities of carbon dioxide. As of 2001, California ranked second in the nation among states, behind Texas, in the production of carbon dioxide.

Members of the California Legislature introduced a bill entitled the Global Warming Solutions Act of 2006, which directly addressed the problem not only associated with gases produced by these power plants, but also the gases produced by oil refineries and cement plants. Under the legislation, the state aimed to reduce industrial carbon dioxide emissions by 25 percent by 2020. Although other states, such as New York, have considered proposals, the California legislation was the most aggressive proposal for attacking the problem of the production of greenhouse gases.

The State of California has taken a number of steps to reduce its energy consumption and to reduce the emission of greenhouse gases. For a number of years, the state has required that home devices such as refrigerators, air conditioners, and water heaters become more energy efficient. The state has also targeted chargers for cell phones and computers, as well as remote-controlled devices. Consumers in California also reportedly have begun to trade in their sport utility vehicles for more energy efficient models, including newer hybrid vehicles.

The proposal was not uniformly applauded. California has introduced several initiatives designed to address the causes of global warming, but critics say that these efforts could hurt consumers in California due to the increase in energy costs. In 2002, California became the first state to enact legislation that regulated emissions of carbon dioxide from automobile tailpipes, but that law has been challenged in federal court by members of the automobile industry. More recently, California Governor Arnold Schwarzenegger approved a proposal that requires builders to offer roofs that can convert sunlight into electricity.

Schwarzenegger signed the Global Warming Solutions Act in September 2006. The specific provisions of the act resulted from negotiations between the Democrat-controlled legislature and the governor, who is a Republican. In addition to establishing the goals for reducing greenhouse gases, the legislation also granted new authority to the California Air Resources Board, which was charged with setting specific emissions targets for various industries.

About four months after the passage of the act, the California Public Utilities Commission considered a proposed rule that would prohibit California utilities from buying electricity from power plants that exceed state emissions standards. Under the rule, California utilities could not make "new long-term commitments" with facilities that produce more than 1,100 pounds of carbon dioxide per kilowatt-hour. Such commitments include new construction, "major investments" in existing plants, and contracts lasting five years or longer. At the time of its adoption, coal-burning plants located outside of California supplied about 20 percent of the state's electricity.

The commission unanimously approved the proposal in January 2007. Members of the commission said that the regulation was necessary in order to implement the provisions of the 2006 legislation. According to commissioner Dian M. Grueneich, "The Emissions Performance Standard is a vital step towards achieving the emissions reduction goals of [the Global Warming Solutions Act] and protecting our ratepayers against the risk of high carbon prices in the not-too-distant future. At the same time, this decision leaves the door open to new, advanced technologies and carbon sequestration projects that will allow the energy industry to develop clean and sustainable sources of power."

Utility companies also praised the new standard. "The CPUC's greenhouse gas emissions performance standard is an essential step to addressing climate change. PG&E applauds the CPUC's vision and leadership in designing an aggressive and pragmatic policy, which encourages all of California's energy providers to invest in long term renewable energy sources," said Thomas B. King, Chief Executive Officer with Pacific Gas and Electric Co. "We are committed to doing our part by continuing to develop our renewable energy portfolio and providing our customers with among the cleanest energy in the nation."

At the time of the signing of the new standards, more than 220 companies had registered their emission levels with the California Climate Action Registry, which is a voluntary project that allows companies to register their levels of greenhouse gas emissions. The legislation passed in 2006 provided incentives for companies to submit these emission levels.

PUNITIVE DAMAGES

Monetary compensation awarded to an injured party that goes beyond that which is necessary to compensate the individual for losses and that is intended to punish the wrongdoer.

Philip Morris USA v. Williams

Since the late 1980s the U.S. SUPREME COURT has issued rulings that seek to limit the amount of **punitive damages** awarded by juries to plaintiffs. The Court has been troubled by the disproportionate ratio between the amount of the punitive damages award and the compensatory damage award. Though punitive damages are to be used to punish the defendant reprehensible conduct, the Court in *Philip Morris USA v. Williams*, __U.S.__, 127 S.Ct. 1057, __L.Ed.2d __ (2007), announced a procedural rule that prohibits the jury from being instructed that it may award punitive damages to punish the defendant for injury to other persons not part of the lawsuit.

Mayola Williams sued Philip Morris, the maker of Marlboro cigarettes, claiming that the company caused the death of her husband, Jesse Williams, a heavy smoker of Marlboros. Williams alleged negligence and deceit by Philip Morris. A jury found that his death was caused by smoking, that Williams smoked because he thought it was safe to do so, and that Philip Morris knowingly and falsely led him to believe that smoking was safe. The jury found that the company was negligent and had used deceit. On the deceit claim the jury awarded Williams in **compensatory damages** of about $821,000 and $79.5 million in punitive damages. The trial judge ruled that the punitive damages award was excessive in light of *BMW of North America v. Gore*, 517 U.S. 559, 116 S. Ct. 1589, 134 L. Ed. 2d 809 (1996), and reduced the award to $32 million. Both sides appealed to the Oregon Court of Appeals, which sided with Williams and restored the $79.5 million jury award. Philip Morris appealed to the U.S. Supreme Court, which remanded the case to the Oregon Court of Appeals to reconsider based on the factors detailed in *State Farm Mutual Automobile Insurance Company v. Campbell*, 538 U.S. 408, 123 S.Ct. 1513, 155 L.Ed.2d 585(2003). In this case the Court used three "guideposts" to determine whether a punitive damages award is excessive.

A court must consider (1) the degree of reprehensibility of the defendant's misconduct; (2) the disparity between the actual harm suffered by the plaintiff and the punitive damages award; and, (3) the difference between the punitive damages award and the civil penalties authorized or imposed in comparable bases. The Oregon Court of Appeals issued a new decision that affirmed the basic conclusions of its first ruling.

The Oregon Supreme Court accepted Philip Morris's appeal. The company argued that the trial court had erred by denying its proposed punitive damages instruction that specified the jury could not seek to punish Philip Morris for injury to other persons not before the court. The Williams' lawyer had argued to that it should think about how many other smokers there had been in Oregon over the past 40 years and that cigarettes were going to kill ten out of every one hundred smokers. Philip Morris asked the trial court to instruct the jury that "you may consider the extent of harm suffered by others in determining what [the] reasonable relationship is" between any punitive award and the "harm caused to Jesse Williams" by Philip Morris' misconduct "but you are not to punish the defendant for the impact of its alleged misconduct on other persons, who may bring lawsuits of their own in which other juries can resolve their claims" The judge rejected the proposed instruction and told the jury it could award punitive damages against Philip Morris "to punish misconduct and to deter misconduct," and "are not intended to compensate the plaintiff or anyone else for damages caused by the defendant's conduct." Philip Morris contended that there was the strong likelihood that part of the $79.5 million award represented punishment for its having harmed others. Such an award would violate the Fourteenth Amendment's Due Process Clause. The Oregon Supreme Court rejected this argument and a claim that the award was excessive in light of the State Farm decision. Philip Morris then appealed to the U.S. Supreme Court.

The Court, in a 5–4 decision, overruled the Oregon Supreme Court ruling. Justice STEPHEN BREYER, writing for the majority, only addressed the jury instruction issue. He stated that the Due Process Clause forbids a state to use a punitive damages award to punish a defendant for injuries inflicted on "strangers to the litigation." To permit such an award would run magnify the due process risks of arbitrariness, uncertainty, and lack of notice. Breyer could find no authority for using punitive damages for the purpose of punishing a defendant for harming others. It was acceptable that a jury consider a punitive damages award "in light of the potential harm the defendant's conduct could have caused." However, the "potential harm at issue was harm potentially caused the plaintiff. The Oregon Supreme Court was correct that the U.S. Supreme Court had never explicitly held that a jury "may not punish for the harm caused others. But we do so now." Therefore, the Court remanded the case to the Oregon Supreme Court so it could apply the correct constitutional standard. Justice Breyer acknowledged that the application of the standard might require a new trial or a change in the amount of punitive damages award. In light of this possibility the Court declined to analyze whether the $79.5 million was excessive.

Justices JOHN PAUL STEVENS, ANTONIN SCALIA, CLARENCE THOMAS, and RUTH BADER GINSBURG dissented. Justice Stevens could not understand the "nuance" between taking third-party harm into account in order to determine the reprehensibility of the defendant's conduct and "doing so in order to punish the defendant 'directly'." Justice Thomas reiterated his view that the Constitution does not constrain the size of punitive damages awards. Justice Ginsburg, in a dissent joined by Justice Scalia, reaffirmed the point that punitive damages are meant to punish the reprehensibility of the defendant's conduct. Ginsburg concluded that the Philip Morris jury instruction would confuse rather than enlighten a jury and that the Court should give more respect to state court proceedings that "sought diligently to adhere to our changing, less than crystalline precedent."

RACIAL DISCRIMINATION

Parents Involved in Community Schools v. Seattle School District No. 1

School districts throughout the United States have employed racial guidelines to insure that schools are racially integrated. These guidelines have prevented white students from selecting the schools of their choice, leading critics to label these plans as an outlawed form of racial discrimination. Parents of white children have filed federal lawsuits challenging various guidelines that expressly use race as a determining factor in school selection procedures. These lawsuits produced mixed results until the U.S. SUPREME COURT, in *Parents Involved in Community Schools v. Seattle School District No. 1*, __U.S.__, 127 S.Ct. __, __L.Ed.2d __ 2007 WL 1836531 (2007), issued a landmark ruling that struck down the guidelines used by the Seattle, Washington and Louisville, Kentucky school districts, finding that such plans violated the **Equal Protection** Clause of the FOURTEENTH AMENDMENT. Though four justices voted to end the use of race in public education to promote diversity, Justice ANTHONY KENNEDY issued a separate opinion that said that race could still be taken into account if the programs were more narrowly tailored. The dissenting four justices countered that the majority had made a disastrous decision that would unsettle decades of decisions that sought to prevent the resegregation of public schools.

In 1998 the Seattle school district established guidelines on high school assignments. Because some schools were more popular than others, a series of "tiebreakers" were used to determine who was given open slots. The first tiebreaker gave preference to students who had a sibling enrolled in the high school. The next tiebreaker was based on the racial composition of the school and the race of the individual student. The racial composition of the Seattle schools was 41 percent white and 59 percent nonwhite. If the school was not within 10 percent of the district's overall racial balance, then the school would admit students whose race would help bring the school into balance. The district employed these tiebreakers because most white students live in the northern section of Seattle, while nonwhites mostly live in southern areas of the city. By 2000 many white students were not admitted to one of the four high schools in northern Seattle, leading to the formation of Parents Involved in Community Schools. This organization filed a federal lawsuit, arguing that the tiebreaker system violated the Equal Protection Clause of the Fourteenth Amendment. The federal **district court** ruled against the organization as did the Ninth **Circuit Court** of Appeals. Both courts found that under the **strict scrutiny** analysis of constitutionality the school district had a compelling interest in maintaining racial diversity and had narrowly tailored its plan to serve this interest.

In the second case, the Jefferson County Schools located in the greater Louisville, Kentucky area, established in 2001 a voluntary school assignment plan. The racial composition of the schools was 34 percent black and 66 percent white. The Louisville plan denied admission to grade schools if the student's race would contribute to the school's racial imbalance. Crystal Meredith filed a federal lawsuit challenging the plan after her son was denied the right to transfer to a grade school that was close to their home because the transfer would have an adverse effect on school desegregation. The federal district court and the Sixth Circuit Court of Appeals dismissed her case, finding that the school district had a compelling interest in insuring that the schools remain integrated and that the plan was narrowly tailored to serve that compelling interest.

The Supreme Court, in a 5–4 decision, overruled both circuit courts, finding that the plans did not survive strict constitutional scrutiny. Chief Justice JOHN ROBERTS, in a opinion announcing the judgment of the Court, found that the plans were "directed only to racial balance, pure and simple," which violated the Equal Protection Clause. He concluded that the "way to stop discrimination on the basis of race is to stop discriminating on the basis of race." Roberts noted that in *Brown v. Board of Education*, 347 U.S. 483, 74 S.Ct. 686, 98 L.Ed. 873 (1954) the Court ruled that schoolchildren could not be told where they could go to school based "on the color of their skin." The school districts had failed to demonstrate that they should be allowed to do this "once again—even for very different reasons." In his view it made no difference if the school districts had worthy goals in mind if they were "free to discriminate on the basis of race to achieve it."

Justice Anthony Kennedy supplied the fifth vote to strike down the two plans but he was not prepared to remove race as a consideration in ensuring diversity. Kennedy disagreed with Roberts' conclusion that race could not be taken into account, stating that "The **plurality** opinion is too dismissive of the legitimate interest government has in ensuring all people have equal opportunity regardless of race." He suggested that schools could take into account race if they did not single out individual students. The drawing of school attendance zones, "strategic site selection of new schools," and directing resources at special programs such as magnet schools were possible ways of avoiding "the status quo of racial isolation in schools." Kennedy's concurring opinion emerged as the basis for analyzing other school diversity plans, which are currently in use by over 1,000 school districts throughout the United States.

Justice STEPHEN BREYER wrote a lengthy dissenting opinion, which was joined by Justice JOHN PAUL STEVENS, DAVID SOUTER, and RUTH BADER GINSBURG. Justice Breyer found little merit in Justice Kennedy's suggested alternatives and argued that the Court had taken a "radical" step away from established law. Without the use of such assignment plans he believed that the resegregation by race of the public schools was inevitable. He concluded that the decision would be one that the Supreme Court "and the nation will come to regret."

RAPE

A criminal offense defined in most states as forcible sexual relations with a person against that person's will.

Servicemen Charged in Brutal Case of Rape and Murder in Iraq

Five U.S. servicemen were charged in 2006 in connection with the brutal rape of a 14-year-old Iraqi girl, followed by the murder of the girl and three members of her family. Another former member of the army, who was discharged from the Army prior to being charged with the crime, was prosecuted in federal court. The story of the rape and slaying has been one of the most gruesome to arise out of the conflict with Iraq. The attacks took place in March 2006

According to court records, five members of the 502nd Infanry, 101st Airborne Division, plotted to attack a family in the area of Khasir Abyad, which is located about six miles north of Mahmoudiya and about 20 miles south of Baghdad. The area is known as the "Triangle of Death," due to the number attacks there by Sunni insurgents. The victims of the crime had just recently moved into the home where the attacks occurred. Affidavits indicated that four Americans entered the house while a fifth remained behind to monitor the radio. The soldiers separated the teenaged girl, Abeer Qassim al-Janabi, from three other family members. At least one member of the group raped the girl; shot her father, mother, and younger sister; and then shot the girl in the head.

After the attack, the men tried to cover up the crime by dousing the girl in a flammable liquid and attempting to burn her. They also burned their own clothes and discarded the murder weapon, an AK-47 rifle. Iraqi officials learned of the crime on about March 13, but a local police captain said that this information was not relayed to American forces. The satellite channel Al Jazeera covered the alleged crimes extensively, while the media in Iraq did not until the official investigation began.

Four of the suspects involved in the murders included specialist James Barker, Pfc. Jesse Spielman, Pfc. Bryan Howard, and Sgt. Paul Cortez. A fifth serviceman, Sgt. Anthony Yribie, was also charged with dereliction of duty for his failure to report the incident. The alleged leader of the group, a private named Steven Green, had been discharged from the Army after a psychological evaluation revealed that he had a "personality disorder," though it was also reported that Green had been diagnosed as a homicidal threat. Stories written about Green after the incident indicated that he had made such statements as "I want to kill and hurt a lot of Iraqis" and "I came over here because I want to kill people."

In June, two soldiers who were part of the same platoon as the men responsible for the murders were killed in Yusufiya. A message attached to a video that show the murders of the two men indicated that the act was one of revenge for the killings of the family. Shortly after these killings occurred, one of the soldiers involved in the murders of the family reportedly became overcome with guilt and admitted to the killing. U.S. officials later said that they were aware of the crimes but thought that the killing of the family had been the result of "sectarian violence."

Military officials admitted in July that it had begun a criminal investigation into the allegations. It was the fifth pending case that involved allegations of slayings of Iraqi civilians. On July 9, the Army charged Barker, Spielman, Howard, and Cortez with participation in the rape of the girl and with the murder of the family, while Yribie was charged with dereliction of duty. Because these men were still on active duty, they faced what is known as an Article 32 investigation, which is similar to a **grand jury** investigation in a civilian court.

Green had returned to the United States after his discharge. Prosecutors filed criminal charges against him in federal court in Kentucky, and Green pleaded not guilty. According to the filings, Green had stalked the girl and her family and had organized the entire attack. Attorneys for Green on July 11 requested a **gag order** that would have prevented federal authorities, including President GEORGE W. BUSH and General Peter Pace, chair of the Joint Chiefs of Staff, from commenting on the case. According to the defense, public comments by Bush, Pace, and others had interfered with the possibility of Green receiving a fair trial due to their public comments. U.S. District Judge Thomas Russell denied the request on August 31.

The Article 32 investigation of the active servicemen began in August. One witness testified that combat stress had crushed the morale of the troops stationed near Mahmudiya. However, Captain Alex Pickands, the military lawyer prosecuting the men, argued vigorously against the argument that this stress was a defense to the actions of the defendants. None of the men testified at the proceeding. At the same time that the Army was holding its hearings, Iraqi Prime Minister Nouri al-Maliki said that he wanted those responsible for the crime to be tried in an Iraqi **tribunal** and ordered an independent investigation.

In October, each of the four men were referred to a general court-martial. Spielman and Cortez could have received the death penalty if they were convicted, because their charges included premeditation. About a month later, Green pleaded not guilty to the charges that he faced in federal court. Prosecutors previously asked for a three-month delay in Green's indictment, citing the problems with using evidence and witnesses simultaneously with the military investigation.

Barker entered into a plea bargain in which he agreed to testify against the other soldiers. He received a 90-year sentence with the possibility of parole. He alleged that Cortez and Spielman both participated in the planning of the incident. Cortez avoided the death penalty by pleading guilty to the charges, for which he received a 100-year sentence and was dishonorably discharged. He will be eligible for parole after serving 10 years. Howard later pleaded guilty to being an accessory to the rape and murder.

WILLIAM H. REHNQUIST

Evidence Surfaces of Justice Rehnquist's Dependency on Prescription Drugs

WILLIAM H. REHNQUIST was first named to the U.S. SUPREME COURT as an **associate justice** in 1971, becoming the Court's 16th Chief Justice in 1986, a position he held until his death in September 2005. In January 2007, the Federal Bureau of Investigation (FBI) released 1,561 pages from its files on Rehnquist, pursuant to a FREEDOM OF INFORMATION ACT (FOIA) request, that raised some questions about his tenure on the Court. (Privacy laws prohibit disclosure of such files during the person's lifetime.)

The first involved Rehnquist's use of the prescription drug Placidyl, originally prescribed to him for insomnia following back surgery in 1971. During a routine investigation of Rehnquist's background in 1986 (following President Ronald Reagan's nomination of him as chief justice), the FBI obtained a medical report that described him as seriously "dependent" on Placidyl from 1977 to 1981. The standard adult dose of this drug, labeled a "sedative-hypnotic," is 500 milligrams, taken at bedtime. Rehnquist initially took 200 milligrams in 1971, but by 1981 was taking 1,500 milligrams a day. The medicine was prescribed by Dr. Freeman H. Cary, the attending physician to Congress.

Most of this was already known prior to the release of the FBI file. Journalists had previously reported Rehnquist's self-admission into GEORGE WASHINGTON University Hospital in December 1981 for treatment of persistent back pain and dependence on Placidyl. The prescription drug, generically known as ethchlorvynol, is a sleep-inducing medication but is not technically a pain-killer. Although it is not an opiate, it can be addictive and withdrawal may cause symptoms such as hallucinations and temporary memory loss.

While media stories widely reported Rehnquist's "bizarre" and "paranoid" behavior while in the hospital, they generally failed to note that he had abruptly stopped taking the medication "cold turkey" and that the symptoms were manifestations of withdrawal rather than medication. Doctors told FBI agents that when Rehnquist stopped taking Placidyl, he developed paranoid delusions, hearing voices outside of his hospital room, fearing a CIA plot against him, and describing changing patterns in the design patterns of the hospital curtains. At one point, Rehnquist attempted to escape in his pajamas, but only made it as far as the hospital lobby. The doctors concluded that the withdrawal symptoms were so severe that they reintroduced the justice to Placidyl in smaller doses and gradually weaned him off until he quit taking them entirely in early February 1982.

All the doctors interviewed by FBI investigators in 1986 proffered their expert opinions that the former dependence on Placidyl should not affect Rehnquist's work performance or capability on the Court, and it did not become an issue during his confirmation hearings. Nor were there any later accusations or suggestions that Rehnquist's role on the Court or his work

had been affected by his dependence during those years. He continued to suffer back pain for the remainder of his life, as well as a bout with thyroid cancer.

What *did* become a media issue after the release of the FBI papers was the apparent interest of the JUSTICE DEPARTMENT, during both of Rehnquist's confirmation hearings in 1971 and 1986, in enlisting the FBI to check out what witnesses lined up by Senate Democrats were intending to say at the hearings.

The FBI files showed that in 1971, an aide to FBI Director J. EDGAR HOOVER and then-Deputy Attorney General Richard Kleindienst requested a "background check" on two Phoenix residents who were planning to testify against Rehnquist's nomination. The media covered the story at the time, and the FBI issued a statement that all questioning was impartial and without intimidation. Then again in 1986, Senator Strom Thurmond (R-SC), chairman of the SENATE JUDICIARY COMMITTEE, asked the FBI to interview two witnesses who were expected to raise allegations that Rehnquist had "challenged" blacks waiting in line to vote in 1962. The request was relayed by a young attorney general, John Bolton (the recent ambassador to the UNITED NATIONS). Years later, after the FBI files were released, Bolton was contacted and told reporters that there was no political motivation behind the request because it had come from Senate Democrats. Further, the FBI found no evidence that Rehnquist had intimidated voters.

RELIGION

Gonzales Initiates Program to Protect Religious Freedom

Attorney General Alberto Gonzales in February 2007 announced that the JUSTICE DEPARTMENT had launched a program entitled the "First Freedom Project," which is designed to aid the protection of religious liberties. The program focuses on educating the public about laws that protect religious freedom. It will also promote improved communication with religious, civil rights, and community leaders so that issues related to religious liberties are brought to the attention of the Justice Department.

The term "First Freedom" is used to describe the freedom of religion, referring specifically to the fact that this is the first freedom listed in the Bill of Rights. President GEORGE W. BUSH has been known to express his faith more openly than any president in history. In his proclamation for Religious Freedom Day in 2006, Bush said, "The right to religious freedom is a foundation of America. Our Founding Fathers knew the importance of freedom of religion to a stable democracy, and our Constitution protects individuals' rights to worship as they choose. We reject religious discrimination in every form, and we continue our efforts to oppose prejudice and to counter any infringements on religious freedom."

The Department of Justice has been delegate responsibility for enforcing a number of civil rights statutes that are designed to protect religious liberty. Among these laws include the following: laws that bar discrimination against individuals on account of religion in the areas of education, housing, credit, public facilities, and public accommodations; laws that prohibit local **zoning** authorities from discriminating against churches, other houses of worship, and religious schools; laws and protect the religious rights of prisoners; and certain criminal statutes that prohibit acts of violence against others based on the victims' religion.

The new initiative charges the Justice Department's Civil Rights Division to sponsor a number of programs that focus on the protection of religious rights. One goal is for the department to work on the continued expansion of the enforcement of civil rights statutes. The department will also create a Task Force on Religious Liberty, which will review the department's policies that impact religious liberty, coordinate religious liberty cases, and improve the department's outreach to various communities.

In addition to those efforts, the department plans to improve education about how the federal government can protect religious freedoms. The Justice Department will initiate a series of regional seminars, where civic and religious leaders, as well as members of the public, can learn about laws protecting religion and can learn how to file complains. The department will also increase efforts to reach out to various civil and religious organizations by holding meetings and speaking engagements, as well as by distributing informational literature.

Gonzales announced the launch of the initiative at a meeting of the Southern Baptist Convention in Nashville, Tennessee on February 20, 2007. At the meeting, Gonzales focused on the historic emphasis on religious freedom in the United States. "Throughout our history, nothing has defined us as a nation more than our respect for religious freedom," Gonzales said. "It is not confined to members of one church or

the followers of one set of beliefs. Through this initiative, the Justice Department continues its vigorous efforts to enforce protections against religious discrimination."

Gonzales later said that he chose the Southern Baptist Convention because the group has been "very interested in the protection of religious freedom." Church leaders praised the attorney general's actions after the meeting. "The attorney general's desire to address the major meeting of SBC leaders to announce this initiative shows both the importance of the issue and the commitment of the Justice Department at the highest levels to defend every individual American's religious freedom rights, particularly their free exercise rights, which are too often infringed," said Richard Land, president of the Southern Baptist Ethics and Religious Liberty Commission. "This initiative is needed and should make a real difference. When individuals find themselves in a confrontation concerning their free exercise rights, it helps to have the attorney general and the Department of Justice on your side."

Not everyone to comment about the announcement were entirely positive about the program. Some Christian leaders noted that Gonzales had failed to address all of the aspects of religious freedom. "The FIRST AMENDMENT has two protections for religious freedom—prohibition on religious establishments and protection for free exercise of religion," said Brent Walker, executive director of the Baptist Joint Committee for Religious Liberty. "The administration has often ignored the importance of the no-establishment principle by supporting attempts of governments to endorse a religious message, using tax dollars to fund pervasively religious organizations, allowing religious discrimination in hiring for federally funded projects, and going to the Supreme Court to cut back on the rights of citizens to challenge such practices."

Gonzales made his announcement at the same time that the department released the release of a report that details efforts of the Justice Department in protecting religious freedoms. According to the report, during the period of 1995 to 2000, the department reviewed only one case of religious discrimination in educational institutions and conducted no investigations. During the same length of time between 2001 and 2006, the department reviewed 82 cases and conducted 40 investigations.

In his speech before the Southern Baptist Convention, Gonzales provided several exam-

Kansas Board of Education member Kathy Martin (left) watches as fellow members Sally Cauble and Jana Shaver vote for evolution-friendly science standard for Kansas public schools, February 2007.

AP IMAGES

ples of cases in which the department had intervened on behalf of those who had experienced discrimination. In a case arising from New Jersey in 2006, the Justice Department argued successfully on behalf of a student who was prohibited by her school from singing the Christian song "Awesome God" at a talent show. In another case, the department defended a sixth-grade girl who had been suspended from school for wearing a headscarf that was required by her Muslim faith.

Kansas School Board Throws Out Anti-Evolution Standards

In 2005, a conservative Kansas School Board made international news for adopting "anti-evolution" science education standards for its public schools. Educational standards are used to develop tests to measure students' understanding of the sciences. The controversial standards had required a critical evaluation of biological evolution. In application, this meant students were instructed that the evolution theory of all life on Earth having a 'common origin' had been challenged by fossils and molecular biology. Further, the standards instructed that scientific controversy existed over whether changes in one species over time can lead to a new species.

The victory was short-lived. In the 2006 state elections, three of the conservative Board members were ousted in favor of a more moderate majority. The new majority of the Board adopted new science standards in February 2007 (again revised in June 2007). The new standards were intended to reflect mainstream scientific views of evolution. Even the standards' definition of science was changed, specifically limiting it to the search for natural explanations of what has been observed in the universe.

The changing anti- and pro-evolution standards were mostly the manifestation of changing political whims, and the 2006 Democratic upheaval in many state and local elections again preordained the most recent version. Part of the new standards, "Teaching With Tolerance and Respect," evidenced a more modern approach:

> "Science studies natural phenomena by formulating explanations that can be tested against the natural world. Some scientific concepts and theories (e.g., blood transfusion, human sexuality, nervous system role in consciousness, cosmological and biological evolution, etc.) may differ from the teachings of a student's religious community or their cultural beliefs. Compelling student belief is inconsistent with the goal of education. Nothing in science or in any other field of knowledge shall be taught as absolute knowledge. A teacher is an important role model for demonstrating respect, sensitivity, and civility. Science teachers should not ridicule, belittle, or embarrass a student for expressing an alternative view or belief. Teachers have the opportunity to display and demand tolerance and respect for the diverse ideas, skills, and experiences of all students."

But this change could be short-lived as well. The controversy over evolution and its counterpart "intelligent design" (which posits that there is intelligent causation [rather than random chance] to explain the complexity and order of the universe) had been going on since 1999. The new standards represented the fifth version adopted in the previous eight years.

Also in question was whether the new standards really reflected the views of a majority of Kansas citizens. The overall voter turnout for the election was only 18 percent, the lowest in 14 years, and the media reported that several groups favoring the teaching of evolution had campaigned heavily to stimulate voter turnout among moderate and liberal voters. According to *USA Today*, an independent poll by the media suggested that about half of Kansans thought evolution should be taught alongside intelligent design. "I feel like if you give two sides of something, most people are intelligent enough to make up their own minds," Ryan Cole, a 26-year-old from Smith County, was reported as saying.

Following the adoption of the new standards, the Intelligent Design Network presented petitions with 4,000 signatures opposing them. This suggested the possibility that if a different group of voters showed up for the next election, the outcome could again be different, and educators remained uncertain if the new standards would again be overturned. (Under Kansas law, the next mandatory review of standards must occur prior to 2014.)

While the controversy fell along political lines (the "conservative" Republicans voting for the old standards; the new Board members being Democrats or (one) moderate Republican), it had philosophical underpinnings as well. Some citizens accused the Board of promoting atheism. Others suggested the new standards undermined families and discredited parents who reject materialism.

In 2006, legal disputes, political, legislative, or school debates over the issue of how evolution should be taught cropped up in no less than seven states, including California, Georgia, Kentucky, Louisiana, Nevada, Ohio, and South Carolina. In Dover, Pennsylvania, voters removed school board members who had required the mention of intelligent design in the biology curriculum, while an Atlanta suburb became embroiled in a legal dispute over the placement of 35,000 stickers in biology textbooks declaring evolution "a theory, not a fact." In South Carolina, however, that approach was approved, along with mention of other theories such as intelligent design.

RICO

A set of federal laws (Racketeer Influenced and Corrupt Organizations Act) (18 U.S.C.A. §1961 et seq. [1970]) specifically designed to punish criminal activity by business enterprises.

Gamboa v. Velez

The Racketeer Influenced and Corrupt Organizations Act (RICO) contains civil provisions that are designed to punish illegal activity through the recovery of damage awards. Plaintiffs find RICO attractive because it enhances the award by allowing treble damages. This means that after the jury awards the plaintiff damages the court automatically triples that amount. In addition, the defendant must pay the

plaintiff's legal fees and costs. Though RICO was originally targeted at organized crime, the courts have broadened its reach to any enterprise that conducts illegal acts through a pattern of racketeering activity. The **federal courts** were called on to decide whether a person falsely accused of murder by a group of detectives could sue the police officers using RICO. The Seventh **Circuit Court** of Appeals, in *Gamboa v. Velez*, 457 F.3d 703 (7th Cir. 2006), ruled that he could not use RICO because he failed to establish a pattern of racketeering activity that went beyond the conduct focused on him.

In 1997 the Chicago police department assigned Carlos Velez and three other detectives to investigate the murder of Sindulfo Miranda. The fruits of this investigation led to the arrest of Ronny Gamboa for murder and **solicitation** of murder for hire. The evidence against Gamboa included an allegation that Miranda was in a bar owned by Gamboa the night of the murder, and the suggestion that Gamboa participated in the kidnapping, beating, and murder of Miranda. Gamboa went on trial in 2000 and was acquitted. Four other defendants implicated in Miranda's murder either were convicted or pleaded guilty to lesser charges. However, each of the convictions and guilty pleas were later overturned and the killers of Miranda have never been identified.

In 2003 Gamboa sued the City of Chicago and the four detectives responsible for his apparently erroneous prosecution. He sued using RICO, federal civil rights law 42 U.S.C.A. §1983, and two state law claims involving **malicious prosecution** and intentional infliction of mental distress. The federal **district court** dismissed the §1983 and state claims on statute-of-limitations grounds; this meant Gamboa had waited too long to file these claims. The RICO claim went forward against the detectives (Gamboa voluntarily dismissed the city from the lawsuit). The detectives asked the court to dismiss this count, arguing that Gamboa had not adequately alleged a pattern of racketeering activity. The court denied the motion to dismiss but allowed the defendants to file an immediate appeal that asked the Seventh Circuit Court of Appeals "whether a single scheme that ends without indication that it will be repeated establishes a pattern of racketeering activity merely because the scheme occurs over several years."

The Seventh Circuit answered in the negative, ruling that a single scheme did not establish a pattern merely because it unfolds over several years, involves a number of acts, and targets more than one victim. Judge Daniel Manion, writing for the three-judge panel, agreed that the detectives fell under three of the four RICO elements needed to support a civil claim: There was (1) conduct (2) of an enterprise (3) involving racketeering activity. The fourth element, the need for a pattern of activity, was the only issue before the court. For this element to be satisfied, Gamboa had to show that the alleged acts were not only related but must "amount to or pose a threat of continued criminal activity." Isolated instances of criminal activity that do not present the threat of future harm did not meet the RICO pattern element. Judge Manion concluded that Gamboa failed to meet his burden under RICO, for all he alleged was a "single, nonrecurring scheme (a frame-up of five individuals for a single murder)" which did not carry a threat of continued criminal activity.

Gamboa alleged the detectives had made false arrests, tampered with witness statements, procured perjured testimony, committed perjury, and engaged in malicious prosecution in order to intimidate and retaliate against him. He further alleged that the officers had filed false reports and coerced witnesses to testify against Gamboa at the **grand jury** in order to cover up the false arrests of Gamboa and the four other individuals. Despite these and other specific allegations the appeals court found that these acts were part of a "one-time endeavor." Gamboa did not allege that the detectives had committed misconduct beyond this one murder investigation nor did he indicate that the detectives would repeat their alleged unlawful conduct. Absent this type of evidence the case lacked the "continuity" required of a RICO claim. Despite the multiple acts occurring over several years, the detectives participated in a "non-reoccurring scheme with a built-in termination point."

The court also noted that this analysis made "particular sense in the context of a frame-up claim against police detectives." Some criminal defendants who are acquitted may have causes of action against under state **tort law** and federal civil rights laws. If Gamboa had filed these claims in a timely fashion he would have had his day in court. The court was unwilling to reformulate RICO to revive untimely claims and make it a substitute for tort and civil rights actions. To permit Gamboa to go forward would open up RICO to "garden variety" cases involving police investigations that develop over the course of several years. Therefore, the RICO claimed could not go forward.

Wilkie v. Robbins

"Racketeering" more generally means the extortive demand, **solicitation**, or receipt of anything of value, by means of a threat or promise, in order to cause persons with an interest in something of value to compromise that interest. Because the most pervasive instances of racketeering were at one time associated with "mob activity," Congress passed the Racketeer Influenced and Corrupt Organizations Act (RICO), 18 USC 1961 *et seq.*, to help officials break up, then prosecute activities associated with organized crime. Since then, RICO has been invoked in all sorts of cases alleging some form of conspiratorial activity to extort, bribe, or otherwise illegally pressure persons against their own interests.

In *Wilkie v. Robbins*, No. 06-219, 551 U.S. ___ (2007), Harvey Frank Robbins charged individual government officials from the Bureau of Land Management (BLM) with RICO violations for allegedly attempting to extort an **easement** of land from him. He also brought a private *Bivens* **cause of action** (after *Bivens v. Six Unknown Federal Narcotics Agents*, 403 U.S. 388 (1971)) (a claim seeking monetary damages from federal agents for constitutional violations), alleging retaliation for exercising his FIFTH AMENDMENT right to exclude government officials from his land. The U.S. SUPREME COURT ultimately ruled, 7–2, that "neither *Bivens* nor RICO [gave] Robbins a cause of action."

Robbins owned a private dude ranch in Wyoming, which had state and federal land surrounding much of it. The previous owner of his ranch had granted the BLM a right-of-way easement along a road on the ranch to access federal land. However, BLM failed to have the easement recorded, and therefore, Robbins had no notice of it when he purchased the land and recorded his interest in it. Under Wyoming law, Robbins took title to the ranch unencumbered by the unrecorded easement, and the easement was extinguished.

When BLM officials learned of the extinguished easement, they contacted Robbins to negotiate a new right-of-way easement, but he refused. According to Robbins and his complaint, BLM officials then attempted to extort a right-of-way from him by refusing to maintain the road providing access to his ranch; by threatening to cancel and then canceling his right-of-way across federal lands; by canceling his special recreation use permit and grazing privileges on federal lands; by stating they "would bury Frank

Robbins"; by trespassing on his land; and by bringing unfounded criminal charges against him.

At the **district court** level, the defendants filed a motion to dismiss the RICO claim based on qualified immunity. The district court refused to dismiss based on immunity, and also allowed one of Robbins' Fifth Amendment claims of retaliation to go forward. The Tenth **Circuit Court** of Appeals affirmed, and the government appealed.

Justice Souter, in delivering the opinion of the Court, first explained why Robbins had no private action for damages under *Bivens*. Asking whether any alternative process exists for protecting the interest at stake, the Court noted that this would be convincing reason alone for the Judicial Branch to refrain from creating a new remedy under case **common law**. The Court found that Robbins indeed had other viable administrative and judicial remedies to use for the government's alleged violations, albeit "patchwork," because each of the instances of alleged misconduct was grounded in a different theory. Notwithstanding, the Court needed to weigh reasons for and against creating a new cause of action.

The Court looked to the essence of Robbins' complaint. Robbins had conceded that any single action taken by the government might have been negligible, but for the fact that when aggregated, they amounted, in his mind, to true retaliation and coercion to extract an easement.

Then the Court looked to the government's alleged actions. Although the government was no ordinary landowner, when its lands bordered those of private parties, it could be expected to negotiate and engage in deals like any other landowner. Thus, since the government had the authority to withhold or withdraw permission for Robbins to use government lands, and authority to enforce trespass and land-use rules on federal lands, it was within its rights to make it plain to Robbins that his willingness to give an easement would determine how forgiving BLM would be about his trespasses.

Further, extending a *Bivens* cause of action to facts like these would open a floodgate of ostensible actions against legitimate governmental actions affecting property rights. The Court concluded that it would not expand *Bivens* to create a cause of action based on these facts.

Likewise, the Court ruled that RICO did not give Robbins a claim against defendants in their individual capacities. Noting that extortion has not normally been understood to include the actions of government officials, even *arguendo*, RICO would not apply to individual government officials who were seeking to obtain property for the government and not for themselves. The cases that Robbins cited in support of his argument were obscure and off-point, said the Court. The decision of the Tenth Circuit was reversed and the case remanded.

Justice Ginsburg filed a separate opinion, concurring in part and dissenting in part, in which she was joined by Justice Stevens. She characterized Robbin's Fifth Amendment claim as this: "Does the Fifth Amendment provide an effective check on federal officers who abuse their regulatory powers by harassing and punishing property owners who refuse to surrender their property to the United States without fair compensation? The answer should be a resounding 'Yes.'"

ROYALTY

Compensation for the use of property, usually copyrighted works, patented inventions, or natural resources, expressed as a percentage of receipts from using the property or as a payment for each unit produced.

BP America Production Co. v. Burton

The U.S. government leases vast tracts of land to companies that extract oil and gas from the ground. The Department of Interior negotiates these leases and receives royalty payments from the companies. These companies are responsible for accurate calculation and payment of the royalty but the government may audit the records if it believes it has been underpaid. A question arose whether an administrative payment order issued by the government was subject to a 6-year **statute of limitations** provision governing government contract actions. The Supreme Court, in *BP America Production Co. v. Burton*, __U.S.__, 127 S.Ct. __, L.Ed.2d __ (2006), ruled that this form of administrative action to recover owed royalty payments was not governed by the **statute** of limitations law.

The Mineral Leasing Act of 1920 (MLA), 30 U.S.C.A. §181 *et seq.*, authorizes the Secretary of Interior to lease public land to private parties for the production of oil and gas. MLA lessees must pya a royalty of at least "12.5 percent in amount or value of the production removed or sold from the lease." In 1982

Congress passed the Federal Oil and Gas Royalty Management act (FOGRMA), 30 U.S.C.A. §1701 *et seq.*, to modernize the system of accounting that tracked the payment of oil and gas royalties. FOGRMA ordered the Secretary of Interior to audit all current and past lease accounts and take actions to make additional collections or refunds as warranted. The secretary delegated this authority to the department's Minerals Management Service (MMS). MMS audits royalty payments and notifies lessees about a perceived deficiency. If the lessees' response is not persuasive, MMS issues an order requiring payment of the amount due. The **lessee** may appeal the MMS payment order to the director of MMS and then to the Interior Board of Land Appeals. If the government wishes to recover royalty payments in a lawsuit filed in court, it must do so within six years because of 6-year statute of limitations.

A dispute over royalty payments arose between BP America Production Co. and the MMS. BP held gas leases in New Mexico's San Juan Basin for over fifty years. The leases required BP to pay the **statutory** 12.5 percent royalty. For years the company had calculated this royalty as a percentage of the value of the gas at the moment it was produced at the well. In 1996, MMS directed BP to calculate the royalties on the value of the gas after it was treated to meet quality requirements for introduction into the main U.S. pipelines. Based on this formula, MMS in 1997 ordered the company to pay additional royalties for the period from January 1989 to December 1996 in order to cover the difference between the value of the treated gas and the lower value at the well. The company appealed the order, arguing that MMS's valuation formula was wrong. In addition, it contended that payment order was barred in party by the 6-year statute of limitations provision. BP lost its administrative appeal and then filed a lawsuit in U.S. **district court**. The district court rejected BP's statute of limitations argument, as did the Court of Appeals for the DISTRICT OF COLUMBIA. The Supreme Court

agreed to hear BP's appeal because the Tenth **Circuit Court** of Appeals had ruled that administrative payment orders were covered by the statute of limitations provision.

The Supreme Court, in a unanimous decision, upheld the ruling of the Court of Appeals for the District of Columbia. Justice Samuel Alito, writing for the Court, looked first to the statutory text and noted that unless otherwise defined, "statutory terms are generally interpreted in accordance with their ordinary meaning." Read in this way, the meaning of the statute of limitations provision was clear. The statute of limitations applied when the government started "any action for money damages" by filing a "complaint" to enforce a contract. The 6-year limit ran from the point when "the **right of action** accrues." Justice Alito seized on the terms "action" and "complaint," for they are ordinarily used in connection with judicial, not administrative proceedings. In 1966, when the statute of limitations provision was enacted, these terms were commonly limited to judicial proceedings. There was nothing in the 1966 provision that suggested that Congress intended to have these terms to apply more broadly to administrative proceedings.

BP cited many statutes and regulations that suggested the term "action" applied to both judicial and administrative proceedings. Justice Alito disagreed, pointing out that none of the cited examples used the word "action" alone; rather, each example included a modifier, such as "civil or administrative action." Therefore, the pattern of usage "buttresses the point that the term 'action,' standing alone, ordinarily refers to a judicial proceeding." In addition, the Court rejected BP's contention that the MMS payment order constituted a "complaint" under the statute of limitations provision. The payment order lacked the "essential attributes of a complaint" and it imposed a legally binding obligation on the lessee to pay. Justice Alito concluded that "absent congressional action changing this rule," the statute of limitations did not apply to administrative proceedings.

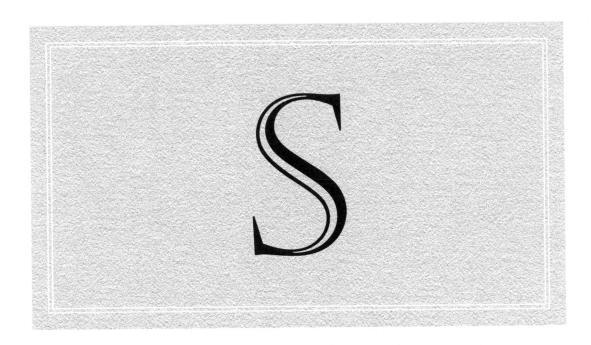

SEARCH AND SEIZURE

A hunt by law enforcement officials for property or communications believed to be evidence of crime, and the act of taking possession of this property

Phaneuf v. Fraikin

The Supreme Court has recognized that high school administrators need the authority to search students for contraband. Searches of student do not have to be based on **probable cause**; instead the legality of a search will depend on the reasonableness, under all circumstances, of the search. The most invasive search is a strip search, where individuals must disrobe and, in some cases, have their body cavities probed. Because of the invasive nature of a strip search, there must be strong reasons for subjecting a person to such an examination. In *Phaneuf v. Fraikin*, 448 F.3d 591 (2nd Cir.2006), the courts had to determine if school officials had reasonable cause to subject a female high school student to a strip search. The Second **Circuit Court** of Appeals held that the school officials appeared not to have reasonable cause, therefore allowing a civil damages suits against the officials to proceed.

In June 2002 the seniors at Plainville High School in Plainville, Connecticut were scheduled to attend their senior class picnic at an off-campus location. Before the students boarded buses for the picnic, school officials conducted a preannounced search of all bags for security reasons. A package of cigarettes was found in Kelly Phaneuf's purse. Though she was over eighteen and legally entitled to possess them, students were prohibited from bringing cigarettes onto school grounds. In addition, a student named Michele Cyr told her physical education teacher that Phaneuf had told her and other students that she had brought marijuana with her and planned to hide it down her pants when teachers performed the mandatory bag check. The teacher, Cindy Birdsall, reported the information to Principal Rose Cipriano. Believing this to be reliable information, Cipriano boarded the bus and asked Phaneuf to come with her to the nurse's office. She informed Phaneuf that a student had told school officials that she possessed marijuana. Phaneuf denied the allegation but Cipriano was skeptical, as Phaneuf had a history of non-drug-related discipline problems.

When they reached the nurse's office, Cipriano instructed the school nurse to conduct a search of Phaneuf's underpants. The nurse, Dorene Fraikin, expressed concerns about conducting a strip search, which led Cipriano to call Phaneuf's mother and ask her to come to the school to conduct the search. After arriving at the school, Phaneuf's mother objected to searching her daughter. She relented after being told that Cipriano would call the police and have an officer conduct the strip search. Phaneuf's mother conducted the search in a small room of the nurse's office, with a curtain separating this area from the main office. Nurse Fraikin was in the small room with the mother and daughter as Kelly disrobed. She claimed she had her back to the Phaneufs during the search but Kelly alleged Fraikin had watched. The search did not reveal any marijuana and Cipriano later drove Phaneuf to the picnic.

Phaneuf filed a civil rights lawsuit for damages against the school district, Cipriano, and Fraikin, claiming that they had violated her

FOURTH AMENDMENT rights when they strip searched her. The defendants contended the search was legal under the reasonableness standard announced by the U.S. SUPREME COURT. Though the federal **district court** found that a strip search conducted by school officials merits a higher level of scrutiny than a search of a student's possessions, the court concluded that the defendants had met the Supreme Court test. The search was both "reasonable at its inception" and "reasonable in scope." The school officials had a reasonable suspicion based on the tip from a reliable student, the prior discipline problems of Phaneuf, the way she denied having the contraband, and the fact she possessed cigarettes. The strip search was reasonable in scope because it was not excessively intrusive in light of her age, the fact that her mother conducted the search, and the nature of the infraction. Therefore, the district court dismissed Phaneuf's lawsuit.

The Second Circuit Court of Appeals disagreed with the district court's decision. The appeals court agreed with the lower court that the two-part reasonableness inquiry was the appropriate measuring stick but it disagreed with the lower court's interpretation of the facts. For the school district to prevail it had to show "a reasonably high level of suspicion that Phaneuf had marijuana to justify an intrusive, potentially degrading strip search." Moreover, this suspicion had to be based on facts known to the school officials prior to the search. Using this approach, the appeals court found the facts offered by school officials to be troubling. The officials could not offer any specific reasons why the informer was judged reliable; despite this uncorroborated tip Cipriano did not investigate the tip before ordering the strip search. Phaneuf's past disciplinary problems were not relevant either, for they did not involve drug abuse. The manner in which Phaneuf denied allegation was also of limited value, for all Birdsall and Cipriano could say was that Phaneuf's denial was "suspicious." Finally, the search of Phaneuf's purse and the discovery of cigarettes appeared to be a justification after school officials decided to conduct the search. Even if not, the possession of cigarettes could not support the suspicion a student is carrying drugs, a firearm, "or is bootlegging gin." The school cannot "vault from the finding of one type of (commonly used) contraband, to a suspicion involving the smuggling of another." Therefore, the appeals court remanded the case to the district court so Phaneuf could proceed with the lawsuit.

SECOND AMENDMENT

Federal Court Strikes Down D.C. Gun Law

The U.S. Court of Appeals for the D.C. Circuit in March 2007 ruled that a 30-year-old ban on the possession of handguns in the DISTRICT OF COLUMBIA violated the SECOND AMENDMENT to the U.S. Constitution. The decision was cheered by those who advocate for the right to bear arms. However, others who are concerned about the relationship between access to guns that could result from the ruling and higher rates of crime, including homicides.

The Second Amendment provides, "A well regulated Militia, being necessary to the security of a free State, the right of the people to keep and bear Arms, shall not be infringed." This right has been the subject of extensive discussion and debate, due largely to the unusual phrasing of the amendment itself. Some argue that the amendment stands for the proposition that "[a] well regulated Militia . . . shall not be infringed." Others argue that the comma preceding "shall" was a mistake, and that the amendment should read that "the right of the people to . . . bear arms . . . shall not be infringed." Under the latter theory, individuals have an absolute, personal right to own firearms.

For more than a century, states have addressed problems with violence by enacting gun control laws. The Supreme Court traditionally has interpreted the Second Amendment to allow states to maintain their own militias separate from a federally-controlled militia. In *United States v. Cruikshank*, 92 U.S. 542, 23 L. Ed. 588 (1875), the Court declared that "the second amendment means no more than that [the right to bear arms] shall not be infringed by Congress, and has no other effect than to restrict the powers of the national government." However, recent cases heard by the lower **federal courts** have reconsidered the scope of this right.

In 1976, the District of Columbia enacted a series of statutes that forbid or severely restricted the possession of firearms. The District required the registration of firearms with the city police department, and the **statute** banned the registration of handguns in most cases. The statute also generally prohibited carrying a pistol without a license. Moreover, lawfully owned firearms had to be kept unloaded and disassembled or bound by a trigger lock. Critics of the law charged that it prevented residents from exercising their rights to possess firearms for self-defense.

Several proposals have been introduced that would have repealed the ban on handgun in the

District. One vocal critic of the law has been Representative Mark Souder (R.-Ind.), who has introduced several such measures. In 2004, Souder introduced the D.C. Personal Protection Act, which would have repealed most of these firearm restrictions. The bill also would have prohibited the mayor or city council of the District of Columbia from enacting limitations that exceeded federal law or "discourage . . . the private ownership or use of firearms." Supporters of the bill noted that the homicide rate in D.C. was 72 percent higher in 2001 than it was in 1976, while the national homicide rate during the same period dropped by 36 percent. Although the bill passed in the House of Representatives by a vote of 250 to 171, it never passed in the Senate.

Six residents of the District of Columbia brought suit to challenge the constitutionality of the handgun law. Plaintiffs Shelley Parker, Tracey Ambeau, Tom G. Palmer, and George Lyon brought suit because they wanted to possess handguns in their home in order to provide self-defense. Another plaintiff, Gillian St. Lawrence, challenged the law because even though he owns a registered shotgun, he wants to keep it assembled and without a trigger lock. A final plaintiff, Dick Heller, wanted to possess a handgun at his home, in addition to the handgun that he was allowed to possess in his position as a special police officer.

The District of Columbia argued that the purpose behind the Second Amendment was only to protect state militias from **encroachment** by the federal government. The appellants stressed that the amendment had to be read to provide an individual right "to keep and bear Arms." U.S. District Judge Emmet G. Sullivan held in favor of the District, finding that individuals do not have a right to bear arms apart from use in a militia and that citizens have no **right of action** to challenge a law based on the Second Amendment. *Parker v. Dist. of Columbia*, 311 F. Supp. 2d 103 (D.D.C. 2004).

The plaintiffs appealed the decision to the D.C. Court of Appeals, which reversed the district court's decision. *Parker v. Dist. of Columbia*, 478 F.3d 370 (D.C. Cir. 2007). In a lengthy opinion by Judge Laurence H. Silberman, the **appellate court** reviewed the history of Supreme Court decisions on the Second Amendment, along with more recent lower federal court decisions and scholarship on the subject. The court identified several theories that have been advanced about the nature of the amendment. Most federal courts have treated the right

to bear arms as a collective right, as opposed to a right possessed by an individual. Under this theory, an individual does not have standing to bring suit against the federal government based on the denial of this collective right. However, the Fifth **Circuit Court** of Appeals ruled otherwise, holding that the Second Amendment establishes an individual right. *United States v. Emerson*, 270 F.3d 203, 218-21 (5th Cir. 2001).

Silberman concluded that the text of the amendment, coupled with language from Supreme Court precedent, guaranteed an individual right as opposed to a collective right. "In sum, the phrase 'the right of the people,' when read intratextually and in light of Supreme Court precedent, leads us to conclude that the right in question in individual," Silberman wrote. "This proposition is true even though 'the people' at the time of the founding was not as inclusive as 'the people' today." Because the District's laws amounted to a "complete prohibition on the lawful use of handguns for self-defense," the court held that the statute violated the Second Amendment.

Judge Karen Lecraft Henderson dissented, arguing that because the District of Columbia is not a "state," the Second Amendment could not apply to it. Other commentators criticized the opinion for its "deplorable citation" of the infamous Supreme Court decision in *Dred Scott v. Sanford*, 60 U.S. (19 How.) 393, 15 L. Ed. 691 (1857). Despite these criticisms, the full D.C. Circuit Court of Appeals denied a request to rehear the case, which could lead to an appeal to the Supreme Court.

SECURITIES

Evidence of a corporation's debts or property.

Tellabs v. Makor Issues & Rights, Ltd.

Congress enacted the Private Securities Litigation Reform Act of 1995 (PSLRA) as a response to a perceived abuse of litigation in private securities **fraud** actions. Under the **statute**, a plaintiff must state with particularity both the facts that constitute the alleged violation as well as the facts that demonstrate the defendant's intent to "deceive, manipulate, or defraud" the plaintiff. In *Tellabs, Inc. v. Makor Issues & Rights, Ltd.*, No. 06-484, 2007 WL 1773208 (June 21, 2007), the Court clarified what a plaintiff must prove under this Act.

Federal antifraud securities laws are generally enforced through criminal prosecutions and civil enforcement actions brought by the Jus-

TICE DEPARTMENT and the SECURITIES AND EXCHANGE COMMISSION. Private actions that are brought to enforce these laws are considered to be an effective supplement to these actions. However, if these types of actions are not appropriately contained, they can be abused in a manner that imposes great costs on companies that are in compliance with securities laws.

Under the PSLRA, a plaintiff must meet exacting pleading requirements in order to bring a private securities action. Under the second prong of the statute, which requires that the defendant has acted with the requisite intent, the statute establishes that that plaintiff must "state with particularity facts giving rise to a strong inference that the defendant acted with the requisite state of mind." Congress did not define the term "strong inference," and the **federal courts** of appeals were split about how the term should be defined. For instance, the Seventh Circuit has held that this strong inference standard is met when the complaint has "allege[d] facts from which, if true, a **reasonable person** could infer that the defendant acted with the required intent."

Tellabs, Inc. is a manufacturer of specialized equipment for fiber optic networks. A group of investors bought Tellabs stock during the period between December 11, 2000 and June 19, 2001. These investors claimed that the chief executive officer of the company, Richard Notebaert, had violated federal law by engaging in securities fraud after the company's stock fell from $67 to $15.87 per share during a short period of time in 2001. These investors brought suit under the PSLRA against both Tellabs and Notebaert in the U.S. **District Court** for the Northern District of Illinois. The defendants moved to dismiss the complaint, arguing that the plaintiffs had not met the standards set forth in the PSLRA.

The district court agreed with the defendants and dismissed the complaint, holding that the plaintiffs had failed to plead the case under the PSLRA's requirements. The shareholders subsequently amended their complaint to add references to 27 confidential sources and making more specific allegations regarding Notebaert's mental state. However, the district court again determined that the plaintiffs had not met the PSLRA standards and dismissed the complaint, this time with prejudice. *Johnson v. Tellabs, Inc.*, 303 F. Supp. 2d 941 (N.D. Ill. 2004).

The shareholders appealed the decision to the Seventh **Circuit Court** of Appeals. The **appellate court** disagreed with the district court

that the plaintiff had not sufficiently alleged that Notebaert had acted with the necessary state of mind under the statute. With respect to the pleading standard, the court said that "courts [should] examine all of the allegations in the complaint and then . . . decided whether collectively they establish" a strong inference that the defendant had the state of mind necessary to support the complaint.

In reaching its decision, the Seventh Circuit did not mandate an assessment of competing inferences in this type of case. This approach conflicted with one adopted by the Sixth Circuit, which established that "plaintiffs are entitled only to the most plausible of competing inferences." According to the Seventh Circuit, this type of assessment of competing inferences could infringe upon the plaintiffs' rights under the SEVENTH AMENDMENT, which preserves a right of trial by jury. *Makor Issues & Rights, Ltd. v. Tellabs, Inc.*, 437 F.3d 588 (7th Cir. 2006). Because the circuit courts had become split on the question of how the courts should treat competing inferences in a private securities fraud case, the Supreme Court granted **certiorari** to resolve the conflict.

In an opinion by Justice RUTH BADER GINSBURG, the Court clarified how the courts should address cases brought under the PSLRA. First, in a motion to dismiss based on Rule 12(b)(6) of the Federal Rules of **Civil Procedure**, the courts should treat all factual allegations in the complaint as true. Second, the court must consider the complaint in its entirety, taking into account all of the facts alleged by a plaintiff, to determine whether the facts taken collectively give rise to a strong inference that the defendant had the necessary state of mind. Third, a court must take into account all plausible opposing inferences, comparing these opposing inferences with those that support a finding that the defendant had the required **scienter**.

In the case before the Court, Tellabs argued that the lack of evidence suggesting that Notebaert had a financial motive in his actions showed that the plaintiff could not prove a strong inference that he had the necessary state of mind. The Court said that though motive could be a factor that is considered in the analysis, but the allegations in the complaint must be taken collectively. Thus, the significance that a court attaches to the lack of motive depends on the contents of the entire complaint itself. The Court also said that the Seventh Circuit's concern about the Seventh Amendment was unwarranted, noting that Congress has the power to prescribe what must be stated in a complaint.

Because the lower courts had not had the opportunity to consider whether the allegations in the complaint warranted a strong inference of Notebaert's state of mind, the Court vacated the Seventh Circuit's decision and remanded the case to the lower court for further consideration.

SEGREGATION

The act or process of separating a race, class, or ethnic group from a society's general population.

District Judge Frees Little Rock Schools from Federal Supervision

A federal judge in Arkansas in February 2007 issued a ruling that released the Little Rock School District from federal supervision related to desegregation. The action occurred nearly 50 years after the first black students enrolled in the school in one of the biggest crises during the civil rights ERA. Despite the decision, representatives of black students in the city said that the district has not done enough to improve the performance of minorities in the district.

The U.S. SUPREME COURT on May 17, 1954 issued its decision in *Brown v. Board of Education*, 347 U.S. 483, 74 S. Ct. 686, 98 L. Ed. 873 in which it held that racially segregated schools were unconstitutional. The Little Rock schools issued a policy statement five days after the decision indicating that they would comply with the Court's order. The School Board subsequently adopted a plan under which the high school would become integrated starting in September 1957. Controversy ensued, however, when 27 black students tried to register for classes in January 1956, but the school refused to admit these students.

The NAACP brought suit against the district, arguing in favor of the students' admission. Federal judge John E. Miller dismissed the suit, and the Eighth **Circuit Court** of Appeals later upheld the dismissal. However, a federal judge in North Dakota named Ronald N. Davies later issued an injunction, ordering the district to begin gradual integration in September 1957. Former Arkansas Governor Orval Faubus called on the Arkansas NATIONAL GUARD to prevent the black students from entering the building. For the first three weeks of school, efforts to allow these students to enter the school failed, due largely to Faubus' actions. The impasse finally ended on September 25, 1957, as the nine students entered the school, accompanied by paratroopers from the Army's 101st Airborne Division, who were called in by President DWIGHT D. EISENHOWER.

Litigation involving the Little Rock district has continued since the 1980s as well. In 1982, the Little Rock School District sued the Pulaski County Special and North Little Rock school districts, arguing that the city should have one unified school district. According to Little Rock, the policies and practices of the various districts had resulted in school segregation and discrimination. A U.S. District Judge in 1984 agreed with Little Rock and ordered the consolidation of the school districts. However, the Eighth Circuit in 1985 reversed the district court's decision and ruled that the Little Rock School District's boundary should coincide with the city limits. *Little Rock Sch. Dist. v. Pulaski County Special Sch. Dist. No. 1*, 778 F.3d 404 (8th Cir. 1985).

In 1998, the Little Rock School District and a group representing black school children (known as the "Joshua Interveners") agreed to a voluntary Revised Desegregation and Education Plan, which required the district to comply with hundreds of obligations in order to be released from federal supervision. Although these requirements were beyond what either the Supreme Court or the Eighth Circuit have mandated, the courts determined that Little Rock was contractually bound to fulfill its obligations under the agreement. The plan called for Little Rock to be released from federal supervision by 2001.

In 2002, U.S. District Judge Bill Wilson agreed to free the Little Rock schools from supervision except in the area of student achievement. *Little Rock Sch. Dist. v. Pulaski County Special Sch. Dist. No. 1*, 237 F. Supp. 2d 988 (E.D. Ark. 2002). Two years later, a panel of the Eighth Circuit affirmed the ruling. *Little Rock Sch. Dist. v. Armstrong*, 359 F.3d 957 (8th Cir. 2004). The Eighth Circuit again revisited the question of federal supervision of Little Rock schools in 2006, and the panel of the **appellate court** again determined that Little Rock had not complied with provisions of a previous court decree. *Little Rock Sch. Dist. v. N. Little Rock Sch. Dist.*, 451 F.3d 528 (8th Cir. 2006).

Little Rock renewed its efforts to be released from federal supervision in October 2006 by submitting a series of evaluations showing that the district had complied with its obligations under a previous order that Wilson had issued. The Joshua Interveners countered by asking Wilson to hold the district in contempt of court for failing to meet these obligations.

Wilson heard testimony in January 2007 from district officials, who provided evidence that the district had complied with the requirements. On February 23, Wilson signed an order that released Little Rock from further supervision. *Little Rock Sch. Dist. v. Pulaski County Special Sch. Dist. No. 1*, No. 4:82CV00866, 2007 WL 624054 (E.D. Ark. Feb. 23, 2007).

One issue that arose from the litigation in the 1980s focused on whether the district had put into place a system that could adequately measure whether test scores of black students were improving. Late in 2006, the district adopted a resolution that required continued assessment of student scores, even if the district was not under court supervision. Critics of the district have pointed out that black students in Little Rock score significantly lower on their standardized tests compared with white students. According to one of the attorneys for the Joshua Interveners, "We're certainly disappointed in view of the lack of progress this district has made in addressing the needs of African-American students. The standard was not high for the district to meet, but they certainly have not met it. We will have to pursue other means."

Officials with the Little Rock School District, however, said that the schools would continue to make progress in improving the education of its students. "The district has been given back to the people of this community, and my pledge to them is to continue to work hard and recognize that we're all going to work hard," said Roy Brooks, superintendent for the school district.

SENTENCING

The postconviction stage of the criminal justice process, in which the defendant is brought before the court for the imposition of a penalty.

Claiborne v. United States

The U.S. SUPREME COURT in the case of *Claiborne v. United States* was expected to issue a ruling that would shed light on how much discretion federal judges have when they apply sentencing guidelines. However, before the Court could issue its ruling, the petitioner in the case was shot and killed while following a stolen truck in St. Louis. His death rendered the case moot and forced the Court to take up another Eighth Circuit case as a replacement.

The Court in *United States v. Booker*, 543 U.S. 220, 125 S. Ct. 738, 160 L. Ed. 2d 621 (2005) established that the Federal Sentencing Guidelines were no longer mandatory. A federal **district court** instead must use these guidelines as advisory in nature, while also taking account of factors that are enumerated in a federal **statute**. **Federal courts** have since struggled to apply the guidelines appropriately.

In light of the decision in *Booker*, the Eighth Circuit has ruled that in determining which sentence is appropriate, the district court must first calculate the applicable sentencing range under the guidelines. *United States v. Haack*, 403 F.3d 994 (8th Cir. 2005). The district court may impose a sentence outside of the range of the guidelines in light of other concerns set forth in the statute. When a district court has correctly determined the appropriate range to apply, the **appellate court** reviews the court's sentence for reasonableness, a test that is similar to a review to determine whether a district court has abused its discretion.

The Eighth **Circuit Court** of Appeals has also held that because the guidelines were drafted to take into account factors in the statute and were produced after years of careful study, the court presumes that the range produced by the sentencing guidelines are reasonable. *United States v. Lincoln*, 413 F.3d 716 (8th Cir. 2005). The Eighth Circuit has also ruled that if the district court varies its sentence from the range established under the guidelines, the **appellate** court reviewing the sentence must determine whether the variance is reasonable. According to a ruling in the Seventh Circuit, the judge that varies a sentence from the range set forth in the guidelines must provide an appropriate justification for the variance.

The level of discretion that district courts have in varying from the guidelines was the primary issue in a case involving Mario Claiborne of St. Louis. Police arrested Claiborne in 2003 for attempting to sell less than one gram of cocaine base to an undercover police officer. Six months after his arrest, police observed him in what appeared to be another drug deal. He attempted to flee, and in the process discarded a bag containing 5.03 grams of cocaine base. He was charged with distributing cocaine in the first incident and with possessing cocaine in the second incident. He pleaded guilty to both charges.

The trial court rejected an argument that Claiborne should receive an increase in his sentencing level because he had fled through a nearby residence when evading the police. The court also determined that he was entitled to relief from a mandatory five-year minimum sentence established by the Controlled Substances Act, 18 U.S.C. §844(a). After issuing these rulings, the court determined that the appropriate range under the sentencing guidelines was 37 to 46 months. However, the judge in the case believed that 37 months was excessive due to such factors as the defendant's young age, lack of criminal history, and the small amount of drugs involved in the case. Moreover, the court determined that Claiborne was not likely to commit similar crimes in the future. Based on these considerations, the court sentenced Claiborne to 15 months in prison.

The government appealed the case, arguing that the variance was unreasonable. On appeal, the Eighth Circuit observed that the district court's imposition of the 15-month sentence was a 60 percent departure from the advisory guidelines range. This represented what the court determined to be an extraordinary reduction that "must be supported by extraordinary circumstances." This case did not present extraordinary circumstances because most of these circumstances were already taken into consideration in the sentencing guidelines themselves. For instance, the fact that only a small amount of cocaine was seized was a factor in determining the appropriate range under the guidelines. Moreover, the court noted that even though the district court had properly focused on whether Claiborne was likely to commit the crime again, "the fact that he committed a second serious drug offense six month after his first arrest demonstrates that Claiborne has not earned an extraordinary downward variance from a guidelines sentence that already reflects substantial leniency." The court thus remanded the case to the district court for resentencing.

Claiborne sought to appeal the decision to the U.S. Supreme Court, which granted **certiorari** on November 6, 2006. The Court heard oral arguments in the case on February 20, 2007, and commentators expected the Court to issue a decision in June 2007. However, on May 29, Claiborne was shot and killed during an altercation that resulted from an attempted car theft. Because Claiborne's death negated the "case or controversy" requirement for the Court to hear a case, the Court on June 4, 2007 dismissed the case as moot.

After its dismissal of *Claiborne*, the Court in June agreed to review two more sentencing cases, including *Gall v. United States* (06-7949) from the Eighth Circuit and *Kimbrough v. United States* (06-6330). The Court will not likely decide these cases until the fall of 2007.

Cunningham v. California

The U.S. SUPREME COURT in series of cases since 2000 has addressed the constitutionality of various schemes that authorized judges to increase criminal sentences. The Court has prohibited the use of any sentencing scheme that allows a judge to impose a sentence above the **statutory** maximum based on a fact, other than a prior conviction, not found by a jury. The Sixth and Fourteenth Amendments have been the foundation for these rulings, which have addressed both state and federal sentencing policies. State **appellate** courts have been forced to reexamine sentencing laws and make changes to comport with these rulings. However, the California Court of Appeals upheld its determinate sentencing law (DSL) despite the fact it gave judges the ability to raise the maximum sentence based on additional facts. The Supreme Court, in *Cunningham v. California*, __U.S.__, 127 S.Ct. 856, 166 L.Ed.2d 856 (2007), overturned this ruling, reaffirming its precedent that only juries can decide facts that affect a defendant's sentence.

John Cunningham was convicted by a jury for sexually abusing a child under the age of 14. Under the DSL the offense was punishable by imprisonment for 6, 12, or 16 years (lower term, middle term, and upper term). The 12-year term was the presumed sentence unless the judge found one or more additional facts in **aggravation**. Following a post-trial sentencing hearing the judge found by a preponderance of the evidence six aggravating circumstances. These included the particular vulnerability of Cunningham's victim and his violent conduct that would be serious danger to the community. The only mitigating factor was that Cunningham did not have a prior criminal record. The judge determined the aggravating circumstances outweighed the mitigating circumstance and sentenced Cunningham to the maximum term of 156 years. Cunningham appealed his sentence but the California Court of Appeals upheld both his conviction and the maximum sentence. The California Supreme Court denied review less than two weeks after it issued a decision upholding the DSL law as constitutional under the SIXTH AMENDMENT. Cunningham the petitioned the U.S. Supreme Court to strike down the DSL sentencing scheme.

The Supreme Court, in a 6–3 decision, struck down the DSL as unconstitutional. Justice RUTH BADER GINSBURG, writing for the majority, noted that the DSL was enacted in 1977 to replace an indeterminate sentencing system that had been in force in California for 60 years. Under the indeterminate scheme the judge sentenced the defendant to an open-ended prison term and the parole board decided if and when the felon would be released from prison. The DSL fixed the terms of imprisonment for most crimes and eliminated the possibility of early release on parole. The state sought to install uniform and proportionate punishment. The DSL directed California's Judicial Council to adopt rules that would guide the judge on whether to impose the lower or upper prison term. The Council rule defined aggravating circumstances to mean "facts which justify the imposition of the upper prison term. The facts had to be established by preponderance of the evidence, an evidentiary standard less than **beyond a reasonable doubt** standard. A fact that was an element of the crime could not be used to impose the upper term. Therefore, an upper prison term could only be ordered if the judge found and placed on the record facts beyond the elements of the charged offense.

Justice Ginsburg concluded in light of the Court's recent cases on sentencing that this scheme violated the Sixth Amendment. Each of these cases made clear that only "any fact that exposes a defendant to a greater potential sentence must be found by a jury, not a judge, and established beyond a reasonable doubt, not merely by a preponderance of the evidence." This standard was first announced in *Apprendi v. New Jersey*, 530 U.S. 466, 120 Ct. 2348, 147 L.Ed.2d 435 (2000). In *Blakely v. Washington*, 542 U.S. 296, 124 S.Ct. 2531, 159 L.Ed.2d 403 (2005) the Court struck down the state of Washington's sentencing guidelines system as violating the Sixth Amendment. One year later the Court struck down the Federal Sentencing Guidelines in *United States v. Booker*, 543 U.S. 220, 125 S.Ct. 738, 160 L.Ed.2d 621(2005). Although the guidelines were no longer mandatory, the Court also ruled that they must be consulted by judges, even if they are advisory, when they sentence federal criminals. In the future, federal criminal sentences would be judged using a reasonableness standard, though few details were given as to what constituted a "reasonable" sentence.

Based on these precedents Justice Ginsburg found that the DSL violated the *Apprendi* bright-line rule that any fact that increases a sentence must be submitted to the jury and proved beyond a reasonable doubt. The California Supreme Court had rejected the application of these precedents to the DSL because in its "operation and effect" it gave judges the same type of fact-finding function that has always been used by judges to select an appropriate statutorily prescribed sentence. The state supreme court characterized the upper term as the "statutory maximum" which did not violate a defendant's right to a jury trial as outline by *Apprendi* and the other cases. It equated this system with the discretion given to federal judges after *Booker*. Justice Ginsburg disagreed, finding that the DSL did not resemble the advisory system set out in *Booker*. Finally, the California system did not employ the reasonableness standard found in the federal system, for the federal system now operated "within the Sixth Amendment constraints delineated in our precedent, not as a substitute for those constraints."

Justices ANTHONY KENNEDY, STEPHEN BREYER, and Samuel Alito dissented. Justice Kennedy scolded the Court for its "wooden, unyielding insistence on expanding the *Apprendi* doctrine far beyond its necessary boundaries. He suggested the Court should distinguish between sentencing enhancements based on the nature of the offense, where *Apprendi* would apply, and sentencing enhancements "based on the nature of the offender, where it would not."

James v. United States

It is a fundamental principle that criminal laws must be written with enough specificity to give notice to the public what actions constitute crimes and what penalties may follow a conviction. The federal Armed Career Criminal Act (ACCA), 18 U.S.C.A. §924, however, has given the courts a difficulty because of the way it has been written. ACCA states that defendants convicted of possession of a firearm by a felon be sentenced to a mandatory term of 15 years imprisonment if the defendant has three prior convictions "for a violent **felony** or a serious drug offense." **Burglary** qualified as a violent felony but left unresolved was whether attempted burglary was also a violent felony under ACCA. The U.S. SUPREME COURT, in *James v. United States*, _U.S._, 127 S.Ct. 1586, _L.Ed.2d _ (2007), ruled that attempted burglary, as defined by Florida Law, was included within ACCA's provisions.

Alphonso James pleaded guilty in federal **district court** to one count of possession a firearm after being convicted of a felony. In his plea, James admitted to three prior felony convictions, including attempted burglary of a dwelling, which is crime under Florida law. The court applied ACCA and sentenced James to a mandatory minimum term of 15 years imprisonment, concluding that attempted burglary was a violent felony under ACCA. The Eleventh **Circuit Court** of Appeals upheld the ruling.

The Supreme Court, in a 5–4 decision, agreed with the lower **federal courts**. Justice Samuel Alito, writing for the majority, noted that ACCA lists only five specific violent felonies: **robbery**, burglary, arson, extortion, or use of explosives. However, Congress included a residual clause that applied ACC to "conduct that presents a serious potential risk of physical injury." Both sides agreed that the sole question was whether attempted burglary, as defined by Florida law, fell within the ACCA residual clause. James had argued that the plain text of ACCA categorically excluded attempted offenses from the residual clause, citing another ACCA clause that includes attempted use of force as a basis for applying the 15-year sentence. James believed that this was the only part of ACCA that specifically dealt with attempted crimes. Justice Alito disagreed, concluding that such a reading would "unduly narrow" the language of the residual clause. The whole point of the residual clause was to broaden the reach of ACCA beyond the defined violent crimes. Congress did not intend to limit ACCA to only to completed offenses.

James also looked to legislative history to buttress his argument. He pointed out that a version of ACCA was rejected in the House of Representatives in 1984 that included attempted violent offenses including burglary. This language was removed from the bill before its adoption, leading James to claim that this showed evidence of congressional intent to exclude attempted burglary. The Court was not persuaded. Justice Alito cited a 1986 amendment to ACCA that included the residual clause that was in dispute. This was compelling evidence that Congress wanted a "broadly worded residual clause that does not by its terms exclude attempt offenses."

Having disposed of these issues, the Court moved on to consider whether attempted burglary, as defined by Florida law, was an offense that applied to "conduct that presents a serious potential risk of physical injury." The Florida Supreme Court defined attempted burglary as requiring an "overt act directed toward entering or remaining in a structure or conveyance." Mere preparation did not qualify as attempted burglary. Using the Florida supreme court definition, Justice Alito looked to what risk of physical injury could be attributed to attempted burglary. Attempted burglary posed the same kind of risk as burglary—a confrontation between the would-be burglar and a **third party**. Interrupting an intruder before the person entered the home created "a risk of violent confrontation comparable to that posed by finding him inside the structure itself." Alito went even further, concluding that attempted burglary may pose even a greater risk of physical injury," for the burglar is "thwarted by some outside intervenor." He backed up his analysis by citing federal appeals court and U.S. Sentencing Commissions rulings that equate attempted burglary with a violent felony.

James contended that generalizing the conclusion that attempted burglary will create a risk of physical injury to others was not sufficient. The Court should only do so when all cases present this risk. Instead, all the Court could say was that this might happen in "most cases." Justice Alito countered that ACCA did not require "metaphysical certainty;" the residual clause showed that Congress intended to deal with possibilities "even more contingent or remote than a simple 'risk', much less certainty." As long as an offense by its nature presents a serious potential risk of injury to another, it satisfied the ACCA residual provision.

Justice ANTONIN SCALIA, in a dissenting opinion joined by Justices JOHN PAUL STEVENS and RUTH BADER GINSBURG, argued that the Court had failed to provide concrete guidance that would give ensure the ACCA residual provision would be "applied with an acceptable degree of consistency by hundreds of district court judges that impose sentences every day." Scalia concluded that the majority's case-by-case approach for applying ACCA would create more work for the courts and enable judges to apply it inconsistently. He preferred that ACCA be applied in a "relatively predictable and administrable fashion to a smaller subset of crimes." Attempted burglary would not be on his list.

Rita v. United States

The U.S. SUPREME COURT in 2007 issued a opinion concluding that federal **appellate** courts may apply a presumption that a sentence complying with the Federal Sentencing Guidelines is a reasonable sentence. The case was one of several involving questions of the role of the guidelines that the Court agreed to hear during its 2006 term. The result in the case allowed a sentence given to a former member of a military who had been convicted of perjury to stand.

By **statute**, a federal judge must consider several factors when handing down a sentence.

These include the following: (1) the offense and characteristics of the offender; (2) the need for the sentence to consider the goals of sentencing, which include retribution, deterrence, and incapacitation; (3) the sentences that are legally available; (4) the Federal Sentencing Guidelines; (5) policy statements issued by the Sentencing Commission; (6) the need to avoid unwarranted disparities; and (7) the need for **restitution**. 18 U.S.C. §3553(a). Congress instructed the Sentencing Commission to write the guidelines to "assure the meeting of the purposes of sentencing" established under §3553.

Federal courts have had difficulty applying the Federal Sentencing Guidelines since the Supreme Court issued its opinion in *United States v. Booker*, 543 U.S. 220, 125 S. Ct. 738, 160 L. Ed. 2d 621 (2005). In *Booker*, the Court determined that the federal judges could not be required to follow these guidelines, but rather that the guidelines were only advisory in nature. Since that decision, federal courts have looked to the guidelines for guidance, but have also looked to other factors established by federal statute in order to hand down sentences.

When a federal **appellate court** reviews a sentence from a federal **district court**, the court of appeals will set aside a sentence if it is unreasonable. Several federal circuits have ruled that when a district court has issued a sentence pursuant to the guidelines that such a sentence is presumptively reasonable. Courts that have adopted this presumption include the following circuits: Fourth, Fifth, Sixth, Seventh, Eighth, Tenth, and DISTRICT OF COLUMBIA. The First, Second, Third, and Eleventh Circuits have not applied this presumption.

The case of *United States v. Rita* arose when Victor Rita purchased a machinegun parts kit. He was later contacted by the Alcohol, Tobacco, Firearms, and Explosives Bureau (ATF) regarding the purchase, and Rita agreed to allow an agent inspect this kit. However, prior to visiting with the ATF agent, Rita exchanged the kit for another one. The contents of the new kit did not amount to a machinegun. A prosecutor later brought Rita before a **grand jury**, and while under oath Rita denied that he had spoken to the agent or that he had contacted the company that sold him the kit. The government thereafter charged Rita with perjury, making false statements, and obstructing justice. A jury convicted Rita on all counts.

During the sentencing phase, a probation officer completed a presentence report. The report established a base level for the combination of offenses that Rita had committed. It also noted that though Rita had previously been convicted of making false statements, the conviction had taken place more than 10 years prior. Thus, it did not count against Rita when the judge calculated the sentence. Other parts of the report focused on Rita's personal characteristics, including personal and family data, physical condition, mental and emotional health, education, employment record, and lack of a history of substance abuse. Based on this information, the report determined that the Sentencing Guidelines called for a sentence of 33 to 41 months.

At his sentencing hearing, Rita argued that his sentence should be lower than the one called for by the guidelines. The judge said that he could lower Rita's sentence if something in the guidelines allows for a downward departure or if Rita could show that something in the sentencing statute would allow for a lower sentence. However, the judge could not find a sufficient justification to reduce the sentence below the guideline number. Accordingly, the judge issued a sentence of 33 months.

Rita appealed the decision to the Fourth **Circuit Court** of Appeals, arguing that the 33-month sentence was unreasonable. According to Rita, the sentence was unreasonable because (1) it did not adequately consider the history and characteristics of the defendant, and (2) it was "greater than necessary to comply with the purposes of sentencing" set forth in §3553. The Fourth Circuit noted that it should set aside a sentence that is unreasonable, but the court also noted that it considers a sentence within the guidelines range to be presumptively reasonable. The court also stated that "while we believe that the appropriate circumstances for imposing a sentence outside the guideline range will depend on the facts of the individual cases, we have no reason to doubt that most sentences will continue to fall within the applicable guideline range." Based on the presumption of reasonableness, the court upheld Rita's sentence.

The Supreme Court granted **certiorari**, and in an opinion by Justice STEPHEN BREYER, affirmed the Fourth Circuit's decision. According to the Court, a federal court of appeals may presume that a sentence within the guidelines range is reasonable. Such a presumption does not bind the court, but rather reflects the nature of the guidelines themselves, which were produced after years of studies and consideration by the Sentencing Commission. Thus, the presumption of reasonableness is appropriate by appellate courts reviewing sentences. After making this determination, the Court ruled that the Fourth Circuit had correctly found that the sentence was not unreasonable. *Rita v. United States*, No. 06-5754, 2007 WL 1772146 (June 21, 2007).

Justice DAVID SOUTER filed the lone dissent in the case. According to Souter, instead of the federal courts fashioning their own doctrines surrounding the Sentencing Guidelines that are now advisory, Congress should take action to reenact the guidelines to address the concerns in *Booker*.

SEPTEMBER 11TH ATTACKS

Departments Fudged Data on Anti-Terrorism Investigations, According to Audit

A report issued by the Office of the Inspector General in 2007 revealed that federal investigators and prosecutors misstated data about the number of anti-terrorism cases that arose after the SEPTEMBER 11TH ATTACKS in 2001. According to the report, prosecutors counted such instances as immigration violations, marriage **fraud**, and drug trafficking as anti-terror cases, even though no evidence linked these types of cases with terrorist activities. The JUSTICE DEPARTMENT responded by noting that some of the figures were either accurately reported or unreported, stressing that the department had not attempted to inflate figures.

The terrorist attacks that occurred in New York and Washington on September 11, 2001 led the Justice Department to alter its priorities to focus on the deterrence, detection, and prevention of potential future acts of terrorism. The department gauges its counterterrorism success based on the reporting of hundreds of terrorism-related statistics. Reports of the statistics focus on such occurrences as the following: the number of individuals charged following terrorism investigations; the number of convictions related to terrorist activities; and the number of terrorism-related threats to transportation, facilities, cities, and people. Components of the Justice Department that are involved in counterterrorism strategies include the FEDERAL BUREAU OF INVESTIGATION, the Executive Office for United States Attorneys (EOUSA), the United States Attorney's Offices (USAO), and the Criminal Division of the Justice Department.

Both Congress and the Justice Department use these statistics to make decisions about counterterrorism operations as well as decisions about funding. In **fiscal** year 2006, the Justice Department received a 400 percent increase in funding for counterterrorism activities compared with the previous fiscal year. Because funding and other decisions are based on these statistics, accurate reporting is essential. Thus, the Office of Inspector General (OIG) decided to initiate an audit to determine the accuracy of the terrorism-related statistics that were being reported.

The OIG identified a total of 209 unique statistics related to terrorism that were reported by the Justice Department between October 1, 2000 and September 30, 2005. Seventeen of the statistics were reported by agencies outside of the department and were not included as part of OIG's study. The OIG conducted interviews with officials from various positions within the Justice Department to determine whether the remaining 192 statistics had been gathered, classified, and reported accurately. "Through these interviews, we learned that the collection and reporting of terrorism-related statistics within the Department is decentralized and haphazard," the OIG's final report noted. "Often, the official who reported the statistic gathered it through telephone requests or e-mail to other Department staff. Also, for many of the statistics reported, Department officials either had not established internal controls to ensure the statistics were accurately gathered, classified, and reported, and did not document the internal controls used."

The OIG chose 26 statistics to test whether the statistical reporting was accurate. "To test the accuracy of these 26 statistics, we analyzed documentation and conducted interviews with Department officials to determine if the information reported for each statistic was accurate," the report said. "In some cases we reviewed documentation for each item counted in the statistic reported. In other cases we reviewed documentation for a sample of the items counted."

Ten of the statistics were reported primarily by the FBI, which failed to report eight of the statistics accurately. Some of these statistics were significantly understated. For example, the FBI provided information that 1,657 intelligence products were produced or disseminated in Fiscal Year 2004, whereas the OIG found evidence that this number was 6,739. Other statistics were overstated, including the number of terrorism-related threats tracked in fiscal year 2004. According to the FBI, the bureau tracked 4,499, but the OIG found evidence supporting only 4,049 such instances.

The audit report identified a number of reasons why the numbers were overstated or understated. In some instances, the FBI incorrectly coded the nature of some of its investigative cases. Other errors occurred as a result of data-entry into various databases. In some instances, the FBI did not follow formalized procedures, nor did the FBI establish internal controls for tracking the statistics. Moreover, some of the numbers were incorrect because certain activities, such as terrorist threats, were counted multiple times.

The EOUSA and the USAO misreported all of the statistics that were included in the study. The audit indicated that most of these mistakes were made because the USAO did not code the statistics correctly. One of the biggest problems identified in the report was that the EOUSA reported that hundreds of cases were terrorism cases when in fact they involved minor crimes with no connection to terrorist activities. In addition, statistics reported by the Criminal Division were also erroneous due largely to the fact that its database was incomplete and not kept up-to-date. According to the audit, "[t]his database was incomplete because the Criminal Division had not established formalized procedures to: (1) instruct the staff on what data should be reported in the database, and how and when the data should be reported; or (2) validate the accuracy of the information reported in the database."

The audit offered several recommendations to improve the accuracy of the reporting by the agencies within the Justice Department. Among these recommendations were suggestions that each agency establish and document internal control procedures for gathering, verifying, and reporting terrorism-related statistics. Other recommendations related to maintenance of documentation regarding the methods used to report the statistics, as well as to the maintenance of evidence that supports these statistics.

The OIG's audit was not the first report to show that terrorism-related statistics provided by the Justice Department were not correct. In 2005, the *Washington Post* analyzed the number of cases reported by the Criminal Division and determined that most defendants included in those statistics were charged only with minor crimes that were not related to terrorist activities. Despite evidence that the information has been reported incorrectly, both President GEORGE W. BUSH and other members of the administration have cited these statistics in support of the threat of terrorism to the United States.

SEX OFFENSES

A class of sexual conduct prohibited by the law.

Class-Action Appeal for 11,000 Registered Sex Offenders in Georgia

As background, Georgia's General Assembly passed legislation in 2003 prohibiting persons on the state's sex offender registry from living in certain locations. This law, still in effect in 2007, specifically prohibited offenders from living within 1,000 feet (measured from property line to property line) of schools, child care facilities, and areas where minors congregate, such as public and private parks, recreation facilities, playgrounds, skating rinks, gymnasiums, neighborhood centers, and similar facilities providing services or programs geared toward persons under the age of 18. Several persons challenged the law, but without success.

In April 2006, the General Assembly passed another law, HB 1059, which actually imposed more restrictions. It added a provision that persons on the registry were prohibited from living within 1,000 feet of churches, public or community swimming pools, and school bus stops. Moreover, the new bill prohibited persons on the registry from *working* at or within 1,000 feet of a school, church, or child-care center. The penalty for knowingly living or working in any of the prohibited locations ranged from a minimum of ten and a maximum of 30 years' imprisonment.

Some of the bill's controversy centered on relatively severe provisions. HB 1059 uniformly applied to everyone, without exception. Unlike other states, it did not allow variances for persons who already owned or rented homes in restricted areas. It provided no procedure to apply for hardship exemptions for illness, advanced age, financial hardship, or disability. It made no distinction between people who were dangerous to children and those who were not known to be. It applied the same restrictions to teenagers convicted of consensual sex as it did to repeat felons convicted of rape.

The law was to take effect on July 1, 2006. However, in June 2006, the Southern Center for Human Rights (SCHR) and the AMERICAN CIVIL LIBERTIES UNION (ACLU) filed a class-action lawsuit on behalf of all persons listed on the registry. The suit, filed in the U.S. **District Court** for the Northern District of Georgia (in Atlanta), challenged the constitutionality of the residency and work restrictions of HB 1059, including the Ex Post Facto Clause, the Due Process Clause, the Free Exercise Clause, the

Takings Clause, and the EIGHTH AMENDMENT. It also alleged that the law violated the federal Religious Land Use and Institutionalized Persons Act. The named defendants were the state governor, attorney general, and all Georgia sheriffs. In July 2006, the court certified the plaintiff class, potentially affecting some 11,000 persons.

The case, still pending as of June 2007 (having survived defendants' motion to dismiss in March 2007), is captioned *Whitaker v. Perdue*, No. 4:06-CV-140-CC (N.D. Ga). Wendy Whitaker, one of the named plaintiffs representing the class, was sentenced to five years' probation for having consensual oral sex with a 15-year-old when she was 17 and they were both high school sophomores. One of the key challenges to the new law was that it imposed punishments beyond the sentences originally meted out to sex offenders before it was enacted (the ex post facto challenge).

Despite the pendency of a **final decision** in the case, several key rulings have been rendered to keep the case moving forward. Shortly after the case was filed, U.S. District Court Judge Clarence Cooper granted a temporary restraining order to stop the enforcement of that portion of HB 1059 that prohibited persons from living within 1,000 feet of a school bus stop or church.

In his order, the judge noted that the contested provision would likely force persons from their homes before the court could ultimately determine the law's constitutionality. After full briefing and hearing on the matter, the judge later removed the temporary restraining order, finding plaintiffs' argument premature, in that there was no evidence that any school board in Georgia had yet officially designated the location of school bus stops. However, the judge noted that the school bus restriction was essentially unenforceable until the actual members of school boards officially identified the locations of school bus stops. Plaintiffs were later able to negotiate and enter a 'consent order' with three Georgia counties that agreed not to enforce the school bus provision until a final decision on its constitutionality was reached. As of June 2007, three county school boards had designated their school bus stops, but sheriffs in those counties were enjoined by the court from enforcing that provision of the law until final decision on its constitutionality was reached.

In a separate but related matter, a Georgia state judge reversed a ten-year sentence for aggravated child molestation given to Genarlow

Wilson for having consensual oral sex when he was 17 with a 15-year-old girl during a 2003 New year's Eve party involving alcohol and marijuana. Instead, the judge reduced the charge to a **misdemeanor**, sentenced Wilson to 12 months, gave him credit for time served, ordered that he not be placed on the state's sexual offender registry, and released him. The case received wide media attention for what appeared to be a grossly disproportionate sentence in relation to the crime. Wilson had already served 27 months in prison, and had garnered much support from outsiders, including former President Jimmy Carter.

Majority Leader Jerry Keen, center, discusses details of a proposed bill that would strengthen Georgia law against sex offenders.
AP IMAGES

SEXUAL ABUSE

Illegal sex acts performed against a minor by a parent, guardian, relative, or acquaintence.

Congressman Mark Foley Resigns Amid Scandal

In October 2006, just days before the national elections, six-term Republican Congressman Mark Foley of Florida's 16th District abruptly resigned his seat. The media, particularly ABC News, had been tracking him down for days, trying to confront him with sexually-explicit text messages he had exchanged with 16-and 17-year old male former congressional pages. (Pages are high school students selected from across the nation to work on Capitol Hill as messengers.)

A former page from Louisiana had previously contacted the office of Representative Rodney Alexander, his local Congressman in Louisiana, who had sponsored the 16-year-old

page in Washington. The page forwarded e-mail and instant-message (IM) text messages sent to him by Foley, including a request that he send a picture of himself to Foley. Although the message was not sexual in content and his parents did not want to pursue the matter, the boy had been uncomfortable with it and decided to forward it. ABC News later reported that Foley had engaged in sending sexually-explicit instant messages to other current and former pages, all male.

When confronted, Foley neither admitted nor denied the accusations. In a brief letter of resignation, he simply stated, "I am deeply sorry and I apologize for letting down my family and the people of Florida I have had the privilege to represent."

However, after resigning, Foley checked himself into an alcohol rehabilitation facility in Florida, citing alcoholism and "other behavioral issues" in a press statement. Through his lawyer, he also acknowledged that he was gay, that he had been sexually abused by a clergyman as a young teenager, and that he "never attempted to have sexual contact with a minor."

The scandal reverberated well beyond Foley's congressional seat lost to a Democrat a few weeks later. Amid accusations by Republicans that Democrats carefully timed the story to leak just before the election, Democrats responded that Republicans were trying to cover up Foley's conduct until after the election.

Meanwhile, as fallout from the scandal rippled through Washington, Father Anthony Mercieca, a priest who had worked at Sacred Heart Church in Lake Worth, Florida in the 1960s, publicly admitted having sexual encounters with a teenaged Foley. These included skinny-dipping on camping trips and massaging Foley in the nude. However, the priest denied forcing himself on Foley or that Foley was abused, stating that what they did together was "natural" and probably enjoyable for Foley.

Back in Washington, New House Speaker Nancy Pelosi took the floor to demand an immediate investigation by the ethics committee to determine who knew about the messages, whether Foley had contacts with other pages, and when the Republican leadership had first been notified of Foley's conduct. The House Ethics Committee launched an investigation and approved nearly 50 subpoenas for witnesses and documents. The FBI and Florida law enforcement also started preliminary inquiries, and House officials were ordered to "preserve all records" relevant to the matter. However, it was unclear as to whether Foley actually violated any laws.

Staff at Congressman Alexander's (LA) office forwarded the matter to the office of Former House Speaker Dennis Hastert. Hastert denied knowing of the allegations against Foley, although his office forwarded the matter to the office of Representative John Shimkus, chairman of the House Page Board that oversees the congressional work-study program. Shimkus and the clerk of the House investigated, questioned Foley, and told him not to contact the boy again. Meanwhile, Kirk Fordham, chief of staff for Representative Tom Reynolds (R-NY, who headed the GOP House Campaign Committee) and formerly Foley's chief of staff for ten years, abruptly resigned following a dispute with Hastert's chief of staff, Scott Palmer. Fordham told reporters that he had brought concerns about Foley's conduct to Palmer as early as late 2003. The congressional finger-pointing continued through the November elections, and then was lost to other priorities. Calls for Hastert's resignation also withered away.

Foley was a popular, outgoing, and competent politician who made no secret of his homosexuality. His constituency seemed not to care. Representing the prosperous Palm Beach district in Florida, he was virtually assured of re-election prior to the Washington scandal.

Ironically, Foley served as chairman of the Missing and Exploited Children's Caucus and had introduced legislation in July 2006 to protect children from exploitation by adults over the Internet. He attended the signing ceremony at the White House for the Child Protection and Safety Act of 2006. "We track library books better than we do sexual predators," he argued in support of the bill. His staff and attorney were clear to point out that he, in no way, was a pedophile.

This was not the first scandal involving congressional pages. In 1983, no less than two congressmen admitted to sexual relations with under-aged pages, one with a girl and one with a boy. Following this, congressional pages were housed in a central dormitory and chaperoned.

The scandal clearly hurt the REPUBLICAN PARTY. At least nine seats suffered from scandals around the country, and it has been said that the Democratic takeover of the House could have happened solely on that basis. Four GOP seats alone were affected by the Jack Abramoff lobbying scandal (although Democrats were implicated as well). Other well-publicized scandals included those involving Representatives Tom Delay (TX), Robert W. Ney (OH), Curl Weldon (PA), Don Sherwood (PA), and Jon Porter (NV)

After elections, Democrats had to deal with their own problems, including the indictment of Representative William Jefferson (LA) and ongoing investigations of Allan B. Mollohan (WV), Jane Harman (CA), as well as Senators Robert Menendez (NJ) and Conrad Burns (MT).

After leaving the Arizona rehabilitation center in November 2007, Foley spent time with his sister in Los Angeles, where he underwent additional treatment at an outpatient facility. He was seen briefly in Washington, for the sale of his prior house. In February 2007, Foley was spotted waiting for his luggage at Palm Beach International Airport.

SEXUAL HARASSMENT

Unwelcome sexual advances, requests for sexual favors, and other verbal or physical conduct of a sexual nature that tends to create a hostile or offensive work environment.

L.W., a minor by His Parent and Guardian, L.G. v. Toms River Regional Schools Board of Education

In the last ten years the bullying and sexual harassment of school children by other students has been recognized as a significant problem by parents, educators, and psychologists. Parents of harassed children have been frustrated when school administrators have not moved aggressively to end the harassment. This has led to lawsuits against school districts based on federal and state anti-discrimination laws. The New Jersey Supreme Court clarified the standards of legal liability for schools in its state in *L.W., a minor by His Parent and Guardian, L.G. v. Toms River Regional Schools Board of Education*, 189 N.J. 381, 915 A.2d 535(2007). The court held that school districts could be held liable under the New Jersey Law Against Discrimination (LAD), N.J.S.A. 10:5-1 to -49, if the plaintiff could show the district knew or should have known of the harassment but failed to take actions reasonably calculated to end the offensive conduct. This "hostile work environment" standard, which was developed for employment discrimination, served the same purpose when applied to education.

L.W., was a fourth-grade boy at South Toms River Elementary when he first was taunted as being gay, a "homo", and a "fag." He did not understand the teasing and had to ask his aunt what these terms meant. In fifth and sixth grade the taunting increased from once a month or once a week to daily ridicule. L.W. at one point refused to attend school, which led his mother, L.G., to talk with school officials. L.W.'s classmates wrote apologies but the harassment continued and then worsened when he entered Intermediate West middle school in 1998. Almost everyday he heard homophobic slurs directed against him in the halls and cafeteria. He was physically assaulted in the cafeteria and several other incidents took place. Despite his mother's complaints to the assistant principal, this administrator did nothing more than issue warnings to the harassers. At another point a school counselor told L.W. to "toughen up and turn the other cheek." After L.W. was again assaulted in the cafeteria the principal of the middle school finally took charge. When the next few incidents occurred the principal suspended students and made clear that there would be serious consequences for harassment. The harassment subsided and L.W. had a better year in eighth grade. However, L.W. noted that a school security guard monitored him between classes most of the time.

L.W. entered High School South and soon discovered that he would be again be subjected to slurs and violence. He decided not to ride the school bus to avoid taunting but on his walk home one afternoon a group of high school boys cornered him and punched him. His mother notified school administrators and told them about L.W.'s history of mistreatment; they seemed unaware of his past difficulties. After

L.W. was assaulted by a student in downtown Toms River withdrew from the high school. L.G. succeeded in having the school district pay for L.W.'s transfer to a regional arts high school. L.W. did not encounter any harassment at the school. However, the lengthy maltreatment had changed L.W. He went from a happy child to one who was depressed, fearful, and withdrawn. Because of these injuries L.G. filed suit on behalf of L.W. against the school district, contending that the harassment by L.W.'s peers for his perceived sexual orientation violated the LAD. The administrative law judge rejected L.W.'s case, believing that student-on-student harassment was not covered by the LAD. The Director of the Division on Civil Rights reviewed and rejected this holding. The director concluded that the LAD recognized hostile environment claims against a school district and awarded L.W. $50,000 in emotional distress damages. The district was also ordered to change its policies and procedures regarding the prevention of peer sexual harassment. The district then moved the case into a state trial court, which ruled that a school district could be held liable for such harassment. The district then appealed to the New Jersey Supreme Court.

The Court, in a unanimous decision, upheld the lower court ruling. Chief Justice Zazzali, writing for the Court, stated that the LAD recognized a **cause of action** against a school district for student-on-student harassment based on perceived sexual orientation. The plain language of the **statute** prohibits discrimination based on "affectional or sexual orientation" in place of public accommodation, which include primary and secondary schools. The application of the LAD to this type of harassment would address "the insidious existence and detrimental effects of peer sexual harassment in our schools." School districts would be held liable if they failed to "reasonably address" that harassment. However, the court went out of its way to disclaim the possibility of school liability for "isolated insults or classroom taunts." An aggrieved student must allege discriminatory conduct that for a reasonable student of the same age and maturity level "would consider sufficiently severe or pervasive enough to create an intimidating, hostile, or offensive school environment."

The school district could be held liable if it had actual or constructive knowledge of the harassment and failed to take effective measures to end the discrimination. Toms River alleged that this hostile environment standard of proof was

wrong. Under Title IX of the federal civil rights laws, schools could be held liable only if they acted with "deliberate indifference," a standard of proof that was stricter than mere negligence. Chief Justice Zazzali rejected this argument, electing to apply state law precedent based on workplace discrimination to the schools. Moreover, the court required school districts to "implement effective preventive and remedial measures to curb severe or pervasive discriminatory treatment." The court sent the case back to the administrative law judge to determine if the school district acted reasonably during the relevant timeframe when policies concerning harassment were not yet in place.

SIXTH AMENDMENT

Carey v. Musladin

The SIXTH AMENDMENT protects the rights of criminal defendants at trial. Most defendants convicted of crimes who raise Sixth Amendment issues target the actions of prosecutors, police officers, and judges. However, in *Carey v. Musladin*, __U.S.__, 127 S.Ct. 649, 166 L.Ed.2d 482(2006), the defendant contended that the allowing members of the victim's family to wear buttons displaying the victim's image into the courtroom deprived the defendant of a fair trial. The Supreme Court upheld his conviction but declined to rule on whether the wearing of buttons was permitted. Though all nine members of the Court agreed with this judgment, three justices filed concurring opinions in which they expressed the desire for the Court to issue a substantive rule on courtroom attire that might be prejudicial to the defendant.

In 1994 Mathew Musladin shot and killed Tom Studer outside the house of Musladin's estranged wife. Musladin admitted he shot Studer but claimed he did so in self-defense. The jury convicted Musladin of first-degree murder. During his trial several members of Studer's family sat in the front row of the spectator's gallery. On some of the trial's 14 days, some members wore buttons with a photo of Studer on them. Before opening statements Musladin's lawyer asked the judge to order the Studer family not to wear the buttons during the trial. The judge rejected this motion, ruling that there was "no possible prejudice" to Musladin.

Following his conviction Musladin appealed to the California Court of Appeals. He contended that the buttons deprived him of his Fourteenth and Sixth Amendment rights to a fair trial. The court of appeals reasoned that he

Jim Studer displays the button with the picture of his slain brother worn during the trial of Matthew Musladin, whose conviction was overturned due to the buttons.
AP IMAGES

had to show actual or inherent prejudice to succeed on his claim. The court cited a U.S. SUPREME COURT case, *Holbrook v. Flynn*, 475 U.S.560, 106 S.Ct. 1340, 89 L.Ed.2d 535(1986), to support this reasoning. Although the court believed the wearing of such buttons should be discouraged the buttons had not "branded" Musladin "with 'an unmistakable mark of guilt' in the eyes of the jurors." The photograph of Studer was "unlikely to have been taken as a sign of anything other than the normal grief occasioned by the loss of a family member."

Musladin then filed an application for a **writ of habeas corpus** with the U.S. **district court**, again asserting that his constitutional rights had been violate by the wearing of the buttons and that he had been denied a fair trial. The district court rejected his application but the Ninth **Circuit Court** of Appeals reversed this decision. The appeals court ruled that under a provision of the Antiterrorism and Effective Death Penalty Act of 1996 (AEDPA), 28 U.S.C.A. §2254(d)(1), the California appeals court decision "was contrary to, or involved an unreasonable application of, clearly established Federal law, as determined by the Supreme Court of the United States." The Ninth Circuit concluded that the *Flynn* decision and another Supreme Court decision had clearly established a rule of federal law applicable to Musladin's case. The Californian appeals court had failed to apply the correct test for inherent prejudice.

The Supreme Court unanimously reversed the Ninth Circuit decision. Justice CLARENCE THOMAS, writing for six justices, made clear that the Court would not look at the underlying issue of wearing buttons into a murder trial. Instead, he looked to a narrower question: Had the state court ruled contrary to "clearly established federal law? Under the AEDPA Musladin's habeas application must be denied if the law was not clearly established. In *Flynn* and the other case the Court had addressed conduct by government officials. The Court ruled in *Flynn* that the presence of four uniformed state troopers sitting in the gallery directly behind the defendant was no so inherently prejudicial that it denied the defendant a fair trial. In contrast, Musladin alleged misconduct on the part of spectators. The effect of spectator conduct on a defendant's right to a fair trial had never been addressed by the Court. Justice Thomas stated that the inherent prejudice test articulated in *Flynn* had never been applied to test spectators' conduct.

Justice Thomas reinforced this claim by noting that lower courts have "diverged widely in their treatment of defendants' spectator-conduct claims." Some courts have applied *Flynn* to spectators' conduct while other courts have declined to do so. Some courts have distinguished *Flynn* on the facts and other courts have come up with their own test without relying, discussing, or distinguishing *Flynn*. Based on this lack of unanimity it could not be said that the California Court of Appeals unreasonably applied clearly established Federal law. Therefore, under AEDPA, Musladin was not entitled to habeas relief.

Justices JOHN PAUL STEVENS, ANTHONY KENNEDY, and DAVID SOUTER filed concurring opinions. Though they all agreed Musladin was not entitled to relief, each of the justice expressed concerns about the Justice Thomas's reasoning. Justice Stevens contended that the lower courts are entitled to take into account the court's discussion (legal **dicta**) of a ruling as well as the ruling itself. Justice Kennedy believed the Court should issue a ruling that would describe the limits of spectator conduct. Finally, Justice Souter urged the Court to consider the substantive issues surrounding spectator rights, including FIRST AMENDMENT rights.

Schriro v. Landrigan

The U.S. SUPREME COURT in 2007 considered a case involving a question of the proper standard by which the courts should consider claims of ineffective assistance of counsel under the SIXTH AMENDMENT of the U.S. Constitution. The case involved a request for habeas relief by a man who had been convicted of multiple murders and who had been sentenced to death. The defendant, Jeffrey Timothy Landrigan, argued that he had been denied effective assistance of counsel, but a federal **district court** denied relief. On appeal, the Ninth **Circuit Court** of Appeals held that the district court had abused its discretion in denying relief. The Supreme Court, in a 5–4 decision, reversed the Ninth Circuit, holding that Landrigan had not been deprived effective counsel. In so ruling, the Court clarified the proper standard by which federal district courts should consider petitions for **habeas corpus** relief.

The general principle that governs whether a federal district court should grant an evidentiary hearing in considering a petition for habeas **corpus** relief is that such as a decision is within the sound discretion of the court. However, the Antiterrorism and Effective Death Penalty Act of 1996 (AEDPA), Pub. L. No. 104-132, 110 Stat. 1214 altered the standard by which a court can grant federal habeas relief. Under this **statute**, the court cannot grant habeas relief unless a state court's decision either (1) "resulted in a decision that was contrary to, or involved an unreasonable application of, clearly established federal law, as determined by the Supreme Court of the United States;" or (2) "was based on an unreasonable determination of the facts in light of the evidence presented in the State court proceeding." 28 U.S.C. §2254(d)(1),(2). More-

over, the AEDPA also requires a federal district court to presume that the factual determination made by a state court is correct unless the petitioner for habeas relief can rebut the presumption with clear and convincing evidence. 28 U.S.C. §2254(e)(1).

Landrigan was first convicted of murder in 1982. Four years later, while he was incarcerated for that crime, he stabbed another inmate and was convicted of **assault and battery** with a deadly weapon. In 1989, he escaped from prison and committed the murder of Chester Dean Dyer during the act of committing a **burglary** in Arizona. An Arizona jury found Landrigan guilty of theft, second-degree burglary, and **felony** murder.

At Landrigan's sentencing hearing, his counsel tried to present the testimony of his ex-wife and his birth mother in order to establish mitigating circumstance surrounding his acts of violence. However, Landrigan asked that neither be permitted to testify. His attorney explained to the court that he had advised Landrigan that it was in his best interest for the two women to present mitigating evidence, and the court questioned Landrigan about his decision. At that time, Landrigan acknowledged that he was acting contrary to his attorney's advice and that he had no mitigating evidence to produce. The trial judge then asked both women if they would take the stand, but both refused.

During the hearing the judge asked Landrigan's counsel to explain what the women would have said had they testified. However, Landrigan continually interrupted his attorney as the latter tried to explain the circumstances surrounding Landrigan's upbringing and the nature of the crimes that he committed. During this time, Landrigan acknowledged that he committed robberies in order to support his family, and he denied that he acted in self-defense when he committed his first murder. Landrigan also explained that he stabbed the inmate in the 1986 incident because the two had begun an argument. Landrigan concluded the sentencing phase by telling the judge, "I think if you want to give me the death penalty, just bring it right on. I'm ready for it."

The trial judge identified two facts that were considered to be aggravating circumstances under the statute: first, Landrigan murdered Dyer in 1989 with the expectation of **pecuniary** gain; and second, Landrigan had previously been convicted of two felonies that had involved the use or threat of violence on another person. Although the judge found some mitigating evidence, she determined that Landrigan was a "person who had no scruples and no regard for human life and human beings." She sentenced Landrigan to death. The case was appealed directly to the Arizona Supreme Court, which affirmed the sentence. *State v. Landrigan*, 176 Ariz. 1, 859 P.2d 111 (1993).

Landrigan petitioned for postconviction relief, arguing that his attorney had failed to identify potential mitigating evidence that might have been presented at trial. The postconviction court, which was presided over by the same judge who had tried and convicted him, rejected his claim as "frivolous." According to the judge, because Landrigan had refused to allow his counsel to present other mitigating evidence at trial, "it is difficult to comprehend how he can claim counsel should have presented other evidence at sentencing." The Arizona Supreme Court thereafter denied his appeal.

Landrigan then filed an application for habeas corpus relief with the U.S. District Court for the District of Arizona. According to the district court, he could not make out even a "colorable" claim for ineffective assistance of counsel because he could not prove that he had been prejudiced by any error that his attorney might have made. After a panel of the Ninth Circuit Court of Appeals affirmed the district court's decision, the full court granted a rehearing, reversed the district court's decision, and remanded the case for a full evidentiary hearing. *Landrigan v. Stewart*, 441 P.3d 638 (9th Cir. 2006). According to the Ninth Circuit, when Landrigan said that he did not want his counsel to present mitigating evidence, he was only referring to the testimony of his ex-wife and birth mother. Moreover, the Ninth Circuit determined that Landrigan's counsel's performance fell below the standard established by the U.S. Supreme Court in *Strickland v. Washington*, 466 U.S. 668, 104 S. Ct. 2052, 80 L. Ed. 2d (1984).

The Court granted **certiorari** to review the case. In an opinion by Justice CLARENCE THOMAS, the Court reversed the decision of the Ninth Circuit. *Schriro v. Landrigan*, No. 05-1575, 2007 WL 1387923 (2007). Thomas determined that the federal district court continued to have broad discretion under the AEDPA in determining whether to grant an evidentiary hearing. If the record before the court refutes an applicant's factual allegations or otherwise precludes habeas relief, then the district court is not obligated to order an evidentiary hearing. The Court also determined that the Ninth Circuit had erred in it application of the standard

established in *Strickland*. According to the Court, the state courts' determination of the facts surrounding his counsel's actions was not unreasonable, and so the district court could properly deny the request for an evidentiary hearing.

Justice JOHN PAUL STEVENS, joined by three other justices, dissented. According to the dissent, Landrigan did not know at the time of his hearing that he suffered from a psychological condition that "sheds important light on his earlier actions." Stevens argued that had Landrigan's counsel conducted a constitutionally adequate background investigation, he could have discovered mitigating evidence. Moreover, the dissent said that the fact that Landrigan had instructed his attorney not to present mitigating evidence was not enough to deny Landrigan's claim that he had received effective counsel.

STATUTE OF LIMITATIONS

A type of federal or state law that restricts the time within which legal proceedings may be brought.

Savory v. Lyons

Statutes of limitations are intended to put potential litigants on notice that a lawsuit must be filed within a specified time following the action that caused an alleged injury. These deadlines serve as an absolute bar and therefore must be clearly defined so litigants have a fair change of complying with these deadlines. Occasionally the courts are called upon to settle a dispute over when the clock starts running for an appeal. The federal civil rights law 42 U.S.C.A. §1983 does not have a **statutory** limitations period. Therefore, the U.S. SUPREME COURT ruled that the personal injury **statute of limitations** of the state in which the plaintiff resides will govern the time period. In *Savory v. Lyons*, 469 F.3d 667 (7th. Cir.2006), the Seventh **Circuit Court** of Appeals ruled that an Illinois prisoner convicted of murder had waited too long to sue under §1983 seeking the release of physical evidence for DNA testing. The Illinois personal injury **statute** of limitations was two years. The prisoner's attempts to qualify for exceptions to this time period proved fruitless.

Johnny Lee Savory II was convicted of murdering a man and a woman in 1977 and was sentenced to a term of 40 to 80 years in prison. Savory, who was fourteen at the time of the murders, was convicted in part on the testimony of three of his friends and in part on the physical evidence. This evidence included hairs found at the crime scene that were similar to Savory's, a knife found in his home with a trace of blood on it, and a pair of pants Savory may have worn bearing a bloodstain of the same type as the female victim's blood. Savory challenged his conviction and sentence on direct appeal and then in state post-conviction proceedings and federal **habeas corpus** proceedings. All his efforts were unsuccessful.

In 1998 he changed course and filed a motion in state court seeking DNA testing of the physical evidence presented at trial. The Illinois circuit court denied his request in July 1998. The Illinois Court of Appeals upheld the decision in December 1999 and the Illinois Supreme Court affirmed the appeals court decision in October 2001. There things stood until April 2005, when Savory filed a §1983 lawsuit in Illinois federal **district court**. In his complaint he alleged his procedural and **substantive due process** rights had been violated by the Peoria prosecutor, the clerk of court, the chief of police, the city, and the county by refusing to give him access to the physical evidence. He sought from the court an order that would compel the production of hair samples, pants, pocketknife, and blood samples taken from Savory, his father, and others. The district court dismissed his lawsuit after determining that the statute of limitations had expired. The court concluded that the two-year statute of limitations began to run in July 1998, after the circuit court denied his motion for access to testing. Based on this date, Savory's action was almost five years too late.

The Seventh Circuit Court of Appeals upheld the lower court decision. The appeals court first looked at whether Savory had a right to file a §1983 action seeking this particular type of relief. The Supreme Court has ruled that claims by state prisoners challenging the fact or duration of their confinement cannot be heard using §1983. Such challenges are limited to the habeas process. The court concluded that Savory could use §1983 because if he prevailed he would not be released from prison or have his sentence shortened. At best he would gain access to the physical evidence for DNA testing that might be used in a future proceeding. As to the statute of limitations question, Savory tried to escape the

1998 accrual date by arguing that the denial of access to the physical evidence was a continuing violation, one that constituted a fresh act each day. Therefore, his action was timely when he filed in 2005. The appeals court agreed with the district court that the clock started ticking in July 1998 and rejected the continuing violation doctrine. This doctrine could only be applied when "the plaintiff could not reasonably be expected to perceive the alleged violation before the limitations period has run, or when the violation only becomes apparent in light of later events." In this case Savory was notified on a specific day, July 7, 1998, that his request for testing had been denied. He was "certainly aware of it on that date" and his "continued lack of access to the evidence is not a fresh act on the part of Peoria. Rather, it was the natural consequence of the discrete act that occurred when Peoria first denied access to the evidence."

Savory also offered an alternative theory called "equitable tolling." This is a court-ordered suspension of the statute of limitations where the plaintiff, through no fault of his own or lack of diligence, was unable to sue before the expiration of the time period. Typical situations justifying equitable tolling include the inability of the plaintiff to determine who caused his injury, inadequate notice, or the pending appointment of legal counsel. If such extraordinary circumstances are found, the court must balance the plaintiff's rights against any prejudice that the delay might cause the defendant. The appeals court found that Savory had failed to identify any extraordinary circumstances. Savory argued that the recent developments in DNA testing technology was an extraordinary circumstance but the court concluded that his claim "did not accrue until after he surely was aware of how DNA technology might apply to his case." By waiting seven years Savory undercut his argument for equitable tolling. The court also pointed out that a plaintiff in a §1983 action is not required to exhaust all remedies in state court before filing the federal action. Even if the appeals court agreed with his point, the **final decision** of the Illinois Supreme Court occurred in 2001. Savory would still be over two years late in filing his action. Therefore, the appeals upheld the dismissal of his lawsuit.

TAXATION

The process whereby charges are imposed on individuals or property by the legislative branch of the federal government and by many state governments to raise funds for public purposes.

EC Term of Years Trust v. United States

The U.S. SUPREME COURT on April 30, 2007 ruled that a **statute of limitations** contained in the INTERNAL REVENUE CODE was the exclusive remedy for a trust that wanted to recover funds that had been seized from its account by the INTERNAL REVENUE SERVICE. The taxpayers who brought the suit had argued that another limitations period should apply and allow the case to proceed. A unanimous Supreme Court disagreed, holding that the case was barred.

Under the Internal Revenue Code, where a person is liable to pay a tax neglects or refuses to do so, a **lien** may attach to all real and personal property that belongs to the taxpayer. This lien is not **self-executing**, meaning that the IRS must take affirmative steps in order to enforce the collection of unpaid taxes. One of the means by which the IRS can collect the tax is through a levy, which allows the government to seize and sell a taxpayer's property in order to satisfy the tax liability.

In 1966, Congress enacted the Federal Tax Lien Act, which provides that "[i]f a levy has been made on property . . . any person (other than the person against whom is assessed the tax out of which such levy arose) who claims an interest in . . . such property and that such property was wrongfully levied upon may bring a **civil action** against the United States in a dis-

trict court." However, the same provision establishes that this type of action must be brought before the expiration of nine months after the date in which the IRS makes the levy against a taxpayer's property. I.R.C. §7426(a)(1). Congress intended for this period of time to be quite short. During the hearings that were held in 1966 when Congress considered the proposed law, an assistant secretary to the TREASURY DEPARTMENT said that because an IRS district director is likely to suspend collection efforts after seizing property, "it is essential that he be advised promptly if he has seized property which does not belong to the taxpayer."

Under another federal **statute**, a taxpayer may bring a tax refund action when the government has assessed a tax erroneously or illegally. 28 U.S.C. §1346(a)(1). In order to bring this type of action, the taxpayer must bring an administrative claim with the Service. The taxpayer must file the refund claim with the service within two years of the date that the tax was paid or within three years that the tax return was filed, whichever is later. If the IRS denies the taxpayer's refund claim, then the taxpayer has two years to bring a judicial action.

Elmer W. and Dorothy Culler allegedly took unwarranted income tax deductions during the 1980s. Before the IRS attempted to collect these taxes, the couple in 1991 established a the EC Term of Years Trust. The IRS assumed that the couple had transferred funds to the trust so that they could evade taxes. In August 1999, the IRS filed a tax lien against the trust. Although the trust denied liability, it deposited funds into a bank account. The government in October 1999 levied on the account.

Nearly a year after the government seized its funds, the trust brought an action under §7426(a)(1) in the U.S. **District Court** for the Western District of Texas, claiming that the government's had wrongfully levied on the account. The trust brought the suit after the expiration of the nine-month period that followed the action. The district court held that the claim was barred because the nine-month period had expired. Moreover, the court held that the provisions of 28 U.S.C. §1346(a)(1) did not apply to the trust because §7426(a)(1) "affords the exclusive remedy for an innocent **third party** whose property is confiscated by the IRS to satisfy another person's tax liability." *BSC Term of Years Trust v. United States*, 2000 WL 33155870 (W.D. Tex. 2000).

The trust later filed a second action, seeking a refund under §1346. The district court again held that §7426 of the Internal Revenue Code was the exclusive remedy for a wrongful levy claim. *EC Term of Years Trust v. United States*, No. EP03-CA-363KC, 2004 WL 5264837 (W.D. Tex. 2004). The trust appealed the decision to the Fifth **Circuit Court** of Appeals, which affirmed the district court's decision. *EC Term of Years Trust v. United States*, 434 F.3d 807 (5th Cir. 2006).

The application of these federal statutes has caused a conflict among the **federal courts**. The Ninth Circuit Court of Appeals has held that §7426(a)(1) is not the exclusive remedy for a wrongful levy claim, meaning that a taxpayer under that circuit's prior rulings could seek a refund under §1346(a)(1). *WWSM Investors v. United States*, 64 F.3d 456 (9th Cir. 1995). Because of this conflict, the Supreme Court in 2006 granted **certiorari** to consider the case.

A unanimous Supreme Court affirmed the decisions of the lower courts. In an opinion by Justice DAVID SOUTER, the Court said that Congress had "specifically tailored" §7426(a)(1) to third-party wrongful levy claims, and if a party had the option of filing a general tax refund claim, the party could easily avoid the nine-month limitations period in §7426. The Court also said that the trust tried to read its prior cases too broadly, noting that previous Supreme Court cases have considered the application of §1346 in the context of a lien but not in the context of a levy.

Hinck v. United States

In 2007, the U.S. SUPREME COURT reviewed a case that involved the application of a Tax Code provision that applies to the **abatement** of interest collected by the federal govern-

ment on unpaid taxes. The section in question was enacted as part of the Taxpayers Bill of Rights in 1996. Under this section, Congress gave the U.S. **Tax Court** authority to review cases involving decisions about whether such interest should be abated. A unanimous Supreme Court determined that the Tax Court had exclusive jurisdiction to review these claims.

When a taxpayer fails to pay taxes when they become due, interest accrues on the amount of the unpaid taxes. The INTERNAL REVENUE SERVICE may take a significant period of time to decide whether the taxpayer indeed owed the tax, and during the period of time, interest may continue to accrue. Under §6404 of the INTERNAL REVENUE CODE, the Secretary of the Treasury may decide to abate, or forgive, any tax or related liability. In 1986, Congress enacted §6404(e)(1), which provides that "[i]n the case of any assessment of interest on . . . any deficiency attributable in whole or in part to any error or delay by an officer or employee of the Internal Revenue Service (acting in his official capacity) in performing a **ministerial** act . . . the Secretary may abate the assessment of all or any part of such interest for any period."

Following the passage of this section, several parties attempted to challenge decisions by the Secretary not to abate interest on taxes that were owed. The **federal courts** that considered these claims uniformly held that these decisions were not subject to **judicial review**. According to these courts, this decision was within the discretion of the Secretary alone, and so the decision was insulated from judicial review.

As part of the **Taxpayer Bill of Rights** approved in 1996, Congress allowed taxpayers to review cases in which the Secretary refused to abate interest. Under §6404(h), Congress gave the U.S. Tax Court jurisdiction over any action brought by a taxpayer who bring suit to "determine whether the Secretary's failure to abate interest . . . was an **abuse of discretion**. . . ." Moreover, the section allows the Tax Court to order an abatement, so long as the suit is brought within 180 days of the date in which the Secretary mails the final determination not to abate the interest.

John Hinck was a limited partner in a company called Agri-Cal Venture Associates (ACVA). In 1986, he and his wife filed a joint tax return, reporting losses that resulted from the partnership. The IRS reviewed Hinck's return and decided that deductions for several years needed to be adjusted, and in 1990, notified the partnership that the Service would disallow tens of millions of dollars in deductions. Hinks and his wife paid $93,890 to the IRS in 1996 to cover any personal deficiencies that would result from the adjustment of the deductions. After the IRS settled with ACVA in 1999 with respect to adjustments that would affect Hinck's return, the Service imposed additional liability against Hinck in both tax and interest.

The Hincks requested that the IRS abate the interest due to errors and delays that allegedly occurred between 1989 and 1993. After the IRS denied this request, the Hincks brought suit in the U.S. Court of Federal Claims, asking the court to review the denial of the abatement request. Judge Francis Allegra granted the government's motion to dismiss, holding that §6404(e)(1) did not provide a basis to allow the court to exercise jurisdiction over the claim. *Hinck v. United States* 64 Fed. Cl. 71 (Fed. Cl. 2005). The Hincks then appealed the decision to the Federal **Circuit Court** of Appeals, which affirmed the lower court's decision. *Hinck v. United States*, 446 F.3d 1307 (Fed. Cir. 2006).

In 2003, the Fifth Circuit Court of Appeals determined that §6404(e)(1) granted **concurrent jurisdiction** to the Tax Court as well as federal district courts and the U.S. Court of Federal Claims. *Beall v. United States*, 336 F.3d 419 (5th Cir. 2003). Federal district courts also reached different results on the issue. To resolve the split among the lower courts, the Supreme Court granted **certiorari** to review the case.

A unanimous Court affirmed the lower court's decision. *Hinck v. United States*, No. 06-376, 2007 WL 1641153 (May 21, 2007). In an opinion by Chief Justice JOHN ROBERTS, the Court emphasized that "a precisely drawn, detailed **statute** pre-empts more general remedies." The Court also noted the principle that "when Congress enacts a specific remedy when no remedy was previously recognized, or when previous remedies were 'problematic,' the remedy provided is generally regarded as exclusive."

According to Roberts' opinion, both of these principles apply to §6404(h). Even though Congress did not expressly state that the Tax Court's jurisdiction under this section, Congress addressed a specific need by enacting the statute; that is, Congress allowed a taxpayer to challenge an abatement decision made by the Secretary by giving jurisdiction to the Tax Court. The Hincks argued that Congress had removed impediments to review by district courts, and so Congress had only given concurrent jurisdiction to the various federal courts. The Court rejected this and other arguments, noting that Congress

"set out a carefully circumscribed, time-limited, plaintiff-specific provision, which also precisely defined the appropriate forum."

Limtiaco v. Camacho

Being a U.S. territory, the island of Guam has **appellate** rights through the United States' judicial system. Originally, appeals were channeled through the U.S. **Circuit Court** of Appeals for the Ninth Circuit. However, in 2004, Congress amended 48 USC §1424-2 to now provide that the U.S. SUPREME COURT, and not the Ninth Circuit, has **certiorari** (review) jurisdiction over decisions of the Guam Supreme Court.

The long-running dispute which became the subject matter of *Limtiaco, Attorney General of Guam v. Camacho, Governor of Guam*, No. 06-116, 549 U.S. ___ (2007) (originally captioned as *Moylan v. Camacho*, referring to the prior attorney general), began in 2003, when Guam had insufficient revenues to pay its obligations. To remedy the situation, the legislature of Guam authorized Guam's Governor Camacho to issue bonds worth approximately $400 million. The governor signed the law and prepared to issue the bonds.

Under Guam's law, the attorney general must review and approve all government contracts prior to their execution. Section 11 of the Organic Act of Guam provided in relevant part that the government of Guam could issue "bonds and other obligations" as needed "to anticipate taxes and revenues." However, within the same Section 11 (48 USC §1423a), Congress limited Guam's debt to ". . . 10 per centum of the aggregate tax valuation of the property in Guam." The attorney general concluded that issuing bonds in the requested amount ($400 million) would raise Guam's debt above the permitted level, and he refused to approve the bond contracts.

The governor then sought a declaration from the Guam Supreme Court that issuance of the bonds would not raise Guam's debt above the limitation. In order to make that determination, the court needed to ascertain the meaning of the term "aggregate tax valuation" as used in Section 11 of the Organic Act. The attorney general interpreted this to mean 10 percent of the **assessed valuation**, while the governor argued that it meant 10 percent of the appraised valuation. The Guam Supreme Court agreed with the governor and concluded that 48 USC §1423a prohibited debt greater than 10 percent of the appraised valuation of property in Guam.

The attorney general sought review in the Ninth Circuit. While the appeal was pending, Congress amended §1424-2, removing language that vested appellate jurisdiction for Guam controversies in the Ninth Circuit. The Ninth Circuit, citing one of its earlier cases addressing the effect of the amendment on its jurisdiction, dismissed the attorney general's appeal on March 6, 2006. The attorney general then filed a petition for certiorari to the U.S. Supreme Court.

As the case came to it, the Supreme Court now had two issues before it: the substantive issue relating to the definition of "aggregate tax valuation" and a new issue of whether the time for filing petition for certiorari had expired, rendering the substantive arguments moot.

Justice Thomas delivered the opinion of the Court. The jurisdictional issue needed to be addressed first. Under 21 USC §2101(c), petitions for certiorari must be filed within 90 days after the entry of a lower court's "genuinely final judgment." There are some circumstances that serve to "suspend" the finality of judgments by "rais[ing] the question whether the court will modify the judgment and alter the parties' rights." (*Hibbs v. Winn*, 542 U.S. 88).) The Supreme Court held that the Ninth Circuit, by granting the petition for certiorari, raised the possibility that "the court will modify the judgment and alter the parties' rights." Therefore, until it issued its order dismissing the case for lack of jurisdiction, the appeal remained "pending," and the "finality" of the judgment remained suspended. Limiting its holding to the unique procedural circumstances presented in this case only, the Court found the petition timely filed and moved on to the merits.

The Court resolved the meaning of "aggregate tax valuation" by noting that it most naturally and meaningfully correlated with the value to which the tax rate is applied. Tax rates are generally applied to properties according to their assessed values, not their appraised values (which simply reflect **market value**). Further, the Guam Supreme Court had reasoned that, because the debt-limitation provision contained in the Virgin Islands' law explicitly referred to "assessed value," Congress must have intended, by absence of similar language, to base Guam's limitation on some other value. The Court rejected this reasoning. By not including the word "assessed," Congress also chose not to insert the words "actual" or "appraised," so one meaning cannot be **imputed** more than another. But, said the Court, interpreting it to mean "assessed value" comported with most states' practice of holding debt limitations of municipalities to assessed valuation. The U.S. Supreme Court accordingly reversed the decision of the Guam Supreme Court and remanded the case.

The Court's **plurality** opinion included Chief Justice Roberts, as well as Justices Scalia, Kennedy, and Breyer. Justice Souter concurred in part and dissented in part, in which Justices Stevens, Ginsburg, and Alito joined. The dissent agreed with the Court's finding of timeliness of the petition for **writ** of certiorari. However, the dissent disagreed that the phrase "tax valuation" in the Organic Act of Guam referred unambiguously to assessed value. Since **statutory** text and sources gave no dispositive finality to the meaning, the dissent opined that congressional purpose may have indicated that appraised, rather than assessed value was the intended meaning of the term.

Permanent Mission of India v. City of New York

The Permanent Mission of India to the UNITED NATIONS (the Mission) is the diplomatic delegation of India to the United Nations. It owned real property (a 26-floor building) in New York City, which housed not only its diplomatic offices but also residential units (filling about 20 floors) for its lower-level employees and their families. Similarly, the Ministry for Foreign Affairs of the People's Republic of Mongolia was housed in a six-story building in New York City owned by the Mongolian government. Like the Mission, the Ministry Building also used much of its floor space to house lower-level employees and their families.

Under New York law, real property owned by foreign governments is exempt from taxation when used exclusively for diplomatic offices or residential quarters for ambassadors or ministers to the United Nations.

For years, New York City levied property taxes on the Mission and the Ministry for that portion of their real property that was used to house lower levels of employees and their families. The Mission and the Ministry refused to pay. By **operation of law**, the unpaid taxes converted to tax liens against the property. By 2003, the taxes in **arrears** reached over $16 million for the Mission and $2 million for the Ministry.

In April 2003, the City of New York filed complaints in state court to establish the validity of the tax liens. The Mission and Ministry, defendants, removed the cases to federal court, then petitioned for dismissal based on **sover-**

eign immunity. In *Permanent Mission of India to the United Nations v. City of New York*, No. 06-134, 551 U.S. ___ (2007), the U.S. SUPREME COURT was ultimately asked to determine whether the Foreign Sovereign Immunities Act of 1976 (FSIA), 28 USC §1602 *et seq.*, provided immunity from a lawsuit to declare the validity of tax liens on property held by the sovereigns to house their employees. The Court concluded that the FSIA did not provide immunity from such a suit.

At the **district court** level, the court denied dismissal based on immunity, citing an exception contained within the FSIA expressly providing that a foreign state shall not be immune from jurisdiction in any case in which "rights in immovable property situated in the United States are in issue" (§1605(a)(4)). The Second **Circuit Court** of Appeals affirmed, holding that the above exception did apply to the present case.

The Supreme Court affirmed the decision and agreed that the FSIA's exception applied to the Mission and the Ministry, and that they were not immune from a suit of this nature. Starting with the text of the FSIA, the Court determined the scope of the "immovable property" exception. The defendants had argued that the exception only applied to cases in which the specific right at issue involved title, ownership, or possession. The Court rejected this narrow application, finding that the plain language refers generally to "rights in" immovable property, and did not enumerate any specific rights. Next, looking to liens, the Court noted that liens are interests in property that run with the land. Therefore, a suit to establish validity of a tax **lien** necessarily implicates "rights in immovable property."

Moreover, looking to the stated purposes of the FSIA, the Court noted that Congress intended the FSIA to adopt a restrictive theory of sovereign immunity as one that recognized immunity "with regard to sovereign or public acts ... of a state, but not ... private acts" *Alfred Dunhill of London, Inc. v. Republic of Cuba*, 425 U.S. 682). Property ownership is not an inherently sovereign function, said the Court. There is no foreign sovereign immunity to attach, it concluded. The Second Circuit's decision was affirmed and the case remanded.

Justice Breyer joined Justice Stevens in dissent. They felt that tax actions fell outside the **purview** of the FSIA. They also expressed concern for the possibility of increased incidence of pierced immunity, since New York City also applies liens to compel landowners to pay for pest control, emergency repairs, and sidewalk upkeep.

As a footnote, New York City had conceded that even if a court of competent jurisdiction found the tax liens valid, the Mission and the Ministry would be immune (as sovereigns) from **foreclosure** proceedings. However, valid tax liens often cause foreign sovereigns to concede and pay. If they still refuse to pay in the face of a valid court judgment, the sovereign's foreign aid may be reduced by the United States by as much as 110 percent of the outstanding debt. Third, the liens would "run with the land" and be enforceable as against subsequent purchasers.

TERRORISM

The unlawful use of force or violence against persons or property in order to coerce or intimate a government or the civilian population in furtherance of political or social objectives.

New Airport Rules to Combat Terrorism

In August 2006, a sobering international news release revealed a thwarted Islamist terrorist plot to bomb ten U.S.-bound airplanes leaving London. In immediate response, the U.S. Secretary of Homeland Security elevated the Homeland Security Advisory System Threat Condition to High (Orange) for all inbound commercial flights from the United Kingdom, as well as all other international flights and domestic commercial aviation.

Pursuant to that announcement, the Transportation Security Administration (TSA) implemented changes to airport screening procedures, effective September 26, 2006, to ensure the continued safety and security of the traveling public and the national transportation system.

Travelers may now carry through security checkpoints *travel size* toiletries (3 oz. or less) that fit comfortably in a single, clear-plastic, zip-top bag. Moreover, after passing through security checkpoints, travelers may now bring beverages and other items purchased in the secure boarding area. This modified rule replaces the absolute ban on all liquids implemented immediately following the revealed London plot.

In addition, larger amounts of liquid prescription medications, baby formulas, and diabetic glucose treatments must be declared at the checkpoint for additional screening. Also needing to be declared are all liquids, including water, juice, or liquid nutrition or gels for passengers with disabilities or medical conditions, as well as life-support and life-sustaining items such as blood products, transplant organs, or items used to augment the body for medical or cosmetic reasons, such as mastectomy products, prosthetic breasts, bras or shells containing gels, saline, or other solutions, and gels or liquids used to cool disability or medically-related items used by persons with disabilities or medical conditions.

Other enhanced security measures are less visible to the public, including expanded mission coverage by the Federal Air Marshals Service (FAMS) and enhanced border control.

TSA also employs (since 2003)a passenger profiling system known as Screening of Passengers by Observation Techniques, or SPOT. Referred to as the antidote to **racial profiling**, SPOT discerns extremely high levels of stress, fear, and deception through "behavioral pattern recognition." SPOT agents are situated throughout airports and observe passengers moving about, with trained TSA agents specifically looking for physical symptoms such as sweating, rigid posture, or clenched fists. A screener then engages "selectees" in conversation, looking for body language or unnatural responses. Although SPOT has successfully identified passengers with forged visas, fake IDs, stolen air tickets, and other forms of contraband, its use to combat terrorism is less promising. Professionally-trained terrorists can easily learn how to control physical symptoms and answer questions convincingly, in much the same manner as those who have mastered lie-detector machinery technology.

New X-ray machines were implemented at 12 U.S. airports that employ a state-of-the-art electronic technology referred to as digital scanning, or "backscatter" screening. While originally used to search air travelers that U.S. Customs agents suspected of drug trafficking, the machines were expanded in use to search all air passengers at London's Heathrow Airport, and TSA planned for more comprehensive use of the technology in an increasing number of airports as well. While the technology has evoked some privacy concerns among passengers, they are warned in advance, and persons other than TSA officials cannot view the resulting images.

In the wake of the London threats, House Homeland Security Chairman Peter King publicly declared his endorsement of terrorism profiling based on race, ethnicity, and religion. King reminded the public at large that, while all Muslims were not terrorists, all recent terrorists were Muslim.

Notwithstanding that endorsement, the U.S. JUSTICE DEPARTMENT had issued a policy in 2003 banning racial profiling, and U.S. Attorney General Alberto Gonzales also disfavored the practice. But Marvin Badler, former head of security for Israeli airline El Al, warned that the United States was taking a big risk by not allowing racial profiling. Badler reminded CBS News correspondent Bob Orr that all 19 hijackers in the September 2001 terrorist attack were young Muslim males, and the suspects in the London bomb plot also shared the same ethnic and religious background.

Biometric technology (not based on race or ethnicity) has already been employed in the United States, Canada, and Australia. In October 2006, the use of *e-Passports* for all travel between Visa Waiver Program (VWP) countries (primarily 27 countries in Western Europe) or travel to the United States from a VWP country was implemented. E-Passports contain electronic chips holding the same information as that found on a passport's data page, including name, date of birth, and other biographic information. Uniquely, the e-Passports are equipped with biometric identifiers. The United States requires that the electronic chip contain a digital photograph of the passport-holder as well.

All e-Passports issued by VWP countries and the United States have special security features designed to prevent the unauthorized reading or "skimming" of data stored on the e-Passport chip. The inspection process upon entry into the United States is different for holders of e-Passports than previously-issued ones, and all U.S. ports of entry are now equipped with signs and/or special personnel to direct e-Passport holders to the appropriate U.S. Customs and Border Protection booth to process through.

White House Halts Terrorist Surveillance Program

Faced with significant pressure from critics, as well as litigation over the issue, the administration of President GEORGE W. BUSH in January 2007 announced that it would not reauthorize the terrorist surveillance program that had been in place since shortly after the SEPTEMBER 11TH ATTACKS in 2001. Under this program, the National Security Agency had collected a massive amount of information about ordinary people and businesses in an effort to identify communications related to terrorist activities.

Following the terrorist attacks on September 11, 2001, President Bush addressed a joint session of Congress. At this session he announced that he would use "every means of diplomacy, every tool of intelligence, every tool of law enforcement, every financial influence, and every weapon of war" to put an end to the threat of terrorism. One program that was initiated as a tool for fighting the terrorist threat was the terrorist surveillance program. This program was designed to focus on communications where one party to the communication was outside of U.S. borders and the government had reason to believe that at least one person involved in the communication was a member of al Qaeda or another terrorist group. The President reviewed the program regularly and could reauthorize the program every 45 days.

The surveillance program began to come under attack when the *New York Times* reported its existence in December 2005. Members of Congress, such as Senator John Kerry (D.-Mass.), argued that the program was unlawful because it was not authorized under the Foreign Intelligence Surveillance Act (FISA), Pub. L. No. 95-511, 92 Stat. 1976 (1978). The White House countered that the program was legal because as Commander-in-Chief, the President has inherent authority to approve this type of program. White House Press Secretary Scott McClellan addressed these criticisms by saying, "The NSA's terrorist surveillance program is targeted at al Qaeda communications coming into or going out of the United States. It is a limited, **hot pursuit** effort by our intelligence community to detect and prevent attacks. Senate Democrats continue to engage in misleading and outlandish charges about this vital tool that helps us do exactly what the 9/11 Commission said we needed to do—connect the dots."

Attorney General Alberto Gonzales also defended the program but declined to engage in an open discussion about the operational aspects of the program. In a prepared statement, he said, "The terrorist surveillance program remains highly classified, as it should be. We must protect this tool, which has proven so important to protecting America. An open discussion of the operational details of this program would put the lives of Americans at risk."

In May 2006, activities of the NSA again caused concern when reporters learned that the agency was collecting phone call records from tens of millions of Americans. Although the agency did not listen to or record telephone conversations, it collected information about calling patterns that ordinary citizens made in an effort to identify calling patterns that may suggest terrorist activity. According to one person who spoke about the program anonymously, the agency's goal was "to create a database of every call every made" within U.S. borders. The NSA was able to collect this data through agreements with AT&T, Verizon, and BellSouth.

The AMERICAN CIVIL LIBERTIES UNION and several other organizations brought suit against the NSA in the U.S. **District Court** for the Eastern District of Michigan, asking the court to strike down the program due to violations with the U.S. Constitution and with **statutory** law. Several of the plaintiffs in the case were U.S. citizens who regularly made international telephone calls for such purposes as the practice of law, journalism, and scholarship. U.S. District Judge Anna Diggs Taylor reviewed the program in light of the provisions of the FIRST AMENDMENT, FOURTH AMENDMENT, the Separation of Powers doctrine, and acts of Congress authorizing military force against terrorists and terrorist organizations. On August 17, 2006, Taylor issued an opinion ruling that the surveillance program violated the Constitution and had not otherwise been authorized by Congress. *ACLU v. Nat'l Security Agency*, 438 F. Supp. 2d 754 (E.D. Mich. 2006).

The JUSTICE DEPARTMENT immediately disputed the decision and said it would appeal. The White House issued a statement indicating that "United States intelligence officials have confirmed that the program has helped stop terrorist attacks and saved American lives. The program is carefully administered, and only targets international phone calls coming into or out of the United States where one of the parties on the call is a suspected Al Qaeda or affiliated terrorist. The whole point is to detect and prevent terrorist attacks before they can be carried out." On October 4, 2006, the Sixth **Circuit Court** of Appeals granted a stay of the district court's decision, pending a review by the **appellate court**.

Before the case could be appealed, however, the administration announced that the President would not reauthorize the surveillance program. In a letter to members of the SENATE JUDICIARY COMMITTEE, Gonzales said that a judge with the Foreign Intelligence Surveillance Court had issued orders that authorized the federal government to target communications where investigators have **probable cause** to believe that one of the communicants is a member of al Qaeda or another terrorist group. Gonzales said in the letter that "any electronic surveillance that was occurring as part of the Terrorist Surveillance Program will be conducted subject to the approval of the Foreign Intelligence Surveillance Court."

Gonzales again came under fire in May 2007 when former U.S. Deputy Attorney General James Comey testified that Gonzales had tried to pressure former Attorney General JOHN ASHCROFT to reauthorize the warrantless domestic surveillance program. Ashcroft at the time had been hospitalized with pancreatitis. The revelation led Senator Chuck Hagel (R.-Neb.) to call for Gonzales to resign.

Update on Terrorist Trials

Nearly five years after then-Attorney General JOHN ASHCROFT declared the United States had thwarted an al-Qaeda terrorist plot to detonate a "dirty bomb," trial for the man arrested and accused in connection with that attempt finally commenced in April 2007. Jose Padilla, a U.S. citizen, was initially arrested in 2002 at Chicago's O'Hare International Airport and subsequently detained as an "enemy combatant" at a Navy facility in Charleston, South Carolina. He remained held as an enemy combatant for more than three years until finally charged in 2005. In January 2006, he was transferred to civilian custody and held as a criminal defendant.

However, in the trial captioned *United States v. Padilla, et al*, which commenced in the U.S. **District Court** for the Southern District of Florida in Miami, Padilla was not charged with involvement in the "dirty bomb" attempt. Instead, he and co-defendants Adham Amin Hassoun and Kifah Wael Jayyousi faced charges of conspiracy to "murder, kidnap and maim" U.S. nationals overseas, in addition to charges of providing support to terrorist groups and activities. All three were accused of being part of a North American terrorist cell that funneled money, supplies, and fighters to Islamic extremist groups fighting "jihad," or Muslim holy war in several battles across the globe.

Earlier, in March, U.S. District Judge Marcia Cooke denied Padilla's motion to dismiss charges based on his allegations that he had been tortured while detained as an enemy combatant. Padilla had alleged that he had been abused, threatened, administered psychotropic PCP or LSD as a truth serum, and subjected to sleep deprivation while in military custody. Judge Cooke ruled that the standards for "outrageous government conduct" were not satisfied to entitle him to dismissal of the indictment. In an earlier competency hearing in February, Padilla was found competent to stand trial, despite his claims of **incompetency** based on post-traumatic stress from his lengthy detention.

There was no evidence directly connecting Padilla and his co-defendants to the September 11, 2007 terrorist attack, and Judge Cooke cautioned prosecutors that she would permit only limited reference to that event. Other evidence ostensibly inadmissible was the claim by federal officials that Padilla admitted involvement with the "dirty bomb" plot as well as plans to blow up apartment buildings, and he further admitted that he trained with al-Qaeda. However, these statements/confessions were made during his detention at the Navy facility, where, as an enemy combatant, he had no lawyer present and was not read his Miranda rights.

Notwithstanding, prosecutors intended to introduce at trial a key piece of evidence: a "mujahedeen data form" that Padilla completed in 2000 to join an al-Qaeda training camp in Afghanistan. Padilla's fingerprints were still on it. Additionally, Padilla's voice is heard on eight FBI wiretaps, and he is mentioned in about 20 others. One of the recordings mentions that Padilla had gone to "the area of Osama," apparently referencing bin Laden's al-Qaeda training camps in Afghanistan.

As to his co-defendants, Hassoun allegedly acted as a South Florida recruiter and fundraiser for violent Muslim causes, prosecutors charged. Padilla, who was previously a member of Chicago's Latin Disciples street gang, became one of Hassoun's recruits and warriors after moving to Florida. He converted to Islam while serving time in a Florida prison for a 1991 weapons conviction.

The other co-defendant, Jayyousi, was responsible for publishing the "Islam Report," which was used to spread Islamic ideology and promote terror support and fundraising. Defense counsel contended that he was only reporting on global events of Muslim interest.

The Bush Administration had already suffered a major legal setback with the U.S. SUPREME COURT decision of *Hamdan v. Rumsfeld*, 126 S.Ct. 2749 (2005), wherein the Court held that neither the U.S. Constitution (including the inherent powers of the Executive) nor any act of Congress expressly authorized the type of "military commissions" created by the Bush Administration to try detained enemy combatants for war crimes.

In response to the Court's ruling, Congress enacted the U.S. Military Commissions Act,

Pub. L. 109-366, 120 Stat. 2600, on September 29, 2006 (the "Act"). (President Bush signed it on October 10, 2006.) Its stated purpose was to "facilitate bringing to justice terrorists and other unlawful enemy combatants through full and fair trials by military commissions, and for other purposes."

One of the more controversial provisions of the Act was its amendment of the federal *habeas corpus* statute, 28 USC §2241. The new subsection (e) prevents courts from exercising jurisdiction to consider applications for writs of habeas **corpus** filed by or on behalf of aliens detained by the United States who have been determined to be detained as enemy combatants or those who are awaiting such determination.

Almost immediately upon its enactment, legal challenges to some of the Act's provisions were filed. On April 30, 2007, the Court denied **certiorari** of two more Guantanamo Bay detainees in *Hamdan v. Gates*, and *Khadr v. Bush*. These latter cases had a new twist. The same Salim Ahmed Hamdan who had prevailed in the 2005 case of *Hamdan v. Rumsfeld*, (see above) was now facing the possibility of being tried under the new Act. This time he attempted to challenge the *constitutionality* of Congress' decision to deny habeas relief under the Act. His lawyers unsuccessfully argued that the new **tribunal** system was substantially similar to the old one. As of June 2007, several cases were still pending in lower courts in which detainees were challenging their status as "enemy combatants" under the Act.

TRADEMARKS

Distinctive symbols of authenticity through which the products of particular manufacturers or the salable commodities of particular merchants can be distinguished from those of others.

Cisco and Apple Settle Trademark Dispute Over iPhone

Cisco and Apple, Inc. in February 2007 settled a dispute over Apple's use of the term iPhone, for which Cisco has held the trademark. The controversy erupted less than two months earlier when Apple introduced a new product called the iPhone, which had the same name as a product that had been introduced by Cisco in 2006. Experts on intellectual property said that they thought Cisco would win its trademark infringement suit against Apple, but the two companies reached an agreement before lengthy litigation ensued.

Apple CEO Steve Jobs demonstrates the new Apple iPhone, January 9, 2007.

AP IMAGES

The name iPhone was first registered as a trademark by InfoGear Technology Corp. in 1996. Cisco acquired the trademark in 2000 when it acquired InfoGear. Cisco did not put the trademark into use until the spring of 2006, when it announced the release of its new iPhone, which is an Internet phone that uses the popular Voice over Internet Protocol, or VoIP. Cisco launched the produce through its Linksys division, which expanded iPhone with additional products late in 2006.

Apple began in 1977 as a computer company, but by the beginning of the new millennium had transformed itself into a manufacturer of a broader range of electronic devices. The company's popular products include the iMac and the iPod. In 2006, rumors swirled on the Internet that Apple was developing a new mobile phone product that would also be capable of playing music, surfing the Internet, and running the Macintosh operation system. Apple confirmed these rumors in January 2007 when it announced the introduction of the iPhone. Apple CEO commented, "Every once in a while a revolutionary product comes along that changes everything. It's very fortunate if you can work on just one of these in your career."

Apple's iPhone, which was first retailed at a cost starting at $499, works with a new touch-screen technology that Jobs described as "far more accurate than any touch display every shipped." The half-inch device automatically synchronizes a user's media, including movies, music, photos, and e-mail, so that users can access their files on their phones. The phones operate on AT&T's Cingular wireless network and supports technologies such as Wi-Fi and Bluetooth. At the time that the company introduced is iPhone, Jobs also announced the release of other products, including one that would allow computer users to watch movies on their televisions.

Just one day after Apple announced its new product, Cisco filed a lawsuit in federal court in San Francisco, alleging that Apple had infringed Cisco's trademark in the use of the term iPhone. Cisco acknowledged that it had approached Apple in the years prior to the launch of the products to negotiate a licensing agreement that would allow Apple to use the name. However, when Apple made its announcement in January, Cisco assumed that the companies could not reach and agreement.

According to Mark Chandler, Cisco's senior vice president and general counsel, "Cisco entered into negotiations with Apple in **good faith** after Apple repeatedly asked permission to use Cisco's iPhone name. There is no doubt that Apple's new phone is very exciting, but they should not be using our trademark without our permission." Chandler also added, "We certainly expected that since [Apple] had gone ahead and announced a product without receiving permission to use the brand, that meant that the negotiation was concluded."

Apple countered that it was entitled to use the term iPhone because its product is materially different than the Cisco product. Apple spokesperson Natalie Kerris referred the lawsuit as "silly," stressing that several other companies using the VoIP products were using the name iPhone. "We believe that Cisco's U.S. trademark registration is tenuous at best," Kerris said. "Apple's the first company to use the iPhone name for a cell phone. And if Cisco wants to challenge us on it, we're very confident we will prevail."

Under federal trademark law, both companies could share the iPhone trademark so long as the uses of the products are not confusingly similar. Apple has endured other controversies over its own name. For example, the company waged a battle with Apple Corps., which is owned by the Beatles, for several decades. This ongoing dispute was not settled until early 2007. At the launching, Jobs chose to demonstrate the capabilities of the iPhone by playing two Beatles songs.

Cisco said that even though the products may have been dissimilar at the time of the dispute, both products could later incorporate new features or work in different networks after further development. Industry analysts said that Cisco's argument had merit, because Cisco could add new features to its iPhone to make it more comparable to Apple's iPhone. For instance, Cisco could add cellular functionality to convert its product to a cell phone, or it could add memory to allow the device to support additional media functions.

Some commentators also noted that Cisco's move was strategic, emphasizing that the company had been aggressive in making new acquisitions. Company CEO John Chambers had been ambitious about increasing Cisco's production of consumer electronic products. Chambers also wanted to enhance the company's brand name. Other commentators questioned the move, noting that Cisco had little to gain through litigation over the use of the name of a product. Nevertheless, intellectual property experts said that Cisco was likely to prevail in its suit. In early February, Cisco took out a full-age ad in the *New York Times* to promote its iPhone and included the small "R" next to the name to indicate that it was a registered trademark.

Just weeks after Cisco filed its lawsuit, the companies agreed to suspend the litigation and return to the negotiating table. At this time, Cisco agreed to extend the time during which Apple could respond to the filing. On February 21, the companies announced that they had reached a settlement. Under the terms of the settlement, Apple could use the term iPhone and agreed to explore interoperability between the two companies' products in the areas of security and consumer and enterprise communications.

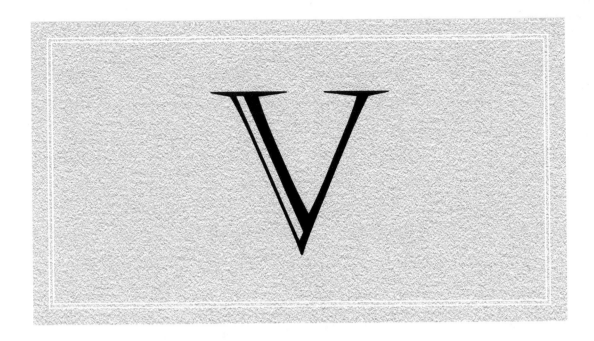

VOTING

California Court Restores Voting Rights to Prisoners

The California 1st **District Court** of Appeals in December 2006 restored voting rights to about 100,000 inmates serving a year or less for **felony** convictions in local jails. These rights had been suspended when Secretary of State Bruce McPhearson determined that those who served short-term sentences in county jails were not eligible to vote under the California Constitution. These rights were restored permanently when the State of California decided not to appeal the decision.

The first California Constitution in 1849 included a provision that permanently disenfranchised anyone who was "convicted of any infamous crime." The courts struggled in several cases with the meaning of "convicted." In *Stephens v. Toomey*, 51 Cal. 2d 864, 338 P.2d 182 (1959), the California Supreme Court determined that a person against whom a guilty verdict had been rendered, but whose sentence had been suspended, had not been "convicted" for purposes of determining whether the convicted person was disenfranchised. In 1960, a proposed amendment to the constitution would have eliminated voting rights for those who were on parole or probation but would have reinstated voting rights to those who had paid the penalties imposed by law. The California Legislature never adopted this proposal.

A 1972 amendment to the constitution established that persons who were "under court order" but who were not "under sentence" retained their voting rights. This amendment also retained the "infamous crime" language, which had begun to give the courts problems. In 1973, the California Supreme Court considered whether the state could continue to disenfranchise those who had been convicted of an "infamous crime." In *Ramirez v. Brown*, 9 Cal. 3d 199, 107 Cal. Rptr. 137, 507 P.2d 1345 (1973), the court held that the California provision violated the FOURTEENTH AMENDMENT to the U.S. Constitution because its denial of the right to vote of all ex-felons was not the least restrictive method of protecting the ballot box against voters who may be morally corrupt or dishonest.

In response to *Ramirez* in 1974, California approved article II, section 4, which established the modern restrictions on the voting power of certain prisoners. The text of the provision provides as follows: "The Legislature shall prohibit improper practices that affect elections and shall provide for the disqualification of electors while mentally incompetent or imprisoned or on parole for the conviction of a felony." Previous secretaries of state established that this provision only disenfranchised those persons who were serving time in a state prison as a result of a felony conviction, or who were on parole from a felony conviction. Opinions issued by former officials indicated that the law did not apply to those who were on probation due to a felony conviction.

McPhearson in November 2005 asked the California Attorney General Bill Lockyer for an opinion about whether a person who is incarcerated in a local detention facility for the conviction of a felony was eligible to vote. Lockyer departed from prior interpretations and determined that article II, section 4 applied not only to those felons who were serving time in state prisons or who were on parole, but also to those who were confined at a local jail as a condition of probation. Lockyer's opinion focused on the term "imprisoned" in the constitution and concluded that the meaning of the term should not exclude those who served time in a local jail. Moreover, the attorney general determined that the California Legislature never gave an indication that it intended to grant voting rights to those who were in custody, even if custody meant a local detention facility.

McPherson responded to the opinion in December 2005 by issuing a memorandum to all county clerks and registrars of voters, ordering them to cancel voter registrations for all person who were imprisoned or on parole for conviction of a felony. According to the memo, "Where the sentence is physically served is immaterial with respect to voting eligibility, the fact of a felony conviction is what triggers the restriction on the felon's voting rights."

The League of Women Voters of California (represented by the AMERICAN CIVIL LIBERTIES UNION), along with other voter and groups who advocate prisoners' rights brought suit against McPherson and others in the First District **Court of Appeal** of California. This type of case fell within a limited category of cases where the **appellate court** had **original jurisdiction** to hear the case. The petitioners asked the court to issue an order directing the Secretary of State and the San Francisco Director of Elections to allow prisoners held in local jails to register to vote. According to these petitioners, the opinion adopted by McPherson and Lockyer was overly broad.

The court, in an opinion by **Associate Justice** William Stein, agreed with the petitioners. According to Stein, the Attorney General's opinion focused too heavily on the definition of the term "imprisoned" and disregarded the distinction between a person who is confined to a local jail as condition of probation and a person who is imprisoned in a state prison for a felony conviction. Stein noted that the history of the 1974 amendment shows that the legislature intended not to disenfranchise those who are on probation and that the Attorney General's opinion "ignored decades of judicial construction without regard for the history of the constitutional provision or the purpose of the 1974 amendment." Accordingly, the court ordered McPherson to inform various clerks and registrars that the constitution's prohibition only ap-

plies to those imprisoned in state prison or those who are on parole for the conviction of a felony. *League of Women Voters of Cal. v. McPherson*, 145 Cal. App. 4th 1469, 52 Cal. Rptr. 3d 585 (Ct. App. 2006).

Spokespersons for the ACLU said that most of the people affected by McPherson's actions were young men, often racial or ethnic minorities, who had not committee violent crimes. Probation officers also noted that the restoration of these voter's rights would help in the rehabilitation of these inmates.

Voter Identification Laws Receive Court Scrutiny

Following the 2000 national elections, Congress passed the 2002 Help America Vote Act (HAVA), P.L. 107-252, 116 Stat. 1666. The new law, addressing all aspects of the election and voting process, was implemented with sequential deadlines that started in December 2002 and ended in January 2007.

HAVA Title III set minimum national standards for the kind of identification voters must present at the polls before being allowed to vote. HAVA mandated that states require identification at the polls for all first-time voters who registered by mail, if the registration did not require identification. In addition, voters who had not voted in the previous election would now be required to provide identification.

Under HAVA, there are two approved forms of identification: photo and non-photo. Any current and valid government-issued photo identification (e.g., driver's license, passport, etc.) meets the photo ID requirement. Otherwise, a copy of a current utility bill, bank statement, government check, or other government document that shows a voter's name and address meets the non-photo ID requirement.

Originally, the Commission on Federal Election Reform (commonly known as the Carter-Baker Commission, named for the co-chairs, former President Jimmy Carter and former Secretary of State James Baker III) contemplated a national voter identification card, *Real ID*. However, amid resistance and objections from many influential citizen organizations, a national ID card was, at least for 2007, shelved.

As new voter ID laws were implemented in compliance with HAVA, the National Conference of State Legislatures reported that by February 2007, a minimum of 24 states had opted for broader voter identification requirements than what HAVA mandated. In these states, all voters must present identification prior to voting, and a minimum of seven of these states require photo ID. Notwithstanding, no voters are turned away if they fail to produce appropriate ID; all states have individual procedures to address this.

Several states had their laws challenged in court. In Arizona v. Gonzalez, consolidated Nos. 06-532 and 06-533, 549 U.S. ___ (2006), the U.S. SUPREME COURT upheld Arizona's photo ID requirement as well as its requirement that voters prove their U.S. citizenship. The ruling vacated a decision by the Ninth **Circuit Court** of Appeals that had suspended those requirements pending further litigation.

In October 2006, the Eleventh Circuit Court of Appeals came to the opposite conclusion in *Perdue v. Lake*, upholding an injunction *barring* the state of Georgia from enforcing its photo ID requirement, at least through the November 2006 elections. However, when the case was considered on the merits in June 2007, the Supreme Court of Georgia found that the sole plaintiff in the case did not have legal *standing* to challenge the law. This was because the plaintiff failed to show harm. She presented no evidence as to why she could not have voted in person without showing a photo ID, since she qualified as a first-time voter who had registered by mail and therefore needed only to show an acceptable document identifying her. She showed no evidence that she lacked such an acceptable document. Second, the plaintiff did possess an acceptable form of photo ID under the 2006 Voter ID law, a public transportation pass card that she had been using. The Court ordered the case dismissed. Meanwhile, Georgia's list of acceptable forms of ID is now much broader and includes some forms without photo identification.

In *Indiana DEMOCRATIC PARTY v. Rokita*, the Seventh Circuit Court of Appeals upheld Indiana's Photo ID law as constitutional in January 2007. It upheld a lower court decision that the law did not unduly burden the right to vote. The AMERICAN CIVIL LIBERTIES UNION and the Indiana Democratic Party had claimed that the law would discourage voters from casting ballots, an argument that the **appellate court** discounted.

In October 2006, the Missouri State Supreme Court struck down that state's photo ID law. Earlier in the year, the state legislature had tightened its existing law by adding the requirement for photo ID, which was immediately challenged. But the state's high court found the law burdened the fundamental right to vote and violated the **equal protection** provisions of the

Missouri Constitution. The problem was that the law allowed only four types of acceptable identification. *Weinschenk v. State of Missouri, et al.* The list of acceptable forms of ID has since been broadened and includes some forms without photo identification.

Ohio's photo ID law was temporarily suspended by the secretary of state for the 2006 national elections, but would be effective for future elections. The case that triggered the hold, *Northeast Ohio Coalition for the Homeless and Service Employees International Union v. Blackwell* case was ultimately settled. Terms of the settlement still required absentee voters to show proof of identification when applying for an absentee ballot, but absentee ballots already obtained without ID would be counted for the November 2006 elections. As to future elections, voters at polls may provide other forms of identification (e.g., ID cards from county or local governments and university ID cards) instead of just government-issued ID cards.

Voter Registration Statutes

Congress enacted the National Voter Registration Act (NVRA) in 1993 not only to increase the number of citizens who register to vote, but also to enhance voter participation in elections and protect the electoral process. One of the ways the law did this was by effecting a variety of means to allow Americans to obtain and fill out voter registration forms. These included mail-in forms as well as the ability to register at state motor vehicle departments (while getting or renewing drivers' licenses) and at public assistance agencies.

While most states easily implemented voter registration programs in conjunction with state motor vehicle departments and mail-in procedures, registration through public assistance programs lagged behind. This resulted in the growth of third-party civil rights and ostensibly non-partisan groups that mobilized and attempted to enhance voter turnout, particularly in under-represented groups of the general population.

New problems and controversies arose for these "voter registration" groups in their efforts to recruit new voting registrants. For example, in the weeks leading up to the 2006 national elections, the media televised several instances of third-party groups bestowing money and gifts on inner-city and/or homeless persons in return for their efforts to register and vote, many times with a commitment to vote for a certain party or issue. In other instances, the media covered stories of groups losing registration forms, not checking them for correctness, or submitting them too late, thereby disenfranchising the very persons they were purporting to empower. Even worse were isolated reports of third-party groups selectively destroying registration forms filled out by certain persons, -perhaps from the wrong political party or opposing viewpoint.

This, in turn, raised issues regarding a state's responsibility for counting or not counting 'provisional ballots' cast by voters whose registration forms had been rejected for these errors or allegedly lost. Before the next national election, many states vowed to create new laws addressing these issues.

The states themselves then became defendants in several lawsuits around the country. Two of the most publicized suits involved the states of Florida and Ohio. In Florida, the League of Women Voters filed suit, claiming that under the new Third-Party Voter Registration Organization law, the mandatory fines charged for losing forms ($5000 per form) or submitting them more than 10 days after they were collected ($250 per form) were unfair, excessive, and allowed for no exceptions. The group challenged the law's unequal treatment of political parties and non-partisan groups. It halted all efforts in Florida, fearing the possibility of facing criminal sanctions for any errors. Also joining the League as plaintiffs were the Florida AFL-CIO, the American Federation of State, County and Municipal Employees, and other groups.

In September 2006, U.S. **District Court** Judge Patricia Seitz declared the new law unconstitutional, saying that criminal penalties for violations threatened free speech rights. She also took exception to the fact that political parties were exempted from the law. The state defendants appealed her decision. As of June 2007, the case was still on appeal before the U.S. **Circuit Court** of Appeals for the Eleventh Circuit. *League of Women Voters v. Cobbs, No. 06-14836D.*

Likewise, in Ohio, civil rights groups protested the new rule that individuals who participated in voter registration drives and collected completed forms must personally deliver or mail the forms directly to election officials. Prior to the new law, they could return forms to a church or institution promoting a voter registration drive. The plaintiffs complained that the new rules were intimidating, particularly in low-income and minority areas, because criminal penalties were also imposed for violations. Plaintiffs alleged that the new rules violated their constitutional rights of **equal protection**, **substantive due process**, and procedural due process.

Defendants in the Ohio case (including the secretary of state and governor) asserted **sovereign immunity** under the ELEVENTH AMENDMENT, and further asserted that the violations were not within the **purview** of defendants, but rather, of local boards of elections.

In September 2006, U.S. District Court Judge Kathleen O'Malley declared the new law unconstitutional, saying that criminal penalties for violations threatened free speech rights. Only the parts of the election law that dealt with voter registration were struck and the remainder of the law remained in effect. Judge O'Malley stated that voters should ignore the references to criminal penalties that were printed on the forms used to register new voters. Defendant appealed, arguing on appeal that the matter had become moot with the passage of Ohio's Amended Substitute House Bill 3. As of June 2007, this case was also on appeal before the U.S. Circuit Court of Appeals for the Sixth Circuit. *League of Women Voters v. Blackwell, No. 06-3335.*

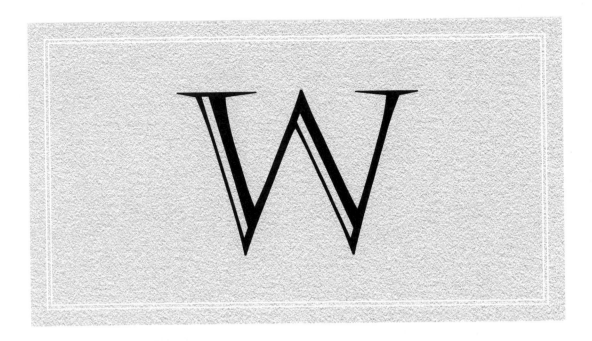

WOODS AND FORESTS

A comprehensive term for a large collection of trees in their natural setting and the property on which they stand.

Reinstatement of the Roadless Area Conservation Rule

The U.S. Forest Department's Roadless Area Conservation Rule (the "Roadless Rule"), 66 Fed. Reg. 3244; codified at 36 CFR pt. 212 (2001) prohibited logging, mining, and other development on approximately 58 million acres of America's wilderness in 38 states and Puerto Rico. Its main objective was to keep "roadless" certain areas of pristine woodlands and forests. Research has shown that roads running through wilderness areas create barriers that separate and fragment some populations of wildlife (that will not cross or breach human paths or roads). Roads going through wilderness areas also have been shown to detrimentally increase erosion and siltation of wetlands. Moreover, roadways that penetrate pristine lands often introduce invasive species to the forests that would not normally be found there, including certain weeds, pathogens (that may infect wildlife with no natural immunity to them) and fish illegally dumped by fishers.

As good as it sounded (polls showed that the general public supported the ban), there was plenty of controversy. Nearly 97 percent of the subject pristine wilderness (albeit federally-owned land) was located in 12 western states, and many governors and congressional delegations from those states opposed the ban on road construction. Professional foresters and forest products groups objected that it would be harder to man-

age the national forests or restore the millions of acres in poor ecological health without roads. And how would firefighters reach forest fires?

Those concerns found their common voice in government when in 2005, the U.S. DEPARTMENT OF AGRICULTURE issued the State Petitions for Inventoried Roadless Area Management Rule (the "State Petitions Rule") (70 Fed. Reg. 25,654; codified at 36 CFR pt. 294). Under this Rule, governors in affected states were given 18 months to affirmatively petition the Secretary of Agriculture to request continued protection from road construction. (Originally slated for expiration on January 16, 2006, the Rule was extended for another 18-month period effective January 16, 2006.)

Upon its enactment, four states (California, New Mexico, Oregon, and Washington) and 20 environmental groups filed suit in the U.S. **District Court** for the Northern District of California. They sought **repeal** of the 2005 State Petitions Rule and reinstatement of the 2001 Roadless Rule. In September 2006, they won their case. U.S. District Court Judge Elizabeth D. LaPorte granted plaintiffs' motion for **summary judgment**. In so ruling, she set aside the State Petitions Rule, and reinstated the 2001 Roadless Rule. *People of the State of California, ex rel. Lockyer v. U.S. Department of Agriculture, et al.*, No. 3:05-CV-03508-EDL (N.D.Ca. 2006). (This was the caption for two consolidated cases, *California, et al. v. U.S. Department of Agriculture, et al.*, and *Wilderness Society, et al. v. U.S. Forest Service, et al.*)

The quintessential question before the court was whether the State Petitions Rule was merely procedural fine-tuning of the Roadless

Rule, or whether it constituted a substantive repeal of the Roadless Rule. This determination would dictate whether or not defendants had violated federal law prior to enacting the State Petitions Rule.

Under the National Environmental Protection Act (NEPA) and the ENDANGERED SPECIES ACT (ESA), governmental agencies are required to conduct research and issue a Final Environmental Impact Statement (FEIS) prior to implementing new rules affecting the environment. Although the Forest Service had incorporated numerous studies before implementing the 2001 Roadless Rule, the Department of Agriculture had not done this prior to implementing the State Petitions Rule. Judge LaPorte agreed with the consolidated plaintiffs that the 2005 State Petitions Rule violated federal law. Specifically, she ruled that the administrative department failed to undergo environmental impact studies before implementing the new rule. But this was not the final chapter in the Rules litigation.

As background, just when the Roadless Rule (that Judge LaPorte reinstated) was about to take effect in 2001, the U.S. District Court in Idaho granted a **preliminary injunction** that stopped its implementation. Environmental groups appealed the Idaho injunction and in December 2002, the Ninth **Circuit Court** of Appeals reversed the injunction. Two years later, in 2003, the Ninth Circuit issued a mandate ending the injunction and the Roadless Rule went into effect.

Not more than three months later, in July 2003, the Wyoming federal district court issued a nationwide permanent injunction stopping the Roadless Rule. In its ruling, it acknowledged the Ninth Circuit's decision (above), but noted that it had "limited persuasive value." (Wyoming falls within the jurisdiction of the Tenth Circuit Court of Appeals.) Again, the environmental groups appealed. But in 2005, before the Tenth Circuit could render an opinion, the State Petitions Rule went into effect. Bases on this, the Forest Service petitioned the Tenth Circuit to simply dismiss the appeal as moot, without rendering a decision. The Tenth Circuit agreed and dismissed without ruling (*Wyoming v. U.S. Department of Agriculture, 414 F.3d. 1207 (2005).*

The environmental groups then reorganized, joined with the four states, and the present consolidated cases (ruled on by Judge LaPorte) followed in the California district court.

Following LaPorte's judgment, the State of Wyoming began procedural initiatives to rein-

state the district court's 2003 injunction of the Roadless Rule (never decided on by the Tenth Circuit). Meanwhile, the states of Idaho and Alaska also appeared to side with Wyoming. The governor of Idaho filed a petition to reopen much of its unroaded wilderness to logging and road-building. Additionally, Several anti-Roadless Rule organizations, e.g., American Council of Snowmobile Associations, Silver Creek Timber Company, United Four Wheel Drive Associations, etc., were expected to join. The states of North Carolina, South Carolina, and Virginia, which had smaller tracts of wilderness at stake, timely filed their petitions for continued protection under the newer Rule and had been approved.

WRONGFUL DISCHARGE

An at-will employee's cause of action against his former employer, alleging that his dischargee was in violation of state or federal antidiscrimination statutes, public policy, an implied contract or an implied covenant of good faith and fair dealing.

Office of Senator Mark Dayton v. Hanson

Rarely does the U.S. SUPREME COURT issue more than a paragraph when it denies **certiorari** (review) of a case. Not so in *Office of Senator Mark Dayton v. Hanson*, No. 06-618, 550 U.S. ___ (2007). In a pointed but unanimous six-page opinion, the high court took the time to explain why it lacked jurisdiction to review the case. (Chief Justice Roberts recused himself, as he had previously participated in the case while sitting as a judge on the D.C. Circuit.)

U.S. Senator Mark Dayton's office was appealing an adverse decision by the local federal **district court** of its motion for **summary judgment** based on immunity from suit. The office had been sued for wrongful termination by a former employee, Brad Hanson, who had worked for the one-term Senator's 2000 campaign in Minnesota. He eventually became Dayton's State Office Manager, but in 2002, requested three weeks' medical leave for heart surgery and recuperation. While on medical leave, Hanson was contacted by a fellow staffer and told not to return to work.

Hanson subsequently sued the Senator's office for wrongful employment termination under the Family and Medical Leave Act (FMLA) and the Americans with Disabilities Act (ADA). (He also added a charge for unpaid overtime under the Fair Labor Standards Act.) Hanson claimed that the district court had jurisdiction over the case under the Congressional Accountability Act of 1995, 109 Stat. 3, as amended, 2 USC §1301 *et seq*. The Act is part of the "Contract with America" initiative of the Bush Administration; under its provisions, Congress subjected itself to 11 labor and employment laws that it had previously passed for private-sector employers.

In response, Dayton's office asserted immunity from suit based upon the Speech and Debate Clause of the U.S. Constitution. Article I,§6 of the U.S. Constitution states, in part, that "[f]or any Speech or Debate in either House, [the Senators and Representatives] shall not be questioned in any other Place." (The main objective of this clause is to afford members of Congress the ability to engage in legislative matters and other constitutional duties without fear of private retaliatory action or questioning by constituents.) In this case, argued the Senator's office, since Hanson worked as an assistant to Senator Dayton in performing legislative duties, forcing Dayton's office to defend against allegations would necessarily "contravene" the SPEECH OR DEBATE CLAUSE. Any personnel decisions regarding Hanson were shielded by the Clause. Dayton's office moved to dismiss the suit based on lack of **subject matter jurisdiction**.

The U.S. District Court for the DISTRICT OF COLUMBIA denied the motion, and its decision was affirmed by the Court of Appeals for the District of Columbia Circuit. The court essentially held that the personal office of any member of Congress could be liable under the Accountability Act for misconduct, if the plaintiff could prove his or her case without inquiring into "legislative acts or the motivation for legislative acts."

On appeal to the U.S. Supreme Court, Justice Stevens, who authored the Court's opinion, first looked at §412 of the Congressional Accountability Act, which states that the U.S. Supreme Court shall have jurisdiction for direct review "from any **interlocutory** or final judgment, decree, or order of a court upon the constitutionality of any provision" of the Act. But, noted Justice Stevens, "Neither the order of the District Court denying appellant's motion to dismiss nor the judgment of the Court of Appeals affirming that order can fairly be characterized as a ruling 'upon the constitutionality' of any provision of the Act." Therefore, (treating appellant's jurisdictional statement as a petition for **writ** of certiorari), the Court found that it

Former Senator Mark Dayton, May 2006.
AP IMAGES

did not have jurisdiction under §412, denied review and dismissed the appeal.

Senator Dayton' office (the **appellant**) also had argued that the Court of Appeals' holding amounted to a ruling that the Act was constitutional "as applied;" in other words, because the Court of Appeals addressed the issue, this was tantamount to acknowledging that an "as applied" constitutional holding was rendered, thereby satisfying the jurisdictional requirement. However, the Supreme Court did not embrace that interpretation. Just because the Court of Appeals determined that jurisdiction attached, despite a claim of Speech or Debate Clause immunity, did not mean that it was ruling on an issue relating to the Act's *constitutionality*. At best, the Court of Appeals was merely ruling on the Act's *scope*.

Moreover, there were no special circumstances that would justify the exercise of discretionary review by the Supreme Court. The high court expressed no opinion on the merits of the case, nor did it decide whether the entire action became moot upon the expiration of Senator Dayton's term in office (January 3, 2007).

Several lawyers, legal scholars, and professors were disappointed that the Court did not take this opportunity to shed some light on the extent of the Speech and Debate Clause, through discretionary review. The Court obviously decided this was not an appropriate case to do so. The case was returned to the district court for consideration on the merits.

YOO, JOHN CHOON

Lawyer and scholar John Yoo came to national prominence as one of the primary thinkers behind the Department of Justice's so-called "torture memo," which laid out the Bush administration's legal reasoning for committing acts of torture in the war on terror. Yoo, a South Korean-born professor of law at University of California-Berkeley, worked as a member of the Office of Legal Counsel when the infamous memo was drafted.

Yoo earned degrees from Harvard and Yale prior to taking his position at Berkeley. He clerked for Judge Laurence Silberman of the U.S. Court of Appeals, D.C. Circuit, from 1992 to 1993, and then for U.S. Supreme Court Justice Clarence Thomas from 1994 to 1995. He is the author of numerous articles and two books, *The Powers of War and Peace: Foreign Affairs and the Constitution after 9/11* and *War by Other Means: An Insider's Account of the War on Terror*. The first book laid out Yoo's view of the presidency in a wartime environment, leading one legal scholar to write that "Yoo concludes that for all intents and purposes we have an elected king," referring to Yoo's assertion that the president possesses broad powers given by the Constitution to conduct a war as he sees fit, without intereference from Congress.

This view has proven, unsurprisingly, to foster highly divisive views based on political alliance. His second book sparked further support and anger, leading a *Washington Post* review to write that Yoo's view of the presidency was "extreme, reckless and dangerous. . . . That it has shaped the policies of our government is nothing short of irresponsible. Even U.S. Court of Appeals Judge Richard A. Posner, no slouch when it comes to advocating the aggressive use of government power to combat terrorism, has charged that Yoo's 'extravagant interpretation of presidential authority . . . confuses commanding the armed forces with exercising dictatorial control' of the sort exercised by 'a Hitler or a Stalin.'"

Yoo, for his part, has been outspoken in supporting his work. In a *Washington Post* article, he commented that "The worst thing you could do, now that people are critical of your views, is to run and hide. I agree with the work I did. I have an obligation to explain it. I'm one of the few people who is willing to defend decisions I made in government."

John Yoo.
AP IMAGES

JOHN CHOON YOO

1967: Born, South Korea

1993: Joined faculty at University of California at Berkeley

2001–03: Served in Office of Legal Counsel

2005: First book, The Powers of War and Peace, published

2006: Second book, War By Other Means, published

ABORTION

GONZALES V. CARHART

Branigan, William, and Barnes, Robert. "Court Backs Ban on Abortion Procedure." *The Washington Post.* April 18. 2007.

Savage, David. "Abortion Ruling Marks a First for High Court." *The Los Angeles Times.* April 18, 2007.

Stout, David. "Supreme Court Upholds Ban on Abortion Procedures." *The New York Times.* April 18, 2007.

SOUTH DAKOTA ANTI-ABORTION LAW DEFEATED

Bailey, Ronald. "Some Questions About South Dakota's Anti-Abortion Law." *San Francisco Gate*, 12 March 2006. Available at http://sfgate.com/cgi-bin/article.cgi?f=/chronicle/archive/2006/03/12/ING4THKSUR1.DTL

Davey, Monica. "South Dakota Bans Abortion, Setting Up Battle." *International Herald Tribune*, 7 March 2006. Available at: http://www.iht.com/bin/print_ipub.php?file=/articles/2006/03/07/america/web.0307abortion.php

"South Dakota Abortion Ban Rejected." *USA Today*, 8 November 2006. Available at http://www.usatoday.com/news/politicselections/vote2006/SD/2006-11-08-abortion-ban_x.htm

ADMINISTRATIVE LAW AND PRACTICE

PRESIDENT APPROVES EXECUTIVE ORDER ON FEDERAL ENVIRONMENTAL, ENERGY, AND TRANSPORTATION MANAGEMENT

"Executive Order 13423: Strengthening Federal Environmental, Energy, and Transportation Management," January 24, 2007. Available at http://www.whitehouse.gov/news/releases/2007/01/print/20070124-2.html

Office of the Federal Environmental Executive, "Fact Sheet: Executive Order 13423: Strengthening Federal Environmental, Energy, and Transportation Management." Available at http://www.ofee.gov/eo/EO_FactSheetOFEE%20_6.pdf.

ADOPTION

CUSTODY RETURNED TO BIOLOGICAL PARENTS AFTER SEVEN YEARS

Baird, Woody. "Chinese Parents Reunited With Daughter." Federal News Radio (WFED), 15 March 2007.

"Court Sends Foster Child Back to Chinese Parents." CBS News, 24 January 2007. Available at http://kutv.com/topstories/topstories_story_024221955.html

AGRICULTURAL LAW

JONES V. GALE

Coenen, Dan. *Constitutional Law: The Commerce Clause.* Foundation Press, 2003.

Drahozal, Christopher. *The Supremacy Clause: A Reference Guide to the United States Constitution.* Praeger, 2004.

Kallanbach, Joseph. *Federal Cooperation with the States under the Commerce Clause.* Greenwood Press, 1970.

TAINTED SPINACH LEADS TO SICKNESS AND DEATH

Associated Press, "Sou, rce of Tainted Spinach Finally Pinpointed," MSNBC.com, March 23, 2007. Available at http://www.msnbc.msn.com/id/17755937.

Hoffman, Barry and Jeff Walse, "E. Coli Cases Hit 114 in 21 States," *Health Day*, September 19, 2006.

ANTITERRORISM AND EFFECTIVE DEATH PENALTY ACT OF 1996

ROPER V. WEAVER

Altman, Alex. "Does Law Limiting Death Penalty Appeals Go Too Far?" *On the Docket*, Medill News Service, 26 March 2007.

Roper v. Weaver, No. 06-313, 550 U.S. ___ (2007). Available at www.supremecourtus.gov/opinions/06slipopinion.html

"Roper v. Weaver Dismissed" *Supreme Court Times*, 27 May 2007. Available at: http://www.lawmemo.sct/blog/roper_v_weaver/index.html

ANTITRUST

BELL ATLANTIC CORPORATION V. TWOMBLY

American Bar Association. *Market Power Handbook: Competition Law and Economic Foundation.* American Bar Association, 2006.

Gellhorn, Ernset. *Antitrust Law And Economics In A Nutshell, 5th Ed.* West Group, 2004.

Macavoy, Christopher. *A Primer on the Federal Price Discrimination Laws: A General Review of the Robinson-Patman Act for Business Managers.* American Bar Association, 1999.

CREDIT SUISSE FIRST BOSTON V. BILLING

"Credit Suisse First Boston v. Billing," *Point of Law,* 19 June 2007. Available at http://www.PointofLaw .com/PointofLaw.Forum/

"Credit Suisse Securities v. Billing." Duke University School of Law, available at: http://www.law.duke .edu/publiclaw/supremecourtonline/certgrants/2006/

The OYEZ Project, "Credit Suisse First Boston v. Billing." Available at: www.oyez.org/cases/2000-2009/2006/2006_5_1157

LEEGIN CREATIVE LEATHER PRODUCTS V. PSKS

Greenhouse, Linda. "U.S. Supreme Court Case Tests Minimum Price Rule." *International Herald Tribune,* 27 March 2007. Available at http://www.iht.com/ articles/2007/02/27/business/pricing.php

Leegin Creative Leather Products v. PSKS, No. 06-480, 551 U.S. ___ (2007). Available at www.supreme courtus.gov/opinions/06slipopinion.html

Nguyen, Giang. "Leegin Creative Leather Products v. PSKS." *On the Docket,* Medill News Service, 28 June 2007.

WEYERHAEUSER COMPANY V. ROSS-SIMMONS HARDWOOD LUMBER CO., INC.

American Bar Association. *Market Power Handbook: Competition Law and Economic Foundation.* Chicago, Ill.: 2006.

Gellhorn, Ernset. *Antitrust Law And Economics In A Nutshell.* Saint Paul, MN. West Group. Fifth Edition, 2004.

Kwoka, John and White, Lawrence. *The Antitrust Revolution. 4th Edition.* Oxford University Press, 2003.

APPELLATE REVIEW

OSBORN V. HALEY

Chemerinsky, Erwin. *Federal Jurisdiction.* New York: Aspen Publishers. 2003. Fourth Edition.

Currie, David. *Federal Jurisdiction in a Nutshell.* Saint Paul, MN: West Group. 1999.

Wright, Charles Alan. *Law of Federal Courts.* Saint Paul, MN: West Group. 2002. Sixth Edition.

ASYLUM

U.S. ASYLUM PROCESS NEEDS FURTHER REFORM, ACCORDING TO COMMISSION REPORT

Rooney, John Flynn, "U.S. Needs to Revamp Its Asylum System, Groups Say," *Chicago Daily Law Bulletin,* Feb. 12, 2007.

United States Commission on International Religious Freedom, *Expedited Removal Study Report Card: 2 Years Later* (2007). Available at http://www.uscirf .gov/reports/scorecard_FINAL.pdf.

BANKING

WATTERS V. WACHOVIA BANK, N.A.

Barnes, Robert. "High Court Sides with Banks on Mortgage Rules." *The Washington Post.* April 18, 2007.

Greenhouse, Linda. "Ruling Limits State Control of Big Banks." *The New York Times.* April 18, 2007.

Yost, Pete. "Court: Feds Lead in Bank Subsidiaries." *The Los Angeles Times.* April 17, 2007.

BANKRUPTCY

MARRAMA V. CITIZENS BANK OF MASSACHUSSETTS

Epstein, Richard. *Bankruptcy and Related Law in a Nutshell. 7th Ed.* West, 2005.

TRAVELERS CASUALTY & SURETY CO. OF AMERICA V. PACIFIC GAS & ELECTRIC CO.

Dreher, Nancy C., *Bankruptcy Service Current Awareness Alert,* No. 5, May 2007, at 8.

McFadden, Zena, "Travelers Casualty & Surety Co. of America v. Pacific Gas & Electric Co.," *Medill News Service,* October 7, 2006. <http://docket .medill.northwestern.edu/archives/003979.php>.

BRIBERY

REPRESENTATIVES ROBERT NEY, WILLIAM JEFFERSON FACE BRIBERY CHARGES

"Ex-Rep. Bob Ney Gets 30 Months in Jail." *CBS News,* 19 January 2007. Available at www.cbsnews .com/stories/2007/01/19/politics/printable2374241 .shtml

"Louisiana Congressman Pleads Not Guilty in Bribery Case." *The New York Times.* (June 9, 2007): A10(L).

Rulon, Malia. "Ney to Admit Guilt in Corruption Probe," *USA Today,* 15 September 2006. Available at www.usatoday.com/news/washington/2006-09-15-ney_x.htm

CAMPAIGN FINANCING

2008 RACE COULD BE THE FIRST BILLION DOLLAR CAMPAIGN

Kirkpatrick, David D., "Death Knell May Be Near for Public Election Funds," *New York Times,* January 23, 2007.

Kirkpatrick, David D., "Obama Proposes Candidates Limit General Election Spending," *New York Times*, February 7, 2007.

Solomon, John, "One Time Reformer Taps Big Donors," *Washington Post*, February 11, 2007.

CAPITAL PUNISHMENT

AYERS V. BELMONTES

Cohen, Stanley. *The Wrong Men: America's Epidemic of Wrongful Death Row Convictions*. New York: Carroll and Graf. 2003.

BREWER V. QUARTERMAN

Brewer v. Quarterman, No. 05-11287, 550 U.S.___ (2007). Available at www.supremecourtus.gov/opinions/06slipopinion.html

The OYEZ Project, "Brewer v. Quarterman," (No. 05-11287), available at: www.oyez.org/cases/2000-2009/2006/2006_5_11287/

ABDUL-KABIR V. QUARTERMAN

Abdul-Kabir v. Quarterman, No. 05-11284, 550 U.S.___ (2007). Available at www.supremecourtus.gov/opinions/06slipopinion.html

The OYEZ Project, "Abdul-Kabir v. Quarterman," (No. 05-11284), available at: www.oyez.org/cases/2000-2009/2006/2006_5_11284/

"Supreme Court Throws Out 3 Death Sentences." *CBS News*, 25 April 2007. Available at http://www.cbsnews.com/stories/2007/04/25/supremecourt/printable2726686.shtml

PANETTI V. QUARTERMAN

Hertz, Randy and James S. Liebman, *Federal Habeas Corpus Practice and Procedure*, Newark, N.J.: Matthew Bender, 2005.

Sorenson, Jon and Rocky LeAnn Pilgrim, *Lethal Injection: Capital Punishment in Texas During the Modern Era*, Austin, Tex.: University of Texas Press, 2006.

SMITH V. TEXAS (SMITH II)

The OYEZ Project, Smith v. Texas." (No. 05-11304), available at: www.oyez.org/cases/2000-2009/2006/2006_5_11304/

"Smith v. Texas." Duke University School of Law, available at: http://www.law.duke.edu/publiclaw/supremecourtonline/certgrants/2006/smivtex

CIVIL RIGHTS

ANDREWS V. CITY OF WEST BRANCH IOWA

Currie, David. *Federal Jurisdiction in a Nutshell*. West Group, 1999.

CLEAN AIR ACT

ENVIRONMENTAL DEFENSE V. DUKE ENERGY CORPORATION

Novello, David, and Martineau, Robert. *The Clean Air Act Handbook, 2nd ed.* American Bar Association, 2005.

MASSACHUSETTS V. ENVIRONMENTAL PROTECTION AGENCY (EPA)

"Court Rules 5–4 in Massachusetts versus EPA." Environmental Defense Web article, April 3, 2007. Available at http://www.environmentaldefense.org/article.cfm?contentID=5623

Massachusetts v. Environmental Protection Agency (EPA), No. 05-1120, 549 U.S.___ (2007), Available at www.supremecourtus.gov/opinions/06slipopinion.html

"Massachusetts v. EPA." National Environmental Trust (NET) Web article, undated. Available at http://www.net.org/proactive/newsroom/release.vtml?id=29154

COMMERCE CLAUSE

UNITED HAULERS ASS'N V. ONEIDA-HERKIMER SOLID WASTE MANAGEMENT AUTHORITY

McGowan, Elizabeth, "Results of Supreme Court's United Haulers Ruling Begin to Sink In," *Waste News*, May 14, 2007, at 1.

Ufner, Julie, "Counties Victorious in Supreme Court Flow Control Case," National Association of Counties, May 1, 2007. http://www.naco.org/

CONSTITUTIONAL LAW

JUSTICE SCALIA DEBATES PRESIDENT OF AMERICAN CIVIL LIBERTIES UNION

Biskupic, Joan, "Conservative Justice Defends Views at Annual ACLU Meeting," *New York Times*, February 7, 2007.

Yen, Hope, "Scalia Defends Positions in TV Debate," *ABCNews*, October 15, 2006.

CONSUMER CREDIT

SAFECO INSURANCE CO. OF AMERICA V. BURR

"Higher Rates 'Adverse Actions' Under Credit Law, High Court Rules," *Andrews Insurance Coverage Litigation Reporter*, June 15, 2007.

Rodriguez, Anthony, Carolyn L. Carter, Willard P. Ogburn *Fair Credit Reporting*, Boston, Mass.: National Consumer Law Center, 2002.

COPYRIGHT

VIDEO SHARING SITES FACE MAJOR COPYRIGHT ISSUES

Diaz, Sam, "YouTube Forced to Restrategize," *Miami Herald*, March 24, 2007.

Lee, Ellen, "Firms Working to Halt Pirates," *San Francisco Chronicle*, March 19, 2007.

COURT MARTIAL

COURT MARTIAL OF MILITARY OFFICER IN ABU GHRAIB PRISON SCANDAL

Benjamin, Mark. "First Officer is Charged in Abu Ghraib Scandal." 29 April 2006. Available at http://www.salon.com/news/feature/2006/04/29/jordan/print.html

Joshi, Jitendra. "Sole US Officer Charged Over Abu Ghraib to Face Trial." *Agence France Presse*, 16 May 2007. As appears at http://sg.news.yahoo.com/070515/1/48kom.html

"More Charges in Abu Ghraib Scandal." *CBS News*, 26 April 2006. Available at http://www.cbsnews.com/stories/2006/04/28/iraq/printable1560925.shtml

Sung, Michael. "US Army Officer to be Court-Martialed for Role in Abu Ghraib Abuses." *The Jurist*, 27 January 2007. University of Pittsburgh School of Law publication available at http://jurist.law.pitt.edu/paperchase/2007/01/us-army-officer-to-be-court-martialed.php

Tyson, Ann Scott. "Army Officer Charged in Abu Ghraib Prison Abuse." *The Seattle Times*, 29 April 2006.

CRIMINAL LAW

WHORTON V. BOCKTING

Freedman, Eric. *Habeas Corpus: Rethinking the Great Writ of Liberty*. New York: New York Univ. Press. 2003.

LAW ENFORCEMENT USING YOUTUBE TO CATCH CRIMINALS

Austen, Ian, "Fighting Crime Using Videos on YouTube," *New York Times*, December 18, 2006.

Tucker, Eric, "Police Turn to YouTube to Catch Suspects," *USA Today*, March 4, 2007.

CUOMO, ANDREW

"Andrew Cuomo." *Biography Resource Center Online*. Gale, 2003. Reproduced in Biography Resource Center. Farmington Hills, Mich.: Thomson Gale. 2007. http://galenet.galegroup.com/servlet/BioRC

DAMAGES

CHRISTOPHER V. FLORIDA

Vieira, Norman. *Constitutional Civil Rights in a Nutshell*. West, 1998.

DECLARATORY JUDGMENT

MEDIMMUNE, INC. V. GENENTECH, INC.

Borchard, Edwin. *Declaratory Judgments*. William S. Hein and Co., 2000.

Miller, Arthur R., and Davis, Michael H. *Intellectual Property: Patents, Trademarks, and Copyright, 3rd Edition*. West Group, 2000.

Poltorak, Alexander, and Lerner, Paul. *Essentials of Intellectual Property*. Wiley, 2002.

DEPARTMENT OF JUSTICE

FIRING OF NINE U.S. ATTORNEYS

Eggen, Dan. "GOP Lawmaker Told of Plan to Fire U.S. Attorney." *The Washington Post*, 28 April 2007.

Eggen, Dan. "Justice Dept.'s No. 2 to Counter Claims of Untruths Over Firings." *The Washington Post*, 21 June 2007, p. A04.

Gallagher, Mike. "Domenici Sought Iglesias Ouster." *The Albuquerque (NM) Journal*, 15 April 2007.

Goldstein, Amy. "Fired Prosecutor Says Gonzales Pushed Death Penalty." *The Washington Post*, 28 June 2007, p. A07.

Greenburg, Jan Crawford. "E-Mails Show Rove's Role in U.S. Attorney Firings." ABC News, 15 March 2007. Available at http://abcnews.go.com/print?id=2954988

Schmitt, Richard B. "Bush's Executive Privilege Claim Leaves Congress With Tough Options." *Los Angeles Times*, 9 July 2007.

"U.S. Attorney Firings Investigation." *The Washington Post*, 9 July 2007. Available at http://www.washingtonpost.com

DISCRIMINATION

JURY VERDICT ENHANCED TO $334 MILLION IN CORPORATE DISCRIMINATION CASE

"Amerigroup Corp-AGP Quarterly Report 10-Q) Item 1. Legal Proceedings." *Edgar Reports*, 4 November 2005. Available at http://sec.edgar-online.com/2005/11/04/0000950133-05-004984/Section9.asp

"Amerigroup Fined $48M for Discrimination." *Forbes*, 31 October 2006.

"Health Plan Lawsuit Watch." Health Care Practice Group of Crowell & Moring LLP Legal Professionals' website at http://www.aishealth.com/ManagedCare/HMOLawsuitWatch/US_ex_rel_Cleveland_Tyson_v_Amerigroup_Illinois.html

"Jury Returns $48 Million Verdict Against Amerigroup in Discrimination Suit." *The Jurist*, 31 October 2006.

"Madigan and Fitzgerald Praise $144 Million Fraud Verdict Against Medicaid HMO." Press Release of Illinois Attorney General, 31 October 2006. Available at http://www.illinoisattorneygeneral.gov/pressroom/2006_10/2006/31c.html

DRUGS AND NARCOTICS

RAID OF DRUG RING COULD EXPOSE ATHLETES' USE OF STEROID USE

Lyons, Brendan J., "Judge Offers Steroid Buyers a Shot at Privacy," *Albany Times-Union*, April 6, 2007.

"NY Investigation Leads to Raid of Orlando Pharmacy," ESPN.com, March 1, 2007. Available at http://myespn.go.com/conversation/story?id=2781674&section=gen

VIOXX PRODUCER CONTINUES TO FACE LITIGATION

Associated Press, "Fast Facts: Timeline of Vioxx Litigation," *FOXNews.com*, July 13, 2006.

Jadhav, Adam, "Vioxx Maker Wins First Case in Madison County, but Others Await," *St. Louis Post Dispatch*, April 9, 2007.

DUE PROCESS

BROWN V. CITY OF MICHIGAN CITY, INDIANA

Vieira, Norman. *Constitutional Civil Rights in a Nutshell.* West Group, 1998.

EDUCATION LAW

WINKELMAN V. PARMA CITY SCHOOL DISTRICT

Stout, David. "Supreme Court Rules on Education Lawsuits." *The New York Times.* May 21, 2007.

ZUNI PUBLIC SCHOOL DISTRICT 89 V. DEPT. OF EDUCATION

Ruffins, Ebonne and Jennifer Koons. "Zuni Public School District No. 89, et al. v. Department of Education, et al." *On the Docket*, Medill School of Journalism, Northwestern University, 17 April 2007.

Zuni Public School District No. 89 v. Department of Education, No. 05-1508 (2007). Available at www.supremecourtus.gov/opinions/06slipopinion.html

ELECTION CAMPAIGN FINANCING

WISCONSIN RIGHT TO LIFE V. FEDERAL ELECTION COMMISSION

Kriva, Christopher. "Wisconsin Right to Life v. FEC." *On the Docket*, Medill News Service, 23 January 2006.

ELEVENTH AMENDMENT

THOMAS V. ST. LOUIS BOARD OF POLICE COMMISSIONERS

Wright, Charles Alan. *Law of Federal Courts, 6th Ed.* West Group, 2002.

EMINENT DOMAIN

MENDOTA GOLF V. CITY OF MENDOTA HEIGHTS

"Another Big Win for Comprehensive Plans." *Community Rights Report*, Monthly Newsletter, January 2006. Available at http://www.communityrights.org/PDFs/Newsletters/Jan2006.pdf

"Mendota Heights Approves Golf Course Referendum." *Mendota Heights News*, 26 April 2006. Available at http://www.mendota-heights.com

Ripple, Adam. "Environmental Case Law Summaries." *ENR Law News*, Winter 2006.

"Zone and Land Use: Comprehensive Plan Amendment," *State Digest*,

KELO DECISION CONTINUES TO CAUSE CONTROVERSY

Boulard, Garry, "Eminent Domain—For the Greater Good?," *NCSL State Legislatures Magazine*, January 2006.

Garrett, Thomas A. and Paul Rothstein, "The Taking of Prosperity? *Kelo v. New London* and the Economics of Eminent Domain," *Regional Economist*, January 1, 2007.

Somin, Ilya, "Post- *Kelo* America," *Reason Magazine*, April 20, 2007.

EMPLOYMENT LAW

LEDBETTER V. GOODYEAR TIRE & RUBBER COMPANY, INC.

Savage, David. "High Court Narrows Rules for Claims of Unfair Pay." *The Los Angeles Times.* May 30, 2007.

BCI COCA-COLA BOTTLING CO. OF L.A. V. EEOC

Glover, Katherine, "BCI Coca-Cola Bottling Co. of Los Angeles v. EEOC," *Medill News Service*, January 9, 2007. <http://docket.medill.northwestern.edu/archives/004244.php>.

Yost, Pete, "Company Asks Top Court to Dismiss Appeal," Associated Press Wire Reports, April 11, 2007.

ENVIRONMENTAL LAW

UNITED STATES V. ATLANTIC RESEARCH CORPORATION

Best, Michael. "Land and Resources Alert: United States v. Atlantic Research Corp." *Outside the Box*, June 2007.

The OYEZ Project, "United States v. Atlantic Research Corp., 551 U.S. ___ (No. 06-562)", available at: www.oyez.org/cases/2000-2009/2006/2006_06_562/

United States v. Atlantic Research Corporation, No. 06-562, 551 U.S. ___ (2007) Available at www.supremecourtus.gov/opinions/06slipopinion.html

EPA ISSUES NEW RULES TO CUT TOXIC EMISSIONS

Control of Hazardous Air Pollutants from Mobile Sources, (72 FR 8428), and appurtenant regulatory documentation, 26 February 2007, available at: http://www.epa.gov/otaq/toxics.htm

Daly, Matthew. "EPA Toughens Toxic Emissions Standards." *Washington Post*, 9 February 2007.

"EPA Finalizes Rule to Cut Toxic Emissions." *The Jurist*, University of Pittsburgh School of Law, 9 February 2007.

Pew, James. "EPA Greenlights Troublesome Benzene Program, Creating Dangerous Hot Spots." *Environmental Law Update*, Earthjustice Law Firm, 9 February 2007. www.earthjustice.com

U.S. EPA, "What is EPA Doing About Mobile Source Air Toxics?" *Overview: Pollutants and Programs*, undated. Available at www.epa.gov/otag/toxics.html #mobile

NATIONAL ASSOCIATION OF HOME BUILDERS V. DEFENDERS OF WILDLIFE

Glicksman, Robert L. *Environmental Protection: Law and Policy*, Austin, Tex.: Aspen Publishers, 2007.

Salzman, James and Barton H. Thompson, Jr. *Environmental Law and Policy* St. Paul, Minn.: Foundation Press 2007.

ERISA

BECK V. PACE INTERNATIONAL UNION

Whipp, Emily. "Beck, Jeffrey & Crown Paper Co. v. PACE International Union, et al ." *On the Docket*, Medill School of Journalism, Northwestern University, 17 January 2007.

RETAIL INDUSTRY LEADERS ASSOCIATION V. FIELDER

Ziesenheim, Ken. *Understanding ERISA: A Compact Guide to the Landmark Act*. Marketplace Books, 2002.

ESTABLISHMENT CLAUSE

HEIN V. FREEDOM FROM RELIGION FOUNDATION

Hein v. Freedom From Religion Foundation, No. 06-157, 551 U.S. __ (2007), Available at www .supremecourtus.gov/opinions/06slipopinion.html

"Hein v. Freedom From Religion Foundation." Duke University School of Law, available at: http://www .law.duke.edu/publiclaw/supremecourtonline/cert grants/2006/heivfre

"Hein v. Freedom From Religion Foundation." Cornell University School of Law, 26 February 2007. Available at http://www.law.cornell.edu.supct.cert/ 05-1631.html

Mauro, Tony. "'Faith-based' Case Tests Establishment-Clause Lawsuit Standing." First Amendment Center press release, 6 December 2006. Available at http://www.firstamendmentcenter .org/analysis.aspx?id = 17851

The OYEZ Project, "Hein v. Freedom From Religion Foundation," available at: www.oyez.org/cases/ 2000-2009/2006/2006_06_157/

EXTRADITION

UNITED STATES AND UNITED KINGDOM RATIFY NEW EXTRADITION TREATY

Branick, Margaret I., "Extradition and the Conflict in Northern Ireland: The Past, the Present, and the Future of an Intractable Problem," *Hastings International and Comparative Law Review*, Spring 2002, at 169.

Doyle, Charles, *Extradition Between the United States and Great Britain: The 2003 Treaty*. Congressional Research Service, October 10, 2006.

FALSE CLAIMS ACT

ROCKWELL INTERNATIONAL, CORP. V. UNITED STATES

"Flats Whistleblower Skunked." *The Denver Post*. March 27, 2007.

FEDERAL COMMUNICATIONS COMMISSION

GLOBAL CROSSING TELECOMMUNICATIONS, INC. V. METROPHONES TELECOMMUNICATIONS, INC.

Zarkin, Kimberly and Zarkin, Michael. *The Federal Communications Commission*. Greenwood Press, 2006.

FEDERAL TORT CLAIMS ACT

BARRETT V. UNITED STATES

Wright, Charles Alan. *Law of Federal Courts. 6th ed.* West Group, 2002.

FIRST AMENDMENT

DAVENPORT V. WASHINGTON EDUCATION ASSOCIATION

"What a Union Is Due," *Chicago Tribune*, June 18, 2007.

Savage, David S., "Justices Curb Unions' Use of Fees for Politics," *Los Angeles Times*, June 15, 2007.

LEONARD V. ROBINSON

Sunstein, Cass. *Democracy and the Problem of Free Speech*. Free Press, 1995.

MORSE V. FREDERICK

Barnes, Robert. "Justices to Hear Landmark Free-Speech Case." *Washington Post*, 13 March 2007.

"Morse v. Frederick." Duke University School of Law, available at: http://www.law.duke.edu/publiclaw/ supremecourtonline/certgrants/2006/morvfre

Morse v. Frederick, No. 06-278, 551 U.S. __ (2007). Available at www.supremecourtus.gov/opinions/ 06slipopinion.html

The OYEZ Project, "Morse v. Frederick," available at: www.oyez.org/cases/2000-2009/2006/2006_06_278

TENNESSEE SECONDARY SCHOOL ATHLETIC ASSN. V. BRENTWOOD

First Amendment Center, "Tennessee Secondary School Association v. Brentwood." First Amendment Center Library, 21 June 2007. Available at http://www.firstamendmentcenter.org/case.aspx?case = Tennessee_Secondary_School_Athletic_ Association_v_Brentwood_Academy

The OYEZ Project, "Tennessee Secondary School Association v. Brentwood," available at: www.oyez .org/cases/2000-2009/2006/2006_06_427

Weinstein, Jonathan. "Tennessee Secondary School Association v. Brentwood Academy." *On the Docket*, Medill News Service, 21 June 2007.

FITZGERALD, PATRICK

"Patrick Fitzgerald." *Newsmakers*, Issue 4. Thomson Gale, 2006. Reproduced in Biography Resource Center. Farmington Hills, Mich.: Thomson Gale. 2007. http://galenet.galegroup.com/servlet/BioRC

FOOD AND DRUG ADMINISTRATION

FDA APPROVES SILICONE BREAST IMPLANTS AFTER 14-YEAR BAN

Brown, David and Christopher Lee, "FDA Ends Silicone-Implant Ban," *Seattle Times*, November 18, 2006, at A4.

Hendrick, Bill, "Silicone Implants Back, for Better or Worse," *Atlanta Journal and Constitution*, November 24, 2006, at F1

Perkes, Courtney, "Women Expected to Select Silicone Instead of Saline," *Chicago Tribune*, December 26, 2006, at 5.

FORUM NON CONVENIENS

SINOCHEM INTERNATIONAL V. MALAYSIA INTERNATIONAL SHIPPING

Anand, Moushumi, "Sinochem International Co., Ltd. v. Malaysia International Shipping Corp." *On the Docket*, Medill School of Journalism, 20 February 2007.

The OYEZ Project, "Sinochem International Co. v. Malaysia International Shipping," No. 06-102, available at: www.oyez.org/cases/2000-2009/2006/2006/

Sinochem International Co. v. Malaysia International Shipping, No. 06-102, 549 U.S. ___ (2007), Available at www.supremecourtus.gov/opinions/06slipopinion.html

"Sinochem International Co. v. Malaysia International Shipping." Available at http://www.law.duke.edu/publiclaw/supremecourtonline/certgrants/2006/sinvmal

FOURTH AMENDMENT

UNLAWFUL SHOOTING OF PET DOG CONSTITUTES FOURTH AMENDMENT SEIZURE

Andrews v. City of West Branch (IA), No. 05-1188 (2006). Available at http://www.findlaw.com.

Fleck, Terry. "Case: Andrews v. City of West Branch, Iowa." *Patrol Canine Legal Update and Opinions.* Available at http://www.law.cornell.edu.supct.cert/05-1631.html

SANCHEZ V. COUNTY OF SAN DIEGO

Long, Carolyn. *Mapp V. Ohio: Guarding Against Unreasonable Searches And Seizures.* Lawrence, KS: University Press of Kansas. 2006.

FRAUD

LEGAL WOES OF FORMER CEO OF WESTAR ENERGY CONTINUE

"Former Westar Execs Guilty in Federal Fraud Trial," *USA Today*, September 12, 2005.

Twiddy, David, "Judge Cuts Wittig's Sentence," *Lawrence Journal-World.* February 6, 2007.

FREEDOM OF INFORMATION ACT

DAVIS V. DEPARTMENT OF JUSTICE

Henry, Christopher. *Freedom of Information Act.* Novinka Press, 2003.

FREEDOM OF THE PRESS

THE NEW YORK TIMES COMPANY V. GONAZALES

Schmidt, Susan. "Reporters' Files Subpoened." *Washington Post.* September 10, 2004.

FREEDOM OF SPEECH

VIDEO GAME INDUSTRY DEFEATS BANS ON SALES OF VIDEO GAMES

Press Release, "Video Game Industry Wins Over Half a Million Dollars in Attorney's Fees from State of Illinois," Entertainment Software Association, August 10, 2006.

Price, Marie, "Federal Judge Blocks Enforcement of Violent Video Game Law," *Journal Record*, October 13, 2006.

GAY AND LESBIAN RIGHTS

NEW JERSEY PASSES LAW OFFERING CIVIL UNIONS

Maguire, Ken. Next Battle Ready for Mass. Gay Marriage." *The Guardian Unlimited (UK)*, 15 June 2007.(

"New Jersey Begins Offering Civil Unions." CBS News, 19 February 2007. Available at http://www CBSNews.com

"New Jersey Rules Neither For, Against Gay Marriage." NBC News, 11 January 2007. Available at http://www.MSNBC.com.

HABEAS CORPUS

BOWLES V. RUSSELL

"Bowles v. Russell." Duke University School of Law, available at: http://www.law.duke.edu/publiclaw/supremecourtonline/certgrants/2006/bowvrus

"Bowles v. Russell." Law Professor Blogs Network, available at http://lawprofessors.typepad.com/civpro/2007/06/bowles_v_russel.html

The OYEZ Project, "Bowles v. Russell," available at: www.oyez.org/cases/2000-2009/2006/2006_5_11284/

BURTON V. STEWART

Freedman, Eric. *Habeas Corpus: Rethinking the Great Writ of Liberty.* New York: New York Univ. Press. 2003.

LAWRENCE V. FLORIDA

Freedman, Eric. *Habeas Corpus: Rethinking the Great Writ of Liberty.* New York: New York Univ. Press. 2003.

HARMLESS ERROR

FRY V. PLILER

Dye, Jessica. "Fry, John Francis c. Pliler, Cheryl (Warden)." *On the Docket*, Medill News Service, March 2007.

Fry v. Pliler, No. 06-5247, 551 U.S. ___ (2007). Available at www.supremecourtus.gov/opinions/06slipopinion.html

The OYEZ Project, "Fry v. Pliler," available at: www.oyez.org/cases/2000-2009/2006/2006_06_5247/

IMMIGRATION LAW

BUSH ADMINISTRATION'S IMMIGRATION REFORM FAILS

Babington, Charles. "Senate Rejects Bush Immigration Plan." *Washington Post*, 29 June 2007.

"Immigration Bill Dies in Senate." CBS News,, 28 June 2007.

Martinez, Mai. "Senate Blocks Bush's Immigration Plan." CBS News Interactive, 28 June 2007.

Pear, Robert and David Stout. "Doubts Emerge About Passage of Immigration Bill." *New York Times*, 27 June 2007.

"President Bush's Plan for Comprehensive Immigration Reform." Office of the White House, 2007 State of the Union Initiatives, available at http://www.whitehouse.gov/stateoftheunion/2007/initiatives/print/immigration.html

GONZALES V. DUENAS-ALVAREZ

Weissbrodt, David and Danielson, Laura. *Immigration Law and Procedure in a Nutshell, 5th Edition.* West Group, 2005.

LOPEZ V. GONZALES

"Supreme Court Rules in Favor of Immigrant on Deportation Issue." *FoxNews.com* http://www.foxnews.com/story/0,2933,234642,00.html December 5, 2006.

IMMUNITY

ROGERS V. CITY OF KENNEWICK

Currie, David. *Federal Jurisdiction in a Nutshell.* West Group, 1999.

SCOTT V. HARRIS

Crane, Catherine. "Scott, Timothy v. Harris, Victor." *On the Docket*, Medill School of Journalism, Northwestern University, 30 April 2007.

Scott v. Harris, No. 05-1631, 550 U.S. ___ (2007). Available at http://www.supremecourtus.gov/opinions/06slipopinion.html

"Scott v. Harris (05-1631)." Cornell University School of Law, 26 February 2007. Available at http://www.law.cornell.edu.supct.cert/05-1631.html

INDICTMENT

UNITED STATES V. RESENDIZ-PONCE

Sprack, John. *A Practical Approach to Criminal Procedure, 11th Edition.* Oxford University Press, 2006.

INSURANCE

$2.5 MILLION IN PUNITIVE DAMAGES AGAINST STATE FARM

"Class-Action Status is Denied to Katrina Suits in Mississippi." *New York Times*, 23 March 2007.

"Judge Reduces State Farm's Punitive Damages in Miss. Katrina Case." *Insurance Journal*, 31 January 2007.

"Mississippi Attorney General Sues State Farm Over Katrina Claims." *New York Times*, 12 June 2007.

Pantesco, Joshua. "Mississippi Jury Awards $2.5 Million Katrina Punitive Damages Against State Farm." *The Jurist*, University of Pittsburgh School of Law, 11 January 2007.

"State Farm Liable in Katrina Case." 11 January 2007. Available at http://www.MSNBC.com

"State Farm Settles Katrina Lawsuit In Mississippi on Day of Trial." *Insurance Journal*, 7 June 2007.

"State Farm Skirts Judge in New Hurricane Plan." *New York Times*, 20 March 2007.

JUDGE

ABA HOUSE OF DELEGATES APPROVES NEW MODEL CODE OF JUDICIAL CONDUCT

"American Bar Association Adopts New Policies," *Daily Record*, February 15, 2007.

Toutant, Charles, "Appearance-of-Impropriety Standards for Judges Holds Ground in ABA," *New Jersey Law Journal*, February 19, 2007, at 11.

LOPEZ TORRES V. NEW YORK STATE BOARD OF ELECTIONS

Streb, Matthew. *Running for Judge: The Rising Political, Financial, and Legal Stakes of Judicial Elections.* New York University Press, 2007.

JUSTICE KENNEDY URGES CONGRESS TO RAISE JUDICIAL SALARIES

Mauro, Tony, "Kennedy Makes Plea for Higher Judicial Salaries and No Cameras at the Supreme Court," *Legal Times*, February 14, 2007.

Sherman, Mark, "Justice Kennedy Says Morale Low Over Pay," *Washington Post*, February 14, 2007.

SOUTH DAKOTA VOTERS DEFEAT JUDICIAL ACCOUNTABILITY PROPOSAL

Garrison, Sica, "Activist Wants to See Judges Judged," *Los Angeles Times*, April 24, 2006, at 1.

Pordum, Matt, "J.A.I.L. Group Goes After Judges," *Las Vegas Sun*, February 24, 2006, at A3.

JURISDICTION

POWEREX CORP. V. RELIANT ENERGY SERVICES, INC.

Wright, Charles Alan. *Law of Federal Courts*. Saint Paul, MN: West Group. 2002. Sixth Edition.

JURY

UTTECHT V. BROWN

The OYEZ Project, "Uttecht v. Brown," (No. 06-413), available at: www.oyez.org/cases/2000-2009/2006/2006_6_413

Russell, Ross. "Uttecht v. Brown - Jury Selection." *Supreme Court Times*, 6 June 2007. Available at http://www.cnn.com.

Uttecht v. Brown, No. 06-413, 551 U.S. ___ (2007). Available at www.supremecourtus.gov/opinions/06slipopinion.html

Wiggins and Dana, LLP. "Uttrecht (sic) v. Brown." *Supreme Court Updates*, 8 June 2007. Available at http://www.wiggin.com/pubs/scupdate_template.asp?ID=173322672007&groupid=5

Hirsh, Michael, and Mark Hosenball. "The Next Top Spy." *Newsweek.com* <http://www.msnbc.msn.com/id/16475979/site/newsweek/page/0/> January 4, 2007.

McConnell, Michael. "Overhauling Intelligence." *Foreign Affairs*. <http://www.foreignaffairs.org/20070701faessay86404-p0/mike-mcconnell/overhauling-intelligence.html> July/August 2007.

"Mike McConnell." *Marquis Who's Who*. Marquis Who's Who, 2007. Reproduced in Biography Resource Center. Farmington Hills, Mich.: Thomson Gale. 2007. <http://galenet.galegroup.com/servlet/BioRC>

MILITARY LAW

U.S. SOLDIERS GUILTY OF MURDER AND RAPE IN IRAQ

"Five Soldiers Charged In Iraq Rape-Murder Case," CNN News, 9 July 2006. Available at http://www.cnn.com/2006/LAW/07/09/soldiers.charged/index.html

"Four Soldiers Charged With Rape and Murder." CNN News, 18 October 2006. Available at http://www.cnn.com/2006/LAW/10/18/soldiers.court

"Investigator: U.S. Soldier Poured Kerosene on Raped, Slain Iraqi." CNN News, 7 August 2006. Available at http://www.cnn.com/2006/WORLD/meast/08/07/iraq.familyslain/index.html

Jervis, Rick and Andrea Stone. "Four More Soldiers Accused of Rape, Murder in Iraq." *USA Today*, 9 July 2006.

"Judge Accepts Second Soldier's Guilty Plea to Raping, Killing Iraqi Teen Girl." 21 February 2007. Available at http://www.FOXnews.com

"Soldier Who Pleaded Guilty of Rape Sentenced to 90 Years." FOX News Country Watch: Iraq, 17 November 2006. Available at http://www.FOXnews.com

THE MILITARY COMMISSIONS ACT OF 2006

Addicott, Jeffrey. "The Military Commissions Act: Congress Commits to the War on Terror." *The Jurist Forum*, University of Pittsburgh School of Law, 9 October 2006.

"Appeals Court Hears Challenge to Guantanamo 'Enemy Combatant' Status." *The Jurist*, University of Pittsburgh School of Law, 15 May 2007. http://jurist.law.pitt.edu/paperchase/2007/05/appeals-court-hears-challenge-to.php

"Supreme Court Declines to Hear Guantanamo Detainee Habeas Appeals." *The Jurist*, University of Pittsburgh School of Law, 2 April 2007. http://jurist.law.pitt.edu/paperchase/2007/04/supreme-court-declines-to-hear.php

Notar, Susan and Carson Clements. "United States: Military Commissions Act of 2006." *International Law in Brief*, 29 September 2006.

MONOPOLY

FTC RULES THAT RAMBUS ILLEGALLY ACQUIRED MONOPOLY POWER

Hadjis, Alexander J. and Matthew J. Vlissides, "FTC Targets Abuse of Standard Setting Bodies," *National Law Journal*, October 12, 2006, at S2.

Poletti, Theresa, "FTC Ruling Restricts Rambus Royalties," *San Jose Mercury News*, February 6, 2007, at 1.

MURDER

WISCONSIN MAN EXONERATED THROUGH DNA EVIDENCE SUBSEQUENTLY CONVICTED OF MURDER

Antlfinger, Carrie, "Avery First To Be Freed, Convicted of Murder," *Wisconsin State Journal*, March 20, 2007, at B1.

Kertscher, Tom, "Steven Avery Trial Begins," *Milwaukee Journal Sentinel*, February 13, 2007, at 1.

VIRGINIA TECH MASSACRE

Craig, Tim. "Virginia Tech Families Fear Investigators Have Conflicts." *The Washington Post*, 23 June 2007, p.B1.

Hauser, Christine and Anahad O'Connor. "Virginia Tech Shooting Leaves 33 Dead." *New York Times*, 16 April 2007.

Urbina, Ian. "Lawyer Who Directed September 11 Compensation to Oversee Virginia Tech Program." *New York Times*, 5 July 2007

"Virginia Tech Shootings-News." *New York Times*, 10 July 2007.

"Virginia Tech Shooting Victims' Family Members Outraged Over No Representation on Panel Studying Killings." 12 June 2007. Available through Fox News at http://www.FOXNews.com

NATIVE AMERICAN RIGHTS

SAN MANUEL INDIAN BINGO AND CASINO V. NATIONAL LABOR RELATIONS BOARD

Wilkins, David. *American Indian Sovereignty and the U.S. Supreme Court.* Austin, TX: University of Texas Press. 1997.

NEGLIGENCE

NORFOLK SOUTHERN RAILWAY COMPANY V. SORRELL

Savage, Ian. *The Economics of Railroad Safety.* Springer, 2006.

PASSPORTS

NEW U.S. PASSPORT REQUIREMENTS

U.S. Department of State. Travel Accommodation Announced June 8, 2007." Available at: http://travel.state.gov/travel/cbpmc_2223.html

"U.S. Puts New Passport Requirements On Hold." CBS News, 15 June 2007. Available at http://www.cbsnews.com/stories/2007/06/15/travel/printable2935772.sghtml

PATENTS

KSR INTERNATIONAL CO. V. TELEFLEX INC.

Puzzanghera, James. "Supreme Court Reins in Patent Power." *Seattle Times.* May 1, 2007.

MICROSOFT CORP. V. AT&T CORP.

"High Court Rules on Patent Protections Here and Abroad," *Congress Daily*, April 30, 2007.

Romano, Benjamin J., "Patent Case Hits Microsoft with $1.5 Billion Penalty," *Seattle Times*, February 22, 2007.

PELOSI, NANCY

"Nancy Pelosi." *Encyclopedia of World Biography Supplement*, Vol. 25. Thomson Gale, 2005. Reproduced in Biography Resource Center. Farmington Hills, Mich.: Thomson Gale. 2007. http://galenet.galegroup.com/servlet/BioRC

PERJURY

LIBBY CONVICTED FOR LYING ABOUT HIS ROLE IN CIA LEAK

"Juror: Libby is Guilty, but He was Fall Guy," CNN.com, March 6, 2007.

Leonnig, Carol D. and Amy Goldstein, "Libby Found Guilty in CIA Leak Case," *Washington Post*, March 7, 2007, at A1.

PREVAILING PARTY

SOLE V. WYNER

"Sole v. Wyner (No. 06-531)." Cornell University School of Law, 17 April 2007. Available at http://www.law.cornell.edu.supct.cert/05-1631.html

"Sole v. Wyner." Duke University School of Law, 26 February 2007. Available at http://www.law.duke.edu/publiclaw/supremecourtonline/cert/Grants/2006/schvlan.html

PRISONERS' RIGHTS

JONES V. BOCK

Vieira, Norman. *Constitutional Civil Rights in a Nutshell.* Saint Paul, MN.: West Group. 1998.

PRISONS

CALIFORNIA JUDGE BLOCKS EFFORT TO TRANSFER PRISONERS OUT OF THE STATE

Furillo, Andy, "Democrats Offer Own Prison Plan," *Sacramento Bee*, August 30, 2006.

Mendel, Ed, "Guard Pact Could Bedevil Prison-Relief Negotiations," *San Diego Union-Tribune*, April 16, 2007.

U.S. PRISON POPULATION CONTINUES TO RISE

Harrison, Paige M. and Allen J. Beck, "Prisoners in 2005," *Bureau of Justice Statistics Bulletin*, November 2006.

"Rising Prison Problems Begin to Trickle Into Society" *USA Today*, June 11, 2006.

PRIVACY

ANDERSON V. BLAKE

TEXAS LEGISLATURE BLOCKS EFFORT TO REQUIRE VACCINES FOR CERVICAL CANCER

Elliott, Janet, "Perry's Vaccination Order Still Stoking Fires," *Houston Chronicle*, February 8, 2007.

Hoppe, Christy, "Bell Backs Perry on Vaccine," *Dallas Morning News*, February 8, 2007.

CONGRESS PASSES THE TELEPHONE RECORDS AND PRIVACY PROTECTION ACT OF 2006

Jones, K.C., "Senate Passage of Phone Records Privacy Bill Likely," *Information Week*, December 8, 2006, http://www.informationweek.com/news/showArticle.jhtml?articleID=196602803

Law Enforcement and Phone Privacy Protection Act of 2006, H.R. Rpt. No. 109-395 (Committee on the Judiciary), March 16, 2006.

PROBATE LAW

DEATH OF ANNA NICOLE SMITH LEADS TO NUMEROUS LEGAL DISPUTES

Deutsch, Linda, "Anna Nicole Smith Leaves Behind Legal Tangle," Law.com, February 12, 2007.

Puente, Maria, "In the Smith Case, the Mystery Will Linger and the Weirdness Will Continue," *USA Today*, February 10, 2007.

PUBLIC UTILITIES

CALIFORNIA APPROVES MEASURES DESIGNED TO REDUCE GREENHOUSE GASES

Barringer, Felicity, "California, Taking Big Gamble, Tries to Curb Greenhouse Gases," *N.Y. Times*, September 15, 2006.

Press Release, "PUC Sets GHG Emissions Performance Standard to Help Mitigate Climate Change," California Public Utilities Commission, January 25, 2007.

PUNITIVE DAMAGES

PHILIP MORRIS USA v. WILLIAMS

Kmiec, Douglas. "Up in Smoke." Slate.com.February 21, 2007. http://www.slate.com/id/2160286

Sherman, Mark. "Court Nixes Award Against Philip Morris."Washington Post.February 20, 2007.

RACIAL DISCRIMINATION

PARENTS INVOLVED IN COMMUNITY SCHOOLS v. SEATTLE SCHOOL DISTRICT NO. 1

Savage, David. "Justices Reject School Integration Efforts." *The Los Angeles Times*. June 29, 2007.

RAPE

SERVICEMEN CHARGED IN BRUTAL CASE OF RAPE AND MURDER IN IRAQ

Associated Press, "U.S. Soldier Gets 100 Years for Rape-Slay," CBS News.com, February 22, 2007.

"Five Soldiers Charged in Iraq Rape-Murder Case," *CNN.com*, July 9, 2006.

REHNQUIST, WILLIAM H.

EVIDENCE SURFACES OF JUSTICE REHNQUIST'S DEPENDENCY ON PRESCRIPTION DRUGS

Cooperman, Alan. "Sedative Withdrawal Made Rehnquist Delusional in '81." *Washington Post*, 5 January 2007.

Dirf, Michael C. "The Big News in the Rehnquist FBI File: There is None." *FindLaw Writ*, 15 January 2007.

Shafer, Jack. "Rehnquist's Drug Habit: The Man in Full," *Slate Magazine*, 5 January 2007.

RELIGION

GONZALES INITIATES PROGRAM TO PROTECT RELIGIOUS FREEDOM

U.S. Department of Justice, *Report on Enforcement of Laws Protecting Religious Freedom, Fiscal Years 2001-2006* (February 20, 2007).

Wilkey, Lonnie and Robert Marus, "Gonzales Touts Religious-Freedom Plan to SBC," *Associated Baptist Press*, February 22, 2007.

KANSAS SCHOOL BOARD THROWS OUT ANTI-EVOLUTION STANDARDS

Davey, Monica. "Evolution Opponents Lose Kansas School Board Majority." *Austin (TX) American-Statesman*, 3 August 2006.

Evolution Opponents Lose Control of Kansas School Board." *USA Today*, 2 August 2006. Available at http://www.usatoday.com/news/nation/2006-08-01-kansas-evolution-vote_x.htm

Hanna, John. "Kansas Rewrites Science Standards Again." 14 February 2007. Available at http://www.abcnews.go.com/Technology/wireStory?id=2872167

"Kansas School Board Repeals Guidelines Questioning Evolution." 15 February 2007. Available at http://www.FOXnews.com

"Kansas Science Education Standards." 7 June 2007. Available at http://www.ksde.org

RICO

GAMBOA v. VELEZ

Batista, Paul. *Civil RICO Practice Manual, 2nd. Ed.* Aspen Publishers, 2005.

Shapo, Marshall. *Principles of Tort Law, 2nd Ed.* West Group, 2003.

WILKIE v. ROBBINS

The OYEZ Project, "Wilkie v. Robbins," available at: www.oyez.org/cases/2000-2009/2006/2006_06_219/

"Wilkie v. Robbins." Duke University School of Law, available at: http://www.law.duke.edu/publiclaw/supremecourtonline/certgrants/2006/wilvrob

Wilkie v. Robbins, No. 06-219, 551 U.S. ___ (2007). Available at www.supremecourtus.gov/opinions/06slipopinion.html

"Wilkie v. Robbins." Cornell University School of Law, 26 February 2007. Available at http://www.law.cornell.edu.supct.cert/06-219.html

ROYALTY

BP AMERICA PRODUCTION CO. v. BURTON

Lowe, John S. *Oil and Gas Law in a Nutshell. 4th Edition.* West Group, 2003.

SEARCH AND SEIZURE

PHANEUF v. FRAIKIN

Long, Carolyn. *Mapp V. Ohio: Guarding Against Unreasonable Searches And Seizures.* Lawrence, KS: University Press of Kansas. 2006.

SECOND AMENDMENT

FEDERAL COURT STRIKES DOWN D.C. GUN LAW

Lanier, Cathy and Vincent Schiraldi, "Give Us Back Our Gun Law," Washington Post, March 15, 2007.

Wallance, Gregory J., "A Deplorable Citation," *New Jersey Law Journal*, April 2, 2007, at 23.

SECURITIES

TELLABS V. MAKOR ISSUES & RIGHTS, LTD.

Soderquist, Larry D. and Theresa A. Gabaldon, *Securities Law*, New York: Foundation Press, 20078.

Steinberg, Mark I. and Ralph C. Ferrara, *Securities Practice: Federal and State Enforcement* St. Paul, Minn.: West Group, 2001.

SEGREGATION

DISTRICT JUDGE FREES LITTLE ROCK SCHOOLS FROM FEDERAL SUPERVISION

Associated Press, "Little Rock Schools Freed from Federal Supervision 50 Years After Crisis," *USA Today*, February 23, 2007.

DeMillo, Andrew, "Little Rock Schools Freed from Court," *Washington Post*, February 24, 2007.

SENTENCING

CLAIBORNE V. UNITED STATES

Patrick, Robert, "Man's Death Has 'Far-Reaching' Effect," *St. Louis Post-Dispatch*, June 7, 2007.

Retka, Allison, "U.S. Supreme Court Picks Up Replacements for St. Louis Man," *Daily Record*, June 12, 2007.

CUNNINGHAM V. CALIFORNIA

Sentencing Law and Policy. http://sentencing.typepad .com/sentencing_law_and_policy/2007/week4/index .html. Accessed April 20, 2007.

Tonry, Michael. *Sentencing Matters.* Oxford University Press, 2004.

RITA V. UNITED STATES

Bamberger, Phylis Skloot and David J. Gottlieb, *Practice Under the Federal Sentencing Guidelines*, Gaithersburg, Maryland.: Aspen Law and Business, 2001.

Branham, Lynn S., *The Law and Policy of Sentencing and Corrections in a Nutshell* St. Paul, Minn.: West Group, 2007.

SEPTEMBER 11TH ATTACKS

DEPARTMENTS FUDGED DATA ON ANTI-TERRORISM INVESTIGATIONS, ACCORDING TO AUDIT

Eggen, Dan, "Justice Dept. Statistics on Terrorism Faulted," Washington Post, February 21, 2007, at A8.

Office of the Inspector General, U.S. Department of Justice, *The Department of Justice's Internal Controls Over Terrorism Reporting* (2007).

SEX OFFENSES

CLASS-ACTION APPEAL FOR 11,000 REGISTERED SEX OFFENDERS IN GEORGIA

Campos, Carlos. "Judge Cooper's Order on Defendants' Motion to Dismiss the Case." 31 March 2007. Available at http://www.schr.org/aboutthe center/pressreleases/HB1059_litigation/Legal Documents/Cooper_3.30.07.html

Georgia General Assembly, "HB 1059." Available at official website http://wwww/legis.state.ga.us/legis/ 2005_06/sum/hb1059.htm

McCaffrey, Shannon. "Judge Voids Teen Sex Offender's Ten-Year Sentence." ABC News, 11 June 2007. Available at http://www,abcnews.go.com/The Law/story?ide=3266087

"SCHR: Litigation Challenging HB 1059: Georgia's Sex Offender Law." Southern Center for Human Rights (SCHR) Website at http://www.schr.org/ aboutthecenter/pressreleases/HB1059_litigation/

SEXUAL ABUSE

CONGRESSMAN MARK FOLEY RESIGNS AMID SCANDAL

Babington, Charles and Jonathan Weisman. "Rep. Foley Quits in Page Scandal." *Washington Post*, 30 September 2006.

Feldman, Linda. "How the Foley Scandal Unfolded." *Christian Science Monitor*, 06 Ocyober 2006.

"Fla. Congressman Mark Foley Resigns Over E-Mails to Male Page." Undated. Available at http://www .FOXnews.com

"Mark Foley Blows Town." *Capitol Hill Blue*, 23 February 2007.

Weisman, Jonathan and Jeffrey H. Birnbaum. "Scandals Alone Could Cost Republicans Their House Majority." *Washington Post*, 2 November 2006.

SEXUAL HARASSMENT

L.W., A MINOR BY HIS PARENT AND GUARDIAN, L.G. V. TOMS RIVER REGIONAL SCHOOLS BOARD OF EDUCATION

Vieira, Norman. *Constitutional Civil Rights in a Nutshell.* Saint Paul, MN.: West Group. 1998.

SIXTH AMENDMENT

CAREY V. MUSLADIN

Freedman, Eric. *Habeas Corpus: Rethinking the Great Writ of Liberty.* New York: New York Univ. Press. 2003.

SCHRIRO V. LANDRIGAN

Savage, David G., "Supreme Court Restores Death Sentence for Two-Time Murderer," *L.A. Times*, May 15, 2007.

STATUTE OF LIMITATIONS

SAVORY V. LYONS

Currie, David. *Federal Jurisdiction in a Nutshell.* West Group, 1999.

TAXATION

EC Term of Years Trust v. United States

"EC Term of Years Trust v. United States," *Legal Times*, May 14, 2007.

Ruffins, Ebonne, "EC Term of Years Trust v. U.S.," *On the Docket* (Medill News Service), October 27, 2006, http://docket.medill.northwestern.edu/archives/004068.php

Hinck v. United States

Posin, Daniel Q. and Donald B. Tobin, *Principles of Federal Income Taxation of Individuals*, St. Paul, Minn.: Thomson/West 2005.

Bankman, Joseph et al., *Federal Income Tax: Examples and Explanations*, New York: Aspen Publishers 2005.

Limtiaco v. Camacho

Limtiaco, Attorney General of Guam v. Camacho, Governor of Guam, No. 06-116, 549 U.S. ___ (2007). Available at www.supremecourtus.gov/opinions/06slipopinion.html

"Moylan v. Camacho." Cornell University School of Law, 26 February 2007. Available at http://www.law.cornell.edu.supct.cert/06-116.html

The OYEZ Project, "Limtiaco v. Camacho," (available at: www.oyez.org/cases/2000-2009/2006/2006_06_116/

Permanent Mission of India v. City of New York

Pudelski, Christopher. "Preview: Perm. Mission of India v. New York on 4/24." *SCOTUSblog*, 23 April 2007.

The OYEZ Project, "Permanent Mission of India to the United Nations v. City of New York," available at: www.oyez.org/cases/2000-2009/2006/2006_06_134/

"Permanent Mission of India to the United Nations v. City of New York." Duke University School of Law, available at: http://www.law.duke.edu/public law/supremecourtonline/certgrants/2006/pervnyc/

Permanent Mission of India to the United Nations v. City of New York, No. 06-134, 551 U.S. ___ (2007). Available at www.supremecourtus.gov/opinions/06slipopinion.html

"Permanent Mission of India to the United Nations v. City of New York." Cornell University School of Law, 26 February 2007. Available at http://www.law.cornell.edu.supct.cert/06-134.html

TERRORISM

New Airport Rules to Combat Terrorism

Electronic Privacy Information Center (EPIC). "Spotlight on Surveillance: Transportation Agency's Plan to X-Ray Travelers Should Be Stripped of Funding." June 2005. Available at http://www.epic.org/privacy/surveillance/spotlight/0605/

Orr, Bob. "London Plot Revives Profiling Debate." 23 August 2006. Available at http://www.cbsnews.com/stories/2006/08/23/eveningnews/printable1931405.shtml

Peev, Gerri. "Every Airport Traveler 'will be Finger-printed.'" *The Scotsman*, 17 August 2006.

Pipes, Daniel. "Calls for Racial Profiling Increase After London Plot." *The New York Sun*, 22 August 2006.

Palmer, J. Jioni. "King Endorses Ethnic Profiling." *Newsday*, 17 August 2006.

Transportation Security Administration. "Where We Stand." http://www.tsa.gov.us.org/

White House Halts Terrorist Surveillance Program

Cauley, Leslie, "NSA Has Massive Database of Americans' Phone Calls," USA Today, May 11, 2006.

Zajac, Andrew, "Wiretaps Not Legal, Ex-Justice Aid Says," *Chicago Tribune*, May 16, 2007.

Update on Terrorist Trials

Anderson, Curt. "Terrorism Trial Begins for Padilla, Once Dubbed 'Dirty Bomber." *The San Diego Union-Tribune*, 15 April 2007.

"Padilla Judge Refuses to Dismiss Terror Charges Over Torture Allegations." *The Jurist*, University of Pittsburgh School of Law, 23 March 2007. http://jurist.law.pitt.edu/paperchase/2007/03/padilla-judge-refuses-to-dismi.php

"Padilla Jury Hears Co-Defendant Wiretap Conversations Supporting bin Laden." *The Jurist*, University of Pittsburgh School of Law, 26 June 2007. http://jurist.law.pitt.edu/paperchase/2007/04/padilla-jury-hears-co-defendant-wiretap.php

"Supreme Court Declines to Hear Guantanamo Detainee Habeas Appeals." *The Jurist*, University of Pittsburgh School of Law, 2 April 2007. http://jurist.law.pitt.edu/paperchase/2007/04/supreme-court-declines-to-hear.php

TRADEMARK

Cisco and Apple Settle Trademark Dispute Over iPhone

Associated Press, "Cisco, Apple Settle Over Right to iPhone Name," MSNBC.com, February 21, 2007.

Stone, Brad, "Settlement Lets Apple Use 'iPhone'," *New York Times*, February 22, 2007.

VOTING

California Court Restores Voting Rights to Prisoners

Egelko, Bob, "Voting Rights Restored for Thousands in State on Probation," *San Francisco Chronicle*, December 28, 2006.

Richmond, Josh, "Voting Rights for Jail Inmates Reinstated," *Oakland Tribune*, December 22, 2006.

Voter Identification Laws Receive Court Scrutiny

Davenport, Paul. "Judge Won't Block Arizona Voter ID Law." Associated Press Release, 11 September 2006. Available at http://www.truthout.org/cgi-bin/artman/exec/view.cgi/64/22447

"Help America Vote Act of 2002." Available at: www
.fec.gov/hava

Palmer, Alyson M. "Justices Sidestep Voter ID Law
Challenge." *Daily Report*, 12 June 2007.

"Requirements for Voter Identification." National
Conference of State Legislatures. 1 February 2007.
Available at: http://www.ncsl.org/programs/
legismgt/elect/taskfc/voteridreq.htm

Slater, Michael and Nathan Henderson-James. "The
Fraud of Voter ID Laws." Institute for America's
Future, 6 March 2007. Available at http://www.tom
paine.com/print/the_fraud_of_voter_id_laws.php

VOTER REGISTRATION STATUTES

Kropko, M.R. "AAPD Wins in Federal Court." Ohio
Statewide Independent Living Council News, 2
September 2006. Available at http://www.ohiosilc
.org/web06//news

"Judge Blocks Florida Voter Registration Law." Associated Press news release, 28 August 2006. Available at: www.truthout.org/docs_226/08/2806S
.shtml

Anderson, Curt. "Judge Raises Questions About New
Voter Registration Law." Associated Press news release, undated. Available at http://FirstCoast.News
.com

WOODLANDS AND FORESTS

REINSTATEMENT OF THE ROADLESS AREA CONSERVATION RULE

Greater Yellowstone Coalition. "Where Are We
Now?" June 2007. Available at http://www.gyc.org

Griffith, Martin. "Ex-Forest Service Chief Backs Most
of Clinton-era 'Roadless Rule'." *Las Vegas Sun*, 25
February 2007.

Hatch, Cory. "Roadless Rule Reinforced." *Jackson Hole
News & Guide*, 8 February 2007.

Young, Samantha. "Federal Court Weighs Legality of
Road Plan." *The Casper (WY) Star-Tribune*, 3 August 2006.

WRONGFUL DISCHARGE

OFFICE OF SENATOR MARK DAYTON v. HANSON

Barnes, Robert. "Justices Weigh Legislators' Right to
Fire." *Washington Post*, 25 April 2007. p.A15.

"Dayton v. Hanson." *The OYEZ Project*, U.S. Supreme
Court Media, 24 April 2007. Available at: www
.oyez.org/cases/2000-2009/2006/2006_06_618/

YOO, JOHN

"John Yoo." *Contemporary Authors Online*. Gale, 2007.
Reproduced in Biography Resource Center. Farmington Hills, Mich.: Thomson Gale. 2007. <http://
galenet.galegroup.com/servlet/BioRC>

"John Yoo Profile." University of Calfornia-Berkeley.
<http://www.law.berkeley.edu/faculty/yooj/>

Slevin, Peter. "Scholar Stands by Post-9/11 Writings
On Torture, Domestic Eavesdropping" *Washington
Post*. <http://www.washingtonpost.com/wp-dyn/
content/article/2005/12/25/AR2005122500570
.html> December 26, 2005.

Stone, Geoffrey. "A Review of John Yoo's 'War By
Other Means: An Insider's Account of the War on
Terror'" *Washington Post*. November 4, 2006.

AMERICAN ASSOCIATION OF LAW SCHOOLS

Founded in 1900, the American Association of Law Schools (AALS) is a nonprofit organization with a stated purpose of "the improvement of the legal profession through legal education." Beginning with 32 schools, AALS now serves 168 schools from its headquarters in Washington, D.C. Its web site is found at www.aals.org.

AALS "serves as the learned society for law teachers and is legal education's principal representative to the federal government and to other national higher education organizations and learned societies." It serves law teachers in a number of ways. For example, it publishes an annual directory of all full-time law school faculty and professional staff of its member schools. The directory includes biographical information of more than 10,000 teachers and law librarians. The directory also lists subjects taught and provides separate listings for minority, gay, lesbian, and other classifications of faculty and professional staff of the schools. Moreover, AALS publishes the quarterly Journal of Legal Education to address legal education issues.

Persons interested in becoming law professors also may benefit from AALS services. For a fee, a potential professor can have biographical information listed in the organization's Faculty Appointments Register. Schools are able to access this information on line or on paper. Although AALS does not provide career counseling, the organization also sends position advertisements to candidates. In the fall of each year, AALS sponsors a Faculty Recruitment Conference where schools and candidates can meet. In addition, AALS sponsors an annual conference for new law teachers.

AALS also maintains women and minority deans' databanks. These databanks are compiled by soliciting names of women and minority professors who possess deanship qualifications. Nominations come from present deans and colleagues, as well as through self-nomination. Once candidates have been identified, AALS contacts each person to determine whether he or she wishes to be included in the databank. This information is released to dean search committees.

A visiting faculty register is distributed to law schools twice a year, in February and October. This register is the networking vehicle for professors who are interested in becoming visiting professors at other schools.

AALS has 85 sections of interest groups for faculty of member schools. These interest groups cover a wide range of academic topics, from administrative law to torts. In addition, groups on other topics, such as academic support and new law professors, are available. The groups conduct various activities, including providing newsletters for members, programs at the AALS annual meeting, exam exchanges, mentoring programs, and listservs.

AMERICAN INNS OF COURT

The American Inns of Court (AIC) "are designed to improve the skills, professionalism and ethics of the bench and bar," according to information presented on the organization's web site, found at http://www.inssofcourt.org. The first Inn was formed in Provo, Utah, in 1980.

The AIC explains, "An American Inn of Court is not a fraternal order, a social club, a course in continuing legal education, a lecture series, an apprenticeship system, or an adjunct of a law school's program. While an AIC partakes of some of each of these concepts, it is quite different in aim, scope, and effect." Inns are distinct from bar associations. The AIC is not a lobbying organization and does not take positions on political issues.

The American Inns of Court are modeled on the tradition of English legal apprenticeships. Inns of England date back 800 years. There is no formal connection between American Inns of Court and English Inns, however. Nevertheless, a member of an American Inn is welcome to visit an English Inn. Active members need a letter of introduction from the national office, and then are welcome to visit the King's Inn in Dublin or the four London Inns: Gray's Inn, Inner Temple, Lincoln's Inn, and Inner Temple. Members from the London Inns or Dublin are welcome to visit American Inns, as well.

Individual Inns meet approximately once a month from September to May. Nationwide membership totals more than 20,000 members. These members are divided into Inns with a suggested membership of 80 members. Members fall into the following categories: Masters of the Bench, Barristers, Associates, and Pupils. Masters of the Bench are those members who are judges, experienced lawyers, and law professors. Barristers are higher ranking than Associates; both refer to lawyers with a certain amount of experience. Law students make up the Pupils category. More than 100 law schools participate in Inns.

Within an individual inn are pupilage teams. A pupilage team has a few members from each category. Each team is expected to get together each month in groups of two or more, in addition to the monthly Inn meeting. The purpose of these teams is to foster more effective advocacy by having more experienced members mentor less experienced members. In addition to this group mentoring approach, each less experienced Inn member is paired with a more experienced member who is expected to encourage conversations about the practice of law.

Inns typically address both civil and criminal litigation. However, some Inns have a more specialized membership and focus, such as bankruptcy, intellectual property, or tax law.

BETTER BUSINESS BUREAU

The Better Business Bureau (BBB) was founded in 1912. Headquartered in Arlington, Virginia, its purpose is to solve problems in the marketplace through self-regulation and consumer education. According to the BBB, its purpose "is not to act as an advocate for businesses or consumers, but to act as a mutually trusted intermediary to resolve disputes, to facilitate communication, and to provide information on ethical business practices."

The organization's web site is www.bbb .org. The BBB is a private, nonprofit organization. Its funding comes from member businesses. The BBB provided more than 105 million instances of consumer service in 2006. This was the highest number ever reported and a significant increase from the 41.5 million instances in 2002.

The BBB provides five main services: business reliability reports, dispute resolution, truth-in-advertising, consumer and business education, and charity review.

The BBB issues business reliability reports on member and nonmember businesses. The BBB does not recommend any company, service, or product. Companies with a bad report are disqualified from BBB membership. The report does not include credit information, but does include a three-year history of complaints to the BBB. In addition, the report notes any government involvement regarding the company's marketplace practices. A typical report will also provide information regarding BBB membership and whether the company participates in BBB programs on customer satisfaction. Business reliability reports are available on-line.

When a consumer complains to the BBB about a business, the organization contacts the business and seeks assistance in resolving the issue. The BBB cannot force companies to respond to customer complaints. However, BBB member businesses will lose their membership if they do not. Moreover, companies who do not agree to respond to the BBB will have their response noted in the BBB's public reliability reports. This applies to both member and nonmember businesses.

Methods for dispute resolution employed by the BBB include binding arbitration, conditional binding arbitration, informal dispute settlement, and mediation. In arbitration, a neutral party or a board determines the outcome of a business dispute. An arbitrator may award any legal remedy, but if the parties agree that something may not be awarded, the arbitrator is prohibited from making that award. Informal dispute settlement means that a neutral party makes a non-binding decision regarding the dispute. In mediation, a neutral party helps disputants negotiate a settlement.In mediation situations the neutral party does not make a determination of who is right and who is wrong.

The BBB Auto Line is intended for disputes involving alleged manufacturing defects in automobiles. It is a service only applicable to automobile manufacturers. It does not cover issues with automobile dealerships, repair shops, or vehicle insurance companies. Most auto manufacturers participate in the program.

Truth in advertising is another keystone of the BBB's work. The objective is to promote self-regulation of advertising. The National Advertising Division administers national advertising, while the Children's Advertising Unit addresses advertising directed at children.

BBB education covers both consumer and business issues. Areas of interest include identity theft and on-line shopping tips. Working with the United States Department of Commerce, the BBB also provides information to businesses to encourage them to expand their on-line businesses internationally.

The fifth major emphasis of the BBB is charitable review. The BBB's Wise Giving Alliance encourages consumers to investigate a charity before giving. Although linked to the BBB web site, this component has its own web site at www.give.org. The BBB has also set up voluntary standards for charity accountability. To help them make sound giving decisions, donors can research nationally soliciting charitable organizations for reports. The reporting does not cover all of the one million plus charities that have received charitable tax exempt status from the Internal Revenue Service. The Alliance first seeks to report on charities that it has received inquiries on and charities that have approached the Alliance asking to have a report completed.

The BBB has been criticized for having business as its source of funding. Another criticism is that because it is not a government agency, it lacks any enforcement strength. It relies on reporting complaints to the public.

CAMPAIGN FINANCE INSTITUTE

The Campaign Finance Institute (CFI) is a watchdog organization affiliated with The George Washington University in Washington, D.C. This nonpartisan, nonpolitical organization "conducts objective research and education, empanels task forces and makes recommendations for policy change in the field of campaign finance," according to the group's web site at http://www.cfinst.org/.

Campaign finance reform has several purposes. One purpose of campaign finance reform is to limit certain individuals and groups from having a disproportionate influence on elections. Other purposes include prohibiting certain sources of funds for campaigns, controlling campaign spending, and requiring public disclosure of campaign finances.

Controversies over how candidates should handle campaign finances are nearly as old as the country itself. In 1867, the federal government enacted its first campaign finance legislation. The law prohibited federal officers from soliciting contributions by Navy Yard workers.

Campaign finance reform has been in the news frequently in the past several decades. In 1974, partially spurred on by the abuses in the 1972 presidential election, Congress created the Federal Election Commission (FEC). Strict limits for contributions and expenditures were also put in place, and were swiftly challenged in Buckley v. Valeo, 424 U.S. 1 (1976). The United States Supreme Court upheld contribution limits as a valid government interest in safeguarding the integrity of elections. Expenditure limits, on the other hand, were overturned. This ruling prompted Congress to further amend campaign finance laws.

Congress has continued to tinker with campaign finance laws. In 2002, the Bipartisan Campaign Reform Act was signed into law. Also known as the McCain-Feingold law, it is the most recent major federal campaign legislation.

The Campaign Finance Institute has been a strong advocate for the past several years for electronic filing of campaign finance reports. Since 2001, House of Representatives members, candidates for the House, and House and national party committees, have been required to report contributions and expenditures electronically. In addition, Congress has approved legislation requiring lobbyists to file electronic reports. However, no such requirement exists for senators, senate candidates, or senate campaign committees.

According to the Capitol Hill newspaper, Roll Call, this senate campaign finance information is actually already available electronically. Instead of sending the files electronically to the Federal Election Commission, senators print the files. Then they send them to the Office of the Secretary of the Senate. There, the pages are scanned, page by page, for e-mailing to the FEC.

Next, the files are printed at the FEC, but at this stage are not yet available for the general public. In 2006, the Senate reports amounted to more than 10,000 pages of information. The FEC sends the information to a private contractor, whose employees type the information back into the computer. The private contractor costs taxpayers about $250,000 per year. Finally, the information is sent back to the FEC and posted on the Internet.

Only the Senate's contribution information is eventually posted. The expenditure data does not get posted electronically. In 2003, Senators John McCain (R-AZ) and Russ Feingold (D-WI) sought to close this loophole. However, to date, the loophole remains open. The Campaign Finance Institute and many other critics point out that this means that information that is available for the House is unavailable until weeks after an election or key vote.

CFI noted that just one week before the 2006 election, information dating from June 30 was still not available via the Internet for six of the ten most hotly contested Senate races. Moreover, because of the Senate's system, no information was available on any Senate candidate for the weeks just prior to election.

The latest version of the 2003 Feingold-McCain proposal has 38 co-sponsors. Fifteen are Republican senators, 21 are Democratic, and two are Independents. Despite the broad partisan support, opposition remains, and CFI continues to seek transparency in campaign financial matters. In April 2007, Senate Rules and Administration Chairwoman Dianne Feinstein (D-CA) asked for unanimous consent to bring up the bill. On at least two occasions, Republican senators opposed unanimous consent on behalf of unnamed Republican senators. On one occasion, Senator Lamar Alexander (R-TN) opposed bringing up the bill; on another, Senator Jim Bunning (R-KY) spoke against it "on behalf of the Republican side." The Campaign Finance Institute promptly issued a press release urging members of the public, including bloggers, to contact senators to solicit support for the change.

In addition to advocating legislative reform, CFI also works to disseminate information about other campaign finance matters. For example, in April 2007, CFI reported that donations in excess of $1,000 make up 79 percent of the presidential candidates' fundraising to date. On the other hand, only 14 percent come from donations of $200 or less.

FEDERALIST SOCIETY

The Federalist Society for Law and Public Policy Studies was founded in 1982 by a group of law students at Yale, Harvard, and the University of Chicago. The Federalist Society "is a group of conservatives and libertarians dedicated to reforming the current legal order," according to the group's web site at http://www.fed-soc.org. The Society is a tax-exempt nonprofit organization and is forbidden from political or lobbying activities.

Reformation of the current legal order "entails reordering priorities within the legal system to place a premium on individual liberty, traditional values, and the rule of law." The group is "committed to the principles that the state exists to preserve freedom, that the separation of governmental powers is central to our Constitution, and that it is emphatically the province and duty of the judiciary to say what the law is, not what it should be."

The name of the organization comes from the Federalist Papers, the series of articles by James Madison, Alexander Hamilton, and James Jay that explained the new United States Constitution to residents of New York to persuade them to ratify it. Federalist Paper number 78, written by Alexander Hamilton, addresses judicial restraint. Its argument forms a lynchpin of the Federalist Society's ideals. Madison, often called the Father of the Constitution, provides the silhouette of the Society's logo.

The 40,000-member society is made up of lawyers, law students, scholars, and other interested people. The organization is comprised of 180 law school chapters, 60 metropolitan lawyers' chapters, and 15 nationwide practice groups. The organization's stated purpose is "ideas." The Society does not endorse candidates for public office. The Federalist Society supports a limited government, but claims its members often hold conflicting views about controversial issues involving tort reform, privacy rights, and criminal justice.

Steven G. Calabresi is a co-founder of the Federalist Society and presently serves as its Chair. Calabresi is the George C. Dix Professor of Constitutional Law at Northwestern University's School of Law. A graduate of Yale Law School, he worked in both Ronald Reagan and George H. Bush's administrations, from 1985 to 1990.

Supreme Court Justice Antonin Scalia served as a faculty member when the organization was being formed. In addition, Justices Samuel Alito and Clarence Thomas are members. Evidence suggests that Chief Justice John Roberts has been a member, although the membership rolls of the organization are not made public. Other easily-recognizable names on the roster are Robert Bork (former United States Circuit Court Judge); Edwin Meese (former United States Attorney General); Ted Olson and Kenneth Starr (former Solicitors General); and Senator Orrin Hatch (R-UT).

Libertarians, who advocate maximizing individual rights and minimizing the role of the state, also find a home in the Federalist Society. Prominent libertarian members include University of Chicago Law School professor Richard Epstein, Professor Randy Barnett from Georgetown Law School, and the Cato Institute's Director of Constitutional Studies, Roger Pilon.

By sponsoring "fair, serious, and open debate," the Federalist Society believes it will be more successful at promoting its agenda than if it used other methods. Scholars and jurists opposed to the Federalist Society's aims often appear at its events. For example, in mid-June, 2007, the Boston Lawyers Chapter of the Federalist Society and other organizations sponsored United States Supreme Court Justice Stephen Breyer as the chair of a debate on the art and practice of judging. Alan Dershowitz, a professor at Harvard Law School, is another prominent figure who has appeared at Federalist Society events to provide a different perspective. Anyone may attend Federalist Society events.

One feature of the Federalist's Society's on-line presence is its on-line roundtable discussion. Up for discussion in May 2007 was the April 18, 2007, Supreme Court decision in Gonzales v. Carhart. In Carhart, the Supreme Court upheld the constitutionality of the Partial Birth Abortion Ban Act. The Society's web site began an on-line debate between noted legal scholars who either supported or disagreed with the Court's decision.

The Federalist Society publishes a journal, Engage, that covers the work of the Society's fifteen Practice Groups. The Practice Groups cover the following topics: administrative law, civil rights, corporations, criminal law and procedure, environmental law and property rights, federalism and separation of powers, financial services and e-commerce, free speech and election law, intellectual property, international and national security law, labor and employment law, litigation, professional responsibility, religious liberties, and telecommunications.

INNOCENCE PROJECT

Lawyers Barry C. Scheck and Peter J. Neufeld started the Innocence Project at Benjamin Cardozo School of Law in 1992. The nonprofit group's goal, according to its web site, is to exonerate "wrongfully convicted people through DNA testing and [reform] the criminal justice system to prevent future injustice." The group's web site is found at http://www.innocenceproject.org.

DNA (deoxyribonucleic acid) is a molecule in an organism's cells. DNA contains genetic information. Blood, saliva, sweat, semen, hair, and skin are all potential types of evidence in a criminal case; all contain DNA. Every person has a distinct DNA profile (except for identical twins).

The Innocence Project was not the first organization dedicated to freeing the wrongly convicted, but it was the first to base its work on DNA technology. According to the group's web site, the first DNA exoneration took place in 1989, three years before establishment of the Innocence Project. In its 15 years of operation, the Innocence Project's efforts have resulted in the release of 201 falsely convicted persons. These 201 people served a combined total of nearly 2,500 years of incarceration before DNA testing brought about their release.

In addition to co-directors Scheck and Neufeld, the legal clinic at Yeshiva University employs full-time staff attorneys, a social worker, paralegals, and others; law students handle much of the work. The organization has a caseload of 160 active cases. Resolution of a case takes anywhere from one to ten years. The Innocence Project receives about 200 requests for representation per month. Cases are only accepted where post-conviction DNA testing could lead to exoneration. However, the Innocence Project does not require production of the possible DNA evidence as a prerequisite for acceptance of a case.

One high-profile member of the Innocence Project's Board of Directors is John Grisham, an attorney turned writer known for his legal thrillers. Grisham has called for a moratorium on all executions. He has stated he is opposed to capital punishment both because he believes the system is badly flawed, and because as a Christian, he believes the death penalty is immoral.

Others on the board include Calvin Johnson and Janet Reno. Johnson was an Innocence Project client who was exonerated in 1999. He is the author of the book, Exit to Freedom. Reno was the first woman Attorney General in the United States. Appointed by President William J. Clinton, Reno held office from 1993 to 2001.

According to the organization, 11 percent of those wrongly convicted were less than 17 years old at the time of conviction; 27 percent were less than 21 years of age. The average age was 26 years old. The breakdown, according to race: 62 percent of the exonerated persons are African American; 10 percent are Latino, and 28 percent are Caucasian. Fourteen served time on death row.

According to the Innocence Project, 74 suspects and/or perpetrators have been identified during the exoneration process. In addition, a 1995 study by the National Institute of Justice of more than 10,000 cases involving FBI testing, concluded that 25 percent of suspects were cleared when the DNA testing was completed during the investigation stage of a crime. Potential obstacles for Innocence Project cases includes "degraded evidence that cannot be accurately tested; lost or destroyed evidence; and prosecutorial objections."

In some cases, the Innocence Project has reaffirmed guilt of a defendant. Potential clients are informed that any DNA results will be made public.

Slightly fewer than half of those exonerated have been compensated for their wrongful incarceration. The federal government, the District of Columbia, and 21 states have enacted compensation laws.

Wrongful convictions fall into several broad categories, according to the Innocence Project. Those categories are: mistaken identity; lab error and junk science; false confessions and incriminating statements; and erroneous testimony by snitches.

Mistaken identification is the largest category of wrongful convictions. According to the Innocence Project, "Seventy-seven percent of post-conviction DNA exoneration cases in the U.S. involve mistaken eyewitness identification testimony." The Innocence Project has recommended guidelines to improve the reliability of eyewitness testimony; a number of jurisdictions now employ these guidelines.

The next largest category leading to DNA exoneration is lab error and junk science, a factor in 65 percent of cases. This category includes both honest mistakes (such as an inadvertent misanalysis of fingerprints or bite marks) and fraudulent, exaggerated, or otherwise tainted forensic evidence.

False confessions and incriminating statements are a factor in 25 percent of DNA exoneration cases. Not surprisingly, many of these cases arise where the defendant is under the age of 18 and/or is developmentally disabled. The issue of false confessions has led many jurisdictions to record interrogations. About 350 jurisdictions have adopted this practice voluntarily. Moreover, a number of states mandate taped interrogations in homicide cases.

In 15 percent of DNA exonerations, snitches (also known as jailhouse informants) are an issue. The Innocence Project recommends full disclosure of any incentives the snitch may receive in exchange for testimony, as well as a jury instruction that the informant's testimony may be unreliable.

Many states now have their own innocence organizations. Canada, Great Britain, and Australia also have innocence projects.

The Innocence Project advocates on behalf of criminal justice reform related to wrongful convictions. The organization encourages the formation of "Innocence Commissions" to "to investigate and understand the circumstances that lead to wrongful convictions." California, Connecticut, Wisconsin, Illinois, North Carolina, and Pennsylvania have all formed criminal justice reform commissions. Each jurisdiction has set up its commission differently, but the Innocence Project recommends that such commissions need the following to be effective: "subpoena power, access to first-rate investigative resources, and political independence."

LEAGUE OF WOMEN VOTERS

The League of Women Voters was founded in 1920. This nonpartisan political organization works "to improve our systems of government and impact public policies through citizen education and advocacy," according to its web site at http://www.lwv.org. Calling itself a grassroots organization, the group has Leagues in every state in the U.S., as well as the District of Columbia, Puerto Rico, the Virgin Islands, and Hong Kong. In addition, hundreds of localities have their own Leagues. There are 900 state and local Leagues.

Membership in the League is open to women and men age 18 and older. A person may join at any level: local, state, or national. The League has approximately 150,000 members.

The League of Women Voters was founded by Carrie Chapman Catt, the head of the National American Woman Suffrage Association. Catt's "Winning Plan" laid the groundwork for the passage and ratification of the Nineteenth Amendment, awarding suffrage to women after a struggle of 72 years. Catt formed the League six months before the amendment was ratified, as a way to aid the 20 million women who would soon gain suffrage to carry out their new responsibilities. Catt and other leaders intended that the League would stay out of party politics, while advocating for government and social reform legislation.

Just as when it was founded, the League today does not support any candidates for office. Its stated purpose is to make democracy work for all citizens. The League's priorities include: campaign finance reform; civil liberties, voting rights for the District of Columbia; election administration; ethics and lobbying reform; climate change; and health care reform. The League's issues are member-studied and member-approved.

The high cost of campaigns is a campaign finance issue for the League. The League supports proposed legislation known as the McCain-Feingold-Durbin Free Air Time Legislation. This legislation would make free television and radio air time available for candidates and political parties for debates before elections. The League recently filed an amicus (friend of the court) brief in a campaign finance case before the Supreme Court. In addition, the League is urging all candidates to commit to public financing for the 2008 presidential race. Moreover, the League supports legislation that calls for electronic filing disclosure of campaign finance information in the Senate. The House of Representatives and the President already are required to file this information electronically.

In the area of civil liberties, the League is concerned about certain aspects of the Patriot Act, which was passed following the events of September 11, 2001. The League's goal is to ensure the protection of basic civil liberties, while allowing the U.S. to guard against threats to national security. In late 2006, the League joined other groups in voicing its concern of domestic warrantless wiretaps. In addition, in 2005, the League advocated on behalf of the McCain Anti-Torture Amendment.

The League also fights for voting rights for citizens of the District of Columbia. District residents have a non-voting delegate in the House of Representatives, and no presence in the Senate. The League notes that residents pay U.S. taxes, fight on behalf of the country, and are governed by U.S. laws. In May 2007, it urged citizens to contact senators for support of the "District of Columbia Voting Rights Act" that passed the House earlier in the year.

Election issues captured the League's attention following the controversies of the 2000 presidential election between George W. Bush and Al Gore. The League advocated on behalf of improved voting systems and machines. It sought safeguards such as provisional balloting, improved voter registration methods, and training for poll workers.

The League supports fundamental changes to the lobbying and ethics processes of the government, stating that many aspects "are simply inadequate to protect against corruption." It is advocating for new "contribution and fundraising limits on lobbyists and lobbying firms" and changes to the gift, travel, and employment relationships. The League supports an independent office or commission to oversee, enforce, and investigate ethics issues and lobbying laws for Congress.

In recent years, the League has added global climate change to its agenda of concerns. According to the web site, the League believes "global climate change is one of the most serious threats to the environment, health and economy of our nation." It is urging federal action aimed at reducing pollutants causing global warming.

The League advocates measures to ensure the availability of quality, affordable health care for all Americans. This includes a basic level of care for prevention of disease, health education, prenatal care, mental health care, acute care, and long-term care. The organization also supports advancing medical research and technology.

In October 2006, the League launched its Vote411.org project. The League calls this new destination "a 'one-stop-shop' for election related information." It provides visitors with general and specific voting information, including location of polling places, voter registration requirements, absentee ballot information, ballot measure information, and factual data on candidates in state, local, and federal elections. The site allows a person to type in an address and locate the applicable polling place.

In September 2006, the League launched an immigration study. The study is meant to "explore the underlying values and principles regarding immigration, reasons for immigration, current federal immigration policy, and the impact of immigration in American society." The League expects to release its findings in 2008.

Through its League of Women Voters Education Fund, in 2006, the League also launched an educational program to promote an independent judiciary. Other issues that the League explores and educates on are: redistricting reform, and encouraging discussion on the system and effectiveness of homeland security. In addition, the League is involved in a global democracy project. This project works with people worldwide to increase "transparency, accountability, and good government" in other countries.

NATIONAL BOARD OF TRIAL ADVOCACY

The National Board of Trial Advocacy (NBTA) was founded in 1977. Its purpose is to improve the quality of trial advocacy in the nation's courtrooms. In addition, it is intended to help consumers locate highly qualified trial lawyers. The organization certifies lawyers in civil, criminal, family, and social security disability law trial advocacy.

Certification is a voluntary undertaking and is not required of any attorney. According to the NBTA web site, more than 2400 attorneys are certified in the various areas. The overwhelming majority of certifications are in the civil trial advocacy area.

In order to be certified, an applicant must meet a number of requirements. First, the applicant must be a member of a bar in good standing. The attorney must also practice at least 30

percent in the field in which certification is sought, and have done so for the past three years. A writing sample is also required. This requirement is satisfied by submitting a trial brief that the applicant submitted to a court of law within the last three years. Next, applicants must have amassed at least 45 hours of continuing legal education in the last three years. This continuing education must be in the field in which certification is sought.

Three judges and three attorneys who are familiar with the applicant's courtroom abilities must provide references. Moreover, the applicant must provide evidence of courtroom skills in a number of trials that went as far as a verdict or judgment. He or she must have been the lead counsel in at least 40 contested matters as well. Finally, applicants must pass a six-hour examination that is graded by trial attorneys and law professors.

A member in good standing must apply for recertification after five years. No exam is required for recertification.

NBTA's headquarters is located in Boston. Its web site is found at http://www.NBTAnet.org. A feature on the web site allows visitors to search for certified NBTA attorneys in any of the four areas.

NATIONAL CONFERENCE OF STATE LEGISLATURES

The National Conference of State Legislatures (NCSL) was established in 1975 to provide bipartisan support to state legislatures, commonwealths, and territories. It provides research for legislators and legislative staff, technical assistance, and opportunities for networking on issues. In addition, NCSL provides advocacy for state governments before Congress and federal agencies. The web site is located at http://www.ncsl.org. NCSL has offices in Washington, D.C., and Denver, Colorado.

NCSL is governed by a 60-member executive committee. Half of the elected members are legislators; another significant portion is made up of legislative staff. The committee meets at least four times per year.

NCSL is available to help state legislators craft legislation. Its staff will also supply expert witnesses who can testify before legislative committees on a wide variety of topics. In addition, NCSL staff will come to a state and work directly with legislators and staff on issues. NCSL answers more than 20,000 requests for information each year.

NCSL is meant to be a clearinghouse for information. It has a magazine, State Legislatures. NCSL also sends out several dozen briefing papers each year on current issues. The organization strives to provide networking opportunities through its web site. Its web site content includes state statutes, constitutions, and research.

Further networking opportunities arise during the twenty or so meetings and seminars conducted by NCSL each year. An annual meeting is held each summer. This meeting includes more than 150 sessions on various issues. NCSL also provides opportunities for legislative staff to learn and network. Moreover, NCSL provides lobbying services on behalf of state governments in the United States Congress.

NCSL has 11 standing committees that address both state and federal issues. The committees are: Agriculture, Environment and Energy; Budgets and Revenue; Communications, Financial Services and Interstate Commerce; Education; Health; Human Services and Welfare; Labor and Economic Development; Law and Criminal Justice; Legislative Effectiveness; Redistricting and Elections; and Transportation. Appointed members are legislators and legislative staff, but committee meetings are open to anyone.

According to the NCSL web site, the "Standing Committees allow legislators and staff to benefit from the experiences of other states in shaping public policy, experimenting with new laws, and managing the legislative institutions. Committee members explore issues . . . but committees do not recommend policy to the legislatures on issues that are internal to the states." However, the committees do develop policies on issues that have both state and federal components.

SHRIVER NATIONAL CENTER OF POVERTY LAW

The Shriver National Center of Poverty Law was established in 1967 by Sargent Shriver. The organization's mission is to help lawyers better serve low-income clients. The Shriver Center calls poverty "our most populous state," with 37 million residents.

Sargent Shriver, who is married to Eunice Kennedy Shriver, is a graduate of Yale, both as an undergraduate and from the law school. Under President John F. Kennedy, he served as the first director of the Peace Corps. In addition to involvement in a multitude of social service organizations, he also served as ambassador to France from 1968 to 1970, and was George McGovern's vice-presidential running mate in 1972. He received the Presidential Medal of Freedom in 1994. One of his five children, Maria Shriver, is married to California governor, Arnold Schwarzenegger.

The Shriver Center is responsible for a number of print and on-line publications that are intended to further the organization's aims. The Clearinghouse Review: The Journal of Law and Policy, has been published since nearly the founding of the organization. It acts as a forum "to share ideas and plant seeds for legal and policy innovation," according to the Shriver Center's web site at http://www.povertylaw.org.

The Poverty Law Library is a collection of 500,000 legal documents intended to provide valuable assistance to legal aid attorneys. Information is divided into numerous categories, ranging from food programs to migrants to veterans' issues. In addition, the Shriver Center has made the Federal Practice Manual for Legal Aid Attorneys available on-line. This manual allows readers to search by key word or link to federal statutes, Supreme Court case citations, and pleadings. The Shriver Center also distributes a number of electronic newsletters covering various topics, including women's poverty issues and policy developments in poverty law.

In addition to helping legal aid attorneys serve their clients, the Shriver Center also strives to influence policy at the state and national levels. It does this by disseminating information and taking stances on issues that affect the nation's poor. For example, in 2007, the Center sponsored a roundtable on a Medicaid rule called the Citizenship Documentation Rule. The Shriver Center has also taken a stance against Senate Bill 1348 (the Comprehensive Immigration Reform Act of 2007). The Shriver Center maintains that the proposed legislation is "a failed attempt to reform our nation's immigration laws."

*This section includes difficult or uncommon legal terms (**bolded** in the essays) and their definitions from West's Encyclopedia of American Law (WEAL). Simple or common legal terms such as "lawsuit" and "plaintiff" are not **bolded** in the text and do not appear in this glossary; they do, however, have full entries in WEAL. Furthermore, terms that appear in* SMALL CAPS *within the essays—such as acts, cases, events, organizations, and persons—also appear in WEAL.*

A

Abatement: A reduction, a decrease, or a diminution. The suspension or cessation, in whole or in part, of a continuing charge, such as rent.

Abuse of Discretion: A failure to take into proper consideration the facts and law relating to a particular matter; an arbitrary or unreasonable departure from precedents and settled judicial custom.

Ad Hoc: [*Latin, For this; for this special purpose.*] An attorney ad hoc, or a guardian or curator ad hoc, is one appointed for a special purpose, generally to represent the client or infant in the particular action in which the appointment is made.

Adjudication: The legal process of resolving a dispute. The formal giving or pronouncing of a judgment or decree in a court proceeding; also the judgment or decision given. The entry of a decree by a court in respect to the parties in a case. It implies a hearing by a court, after notice, of legal evidence on the factual issue(s) involved. The equivalent of a determination. It indicates that the claims of all the parties thereto have been considered and set at rest

Administrative Agency: An official governmental body empowered with the authority to direct and supervise the implementation of particular legislative acts. In addition to *agency*, such governmental bodies may be called commissions, corporations (e.g., FDIC), boards, departments, or divisions.

Affirmative Defense: A new fact or set of facts that operates to defeat a claim even if the facts supporting that claim are true.

Aggravation: Any circumstances surrounding the commission of a crime that increase its seriousness or add to its injurious consequences.

Animus: [*Latin, Mind, soul, or intention.*] A tendency or an inclination toward a definite, sometimes unavoidable, goal; an aim, objective, or purpose.

Annuity: A right to receive periodic payments, usually fixed in size, for life or a term of years that is created by a contract or other legal document.

Antitrust Law: Legislation enacted by the federal and various state governments to regulate trade and commerce by preventing unlawful restraints, price-fixing, and monopolies, to promote competition, and to encourage the production of quality goods and services at the lowest prices, with the primary goal of safeguarding public welfare by ensuring that consumer demands will be met by the manufacture and sale of goods at reasonable prices.

Appellant: A person who dissatisfied with the judgment rendered in a lawsuit decided in a lower court or the findings from a proceeding before an administrative agency, asks a superior court to review the decision.

Appellate: Relating to appeals; reviews by superior courts of decisions of inferior courts or administrative agencies and other proceedings.

Appellate Court: A court having jurisdiction to review decisions of a trial-level or other lower court.

Arbiter: [*Latin, One who attends something to view it as a spectator or witness.*] Any person who is given an absolute power to judge and rule on a matter in dispute.

Arrears: A sum of money that has not been paid or has only been paid in part at the time it is due.

Assault and Battery: Two separate offenses against the person that when used in one expression may be defined as any unlawful and unpermitted touching of another. *Assault* is an act that creates an apprehension in another of an imminent, harmful, or offensive contact. The act consists of a threat of harm accompanied by an apparent, present ability to carry out the threat. *Battery* is a harmful or offensive touching of another.

Assessed Valuation: The financial worth assigned to property by taxing authorities that is used as a basis or factor against which the tax rate is applied.

Associate Justice: The designation given to a judge who is not the chief or presiding justice of the court on which he or she sits.

Assumption of Risk: A defense, facts offered by a party against whom proceedings have been instituted to diminish a plaintiff's cause of action or defeat recovery to an action in negligence, which entails proving that the plaintiff knew of a dangerous condition and voluntarily exposed himself or herself to it.

B

Backdating: Predating a document or instrument prior to the date it was actually drawn. The negotiability of an instrument is not affected by the fact that it is backdated.

Bad Faith: The fraudulent deception of another person; the intentional or malicious refusal to perform some duty or contractual obligation.

Bargaining Agent: A union that possesses the sole authority to act on behalf of all the employees of a particular type in a company.

Battery: At common law, an intentional unpermitted act causing harmful or offensive contact with the person of another.

Beyond A Reasonable Doubt: The standard that must be met by the prosecution's evidence in a criminal prosecution: that no other logical explanation can be derived from the facts except that the defendant committed the crime, thereby over-coming the presumption that a person is innocent until proven guilty.

Bill of Lading: A document signed by a carrier (a transporter of goods) or the carrier's representative and issued to a consignor (the shipper of goods) that evidences the receipt of goods for shipment to a specified designation and person.

Breach of The Peace: A comprehensive term encompassing acts or conduct that seriously endanger or disturb public peace and order.

Burden of Persuasion: The onus on the party with the burden of proof to convince the trier of fact of all elements of his or her case. In a criminal case the burden of the government to produce evidence of all the necessary elements of the crime beyond a reasonable doubt.

Burglary: The criminal offense of breaking and entering a building illegally for the purpose of committing a crime therein.

C

Carriers: Individuals or businesses that are employed to deliver people or property to an agreed destination.

Case Law: Legal principles enunciated and embodied in judicial decisions that are derived from the application of particular areas of law to the facts of individual cases.

Case or Controversy: A term used in Article III, Section 2, of the Constitution to describe the structure by which actual, conflicting claims of individuals must be brought before a federal court for resolution if the court is to exercise its jurisdiction to consider the questions and provide relief.

Cause of Action: The fact or combination of facts that gives a person the right to seek judicial redress or relief against another. Also, the legal theory forming the basis of a lawsuit.

Certiorari: [*Latin, To be informed of.*] At common law, an original writ or order issued by the Chancery of King's Bench, commanding officers of inferior courts to submit the record of a cause pending before them to give the party more certain and speedy justice.

A writ that a superior appellate court issues on its discretion to an inferior court, ordering it to produce a certified record of a particular case it has tried, in order to determine whether any irregularities or errors occurred that justify review of the case.

A device by which the Supreme Court of the United States exercises its discretion in selecting the cases it will review.

Character Evidence: Proof or attestations about an individual's moral standing, general nature, traits, and reputation in the general community.

Circuit Court: A specific tribunal that possesses the legal authority to hear cases within its own geographical territory.

Civil Action: A lawsuit brought to enforce, redress, or protect rights of private litigants (the plaintiffs and the defendants); not a criminal proceeding.

Civil Procedure: The methods, procedures, and practices used in civil cases.

Class Action: A lawsuit that allows a large number of people with a common interest in a matter to sue or be sued as a group.

Clerical Error: A mistake made in a letter, paper, or document that changes its meaning, such as a typographical error or the unintentional addition or omission of a word, phrase, or figure.

Closing Argument: The final factual and legal argument made by each attorney on all sides of a case in a trial prior to a verdict or judgment.

Cloture: The procedure by which debate is formally ended in a meeting or legislature so that a vote may be taken.

Collateral: Related; indirect; not bearing immediately upon an issue. The property pledged or given as a security interest, or a guarantee for payment of a debt, that will be taken or kept by the creditor in case of a default on the original debt.

Collateral Attack: An attempt to impeach or overturn a judgment rendered in a judicial proceeding, made in a proceeding other than within the original action or an appeal from it.

Color of Law: The appearance of a legal right.

Commerce Clause: The provision of the U.S. Constitution that gives Congress exclusive power over trade activities between the states and with foreign countries and Indian tribes.

Common Law: The ancient law of England based upon societal customs and recognized and enforced by the judgments and decrees of the courts. The general body of statutes and case law that governed England and the American colonies prior to the American Revolution.

The principles and rules of action, embodied in case law rather than legislative enactments, applicable to the government and protection of persons and property that derive their authority from the community customs and traditions that evolved over the centuries as interpreted by judicial tribunals.

A designation used to denote the opposite of statutory, equitable, or civil; for example, a common-law action.

Compensatory Damages: A sum of money awarded in a civil action by a court to indemnify a person for the particular loss, detriment, or injury suffered as a result of the unlawful conduct of another.

Comptroller: An officer who conducts the fiscal affairs of a state or municipal corporation.

Concurrent Jurisdiction: The authority of several different courts, each of which is authorized to entertain and decide cases dealing with the same subject matter.

Concurrent Resolution: An action of Congress passed in the form of an enactment of one house, with the other house in agreement, which expresses the ideas of Congress on a particular subject.

Congressional Record: A daily publication of the federal government that details the legislative proceedings of Congress.

Consumer Credit: Short-term loans made to enable people to purchase goods or services primarily for personal, family, or household purposes.

Corpus: [*Latin, Body, aggregate, or mass.*]

Court of Appeal: An intermediate federal judicial tribunal of review that is found in thirteen judicial districts, called circuits, in the United States.

A state judicial tribunal that reviews a decision rendered by an inferior tribunal to determine whether it made errors that warrant the reversal of its judgment.

Criminal Law: A body of rules and statutes that defines conduct prohibited by the government because it threatens and harms public safety and welfare and that establishes punishment to be imposed for the commission of such acts.

Criminal Procedure: The framework of laws and rules that govern the administration of justice in cases involving an individual who has been accused of a crime, beginning with the initial investigation of the crime and concluding either with the unconditional release of the accused by virtue of acquittal (a judgment of not guilty) or by the imposition of a term of punishment pursuant to a conviction for the crime.

Cruel and Unusual Punishment: Such punishment as would amount to torture or barbarity, and cruel and degrading punishment not known to the common law, or any fine, penalty, confinement, or treatment so disproportionate to the offense as to shock the moral sense of the community.

D

Declaratory Judgment: Statutory remedy for the determination of a justiciable controversy where the plaintiff is in doubt as to his or her legal rights. A binding adjudication of the rights and status of litigants even though no consequential relief is awarded.

Dicta: Opinions of a judge that do not embody the resolution or determination of the specific case before the court. Expressions in a court's opinion that go beyond the facts before the court and therefore are individual views of the author of the opinion and not binding in subsequent cases as legal precedent. The plural of *dictum*.

Direct Evidence: Evidence in the form of testimony from a witness who actually saw, heard, or touched the subject of questioning. Evidence that, if believed, proves existence of the fact in issue without inference or presumption. That means of proof which tends to show the existence of a fact in question, without the intervention of the proof of any other fact, and which is distinguished from circumstantial evidence, often called *indirect*.

Evidence that directly proves a fact, without an inference or presumption, and which in itself, if true, conclusively establishes that fact.

Disorderly Conduct: A broad term describing conduct that disturbs the peace or endangers the morals, health, or safety of a community.

Disposition: Act of disposing; transferring to the care or possession of another. The parting with, alienation of, or giving up of property. The final settlement of a matter and, with reference to decisions announced by a court, a judge's ruling is commonly referred to as disposition, regardless of level of resolution. In criminal procedure, the sentencing or other final settlement of a criminal case. With respect to a mental state, denotes an attitude, prevailing tendency, or inclination.

District Court: A designation of an inferior state court that exercises general jurisdiction that it has been granted by the constitution or statute which created it. A U.S. judicial tribunal with original jurisdiction to try cases or controversies that fall within its limited jurisdiction.

Documentary Evidence: A type of written proof that is offered at a trial to establish to existence or nonexistence of a fact that is in dispute.

Due Process of Law: A fundamental, constitutional guarantee that all legal proceedings will be fair and that one will be given notice of the proceedings and an opportunity to be heard before the government acts to take away one's life, liberty, or property. Also, a constitutional guarantee that a law shall not be unreasonable, arbitrary, or capricious.

E

Easement: A right of use over the property of another. Traditionally the permitted kinds of uses were limited, the most important being rights of way and rights concerning flowing waters. The easement was normally for the benefit of adjoining lands, no matter who the owner was (an easement appurtenant), rather than for the benefit of a specific individual (easement in gross).

Eminent Domain: The power to take private property for public use by a state, municipality, or private person or corporation authorized to exercise functions of public character, following the payment of just compensation to the owner of that property.

En Banc: [*Latin, French. In the bench.*] Full bench. Refers to a session where the entire membership of the court will participate in the decision rather than the regular quorum. In other countries, it is common for a court to have more members than are usually necessary to hear an appeal. In the United States, the Circuit Courts of Appeal usually sit in panels of judges but for important cases may expand the bench to a larger number, when the judges are said to be sitting *en banc*. Similarly, only one of the judges of the U.S. Tax Court will typically hear and decide on a tax controversy. However, when the issues involved are unusually novel or of wide impact, the case will be heard and decided by the full court sitting *en banc*.

Encroachment: An illegal intrusion in a highway or navigable river, with or without obstruction. An encroachment upon a street or highway is a fixture, such as a wall or fence, which illegally intrudes into or invades the highway or encloses a portion of it, diminishing its width or area, but without closing it to public travel.

Entity: A real being; existence. An organization or being that possesses separate existence for tax purposes. Examples would be corporations, partnerships, estates, and trusts. The accounting entity for which accounting statements are prepared may not be the same as the entity defined by law.

Entity includes corporation and foreign corporation; not-for-profit corporation; profit and not-for-profit unincorporated association; business trust, estate, partnership, trust, and two or more persons having a joint or common economic interest; and state, U.S., and foreign governments.

An existence apart, such as a corporation in relation to its stockholders.

Entity includes person, estate, trust, governmental unit.

Entry of Judgment: Formally recording the result of a lawsuit that is based upon the determination by the court of the facts and applicable law, and that makes the result effective for purposes of bringing an action to enforce it or to commence an appeal.

Equal Protection: The constitutional guarantee that no person or class of persons shall be denied the same protection of the laws that is enjoyed by other persons or other classes in like circumstances in their lives, liberty, property, and pursuit of happiness.

Et Seq.: "An abbreviation for the Latin *et sequentes* or *et sequentia*, meaning 'and the following.'"

Executive Privilege: The right of the president of the United States to withhold information from Congress or the courts.

Extraordinary Remedy: The designation given to such writs as habeas corpus, mandamus, and quo warranto, determined in special proceedings and granted only where absolutely necessary to protect the legal rights of a party in a particular case, as opposed to the customary relief obtained by the maintenance of an action.

F

False Arrest: A tort (a civil wrong) that consists of an unlawful restraint of an individual's personal liberty or freedom of movement by another purporting to act according to the law.

False Imprisonment: The illegal confinement of one individual against his or her will by another individual in such a manner as to violate the confined individual's right to be free from restraint of movement.

Federal Courts: The U.S. judicial tribunals created by Article III of the Constitution, or by Congress, to hear and determine justiciable controversies.

Felony: A serious crime, characterized under federal law and many state statutes as any offense punishable by death or imprisonment in excess of one year.

Fiduciary: An individual in whom another has placed the utmost trust and confidence to manage and protect property or money. The relationship wherein one person has an obligation to act for another's benefit.

Filibuster: A tactic used by a LEGISLATIVE representative to hinder and delay consideration of an action to be taken on a proposed bill through prolonged, irrelevant, and procrastinating speeches on the floor of the House, Senate, or other legislative body.

Final Decision: The resolution of a controversy by a court or series of courts from which no appeal may be taken and that precludes further action. The last act by a lower court that is required for the completion of a lawsuit, such as the handing down of a final judgment upon which an appeal to a higher court may be brought.

First Impression: The initial presentation to, or examination by, a court of a particular question of law.

Fiscal: Relating to finance or financial matters, such as money, taxes, or public or private revenues.

Foreclosure: A procedure by which the holder of a mortgage—an interest in land providing security for the performance of a duty or the payment of a debt—sells the property upon the failure of the debtor to pay the mortgage debt and, thereby, terminates his or her rights in the property.

Fraud: A false representation of a matter of fact—whether by words or by conduct, by false or misleading allegations, or by concealment of what should have been disclosed—that deceives and is intended to deceive another so that the individual will act upon it to her or his legal injury.

Fraudulent: The description of a willful act commenced with the specific intent to deceive or cheat, in order to cause some financial detriment to another and to engender personal financial gain.

Freedom of Speech: The right, guaranteed by the First Amendment to the U.S. Constitution, to express beliefs and ideas without unwarranted government restriction.

Freedom of The Press: The right, guaranteed by the First Amendment to the U.S. Constitution, to gather, publish, and distribute information and ideas without government restriction; this right encompasses freedom from prior restraints on publication and freedom from censorship.

G

Gag Order: A court order to gag or bind an unruly defendant or remove her or him from the courtroom in order to prevent further interruptions in a trial. In a trial with a great deal of notoriety, a court order directed to attorneys and witnesses not to discuss the case with the media—such order being felt necessary to assure the defendant of a fair trial. A court order, directed to the media, not to report certain aspects of a crime or criminal investigation prior to trial.

General Jurisdiction: The legal authority of a court to entertain whatever type of case comes up within the geographical area over which its power extends.

Good Faith: Honesty; a sincere intention to deal fairly with others.

Grand Jury: A panel of citizens that is convened by a court to decide whether it is appropriate for the government to indict (proceed with a prosecution against) someone suspected of a crime.

Guardian: A person lawfully invested with the power, and charged with the obligation, of taking care of and managing the property and rights of a person who, because of age, understanding, or self-control, is considered incapable of administering his or her own affairs.

H

Habeas Corpus: "[*Latin, You have the body.*] A writ (court order) that commands an individual or a government official who has restrained another to produce the prisoner at a designated time and place so that the court can determine the legality of custody and decide whether to order the prisoner's release."

Harmless Error: "A legal doctrine in criminal law that allows verdicts to stand without new trials being ordered despite errors of law at trial as long as all errors were insufficient to affect the final outcome. Rule 52(a) of the Federal Code of Criminal Procedure explains it as, "'Any error, defect, irregularity or variance which does not affect substantial rights shall be disregarded."??

Hearsay: A statement made out of court that is offered in court as evidence to prove the truth of the matter asserted.

Homestead: The dwelling house and its adjoining land where a family resides. Technically, and pursuant to the modern homestead exemption laws, an artificial estate in land, created to protect the possession and enjoyment of the owner against the claims of creditors by preventing the sale of the property for payment of the owner's debts so long as the land is occupied as a home.

Hot Pursuit: A doctrine that provides that the police may enter the premises where they suspect a crime has been committed without a warrant when delay would endanger their lives or the lives of others and lead to the escape of the alleged perpetrator; also sometimes called fresh pursuit.

Husband and Wife: A man and woman who are legally married to one another and are thereby given by law specific rights and duties resulting from that relationship.

I

Imputed: Attributed vicariously.

Incompetency: The lack of ability, knowledge, legal qualification, or fitness to discharge a required duty or professional obligation.

Interlocutory: Provisional; interim; temporary; not final; that which intervenes between the beginning and the end of a lawsuit or proceeding to either decide a particular point or matter that is not the final issue of the entire controversy or prevent irreparable harm during the pendency of the lawsuit.

J

Jeopardy: Danger; hazard; peril. In a criminal action, the danger of conviction and punishment confronting the defendant.

Judicial Immunity: A judge's complete protection from personal liability for exercising judicial functions.

Judicial Review: A court's authority to examine an executive or legislative act and to invalidate that act if it is contrary to constitutional principles.

Jurisprudence: "From the Latin term *juris prudentia,* which means 'the study, knowledge, or science of law'; in the United States, more broadly associated with the philosophy of law."

Justiciable: Capable of being decided by a court.

L

Legal Proceedings: All actions that are authorized or sanctioned by law and instituted in a court or a tribunal for the acquisition of rights or the enforcement of remedies.

Legal Right: An interest that the law protects; an enforceable claim; a privilege that is created or recognized by law, such as the constitutional right to freedom of speech.

Lessee: One who rents real property or personal property from another.

Libelous: In the nature of a written defamation, a communication that tends to injure reputation.

Lien: A right given to another by the owner of property to secure a debt, or one created by law in favor of certain creditors.

Line of Credit: The maximum borrowing power granted to a person from a financial institution.

Liquidation: The collection of assets belonging to a debtor to be applied to the discharge of his or her outstanding debts.

A type of proceeding pursuant to federal bankruptcy law by which certain property of a debtor is taken into custody by a trustee to be sold, the proceeds to be distributed to the debtor's creditors in satisfaction of their claims.

The settlement of the financial affairs of a business or individual through the sale of all assets and the distribution of the proceeds to creditors, heirs, or other parties with a legal claim.

M

Malicious Prosecution: An action for damages brought by one against whom a civil suit or criminal proceeding has been unsuccessfully commenced without probable cause and for a purpose other than that of bringing the alleged offender to justice.

Mandamus: [*Latin, We command.*] A writ or order that is issued from a court of superior jurisdiction that commands an inferior tribunal, corporation, municipal corporation, or individual to perform, or refrain from performing, a particular act, the performance or omission of which is required by law as an obligation.

Market Value: The highest price a willing buyer would pay and a willing seller would accept, both being fully informed, and the property being exposed for sale for a reasonable period of time. The market value may be different from the price a property can actually be sold for at a given time (market price). The market value of an article or piece of property is the price that it might be expected to bring if offered for sale in a fair market; not the price that might be obtained on a sale at public auction or a sale forced by the necessities of the owner, but such a price as would be fixed by negotiation and mutual agreement, after ample time to find a purchaser, as between a vendor who is willing (but not compelled) to sell and a purchaser who desires to buy but is not compelled to take the particular article or piece of property.

Mediation: A settlement of a dispute or controversy by setting up an independent person between two contending parties in order to aid them in the settlement of their disagreement.

Medicaid: A joint federal-state program that provides health care insurance to low-income persons.

Ministerial: Done under the direction of a supervisor; not involving discretion or policymaking.

Misdemeanor: Offenses lower than felonies and generally those punishable by fine, penalty, forfeiture, or imprisonment other than in a penitentiary. Under federal law, and most state laws, any offense other than a felony is classified as a misdemeanor. Certain states also have various classes of misdemeanors (e.g., Class A, B, etc.).

Money Laundering: The process of taking the proceeds of criminal activity and making them appear legal.

Monopoly: An economic advantage held by one or more persons or companies deriving from the exclusive power to carry on a particular business or trade or to manufacture and sell a particular item, thereby suppressing competition and allowing such persons or companies to raise the price of a product or service substantially above the price that would be established by a free market.

N

Natural and Probable Consequences: Those ramifications of a particular course of conduct that are reasonably foreseeable by a person of average intelligence and generally occur in the normal course of events.

O

Operation of Law: The manner in which an individual acquires certain rights or liabilities through no act or cooperation of his or her own, but merely by the application of the established legal rules to the particular transaction.

Ordinance: A law, statute, or regulation enacted by a municipal corporation.

Original Jurisdiction: The authority of a tribunal to entertain a lawsuit, try it, and set forth a judgment on the law and facts.

P

Pander: To pimp; to cater to the gratification of the lust of another. To entice or procure a person, by promises, threats, fraud, or deception to enter any place in which prostitution is practiced for the purpose of prostitution.

Pecuniary: Monetary; relating to money; financial; consisting of money or that which can be valued in money.

Pension: A benefit, usually money, paid regularly to retired employees or their survivors by private business and federal, state, and local governments. Employers are not required to establish pension benefits but do so to attract qualified employees.

Per Curiam: [*Latin, By the court.*] A phrase used to distinguish an opinion of the whole court from an opinion written by any one judge.

Personal Jurisdiction: The power of a court to hear and determine a lawsuit involving a defendant by virtue of the defendant's having some contact with the place where the court is located.

Personal Service: The actual delivery of process to the individual to whom it is directed or to someone authorized to receive it on his or her behalf.

Plurality: The opinion of an appellate court in which more justices join than in any concurring opinion.

The excess of votes cast for one candidate over those votes cast for any other candidate.

Preemption: A doctrine based on the Supremacy Clause of the U.S. Constitution that holds that certain matters are of such a national, as opposed to local, character that federal laws preempt or take precedence over state laws. As such, a state may not pass a law inconsistent with the federal law.

A doctrine of state law that holds that a state law displaces a local law or regulation that is in the same field and is in conflict or inconsistent with the state law.

Preliminary Hearing: A proceeding before a judicial officer in which the officer must decide whether a crime was committed, whether the crime occurred within the territorial jurisdiction of the court, and whether there is probable cause to believe that the defendant committed the crime.

Preliminary Injunction: A temporary order made by a court at the request of one party that prevents the other party from pursuing a particular course of conduct until the conclusion of a trial on the merits.

Prevailing Party: The litigant who successfully brings or defends an action and, as a result, receives a favorable judgment or verdict.

Price-Fixing: The organized setting of what the public will be charged for certain products or services agreed to by competitors in the marketplace in violation of the Sherman Anti-Trust Act (15 U.S.C.A. § 1 et seq.).

Prima Facie: [*Latin, On the first appearance.*] A fact presumed to be true unless it is disproved.

Primary Authority: Law, in various forms, that a court must follow in deciding a case.

Private Law: That portion of the law that defines, regulates, enforces, and administers relationships among individuals, associations, and corporations. As used in distinction to public law, the term means that part of the law that is administered between citizen and citizen, or that is concerned with the definition, regulation, and enforcement of rights in cases where both the person in whom the right inheres and the person upon whom the obligation rests are private individuals.

Probable Cause: Apparent facts discovered through logical inquiry that would lead a reasonably intelligent and prudent person to believe that an accused person has committed a crime, thereby warranting his or her prosecution, or that a cause of action has accrued, justifying a civil lawsuit.

Probative: Having the effect of proof, tending to prove, or actually proving.

Promissory Note: A written, signed, unconditional promise to pay a certain amount of money on demand at a specified time. A written promise to pay money that is often used as a means to borrow funds or take out a loan.

Public Domain: Land that is owned by the United States. In copyright law, literary or creative works over which the creator no longer has an exclusive right to restrict, or receive a royalty for, their reproduction or use but which can be freely copied by the public.

Public Law: A general classification of law concerned with the political and sovereign capacity of a state.

Punitive Damages: Monetary compensation awarded to an injured party that goes beyond that which is necessary to compensate the individual for losses and that is intended to punish the wrongdoer.

Purview: The part of a statute or a law that delineates its purpose and scope.

R

Racial Profiling: The use of race as a determining factor for police searches and traffic stops.

Ratification: The confirmation or adoption of an act that has already been performed.

Reasonable Person: A phrase frequently used in tort and criminal law to denote a hypothetical person in society who exercises average care, skill, and judgment in conduct and who serves as a comparative standard for determining liability.

Recidivism: The behavior of a repeat or habitual criminal. A measurement of the rate at which offenders commit other crimes, either by arrest or conviction baselines, after being released from incarceration.

Recoupment: To recover a loss by a subsequent gain. In pleading, to set forth a claim against the plaintiff when an action is brought against one as a defendant. Keeping back of something that is due, because there is an equitable reason to withhold it. A right of the defendant to have a deduction from the amount of the plaintiff's damages, for the reason that the plaintiff has not complied with the cross-obligations or independent covenants arising under the same contract.

Referendum: The right reserved to the people to approve or reject an act of the legislature, or the right of the people to approve or reject an act of the legislature, or the right of the people to approve or reject legislation that has been referred to them by the legislature.

Registrar: The public official charged with the duty of making and maintaining public records.

Remittitur: The procedural process by which an excessive verdict of the jury is reduced. If money damages awarded by a jury are grossly excessive as a matter of law, the judge may order the plaintiff to remit a portion of the award.

Repeal: The annulment or abrogation of a previously existing statute by the enactment of a later law that revokes the former law.

Repugnancy: An inconsistency or opposition between two or more clauses of the same deed, contract, or statute, between two or more material allegations of the same pleading or between any two writings.

Rescind: To declare a contract void—of no legal force or binding effect—from its inception and thereby restore the parties to the positions they would have occupied had no contract ever been made.

Restitution: In the context of criminal law, state programs under which an offender is required, as a condition of his or her sentence, to repay money or donate services to the victim or society; with respect to maritime law, the restoration of articles lost by jettison, done when the remainder of the cargo has been saved, at the general charge of the owners of the cargo; in the law of torts, or civil wrongs, a measure of damages; in regard to contract law, the restoration of a party injured by a breach of contract to the position that party occupied before she or he entered the contract.

Reversion: Any future interest kept by a person who transfers property to another.

Right of Action: The privilege of instituting a lawsuit arising from a particular transaction or state of facts, such as a suit that is based on a contract or a tort, a civil wrong.

Robbery: The taking of money or goods in the possession of another, from his or her person or immediate presence, by force or intimidation.

Rule of Law: Rule according to law; rule under law; or rule according to a higher law.

S

Scienter: [*Latin, Knowingly.*] Guilty knowledge that is sufficient to charge a person with the consequences of his or her acts.

Scope of Employment: Activities of an employee that are in furtherance of duties that are owed to an employer and where the employer is, or could be, exercising some control, directly or indirectly, over the activities of the employee.

Search and Seizure: In international law, the right of ships of war, as regulated by treaties, to examine a merchant vessel during war in order to determine whether the ship or its cargo is liable to seizure.

A hunt by law enforcement officials for property or communications believed to be evidence of crime, and the act of taking possession of this property.

Self-Executing: Anything (e.g., a document or legislation) that is effective immediately without the need of intervening court action, ancillary legislation, or other type of implementing action.

Settlor: One who establishes a trust—a right of property, real or personal—held and administered by a trustee for the benefit of another.

Sodomy: Anal or oral intercourse between human beings, or any sexual relations between a human being and an animal, the act of which may be punishable as a criminal offense.

Solicitation: Urgent request, plea, or entreaty; enticing, asking. The criminal offense of urging someone to commit an unlawful act.

Solicitor General: An officer of the U.S. Department of Justice who represents the U.S. government in cases before the U.S. Supreme Court.

Solvency: The ability of an individual to pay his or her debts as they mature in the normal and ordinary course of business, or the financial condition of owning property of sufficient value to discharge all of one's debts.

Sovereign Immunity: The legal protection that prevents a sovereign state or person from being sued without consent.

State Action: A requirement for claims that arise under the **Due Process Clause** of the FOUR-TEENTH AMENDMENT and civil rights legislation, for which a private citizen seeks relief in the form of damages or redress based on an improper intrusion by the government into his or her private life.

State Interest: A broad term for any matter of public concern that is addressed by a government in law or policy.

Statute: An act of a legislature that declares, proscribes, or commands something; a specific law, expressed in writing.

Statute of Limitations: A type of federal or state law that restricts the time within which legal proceedings may be brought.

Statutory: Created, defined, or relating to a statute; required by statute; conforming to a statute.

Strict Scrutiny: A standard of judicial review for a challenged policy in which the court presumes the policy to be invalid unless the government can demonstrate a compelling interest to justify the policy.

Subject Matter Jurisdiction: The power of a court to hear and determine cases of the general class to which the proceedings in question belong.

Subrogation: The substitution of one person in the place of another with reference to a lawful claim, demand, or right, so that he or she who is substituted succeeds to the rights of the other in relation to the debt or claim, and its rights, remedies, or securities.

Substantive Due Process: The substantive limitations placed on the content or subject matter of state and federal laws by the Due Process Clauses of the FIFTH and FOURTEENTH AMENDMENTS to the U.S. CONSTITUTION.

Summary Judgment: A procedural device used during civil litigation to promptly and expeditiously dispose of a case without a trial. It is used when there is no dispute as to the material facts of the case and a party is entitled to judgment as a matter of law.

T

Tax Court: A specialized federal or state court that decides cases involving tax-related controversies.

Taxpayer Bill of Rights: A federal or state law that gives taxpayers procedural and substantive protection when dealing with a revenue department concerning a tax collection dispute.

Third Party: A generic legal term for any individual who does not have a direct connection with a legal transaction but who might be affected by it.

Tort Law: A body of rights, obligations, and remedies that is applied by courts in civil proceedings to provide relief for persons who have suffered harm from the wrongful acts of others. The person who sustains injury or suffers pecuniary damage as the result of tortious conduct is known as the plaintiff, and the person who is responsible for inflicting the injury and incurs liability for the damage is known as the defendant or tortfeasor.

Transfer of Assets: The conveyance of something of value from one person, place, or situation to another.

Tribunal: A general term for a court, or the seat of a judge.

Trustee: An individual or corporation named by an individual, who sets aside property to be used for the benefit of another person, to manage the property as provided by the terms of the document that created the arrangement.

V

Venue: A place, such as the territory from which residents are selected to serve as jurors.

A proper place, such as the correct court to hear a case because it has authority over events that have occurred within a certain geographical area.

Vicarious Liability: The tort doctrine that imposes responsibility upon one person for the failure of another, with whom the person has a special relationship (such as parent and child, employer and employee, or owner of vehicle and driver), to exercise such care as a reasonably prudent person would use under similar circumstances.

Voir Dire: [*Old French, To speak the truth.*] The preliminary examination of prospective jurors to determine their qualifications and suitability to serve on a jury, in order to ensure the selection of fair and impartial jury.

W

Writ: An order issued by a court requiring that something be done or giving authority to do a specified act.

Wrongful Death: The taking of the life of an individual resulting from the willful or negligent act of another person or persons.

Wrongful Discharge: An at-will employee's cause of action against his former employer, alleging that his dischargee was in violation of state or federal antidiscrimination statutes, public policy, an implied contract or an implied covenant of good faith and fair dealing.

Z

Zoning: The separation or division of a municipality into districts, the regulation of buildings and structures in such districts in accordance with their construction and the nature and extent of their use, and the dedication of such districts to particular uses designed to serve the general welfare.

A.	Atlantic Reporter
A. 2d	Atlantic Reporter, Second Series
AA	Alcoholics Anonymous
AAA	American Arbitration Association; Agricultural Adjustment Act of 1933
AALS	Association of American Law Schools
AAPRP	All African People's Revolutionary Party
AARP	American Association of Retired Persons
AAS	American Anti-Slavery Society
ABA	American Bar Association; Architectural Barriers Act of 1968; American Bankers Association
ABC	American Broadcasting Companies, Inc. (formerly American Broadcasting Corporation)
ABM	Antiballistic missile
ABM Treaty	Anti-Ballistic Missile Treaty of 1972
ABVP	Anti-Biased Violence Project
A/C	Account
A.C.	Appeal cases
ACAA	Air Carrier Access Act
ACCA	Armed Career Criminal Act of 1984
ACF	Administration for Children and Families
ACLU	American Civil Liberties Union
ACRS	Accelerated Cost Recovery System
ACS	Agricultural Cooperative Service
ACT	American College Test
Act'g Legal Adv.	Acting Legal Advisor
ACUS	Administrative Conference of the United States
ACYF	Administration on Children, Youth, and Families
A.D. 2d	Appellate Division, Second Series, N.Y.
ADA	Americans with Disabilities Act of 1990
ADAMHA	Alcohol, Drug Abuse, and Mental Health Administration
ADC	Aid to Dependent Children
ADD	Administration on Developmental Disabilities
ADEA	Age Discrimination in Employment Act of 1967
ADL	Anti-Defamation League
ADR	Alternative dispute resolution
AEC	Atomic Energy Commission

AECB	Arms Export Control Board
AEDPA	Antiterrorism and Effective Death Penalty Act
A.E.R.	All England Law Reports
AFA	American Family Association; Alabama Freethought Association
AFB	American Farm Bureau
AFBF	American Farm Bureau Federation
AFDC	Aid to Families with Dependent Children
aff'd per cur.	Affirmed by the court
AFIS	Automated fingerprint identification system
AFL	American Federation of Labor
AFL-CIO	American Federation of Labor and Congress of Industrial Organizations
AFRes	Air Force Reserve
AFSC	American Friends Service Committee
AFSCME	American Federation of State, County, and Municipal Employees
AGRICOLA	Agricultural Online Access
AIA	Association of Insurance Attorneys
AIB	American Institute for Banking
AID	Artificial insemination using a third-party donor's sperm; Agency for International Development
AIDS	Acquired immune deficiency syndrome
AIH	Artificial insemination using the husband's sperm
AIM	American Indian Movement
AIPAC	American Israel Public Affairs Committee
AIUSA	Amnesty International, U.S.A. Affiliate
AJS	American Judicature Society
ALA	American Library Association
Alcoa	Aluminum Company of America
ALEC	American Legislative Exchange Council
ALF	Animal Liberation Front
ALI	American Law Institute
ALJ	Administrative law judge
All E.R.	All England Law Reports
ALO	Agency Liaison
A.L.R.	American Law Reports
ALY	*American Law Yearbook*
AMA	American Medical Association
AMAA	Agricultural Marketing Agreement Act
Am. Dec.	American Decisions
amdt.	Amendment
Amer. St. Papers, For. Rels.	American State Papers, Legislative and Executive Documents of the Congress of the U.S., Class I, Foreign Relations, 1832–1859
AMS	Agricultural Marketing Service
AMVETS	American Veterans (of World War II)
ANA	Administration for Native Americans
Ann. Dig.	Annual Digest of Public International Law Cases
ANRA	American Newspaper Publishers Association
ANSCA	Alaska Native Claims Act
ANZUS	Australia-New Zealand-United States Security Treaty Organization
AOA	Administration on Aging
AOE	Arizonans for Official English
AOL	America Online
AP	Associated Press
APA	Administrative Procedure Act of 1946
APHIS	Animal and Plant Health Inspection Service
App. Div.	Appellate Division Reports, N.Y. Supreme Court

Arb. Trib., U.S.-British	Arbitration Tribunal, Claim Convention of 1853, United States and Great Britain Convention of 1853
Ardcor	American Roller Die Corporation
ARPA	Advanced Research Projects Agency
ARPANET	Advanced Research Projects Agency Network
ARS	Advanced Record System
Art.	Article
ARU	American Railway Union
ASCME	American Federation of State, County, and Municipal Employees
ASCS	Agriculture Stabilization and Conservation Service
ASM	Available Seatmile
ASPCA	American Society for the Prevention of Cruelty to Animals
Asst. Att. Gen.	Assistant Attorney General
AT&T	American Telephone and Telegraph
ATFD	Alcohol, Tobacco and Firearms Division
ATLA	Association of Trial Lawyers of America
ATO	Alpha Tau Omega
ATTD	Alcohol and Tobacco Tax Division
ATU	Alcohol Tax Unit
AUAM	American Union against Militarism
AUM	Animal Unit Month
AZT	Azidothymidine
BAC	Blood alcohol concentration
BALSA	Black-American Law Student Association
BATF	Bureau of Alcohol, Tobacco and Firearms
BBS	Bulletin Board System
BCCI	Bank of Credit and Commerce International
BEA	Bureau of Economic Analysis
Bell's Cr. C.	Bell's English Crown Cases
Bevans	United States Treaties, etc. *Treaties and Other International Agreements of the United States of America, 1776–1949* (compiled under the direction of Charles I. Bevans, 1968–76)
BFOQ	Bona fide occupational qualification
BI	Bureau of Investigation
BIA	Bureau of Indian Affairs; Board of Immigration Appeals
BID	Business improvement district
BJS	Bureau of Justice Statistics
Black.	Black's United States Supreme Court Reports
Blatchf.	Blatchford's United States Circuit Court Reports
BLM	Bureau of Land Management
BLS	Bureau of Labor Statistics
BMD	Ballistic missile defense
BNA	Bureau of National Affairs
BOCA	Building Officials and Code Administrators International
BOP	Bureau of Prisons
BPP	Black Panther Party for Self-defense
Brit. and For.	British and Foreign State Papers
BSA	Boy Scouts of America
BTP	Beta Theta Pi
Burr.	James Burrows, *Report of Cases Argued and Determined in the Court of King's Bench during the Time of Lord Mansfield* (1766–1780)
BVA	Board of Veterans Appeals
c.	Chapter
C³I	Command, Control, Communications, and Intelligence
C.A.	Court of Appeals
CAA	Clean Air Act
CAB	Civil Aeronautics Board; Corporation for American Banking

CAFE	Corporate average fuel economy
Cal. 2d	California Reports, Second Series
Cal. 3d	California Reports, Third Series
CALR	Computer-assisted legal research
Cal. Rptr.	California Reporter
CAP	Common Agricultural Policy
CARA	Classification and Ratings Administration
CATV	Community antenna television
CBO	Congressional Budget Office
CBS	Columbia Broadcasting System
CBOEC	Chicago Board of Election Commissioners
CCC	Commodity Credit Corporation
CCDBG	Child Care and Development Block Grant of 1990
C.C.D. Pa.	Circuit Court Decisions, Pennsylvania
C.C.D. Va.	Circuit Court Decisions, Virginia
CCEA	Cabinet Council on Economic Affairs
CCP	Chinese Communist Party
CCR	Center for Constitutional Rights
C.C.R.I.	Circuit Court, Rhode Island
CD	Certificate of deposit; compact disc
CDA	Communications Decency Act
CDBG	Community Development Block Grant Program
CDC	Centers for Disease Control and Prevention; Community Development Corporation
CDF	Children's Defense Fund
CDL	Citizens for Decency through Law
CD-ROM	Compact disc read-only memory
CDS	Community Dispute Services
CDW	Collision damage waiver
CENTO	Central Treaty Organization
CEO	Chief executive officer
CEQ	Council on Environmental Quality
CERCLA	Comprehensive Environmental Response, Compensation, and Liability Act of 1980
cert.	*Certiorari*
CETA	Comprehensive Employment and Training Act
C & F	Cost and freight
CFC	Chlorofluorocarbon
CFE Treaty	Conventional Forces in Europe Treaty of 1990
C.F. & I.	Cost, freight, and insurance
C.F.R	Code of Federal Regulations
CFNP	Community Food and Nutrition Program
CFTA	Canadian Free Trade Agreement
CFTC	Commodity Futures Trading Commission
Ch.	Chancery Division, English Law Reports
CHAMPVA	Civilian Health and Medical Program at the Veterans Administration
CHEP	Cuban/Haitian Entrant Program
CHINS	Children in need of supervision
CHIPS	Child in need of protective services
Ch.N.Y.	Chancery Reports, New York
Chr. Rob.	Christopher Robinson, *Reports of Cases Argued and Determined in the High Court of Admiralty* (1801–1808)
CIA	Central Intelligence Agency
CID	Commercial Item Descriptions
C.I.F.	Cost, insurance, and freight
CINCNORAD	Commander in Chief, North American Air Defense Command
C.I.O.	Congress of Industrial Organizations

CIPE	Center for International Private Enterprise
C.J.	Chief justice
CJIS	Criminal Justice Information Services
C.J.S.	Corpus Juris Secundum
Claims Arb. under Spec. Conv., Nielsen's Rept.	Frederick Kenelm Nielsen, *American and British Claims Arbitration under the Special Agreement Concluded between the United States and Great Britain, August 18, 1910* (1926)
CLASP	Center for Law and Social Policy
CLE	Center for Law and Education; Continuing Legal Education
CLEO	Council on Legal Education Opportunity; Chief Law Enforcement Officer
CLP	Communist Labor Party of America
CLS	Christian Legal Society; critical legal studies (movement); Critical Legal Studies (membership organization)
C.M.A.	Court of Military Appeals
CMEA	Council for Mutual Economic Assistance
CMHS	Center for Mental Health Services
C.M.R.	Court of Military Review
CNN	Cable News Network
CNO	Chief of Naval Operations
CNOL	Consolidated net operating loss
CNR	Chicago and Northwestern Railway
CO	Conscientious Objector
C.O.D.	Cash on delivery
COGP	Commission on Government Procurement
COINTELPRO	Counterintelligence Program
Coke Rep.	Coke's English King's Bench Reports
COLA	Cost-of-living adjustment
COMCEN	Federal Communications Center
Comp.	Compilation
Conn.	Connecticut Reports
CONTU	National Commission on New Technological Uses of Copyrighted Works
Conv.	Convention
COPA	Child Online Protection Act (1998)
COPS	Community Oriented Policing Services
Corbin	Arthur L. Corbin, *Corbin on Contracts: A Comprehensive Treatise on the Rules of Contract Law* (1950)
CORE	Congress on Racial Equality
Cox's Crim. Cases	Cox's Criminal Cases (England)
COYOTE	Call Off Your Old Tired Ethics
CPA	Certified public accountant
CPB	Corporation for Public Broadcasting, the
CPI	Consumer Price Index
CPPA	Child Pornography Prevention Act
CPSC	Consumer Product Safety Commission
Cranch	Cranch's United States Supreme Court Reports
CRF	Constitutional Rights Foundation
CRR	Center for Constitutional Rights
CRS	Congressional Research Service; Community Relations Service
CRT	Critical race theory
CSA	Community Services Administration
CSAP	Center for Substance Abuse Prevention
CSAT	Center for Substance Abuse Treatment
CSC	Civil Service Commission
CSCE	Conference on Security and Cooperation in Europe
CSG	Council of State Governments

CSO	Community Service Organization
CSP	Center for the Study of the Presidency
C-SPAN	Cable-Satellite Public Affairs Network
CSRS	Cooperative State Research Service
CSWPL	Center on Social Welfare Policy and Law
CTA	*Cum testamento annexo* (with the will attached)
Ct. Ap. D.C.	Court of Appeals, District of Columbia
Ct. App. No. Ireland	Court of Appeals, Northern Ireland
Ct. Cl.	Court of Claims, United States
Ct. Crim. Apps.	Court of Criminal Appeals (England)
Ct. of Sess., Scot.	Court of Sessions, Scotland
CTI	Consolidated taxable income
CU	Credit union
CUNY	City University of New York
Cush.	Cushing's Massachusetts Reports
CWA	Civil Works Administration; Clean Water Act
DACORB	Department of the Army Conscientious Objector Review Board
Dall.	Dallas's Pennsylvania and United States Reports
DAR	Daughters of the American Revolution
DARPA	Defense Advanced Research Projects Agency
DAVA	Defense Audiovisual Agency
D.C.	United States District Court; District of Columbia
D.C. Del.	United States District Court, Delaware
D.C. Mass.	United States District Court, Massachusetts
D.C. Md.	United States District Court, Maryland
D.C.N.D.Cal.	United States District Court, Northern District, California
D.C.N.Y.	United States District Court, New York
D.C.Pa.	United States District Court, Pennsylvania
DCS	Deputy Chiefs of Staff
DCZ	District of the Canal Zone
DDT	Dichlorodiphenyltricloroethane
DEA	Drug Enforcement Administration
Decl. Lond.	Declaration of London, February 26, 1909
Dev. & B.	Devereux & Battle's North Carolina Reports
DFL	Minnesota Democratic-Farmer-Labor
DFTA	Department for the Aging
Dig. U.S. Practice in Intl. Law	Digest of U.S. Practice in International Law
Dist. Ct.	D.C. United States District Court, District of Columbia
D.L.R.	Dominion Law Reports (Canada)
DMCA	Digital Millennium Copyright Act
DNA	Deoxyribonucleic acid
Dnase	Deoxyribonuclease
DNC	Democratic National Committee
DOC	Department of Commerce
DOD	Department of Defense
DODEA	Department of Defense Education Activity
Dodson	Dodson's Reports, English Admiralty Courts
DOE	Department of Energy
DOER	Department of Employee Relations
DOJ	Department of Justice
DOL	Department of Labor
DOMA	Defense of Marriage Act of 1996
DOS	Disk operating system
DOT	Department of Transportation
DPT	Diphtheria, pertussis, and tetanus
DRI	Defense Research Institute

DSAA	Defense Security Assistance Agency
DUI	Driving under the influence; driving under intoxication
DVD	Digital versatile disc
DWI	Driving while intoxicated
EAHCA	Education for All Handicapped Children Act of 1975
EBT	Examination before trial
E.coli	Escherichia coli
ECPA	Electronic Communications Privacy Act of 1986
ECSC	Treaty of the European Coal and Steel Community
EDA	Economic Development Administration
EDF	Environmental Defense Fund
E.D.N.Y.	Eastern District, New York
EDP	Electronic data processing
E.D. Pa.	Eastern-District, Pennsylvania
EDSC	Eastern District, South Carolina
EDT	Eastern daylight time
E.D. Va.	Eastern District, Virginia
EEC	European Economic Community; European Economic Community Treaty
EEOC	Equal Employment Opportunity Commission
EFF	Electronic Frontier Foundation
EFT	Electronic funds transfer
Eliz.	Queen Elizabeth (Great Britain)
Em. App.	Temporary Emergency Court of Appeals
ENE	Early neutral evaluation
Eng. Rep.	English Reports
EOP	Executive Office of the President
EPA	Environmental Protection Agency; Equal Pay Act of 1963
ERA	Equal Rights Amendment
ERDC	Energy Research and Development Commission
ERISA	Employee Retirement Income Security Act of 1974
ERS	Economic Research Service
ERTA	Economic Recovery Tax Act of 1981
ESA	Endangered Species Act of 1973
ESF	Emergency support function; Economic Support Fund
ESRD	End-Stage Renal Disease Program
ETA	Employment and Training Administration
ETS	Environmental tobacco smoke
et seq.	*Et sequentes* or *et sequentia* ("and the following")
EU	European Union
Euratom	European Atomic Energy Community
Eur. Ct. H.R.	European Court of Human Rights
Ex.	English Exchequer Reports, Welsby, Hurlstone & Gordon
Exch.	Exchequer Reports (Welsby, Hurlstone & Gordon)
Ex Com	Executive Committee of the National Security Council
Eximbank	Export-Import Bank of the United States
F.	Federal Reporter
F. 2d	Federal Reporter, Second Series
FAA	Federal Aviation Administration; Federal Arbitration Act
FAAA	Federal Alcohol Administration Act
FACE	Freedom of Access to Clinic Entrances Act of 1994
FACT	Feminist Anti-Censorship Task Force
FAIRA	Federal Agriculture Improvement and Reform Act of 1996
FAMLA	Family and Medical Leave Act of 1993
Fannie Mae	Federal National Mortgage Association
FAO	Food and Agriculture Organization of the United Nations
FAR	Federal Acquisition Regulations

FAS	Foreign Agricultural Service
FBA	Federal Bar Association
FBI	Federal Bureau of Investigation
FCA	Farm Credit Administration
F. Cas.	Federal Cases
FCC	Federal Communications Commission
FCIA	Foreign Credit Insurance Association
FCIC	Federal Crop Insurance Corporation
FCLAA	Federal Cigarette Labeling and Advertising Act
FCRA	Fair Credit Reporting Act
FCU	Federal credit unions
FCUA	Federal Credit Union Act
FCZ	Fishery Conservation Zone
FDA	Food and Drug Administration
FDIC	Federal Deposit Insurance Corporation
FDPC	Federal Data Processing Center
FEC	Federal Election Commission
FECA	Federal Election Campaign Act of 1971
Fed. Cas.	Federal Cases
FEHA	Fair Employment and Housing Act
FEHBA	Federal Employees Health Benefit Act
FEMA	Federal Emergency Management Agency
FERC	Federal Energy Regulatory Commission
FFB	Federal Financing Bank
FFDC	Federal Food, Drug, and Cosmetics Act
FGIS	Federal Grain Inspection Service
FHA	Federal Housing Administration
FHAA	Fair Housing Amendments Act of 1998
FHWA	Federal Highway Administration
FIA	Federal Insurance Administration
FIC	Federal Information Centers; Federation of Insurance Counsel
FICA	Federal Insurance Contributions Act
FIFRA	Federal Insecticide, Fungicide, and Rodenticide Act
FIP	Forestry Incentives Program
FIRREA	Financial Institutions Reform, Recovery, and Enforcement Act of 1989
FISA	Foreign Intelligence Surveillance Act of 1978
FISC	Foreign Intelligence Surveillance Court of Review
FJC	Federal Judicial Center
FLSA	Fair Labor Standards Act
FMC	Federal Maritime Commission
FMCS	Federal Mediation and Conciliation Service
FmHA	Farmers Home Administration
FMLA	Family and Medical Leave Act of 1993
FNMA	Federal National Mortgage Association, "Fannie Mae"
F.O.B.	Free on board
FOIA	Freedom of Information Act
FOMC	Federal Open Market Committee
FPA	Federal Power Act of 1935
FPC	Federal Power Commission
FPMR	Federal Property Management Regulations
FPRS	Federal Property Resources Service
FR	Federal Register
FRA	Federal Railroad Administration
FRB	Federal Reserve Board
FRC	Federal Radio Commission
F.R.D.	Federal Rules Decisions

FSA	Family Support Act
FSB	Federal'naya Sluzhba Bezopasnosti (the Federal Security Service of Russia)
FSLIC	Federal Savings and Loan Insurance Corporation
FSQS	Food Safety and Quality Service
FSS	Federal Supply Service
F. Supp.	Federal Supplement
FTA	U.S.-Canada Free Trade Agreement of 1988
FTC	Federal Trade Commission
FTCA	Federal Tort Claims Act
FTS	Federal Telecommunications System
FTS2000	Federal Telecommunications System 2000
FUCA	Federal Unemployment Compensation Act of 1988
FUTA	Federal Unemployment Tax Act
FWPCA	Federal Water Pollution Control Act of 1948
FWS	Fish and Wildlife Service
GAL	Guardian ad litem
GAO	General Accounting Office; Governmental Affairs Office
GAOR	General Assembly Official Records, United Nations
GAAP	Generally accepted accounting principles
GA Res.	General Assembly Resolution (United Nations)
GATT	General Agreement on Tariffs and Trade
GCA	Gun Control Act
Gen. Cls. Comm.	General Claims Commission, United States and Panama; General Claims United States and Mexico
Geo. II	King George II (Great Britain)
Geo. III	King George III (Great Britain)
GHB	Gamma-hydroxybutrate
GI	Government Issue
GID	General Intelligence Division
GM	General Motors
GNMA	Government National Mortgage Association, "Ginnie Mae"
GNP	Gross national product
GOP	Grand Old Party (Republican Party)
GOPAC	Grand Old Party Action Committee
GPA	Office of Governmental and Public Affairs
GPO	Government Printing Office
GRAS	Generally recognized as safe
Gr. Br., Crim. Ct. App.	Great Britain, Court of Criminal Appeals
GRNL	Gay Rights-National Lobby
GSA	General Services Administration
Hackworth	Green Haywood Hackworth, *Digest of International Law* (1940–1944)
Hay and Marriott	Great Britain. High Court of Admiralty, *Decisions in the High Court of Admiralty during the Time of Sir George Hay and of Sir James Marriott, Late Judges of That Court* (1801)
HBO	Home Box Office
HCFA	Health Care Financing Administration
H.Ct.	High Court
HDS	Office of Human Development Services
Hen. & M.	Hening & Munford's Virginia Reports
HEW	Department of Health, Education, and Welfare
HFCA	Health Care Financing Administration
HGI	Handgun Control, Incorporated
HHS	Department of Health and Human Services
Hill	Hill's New York Reports
HIRE	Help through Industry Retraining and Employment
HIV	Human immunodeficiency virus

H.L.	House of Lords Cases (England)
H. Lords	House of Lords (England)
HMO	Health Maintenance Organization
HNIS	Human Nutrition Information Service
Hong Kong L.R.	Hong Kong Law Reports
How.	Howard's United States Supreme Court Reports
How. St. Trials	Howell's English State Trials
HUAC	House Un-American Activities Committee
HUD	Department of Housing and Urban Development
Hudson, Internatl. Legis.	Manley Ottmer Hudson, ed., *International Legislation: A Collection of the Texts of Multipartite International Instruments of General Interest Beginning with the Covenant of the League of Nations* (1931)
Hudson, World Court Reps.	Manley Ottmer Hudson, ea., *World Court Reports* (1934–)
Hun	Hun's New York Supreme Court Reports
Hunt's Rept.	Bert L. Hunt, *Report of the American and Panamanian General Claims Arbitration* (1934)
IAEA	International Atomic Energy Agency
IALL	International Association of Law Libraries
IBA	International Bar Association
IBM	International Business Machines
ICA	Interstate Commerce Act
ICBM	Intercontinental ballistic missile
ICC	Interstate Commerce Commission; International Criminal Court
ICJ	International Court of Justice
ICM	Institute for Court Management
IDEA	Individuals with Disabilities Education Act of 1975
IDOP	International Dolphin Conservation Program
IEP	Individualized educational program
IFC	International Finance Corporation
IGRA	Indian Gaming Regulatory Act of 1988
IJA	Institute of Judicial Administration
IJC	International Joint Commission
ILC	International Law Commission
ILD	International Labor Defense
Ill. Dec.	Illinois Decisions
ILO	International Labor Organization
IMF	International Monetary Fund
INA	Immigration and Nationality Act
IND	Investigational new drug
INF Treaty	Intermediate-Range Nuclear Forces Treaty of 1987
INS	Immigration and Naturalization Service
INTELSAT	International Telecommunications Satellite Organization
Interpol	International Criminal Police Organization
Int'l. Law Reps.	International Law Reports
Intl. Legal Mats.	International Legal Materials
IOC	International Olympic Committee
IPDC	International Program for the Development of Communication
IPO	Intellectual Property Owners
IPP	Independent power producer
IQ	Intelligence quotient
I.R.	Irish Reports
IRA	Individual retirement account; Irish Republican Army
IRC	Internal Revenue Code
IRCA	Immigration Reform and Control Act of 1986
IRS	Internal Revenue Service
ISO	Independent service organization

ISP	Internet service provider
ISSN	International Standard Serial Numbers
ITA	International Trade Administration
ITI	Information Technology Integration
ITO	International Trade Organization
ITS	Information Technology Service
ITT	International Telephone and Telegraph Corporation
ITU	International Telecommunication Union
IUD	Intrauterine device
IWC	International Whaling Commission
IWW	Industrial Workers of the World
JAGC	Judge Advocate General's Corps
JCS	Joint Chiefs of Staff
JDL	Jewish Defense League
JNOV	Judgment *non obstante veredicto* ("judgment nothing to recommend it" or "judgment notwithstanding the verdict")
JOBS	Jobs Opportunity and Basic Skills
John. Ch.	Johnson's New York Chancery Reports
Johns.	Johnson's Reports (New York)
JP	Justice of the peace
K.B.	King's Bench Reports (England)
KFC	Kentucky Fried Chicken
KGB	Komitet Gosudarstvennoi Bezopasnosti (the State Security Committee for countries in the former Soviet Union)
KKK	Ku Klux Klan
KMT	Kuomintang (Chinese, "national people's party")
LAD	Law Against Discrimination
LAPD	Los Angeles Police Department
LC	Library of Congress
LCHA	Longshoremen's and Harbor Workers Compensation Act of 1927
LD50	Lethal dose 50
LDEF	Legal Defense and Education Fund (NOW)
LDF	Legal Defense Fund, Legal Defense and Educational Fund of the NAACP
LEAA	Law Enforcement Assistance Administration
L.Ed.	Lawyers' Edition Supreme Court Reports
LI	Letter of interpretation
LLC	Limited Liability Company
LLP	Limited Liability Partnership
LMSA	Labor-Management Services Administration
LNTS	League of Nations Treaty Series
Lofft's Rep.	Lofft's English King's Bench Reports
L.R.	Law Reports (English)
LSAC	Law School Admission Council
LSAS	Law School Admission Service
LSAT	Law School Aptitude Test
LSC	Legal Services Corporation; Legal Services for Children
LSD	Lysergic acid diethylamide
LSDAS	Law School Data Assembly Service
LTBT	Limited Test Ban Treaty
LTC	Long Term Care
MAD	Mutual assured destruction
MADD	Mothers against Drunk Driving
MALDEF	Mexican American Legal Defense and Educational Fund
Malloy	William M. Malloy, ed., *Treaties, Conventions International Acts, Protocols, and Agreements between the United States of America and Other Powers* (1910–1938)

Martens	Georg Friedrich von Martens, ea., *Noveau recueil général de traités et autres actes relatifs aux rapports de droit international* (Series I, 20 vols. [1843–1875]; Series II, 35 vols. [1876–1908]; Series III [1909–])
Mass.	Massachusetts Reports
MCC	Metropolitan Correctional Center
MCCA	Medicare Catastrophic Coverage Act of 1988
MCH	Maternal and Child Health Bureau
MCRA	Medical Care Recovery Act of 1962
MDA	Medical Devices Amendments of 1976
Md. App.	Maryland, Appeal Cases
M.D. Ga.	Middle District, Georgia
Mercy	Movement Ensuring the Right to Choose for Yourself
Metc.	Metcalf's Massachusetts Reports
MFDP	Mississippi Freedom Democratic party
MGT	Management
MHSS	Military Health Services System
Miller	David Hunter Miller, ea., *Treaties and Other International Acts of the United States of America* (1931–1948)
Minn.	Minnesota Reports
MINS	Minors in need of supervision
MIRV	Multiple independently targetable reentry vehicle
MIRVed ICBM	Multiple independently targetable reentry vehicled intercontinental ballistic missile
Misc.	Miscellaneous Reports, New York
Mixed Claims Comm., Report of Decs	Mixed Claims Commission, United States and Germany, Report of Decisions
M.J.	Military Justice Reporter
MLAP	Migrant Legal Action Program
MLB	Major League Baseball
MLDP	Mississippi Loyalist Democratic Party
MMI	Moslem Mosque, Incorporated
MMPA	Marine Mammal Protection Act of 1972
Mo.	Missouri Reports
MOD	Masters of Deception
Mod.	Modern Reports, English King's Bench, etc.
Moore, Dig. Intl. Law	John Bassett Moore, *A Digest of International Law*, 8 vols. (1906)
Moore, Intl. Arbs.	John Bassett Moore, *History and Digest of the International Arbitrations to Which United States Has Been a Party*, 6 vols. (1898)
Morison	William Maxwell Morison, *The Scots Revised Report: Morison's Dictionary of Decisions* (1908–09)
M.P.	Member of Parliament
MP3	MPEG Audio Layer 3
MPAA	Motion Picture Association of America
MPAS	Michigan Protection and Advocacy Service
MPEG	Motion Picture Experts Group
mpg	Miles per gallon
MPPDA	Motion Picture Producers and Distributors of America
MPRSA	Marine Protection, Research, and Sanctuaries Act of 1972
M.R.	Master of the Rolls
MS-DOS	Microsoft Disk Operating System
MSHA	Mine Safety and Health Administration
MSPB	Merit Systems Protection Board
MSSA	Military Selective Service Act
N/A	Not Available
NAACP	National Association for the Advancement of Colored People
NAAQS	National Ambient Air Quality Standards

NAB	National Association of Broadcasters
NABSW	National Association of Black Social Workers
NACDL	National Association of Criminal Defense Lawyers
NAFTA	North American Free Trade Agreement of 1993
NAGHSR	National Association of Governors' Highway Safety Representatives
NALA	National Association of Legal Assistants
NAM	National Association of Manufacturers
NAR	National Association of Realtors
NARAL	National Abortion and Reproductive Rights Action League
NARF	Native American Rights Fund
NARS	National Archives and Record Service
NASA	National Aeronautics and Space Administration
NASD	National Association of Securities Dealers
NATO	North Atlantic Treaty Organization
NAVINFO	Navy Information Offices
NAWSA	National American Woman's Suffrage Association
NBA	National Bar Association; National Basketball Association
NBC	National Broadcasting Company
NBLSA	National Black Law Student Association
NBS	National Bureau of Standards
NCA	Noise Control Act; National Command Authorities
NCAA	National Collegiate Athletic Association
NCAC	National Coalition against Censorship
NCCB	National Consumer Cooperative Bank
NCE	Northwest Community Exchange
NCF	National Chamber Foundation
NCIP	National Crime Insurance Program
NCJA	National Criminal Justice Association
NCLB	National Civil Liberties Bureau
NCP	National contingency plan
NCSC	National Center for State Courts
NCUA	National Credit Union Administration
NDA	New drug application
N.D. Ill.	Northern District, Illinois
NDU	National Defense University
N.D. Wash.	Northern District, Washington
N.E.	North Eastern Reporter
N.E. 2d	North Eastern Reporter, Second Series
NEA	National Endowment for the Arts; National Education Association
NEH	National Endowment for the Humanities
NEPA	National Environmental Protection Act; National Endowment Policy Act
NET Act	No Electronic Theft Act
NFIB	National Federation of Independent Businesses
NFIP	National Flood Insurance Program
NFL	National Football League
NFPA	National Federation of Paralegal Associations
NGLTF	National Gay and Lesbian Task Force
NHL	National Hockey League
NHRA	Nursing Home Reform Act of 1987
NHTSA	National Highway Traffic Safety Administration
Nielsen's Rept.	Frederick Kenelm Nielsen, *American and British Claims Arbitration under the Special Agreement Concluded between the United States and Great Britain, August 18, 1910* (1926)
NIEO	New International Economic Order
NIGC	National Indian Gaming Commission
NIH	National Institutes of Health

NIJ	National Institute of Justice
NIRA	National Industrial Recovery Act of 1933; National Industrial Recovery Administration
NIST	National Institute of Standards and Technology
NITA	National Telecommunications and Information Administration
N.J.	New Jersey Reports
N.J. Super.	New Jersey Superior Court Reports
NLEA	Nutrition Labeling and Education Act of 1990
NLRA	National Labor Relations Act
NLRB	National Labor Relations Board
NMFS	National Marine Fisheries Service
No.	Number
NOAA	National Oceanic and Atmospheric Administration
NOC	National Olympic Committee
NOI	Nation of Islam
NOL	Net operating loss
NORML	National Organization for the Reform of Marijuana Laws
NOW	National Organization for Women
NOW LDEF	National Organization for Women Legal Defense and Education Fund
NOW/PAC	National Organization for Women Political Action Committee
NPDES	National Pollutant Discharge Elimination System
NPL	National priorities list
NPR	National Public Radio
NPT	Nuclear Non-Proliferation Treaty of 1970
NRA	National Rifle Association; National Recovery Act
NRC	Nuclear Regulatory Commission
NRLC	National Right to Life Committee
NRTA	National Retired Teachers Association
NSA	National Security Agency
NSC	National Security Council
NSCLC	National Senior Citizens Law Center
NSF	National Science Foundation
NSFNET	National Science Foundation Network
NSI	Network Solutions, Inc.
NTIA	National Telecommunications and Information Administration
NTID	National Technical Institute for the Deaf
NTIS	National Technical Information Service
NTS	Naval Telecommunications System
NTSB	National Transportation Safety Board
NVRA	National Voter Registration Act
N.W.	North Western Reporter
N.W. 2d	North Western Reporter, Second Series
NWSA	National Woman Suffrage Association
N.Y.	New York Court of Appeals Reports
N.Y. 2d	New York Court of Appeals Reports, Second Series
N.Y.S.	New York Supplement Reporter
N.Y.S. 2d	New York Supplement Reporter, Second Series
NYSE	New York Stock Exchange
NYSLA	New York State Liquor Authority
N.Y. Sup.	New York Supreme Court Reports
NYU	New York University
OAAU	Organization of Afro American Unity
OAP	Office of Administrative Procedure
OAS	Organization of American States
OASDI	Old-age, Survivors, and Disability Insurance Benefits
OASHDS	Office of the Assistant Secretary for Human Development Services

OCC	Office of Comptroller of the Currency
OCED	Office of Comprehensive Employment Development
OCHAMPUS	Office of Civilian Health and Medical Program of the Uniformed Services
OCSE	Office of Child Support Enforcement
OEA	Organización de los Estados Americanos
OEM	Original Equipment Manufacturer
OFCCP	Office of Federal Contract Compliance Programs
OFPP	Office of Federal Procurement Policy
OIC	Office of the Independent Counsel
OICD	Office of International Cooperation and Development
OIG	Office of the Inspector General
OJARS	Office of Justice Assistance, Research, and Statistics
OMB	Office of Management and Budget
OMPC	Office of Management, Planning, and Communications
ONP	Office of National Programs
OPD	Office of Policy Development
OPEC	Organization of Petroleum Exporting Countries
OPIC	Overseas Private Investment Corporation
Ops. Atts. Gen.	Opinions of the Attorneys-General of the United States
Ops. Comms.	Opinions of the Commissioners
OPSP	Office of Product Standards Policy
O.R.	Ontario Reports
OR	Official Records
OSHA	Occupational Safety and Health Act
OSHRC	Occupational Safety and Health Review Commission
OSM	Office of Surface Mining
OSS	Office of Strategic Services
OST	Office of the Secretary
OT	Office of Transportation
OTA	Office of Technology Assessment
OTC	Over-the-counter
OTS	Office of Thrift Supervisors
OUI	Operating under the influence
OVCI	Offshore Voluntary Compliance Initiative
OWBPA	Older Workers Benefit Protection Act
OWRT	Office of Water Research and Technology
P.	Pacific Reporter
P. 2d	Pacific Reporter, Second Series
PAC	Political action committee
Pa. Oyer and Terminer	Pennsylvania Oyer and Terminer Reports
PATCO	Professional Air Traffic Controllers Organization
PBGC	Pension Benefit Guaranty Corporation
PBS	Public Broadcasting Service; Public Buildings Service
P.C.	Privy Council (English Law Reports)
PC	Personal computer; politically correct
PCBs	Polychlorinated biphenyls
PCIJ	Permanent Court of International Justice
	Series A-Judgments and Orders (1922–30)
	Series B-Advisory Opinions (1922–30)
	Series A/B-Judgments, Orders, and Advisory Opinions (1931–40)
	Series C-Pleadings, Oral Statements, and Documents relating to Judgments and Advisory Opinions (1923–42)
	Series D-Acts and Documents concerning the Organization of the World Court (1922 –47)
	Series E-Annual Reports (1925–45)
PCP	Phencyclidine

P.D.	Probate Division, English Law Reports (1876–1890)
PDA	Pregnancy Discrimination Act of 1978
PD & R	Policy Development and Research
Pepco	Potomac Electric Power Company
Perm. Ct. of Arb.	Permanent Court of Arbitration
PES	Post-Enumeration Survey
Pet.	Peters' United States Supreme Court Reports
PETA	People for the Ethical Treatment of Animals
PGA	Professional Golfers Association
PGM	Program
PHA	Public Housing Agency
Phila. Ct. of Oyer and Terminer	Philadelphia Court of Oyer and Terminer
PhRMA	Pharmaceutical Research and Manufacturers of America
PHS	Public Health Service
PIC	Private Industry Council
PICJ	Permanent International Court of Justice
Pick.	Pickering's Massachusetts Reports
PIK	Payment in Kind
PINS	Persons in need of supervision
PIRG	Public Interest Research Group
P.L.	Public Laws
PLAN	Pro-Life Action Network
PLC	Plaintiffs' Legal Committee
PLE	Product liability expenses
PLI	Practicing Law Institute
PLL	Product liability loss
PLLP	Professional Limited Liability Partnership
PLO	Palestine Liberation Organization
PLRA	Prison Litigation Reform Act of 1995
PNET	Peaceful Nuclear Explosions Treaty
PONY	Prostitutes of New York
POW-MIA	Prisoner of war-missing in action
Pratt	Frederic Thomas Pratt, *Law of Contraband of War, with a Selection of Cases from Papers of the Right Honourable Sir George Lee* (1856)
PRIDE	Prostitution to Independence, Dignity, and Equality
Proc.	Proceedings
PRP	Potentially responsible party
PSRO	Professional Standards Review Organization
PTO	Patents and Trademark Office
PURPA	Public Utilities Regulatory Policies Act
PUSH	People United to Serve Humanity
PUSH-Excel	PUSH for Excellence
PWA	Public Works Administration
PWSA	Ports and Waterways Safety Act of 1972
Q.B.	Queen's Bench (England)
QTIP	Qualified Terminable Interest Property
Ralston's Rept.	Jackson Harvey Ralston, ed., *Venezuelan Arbitrations of 1903* (1904)
RC	Regional Commissioner
RCRA	Resource Conservation and Recovery Act
RCWP	Rural Clean Water Program
RDA	Rural Development Administration
REA	Rural Electrification Administration
Rec. des Decs. des Trib. Arb. Mixtes	G. Gidel, ed., *Recueil des décisions des tribunaux arbitraux mixtes, institués par les traités de paix* (1922–30)

Redmond	Vol. 3 of Charles I. Bevans, *Treaties and Other International Agreements of the United States of America, 1776–1949* (compiled by C. F. Redmond) (1969)
RESPA	Real Estate Settlement Procedure Act of 1974
RFC	Reconstruction Finance Corporation
RFRA	Religious Freedom Restoration Act of 1993
RIAA	Recording Industry Association of America
RICO	Racketeer Influenced and Corrupt Organizations
RLUIPA	Religious Land Use and Institutionalized Persons Act
RNC	Republican National Committee
Roscoe	Edward Stanley Roscoe, ed., *Reports of Prize Cases Determined in the High Court Admiralty before the Lords Commissioners of Appeals in Prize Causes and before the Judicial Committee of the Privy Council from 1745 to 1859* (1905)
ROTC	Reserve Officers' Training Corps
RPP	Representative Payee Program
R.S.	Revised Statutes
RTC	Resolution Trust Corp.
RUDs	Reservations, understandings, and declarations
Ryan White CARE Act	Ryan White Comprehensive AIDS Research Emergency Act of 1990
SAC	Strategic Air Command
SACB	Subversive Activities Control Board
SADD	Students against Drunk Driving
SAF	Student Activities Fund
SAIF	Savings Association Insurance Fund
SALT	Strategic Arms Limitation Talks
SALT I	Strategic Arms Limitation Talks of 1969–72
SAMHSA	Substance Abuse and Mental Health Services Administration
Sandf.	Sandford's New York Superior Court Reports
S and L	Savings and loan
SARA	Superfund Amendment and Reauthorization Act
SAT	Scholastic Aptitude Test
Sawy.	Sawyer's United States Circuit Court Reports
SBA	Small Business Administration
SBI	Small Business Institute
SCCC	South Central Correctional Center
SCLC	Southern Christian Leadership Conference
Scott's Repts.	James Brown Scott, ed., *The Hague Court Reports*, 2 vols. (1916–32)
SCS	Soil Conservation Service; Social Conservative Service
SCSEP	Senior Community Service Employment Program
S.Ct.	Supreme Court Reporter
S.D. Cal.	Southern District, California
S.D. Fla.	Southern District, Florida
S.D. Ga.	Southern District, Georgia
SDI	Strategic Defense Initiative
S.D. Me.	Southern District, Maine
S.D.N.Y.	Southern District, New York
SDS	Students for a Democratic Society
S.E.	South Eastern Reporter
S.E. 2d	South Eastern Reporter, Second Series
SEA	Science and Education Administration
SEATO	Southeast Asia Treaty Organization
SEC	Securities and Exchange Commission
Sec.	Section
SEEK	Search for Elevation, Education and Knowledge
SEOO	State Economic Opportunity Office
SEP	Simplified employee pension plan

Ser.	Series
Sess.	Session
SGLI	Servicemen's Group Life Insurance
SIP	State implementation plan
SLA	Symbionese Liberation Army
SLAPPs	Strategic Lawsuits Against Public Participation
SLBM	Submarine-launched ballistic missile
SNCC	Student Nonviolent Coordinating Committee
So.	Southern Reporter
So. 2d	Southern Reporter, Second Series
SPA	Software Publisher's Association
Spec. Sess.	Special Session
SPLC	Southern Poverty Law Center
SRA	Sentencing Reform Act of 1984
SS	*Schutzstaffel* (German, "Protection Echelon")
SSA	Social Security Administration
SSI	Supplemental Security Income
START I	Strategic Arms Reduction Treaty of 1991
START II	Strategic Arms Reduction Treaty of 1993
Stat.	United States Statutes at Large
STS	Space Transportation Systems
St. Tr.	State Trials, English
STURAA	Surface Transportation and Uniform Relocation Assistance Act of 1987
Sup. Ct. of Justice, Mexico	Supreme Court of Justice, Mexico
Supp.	Supplement
S.W.	South Western Reporter
S.W. 2d	South Western Reporter, Second Series
SWAPO	South-West Africa People's Organization
SWAT	Special Weapons and Tactics
SWP	Socialist Workers Party
TDP	Trade and Development Program
Tex. Sup.	Texas Supreme Court Reports
THAAD	Theater High-Altitude Area Defense System
THC	Tetrahydrocannabinol
TI	Tobacco Institute
TIA	Trust Indenture Act of 1939
TIAS	Treaties and Other International Acts Series (United States)
TNT	Trinitrotoluene
TOP	Targeted Outreach Program
TPUS	Transportation and Public Utilities Service
TQM	Total Quality Management
Tripartite Claims Comm., Decs. and Ops.	Tripartite Claims Commission (United States, Austria, and Hungary), Decisions and Opinions
TRI-TAC	Joint Tactical Communications
TRO	Temporary restraining order
TS	Treaty Series, United States
TSCA	Toxic Substance Control Act
TSDs	Transporters, storers, and disposers
TSU	Texas Southern University
TTBT	Threshold Test Ban Treaty
TV	Television
TVA	Tennessee Valley Authority
TWA	Trans World Airlines

UAW	United Auto Workers; United Automobile, Aerospace, and Agricultural Implements Workers of America
U.C.C.	Uniform Commercial Code; Universal Copyright Convention
U.C.C.C.	Uniform Consumer Credit Code
UCCJA	Uniform Child Custody Jurisdiction Act
UCMJ	Uniform Code of Military Justice
UCPP	Urban Crime Prevention Program
UCS	United Counseling Service
UDC	United Daughters of the Confederacy
UFW	United Farm Workers
UHF	Ultrahigh frequency
UIFSA	Uniform Interstate Family Support Act
UIS	Unemployment Insurance Service
UMDA	Uniform Marriage and Divorce Act
UMTA	Urban Mass Transportation Administration
U.N.	United Nations
UNCITRAL	United Nations Commission on International Trade Law
UNCTAD	United Nations Conference on Trade and Development
UN Doc.	United Nations Documents
UNDP	United Nations Development Program
UNEF	United Nations Emergency Force
UNESCO	United Nations Educational, Scientific, and Cultural Organization
UNICEF	United Nations Children's Fund (formerly United Nations International Children's Emergency Fund)
UNIDO	United Nations Industrial and Development Organization
Unif. L. Ann.	Uniform Laws Annotated
UN Repts. Intl. Arb. Awards	United Nations Reports of International Arbitral Awards
UNTS	United Nations Treaty Series
UPI	United Press International
URESA	Uniform Reciprocal Enforcement of Support Act
U.S.	United States Reports
U.S.A.	United States of America
USAF	United States Air Force
USA PATRIOT Act	Uniting and Strengthening America by Providing Appropriate Tools Required to Intercept and Obstruct Terrorism Act
USF	U.S. Forestry Service
U.S. App. D.C.	United States Court of Appeals for the District of Columbia
U.S.C.	United States Code; University of Southern California
U.S.C.A.	United States Code Annotated
USCCAN	United States Code Congressional and Administrative News
USCMA	United States Court of Military Appeals
USDA	U.S. Department of Agriculture
USES	United States Employment Service
USFA	United States Fire Administration
USGA	United States Golf Association
USICA	International Communication Agency, United States
USMS	U.S. Marshals Service
USOC	U.S. Olympic Committee
USSC	U.S. Sentencing Commission
USSG	United States Sentencing Guidelines
U.S.S.R.	Union of Soviet Socialist Republics
UST	United States Treaties
USTS	United States Travel Service
v.	*Versus*
VA	Veterans Administration
VAR	Veterans Affairs and Rehabilitation Commission

VAWA	Violence against Women Act
VFW	Veterans of Foreign Wars
VGLI	Veterans Group Life Insurance
Vict.	Queen Victoria (Great Britain)
VIN	Vehicle identification number
VISTA	Volunteers in Service to America
VJRA	Veterans Judicial Review Act of 1988
V.L.A.	Volunteer Lawyers for the Arts
VMI	Virginia Military Institute
VMLI	Veterans Mortgage Life Insurance
VOCAL	Victims of Child Abuse Laws
VRA	Voting Rights Act
WAC	Women's Army Corps
Wall.	Wallace's United States Supreme Court Reports
Wash. 2d	Washington Reports, Second Series
WAVES	Women Accepted for Volunteer Service
WCTU	Women's Christian Temperance Union
W.D. Wash.	Western District, Washington
W.D. Wis.	Western District, Wisconsin
WEAL	*West's Encyclopedia of American Law*; Women's Equity Action League
Wend.	Wendell's New York Reports
WFSE	Washington Federation of State Employees
Wheat.	Wheaton's United States Supreme Court Reports
Wheel. Cr. Cases	Wheeler's New York Criminal Cases
WHISPER	Women Hurt in Systems of Prostitution Engaged in Revolt
Whiteman	Marjorie Millace Whiteman, *Digest of International Law*, 15 vols. (1963–73)
WHO	World Health Organization
WIC	Women, Infants, and Children program
Will. and Mar.	King William and Queen Mary (Great Britain)
WIN	WESTLAW Is Natural; Whip Inflation Now; Work Incentive Program
WIPO	World Intellectual Property Organization
WIU	Workers' Industrial Union
W.L.R.	Weekly Law Reports, England
WPA	Works Progress Administration
WPPDA	Welfare and Pension Plans Disclosure Act
WTO	World Trade Organization
WWI	World War I
WWII	World War II
Yates Sel. Cas.	Yates's New York Select Cases
YMCA	Young Men's Christian Association
YWCA	Young Women's Christian Association

INDEX
BY NAME AND SUBJECT

Page numbers appearing in boldface indicate major treatment
of entries. Italicized page numbers refer to photos.

ISBN-13:978-1-4144-0118-8
ISBN-10: 1-4144-0118-3